THE BOOK OF THE DEAD

Above, twelve gods seated in order, as judges, before a table of offerings. Below, the Psychostasia, or Weighing of the Conscience: the jackal-headed Anubis trying in the Balance the heart (conscience) of the deceased against the feather symbolical of Law; on the left, Ani and his wife in an attitude of devotion;

on the right, the ibis-headed Thoth, the scribe of the gods, noting down the result of the trial and behind him the monster Amemit, the Devourer. On the left of the balance, Shai (Destiny) with the two goddesses Renenit and Meschenit behind him; above them, the soul of Ani, as a human-headed hawk, and the symbol of the cradle.

The presentation of Ani, triumphant, to Osiris. The god enthroned within a shrine; behind him, Isis and Nephthys; in front, a lotus-flower, on which are the

four children of Horus, genii of the dead. On the left, Horus leads forward Ani; who again kneels, with whitened hair, and presents offerings.

Above: Funeral procession: the mummy on a boat-shaped hearse, drawn by oxen; beside it kneels the mourning wife; in front, a priest officiates; behind follow mourners, and servants drawing a funeral shrine and bearing articles for the tomb, among which is the deceased's writing pallet.

Below: Funeral procession continued: ministrants carrying sepulchral furniture; a band of female mourners. On the right, the tomb, in front of which Anubis supports the mummy, the mourning wife kneeling before it. Facing the mummy, two priests officiate before a table of offerings; behind them a priest reads the funeral service from a papyrus, and a shaven priest brings forward an offering: the calf and cow above symbolize the rising Sun and Heaven.

Above: Ani, playing at draughts, together with his wife, within a hall. Their two souls, standing above the tomb; in front of them, an altar with a libation-vase and lotus-flowers. The Sun disk in the solar mount, with the canopy of heaven above; on either side the lions "Yesterday" and "The Morrow," otherwise Osiris and Ra. The Heron, identified with Osiris; an altar with vase and lotus-flower before him. The mummy in a shrine, with Isis and Nephthys in the form of twin birds; beneath the bier are jars, the writing pallet, etc.

Below: A seated male figure, with the emblem of "millions of years" in his right hand and on his head; his left hand extended above the Eye of Horus. A male figure standing with arms outstretched above the lakes of "Maaāt" and "Hesmen" (natron). A pylon, or gate with folding doors: "The Door of the Funeral Passages." The Eye of Horus upon a pedestal. The great cow "Mehurit, the Eye of Rā." A funereal chest, surrounded by the four children of Horus, with Rā rising from it holding the Sign of Life in each hand.

Ani adoring a triad of gods. Ani, with his writing pallet in his left hand addressing a god, who with turned head is seated in a boat. The soul of Ani visiting his mummified body, to illustrate the chapter "of reuniting the soul of the dead body." The soul standing before a door-way, to illustrate the chapter "that the soul of a person may not be imprisoned."

Ani and his wife.

Osiris-Seker within a shrine, in mummy form with a hawk's head. The goddess Hathor, as a hippopotamus, crowned with the sun-disk and horns; before her,

a table of offerings; behind, the Meh-urit Cow, symbolizing the same goddess, who gazes forth from the mountain of Amenta, at the foot of which is the tomb.

Isis and Nephthys, the sisters of Osiris, kneeling in adoration on the left and right of the Tat, a symbol of Osiris, which stands upon the Solar Mount and supports the Sign of Life upholding the Sun disk. The ornaments upon the heads of the two goddesses are the hieroglyphic signs of their names. On each side, three cynocephali or dog-headed apes, the transformed openers of the eastern portals of heaven, raising their hands in adoration. Ani and his wife before a table of offerings.

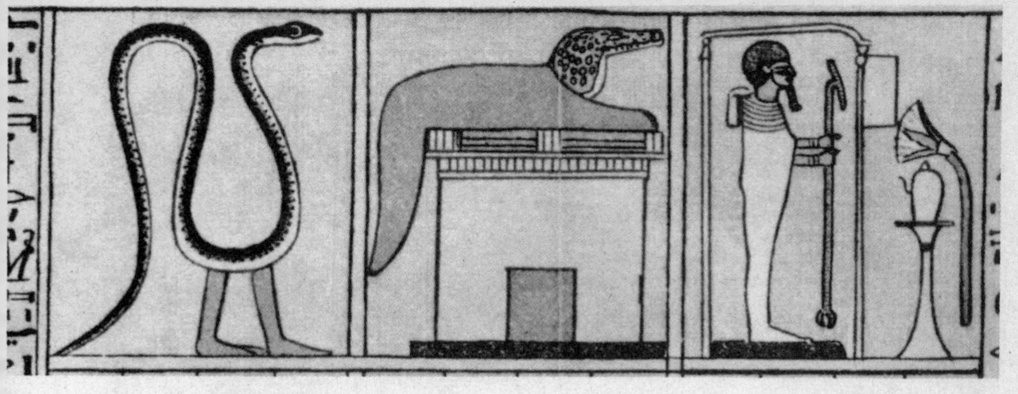

The Serpent Se-ta, the Crocodile Sebak, the god Ptah, the Ram (soul of Tmu), and the Heron, illustrating transformations.

Osiris and Isis within a shrine; before them a lotus-flower on which stand the four children of Horus, genii of the dead.

THE BOOK OF THE DEAD

The Hieroglyphic Transcript and Translation
into English of the Ancient Egyptian Papyrus of Ani

With a Comprehensive Introduction and Commentary by

E. A. WALLIS BUDGE

GRAMERCY BOOKS
NEW YORK

This 1999 edition is published by Gramercy Books,™
an imprint of Random House Value Publishing, Inc.,
201 East 50th Street, New York, New York 10022.

Gramercy Books™ and design are trademarks of
Random House Value Publishing, Inc.

Random House
New York • Toronto • London • Sydney • Auckland
http://www.randomhouse.com/

Printed and bound in the United States of America

Library of Congress Cataloging-in-Publication Data
Book of the dead. English.
The book of the dead / [edited by] E. A. Wallis Budge.
p. cm.
Originally published: 1895
Includes bibliographical references and index.
ISBN 0-517-12283-9
1. Incantations, Egyptian. 2. Future life.
I. Budge, E. A. Wallis (Earnest Alfred Wallis), Sir, 1857–1934.
II. Title
PJ1555.E5B7 1994
299′.31—dc20
94-39049
CIP

10 9 8 7 6 5

FOREWORD

Sir E. A. Wallis Budge was Keeper of Egyptian and Assyrian Antiquities at the British Museum in the late nineteenth and early twentieth centuries. His exhaustive study of ancient Egyptian magic, religion, and ritual resulted in a number of classic books, and among these are several versions of the most famous of Egyptian writings, the Book of the Dead. Budge's books were based on the British Museum's Papyrus of Ani, which he considered "the largest, the most perfect, and the best illuminated" of all the Book of the Dead papyri.

Budge's facsimile editions of the Papyrus of Ani were published in 1890 and 1894. These two versions each encompassed three folio-size volumes. The contents of the first two volumes—the text as well as the black and white vignettes—were basically the same as in the present edition. The third volume consisted of color facsimiles of the papyrus.

The folio books were followed in 1913 by a work of smaller dimensions in two volumes, which was published by the Medici Society. Folding plates of the color facsimiles were placed at the end of volume one. The text included important improvements over that of the folio editions. Supplementary chapters and sections were added from funerary papyri obtained by the British Museum since the acquisition of the Papyrus of Ani. The translation was rewritten and the notes were corrected and amplified in the light of recent discoveries. The greater part of the introduction was also rewritten by Budge, who ended his preface—included in the present edition—with the words, "and the entire work thus becomes truly a New Edition, fully revised to the date of issue." It was the last substantial revision he was ever to make.

There have also been numerous printings of a small-format, one-volume book, in which the English translation is identical with that of the Medici Society edition. However, this version lacks the hieroglyphic transcript and the notes; and the black and white vignettes are inferior in size and quality. The introduction to this volume differs considerably from that in the Medici Society version, which is in all respects superior.

The present volume is identical to the Medici Society edition, except that the reproductions of the plates are in black and white and that one volume now includes the contents previously in two. It should be noted that Budge's introduction is in reality a book in itself. His preface echoes that of the Medici Society edition; but it also incorporates material from other prefaces, as well as a number of paragraphs of great interest from a pamphlet on the Book of the Dead that he prepared for the British Museum in 1920.

GEORGE PALMER BLAKE

CONTENTS

Page

PREFACE ix

INTRODUCTION:

THE RECENSIONS OF THE BOOK OF THE DEAD 1

THE LEGEND OF OSIRIS... 52

APPENDIX I—HYMN TO OSIRIS 59

" II.—OSIRIS AND HIS PRINCIPAL FORMS UNDER THE XVIIITH DYNASTY... 61

THE DOCTRINE OF ETERNAL LIFE 66

EGYPTIAN IDEAS ABOUT GOD AND THE "GODS" 99

APPENDIX. LIST OF THE GODS WHOSE NAMES WERE RECITED BY THE DECEASED TO PERFECT HIS SPIRIT-SOUL ... 125

THE ABODE OF THE BLESSED 130

THE GODS OF THE BOOK OF THE DEAD 161

THE PRINCIPAL GEOGRAPHICAL AND MYTHOLOGICAL PLACES IN THE BOOK OF THE DEAD 202

FUNERAL CEREMONIES 207

THE PAPYRUS OF ANI, ITS DATE AND CONTENTS... 217

DESCRIPTION OF THE PLATES 231

LIST OF HYMNS AND CHAPTERS 331

THE PAPYRUS OF ANI. HIEROGLYPHIC TRANSCRIPT, TRANSLATION AND NOTES:

A HYMN TO RĀ THE SUN-GOD [CHAPTER XV]. **Plate I** ... 339

APPENDIX TO CHAPTER XV 347

HYMN TO OSIRIS UN-NEFER. **Plate II** 350

THE CHAPTERS OF COMING FORTH BY DAY [CHAPTER I]. **Plates V, VI**... 355

APPENDIX TO CHAPTER I 365
CHAPTER XXII 367
„ XXI 368
RUBRIC OF CHAPTER LXXII 368
APPENDIX. CHAPTER LXXII 369

TEXTS RELATING TO THE WEIGHING OF THE HEART OF ANI. Plates III, IV 371

CHAPTER OF PRAISES AND GLORIFYINGS, AND OF COMING FORTH BY DAY [CHAPTER XVII]. Plates VII–X 376
„ CXLVII. THE SEVEN ARITS. Plates XI, XII... 402
„ CXLVI. THE PYLONS OF THE HOUSE OF OSIRIS. Plate XI 409
„ XVII. INTRODUCTION. Plate XII 422
„ XVIII. Plates XIII, XIV 424
„ XXIII. THE CHAPTER OF OPENING OF THE MOUTH. Plate XV 433
CHAPTER XXIV 435
APPENDIX. CHAPTER XXV 436
CHAPTER XXVI 437
„ XXXB 439
APPENDIX. CHAPTER XXXB 440
CHAPTER LXI 442
„ XLIV 446
„ XXIXA 449
APPENDIX 450

CHAPTER XXVII. THE CHAPTER OF NOT LETTING THE HEART-CASE BE TAKEN FROM A MAN. Plates XV, XVI 451
CHAPTER LVIII 456
„ LIX 458
„ XLIV 459
„ XLV 460
„ XLVI 465
„ L 466

CHAPTER XCIII. THE CHAPTER OF NOT BEING TRANSPORTED TO THE EAST. Plate XVII 467
CHAPTER XLIII 470
„ LXXXIX... 471
„ XCI 473
„ XCII 474

CHAPTER LXXIV. THE CHAPTER OF LIFTING UP THE FEET AND OF APPEARING ON THE EARTH. **Plate XVIII** 477
CHAPTER VIII 478
„ II 481
„ IX... 483
„ CXXXII 484
„ X OR XLVIII 485
CHAPTER XV. A HYMN OF PRAISE [TO BE SUNG] TO RĀ WHEN HE RISETH ON THE HORIZON, [AND] WHEN HE SETTETH IN THE [LAND OF] LIFE. **Plate XIX** 487
„ XV. A HYMN OF PRAISE TO RĀ WHEN HE RISETH ON THE EASTERN HORIZON OF HEAVEN, AND TO THOSE WHO ARE IN HIS TRAIN. **Plates XX, XXI** 496
CHAPTER CXXXIII... 504
CHAPTER CXXXIV. A HYMN TO RĀ FOR THE DAY OF THE NEW MOON. **Plate XXII** 508
„ XVIII. **Plates XXIII, XXIV** 513
CHAPTER CXXIV 517
CHAPTER LXXXVI. THE CHAPTER OF CHANGING INTO A SWALLOW. **Plate XXV** 521
CHAPTER LXXVII 523
CHAPTER LXXVIII. THE CHAPTER OF CHANGING INTO A DIVINE HAWK. **Plates XXV, XXVI** 525
APPENDIX 535
CHAPTER LXXIX. APPENDIX. THE CHAPTER OF CHANGING INTO THE PRINCE OF THE TCHATCHAU CHIEFS 541
CHAPTER LXXXVII. THE CHAPTER OF CHANGING INTO THE SERPENT SATA. **Plate XXVII** 544
CHAPTER LXXXVIII 545
„ LXXXII 546
„ LXXXV 549
„ LXXXIII 552
CHAPTER LXXXIV. THE CHAPTER OF CHANGING INTO A HERON. **Plate XXVIII** 554
CHAPTER LXXXIA 557
APPENDIX. CHAPTER LXXXIB 557
CHAPTER LXXX 559

CHAPTER CLXXV. THE CHAPTER OF NOT DYING A SECOND TIME. **Plate XXIX** 561
„ CXXV. INTRODUCTION (A). THE CHAPTER OF ENTERING THE HALL OF MAĀT. **Plate XXX** ... 568
APPENDIX. CHAPTER XXV. INTRODUCTION (B) ... 572
CHAPTER CXXV. THE NEGATIVE CONFESSION. **Plates XXXI, XXXII** 576
APPENDIX. CHAPTER CXXV 585
CHAPTER XLII 597
APPENDIX. CHAPTER OF THE DEIFICATION OF MEMBERS 600
CHAPTER XLII. THE CHAPTER OF REPULSING SLAUGHTER IN HENSU 606
RUBRIC TO CHAPTER CXXV. **Plate XXXIII** 612
APPENDIX TO CHAPTER CXXV 614
CHAPTER CLV 616
APPENDIX TO CHAPTER CLV 616
CHAPTER CLVI 618
„ XXIXc 620
„ CLXVI 621
CHAPTER CLIA. THE TEXTS IN THE FUNERAL CHAMBER. **Plates XXXIII, XXXIV** 624
CHAPTER CX 632
APPENDIX. CHAPTER CX. THE CHAPTERS OF SEKHET-ḤETEPET 634
CHAPTER CXLVIII. THE CHAPTER OF PROVIDING THE DECEASED WITH MEAT, MILK, ETC. **Plate XXXV** 644
ADDRESSES TO THE FOUR RUDDERS OF HEAVEN. **Plate XXXVI** 645
APPENDIX. RUBRIC FROM THE PAPYRUS OF NU ... 646
„ RUBRIC FROM THE SAÏTE RECENSION ... 647
CHAPTER CLXXXV. HYMN TO OSIRIS 650
CHAPTER CLXXXVI. THE CHAPTER OF THE PRAISE OF HATHOR. **Plate XXXVII** 652
APPENDIX. CHAPTER CXXXVII. THE CHAPTER OF THE FOUR TORCHES 653
INDEX 665

PREFACE

The Papyrus of Ani is the largest, the most perfect, and the best illuminated of all the papyri containing copies of the Theban Recension of the Book of the Dead. Its rare Vignettes, Hymns, and Chapters, and its descriptive Rubrics, render it of unique importance for the study of the Book of the Dead, and it holds a very high place among the funerary papyri that were written between 1500 B.C. and 1350 B.C. Although it contains less than one-half of the Chapters which formed the great corpus of texts written for the benefit of the dead, we may conclude that Ani's exalted official position, as chancellor of the ecclesiastical revenues and endowments of all the temples of Thebes and Abydos, ensured the inclusion of all the Chapters which an educated Egyptian deemed essential for salvation. The Papyrus of Ani is, in short, typical of the Book of the Dead in vogue among the Theban nobles of his time.

In recent years there has been a growing demand for the Papyrus of Ani in a form convenient for use by beginners and students, and at a reasonable price. As the second edition of the facsimile in folio, and the edition of the accompanying volume of English text, are exhausted, the Trustees of the British Museum were asked to sanction the issue of the present edition. This they have done, and they have also permitted the use of the black and white vignettes which appeared in the text volume, and the reprinting of any sections which were necessary. The present edition therefore contains:

1. The general Introduction, with chapters on the history of the Book of the Dead and on Egyptian religion.

2. A full description of the Papyrus of Ani, plate by plate.
3. A complete transcript of the Papyrus in hieroglyphic type, with English translations, notes, etc., and an Index.

In preparing the material for this volume a new copy of the text has been made, and supplementary Chapters and Sections have been added from the funerary papyri that have been acquired by the Trustees since the Papyrus of Ani. The translations have been rewritten, and the notes have been corrected and amplified in the light of recent discoveries. The greater part of the Introduction has also been rewritten, and the entire work thus becomes truly a New Edition, fully revised to the date of issue.

"Book of the Dead" is the title now commonly given to the great collection of funerary texts which the ancient Egyptian scribes composed for the benefit of the dead. These consist of spells and incantations, hymns and litanies, magical formulae and names, and words of power and prayers, and they are found cut or painted on walls of pyramids and tombs, and painted on coffins and sarcophagi and rolls of papyri. The title "Book of the Dead" is somewhat unsatisfactory and misleading, for the texts neither form a connected work nor belong to one period; they are miscellaneous in character, and tell us nothing about the lives and works of the dead with whom they were buried. Moreover, the Egyptians possessed many funerary works that might rightly be called "Books of the Dead," but none of them bore a name that could be translated by the title "Book of the Dead." This title was given to the great collection of funerary texts in the first quarter of the nineteenth century by the pioneer Egyptologists, who as yet possessed no exact knowledge of their contents. This title is merely a translation of the name given by the Egyptian tomb-robbers to every roll of inscribed papyrus which they found with mummies, namely, Katâb al-Mayyit, "Book of the dead man," or Kitâb al-Mayyitun, "Book of the dead" (plur.). These men knew nothing of the contents of such a roll, and all they meant to say was that it was "a dead man's book," and that it was found in his coffin with him.

The objects found in the graves of the predynastic Egyptians—i.e., vessels of food, flint knives and other weapons—prove that these early dwellers in the Nile Valley believed in some kind of a future existence. But as the art of writing was unknown to them, their graves contain no inscriptions, and we can only infer from texts of the dynastic period what their ideas about the Other World were. It is clear that they did not consider it of great importance to preserve the dead body in as complete and perfect state as possible, for in many of their graves the heads, hands, and feet have been found severed from the trunks and lying at some distance from them. On the other hand, the dynastic Egyptians, either as the result of a difference in religious belief, or under the influence of invaders who had settled in their country, attached supreme importance to the preservation and integrity of the dead body, and they adopted every means known to them to prevent its dismemberment and decay. They cleansed it and embalmed it with drugs, spices and balsams; they anointed it with aromatic oils and preservative fluids; they swathed it in hundreds of yards of linen bandages; and then they sealed it up in a coffin or sarcophagus, which they laid in a chamber hewn in the bowels of the mountain. All these things were done to protect the physical body against damp, dry rot and decay, and against the attacks of moths, beetles, worms and wild animals. But these were not the only enemies of the dead against which precautions had to be taken, for both the mummified body and the spiritual elements which had inhabited it upon earth had to be protected from a multitude of devils and fiends, and from the powers of darkness generally.

These powers of evil had hideous and terrifying shapes

and forms, and their haunts were well known, for they infested the region through which the road of the dead lay when passing from this world to the Kingdom of Osiris. The "great gods" were afraid of them, and were obliged to protect themselves by the use of spells and magical names, and words of power, which were composed and written down by Thoth. In fact it was believed in very early times in Egypt that Rā, the Sun-god, owed his continued existence to the possession of a secret name with which Thoth had provided him. And each morning the rising sun was menaced by a fearful monster called Āapep which lay hidden under the place of sunrise waiting to swallow up the solar disc. It was impossible, even for the Sun-god, to destroy this "great devil," but by reciting each morning the powerful spell with which Thoth had provided him he was able to paralyze all Āapep's limbs and to rise upon this world. Since the "great gods," even though benevolently disposed towards them, were not able to deliver the dead from the devils that lived upon the "bodies, souls, spirits, shadows and hearts of the dead," the Egyptians decided to invoke the aid of Thoth on behalf of their dead and to place them under the protection of his almighty spells. Inspired by Thoth the theologians of ancient Egypt composed a large number of funerary texts which were certainly in general use under the IVth dynasty (about 3700 B.C.), and were probably well known under the Ist dynasty, and throughout the whole period of dynastic history Thoth was regarded as the author of the Book of the Dead.

Taken together, these texts are generally known as the Theban Recension of the Book of the Dead, that is to say, the Recension of the great national funeral work which was copied by the scribes for themselves and for Egyptian kings and queens, princes and nobles, gentle and simple, rich and poor, from about 1600 B.C. to 900 B.C.

Many of the ideas and beliefs embodied in the texts here translated are coeval with Egyptian civilization, and the actual forms of some of the most interesting of these are identical with those which we now know to have existed in the Vth and VIth dynasties, about 3500 B.C. On the other hand, many of them date from the predynastic period, and in the Introduction an attempt has been made to show how some of the religious views of the north-east African race, which formed the main indigenous substratum of the dynastic Egyptians, found their way into the Book of the Dead and maintained their position there.

The translation has been made as literal as possible, my aim being to let the reader judge the contents of the Theban Recension of the Book of the Dead for himself.

It has been the fashion during the last few years among certain writers on Egyptology to decry the Book of the Dead, and to announce as a great discovery that the hieroglyphic and hieratic texts thereof are corrupt; but that several passages of the work are hopelessly corrupt has been well known to Egyptologists for the last fifty years, and they have never concealed the fact that they could not translate them. The history of the religious literatures of the world shows that when a series of compositions has once attained the position of a recognized national religious work, the corruptions in the text thereof do not in any way affect the minds of their orthodox readers in the general credibility of the passages in which they occur. And the Book of the Dead forms no exception to this rule, for the work, which was very old even in the reign of Semti, a king of the Ist dynasty, and was, moreover, so long at that time as to need abbreviation, was copied and recopied, and added to by one generation after another for a period of nearly five thousand years; and the pious Egyptian, whether king or ploughman, queen or maid-servant, lived with the teaching of the Book of the Dead before his eyes, and he was buried according to its directions, and he based his hope of everlasting life and happiness upon the efficacy of its hymns and prayers, and words of power. By him its Chapters were not regarded as materials for grammatical exercises, but as all-powerful guides along the road which, passing through death and the grave, led into the realms of light and life, and into the presence of the divine being Osiris, the conqueror of death, who made men and women "to be born again." The more the Book of the Dead is read and examined, the better chance there is of its difficult allusions being explained, and its dark passages made clear, and this much-to-be-desired result can only be brought about by the study, and not by the neglect, of its texts.

E. A. WALLIS BUDGE

THE BOOK OF THE DEAD

INTRODUCTION

THE RECENSIONS OF THE BOOK OF THE DEAD

The Recensions of the great body of religious compositions, which were drawn up for the use of dead kings, nobles, priests, and others, and which form the **Book of the Dead** of the Ancient Egyptians may be thus summarized :—

I. The **Heliopolitan Recension,** *i.e.*, that which was edited by the priests of the College of Ȧnu (the On of the Bible, and the Heliopolis of the Greeks), and which was based upon a series of texts now lost. It is found cut in hieroglyphs upon the walls of the chambers and corridors of the pyramid tombs [1] of certain kings [2] of the Vth and VIth dynasties. It represents the system of theology promulgated by the priests of Rā the Sun-god, but all the essential elements in it, with the exception of the solar doctrines, are derived from the primitive, indigenous, and probably predynastic, Egyptians. In the texts of the later kings we find that the priests of Rā were obliged to acknowledge the supremacy of Osiris, whose cult, even under the earliest dynasties, was very general in Upper and Lower Egypt.

Under the XIth and XIIth dynasties sections of the Pyramid Texts, with titles in which they are styled "Chapters," were written in cursive hieroglyphs upon sarcophagi and coffins,[3] and to these were added a number

[1] Hence known as the "Pyramid Texts."

[2] *I.e.*, Unȧs, Tetȧ, Pepi I, Meḥti-em-sa-f, and Pepi II. Their pyramids were cleared out by MM. Mariette and Maspero during the years 1880–84, and the hieroglyphic texts were published, with a French translation, in *Recueil de Travaux*, tt. III–XIV, Paris, 1882–93. A revised edition of the text has been recently published by Sethe, *Pyramidentexte*, Leipzig, 1908–1910.

[3] In the XIth, XIIth, and XIIIth dynasties many monuments are inscribed with sections of the Unȧs text. Thus ll. 206–69 are found in hieroglyphs upon the coffin of Amamu (British Museum, No. 6654;

of Chapters which appear to have been composed during the interval between the VIth and XIth dynasties. The treatment of the older texts, and the character of the newer texts may be studied in the excellent transcripts

---

see Birch, *Egyptian Texts of the Earliest Period from the Coffin of Amamu*, 1886, Plates XVII–XX); ll. 206–14 and 268–84 on the coffin of , Åpå-ānkh, from Ṣaḳḳârah (see Lepsius, *Denkmäler*, II, Bl. 99 *b*; Maspero, *Recueil*, t. III, pp. 200 and 214 ff.); ll. 206–10 and 268–89 on the coffin of Åntef (see Lepsius, *Denkmäler*, II, Bl. 145; Maspero, *Recueil*, t. III, pp. 200, 214); l. 206 on a coffin of Menthu-ḥetep at Berlin (see Lepsius, *Aelteste Texte*, Bl. 5); ll. 269–94 on the sarcophagus of Ḥeru-ḥetep (see Maspero, *Mémoires*, t. I, p. 144). A section is found on the walls of the tomb of Queen Neferu (see Maspero, *Recueil*, t. III, pp. 201 ff.; *Mémoires*, t. I, p. 134); other sections are found on the sarcophagus of , Ṭaḳå (see Lepsius, *Denkmäler*, II, Bll. 147, 148; Maspero, *Guide au Visiteur*, p. 224, No. 1053; *Mémoires*, t. I, p. 134); ll. 5–8 occur on the stele of Åpå (see Ledrain, *Monuments Égyptiens de la Bibl. Nationale*, Paris, 1879, foll. 14, 15); ll. 166 ff. are found on the stele of Neḥi (see Mariette, *Notice des Mon. à Boulaq*, p. 190; Maspero, *Recueil*, t. III, p. 195); and ll. 576–83 on the coffin of Sebek-Āa (see Lepsius, *Aelteste Texte*, Bl. 37; Maspero, *Recueil*, t. IV, p. 68). In the XVIIIth dynasty l. 169 was copied on a wall in the temple of Ḥātshepset at Dêr al-Baharî (see Dümichen, *Hist. Inschriften*, Bll. 25–37; Maspero, *Recueil*, t. I, pp. 195 ff.); and copies of ll. 379–99 occur in the papyri of Mut-ḥetep (British Museum, No. 10010) and Nefer-uben-f (Paris, No. 3092. See Naville, *Todtenbuch*, Bd. I, Bl. 197; *Aeg. Zeitschrift*, Bd. XXXII, p. 3; and Naville, Einleitung, pp. 39, 97). In the XXVIth dynasty we find texts of the Vth dynasty repeated on the walls of the tomb of Peṭa-Åmen-åpt, the chief *kher-ḥeb* at Thebes (see Dümichen, *Der Grabpalast des Patuamenap in der Thebanischen Nekropolis*, Leipzig, 1884–85); and also upon the papyrus written for the lady Sais , about A.D. 200 (see Devéria, *Catalogue des MSS. Égyptiens*, Paris, 1874, p. 170, No. 3155). Signor Schiaparelli's words are:—"Esso è scritto in ieratico, di un tipo paleografico speciale: l'enorme "abbondanza di segni espletivi, la frequenza di segni o quasi demotici "o quasi geroglifici, la sottigliezza di tutti, e l'incertezza con cui sono "tracciati, che rivela una mano più abituata a scrivere in greco che in "egiziano, sono altrettanti caratteri del tipo ieratico del periodo esclusiva-"mente romano, a cui il nostro papiro appartiene senza alcun dubbio.' *Il Libro dei Funerali*, p. 19. On Devéria's work in connection with this MS., see Maspero, *Le Rituel du sacrifice Funéraire* (in *Revue de l'Histoire des Religions*, t. XV, p. 161).

made by M. Lacau from the coffins of Al-Barshah, and published by him in *Recueil de Travaux*, t. 26–27, 28–33.

II. The **Theban Recension,** which was commonly written upon papyri and painted upon coffins in hieroglyphs and was divided into sections or chapters, each of which had its distinct title but no definite place in the series. The version was much used from the XVIIIth to the XXIInd dynasty. This Recension was also written upon papyri in the hieratic character and in hieroglyphs.

III. The so-called **Saïte Recension,** in which, at some period, anterior probably to the XXVIth dynasty, the chapters were arranged in a definite order. It is written upon coffins, papyri, etc., in hieroglyphs, and in hieratic and in demotic, and it was much used from the XXVIth dynasty to the end of the Ptolemaic Period.

The title of **Book of the Dead** has been usually given by Egyptologists to the Theban and Saïte Recensions, but in this Introduction the term is intended to include the general body of religious texts which deal with the welfare of the dead and their new life in the world beyond the grave, and which are known to have existed and to have been in use among the Egyptians from about 4000 B.C. to the early centuries of the Christian era.

The Pyramid Texts represent the oldest form of the Book of the Dead known to us, and although we have only copies of them which were written for kings, and none which were written for priests, officials, and private gentlemen, it is not right to conclude from this fact that copies were not made for persons other than kings and to seek to make a distinction between the Heliopolitan and the later Recensions of the Book of the Dead. The *maṣṭabah* tombs of the IVth dynasty prove that the Liturgy of Funerary Offerings and the Book of Opening the Mouth were recited for the benefit of ecclesiastical and civil officials, and there is no reason for doubting that copies of sections of the Pyramid Texts were made for their benefit.

The earliest tombs found in Egypt prove that the primitive Egyptians disposed of their dead partly by burial, and partly by burning, but there are no grounds whatever for assuming that *all* the dead were buried and burned, for from time immemorial it has always been the custom in Africa, and still is in many parts of that continent, to allow the bodies of all except kings, governors, nobles, and men of high rank, to be devoured by wild animals, or to be consumed by the myriads of flesh-destroying insects which infest the ground. The bodies which were buried were either dismembered or buried whole. Bodies which were buried in graves were laid on their left sides with their heads to the south, and they were sometimes wrapped in skins of animals, or reeds, or grass mats. Bodies were cut in pieces for two reasons, to save space in a country where land was peculiarly valuable, and to prevent the spirits of the dead from returning and re-occupying their old bodies. In cases where fire was used in disposing of the dead, the bodies were only partially burnt, and the bones were collected and thrown into a shallow pit, care being taken to keep the head and the hands together. At this period it is certain that offerings were made to the dead, and it is quite clear that both those to whom the offerings were made, and those who made them, held very definite views about the future life in the Other World. They were quite certain that men did not perish finally when they died, and that some part of a man departed after death to some place where he would renew his life in some form, according to the dictates of some divine being.

The inhabitants of Egypt who disposed of their dead by burial and burning could not write, and therefore they could not have possessed any collection of religious texts which could be regarded as the foundations of the Book of the Dead now known to us, and it is most unlikely that they made use of any religious formulae when they buried or burned their dead. There are many passages in the Book of the Dead containing references to the burial customs of the primitive Egyptians, which indicate that the aborigines possessed a low form of religious belief. They cannot, however, in any way be regarded as the founders of the Book of the Dead, because that work presupposes the existence of ideas which the aborigines did not possess, and refers to an elaborate system of sepulture which they never practised. Whatever views may be held as to the origin of the Egyptians, it is quite certain that the aborigines of

Egypt employed a system of sepulture which was quite different from that which was in use among their latest predynastic and their earliest dynastic descendants.

From what has been said above it is clear that the earliest inhabitants of Egypt made no attempt to mummify their dead in the strict sense of the term. Still, as Dr. Fouquet has found traces of bitumen in some predynastic skeletons, we may assume that the primitive Egyptians would have taken far more elaborate precautions to preserve their dead had they possessed the necessary knowledge. As soon as the Egyptians began to mummify their dead, in other words, to preserve the body in a complete form, they also began to perform funerary ceremonies of a symbolic nature, and to recite formulae and prayers which were believed to cause great benefit to the dead. The greatest importance was attached to such ceremonies and formulae, for it was thought that they would endow the dead body with power to resist corruption, would ensure it a renewed and beatified existence with the gods, and would preserve it for ever. The great change which took place in the religious views of the Egyptians a little before the beginning of dynastic history was, I believe, due entirely to the rise and spread of the cult of Osiris throughout Egypt. Whether it was introduced into Egypt by a people coming from the shores of the Mediterranean, or by a Libyan tribe, or by "proto-Semites" from the east or south-east, or whether it was of purely native growth, need not concern us here. What is all-important to note is that the teachers of the cult of Osiris preached that the dead body of a man was a sacred thing, and that it was not to be devoured by men or beasts, or burnt, or mutilated. On the contrary, it must, if the wish of Osiris was to be considered, be taken the greatest care of, and embalmed, and buried in a carefully concealed tomb. But why? The preservation of the body was of vital importance, because the dogma of Osiris taught that from it would spring the translucent, transparent, immaterial, refulgent and glorious envelope in which the Spirit-soul of the deceased would take up its abode with all his mental and spiritual attributes.

The evidence derived from the enormous mass of new material which we owe to the all-important discoveries of *maṣṭabah* tombs and pyramids by M. Maspero, and to his publication of the early religious texts, proves beyond all doubt that all the essential texts comprised in the Book of the Dead are, in one form or another, far older than the period of Menȧ (Menes), the first historical king of Egypt.[1] Certain sections, indeed, appear to belong to the Predynastic Period.

The earliest texts bear within themselves proofs, not only of having been composed, but also of having been revised, or edited, long before the copies known to us were made, and, judging from many passages in the copies inscribed in hieroglyphs upon the pyramids of Unȧs (the last king of the Vth dynasty, about 3333 B.C.), and Tetȧ, Pepi I., Meḥti-em-sa-f, and Pepi II (kings of the VIth dynasty, about 3300–3166 B.C.), it would seem that, even at that remote date, the scribes were perplexed and hardly understood the texts which they had before them.[2] The most moderate estimate makes certain sections of the Book

[1] " Les textes des Pyramides . . . . . nous reportent si loin dans le " passé que je n'ai aucun moyen de les dater que de dire qu'elles étaient " déjà vieilles cinq mille ans avant notre ère. Si extraordinaire que " paraisse ce chiffre, il faudra bien nous habituer à le considérer comme " représentant une évaluation *à minima* toutes les fois qu'on voudra " rechercher les origines de la religion Égyptienne. La religion et les " textes qui nous la font connaître étaient déjà constitués avant la Ire " dynastie : c'est à nous de nous mettre, pour les comprendre, dans l'état " d'esprit où était, il y a plus de sept mille ans, le peuple qui les a constitués. " Bien entendu, je ne parle ici que des systèmes théologiques : si nous " voulions remonter jusqu'à l'origine des éléments qu'ils ont mis en œuvre, " il nous faudrait reculer vers des âges encore plus lointains." Maspero, *La Religion Égyptienne* (in *Revue de l'Histoire des Religions*, t. XIX, p. 12; and in *Études de Mythologie et d'Archéologie Égyptiennes*, t. II, p. 236). Compare also " dass die einzelnen Texte selbst damals schon einer alten " heiligen Litteratur angehörten, unterliegt keinen Zweifel, sie sind in jeder " Hinsicht alterthümlicher als die ältesten uns erhaltenen Denkmäler. Sie " gehören in eine für uns 'vorhistorische' Zeit und man wird ihnen gewiss " kein Unrecht anthun, wenn man sie bis in das vierte Jahrtausend hinein " versetzt." Erman, *Das Verhältniss des aegyptischen zu den semitischen Sprachen*, in *Z.D.M.G.*, Bd. XLVI, p. 94.

[2] " Le nombre des prières et des formules dirigées contre les animaux " venimeux montre quel effroi le serpent et le scorpion inspirait aux " Égyptiens. Beaucoup d'entre elles sont écrites dans une langue et avec " des combinaisons de signes qui ne paraissent plus avoir été complète- " ment comprises des scribes qui les copiaient sous Ounas et sous Pepi. " Je crois, quant à moi, qu'elles appartiennent au plus vieux rituel et " remontent au delà du règne de Mînî." Maspero, *La Religion Égyptienne* (in *Revue de l'Histoire des Religions*, t. XII, p. 125). See also *Recueil de Travaux*, t. IV, p. 62.

of the Dead as known from these tombs older than three thousand years before Christ. We are in any case justified in estimating the earliest form of the work to be contemporaneous with the foundation of the civilization[1] which we call Egyptian in the valley of the Nile.[2] To fix a chronological limit for the arts and civilization of Egypt is absolutely impossible.[3]

The oldest form or edition of the Book of the Dead as we have received it supplies no information whatever as to the period when it was compiled; but a copy of the hieratic text inscribed upon a coffin of Queen Khnem-Nefert, the wife of Menthu-ḥetep, a king of the XIth dynasty,[4] about 2500 B.C., made by the late Sir J. G. Wilkinson,[5] informs us that the Chapter which, according to the arrangement of Lepsius, bears the number LXIV,[6] was discovered in the reign of Ḥesep-ti,[7] the fifth king of the Ist dynasty, about 4266 B.C. On this coffin are two copies of the Chapter, the one immediately following the other. In the Rubric to the first the name of the king during whose reign the Chapter is said to have been "found" is given as Menthu-ḥetep, which, as Goodwin first pointed out,[8] is a mistake

1 "So sind wir gezwungen, wenigstens die ersten Grundlagen des "Buches den Anfängen der Aegyptischen Civilisation beizumessen." See Naville, *Das Aegyptische Todtenbuch* (Einleitung), Berlin, 1886, p. 18.

2 The date of Menȧ is variously given as 5869 B.C. (Champollion), 5004 B.C. (Mariette), 4455 B.C. (Brugsch), 3893 B.C. (Lieblein), 5510 B.C. (Petrie), 3892 B.C. (Lepsius), 3623 B.C. (Bunsen).

3 See Chabas, *Aeg. Zeitschrift*, 1865, p. 95. On the subject of the Antiquity of Egyptian Civilization generally, see Chabas, *Études sur l'Antiquité Historique d'après les Sources Égyptiennes*, Paris, 1873—Introduction, p. 9, and see especially de Morgan, *Recherches*, Paris, 1897; *L'Âge de la pierre et les Métaux*, Paris, 1896; *Les Premières Civilisations*, Paris, 1909.

4 The name of the queen and her titles are given thus:—

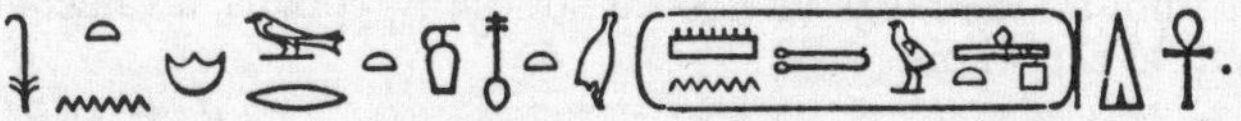

5 It was presented to the British Museum in 1834, and is now in the Department of Egyptian and Assyrian Antiquities. A facsimile of this copy is published by Budge, *Egyptian Hieratic Papyri*, London, 1910.

6 *Todtenbuch*, Bl. 23–25.

7 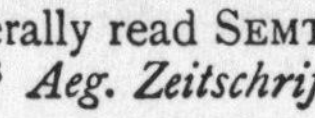 the Οὐσαφαῒς υἱὸς of Manetho. The name is now generally read SEMTI.

8 *Aeg. Zeitschrift*, 1866, p. 54.

for Men-kau-Rā,[1] the fourth king of the IVth dynasty, about 3633 B.C.;[2] but in the Rubric to the second the king's name is given as Ḥesep-ti. Thus it appears that in the period of the XIth dynasty it was believed that the Chapter might alternatively be as old as the time of the Ist dynasty. Further, it is given to Ḥesep-ti in papyri of the XXIst dynasty,[3] a period when particular attention was paid to the history of the Book of the Dead; and it thus appears that the Egyptians of the New Empire believed the Chapter to date from the more remote period. To quote the words of Chabas, the Chapter was regarded as being "very ancient, very mysterious, and very difficult to understand" already fourteen centuries before our era.[4]

The Rubric on the coffin of Queen Khnem-Nefert, which ascribes the Chapter to Ḥesep-ti, states that "this "Chapter was found in the foundations beneath the "Dweller in the *Ḥennu* Boat by the foreman of the builders "in the time of the king of the South and North, Ḥesep-ti, "whose word is truth";[5] the Nebseni Papyrus says that "this Chapter was found in the city of Khemenu "(Hermopolis) on a block of alabaster written in letters of

[1] See Guieyesse, *Rituel Funéraire Égyptien*, chapitre 64ᵉ, Paris, 1876, p. 10, note 2.

[2] The late recension of the Book of the Dead published by Lepsius also gives the king's name as Men-kau-Rā (*Todtenbuch*, B[1] 25, l. 31). In the same recension the CXXXth Chapter is ascribed to the reign of Ḥesep-ti (Bl. 53, l. 28). See also Budge, *The Chapters of Coming Forth by Day*, Chapter LXIV.

[3] Naville, *Todtenbuch* (Einleitung), pp. 33, 139.

[4] Chabas, *Voyage d'un Égyptien*, p. 46. According to M. Naville (Einleitung, p. 138), who follows Chabas's opinion, this Chapter is an abridgment of the whole Book of the Dead; and it had, even though it contained not all the religious doctrine of the Egyptians, a value which was equivalent to the whole.

[5] . See Goodwin, *Aeg. Zeitschrift*, 1866, p. 55, and compare the reading from the Cairo Papyrus of Mes-em-neter given by Naville (*Todtenbuch*, II, p. 139).

"lapis-lazuli, under the feet of the god";[1] and the Turin Papyrus (XXVIth dynasty or later) adds that the name of the finder was Ḥeru-ṭā-ṭā-f, [hieroglyphs], the son of Khufu or Cheops,[2] the second king of the IVth dynasty, about 3733 B.C., who was at the time making a tour of inspection of the temples. Birch[3] and Naville[4] consider the Chapter one of the oldest in the Book of the Dead; the former basing his opinion on the Rubric, and the latter upon the evidence derived from the contents and character of the text: but Maspero, while admitting the great age of the Chapter, does not attach any very great importance to the Rubric as fixing any exact date for its composition.[5]

[1] See Budge, *The Chapters of Coming Forth by Day*, Chapter LXIV.

[2] Lepsius, *Todtenbuch*, Bl. 25, l. 31.

[3] The most remarkable Chapter . . . . . is the 64th . . . . . It is one "of the oldest of all, and is attributed, as already stated, to the epoch of "King Gaga-Makheru [cartouche], or Menkheres . . . . . This "Chapter enjoyed a high reputation till a late period, for it is found on "a stone presented to General Peroffsky by the late Emperor Nicholas, "which must have come from the tomb of Petemenophis,* in "El-Assasif,† and was made during the XXVIth dynasty . . . . "Some more recent compiler of the Hermetic books has evidently para-"phrased it for the Ritual of Turin." Bunsen, *Egypt's Place in Universal History*, London, 1867, p. 142. The block of stone to which Dr. Birch refers is described by Golénischeff, *Ermitage Impérial, Inventaire de la Collection Égyptienne*, No. 1101, pp. 169, 170. There is an electrotype of this stone in the British Museum (No. 29553). I have published a copy of the texts on it (Chapters XXVI, XXXB, and LXIV) in my *Chapters of Coming Forth by Day*, Vol. III, pp. 241 ff., London, 1910. M. Maspero thinks it was meant to be a "prétendu fac-similé" of the original slab, which, according to the Rubric, was found in the temple of Thoth, *Revue de l'Historie des Religions*, t. xv, p. 299, and *Études de Mythologie*, t. I, p. 368.

[4] *Todtenbuch* (Einleitung), p. 139. Sir P. Renouf also held this opinion, *Trans. Soc. Bibl. Arch.*, 1893, p. 6.

[5] "On explique d'ordinaire cette indication comme une marque "d'antiquité extrême; on part de ce principe que le *Livre des Morts* est de "composition relativement moderne, et qu'un scribe égyptien, nommant "un roi des premières dynasties memphites, ne pouvait entendre par là "qu'un personnage d'époque très reculée. Cette explication ne me paraît "pas être exacte. En premier lieu, le chapitre LXIV se trouve déjà sur

---

* *I.e.*, [hieroglyphs], the "chief reader," many of the inscriptions on whose tomb have been published by Dümichen, *Der Grabpalast des Patuamenap;* Leipzig, 1884, 1885.

† *I.e.*, Asasîf al-Baḥrîyah, or Asasif of the North, behind Dêr al-Baḥarî, on the western bank of the Nile, opposite Thebes.

Of Ḥeruṭāṭāf, the finder of the block of stone, we know from later texts that he was considered to be a learned man, and that his speech was only with difficulty to be understood,[1] and we also know the prominent part which he took as a recognized man of letters in bringing to the Court of his father Khufu the Sage Ṭeṭȧ.[2] It is then not improbable that Ḥeruṭāṭāf's character for learning may have suggested the connection of his name with the Chapter, possibly as its literary reviser; at all events as early as the period of the Middle Empire, tradition associated him with it.

Passing from the region of native Egyptian tradition, we touch firm ground with the evidence derived from the

---

" des monuments contemporains de la Xe et de la XIe dynastie, et n'était " certainement pas nouveau au moment où on écrivait les copies les plus " vieilles que nous en ayons aujourd'hui. Lorsqu'on le rédigea sous sa " forme actuelle, le règne de Mykérinos, et même celui d'Housapaïti, " ne devaient pas soulever dans l'esprit des indigènes la sensation de " l'archaïsme et du primitif : on avait pour rendre ces idées des expressions " plus fortes, qui renvoyaient le lecteur au siècles des *Serviteurs d'Horus*, à " la domination de Rā, aux âges où les dieux régnaient sur l'Egypte." *Revue de l'Histoire des Religions*, t. XV, p. 299.

[1] Chabas, *Voyage*, p. 46; Wiedemann, *Aegyptische Geschichte*, p. 191. In the Brit. Mus. Papyrus No. 10060 (Harris 500), Ḥeruṭāṭāf is mentioned together with I-em-ḥetep as a well-known author, and the writer of the dirge says: "I have heard the words of I-em-ḥetep and of Heruṭāṭāf, " whose many and varied writings are said and sung; but now where are " their places?" The hieratic text is published with a hieroglyphic transcript by Maspero in *Journal Asiatique*, Sér. VIIième, t. XV, p. 404 ff., and *Études Égyptiennes*, t. I, p. 173; for English translations, see *Trans. Soc. Bibl. Arch.*, Vol. III, p. 386, and *Records of the Past*, 1st ed., Vol. IV, p. 117.

[2] According to the Westcar Papyrus, Ḥeruṭāṭāf informed his father Khufu of the existence of a man 110 years old who lived in the town of Ṭeṭ-Seneferu: he was able to join to its body again a head that had been cut off, and possessed influence over the lion, and was acquainted with the mysteries of Thoth. By Khufu's command Ḥeruṭāṭāf brought the sage to him by boat, and, on his arrival, the king ordered the head to be struck off from a prisoner that Ṭeṭȧ might fasten it on again. Having excused himself from performing this act upon a man, a goose was brought and its head was cut off and laid on one side of the room and the body was placed on the other. The sage spake certain words of power, whereupon the goose stood up and began to waddle, and the head also began to move towards it; when the head had joined itself again to the body the bird stood up and cackled. For the complete hieratic text, transcript, and translation, see Erman, *Die Märchen des Papyrus Westcar*, Berlin, 1890, p. 11, Plate 6.

monuments of the IInd dynasty. A bas-relief preserved at Aix in Provence mentions Åasen and Ånkef,[1] two of the priests of Senṭ or Senṭå, the fifth king of the IInd dynasty, about 4000 B.C.; and a stele at Oxford[2] and another in the Egyptian Museum at Gîzah[3] record the name of a third priest, Sherå[4] or Sheri, a "royal relative". On the stele at Oxford are represented the deceased and his wife seated, one on each side of an altar,[5] which is covered with funerary offerings of pious relatives; above, in perpendicular lines of hieroglyphs in relief, are the names of the objects offered,[6] and below is an inscription which reads:[7] "thousands of loaves "of bread, thousands of vases of ale, thousands of linen "garments, thousands of changes of wearing apparel, and "thousands of oxen."[8] Now from this monument it is evident that already in the IInd dynasty a priesthood existed in Egypt which numbered among its members

1 Wiedemann, *Aegyptische Geschichte*, p. 170. In a *maṣṭabah* at Ṣaḳḳârah we have a stele of Sheri, a superintendent of the priests of the *ka*, whereon the cartouches of Senṭ and Per-åb-sen both occur. See Mariette and Maspero, *Les Mastaba de l'ancien Empire*, Paris, 1882, p. 92.

2 See Lepsius, *Auswahl*, Bl. 9.

3 See Maspero, *Guide du Visiteur au Musée de Boulaq*, 1883, pp. 31, 32, and 213 (No. 1027).

4 There is also a slab from Sherå's tomb in the British Museum. See *Guide to the Egyptian Galleries*, p. 1, No. 1.

5 A discussion on the method of depicting this altar on Egyptian monuments by Borchardt may be found in *Aeg. Zeitschrift*, Bd. XXXI, p. 1 (*Die Darstellung innen verzierter Schalen auf aeg. Denkmälern*).

6 Among others, (1), (2), (3), (4); the word incense is written twice. Some of these appear in the lists of offerings made for Unås (l. 147) and for Tetå (ll. 125, 131, 133; see *Recueil de Travaux*, 1884, Plate 2).

7 .

8 The sculptor had no room for the belonging to .

relatives of the royal family, and that a religious system which prescribed as a duty the providing of meat and drink offerings for the dead was also in active operation. The offering of specific objects goes far to prove the existence of a ritual or service wherein their signification would be indicated; the coincidence of these words and the prayer for "thousands of loaves of bread, thousands of vases of ale," etc., with the promise, "Ȧnpu-khent-Ȧmenta shall give "thee thy thousands of loaves of bread, thy thousands of "vases of ale, thy thousands of vessels of unguents, thy "thousands of changes of apparel, thy thousands of oxen, "and thy thousands of bullocks," enables us to recognise that ritual in the text inscribed upon the pyramid of Tetȧ in the VIth dynasty, from which the above promise is taken.[1] Thus the evidence of the text on the coffin of the wife of Menthu-ḥetep and the scene on the monument of Sherȧ support one another, and together they prove beyond a doubt that a form of the Book of the Dead was in use at least in the period of the earliest dynasties, and that sepulchral ceremonies connected therewith were duly performed.[2]

[1] 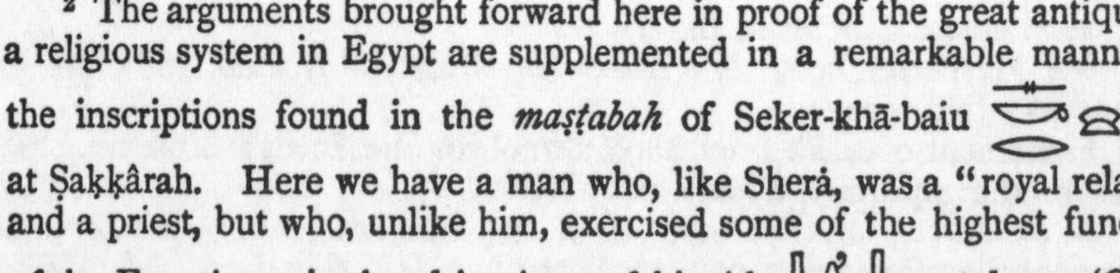, Tetȧ, ll. 388, 389. (*Recueil*, ed. Maspero, t. V, p. 58.)

[2] The arguments brought forward here in proof of the great antiquity of a religious system in Egypt are supplemented in a remarkable manner by the inscriptions found in the *maṣṭabah* of Seker-khā-baiu [hieroglyphs] at Ṣaḳḳârah. Here we have a man who, like Sherȧ, was a "royal relative" and a priest, but who, unlike him, exercised some of the highest functions of the Egyptian priesthood in virtue of his title [hieroglyphs] *χerp ḥem.* (On the [hieroglyphs] * see Max Müller, *Recueil de Travaux*, t. IX, p. 166; Brugsch, *Aegyptologie*, p. 218; and Maspero, *Un Manuel de Hiérarchie Égyptienne*, p. 9.) Among the offerings named in the tomb are the substances [hieroglyphs] and [hieroglyphs] which are also mentioned on the stele of Sherȧ of the IInd dynasty, and in the texts of the VIth dynasty. But the tomb of Seker-khā-baiu is different from any other known to us, both as

* Ptaḥ-shepses bore this title; see Mariette and Maspero, *Les Mastaba*, p. 113.

With the IVth dynasty we have an increased number of monuments, chiefly sepulchral, which give details as to the Egyptian sacerdotal system and the funeral ceremonies which the priests performed.[1] The inscriptions upon the earlier monuments prove that many of the priestly officials were still relatives of the royal family, and the tombs of feudal lords, scribes, and others, record a number of their official titles, together with the names of several of their religious festivals. The subsequent increase in the number of the monuments during this period may be due to the natural development of the religion of the time, but it is very probable that the greater security of life and property which had been assured by the vigorous wars of Seneferu,[2] the first king of this dynasty, about 3766 B.C., encouraged men to incur greater expense, and to build larger and better abodes for the dead, and to celebrate the full ritual at the prescribed festivals. In this dynasty the royal dead were honoured with sepulchral monuments of a greater size and

---

regards the form and cutting of the hieroglyphs, which are in relief, and the way in which they are disposed and grouped. The style of the whole monument is rude and very primitive, and it cannot be attributed to any dynasty later than the IInd, or even to the IInd itself; it must, therefore, have been built during the Ist dynasty, or in the words of MM. Mariette and Maspero, "L'impression générale que l'on reçoit au premier "aspect du tombeau No. 5, est celle d'une extrême antiquité. Rien en "effet de ce que nous sommes habitués à voir dans les autres tombeaux ne "se retrouve ici . . . Le monument . . . . est certainement le plus ancien "de ceux que nous connaissons dans la plaine de Saqqarah, et il n'y a pas "de raison pour qu'il ne soit pas de la Ire Dynastie." *Les Mastaba de l'ancien Empire:* Paris, 1882, p. 73. But because there is no incontrovertible proof that this tomb belongs to the Ist dynasty, the texts on the stele of Sherȧ, a monument of a later dynasty, have been adduced as the oldest evidences of the antiquity of a fixed religious system and literature in Egypt.

[1] Many of the monuments commonly attributed to this dynasty should more correctly be described as being the work of the IInd dynasty; see Maspero, *Geschichte der Morgenländischen Völker im Alterthum* (trans. Pietschmann), Leipzig, 1877, p. 56; Wiedemann, *Aegyptische Geschichte*, p. 170.

[2] He conquered the peoples in the Sinaitic Peninsula, and according to a text of a later date he built a wall to keep out the Aamu from Egypt. In the story of Saneha a "pool of Seneferu" is mentioned, which shows that his name was well known on the frontiers of Egypt. See Golénischeff, *Aeg. Zeitschrift*, p. 110; Maspero, *Mélanges d'Archéologie*, t. III, Paris, 1876, p. 71, l. 2; Lepsius, *Denkmäler*, II, 2*a*.

magnificence than had ever before been contemplated, and the chapels attached to the pyramids were served by courses of priests whose sole duties consisted in celebrating the services. The fashion of building a pyramid instead of the rectangular flat-roofed *maṣṭabah* for a royal tomb was revived by Seneferu,[1] who called his pyramid Khā; and his example was followed by his immediate successors, Khufu (Cheops), Khāf-Rā (Chephren), Men-kau-Rā (Mycerinus), and others.

In the reign of Mycerinus some important work seems to have been undertaken in connection with certain sections of the text of the Book of the Dead, for the Rubrics of Chapters XXXB and CXLVIII[2] state that these compositions were found inscribed upon "a block of alabaster of "the south in letters of real lapis-lazuli under the feet of "the majesty of the god in the time of the King of the "South and North Men-kau-Rā, by the royal son Ḥeru-"ṭāṭāf, whose word is truth." That a new impulse should be given to religious observances, and that the revision of existing religious texts should take place in the reign of Mycerinus, was only to be expected if Greek tradition may be believed, for both Herodotus and Diodorus Siculus represent him as a just king, and one who was anxious to efface from the minds of the people the memory of the alleged cruelty of his predecessor by re-opening the temples and by letting every man celebrate his own sacrifices and discharge his own religious duties.[3] His pyramid is the one now known as the "third pyramid of Gîzah," under which he was buried in a chamber vertically below the apex and sixty feet below the level of the ground. Whether the pyramid was finished or not[4] when the king died, his body was certainly laid in it, and notwithstanding all the attempts made by the Muḥammadan rulers of Egypt[5] to

[1] The building of the pyramid of Mêdûm has usually been attributed to Seneferu, but the excavations made there in 1882 did nothing to clear up the uncertainty which exists on this point; for recent excavations see Petrie, *Medum*, London, 1892, 4to.

[2] For the text see my *Chapters of Coming Forth by Day.* 2nd ed.

[3] Herodotus, II, 129, 1; Diodorus, I, 64, 9.

[4] According to Diodorus, he died before it was completed (I, 64, 7).

[5] According to 'Abd al-Laṭîf the Khalif's name was Mâmûn, but M. de Sacy doubted that he was the first to attempt this work; the authorities on the subject are all given in his *Relation de l'Égypte*, Paris, 1810, pp. 215–221.

destroy it at the end of the twelfth century of our era, it has survived to yield up important facts for the history of the Book of the Dead.

In 1837 Colonel Howard Vyse succeeded in forcing the entrance. On the 29th of July he commenced operations, and on the 1st of August he made his way into the sepulchral chamber, where, however, nothing was found but a rectangular stone sarcophagus[1] without the lid. The large stone slabs of the floor and the linings of the wall had been in many instances removed by thieves in search of treasure. In a lower chamber, connected by a passage with the sepulchral chamber, was found the greater part of the lid of the sarcophagus,[2] together with portions of a wooden coffin, and part of the body of a man, consisting of ribs and vertebrae and the bones of the legs and feet,

---

Tradition, as represented in the "Arabian Nights," says that Al-Mâmûn was minded to pull down the pyramids, and that he expended a mint of money in the attempt; he succeeded, however, only in opening up a small tunnel in one of them, wherein it is said he found treasure to the exact amount of the moneys which he had spent in the work, and neither more nor less. The Arabic writer Idrîsî, who wrote about A.H. 623 (A.D. 1226), states that a few years ago the "Red Pyramid," *i.e.*, that of Mycerinus, was opened on the north side. After passing through various passages a room was reached wherein was found a long blue vessel, quite empty. The opening into this pyramid was effected by people in search of treasure; they worked at it with axes for six months, and they in great numbers. They found in this basin, after they had broken the covering of it, the decayed remains of a man, but no treasure, excepting some golden tablets inscribed with characters of a language which nobody could understand. Each man's share of these tablets amounted to 100 dinars (about £50). Other legendary history says that the western pyramid contains thirty chambers of parti-coloured syenite full of precious gems and costly weapons anointed with unguents that they may not rust until the day of the Resurrection. See Howard Vyse, *The Pyramids of Gizeh*, Vol. II, pp. 71, 72; and Burton, *The Book of the Thousand Nights and a Night*, 1885, Vol. V, p. 105, and Vol. X, p. 150.

[1] Vyse, *The Pyramids of Gizeh*, Vol. II, p. 84. A fragment of this sarcophagus is exhibited in the British Museum, First Egyptian Room, Case B, No. 6646.

[2] With considerable difficulty this interesting monument was brought out from the pyramid by Mr. Raven, and having been cased in strong timbers, was sent off to the British Museum. It was embarked at Alexandria in the autumn of 1838, on board a merchant ship, which was supposed to have been lost off Carthagena, as she never was heard of after her departure from Leghorn on the 12th of October in that year, and as some parts of the wreck were picked up near the former port. The sarcophagus is figured by Vyse, *Pyramids*, Vol. II, Plate facing p. 84.

enveloped in a coarse woollen cloth of a yellow colour, to which a small quantity of resinous substance and gum adhered.[1] It would therefore seem that, as the sarcophagus could not be removed, the wooden case alone containing the body had been brought into the large apartment for examination. Now, whether the human remains[2] there found are those of Mycerinus or of some one else, as some have suggested, in no way affects the question of the ownership of the coffin, for we know by the hieroglyphic inscription upon it that it was made to hold the mummified body of the king. This inscription, which is arranged in two perpendicular lines down the front of the coffin, reads :—

1\. [Hail] Osiris, { King of the South and North, } Men-kau-Rā, living for ever, born of

heaven, conceived of Nut, heir of Ḳeb, his beloved.

Spreadeth herself thy mother 2. Nut over thee in her name of

[1] As considerable misapprehension about the finding of these remains has existed, the account of the circumstances under which they were discovered will be of interest. "Sir, by your request, I send you the " particulars of the finding of the bones, mummy-cloth, and parts of the " coffin in the Third Pyramid. In clearing the rubbish out of the large " entrance-room, after the men had been employed there several days and " had advanced some distance towards the South-eastern corner, some " bones were first discovered at the bottom of the rubbish; and the " remaining bones and parts of the coffin were immediately discovered all " together. No other parts of the coffin or bones could be found in the " room; I therefore had the rubbish which had been previously turned out " of the same room carefully re-examined, when several pieces of the coffin " and of the mummy-cloth were found; but in no other part of the pyramid " were any parts of it to be discovered, although every place was most " minutely examined, to make the coffin as complete as possible. There " was about three feet of rubbish on the top of the same; and from the " circumstance of the bones and part of the coffin being all found together, " it appeared as if the coffin had been brought to that spot and there " unpacked.—H. Raven." Vyse, *Pyramids*, Vol. II, p. 86.

[2] They are exhibited in the First Egyptian Room, Case B, with the fragments of the coffin.

"mystery of heaven," she granteth that thou mayest exist as a god to

thy foes, {O King of the South and North,} Men-kau-Rā, living for ever!

Now it is to be noted that the passage "Thy mother "Nut spreadeth herself over thee in her name of 'Mystery "of Heaven,' she granteth that thou mayest be without "enemies," occurs in the texts which are inscribed upon the pyramids built by the kings of the VIth dynasty,[1] and thus we have evidence of the use of the same version of one religious text both in the IVth and in the VIth dynasties.[2]

Even if we were to admit that the coffin is a forgery of the XXVIth dynasty, and that the inscription upon it was taken from an edition of the text of the Book of the Dead, still the value of the monument as an evidence of the antiquity of the Book of the Dead is scarcely impaired,

[1] See the texts of Tetà and Pepi I, in Maspero, *Recueil de Travaux*, t. V, pp. 20, 38 (ll. 175, 279), and pp. 165, 173 (ll. 60, 103), etc.

[2] So far back as 1883, M. Maspero, in lamenting (*Guide du Visiteur de Boulaq*, p. 310) the fact that the Bûlâq Museum possessed only portions of wooden coffins of the Ancient Empire and no complete example, noticed that the coffin of Mycerinus, preserved in the British Museum, had been declared by certain Egyptologists to be a "restoration" of the XXVIth dynasty, rather than the work of the IVth dynasty, in accordance with the inscription upon it; but like Dr. Birch he was of opinion that the coffin certainly belonged to the IVth dynasty, and adduced in support of his views the fact of the existence of portions of a similar coffin of Seker-em-sa-f, a king of the VIth dynasty. Later, however, another attempt was made (*Aeg. Zeitschrift*, Bd. XXX, pp. 94 ff.) to prove by the agreement of the variants in the text on the coffin of Mycerinus with those of texts of the XXVIth dynasty, that the Mycerinus text is of this late period, or at all events not earlier than the time of Psammetichus. But it is admitted on all hands that in the XXVIth dynasty the Egyptians resuscitated texts of the first dynasties of the Early Empire, and that they copied the arts and literature of that period as far as possible, and, this being so, the texts on the monuments which have been made the standard of comparison for that on the coffin of Mycerinus may be themselves at fault in their variants. If the text on the cover could be proved to differ as much from an undisputed IVth dynasty text as it does from those even of the VIth dynasty, the philological argument might have some weight; but even this would not get rid of the fact that the cover itself is a genuine relic of the IVth dynasty.

for those who added the inscription would certainly have chosen it from a text of the time of Mycerinus.

In the Vth dynasty we have, in an increased number of *maṣṭabahs* and other monuments, evidence of the extension of religious ceremonials, including the celebration of funeral rites; but a text forming the Book of the Dead as a whole does not occur until the reign of Unȧs (3333 B.C.), the last king of the dynasty, who according to the Turin Papyrus reigned thirty years. This monarch built on the plain of Ṣaḳḳârah a stone pyramid about sixty-two feet high, each side measuring about two hundred feet at the base. In the time of Perring and Vyse it was surrounded by heaps of broken stone and rubbish, the result of repeated attempts to open it, and with the casing stones, which consisted of compact limestone from the quarries of Ṭura.[1] In February, 1881, M. Maspero began to clear the pyramid, and soon after he succeeded in making an entrance into the innermost chambers, the walls of which were covered with hieroglyphic inscriptions, arranged in perpendicular lines and painted in green.[2] The condition of the interior showed that at some time or other thieves had already succeeded in making an entrance, for the cover of the black basalt sarcophagus of Unȧs had been wrenched off and moved near the door of the sarcophagus chamber; the paving stones had been pulled up in the vain attempt to find buried treasure; the mummy had been broken to pieces, and nothing remained of it except the right arm, a tibia, and some fragments of the skull and body. The inscriptions which covered certain walls and corridors in the tomb were afterwards published by M. Maspero.[3] The appearance of the text of Unȧs[4] marks an era in the history of the Book of the Dead, and its translation must be regarded as one of the greatest triumphs of Egyptological decipherment, for the want of determinatives in many places in the text, and the archaïc spelling of many of the

[1] Vyse, *Pyramids of Gizeh*, p. 51.

[2] Maspero, *Recueil de Travaux*, t. III, p. 178.

[3] See *Recueil de Travaux*, t. III, pp. 177–224; t. IV, pp. 41–78.

[4] In 1881 Dr. Brugsch described two pyramids of the VIth dynasty inscribed with religious texts similar to those found in the pyramid of Unȧs, and translated certain passages (*Aeg. Zeitschrift*, Bd. XIX, pp. 1–15); see also Birch in *Trans. Soc. Bibl. Arch.* 1881, pp. 111 ff.

words and passages presented difficulties which were not easily overcome.[1] Here, for the first time, it was shown that the Book of the Dead was no compilation of a comparatively late period in the history of Egyptian civilization, but a work belonging to a very remote antiquity; and it followed naturally that texts which were then known, and which were thought to be themselves original ancient texts, proved to be only versions which had passed through two or more successive revisions.

Continuing his excavations at Ṣaḳḳârah, M. Maspero opened the pyramid of Tetȧ,[2] king of Egypt about 3300 B.C., which Vyse thought[3] had never been entered, and of which, in his day, the masonry on one side only could be seen. Here again it was found that thieves had already been at work, and that they had smashed in pieces walls, floors, and many other parts of the chambers in their frantic search for treasure. As in the case of the pyramid of Unȧs, certain chambers, etc., of this tomb were found covered with inscriptions in hieroglyphs, but of a smaller size.[4] A brief examination of the text showed it to be formed of a series of extracts from the Book of the Dead, some of which were identical with those in the pyramid of Unȧs. Thus was brought to light a Book of the Dead of the time of the first king[5] of the VIth dynasty.

The pyramid of Pepi I, king of Egypt about 3233 B.C., was next opened.[6] It is situated in the central group at Ṣaḳḳârah, and is commonly known as the pyramid of

[1] The pyramid which bore among the Arabs the name *Maṣṭabat al-Far'ûn*, or "Pharaoh's Bench," was excavated by Mariette in 1858, and, because he found the name of Unȧs painted on certain blocks of stone, he concluded it was the tomb of Unȧs. M. Maspero's excavations have, as Dr. Lepsius observes (*Aeg. Zeitschrift*, Bd. XIX, p. 15), set the matter right.

[2] The mummy of the king had been taken out of the sarcophagus through a hole which the thieves had made in it; it was broken by them in pieces, and the only remains of it found by M. Maspero consisted of an arm and shoulder. Parts of the wooden coffin are preserved in the Gîzah Museum.

[3] *The Pyramids of Gizeh*, Vol. III, p. 39.

[4] They were copied in 1882, and published by M. Maspero in *Recueil de Travaux*, t. V, pp. 1–59.

[5] The broken mummy of this king, together with fragments of its bandages, was found lying on the floor.

[6] See Vyse, *Pyramids of Gizeh*, Vol. III, p. 51.

Shêkh Abû-Manṣûr.[1] Certain chambers and other parts of the tomb were found to be covered with hieroglyphic texts, which not only repeated in part those which had been found in the pyramids of Unȧs and Tetȧ, but also contained a considerable number of additional sections of the Book of the Dead.[2] In the same neighbourhood M. Maspero cleared out the pyramid of Mer-en-Rā, the fourth king of the VIth dynasty, about 3200 B.C.;[3] and the pyramid of Pepi II, the fifth king of the VIth dynasty, about 3166 B.C.[4]

Thus we have before the close of the VIth dynasty five copies of a series of texts which formed the Book of the Dead of that period, and an extract from a well-known passage of that work on the wooden coffin of Mycerinus; we have also seen from a number of *mastabahs* and stelae that the funeral ceremonies connected with the Book of the Dead were performed certainly in the IInd, and with almost equal certainty in the Ist dynasty. It is easy to show that certain sections of the Book of the Dead of this period were copied and used in the following dynasties down to a period about A.D. 200.

The fact that not only in the pyramids of Unȧs and

[1] It had been partially opened by Mariette in May, 1880, but the clearance of sand was not effected until early in 1881.

[2] The full text is given by Maspero in *Recueil de Travaux*, t. V, pp. 157–58, Paris, 1884; t. VII, pp. 145–76, Paris, 1886; and t. VIII, pp. 87–120, Paris, 1886; and in Sethe, *Pyramidentexte*, 2 vols.

[3] It was opened early in January, 1880, by Mariette, who seeing that the sarcophagus chamber was inscribed, abandoned his theory that pyramids never contained inscriptions, or that if they did they were not royal tombs. The hieroglyphic texts were published by Maspero in *Recueil de Travaux*, t. IX, pp. 177–91, Paris, 1887; t. X, pp. 1–29, Paris, 1888; and t. XI, pp. 1–31, Paris, 1889. The alabaster vase in the British Museum, No. 4493, came from this pyramid.

[4] This pyramid is a little larger than the others of the period, and is built in steps of small stones; it is commonly called by the Arabs *Haram al-Maṣṭabat*, because it is near the building usually called *Maṣṭabat al-Far'ûn*. See Vyse, *Pyramids*, Vol. III, p. 52. The hieroglyphic texts are published by Maspero in *Recueil de Travaux*, t. XII, pp. 53–95, and pp. 136–95, Paris, 1892, and t. XIV, pp. 125–52, Paris, 1892. There is little doubt that this pyramid was broken into more than once in Christian times, and that the early collectors of Egyptian antiquities obtained the beautiful alabaster vases inscribed with the cartouches and titles of Pepi II from those who had access to the sarcophagus chamber. Among such objects in the British Museum collection, Nos. 4492, 22559, 22758, and 22817 are fine examples.

Tetȧ, but also in those of Pepi I and his immediate successors, we find selected passages, suggests that the Book of the Dead was, even in those early times, so extensive that even a king was fain to make from it a selection only of the passages which suited his individual taste or were considered sufficient to secure his welfare in the next world. In the pyramids of Tetȧ, Pepi I, Mer-en-Rā, and Pepi II are found many texts which are identical with those employed by their predecessors, and an examination of the inscription of Pepi II will show that about three-fourths of the whole may be found in the monuments of his ancestors. What principle guided each king in the selection of his texts, or whether the additions in each represent religious developments, it is impossible to say; but, as the Egyptian religion cannot have remained stationary in every particular, it is probable that some texts reflect the changes in the opinions of the priests upon matters of doctrine.[1] The "Pyramid Texts" prove that each section of the religious books of the Egyptians was originally a separate and independent composition, that it was written with a definite object, and that it might be arranged in any order in a series of similar texts. What preceded or what followed it was never taken into consideration by the scribe, although it seems, at times, as if traditions had assigned a sequence to certain texts.

That events of contemporary history were sometimes reflected in the Book of the Dead of the early dynasties is proved by the following. We learn from the inscription upon the tomb of Ḥeru-khuf at Aswân,[2]

[1] A development has been observed in the plan of ornamenting the interiors of the pyramids of the Vth and VIth dynasties. In that of Unȧs about one-quarter of the sarcophagus chamber is covered with architectural decorations, and the hieroglyphs are large, well spaced, and enclosed in broad lines. But as we advance in the VIth dynasty, the space set apart for decorative purposes becomes less, the hieroglyphs are smaller, the lines are crowded, and the inscriptions overflow into the chambers and corridors, which in the Vth dynasty were left blank. See Maspero in *Revue des Religions*, t. XI, p. 124.

[2] The full text from this tomb and a discussion on its contents are given by Schiaparelli, *Una tomba egiziana inedita della VIª dinastia con inscrizioni storiche e geografiche*, in *Atti della R. Accademia dei Lincei*, anno CCLXXXIX, Ser. 4ª, Classe di Scienze Morali, *etc.*, t. X, Rome, 1893, pp. 22–53. This text has been treated by Erman (*Z.D.M.G.*, Bd. XLVI, 1892, pp. 574 ff.), who first pointed out the reference to the pigmy in the Pyramid Texts, and by Maspero in *Revue Critique*, Paris, 1892, p. 366.

that this governor of Elephantine was ordered to bring for King Pepi II[1] a pigmy, [hieroglyphs],[2] from the interior of Africa, to dance before the king and amuse him; and he was promised that, if he succeeded in bringing the pigmy alive and in good health, his Majesty would confer upon him a higher rank and dignity than that which King Ȧssȧ conferred upon his minister Ba-ur-Ṭeṭṭeṭ, who performed this much appreciated service for his master.[3] Now Ȧssȧ was the eighth king of the Vth dynasty, and Pepi II was the fifth king of the VIth dynasty, and between the reigns of these kings there was, according to M. Maspero, an interval of at least sixty-four, but more probably eighty, years. But in the text in the pyramid of Pepi I, which must have been drafted at some period between the reigns of these kings, we have the passage: "Hail thou who [at thy will] "makest to pass over to the Field of Ȧaru the soul that is "right and true, or dost make shipwreck of it. Rā-meri "(*i.e.* Pepi I) is right and true in respect of heaven and "in respect of earth, Pepi is right and true in respect of the "island of the earth whither he swimmeth and where he "arriveth. He who is between the thighs of Nut "(*i.e.*, Pepi) is the pigmy who danceth [like] the god, and "who pleaseth the heart of the god [Osiris] before his great "throne .... The two beings who are over the throne of "the great god proclaim Pepi to be sound and healthy, "[therefore] Pepi shall sail in the boat to the beautiful field "of the great god, and he shall do therein that which is "done by those to whom veneration is due."[4] Here clearly

[1] See Erman in *Aeg. Zeitschrift*, Bd. XXXI, pp. 65 ff.

[2] On the pigmy see Stanley, *Darkest Africa*, Vol. 1, p. 198: Vol. II, pp. 40 f.; Schweinfurth, *Im Herzen von Afrika*, Bd. II, Kap. 16, pp. 131 ff. That the pigmies paid tribute to the Egyptians is certain from the passage [hieroglyphs] "The "pigmies came to him from the lands of the South having things of service "for his palace"; see Dümichen, *Geschichte des alten Aegyptens*, Berlin, 1887, p. 7.

[3] [hieroglyphs].

[4] For the hieroglyphic text see Maspero, *Recueil de Travaux*, t. VII, pp. 162, 163; and t. XI, p. 11.

we have a reference to the historical fact of the importation of a pigmy from the regions south of Nubia; and the idea which seems to have been uppermost in the mind of him who drafted the text was that as the pigmy pleased the king for whom he was brought in this world, even so might the dead Pepi please the god Osiris[1] in the next world. As the pigmy was brought by boat to the king, so might Pepi be brought by boat to the island wherein the god dwelt; as the conditions made by the king were fulfilled by him that brought the pigmy, even so might the conditions made by Osiris concerning the dead be fulfilled by him that transported Pepi to his presence. The wording of the passage amply justifies the assumption that this addition was made to the text after the mission of Ȧssȧ, and during the VIth dynasty.[2]

Like other works of a similar nature, however, the Pyramid Texts, which represent the **Heliopolitan Recension,** afford us no information as to their authorship. In the later versions of the Book of the Dead certain Chapters[3] are stated to be the work of the god Thoth. They certainly belong to that class of literature which the Greeks called "Hermetic,"[4] and it is pretty certain that under some group they were included in the list of the forty-two works which, according to Clement of Alexandria,[5] constituted the sacred books of the Egyptians.[6] As Thoth, whom the Greeks called Hermes, is in Egyptian texts styled "lord of divine books,"[7] "scribe of the Company of the Gods,"[8] and "lord of divine speech,"[9] this ascription is well founded.

1 Pietschmann thinks (*Aeg. Zeitschrift*, Bd. XXXI, pp. 73 f.) that the Satyrs, who are referred to by Diodorus (I, XVIII) as the companions and associates of Osiris in Ethiopia, have their origin in the pigmies.

2 The whole question of the pigmy in the text of Pepi I has been discussed by Maspero in *Recueil de Travaux*, t. XIV, pp. 186 ff.

3 Chapters XXXB, CLXIV, XXXVIIB, and CXLVIII. Although these Chapters were found at Hermopolis, the city of Thoth, it does not follow that they were drawn up there.

4 See Birch, in Bunsen, *Egypt's Place in Universal History*, Vol. V, p. 125; Naville, *Todtenbuch* (Einleitung), p. 26.

5 *Stromata*, VI, 4, 35, ed. Dindorff, t. III, p. 155.

6 On the sacred books of the Egyptians see also Iamblichus, *De Mysteriis*, ed. Parthey, Berlin, 1857, pp. 260, 261; Lepsius, *Chronologie*, pp. 45 ff.; and Brugsch, *Aegyptologie*, p. 149.

7 8 9

The Pyramid Texts are versions of ancient religious compositions which the priests of the College or School of Ȧnu[1] succeeded in establishing as the authorized version of the Book of the Dead in the first six dynasties. Rā, the local form of the Sun-god, usurps the place occupied by the more ancient form Temu, but before the close of the VIth dynasty Osiris had taken his place in the Pyramid Texts as the greatest of the gods. The great influence of the Ȧnu school of priests even in the time of Unȧs is proved by the following passage from the text in his pyramid: "O God, thy Ȧnu is Unȧs; O God, thy Ȧnu is Unȧs. "O Rā, Ȧnu is Unȧs, thy Ȧnu is Unȧs, O Rā. The "mother of Unȧs is Ȧnu, the father of Unȧs is Ȧnu; Unȧs "himself is Ȧnu, and was born in Ȧnu."[2] Elsewhere we are told that Unȧs "cometh to the great bull which cometh "forth from Ȧnu,[3] and that he uttereth words of magical "import in Ȧnu."[4] In Ȧnu the god Temu produced the gods Shu and Tefnut,[5] and in Ȧnu dwelt the great and

[1] *Ȧnu*, the metropolis of the XIIIth Nome of Lower Egypt; see Brugsch, *Dict. Géog.*, p. 41; de Rougé, *Géographie Ancienne de la Basse-Égypte*, p. 81; and Amélineau, *La Géographie de l'Égypte à l'Époque Copte*, p. 287. Ȧnu is אן Genesis xli, 45; און Genesis xli, 50; אָוֶן Ezekiel xxx, 17; and Bêth Shemesh, בֵּית שֶׁמֶשׁ Jeremiah xliii, 13; and the Heliopolis of the Greek writers (Ἡλιούπολις, Strabo, XVII, i, §§ 27, 28; Herodotus, II, 3; Diodorus, I, 57, 4).

[2] Maspero, *Unȧs*, ll. 591, 592; and *cp.* Pepi I, ll. 690, 691.

[3] See l. 596.

[4] (l. 455).

[5] Maspero, *Pepi I*, ll. 465, 466.

oldest Company of the Gods, Temu, Shu, Tefnut, Ḳeb, Nut, Osiris, Isis, Set, and Nephthys.[1] The abode of the blessed in heaven was called Ȧnu,[2] and it was asserted that the souls of the just were there united to their spiritual or glorified bodies, and that they lived there face to face with the deity for all eternity.[3] Judging from the fact that the texts in the tombs of Ḥeru-ḥetep and Neferu, and those inscribed upon the sarcophagus of Ṭaḳȧ, all of the XIth and XIIth dynasties, differ in extent only and not in character or contents from those of the royal pyramids of Ṣaḳḳârah of the Vth and VIth dynasties, it has been declared that the religion as well as the art of the first Theban Empire is nothing but a slavish copy of that of Northern Egypt.[4]

[1] *The Pyramid of Pepi II*, l. 665.

[2] In reading Egyptian religious texts, the existence of the heavenly Ȧnu, which was to the Egyptians what Jerusalem was to the Jews, and what Mecca still is to the Muḥammadans, must be remembered. The heavenly Ȧnu was the capital of the mythological world (see Naville, *Todtenbuch* (Einleitung), p. 27), and was, to the spirits of men, what the earthly Ȧnu was to their bodies, *i.e.*, the abode of the gods and the centre and source of all divine instruction. Like many other mythological cities, such as Ȧbtu, Ṭeṭu, Pe, Ṭep, Khemenu, etc., the heavenly Ȧnu had no geographical position.

[3] The importance of Ȧnu and its gods in the VIth dynasty is well indicated by a prayer from the pyramid of Pepi II (for the texts see Maspero, *Recueil*, t. X, p. 8, and t. XII, p. 146), which reads:—

"Hail, ye Great Nine Gods who dwell in Ȧnu, grant ye that Pepi "may flourish, and grant ye that this pyramid of Pepi, this building built "for eternity, may flourish, even as the name of the god Temu, the chief "of the great Company of the Nine Gods, doth flourish. If the name of "Shu, the lord of the celestial shrine in Ȧnu flourisheth, then Pepi "shall flourish, and this his pyramid shall flourish, and this his work "shall endure to all eternity. If the name of Tefnut, the lady of the "terrestrial shrine in Ȧnu endureth, the name of Pepi shall endure, and "this pyramid shall endure to all eternity. If the name of Ḳeb "flourisheth . . . . . the name of Pepi shall flourish, and this pyramid "shall flourish, and this his work shall endure to all eternity. If the "name of Nut flourisheth in the temple of Shenth in Ȧnu, the name of "Pepi shall flourish, and this pyramid shall flourish, and this his work "shall endure to all eternity. If the name of Osiris flourisheth in This, "the name of Pepi shall flourish, and this pyramid shall flourish, and "this his work shall endure to all eternity. If the name of Osiris Khent-"Ȧmenti flourisheth, the name of Pepi shall flourish, and this pyramid "shall flourish, and this his work shall endure to all eternity. If the name "of Set flourisheth in Nubt, the name of Pepi shall flourish, and this "pyramid shall flourish, and this his work shall endure to all eternity."

[4] Maspero, *La Religion Égyptienne d'après les Pyramides de la Ve et de la VIe dynastie.* (In *Revue des Religions*, t. XII, pp. 138, 139.)

The **Theban Recension,** which was used throughout Egypt by everyone who could afford to be "buried," from the XVIIIth to the XXIst dynasty, was commonly written on papyri in the hieroglyphic character, the scribe invariably beginning his copying at the left-hand end of the papyrus roll, and working towards the right. The text is written in black ink in perpendicular rows of hieroglyphs, which are separated from each other by black lines; the titles of the Chapters or sections, and certain parts of the Chapters and the Rubrics belonging thereto, are written in red ink. A steady development in the illumination of the Vignettes is observable in the papyri of this period. At the beginning of the XVIIth dynasty the Vignettes are in black outline, as we see in the Papyrus of Nebseni; but we see in the Papyrus of Iuåu, a father-in-law of Åmen-ḥetep III, that the Vignettes are painted in reds, greens, yellows, white, and other colours, and that the whole of the text and Vignettes are enclosed in a red and yellow border. Originally the text was the most important part of the work, and both it and its Vignettes were the work of the scribe; gradually, however, the brilliantly illuminated Vignettes were more and more cared for, and when the skill of the scribe failed, the artist was called in. In many fine papyri of the Theban Period it is clear that the whole plan of the Vignettes of a papyrus was set out by artists, who often failed to leave sufficient space for the texts to which they belonged; in consequence many lines of Chapters are often omitted, and the last few lines of some texts are so much crowded as to be almost illegible. The frequent clerical errors also show that, while an artist of the greatest skill might be employed on the Vignettes, the execution of the text was left to a careless, or even ignorant, scribe. Again, the artist at times arranged his Vignettes in wrong order, and it is occasionally evident that neither artist nor scribe understood the matter upon which he was engaged. According to M. Maspero[1] the scribes of the VIth dynasty did not understand the texts which they were drafting, and in the XIXth dynasty the scribe of a papyrus now preserved at Berlin knew or cared so little about the text which he was copying that he transcribed the LXXVIIth Chapter

[1] *Recueil de Travaux*, t. IV, p. 62.

from the wrong end, and apparently never discovered his error, although he concluded the Chapter with its title.[1] Originally each copy of the Book of the Dead was written to order, but soon the custom obtained of preparing copies with blank spaces in which the name of the purchaser might be inserted; and many of the errors in spelling and most of the omissions of words are no doubt due to the haste with which such "stock" copies were written by the members of the priestly caste, whose profession it was to copy them.

The papyri upon which copies of the Theban Recension were written vary in length from about 20 to 90 feet, and in width from 14 to 18 inches; in the XVIIIth dynasty the layers of the papyrus are of a thicker texture and of a darker colour than in the succeeding dynasties. The art of making great lengths of papyrus of light colour and fine texture attained its highest perfection in the XIXth dynasty. An examination of Theban papyri shows that the work of writing and illuminating a fine copy of the Book of the Dead was frequently distributed between two or more groups of artists and scribes, and that the sections were afterwards joined up into a whole. Occasionally by error two groups of men would transcribe the same Chapter; hence in the Papyrus of Ani, Chapter XVIII occurs twice.

The sections or Chapters of the Theban Recension are a series of separate and distinct compositions, which, like the sections of the Pyramid Texts, had no fixed order either on coffins or in papyri. Unlike these texts, however, with very few exceptions each composition has a special title and Vignette which indicate its purpose. The general selection of the Chapters for a papyrus seems to have been left to the individual fancy of the purchaser or scribe, but certain of them were no doubt absolutely necessary for the preservation of the body of the deceased in the tomb, and for the welfare of his soul in its new state of existence. Traditional selections would probably be respected, and recent selections approved by any dominant school of religious thought in Egypt were without doubt accepted.

While in the period of the Pyramid Texts the various sections were said or sung by priests, probably assisted by

[1] Naville, *Todtenbuch* (Einleitung), pp. 41–43.

some members of the family of the deceased, the welfare of his soul and body being proclaimed for him as an established fact, in the Theban Recension the hymns and prayers to the gods were put into the mouth of the deceased. As none but the great and wealthy could afford the ceremonies which were performed in the early dynasties, economy was probably the chief cause of this change, which had come about at Thebes as early as the XIIth dynasty. Little by little the ritual portions of the Book of the Dead disappeared, until finally, in the Theban Recension, the only Chapters of this class which remain are the XXIInd, XXIIIrd, CVth, CXXXVIIth, and CLIst.[1] Every Chapter and prayer of this recension was to be said in the next world, where the words, properly uttered, enabled the deceased to overcome every foe and to attain to the life of the perfected soul which dwelt in a spiritual body in the abode of the blessed.

The common name for the Book of the Dead in the Theban Period, and probably also before this date, is *pert em hru*, which words have been variously translated: "manifested in the light," "coming forth from the day," "coming forth by day," "la manifestation au jour," "la manifestation à la lumière," "[Kapitel von] der Erscheinung im Lichte," "Erscheinen am Tage," "[Caput] egrediendi in lucem," etc. This name, however, had probably a meaning for the Egyptians which has not yet been rendered in a modern language, and one important idea in connection with the whole work is expressed by another title[2] which calls it "the chapter of making strong (*or* perfect) the *Khu*."

In the Theban Recension the main principles of the Egyptian religion which were held in the times when the Pyramid Texts were written are maintained, and the views concerning the eternal existence of the soul remain unaltered. Many passages in the work, however, show that modifications and developments in details have taken place, and

[1] See Naville, *Todtenbuch* (Einleitung), p. 20. On the titles "Book of the Dead" and "Rituel Funéraire" which have been given to these texts, see Lepsius, *Todtenbuch*, p. 3; De Rougé, *Revue Archéologique*, N.S., t. I, 1860, pp. 69–100.

[2] See Naville, Einleitung, p. 24.

much that is not met with in the early dynasties appears, so far as we know, for the first time. The Vignettes, too, are additions to the work; but, although they depict scenes in the life beyond the grave, they do not seem to form a connected series, and it is doubtful if they are arranged on any definite plan. A general idea of the contents of this version may be gathered from the following list of Chapters[1]:—

Chapter I. Here begin the Chapters of "Coming Forth by Day," and of the songs of praise and glorifying,[2] and of coming forth from, and going into, the Underworld.[3] With **Rubric.**

Vignette: The funeral procession from the house of the dead to the tomb.

Chapter Ib. The Chapter of making the Sāḥu, or Spirit-body [hieroglyphs], to go into the Ṭuat [hieroglyphs], on the day of the burial.[4] With **Rubric.**

Vignette: Anubis standing by the bier upon which the mummy of the deceased is laid.

Chapter II. [The Chapter of] coming forth by day and of living after death.

Vignette: A man standing, holding a staff [hieroglyph].

Chapter III. Another Chapter like unto it (*i.e.*, like Chapter II).[5]

This Chapter has no Vignette.

[1] The various Chapters of the Book of the Dead were numbered by Lepsius in his edition of the Turin Papyrus in 1842. This papyrus, however, is a product of the Ptolemaïc Period, and contains a number of Chapters which are wanting in the Theban Recension. For convenience, Lepsius' numbers are retained, and the Chapters which belong to the Saïte Recension are indicated by an asterisk.

[2] Another title reads:—"The Chapter of going in to the divine chiefs of Osiris on the day of the burial, and of going in after coming forth." This Chapter had to be recited on the day of the burial.

[3] [hieroglyphs] Khert-Neter, the commonest name for the tomb.

[4] [hieroglyphs] *sma ta*, "the union with the earth." A copy of this Chapter, with the pictures of the nine worms mentioned in the text, is given in the Papyrus of Iuâu (ed. Naville), as I pointed out in my *Chapters of Coming Forth by Day*, 2nd edition, Vol. I, p. lxxxix, London, 1909.

[5] In some papyri Chapters II and III are united and have only one title; see Naville, *Todtenbuch*, Bd. I, Bl. 6.

Chapter IV. Another Chapter of passing along the way over the earth.

This Chapter has no Vignette.

Chapter V. The Chapter of not allowing the deceased to do work in the Underworld.

Vignette: The deceased kneeling on one knee.

Chapter VI. The Chapter of making *ushabtiu* figures do work for a man in the Underworld.

Vignette: An *ushabti* figure .

Chapter VII. The Chapter of passing over the accursed back of Āapep, the evil one.

Vignette: The deceased spearing a serpent.

Chapter VIII. The Chapter of passing through Åmentet, and of coming forth by day.

Vignette: The deceased standing by .

Chapter IX. The Chapter of Coming Forth by Day after passing through the tomb.

Vignette: The deceased adoring a ram .

Chapter X. (See Chapter XLVIII.)

Chapter XI. The Chapter of a man coming forth against his enemies in the Underworld.

This Chapter has no Vignette, either in the Theban or Saïte Recension.

Chapter XII. Another Chapter of going into, and of coming forth from, the Ṭuat.

This Chapter has no Vignette, either in the Theban or Saïte Recension.

Chapter XIII. The Chapter of going into, and of coming forth, from Åmentet. With **Rubric,** in the Saïte Recension.

This Chapter has no Vignette, either in the Theban or Saïte Recension.

Chapter XIV. The Chapter of driving away shame from the heart of the god in respect of the deceased.

This Chapter has no Vignette, either in the Theban or Saïte Recension.

Chapter XV. A Hymn of praise to Rā when he riseth in the eastern horizon of heaven, Hymn and Litany to Osiris, and a Hymn to Rā.

Vignette: The deceased adoring Rā.

Chapter XVb. **1.** A Hymn of praise to Rā when he setteth in the land of life.

Vignette: The deceased adoring the setting sun.

Chapter XVb. **2.** A Hymn of praise to Rā-Harmakhis when he setteth in the western horizon of heaven.

Vignette: The deceased adoring Rā.

Chapter XVb. **3.** Another hidden Chapter of the *Ṭuat*, and of passing through the secret places of the Underworld, and of seeing the Disk when it setteth in Åmentet.

Vignette: The god or the deceased spearing a serpent.

Chapter XVI. Vignette only, referring to Chapter XV.

Chapter XVII. Here begin the praises and glorifyings of coming out from, and going into, the Underworld in the beautiful Åmenta; of coming out by day, and of making transformations and of changing into any form which he pleaseth; of playing at draughts in the *Seḥ* chamber; and of coming forth in the form of a living soul: to be said by the deceased after his death.

Vignette: The deceased playing at draughts; the deceased adoring the Lion-gods of yesterday and to-day; the bier of Osiris with Isis and Nephthys at the foot and head respectively, etc. See the descriptions of Plates VII–X.

Chapter XVIII. Without title.

Vignette: The deceased adoring the groups of gods belonging to various cities which were centres of the cult of Osiris.

Chapter XIX.* The Chapter of the crown of victory. With **Rubric.**

This Chapter has no vignette.

Chapter XX. Without title in the Theban Recension, but in the Saïte Recension it is called "Another Chapter of the Crown of Victory."

This Chapter has no vignette either in the Theban or Saïte Recension.

Chapter XXI. The Chapter of giving a mouth to a man in the Underworld.

A priest performing the ceremony of opening the mouth on the deceased.

Chapter XXII. The Chapter of giving a mouth to the deceased in the Underworld.

Vignette: The "guardian of the scales" opening the mouth of the deceased.

Chapter XXIII. The Chapter of "opening the mouth" of the deceased in the Underworld.

Vignette: The *Sem* priest "opening the mouth" of the deceased with the *Ur-ḥekau* instrument.

Chapter XXIV. The Chapter of bringing words of magical power to the deceased in the Underworld.

This Chapter has no Vignette in the Theban Recension.

Chapter XXV. The Chapter of causing a man to remember his name in the Underworld.

Vignette: A priest holding up before the deceased.

Chapter XXVI. The Chapter of giving a heart to the deceased in the Underworld.

Vignette: Anubis giving the deceased a necklace to which is attached a pectoral with a heart in it.

Chapter XXVII. The Chapter of not allowing the heart of a man to be taken from him in the Underworld.

Vignette: The deceased adoring his heart in the presence of the Four Sons of Horus.

Chapter XXVIII. [The Chapter of] not allowing the heart of a man to be taken from him in the Underworld.

Vignette: The deceased with his left hand touching the heart upon his breast, kneeling before a demon holding a knife.

Chapter XXIXa. The Chapter of not letting the heart of a man be taken away from him.

Vignette: The deceased holding a staff.

Chapter XXIXb. The Chapter of not letting the heart of a man be taken away dead.

Vignette: Wanting.

Chapter XXIXc. Another Chapter of a heart of carnelian.

Vignette: The deceased sitting on a chair before his heart, which rests on a stand, , or a heart only.

Chapter XXX. The Chapter of not letting the heart of a man be carried off from him. With **Rubric.** [Saïte Recension.]

Vignette: The deceased adoring a beetle.

Chapter XXXa. The Chapter of not allowing the heart of a man to be carried away from him in the Underworld.

Vignette: A heart, .

Chapter XXXb. The Chapter of not allowing the heart of a man to be carried away from him in the Underworld. With **Rubric.**

Vignette: The deceased being weighed against his heart in the balance in the presence of Osiris, "the great god, the prince of eternity."

Chapter XXXI. The Chapter of repulsing the crocodile which cometh to carry the magical words from a man in the Underworld.

Vignette: The deceased slaying three or four crocodiles.

Chapter XXXII.* The Chapter of repulsing the crocodile that cometh to carry the magical words from a man in the Underworld.

Vignette: The deceased spearing four crocodiles.

Chapter XXXIII. The Chapter of repulsing serpents of all kinds.

Vignette: The deceased spearing a snake.

Chapter XXXIV. The Chapter of a man not being bitten by a serpent in the hall of the tomb.[1]

This Chapter has no vignette either in the Theban or Saïte Recension.

Chapter XXXV. The Chapter of not being eaten by worms in the Underworld.

Vignette: Three serpents.

[1] *àmiḥat.*

Chapter XXXVI. The Chapter of repulsing *Āpshai* ( ).

Vignette: The deceased spearing a beetle, or a pig, or about to slay *Apshai.*

Chapter XXXVII. The Chapter of repulsing the two Merti-goddesses .

Vignette: Two uraei, which represent the two eyes of Rā.

Chapter XXXVIIIa. The Chapter of living upon the air which is in the Underworld.

Vignette: The deceased holding a sail , emblematic of air.

Chapter XXXVIIIb. The Chapter of living upon air and of repulsing the two *Merti.*

Vignette: The deceased attacking three serpents, a knife in his right hand and a sail in his left.

Chapter XXXIX. The Chapter of repulsing the serpent in the Underworld.

Vignette: The deceased spearing a serpent.

Chapter XL. The Chapter of repulsing the Eater of the Ass.

Vignette: The deceased spearing a serpent which is biting the neck of an ass.

Chapter XLI. The Chapter of avoiding the slaughterings which are performed in the Underworld.

Vignette: The deceased spearing a serpent.

Chapter XLII. [The Chapter] of avoiding slaughter in Ḥensu (Herakleopolis).

Vignette: A man adjuring a serpent.

Chapter XLIII. The Chapter of not allowing the head of a man to be cut off from him in the Underworld.

Vignette: The deceased addressing three gods.

Chapter XLIV. The Chapter of not dying a second time.

Vignette: The deceased seated on a chair of state.

Chapter XLV. The Chapter of not seeing corruption. With **Rubric.**

Vignette: Anubis holding the mummy of the deceased.

Chapter XLVI. The Chapter of not decaying, and of living in the Underworld.

Vignette: The Heart-soul and Spirit-soul at the door of the tomb.

Chapter XLVII. The Chapter of not letting be carried away the throne from a man in the Underworld.

This Chapter has no Vignette in the Theban Recension.

Chapter XLVIII. [The Chapter of a man coming forth against] his enemies.

Vignette: The deceased spearing a serpent.

Chapter XLIX.* The Chapter of a man coming forth against his enemies in the Underworld.

Vignette: Wanting.

Chapter L. The Chapter of not going in to the chamber of the divine block. Two versions of this Chapter are known, but only one has a Vignette.

Vignette: A man standing with his back to the block.

Chapter LI. The Chapter of not being tripped up in the Underworld.

Vignette: A man standing upright.

Chapter LII. The Chapter of not eating filth in the Underworld.

Vignette: A man seated before a table of food [Saïte Recension].

Chapter LIII. The Chapter of not eating filth and of not drinking polluted water in the Underworld.

Vignette: Wanting.

Chapter LIV. The Chapter of giving air to the deceased in the Underworld.

Vignette: The deceased holding a sail.

Chapter LV. Another Chapter of giving air.

Vignette: The deceased holding a sail in each hand.

Chapter LVI. The Chapter of snuffing the air in the earth.

Vignette: The deceased holding a sail.

Chapter LVII. The Chapter of snuffing the air and of gaining the mastery over the waters in the Underworld.

Vignette: The deceased holding a sail, and standing in a running stream.

Chapter LVIII. The Chapter of snuffing the air and of gaining power over the water which is in the Underworld.

Vignette: The deceased drinking water in a running stream.

Chapter LIX. The Chapter of snuffing the air and of gaining power over the water which is in the Underworld.

Vignette: The deceased receiving meat and drink from Nut or Hathor.

Chapter LX.* Another Chapter.

Vignette: The deceased holding a lotus.

Chapter LXI. The Chapter of not letting the Heart-soul of a man be taken from him.

Vignette: The deceased clasping his Heart-soul.

Chapter LXII. The Chapter of drinking water.

Vignette: The deceased scooping up water with his hands.

Chapter LXIIIa. The Chapter of drinking water, and of not being burnt with fire.

Vignette: The deceased catching water in a bowl.

Chapter LXIIIb. The Chapter of not being boiled (or scalded) in the water.

Vignette: The deceased seated before a table of food.

Chapter LXIV. The Chapter of coming forth by day in the Underworld. Two versions, each with a **Rubric.**

Vignette: The deceased adoring the disk, which stands on the top of a tree.

Chapter LXV. [The Chapter of] coming forth by day, and of gaining the mastery over foes. In two versions.

Vignette: The deceased adoring Rā.

Chapter LXVI. [The Chapter of] coming forth by day.

Vignette: Wanting.

Chapter LXVII. The Chapter of opening the doors of the *Ṭuat* and of Coming Forth by Day.

Vignette: Wanting.

Chapter LXVIII. The Chapter of Coming Forth by day. With **Rubric.**

Vignette: The deceased kneeling by the side of a tree before Hathor.

Chapter LXIX. Another Chapter.

Vignette: Wanting.

Chapter LXX. Another Chapter.

Vignette: Wanting.

Chapter LXXI. The Chapter of Coming Forth by day. With **Rubric.**

Vignette: The deceased with both hands raised in adoration kneeling before the goddess Meḥ-urt.

Chapter LXXII. The Chapter of Coming Forth by Day and of passing through the *Ȧmeḥet.* With **Rubric.**

Vignette: The deceased standing before his tomb.

Chapter LXXIII. See Chapter IX.

Chapter LXXIV. The Chapter of lifting up the legs and coming forth upon earth.

Vignette: The deceased kneeling before the Ḥenu Boat of Seker.

Chapter LXXV. The Chapter of travelling to Ȧnu (On), and of receiving a throne there.

Vignette: The deceased standing before the object *Ȧnu* .

Chapter LXXVI. The Chapter of [a man] changing into whatsoever form he pleaseth.

This Chapter has no Vignette.

Chapter LXXVII. The Chapter of changing into a golden hawk.

Vignette: A golden hawk, .

Chapter LXXVIII. The Chapter of changing into a divine hawk.

Vignette: A hawk, .

Chapter LXXIX. The Chapter of being among the Company of the Gods, and of becoming a prince among the divine powers.

Vignette: The deceased adoring three gods, who represent the Four Sons of Horus.

Chapter LXXX. The Chapter of changing into a god, and of sending forth light into darkness.

Vignette: A god, with the solar disk on his head.

Chapter LXXXIa. The Chapter of changing into a lily.

Vignette: A lily.

Chapter LXXXIb. The Chapter of changing into a lily.

Vignette: The head of the deceased rising out of a lily .

Chapter LXXXII. The Chapter of changing into Ptaḥ, of eating cakes, of drinking ale, of unloosing the body, and of living in Ȧnu (On).

Vignette: The god Ptaḥ in a shrine.

Chapter LXXXIII. The Chapter of changing into a Benu bird.

Vignette: A Benu bird . With **Rubric.**

Chapter LXXXIV. The Chapter of changing into a heron.

Vignette: A heron.

Chapter LXXXV. The Chapter of changing into the Soul, of not going into the place of punishment: whosoever knoweth it will never perish.

Vignette: The Soul-god in the form of a Ram.

Chapter LXXXVI. The Chapter of changing into a swallow. With **Rubric.**

Vignette: A swallow.

Chapter LXXXVII. The Chapter of changing into the serpent Sa-ta.

Vignette: A serpent.

Chapter LXXXVIII. The Chapter of changing into a crocodile.

Vignette: A crocodile.

Chapter LXXXIX. The Chapter of making the Heart-soul to be united to its body. With **Rubric.**

Vignette: The soul visiting the body, which lies on a bier.

Chapter XC. The Chapter of driving evil recollections from a man.

Vignette: The deceased addressing Thoth. (Saïte Recension.)

Chapter XCI. The Chapter of not allowing the soul of a man to be shut in. With **Rubric.**

Vignette: A soul standing at the door of the tomb.

Chapter XCII. The Chapter of opening the tomb to the soul and shadow of a man, so that he may come forth and may gain power over his legs.

Vignette: The soul of the deceased flying through the door of the tomb to the shadow (?).

Chapter XCIII. The Chapter of not sailing to the east in the Underworld.

Vignette: The deceased addressing Ḥer-f-ḥa-f.

Chapter XCIV. The Chapter of praying for an ink jar and palette.

Vignette: The deceased sitting before a stand, upon which are an ink jar and palette.

Chapter XCV. The Chapter of being near Thoth.

Vignette: The deceased standing before Thoth; variant, a goose.

Chapter XCVI. The Chapter of being near Thoth, and of giving glory unto a man in the Underworld.

Vignette: The deceased standing near Thoth.

Chapter XCVII. [No title.]

Vignette: The deceased adoring Rā in his boat.

Chapter XCVIII. The Chapter of bringing a boat in heaven.

Vignette: wanting.

Chapter XCIX. The Chapter of bringing a boat in the Underworld.

Vignette: A boat with the sail hoisted.

Chapter C. The Chapter of making perfect the Spirit-soul, and of making it to enter into the boat of Rā, together with his divine followers. With **Rubric.**

Vignette: A boat containing a Company of Gods.

Chapter CI. [The Chapter of protecting the boat of Rā.] With **Rubric.**

Vignette: The deceased in the boat with Rā. (Saïte Recension.)

Chapter CII. The Chapter of going into the boat of Rā.

Vignette: The deceased in the boat with Rā.

Chapter CIII. The Chapter of being in the following of Hathor.

Vignette: The deceased standing behind Hathor.

Chapter CIV. The Chapter of sitting among the great gods.

Vignette: The deceased seated between two gods.

Chapter CV. The Chapter of providing offerings for the *ka* .

Vignette: The deceased burning incense before his *ka*.

Chapter CVI. The Chapter of giving sepulchral meals each day to a man in Ḥet-ka-Ptaḥ (Memphis).

Vignette: An altar with meat and drink offerings.

Chapter CVII.* The Chapter of going into, and of coming forth from, the gate of the gods of the west among the followers of the god, and of knowing the souls of Åmentet.

Vignette: Three deities: Rā, Sebek, and Hathor.

Chapter CVIII. The Chapter of knowing the souls of the West.

Vignette: Three deities: Temu, Sebek, and Hathor.

Chapter CIX. The Chapter of knowing the souls of the East.

Vignette: The deceased making adoration before Rā-Ḥeru-khuti.

Chapter CX. The beginning of the Chapters of the Field of Offerings, and of the Chapters of Coming Forth by Day, and of going into, and of coming forth from, the Underworld, and of attaining unto the Field of Reeds, and of being in the Field of Offerings.

Vignette: The Field of Offerings.

Chapter CXI. See Chapter CVIII.

Chapter CXII. Another Chapter of knowing the souls of Pe.

Vignette: Horus, Ḳestȧ, and Ḥāpi.

Chapter CXIII. The Chapter of knowing the souls of Nekhen.

Vignette: Horus, Ṭuamutef, and Qebḥsenuf.

Chapter CXIV. The Chapter of knowing the souls of Khemenu (Hermopolis).

Vignette: Three ibis-headed gods.

Chapter CXV. The Chapter of coming forth to heaven, of passing through the hall of the tomb, and of knowing the souls of Ȧnu.

Vignette: The deceased adoring Rā, Shu, and Sekhmet.

Chapter CXVI. [The Chapter of] knowing the souls of Ȧnu. With **Rubric.**

Vignette: The deceased adoring Thoth, Sau, and Tem.

Chapter CXVII. The Chapter of taking a way in Ra-stau.

Vignette: The deceased, holding a staff in his hand, ascending the western hills.

Chapter CXVIII. The Chapter of coming forth from Ra-stau.

Vignette: The deceased holding a staff in his left hand.

Chapter CXIX. The Chapter of knowing the name of Osiris, and of going into, and of coming forth from, Ra-stau.

Vignette: The deceased adoring Osiris, who stands in a shrine.

Chapter CXX. See Chapter XII.

Chapter CXXI. See Chapter XIII.

Chapter CXXII. The Chapter of the deceased going in after coming forth from the Underworld.

Vignette: The deceased bowing before his tomb, which is on a hill. (Saïte Recension.)

Chapter CXXIII. The Chapter of going into the great house (*i.e.*, tomb).

Vignette: The deceased standing before a tomb.

Chapter CXXIV. The Chapter of going in to the princes of Osiris.

Vignette: The deceased adoring Ḳestȧ, Ḥāpi, Ṭuamutef, and Q̣ebḥsenuf.

Chapter CXXV. The words which are to be uttered by the deceased when he cometh to the hall of Maāti, which separateth him from his sins, and which maketh him to see God, the Lord of mankind. With **Rubric.**

A. The Introduction.
B. The Negative Confession.
C. Address of the deceased after the Judgment.

Vignette: The hall of Maāti, in which the heart of the deceased is being weighed in a balance in the presence of the great gods.

Chapter CXXVI. [Without title.]

Vignette: A lake of fire, at each corner of which sits an ape.

Chapter CXXVIIa. The book of the praise of the gods of the Circles .

Vignette: Wanting.

Chapter CXXVIIb. The Chapter of the words to be spoken on going to the Chiefs of Osiris, and of the praise of the gods who are leaders in the *Ṭuat*.

Vignette: Eight pairs of gods, with a table of offerings before each pair.

Chapter CXXVIII.* The Chapter of praising Osiris.

Vignette: The deceased adoring three deities.

Chapter CXXIX. See Chapter C.

Chapter CXXX. The Chapter of making perfect the Spirit-soul. With **Rubric.**

Vignette: The deceased standing between the two boats of the Sun-god, the Maāṭet and the Sektet.

Chapter CXXXI.* The Chapter of having existence nigh unto Rā.

Vignette: Wanting.

Chapter CXXXII. The Chapter of making a man to go about to see his house upon the earth.

Vignette: A man standing before a house or tomb.

Chapter CXXXIII. The Chapter of making perfect the Spirit-soul in the Underworld in the presence of the Great Company of the Gods. With **Rubric.**

Vignette: The deceased adoring Rā who is seated in a boat.

Chapter CXXXIV. The Chapter of entering into the boat of Rā, and of being among those who are in his train. With **Rubric.**

Vignette: The deceased adoring Shu, Tefnut, Ḳeb, Nut, Osiris, Isis, Horus, Hathor.

Chapter CXXXV.* Another Chapter, which is to be recited at the waxing of the moon [each] month.

This Chapter has no Vignette.

Chapter CXXXVIa. The Chapter of sailing in the boat of Rā. In two versions: the second with **Rubric.**

Vignette: The deceased standing with hands raised in adoration.

Chapter CXXXVIb. The Chapter of sailing in the great boat of Rā, to pass over the fiery path of the sun.

Vignette: The head of Rā in a boat.

Chapter CXXXVIIa. The Chapter of the four blazing torches which are to be lighted for the *Khu.* With **Rubrics.**

Vignette: Four men, each holding a lighted torch.

Chapter CXXXVIIb. The Chapter of the deceased kindling the fire.

Vignette: The goddess Taurt kindling a flame.

Chapter CXXXVIII. The Chapter of making the deceased to enter into Abydos.

Vignette: The deceased adoring the standard .

Chapter CXXXIX. See Chapter CXXIII.

Chapter CXL.* The Book which is to be recited in the second month of the season Pert, when the *utchat* is full in the second month of Pert. With **Rubric.**

Vignette : The deceased adoring Ånpu, the *utchat*, and Rā. (Saïte Recension.)

Chapters CXLI-CXLII. The Book which is to be recited by a man for his father and for his son at the festivals of Åmentet. It will make him perfect before Rā and before the gods, and he shall dwell with them. It shall be recited on the ninth day of the festival.

Chapter CXLIII. This is the Vignette of Chapter CXLII.

Vignette : The deceased making offerings before a god.

Chapter CXLIV. The Chapter of entering in. With **Rubric.**

Vignette : Seven pylons, each guarded by a door-keeper, a watchman, and a herald.

Chapter CXLVa. [Without title.]

This Chapter has no Vignette.

Chapter CXLVb. [The Chapter] of coming forth to the hidden pylons.

This Chapter has no Vignette. The Saïte Recension contains many Vignettes,

Chapter CXLVI. [The Chapter of] knowing the pylons in the House of Osiris in the Field of Reeds.

Vignette : A series of pylons guarded each by a god.

Chapter CXLVII. [A Chapter] to be recited by the deceased when he cometh to the first hall of Åmentet. With **Rubric.**

Vignette : A series of doors, each guarded by a god.

Chapter CXLVIII. [The Chapter] of nourishing the *Khu* in the Underworld, and of removing him from every evil thing. With **Rubric.**

Vignette : The Seven Cows and their Bull, and the Four Rudders of Heaven.

Chapter CXLIX. [The Chapter of the Åats.]

Vignette : The Åats of the House of Osiris.

Chapter CL. [Without title.]

Vignette: The Åats of the House of Osiris in tabular form.

Chapter CLI. [Without title.]

Vignette: Scene of the mummy chamber.

Chapter CLIa. [Chapter] of the hands of Ånpu, the dweller in the sepulchral chamber, being upon the lord of life (*i.e.*, the mummy).

Vignette: Anubis standing by the bier of the deceased.

Chapter CLIb. The Chapter of the chief of hidden things.

Vignette: A human head.

Chapter CLII. The Chapter of building a house in the earth.

Vignette: The deceased laying the foundations of his house.

Chapter CLIIIa. The Chapter of coming forth from the net.

Vignette: A net by the side of which stands the deceased.

Chapter CLIIIb. The Chapter of coming forth from the fishing net.

Vignette: Three apes drawing a fishing net.

Chapter CLIV. The Chapter of not allowing the body of a man to decay in the tomb.

Vignette: The sun shining on the body of the deceased. (Saïte Recension.)

Chapter CLV. The Chapter of a Ṭeṭ of gold to be placed on the neck of the *Khu*. With **Rubric.**

Vignette: A Ṭeṭ, *i.e.*, the sacrum bone of Osiris.

Chapter CLVI. The Chapter of a Tet of amethyst to be placed on the neck of the *Khu*. With **Rubric.**

Vignette: A Tet, *i.e.*, the uterus and vagina of Isis.

Chapter CLVII.* The Chapter of a vulture of gold to be placed on the neck of the *Khu*. With **Rubric.**

Vignette: A vulture.

Chapter CLVIII.* The Chapter of a collar of gold to be placed on the neck of the *Khu*. With **Rubric.**

Vignette : A collar.

Chapter CLIX.* The Chapter of a sceptre of mother-of-emerald to be placed on the neck of the *Khu*. With **Rubric.**

Vignette : A sceptre [sceptre sign].

Chapter CLX. [The Chapter] of placing a plaque of mother-of-emerald.

Vignette : Thoth giving a plaque to the deceased.

Chapter CLXI. The Chapter of the opening of the doors of heaven by Thoth, etc. With **Rubric.**

Vignette : Thoth opening the four doors of heaven.

Chapter CLXII.* The Chapter of causing heat to exist under the head of the *Khu*. With **Rubric.**

Vignette : A cow, with a pair of plumes and a disk between her horns.

Chapter CLXIII.* The Chapter of not allowing the body of a man to decay in the Underworld. With **Rubric.**

Vignette : Two *utchats* and a serpent, each on a pair of human legs.

Chapter CLXIV.* Another Chapter. With **Rubric.**

Vignette : A three-headed goddess, winged, standing between two pigmies.

Chapter CLXV.* The Chapter of arriving in port, of not becoming unseen, and of making the body to germinate, and of satisfying it with the water of heaven. With **Rubric.**

Vignette : The god Menu with a beetle's body, and a man with a ram's head on each shoulder.

Chapter CLXVI. The Chapter of the pillow.

Vignette : A pillow or head-rest.

Chapter CLXVII. The Chapter of bringing the *utchat*.

Vignette : An *utchat* resting on [hieroglyph].

Chapter CLXVIIIa. [Without title.]

Vignette : The boats of the sun, etc.

Chapter CLXVIIIb. [Without title.]

Vignette: Men pouring libations, gods, etc.

Chapter CLXIX. The Chapter of setting up the funerary chamber.

Vignette: Wanting.

Chapter CLXX. The Chapter of arranging the funerary chamber.

Vignette: Wanting.

Chapter CLXXI. The Chapter of tying on the garment of purity.

Vignette: Wanting.

Chapter CLXXII. Here begin the Chapters of the praises which are to be recited in the Underworld.

Vignette: Wanting.

Chapter CLXXIII. Addresses by Horus to his father.

Vignette: The deceased adoring Osiris.

Chapter CLXXIV. The Chapter of causing the *Khu* to come forth from the great gate of heaven.

Vignette: The deceased coming forth from a door.

Chapter CLXXV. The Chapter of not dying a second time in the Underworld.

Vignette: The deceased adoring Thoth.

Chapter CLXXVI. The Chapter of not dying a second time in the Underworld. With **Rubric.**

Vignette: Wanting.

Chapter CLXXVII. The Chapter of raising up the *Khu*, and of making the soul to live in the Underworld.

Vignette: The deceased receiving offerings.

Chapter CLXXVIII. The Chapter of raising up the body, of making the eyes to see, of making the ears to hear, of setting firm the head and of giving it its powers.

Vignette: Wanting.

Chapter CLXXIX. The Chapter of coming forth from yesterday, of Coming Forth by Day, and of praying with the hands.

Vignette: Wanting.

Chapter CLXXX. The Chapter of Coming Forth by Day, of praising Rā in Åmentet, and of ascribing praise unto those who are in the *Ṭuat.*

Vignette: The deceased adoring Rā and two other gods.

Chapter CLXXXI. The Chapter of going in to the divine Chiefs of Osiris who are the leaders in the *Ṭuat.* With **Rubric.**

Vignette: The deceased adoring Osiris, etc.

Chapter CLXXXII. The Book of stablishing the backbone of Osiris, of giving breath to him whose heart is still, and of repulsing the enemies of Osiris by Thoth.

Vignette: The deceased lying on a bier in a funeral chest, surrounded by various gods.

Chapter CLXXXIII. A hymn of praise to Osiris; ascribing to him glory, and to Un-nefer adoration.

Vignettes: The deceased, with hands raised in adoration, and the god Thoth.

Chapter CLXXXIV. The Chapter of being with Osiris.

Vignette: The deceased standing by the side of Osiris.

Chapter CLXXXV. The ascription of praise to Osiris, and of adoration to the everlasting lord.

Vignette: The deceased making adoration to Osiris.

Chapter CLXXXVI. A hymn of praise to Hathor, mistress of Åmentet, and to Meḥ-urt.

Vignette: The deceased approaching the mountain of the dead, from which appears the goddess Hathor.

Chapter CLXXXVII. The Chapter of entering into the Company of the Gods.

Vignette: Wanting.

Chapter CLXXXVIII. The Chapter of building a house, and of appearing in a human form.

Vignette: Wanting.

Chapter CLXXXIX. The Chapter of not letting a man suffer hunger.

Vignette: Wanting.

Chapter CXC. The Book of making perfect the *Khu*. With **Rubric.**

Vignette: Wanting.

In the papyri containing the Theban Recension which are written in the hieratic character, the Rubrics, catchwords, and certain accursed names, like that of Āapep, are in red. The vignettes are roughly traced in black outline, and are without ornament; but at the right-hand ends of the best papyri painted scenes, in which the deceased is depicted making adoration to Rā or Horus, are frequently found. The names and titles of the deceased are written in perpendicular rows of hieroglyphs. The finest example of this class of papyri is the Papyrus of Nesitanebtȧshru (the Greenfield Papyrus) in the British Museum (No. 10554). Before opening, this papyrus formed a compact roll about 1 foot 8½ inches in length, which was flatter at one end than the other. With the exception of a few hieroglyphs at the beginning of the papyrus, and portions of the figures of Osiris and the deceased, the document is complete, and text and Vignettes are in a remarkable state of preservation. The papyrus is nearly 123 feet long and 1 foot 6½ inches wide; it contains 2,666 lines of text, hieratic chiefly, arranged in 172 columns. The papyrus is the longest of the Theban codices of the Book of the Dead, and with the exception of the great Harris Papyrus, which measures 133 feet by 1 foot 4½ inches, is the longest papyrus known. All the texts are written in black ink, the titles of the Chapters, the Rubrics, catchwords, etc., being in red; the fine long series of Vignettes are drawn in black outline throughout. The artistic work is of a very high character, and is probably the best example extant of line drawing under the New Empire. The papyrus is written chiefly in hieratic, a script which is both written and read from right to left, and therefore begins at the right-hand end of the papyrus. The so-called "Negative Confession" appears in it in two copies, one in hieratic, and the other in hieroglyphs. The papyrus was written in the second quarter of the tenth century before Christ, and is for all practical purposes a dated document. Its authority for deciding questions concerning hieratic palaeography under the New Empire is very great. It contains eighty-seven Chapters of the

Theban Recension of the Book of the Dead. A facsimile of the papyrus, with a description of its contents, list of Chapters, etc., has been recently published by the Trustees of the British Museum.[1] Other fine examples of the hieratic and hieroglyphic papyri of this period are the copies of the Book of the Dead which were written for Māat-ka-Rā and Nesi-Khensu, and which have been recently published with a luminous introduction by Professor Naville.[2] The character of the handwriting changes in different periods, but within a hundred years, apparently, the fine flowing style disappears, and the writing becomes much smaller and is somewhat cramped; the process of reduction in size continues until the XXVIth dynasty, about 600 B.C., when the small and coarsely written characters are frequently difficult to decipher. The papyri upon which such texts are written vary in length from 3 to about 120 feet, and in width from 9 to 18 inches; as we approach the period of the XXVIth dynasty the texture becomes coarser and the material is darker in colour. The Theban papyri of this period are lighter in colour than those found in the North of Egypt and are less brittle; they certainly suffer less in unrolling.

The **Saïte Recension** was in vogue from the period of the XXVIth dynasty, about 600 B.C., to probably the end of the rule of the Ptolemies over Egypt, about 30 B.C..

[1] *The Greenfield Papyrus in the British Museum, with Introduction and Description* by E. A. Wallis Budge, London, 1912.

[2] *Papyrus Funéraires de la XXIe Dynastie*, Paris, 1912, large 4to. Professor Naville is about to publish the text of the contract between Åmen-Rā and Nesi-Khensu, of which a transcript and translation were given by Professor Maspero in his *Momies Royales*, pp. 600 ff. The text of this remarkable document is divided into paragraphs, which contain neither prayers nor hymns but a veritable contract between the god Åmen-Rā and the princess Nesi-Khensu. After the list of the names and titles of Åmen-Rā with which it begins follow eleven sections, wherein the god declares in legal phraseology that he hath deified the princess in Åmenta and in Khert-Neter; that he hath deified her soul and her body in order that neither may be destroyed; that he hath made her divine like every god and goddess; and that he hath decreed that whatever is necessary for her in her new existence shall be done for her, even as it is done for every other god and goddess. For an English translation see my *Chapters of Coming Forth by Day*, Second Edition, Vol. III, London, 1909.

The Chapters have a fixed and definite order, and it seems that a careful revision of the whole work was carried out, and that several alterations of an important nature were made in it. A number of Chapters which are not found in older papyri appear during this period; but these are not necessarily new inventions, for as the kings of the XXVIth dynasty are renowned for having revived the arts and sciences and literature of the earliest dynasties, it is quite possible that many or most of the additional Chapters are nothing more than new editions of extracts from older works. Many copies of this Recension were written by scribes who did not understand what they were copying, and omissions of signs, words, and even whole passages are very common. In papyri of the Ptolemaïc Period it is impossible to read many passages without the help of texts of earlier periods. The papyri of this period vary in colour from a light to a dark brown, and consist usually of layers composed of strips of the plant measuring about 2 inches in width and 14½ to 16 inches in length. Fine examples of Books of the Dead of this Recension vary in length from about 24½ feet (Brit. Mus. No. 10479, written for the *utcheb* Ḥeru, the son of the *utcheb* Tcheḥrȧ) to 60 feet. Hieroglyphic texts are written in black, in perpendicular rows between rules, and hieratic texts in horizontal lines; both the hieroglyphs and the hieratic characters lack the boldness of the writing of the Theban Period, and exhibit the characteristics of an untrained hand. The titles of the Chapters, catchwords, the words which introduce a variant reading, etc., are sometimes written in red. The Vignettes are usually traced in black outline, and form a kind of continuous border above the text. In good papyri, however, the scene forming the XVIth Chapter, the scene of the Fields of Peace (Chapter CX), the Judgment scene (Chapter CXXV), the Vignette of Chapter CXLVIII, the scene forming Chapter CLI (the sepulchral chamber), and the Vignette of Chapter CLXI, fill the whole width of the inscribed portion of the papyrus, and are painted in somewhat crude colours. In some papyri the disk on the head of the hawk of Horus is covered with gold leaf, instead of being painted red as is usual in older papyri. In the Graeco-Roman period both texts and Vignettes are very carelessly executed, and it is evident that they were written and drawn by ignorant workmen in the quickest and most careless way possible. In this period also certain passages of the text were copied in hieratic and demotic upon small pieces of papyri which were buried with portions of the bodies of the dead, and upon narrow bandages of coarse linen in which they were swathed.[1]

THE LEGEND OF OSIRIS

The essential beliefs of the Egyptian religion remained unchanged from the earliest dynasties down to the period when the Egyptians embraced Christianity, after the preaching of St. Mark the Evangelist in Alexandria, A.D. 69, so firmly had the early beliefs taken possession of the Egyptian mind. And the Christians in Egypt, or Copts as they are commonly called, the racial descendants of the ancient Egyptians, seem never to have succeeded in divesting themselves of the superstitious and weird mythological conceptions which they inherited from their heathen ancestors. It is not necessary here to repeat the proofs of this fact, or to adduce evidence extant in the lives of the saints, martyrs, and ascetics. It is sufficient to note, in passing, that the translators of the New Testament into Coptic rendered the Greek ᾅδης by ⲁⲙⲉⲛϯ,[2] *Amenti*, the name which the ancient Egyptians gave to the abode of man after death,[3] and that the Copts peopled it with beings whose prototypes are found on the ancient monuments.

The chief gods mentioned in the Pyramid Texts are identical with those whose names are given on tomb, coffin, and papyrus in the latest dynasties; and if the names of the great cosmic gods, such as Ptaḥ and Khnemu, are of rare occurrence, this is due to the fact that the gods of the dead must naturally occupy the chief place in this literature which concerns the dead. Furthermore, we find that the

[1] Texts and translations of the principal compositions which took the place of the Book of the Dead in the Ptolemaïc and Roman Periods will be found in my *Chapters of Coming Forth by Day* (Vol. III of text and Vol. III of translation), Second Edition, London, 1909.

[2] *I.e.*, [hieroglyphs].

[3] See St. Matthew xi, 23; Acts ii, 27, etc.

doctrine of eternal life and of the resurrection of a Spirit-body based upon the ancient story of the resurrection of Osiris after a cruel death and horrible mutilation, inflicted by the Power of Evil, was the same in all periods, and that the descriptions of the incidents of the death, mutilation, resurrection, and judgment of Osiris which were written in early dynastic times, were accepted without material alteration or addition by the priests and people of all periods.

The story of Osiris is nowhere found in a connected form in Egyptian literature, but everywhere, and in texts of all periods, the life, sufferings, death, and resurrection of Osiris are accepted as facts universally admitted. Greek writers have preserved in their works traditions concerning this god, and to Plutarch[1] in particular we owe an important version of the legend which was current in his day. It is clear that in some points he errs, but this was excusable in dealing with a series of traditions already some four thousand years old. According to this writer the goddess Rhea [Nut], the wife of Helios [Rā], was beloved by Kronos [Ḳeb]. When Helios discovered the intrigue, he cursed his wife and declared that she should not be delivered of her child in any month or in any year. Then the god Hermes, who also loved Rhea, played at tables with Selene and won from her the seventieth part of each day of the year, which, added together, made five whole days. These he joined to the three hundred and sixty days of which the year then consisted.[2] Upon the first of these five days was Osiris brought forth;[3] and at the moment of his birth a voice was heard to proclaim that the lord of creation was born. In course of time he became king of Egypt, and devoted himself to civilizing his subjects and to teaching

[1] For the text see *De Iside et Osiride*, ed. Didot (Scripta Moralia, t. III, pp. 429–69), §§ XII ff.

[2] The days are called in hieroglyphs, "the five additional days of the year," ἐπαγόμεναι ἡμέραι πέντε; see Brugsch, *Thesaurus Inscriptionum Aegyptiacarum*, Abt. II (*Kalendarische Inschriften*), Leipzig, 1883, pp. 479, 480; Brugsch, *Aegyptologie*, p. 361; Chabas, *Le Calendrier*, Paris (no date), pp. 99 ff.

[3] Osiris was born on the first day, Horus on the second, Set on the third, Isis on the fourth, and Nephthys on the fifth; the first, third, and fifth of these days were considered unlucky by the Egyptians.

them the craft of the husbandman; he established a code of laws and bade men worship the gods. Having made Egypt peaceful and flourishing, he set out to instruct the other nations of the world. During his absence his wife Isis so well ruled the state that Typhon [Set], the evil one, could do no harm to the realm of Osiris. When Osiris came again, Typhon plotted with seventy-two comrades, and with Aso, the queen of Ethiopia, to slay him; and secretly got the measure of the body of Osiris, and made ready a fair chest, which was brought into his banqueting hall when Osiris was present together with other guests. By a ruse Osiris was induced to lie down in the chest, which was immediately closed by Typhon and his fellow conspirators, who conveyed it to the Tanaitic mouth of the Nile.[1] These things happened on the seventeenth day of the month Hathor,[2] when Osiris was in the twenty-eighth year either of his reign or of his age. The first to know of what had happened were the Pans and Satyrs, who dwelt hard by Panopolis: and finally the news was brought to Isis at Coptos, whereupon she cut off a lock of hair[3] and put on mourning apparel. She then set out in deep grief to find her husband's body, and in the course of her wanderings she discovered that Osiris had been united with her sister Nephthys, and that Anubis, the offspring of the union, had been exposed by his mother as soon as born. Isis tracked him by the help of dogs, and bred him up to be her guard and attendant. Soon after she learned that the chest had been carried by the sea to Byblos, where it had been gently

[1] The mouths of the Nile are discussed and described by Strabo, XVII, i, 18 (ed. Didot, p. 681); and by Diodorus, I, 33, 7 (ed. Didot, p. 26).

[2] In the Calendar in the Fourth Sallier Papyrus (No. 10184) this day is marked triply unlucky, and it is said that great lamentation by Isis and Nephthys took place for Un-nefer (Osiris) thereon. See Chabas, *Le Calendrier*, p. 50. Here we have Plutarch's statement supported by documentary evidence. Some very interesting details concerning the festivals of Osiris in the month Choiak are given by Loret in *Recueil de Travaux*, t. III, pp. 43.ff; t. IV, pp. 21 ff.; and t. V, pp. 85 ff. The various mysteries which took place thereat are minutely described.

[3] On the cutting of the hair as a sign of mourning, see W. Robertson Smith, *The Religion of the Semites*, p. 395; and for other beliefs about the hair see Tylor, *Primitive Culture*, Vol. II, p. 364, and Frazer, *Golden Bough*, pp. 193–208.

laid by the waves among the branches of a tamarisk tree (ἐρείκῃ τινὶ), which in a very short time had grown to a magnificent size and had enclosed the chest within its trunk. The king of the country, admiring the tree, cut it down and made a pillar for the roof of his house of that part which contained the body of Osiris. When Isis heard of this she went to Byblos, and, gaining admittance to the palace through the report of the royal maidens, she was made nurse to one of the king's sons. Instead of nursing the child in the ordinary way, Isis gave him her finger to suck, and each night she put him into the fire to consume his mortal parts, changing herself the while into a swallow and bemoaning her fate. But the queen once happened to see her son in flames, and cried out, and thus deprived him of immortality. Then Isis told the queen her story, and begged for the pillar which supported the roof. This she cut open, and took out the chest and her husband's body,[1] and her lamentations were so terrible that one of the royal children died of fright. She then brought the chest by ship to Egypt, where she opened it and embraced the body of her husband, weeping bitterly. Then she sought her son Horus in Buto, in Lower Egypt, first having hidden the chest in a secret place. But Typhon, one night hunting by the light of the moon, found the chest, and, recognizing the body, tore it into fourteen pieces, which he scattered up and down throughout the land. When Isis heard of this she took a boat made of papyrus[2]—a plant abhorred by crocodiles—and sailing about she collected the fragments of Osiris's body.[3] Wherever she found one, there she

[1] The story continues that Isis then wrapped the pillar in fine linen and anointed it with oil, and restored it to the queen. Plutarch adds that the piece of wood is, to this day, preserved in the temple of Isis, and worshipped by the people of Byblos. Prof. Robertson Smith suggests (*Religion of the Semites*, p. 175) that the rite of draping and anointing a sacred stump supplies the answer to the unsolved question of the nature of the ritual practices connected with the Ashera. That some sort of drapery belonged to the Ashera is clear from 2 Kings xxiii, 7. See also Tylor, *Primitive Culture*, Vol. II, p. 150; and Frazer, *Golden Bough*, Vol. I, pp. 304 ff.; see also Mr. Frazer's latest work on the Osiris legends, *Adonis, Attis, and Osiris*, London, 1907.

[2] The ark of "bulrushes" was, no doubt, intended to preserve the child Moses from crocodiles.

[3] Μόνον δὲ τῶν μερῶν τοῦ Ὀσίριδος τὴν Ἶσιν οὐχ εὑρεῖν τὸ αἰδοῖον· εὐθὺς γὰρ εἰς τὸν ποταμὸν ῥιφῆναι, καὶ γεύσασθαι τόν τε λεπιδωτὸν αὐτοῦ καὶ τὸν

built a tomb. But now Horus had grown up, and being encouraged to the use of arms by Osiris, who returned from the Other World, he went out to do battle with Typhon, the murderer of his father. The fight lasted many days, and Typhon was made captive. But Isis, to whom the care of the prisoner was given, so far from aiding her son Horus, set Typhon at liberty. Horus in his rage tore from her head the royal diadem; but Thoth gave her a helmet in the shape of a cow's head. In two other battles fought between Horus and Typhon, Horus was the victor.[1]

This is the story of the sufferings and death of Osiris as told by Plutarch. Osiris was the God-man through whose sufferings and death the Egyptian hoped that he might rise again in a glorified Spirit-body, and to him who had conquered death and had become the king of the Other World the Egyptian appealed in prayer for eternal life through his victory and power. In every funeral inscription known to us, from the Pyramid Texts down to the roughly-written prayers upon coffins of the Roman period, what is done for Osiris is done also for the deceased, the state and condition of Osiris are the state and condition of the deceased; in a word the deceased is identified with Osiris. If Osiris liveth for ever, the deceased will live for ever; if Osiris dieth, then will the deceased perish.

The oldest of the sources of our information about

φάγρον καὶ τὸν ὀξύρυγχον. κ.τ.λ. By the festival celebrated by the Egyptians in honour of Osiris, we are probably to understand the public performance of the ceremony of "setting up the Ṭeṭ in Ṭeṭu", which we know took place on the last day of the month Choiak; see Loret, *Les Fêtes d'Osiris au mois de Khoiak* (*Recueil de Travaux*, t. IV, p. 32, § 87); Plutarch, *De Iside*, § XVIII.

[1] An account of the battle is also given in the IVth Sallier Papyrus, wherein we are told that it took place on the 26th day of the month Thoth. Horus and Set fought in the form of two men, but they afterwards changed themselves into two bears, and they passed three days and three nights in this form. Victory inclined now to one side, and now to the other, and the heart of Isis suffered bitterly. When Horus saw that she loosed the fetters which he had laid upon Set, he became like a "raging panther of the south with fury," and she fled before him; but he pursued her, and cut off her head, which Thoth transformed by his words of magical power and set upon her body again in the form of that of a cow. In the calendars the 26th day of Thoth was marked triply deadly. See Chabas, *Le Calendrier*, pp. 28 ff.

Osiris is the Pyramid Texts, and a careful examination of these proves that nearly all the statements made by classical writers about the murder and mutilation of Osiris are substantially correct. All the important passages in the Pyramid Texts which illustrate the Legend of Osiris are given with English renderings in my *Osiris and the Egyptian Resurrection*, London, 1911, and it is therefore unnecessary to repeat them here.

In the XVIIIth, or early in the XIXth dynasty, we find Osiris called "the king of eternity, the lord of "everlastingness, who traverseth millions of years in the "duration of his life, the firstborn son of the womb of Nut, "begotten of Ḳeb, the prince of gods and men, the god of "gods, the king of kings, the lord of lords, the prince of "princes, the governor of the world, from the womb of "Nut, whose existence is for everlasting,[1] Unnefer of many "forms and of many attributes, Temu in Ȧnu, the lord of "Ȧkert,[2] the only one, the lord of the land on each side "of the celestial Nile."[3]

In the XXVIth dynasty and later there grew up a class of literature represented by such works as "The Book of Breathings,"[4] "The Lamentations of Isis and Nephthys,"[5] "The Festival Songs of Isis and Nephthys,"[6] "The

[1] For the text see the *Papyrus of Ani*, Plate II, and Plate XXXVI, l. 2.

[2] *I.e.*, the Underworld.

[3] [hieroglyphs] *neb ȧṭebui*; see *Ani*, Plate XIX, l. 9.

[4] [hieroglyphs]. A text of this work, transcribed into hieroglyphs, was published, with a Latin translation, by Brugsch, under the title, *Sai an Sinsin sive liber Metempsychosis veterum Aegyptiorum*, Berlin, 1851; and an English translation of the same work, but made from a Paris MS., was given by P. J. de Horrack in *Records of the Past*, 1st series, Vol. IV, pp. 121 ff. See also Birch, *Facsimiles of Two Papyri*, London, 1863, p. 3; Devéria, *Catalogue des MSS. Égyptiens*, Paris, 1874, pp. 130 ff., where several copies of this work are described. Another version of the text from a papyrus in the British Museum (Papyrus of Ḳerāsher, No. 9995) was published, with a hieroglyphic transcript and translation, by me in *Facsimiles of the Papyri of Hunefer*, etc., and see Pellegrini, *Il libro secondo della respirazione*, Rome, 1904.

[5] The hieratic text of this work was published with a French translation by P. J. de Horrack, *Les Lamentations d'Isis et de Nephthys*, Paris, 1886.

[6] A hieroglyphic transcript of these works, with an English translation, was given by me in *Archæologia*, Vol. LII, London, 1891. For the hieratic texts see Budge, *Hieratic Papyri in the British Museum*, London, 1910.

Litanies of Seker,"[1] "The Book of Traversing Eternity,"[2] and the like, the hymns and prayers of which are addressed to Osiris rather as the god of the dead and type of the resurrection than as the successor of the great cosmic god Temu-Rā. He is called "the soul that liveth again,"[3] "the being who becometh a child again,"[4] "the firstborn son of "the primeval god, the lord of multitudes of aspects and "forms, the lord of time and bestower of years, the lord of "life for all eternity."[5] He is the "giver of life from the beginning,"[6] life "springs up to us from his destruction,"[7] and the germ which proceeds from him engenders life in both the dead and the living.[8]

[1] What Devéria says with reference to the Book of Respirations applies to the whole class: "Toutefois, on remarque dans cet écrit une tendance à "la doctrine de la résurrection du corps plus marquée que dans les com- "positions antérieures" (*Catalogue*, p. 13).

[2] See Bergmann, *Das Buch vom Durchwandeln der Ewigkeit*, Vienna, 1877; an English rendering of it will be found in my *Chapters of Coming Forth by Day*, 2nd ed., Vol. III, p. 678.

[3] , *Festival Songs*, IV, 23.

[4] . *Ibid.*, VIII, 21; IX, 8.

[5] *Litanies of Seker*, Col. XVIII.

[6] . *Festival Songs*, VI, 1.

[7] . *Ibid.*, III, 18.

[8] . *Ibid.*, IX, 26.

APPENDIX

I.—HYMN TO OSIRIS[1]

" Homage to thee, Osiris, Lord of eternity, King of the " Gods, whose names are manifold, whose forms are holy, " thou being of hidden form in the temples, whose *Ka* is " holy. Thou art the governor of Ṭaṭṭu (Busiris), and also " the mighty one in Sekhem (Letopolis). Thou art the " Lord to whom praises are ascribed in the nome of Ati, " thou art the Prince of divine food in Ȧnu. Thou art the " Lord who is commemorated in Maāti, the Hidden Soul, " the Lord of Qerrt (Elephantine), the Ruler supreme in " White Wall (Memphis). Thou art the Soul of Rā, his " own body, and hast thy place of rest in Ḥenensu (Herakle-" opolis). Thou art the beneficent one, and art praised in " Nārt. Thou makest thy soul to be raised up. Thou art " the Lord of the Great House in Khemenu (Hermopolis). " Thou art the mighty one of victories in Shas-ḥetep, the " Lord of eternity, the Governor of Abydos. The path " of his throne is in Ta-tcheser (*i.e.*, a part of Abydos). " Thy name is established in the mouths of men. Thou " art the substance of the Two Lands (Egypt). Thou art " Tem, the feeder of the *Kau* (Doubles), the Governor of " the Companies of the gods. Thou art the beneficent " Spirit among the spirits. The god of the Celestial Ocean " (Nu) draweth from thee his waters. Thou sendest forth " the north wind at eventide, and breath from thy nostrils " to the satisfaction of thy heart. Thy heart reneweth its " youth, thou producest the . . . . The stars in the celestial " heights are obedient unto thee, and the great doors of the " sky open themselves before thee. Thou art he to whom " praises are ascribed in the southern heaven, and thanks " are given for thee in the northern heaven. The imperish-" able stars are under thy supervision, and the stars which

[1] For the hieroglyphic text see Ledrain, *Les Monuments Égyptiens de la Bibliothèque Nationale*, Paris, 1879, Plates XXI–XXVII. A French rendering was given by Chabas in *Revue Arch.*, Paris, 1857, t. XIV, pp. 65 ff., and an English rendering in *Records of the Past*, 1st series, Vol. IV, pp. 99 f. See also Budge, *First Steps*, pp. 179–188, and Budge, *Osiris and the Egyptian Resurrection*. Vol. II, p. 75.

"never set are thy thrones. Offerings appear before thee "at the decree of Ḳeb. The Companies of the Gods praise "thee, and the gods of the Ṭuat (Other World) smell the "earth in paying homage to thee. The uttermost parts of "the earth bow before thee, and the limits of the skies "entreat thee with supplications when they see thee. The "holy ones are overcome before thee, and all Egypt offereth "thanksgiving unto thee when it meeteth Thy Majesty. "Thou art a shining Spirit-body, the Governor of Spirit- "bodies; permanent is thy rank, established is thy rule. "Thou art the well-doing Sekhem (Power) of the Company "of the Gods, gracious is thy face, and beloved by him that "seeth it. Thy fear is set in all the lands by reason of thy "perfect love, and they cry out to thy name making it the "first of names, and all people make offerings to thee. "Thou art the lord who art commemorated in heaven and "upon earth. Many are the cries which are made to thee "at the Uak[1] festival, and with one heart and voice Egypt "raiseth cries of joy to thee.

"Thou art the Great Chief, the first among thy brethren, "the Prince of the Company of the Gods, the stablisher of "Right and Truth throughout the World, the Son who "was set on the great throne of his father Ḳeb. Thou art "the beloved of thy mother Nut, the mighty one of valour, "who overthrew the Sebȧu-fiend. Thou didst stand up "and smite thine enemy, and set thy fear in thine adversary. "Thou dost bring the boundaries of the mountains (?). "Thy heart is fixed (or, determined), thy legs are set firm. "Thou art the heir of Ḳeb and of the sovereignty of the "Two Lands (Egypt). He (Ḳeb) hath seen his splendours, "he hath decreed for him the guidance of the world by thy "hand as long as times endure. Thou hast made this "earth with thy hand, and the waters, and the winds, and "the vegetation, and all the cattle, and all the feathered "fowl, and all the fish, and all the creeping things, and all "the wild animals thereof. The desert is the lawful posses- "sion of the son of Nut. The Two Lands (Egypt) are "content to crown thee upon the throne of thy father, "like Rā.

[1] This festival took place on the 17th and 18th days of the month Thoth; see Brugsch, *Kalendarische Inschriften*, p. 235.

"Thou rollest up into the horizon, thou hast set light "over the darkness, thou sendest forth air (or, light) from "thy plumes, and thou floodest the Two Lands like the "Disk at daybreak. Thy crown penetrateth the height of "heaven, thou art the companion of the stars, and the "guide of every god. Thou art beneficent in decree and "speech, the favoured one of the Great Company of the "Gods, and the beloved of the Little Company of the Gods.

"His sister [Isis] hath protected him, and hath repulsed "the fiends, and turned aside calamities (or, times [of evil]). "She uttered the spell with the magical power of her "mouth. Her tongue was perfect (or, well-trained), and it "never halted at a word. Beneficent in command and "word was Isis, the woman of magical spells, the advocate "of her brother. She sought him untiringly, she wandered "round and round about this earth in sorrow, and she "alighted[1] not without finding him. She made light (or, "air) with her feathers, she created air with her wings, and "she uttered the death wail for her brother. She raised "up the inactive members of him whose heart was still, "she drew from him his essence, she made an heir,[2] she "reared the child in loneliness, and the place where he was "was not known, and he grew in strength and stature, "and his hand waṣ mighty in the House of Ḳeb. The "Company of the Gods rejoiced, rejoiced, at the coming "of Horus, the son of Osiris, whose heart was firm, the "triumphant, the son of Isis, the heir of Osiris."[3]

[1] Literally, "she alighted not," ; the whole passage here justifies Plutarch's statement (*De Iside et Osiride*, 16) concerning Isis: Αὐτὴν δὲ γενομένην χελιδόνα τῇ κίονι περιπέτεσθαι καὶ θρηνεῖν.

[2] Compare Plutarch, *op. cit.*, § 19: Τὴν δ' Ἶσιν μετὰ τὴν τελευτὴν ἐξ Οσίριδος συγγενομένου, τεκεῖν ἠλιτόμηνον καὶ ἀσθενῆ τοῖς κάτωθεν γυίοις τὸν Ἁρποκράτην.

[3] The remainder of the hymn refers to Horus.

II.—OSIRIS AND HIS PRINCIPAL FORMS UNDER THE XVIIIth DYNASTY

1. Unn-Nefer
2. Osiris Ānkhti
3. Osiris, Lord of Life
4. Osiris Nebertcher
5. Osiris Khenti . . . . .
6. Osiris Orion (Saḥ)
7. Osiris Saa
8. Osiris, Governor of Temples
9. Osiris in Resnet
10. Osiris in Meḥnet
11. Osiris Everlasting Gold
12. Osiris Bati-erpit
13. Osiris Ptaḥ-neb-Ānkh
14. Osiris, Governor of Rasta
15. Osiris, Dweller in Set(?)

16. Osiris in Åti

17. Osiris in Seḥtet

18. Osiris in Netchfet

19. Osiris in Resu

20. Osiris in Pe

21. Osiris in Netru

22. Osiris in Lower Saïs

23. Osiris in Båkt

24. Osiris in Sunnu

25. Osiris in Reḥnent

26. Osiris in Åper

27. Osiris in Qefṭenu

28. Osiris Sekri in Peṭ-she

29. Osiris, Governor of his City

30. Osiris in Pesḳ-ra

31. Osiris in his Shrines in the Land of the North

32. Osiris in Heaven

33. Osiris in his Shrines in Rasta

34. Osiris Netchesti

35. Osiris Ṭesur

36. Osiris Sekri

37. Osiris, Governor of Eternity

38. Osiris the Begetter

39. Osiris in Åter

40. Osiris with the Plumes(?)

41. Osiris, Lord of Eternity

42. Osiris King (Åti)

43. Osiris Taiti

44. Osiris in Rasta

45. Osiris on his Sand

46. Osiris, Governor of the Chamber of the Cows

47. Osiris in Tanent

48. Osiris in Neṭbit

49. Osiris in Sȧti

50. Osiris in Beṭshu

51. Osiris in Ṭepu

52. Osiris in Upper Sau

53. Osiris in Nepert

54. Osiris in Shennu

55. Osiris in Ḥenket

56. Osiris in Ta-Sekri

57. Osiris in Shau

58. Osiris in Fat-Ḥeru

59. Osiris in Maāti

60. Osiris in Henȧ

THE DOCTRINE OF ETERNAL LIFE

The ideas and beliefs which the Egyptians held in reference to a future existence are not easily to be described in detail, owing to the many difficulties in translating religious texts and in harmonizing the statements made in different works of different periods. Some confusion of details also seems to have existed in the minds of the Egyptians themselves, which cannot be cleared up until the literature of the subject has been further studied and until more texts have been published. That the Egyptians believed in a future life is certain; and the doctrine of eternal existence is the leading feature of their religion, and is enunciated with the utmost clearness in all periods. And it is quite certain that the belief in immortality among the Egyptians is one of the oldest of their religious beliefs. The attainment of a renewal of life in the Other World was the aim and object of every Egyptian believer. To this end all the religious literature of Egypt was composed. Let us take the following extracts from texts of the VIth dynasty as illustrations:—

1. Hail Unȧs, not hast thou gone, behold, [as] one dead,

thou hast gone [as] one living to sit upon the throne of Osiris.[1]

2. O Rā-Tum, cometh to thee thy son, cometh to thee Unȧs .....

thy son is this of thy body for ever.[2]

[1] *Recueil de Travaux*, t. III, p. 201 (l. 206). The context runs "Thy "Sceptre is in thy hand, and thou givest commands unto the living ones. "The *Mekes* and *Neḥbet* sceptres are in thy hand, and thou givest com-"mands unto those whose abodes are secret."

[2] *Ibid.*, t. III, p. 208 (ll. 232, 233).

3. O Tum, thy son is this Osiris; thou hast given his sustenance

and he liveth; he liveth, and liveth Unȧs this; not dieth he, not

dieth Unȧs this.[1]

4. Setteth Unȧs in life in Ȧmenta.[2]

5. He[3] hath eaten the knowledge of god every, [his] existence

eternity, his limit everlastingness in his *sāḥ*[4] this; what

he willeth he doeth, [what] he hateth not doth he do.[5]

6. Live life, not shalt thou die.[6]

In the Papyrus of Ani (Chapter CLXXV) the deceased is represented as having come to a place remote and far away, where there is neither air to breathe nor water to drink, but where he holds converse with Temu. In answer to his question, "How long have I to live?"[7] the great god of Ȧnu answers:—

[1] *Recueil de Travaux*, t. III, p. 209 (l. 240).

[2] *Ibid.*, t. IV, p. 50 (l. 445). The allusion here is to the setting of the sun.

[3] *I.e.*, Unȧs.

[4] *I.e.*, his Spirit-body.

[5] *Ibid.*, t. IV, p. 61 (ll. 520, 521).

[6] *Ibid.*, t. V, p. 170 (Pepi, l. 85).

[7] . Plate XXIX, l. 16. (Book of the Dead, Chapter CLXXV.)

Thou shalt exist for millions of millions of years, a period of millions of years.

In the LXXXIVth Chapter, as given in the same papyrus, the infinite duration of the past and future existence of the soul, as well as its divine nature, is proclaimed by Ani in the words:—

I am Shu of divine company. My soul is God my soul is eternity.[1]

When the deceased identifies himself with Shu, he makes the period of his existence coeval with that of Temu-Rā, *i.e.*, he existed before Osiris and the other gods of his company. These two passages prove the identity of the belief in eternal life in the XVIIIth dynasty with that in the Vth and VIth dynasties.

But while we have this evidence of the Egyptian belief in eternal life, we are nowhere told that man's corruptible body will rise again; indeed, the following extracts show that the idea prevailed that the body lay in the earth while the soul or spirit lived in heaven:—

1. Soul to heaven body to earth.[2] (Vth dynasty.)

2. Thy essence is in heaven, thy body to earth.[3] (VIth dynasty.)

3. Heaven hath thy soul, earth hath thy body.[4] (Ptolemaïc Period.)

Plate XXVIII, l. 15.
Recueil de Travaux, t. IV, p. 71 (l. 582).
Ibid., t. V, p. 45 (l. 304).
Horrack, *Lamentations d'Isis et de Nephthys*, Paris, 1866, p. 6.

There is, however, no doubt that from first to last the Egyptians firmly believed that besides the soul there was some other element of the man that would rise again. The preservation of the corruptible body, too, was in some way connected with the life in the world to come, and its existence was necessary to ensure eternal life; otherwise the prayers recited to this end would have been futile, and the time-honoured custom of mummifying the dead would have had no meaning. The never-ending existence of the soul is asserted in a passage quoted above without reference to Osiris; but the frequent mention of the uniting of his bones, and of the gathering together of his members,[1] and the doing away with all corruption from his body, seems to show that the pious Egyptian connected these things with the resurrection of his own body in some form, and he argued that what had been done for him who was proclaimed to be giver and source of life must be necessary for mortal man.

The physical body of man considered as a whole was called *khat*, a word which seems to be connected with the idea of something which is liable to decay. The word is also applied to the mummified body in the tomb, as we know from the words "My body (*khat*) is buried."[2] Such a body was attributed to the god Osiris;[3] in the CLXIInd Chapter of the Book of the Dead "his great divine body rested in Ȧnu."[4] In this respect the god and the deceased were on an equality. As we have seen above, the body neither leaves the tomb nor reappears on earth; yet its preservation was necessary. Thus the

[1] Already in the Pyramid Texts we have "Rise up, O thou Tetȧ! Thou hast received thy head, thou hast knitted together thy bones, thou hast collected thy members." *Recueil de Travaux*, t. V, p. 40 (l. 287).

[2] Book of the Dead, Chapter LXXXVI, l. 11.

[3] *Papyrus of Ani*, Plate VII, l. 28, and Plate XIX, l. 8.

[4] Lepsius, *Todtenbuch*, Bl. 77, l. 7.

deceased addresses Temu[1]: "Hail to thee, O my father "Osiris, I have come and I have embalmed this my flesh "so that my body may not decay. I am whole, even as "my father Kheperȧ was whole, who is to me the type of "that which passeth not away, Come then, O Form, and "give breath unto me, O lord of breath, O thou who art "greater than thy compeers. Stablish thou me, and form "thou me, O thou who art lord of the grave. Grant thou "to me to endure for ever, even as thou didst grant unto "thy father Temu to endure; and his body neither passed "away nor decayed. I have not done that which is hateful "unto thee, nay, I have spoken that which thy KA loveth; "repulse thou me not, and cast thou me not behind thee, "O Temu, to decay, even as thou doest unto every god and "unto every goddess and unto every beast and creeping "thing which perisheth when his soul hath gone forth from "him after his death, and which falleth in pieces after his "decay . . . . . Homage to thee, O my father Osiris, thy "flesh suffered no decay, there were no worms in thee, "thou didst not crumble away, thou didst not wither away, "thou didst not become corruption and worms; and I "myself am Kheperȧ, I shall possess my flesh for ever and "ever, I shall not decay, I shall not crumble away, I shall "not wither away, I shall not become corruption."

But the body does not lie in the tomb inoperative, for by the prayers and ceremonies on the day of burial it is endowed with the power of changing into a *sāḥu*, or spiritual body. Thus we have such phrases as, "I flourish (literally, "'sprout') like the plants,"[2] "My flesh flourisheth,"[3] "I "exist, I exist, I live, I live, I flourish, I flourish,"[4] "thy

[1] This Chapter is inscribed upon one of the linen wrappings of the mummy of Thothmes III, and a copy of the text is given by Naville (*Todtenbuch*, Bd. I, Bl. 179); for a later version see Lepsius, *Todtenbuch*, Bl. 75, where many interesting variants occur.

[2] . Chapter LXXXIII, 3.

[3] . Chapter LXIV, l. 49.

[4] . Chapter CLIV, l. 12.

"soul liveth, thy body flourisheth by the command of "Rā himself without diminution, and without defect, like "unto Rā for ever and ever."[1] The word *sāḥu* , though at times written with the determinative of a mummy lying on a bier like *khat*, "body," indicates a Spirit-body which is lasting and incorruptible. The body which has become a *sāḥu* has the power of associating with the soul and of holding converse with it. In this form it can ascend into heaven and dwell with the gods, and with the *sāḥu* of the gods, and with the souls of the righteous. In the Pyramid Texts we have these passages :—

1. Rise up thou Tetȧ this. Stand up thou mighty one being strong. Sit thou with the gods, do thou that which did Osiris in the great house in Ȧnu. Thou hast received thy *sāḥ*, not shall be fettered thy foot in heaven, not shalt thou be turned back upon earth.[2]

[1] Brugsch, *Liber Metempsychosis*, p. 22.

[2] *Recueil de Travaux*, t. V, p. 36 (l. 271). From l. 143 of the same text it would seem that a man had more than one *sāḥu*, for the words "all thy *sāḥu*," , occur. This may, however, be only a plural of majesty.

2. Hail to thee, Tetȧ on this thy day [when] thou art standing before Rā [as] he cometh from the east, [when] thou art endued with this thy *sāḥ* among the souls.[1]

3. [His] duration of life is eternity, his limit of life is everlastingness in his *sāḥ*.[2]

4. I am ..... a *sāḥ* with his soul.[3]

In the late Recension of the Book of the Dead published by Lepsius the deceased is said to "look upon his body and to rest upon his *sāḥu*,"[4] and souls are said "to enter into their *sāḥu*";[5] and a passage extant both in this and the older Theban Recension makes the deceased to receive the *sāḥu* of the god Osiris.[6] But that Egyptian writers at times confused the *khat* with the *sāḥu* is clear from a passage in the Book of Respirations, where it is said: "Hail, Osiris, thy name endureth, thy body is stablished, thy *sāḥu* flourisheth";[7]

1 *Recueil de Travaux*, t. V, p. 59 (l. 384).
2 *Ibid.*, t. IV, p. 61 (l. 521).
3 Book of the Dead, Chapter LXXVIII, l. 14.
4 Chapter LXXXIX, l. 6.
5 *Ibid.*, l. 5.
6 Chapter CXXX, l. 38 (ed. Naville).
7 See Brugsch, *Liber Metempsychosis*, p. 15.

in other texts the word "flourish" is applied only to the natural body.

In close connection with the natural and spiritual bodies stood the heart, or rather that part of it which was the seat of the power of life and the fountain of good and evil thoughts. And in addition to the Natural-body and Spirit-body, man also had an abstract individuality or personality endowed with all his characteristic attributes. This abstract personality had an absolutely independent existence. It could move freely from place to place, separating itself from, or uniting itself to, the body at will, and also enjoying life with the gods in heaven. This was the KA 𓂓,[1] a word which at times conveys the meanings of its Coptic equivalent

[1] The general meaning of the word KA was first discovered by Nestor L'Hôte, and his discovery was published in his *Lettres* in 1840. The first Egyptologist who seriously examined the meaning of the word 𓂓 was Dr. Birch, who collected several examples of the word and discussed them in his *Mémoire sur une Patère Égyptienne du Musée du Louvre*, Paris, 1858, pp. 59 ff. (Extrait du t. XXIV des *Mémoires de la Société impériale des Antiquaires de France*). Dr. Birch translated the word by être, personne, emblème, divin, génie, principe, esprit. In September, 1878, M. Maspero explained to the Members of the Congress of Lyons the views which he held concerning this word, and which he had for the past five years been teaching in the Collège de France, and said "le *ka* est une sorte de double de la personne "humaine d'une matière moins grossière que la matière dont est formé le "corps, mais qu'il fallait nourrir et entretenir comme le corps lui-même; ce "double vivait dans le tombeau des offrandes qu'on faisait aux fêtes "canoniques, et aujourd'hui encore un grand nombre des génies de la "tradition populaire égyptienne ne sont que des *doubles*, devenus démons au "moment de la conversion des fellahs au christianisme, puis à l'islamisme." These views were repeated by him at the Sorbonne in February, 1879. See *Comptes Rendus du Congrès provincial des Orientalistes*, Lyons, 1878, t. I, pp. 235–263; *Revue Scientifique de la France et de l'Étranger*, 2ᵉ série, 8ᵉ année, No. 35, March, 1879, pp. 816–820; *Bulletin de l'Association Scientifique de France*, No. 594, 1879, t. XXIII, p. 373–384; Maspero, *Études de Mythologie et d'Archéologie*, t. I, pp. 1, 35, 126. In March, 1879, Mr. Renouf read a paper entitled "On the true sense of an important Egyptian word" (*Trans. Soc. Bibl. Arch.*, Vol. VI, London, 1879, pp. 494–508), in which he arrived at conclusions similar to those of M. Maspero; and in September of the same year M. Maspero again treated the subject in *Recueil de Travaux*, t. I, pp. 152 f. The various shades of meaning in the word have been discussed subsequently by Brugsch, *Wörterbuch* (Suppl.), pp. 997, 1230; Dümichen, *Der Grabpalast des Patuamenap*, Abt. I, p. 10; Bergmann, *Der Sarkophag des Panehemisis* (in *Jahrbuch der Kunsthistorischen Sammlungen des allerhöchsten Kaiserhauses*, Vienna, 1883, p. 5); Wiedemann, *Die Religion der alten Aegypter*, p. 126.

κω, and of *εἴδωλον*, image, genius, double, character, disposition, and mental attributes. What the Ka really was has not yet been decided, and Egyptologists have not yet come to an agreement in their views on the subject. Mr. Griffith thinks (*Hieroglyphs*, p. 15) that "it was from "one point of view regarded as the source of muscular "movement and power, as opposed to '*ba*,' the will or soul "which set it in motion." This view is substantially that of Erman (*Religion*, p. 102). Dr. Steindorff (*A.Z.*, 1910, pp. 152 ff.) thinks that the Ka was a genius, and not a "double." His views are traversed by Maspero in his paper *Le* Ka *des Égyptiens, est-il un génie ou un double* (*Zeitschrift für Kunst. . . . . des Alten Orients*, Bd. VI, pp. 125 ff.) who thinks that his own views on the subject are rather strengthened than weakened by Dr. Steindorff's arguments. Mr. Breasted (*Development*, p. 52) thinks that the Ka was a "superior genius intended to guide the fortunes of the individual in *the hereafter*." The relation of the Ka to the funerary offerings has been ably discussed by Baron Fr. W. v. Bissing (*Versuch einer neuen Erklärung des Ka'i der alten Aegypter* in the *Sitzungsberichte der Kgl. Bayer. Akad.*, Munich, 1911), and it seems as if the true solution of the mystery may be found by working on the lines of his idea, which was published in the *Recueil*, 1903, p. 182, and by comparing the views about the "double" held by African peoples throughout the Sûdân. The funeral offerings of meat, cakes, ale, wine, unguents, etc., were intended for the Ka; the scent of the burnt incense was grateful to it. The Ka dwelt in the man's statue just as the Ka of a god inhabited the statue of the god. In the remotest times the tombs had special chambers wherein the Ka was worshipped and received offerings. The priesthood numbered among its body an order of men who bore the name of "priests of the Ka", and who performed services in honour of the Ka in the "Ka chapel".

In the text of Unȧs the deceased is said to be "happy with his Ka"[1] in the next world, and his Ka is joined unto

[1] , l. 472.

his body in "the great dwelling";[1] his body having been buried in the lowest chamber, "his KA cometh forth to him."[2] Of Pepi I it is said:—

Washed is thy KA, sitteth thy KA [and] it eateth bread

with thee unceasingly for ever.[3]

Thou art pure, thy KA is pure, thy soul is pure,

thy form is pure.[4]

The KA, as we have seen, could eat food, and it was necessary to provide food for it. In the XIIth dynasty and in later periods the gods are entreated to grant meat and drink to the KA of the deceased; and it seems as if the Egyptians thought that the existence of the KA depended upon a constant supply of sepulchral offerings. When circumstances rendered it impossible to continue the material supply of food, the KA fed upon the offerings painted on the walls of the tomb, which were transformed into suitable nourishment by means of the prayers of the living. When there were neither material offerings nor painted similitudes to feed upon, it seems as if the KA must have perished; but the texts are not definite on this point.

The following is a specimen of a petition for food for the KA written in the XVIIIth dynasty:—

"May the gods grant that I go into and come forth

1 [hieroglyphs], l. 482.

2 [hieroglyphs], l. 483.

3 *Recueil de Travaux*, t. V, p. 166, l. 67.

4 *Ibid.*, l. 112.

"from my tomb, may the Majesty refresh its shade, may I "drink water from my cistern every day, may all my limbs "grow, may Ḥāpi give unto me bread and flowers of all "kinds in their season, may I pass over my estate every "day without ceasing, may my soul alight upon the branches "of the groves which I have planted, may I make myself "cool beneath my sycamores, may I eat the bread which "they provide. May I have my mouth that I may speak "therewith like the followers of Horus, may I come forth "to heaven, may I descend to earth, may I never be shut "out upon the road, may there never be done unto me that "which my soul abhorreth, let not my soul be imprisoned, "but may I be among the venerable and favoured ones, "may I plough my lands in the Field of Åaru, may I "arrive at the Field of Peace, may one come out to me "with vessels of ale and cakes and bread of the lords of "eternity, may I receive meat from the altars of the great, "I the KA of the prophet Menu."[1]

To that part of man which beyond all doubt was believed to enjoy an eternal existence after the death of the body, the Egyptians gave the name BA, a word which has been thought to mean something like "sublime," "noble," and which has always hitherto been translated by "soul," or "heart-soul." It was closely associated with the KA and the ÅB, or heart, and it was one of the principles of life in man. In form it is depicted as a human-headed hawk, and in nature and substance it is stated to be exceedingly refined or ethereal. It revisited the body in the tomb and re-animated it, and conversed with it; it could take upon itself any shape that it pleased; and it had the power of passing into heaven and of dwelling with the perfected souls there. It was eternal. As the BA was closely associated with the KA, it partook of the funeral offerings, and in one aspect of its existence at least it was liable to decay if not properly and sufficiently nourished. In the Pyramid Texts the permanent dwelling-place of the BA or soul is heaven with the gods, whose life it shares:—

[1] See *Trans. Soc. Bibl. Arch.*, Vol. VI, pp. 307, 308.

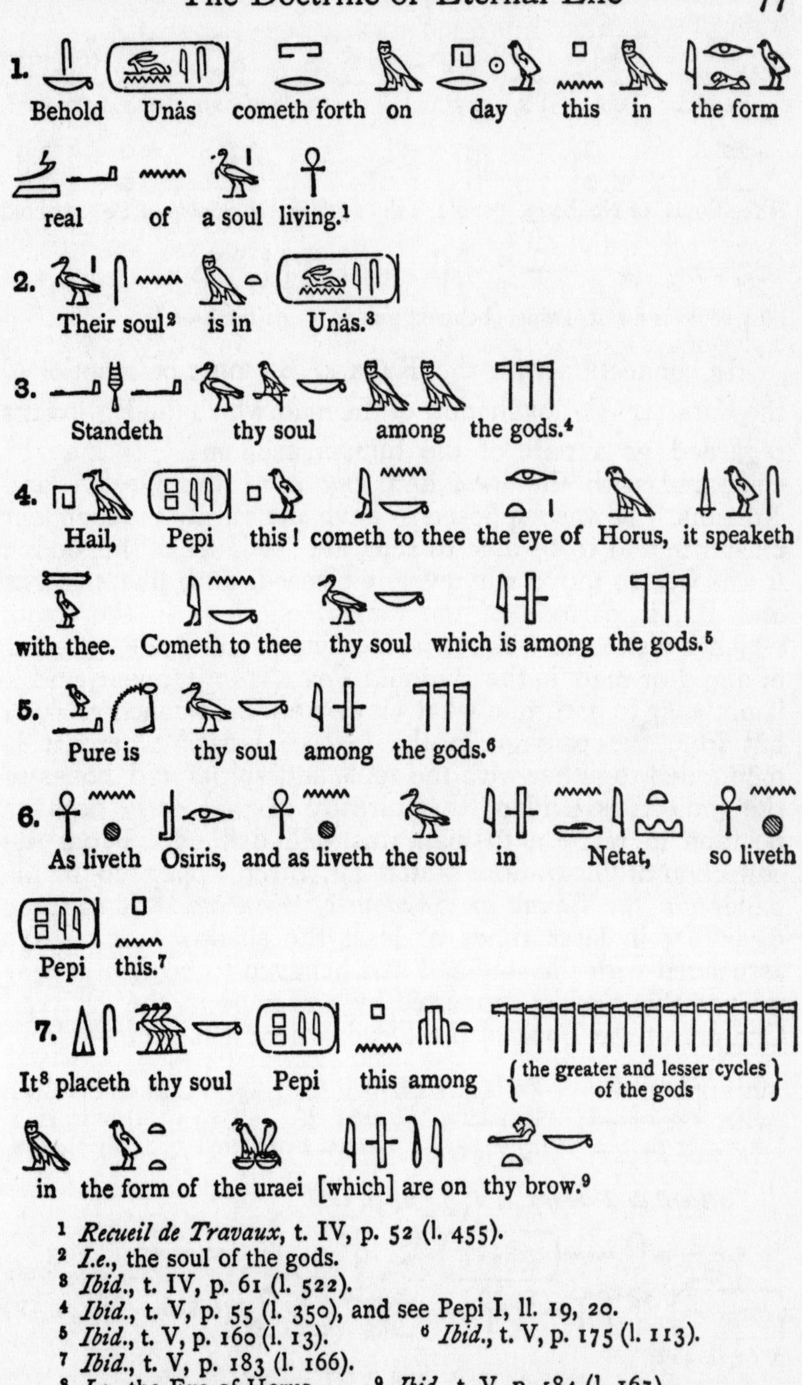

1. Behold Unȧs cometh forth on day this in the form
real of a soul living.[1]
2. Their soul[2] is in Unȧs.[3]
3. Standeth thy soul among the gods.[4]
4. Hail, Pepi this! cometh to thee the eye of Horus, it speaketh
with thee. Cometh to thee thy soul which is among the gods.[5]
5. Pure is thy soul among the gods.[6]
6. As liveth Osiris, and as liveth the soul in Netat, so liveth
Pepi this.[7]
7. It[8] placeth thy soul Pepi this among {the greater and lesser cycles of the gods}
in the form of the uraei [which] are on thy brow.[9]

[1] *Recueil de Travaux*, t. IV, p. 52 (l. 455).
[2] *I.e.*, the soul of the gods.
[3] *Ibid.*, t. IV, p. 61 (l. 522).
[4] *Ibid.*, t. V, p. 55 (l. 350), and see Pepi I, ll. 19, 20.
[5] *Ibid.*, t. V, p. 160 (l. 13). [6] *Ibid.*, t. V, p. 175 (l. 113).
[7] *Ibid.*, t. V, p. 183 (l. 166).
[8] *I.e.*, the Eye of Horus. [9] *Ibid.*, t. V, p. 184 (l. 167).

8. Behold Pepi this, thy soul is the Souls of Ȧnu; behold thy soul is the Souls of Nekhen; behold thy soul is the Souls of Pe; behold thy soul is a star living, behold, among its brethren.[1]

In connection with the KA and BA must be mentioned the KHAIBIT, or shadow of the man, which the Egyptians regarded as a part of the human economy. It may be compared with the σκιά and *umbra* of the Greeks and Romans. It was supposed to have an entirely independent existence and to be able to separate itself from the body; it was free to move wherever it pleased, and, like the KA and BA, it partook of the funeral offerings in the tomb, which it visited at will. The mention of the shade, whether of a god or man, in the Pyramid Texts is unfrequent, and it is not easy to ascertain what views were held concerning it; but from the passage in the text of Unȧs,[2] where it is mentioned together with the souls and spirits and bones of the gods, it is evident that already at that early date its position in relation to man was well defined. From the collection of illustrations which Dr. Birch appended to his paper *On the Shade or Shadow of the Dead*,[3] it is quite clear that in later times at least the shadow was always associated with the soul and was believed to be always near it; and this view is supported by a passage in the XCIInd Chapter of the Book of the Dead, where it is said:—

Let not be shut in my soul, let not be fettered my shadow,

[1] *Recueil de Travaux*, t. V, p. 184 (l. 168).

[2] *Ibid.*, t. IV, p. 62 (l. 523).

[3] See *Trans. Soc. Bibl. Arch.*, Vol. VIII, pp. 386-97.

let be opened the way for my soul and for my shadow, may it see

the great god.

And again, in the LXXXIXth Chapter the deceased says:—

May I look upon my soul and my shadow.[1]

Another important and apparently eternal part of man was the KHU, , which, judging from the meaning of the word, may be defined as a "shining" or translucent Spirit-soul. For want of a better word KHU has often been translated "shining one," "glorious," "intelligence," and the like, but its true meaning must be Spirit-soul. The Pyramid Texts show us that the KHU's of the gods lived in heaven, and thither wended the KHU of a man as soon as ever the body died. Thus it is said, "Unȧs standeth with the KHU's,"[2] and one of the gods is asked to "give him his sceptre among the KHU's";[3] when the souls of the gods enter into Unȧs, their KHU's are with and round about him.[4] To King Tetȧ it is said:—

He[5] hath plucked his eye from himself, he hath given it unto thee

to strengthen thee therewith, that thou mayest prevail with it among

the KHU's.[6]

[1] *Todtenbuch*, Bd. I, Bl. 101.

[2] *Recueil de Travaux*, t. III, p. 188 (l. 71).

[3] *Ibid.*, t. III, p. 215 (l. 274).

[4] *Ibid.*, t. IV, p. 61 (l. 522).

[5] *I.e.*, Horus.

[6] *Ibid.*, t. V, p. 19 (l. 174).

And again, when the god Khent-mennut-f has transported the king to heaven, the god Ḳeb, who rejoices to meet him, is said to give him both hands and welcome him as a brother and to nurse him and to place him among the imperishable KHU's.[1] In the XCIInd Chapter the deceased is made to pray for the liberation of his soul, shadow, and KHU from the bondage of the tomb, and for deliverance from those "whose dwellings are hidden, who fetter the "souls, who fetter souls and KHU's and who shut in the "shadows of the dead"; and in the XCIst Chapter is a formula specially prepared to enable the KHU to pass from the tomb to the domains where Rā and Hathor dwell.

Yet another part of a man was supposed to exist in heaven, to which the Egyptians gave the name SEKHEM, [hieroglyphs]. The word has been rendered by "vital power," and the like, but it is very difficult to find any expression which will represent the Egyptian conception of the SEKHEM. It is mentioned in connection with the soul and KHU, as will be seen from the following passages from the Pyramid Texts:—

1. [hieroglyphs]
Cometh to thee thy SEKHEM among the KHU's.[2]

2. [hieroglyphs]
Pure is thy SEKHEM among the KHU's.[3]

3. [hieroglyphs]
Thou art pure, pure is thy KA, pure is thy soul, pure is thy SEKHEM.[4]

[1] [hieroglyphs] *Recueil de Travaux*, t. V, p. 41 (l. 289).
[2] *Ibid.*, t. V, p. 160 (l. 14).
[3] *Ibid.*, t. V, p. 175 (l. 113).
[4] *Ibid.*, t. V, p. 175 (l. 112).

A name of Rā was [hieroglyphs][1] SEKHEM UR, the "Great Sekhem," and Unȧs is identified with him and called:—

[hieroglyphs]
Great SEKHEM, SEKHEM among the SEKHEMU.[2]

Finally, the name, [hieroglyphs], REN, of a man was believed to exist in heaven, and in the Pyramid Texts we are told that

[hieroglyphs]
Happy is Pepi this with his name, liveth Pepi this with his KA.[3]

Thus, as we have seen, the whole man consisted of a natural body, a Spirit-body, a heart, a double, a Heart-soul, a shadow, a Spirit-soul, and a name. All these were, however, bound together inseparably, and the welfare of any single one of them concerned the welfare of all. For the well-being of the spiritual parts it was necessary to preserve from decay the natural body; and certain passages in the Pyramid Texts seem to show that a belief in the resurrection of the natural body existed in the earliest dynasties.[4]

The texts are silent as to the time when the immortal part began its beatified existence; but it is probable that the Osiris [5] of a man only attained to the full enjoyment of

[1] *Recueil de Travaux*, t. IV, p. 44 (l. 393).

[2] *Ibid.*, p. 60 (ll. 514, 515).

[3] *Ibid.*, t. V, p. 185 (l. 169).

[4] *E.g.*, [hieroglyphs] "This Pepi goeth forth with his flesh." *Ibid.*, t. V, p. 185 (l. 169).

[5] The Osiris consisted of all the spiritual parts of a man gathered together in a form which resembled him exactly. Whatever honour was paid to the mummified body was received by its Osiris, the offerings made to it were accepted by its Osiris, and the amulets laid upon it were made use of by its Osiris for its own protection. The *sāḥu*, the *ka*, the *ba*, the *khu*, the *khaibit*, the *sekhem*, and the *ren* were in primeval times separate and independent parts of man's immortal nature; but in the Pyramid Texts

spiritual happiness after the funeral ceremonies had been duly performed and the ritual recited. Comparatively few particulars are known of the manner of life of the soul in heaven, and though a number of interesting facts may be gleaned from the texts of all periods, it is very difficult to harmonize them. This result is due partly to the different views held by different schools of thought in ancient Egypt, and partly to the fact that on some points the Egyptians themselves seem to have had no decided opinions. We depend upon the Pyramid Texts for our knowledge of their earliest conceptions of a future life.

The life of the Osiris of a man in heaven is at once material and spiritual; and it seems as if the Egyptians never succeeded in breaking away from their very ancient habit of confusing the things of the body with the things of the soul. They believed in an incorporeal and immortal part of man, the constituent elements of which flew to heaven after death; yet the theologians of the VIth dynasty had decided that there was some part of the deceased which could only mount to heaven by means of a ladder. In the pyramid of Tetȧ it is said: "When Tetȧ hath purified "himself on the borders of this earth where Rā hath "purified himself, he prayeth and setteth up the ladder, and "those who dwell in the great place press Tetȧ forward "with their hands."[1] In the pyramid of Pepi I the king is identified with this ladder: "Isis saith, 'Happy are they "who see the father,' and Nephthys saith, 'They who see "the father have rest,' speaking unto the father of this "Osiris Pepi when he cometh forth into heaven among the "stars and among the luminaries which never set. With "the uraeus on his brow, and his book upon both his sides,

---

they are welded together, and the dead king Pepi is addressed as "Osiris Pepi." The custom of calling the deceased Osiris continued until the Roman Period. On the Osiris of a man, see Wiedemann, *Die Osirianische Unsterblichkeitslehre* (in *Die Religion der alten Aegypter*, p. 128).

[1] Maspero, *Recueil de Travaux*, t. V, p. 7 (l. 36).

" and magic words at his feet, Pepi goeth forward unto his " mother Nut, and he entereth therein in his name Ladder."[1] The gods who preside over this ladder are at one time Rā and Horus, and at another Horus and Set. In the pyramid of Unȧs it is said: " Rā setteth upright the ladder for Osiris, " and Horus raiseth up the ladder for his father Osiris, " when Osiris goeth to [find] his soul; one standeth on the " one side, and the other standeth on the other, and Unȧs " is betwixt them. Unȧs standeth up and is Horus, he " sitteth down and is Set."[2] And in the pyramid of Pepi I we read: " Hail to thee, O Ladder of God, hail to thee, " O Ladder of Set. Stand up, O Ladder of God, stand " up, O Ladder of Set, stand up, O Ladder of Horus, " whereon Osiris went forth into heaven. . . . . . This " Pepi is thy son, this Pepi is Horus, thou hast given birth " unto this Pepi even as thou hast given birth unto the god " who is the lord of the ladder. Thou hast given him the " Ladder of God, and thou hast given him the Ladder of " Set, whereon this Pepi hath gone forth into heaven. . . . . " Every KHU and every god stretcheth out his hand unto " this Pepi when he cometh forth into heaven by the " Ladder of God . . . . that which he seeth and that which " he heareth make him wise, and serve as food for him " when he cometh forth into heaven by the Ladder of God. " Pepi riseth up like the uraeus which is on the brow of " Set, and every KHU and every god stretcheth out his " hand unto Pepi on the Ladder. Pepi hath gathered " together his bones, he hath collected his flesh, and Pepi " hath gone straightway into heaven by means of the two " fingers of the god who is the Lord of the Ladder."[3] Elsewhere we are told that Khensu and Set "carry the Ladder of Pepi, and they set it up."

When the Osiris of a man has entered into heaven as a living soul,[4] he is regarded as one of those who "have eaten the eye of Horus";[5] he walks among the living ones,

1 *Recueil de Travaux*, t. V, p. 190 (ll. 181, 182).

2 *Ibid.*, t. IV, p. 70 (ll. 579 ff.).

3 *Etudes de Mythologie et d'Archéologie*, t. I, p. 344, note 1.

4 *Recueil de Travaux*, t. V, p. 52 (l. 456).

5 *Ibid.*, t. III, p. 165 (line 169).

[hieroglyphs],[1] he becomes "God, the son of God,"[2] and all the gods of heaven become his brethren.[3] His bones are the gods and goddesses of heaven;[4] his right side belongs to Horus, and his left side to Set;[5] the goddess Nut makes him to rise up as a god without an enemy in his name "God";[6] and God calls him by his name.[7] His face is the face of Up-uat, his eyes are the great ones among the souls of Ȧnu, his nose is Thoth, his mouth is the great lake, his tongue belongs to the boat of right and truth, his teeth are the spirits of Unu, his chin is Khert-khent-Sekhem, his backbone is Sema, his shoulders are Set, his breast is Beba,[8] etc.; every one of his members is identified with a god. Moreover, his body as a whole is identified with the God of Heaven. For example it is said concerning Unȧs:—

[hieroglyphs]
Thy body is the body of Unȧs this. The flesh is the flesh of

[hieroglyphs]
Unȧs this. Thy bones are the bones of Unȧs this.

[hieroglyphs]
Thy passage is the passage of Unȧs this. The passage of Unȧs

[hieroglyphs]
this is thy passage.[9]

1 *Recueil de Travaux*, t. V, p. 183 (l. 166).

2 [hieroglyphs]. *Ibid.*, t. VIII, p. 89 (l. 574).

3 [hieroglyphs]. See Pyramid of Tetȧ (*Recueil*, t. V), ll. 45, 137, 197, 302.

4 [hieroglyphs]. *Ibid.*, t. III, p. 202 (l. 209).

5 *Ibid.*, t. V, p. 23 (l. 198).

6 [hieroglyphs]. *Ibid.*, t. V, p. 38 (l. 279).

7 *Ibid.*, p. 26 (l. 222).

8 *Ibid.*, t. VIII, p. 88 (ll. 565 ff.).

9 *Ibid.*, t. III, p. 214 (l. 268).

Further, this identification of the deceased with the God of Heaven places him in the position of supreme ruler. For example, we have the prayer that Unȧs "may rule the nine gods and complete the company of the nine gods,"[1] and Pepi I, in his progress through heaven, comes upon the double company of the gods, who stretch out their hands, entreating him to come and sit down among them.[2]

Again, the deceased is changed into Horus, the son of Osiris and Isis. It is said of Pepi I, "Behold it is not "Pepi who entreateth to see thee in the form in which thou "art, O Osiris, who entreateth to see "thee in the form in which thou art, O Osiris; but it is thy "son who entreateth to see thee in the form in which thou "art, O Osiris, it is Horus who entreateth to see thee in "the form in which thou art";[3] and Horus does not place Pepi at the head of the dead, but among the divine gods.[4] Elsewhere we are told that Horus has taken his Eye and given it to Pepi, and that the odour of Pepi's body is the odour of the Eye of Horus.[5] Throughout the Pyramid Texts the Osiris of the deceased is the son of Temu, or Temu-Rā, Shu, Tefnut, Ḳeb, and Nut, the brother of Isis, Nephthys, Set, and Thoth, and the father of Horus;[6] his hands, arms, belly, back, hips and thighs, and legs are the god Temu, and his face is Anubis.[7] He is the brother of the moon,[8] he is the child of the star Sothis,[9] he revolves in

1 *Recueil de Travaux*, t. III, p. 217 (l. 283).

2 *Ibid.*, t. VII, p. 150 (l. 263).

3 *Ibid.*, t. VII, p. 155 (ll. 315 f.).

4 *Ibid.*, t. V, p. 194 (l. 190).

5 *Ibid.*, t. VII, p. 169 (l. 457).

6 *Ibid.*, t. III, pp. 209–211.

7 *Ibid.*, p. 201 (l. 207).

8 *Ibid.*, t. V, p. 198 (l. 203).

9 *Ibid.*, t. IV, p. 44, l. 390.

heaven like Orion [hieroglyphs] and Sothis [hieroglyphs],[1] and he rises in his place like a star.[2] The gods, male and female, pay homage to him,[3] every being in heaven adores him; and in one interesting passage it is said of Pepi I that "when he "hath come forth into heaven he will find Rā standing face "to face before him, and, having seated himself upon the "shoulders of Rā, Rā will not let him put himself down "again upon the ground; for he knoweth that Pepi is more "shining than the shining ones, more perfect than the "perfect, and more stable than the stable ones . . . . . . "When Pepi standeth upon the north of heaven with Rā, "he becometh lord of the universe like unto the king of the "gods."[4] To the deceased Horus gives his own KA,[5] and also drives away the KA's of the enemies of the deceased from him, and hamstrings his foes.[6] By the divine power thus given to the deceased he brings into subjection the KA's of the gods[7] and other KA's,[8] and he lays his yoke upon the KA's of the triple company of the gods.[9] He also becomes Thoth,[10] the intelligence of the gods, and he judges hearts;[11] and the hearts of those who would take away his food and the breath from his nostrils become the prey of his hands.[12]

[1] *Recueil de Travaux*, t. III, p. 205 (ll. 221 f.).
[2] *Ibid.*, t. IV, p. 44 (l. 391).
[3] [hieroglyphs]. *Ibid.*, t. V, p. 23 (l. 197).
[4] *Ibid.*, t. V, p. 171 (ll. 91 ff.).
[5] [hieroglyphs]. *Ibid.*, t. V, p. 33 (l. 265).
[6] *Ibid.*, t. V, p. 40 (l. 287).
[7] [hieroglyphs]. *Ibid.*, p. 45 (l. 306).
[8] [hieroglyphs]. *Ibid.*, t. IV, p. 51 (l. 451); t. III, p. 208 (l. 234).
[9] *Ibid.*, t. V, p. 46 (l. 307).
[10] *Ibid.*, t. VII, p. 168 (l. 452).
[11] *Ibid.*, t. III, p. 208 (l. 233), [hieroglyphs].
[12] *Ibid.*, t. IV, p. 49 (l. 430), [hieroglyphs].

The place of the deceased in heaven is by the side of God[1] in the most holy place,[2] and he becomes God and an angel of God;[3] he himself is a speaker of the truth,[4] and his KA is triumphant.[5] He sits on a great throne by the side of God.[6] The throne is of iron, or alabaster,

[1] *un-k àr ḳes neter.* *Recueil de Travaux*, t. III, p. 202 (l. 209).

[2] *Ibid.*, t. V, p. 189 (l. 178).

[3] *Ibid.*, t. V, p. 187 (l. 175).

[4] *maā-kheru.* *Ibid.*, t. V, p. 186 (l. 172). These words are in later times always added after the name of the deceased, and seem to mean something like "he whose voice, or speech, is right and true"; the expression has been rendered by "disant la vérité," "véridique," "juste," "justifié," "vainqueur," "waltend des Wortes," "mächtig der Rede," "vrai de voix," "juste de voix," "victorious," "triumphant," and the like. See on this subject Maspero, *Études de Mythologie et d'Archéologie*, t. I, pp. 93–114; Devéria, *L'Expression Màâ-χerou* (in *Recueil de Travaux*, t. I, pp. 10 ff.). As to the general meaning of *maākheru* there can be no doubt. When Set made accusations against Osiris, which Osiris denied, the gods of Ȧnu tried Osiris to find out which of the two was speaking the truth. Thoth proved conclusively that Osiris was innocent of the charges made by Set, and therefore that he was *maākheru*, *i.e.*, true of word, or truth-speaker, or innocent. A somewhat different view of the signification of *maākheru* is given by Virey (*Tombeau de Rekhmara*, Paris, 1889, p. 101. Published in *Mémoires publiés par les Membres de la Miss. Arch. Française au Caire*, t. V, fasc. I). The offerings which were painted on the walls of the tomb were actually enjoyed by the deceased in his new state of being. The Egyptians called them "*per kheru*," that is to say, "the things which *the word* or *the demand made to appear*," or "*per hru kheru*," that is to say, "*the things which presented themselves at the word*" or "*at the demand*" of the deceased. The deceased was then called "*maākheru*," that is to say, "*he who realizes his word*," or "*he who realizes while he speaks*," or "*whose voice or demand realizes*," or "*whose voice* or *demand makes true*, or *makes to be really and actually*" that which only appears in painting on the walls of the tomb. M. Amélineau combats this interpretation, and agrees with M. Maspero's rendering of "*juste de voix*"; see *Un Tombeau Égyptien* (in *Revue de l'Histoire des Religions*), t. XXIII, pp. 153, 154.

[5] *Ibid.*, t. V, p. 189 (l. 179).

[6] *Ibid.*, t. IV, p. 58 (l. 494).

ornamented with lions' faces and having the hoofs of bulls.[1] He is clothed in the finest raiment, like unto the raiment of those who sit on the throne of living right and truth.[2] He receives the *Urrt* Crown from the gods,[3] and from the Great Company of the Gods of Ȧnu.[4] He thirsts not, nor hungers, nor is sad;[5] he eats the bread of Rā and drinks what he drinks daily,[6] and his bread also is that which is the word of Ḳeb, and that which comes forth from the mouths of the gods.[7] He eats what the gods eat, he drinks what they drink, he lives as they live, and he dwells where they dwell;[8] all the gods give him their food that he may not die.[9] Not only does he eat and drink of their food, but he wears the apparel which they wear,[10] the white linen and sandals;[11] he is clothed in white,[12] and "he goeth to the great lake in the midst of the Field of "Offerings whereon the great gods sit; and these great and "never-failing gods give unto him [to eat] of the tree of "life of which they themselves do eat "that he likewise may live."[13] The bread which he eats never decays, and his beer

1 . *Recueil de Travaux*, t. VII, p. 154 (ll. 309, 310).

2 *Ibid.*, t. V, p. 148 (l. 239).
3 *Ibid.*, t. IV, p. 56 (l. 480).
4 *Ibid.*, t. V, p. 176 (l. 117).
5 *Ibid.*, t. III, p. 195 (l. 172).
6 *Ibid.*, t. V, p. 52 (l. 335).

7 . *Ibid.*, t. III, p. 208 (l. 234).

8 *Ibid.*, t. III, p. 198 (ll. 191 f.).

9 *Ibid.*, t. V, p. 164 (l. 56).

10 . *Ibid.*, t. V, p. 190 (l. 180).

11 .. *Ibid.*, t. V, p. 163 (l. 408).

12 *Ibid.*, t. IV, p. 45 (l. 394).
13 *Ibid.*, t. VII, p. 165 (l. 430).

never grows stale.[1] He eats of the "bread of eternity" and drinks of the "beer of everlastingness" which the gods eat and drink;[2] and he nourishes himself upon that bread which the Eye of Horus has shed upon the branches of the olive tree.[3] He suffers neither hunger nor thirst like the gods Shu and Tefnut, for he is filled with the bread of wheat of which Horus himself has eaten; and the four children of Horus, Ḥāpi, Ṭuamutef, Qebḥsenuf, and Åmset, have appeased the hunger of his belly and the thirst of his lips.[4] He abhors the hunger which he cannot satisfy, and he loathes the thirst which he cannot slake;[5] but he is delivered from the power of those who would steal away his food.[6] He is washed clean, and his KA is washed clean, and they eat bread together for ever.[7] He is one of the four children of Horus who live on right and truth,[8] and they give him his portion of the food with which they have been so abundantly supplied by the god Ḳeb that they have never yet known what it is to hunger. He goes round about heaven even as they do, and he partakes of their food of figs and wine.[9]

Those who would be hostile to the deceased become thereby foes of the god Temu, and all injuries inflicted on him are inflicted on that god;[10] he dwells without fear under the protection of the gods,[11] from whose loins he has come forth.[12] To him "the earth is an abomination, and he will "not enter into Ḳeb; for his soul hath burst for ever the "bonds of his sleep in his house which is upon earth. His "calamities are brought to an end, for Unås hath been "purified with the Eye of Horus; the calamities of Unås

1 *Recueil de Travaux*, t. V, p. 41 (l. 288), and t. VII, p. 167 (l. 442).

2 *Ibid.*, t. VII, p. 160 (l. 390).

3 *Ibid.*, t. III, p. 199 (l. 200).

4 *Ibid.*, t. V, p. 10 (ll. 54 ff.).

5 *Ibid.*, t. III, p. 199 (ll. 195 f.).

6 *Ibid.*, t. IV, p. 48 (l. 429).

7 *Ibid.*, t. V, p. 167 (l. 66).

8 *Ibid.*, t. VIII, p. 106 (l. 673).

9 *Ibid.*, t. VIII, p. 110 (l. 692).

10 *Ibid.*, t. IV, p. 74 (l. 602).

11 *Ibid.*, t. IV, p. 46 (l. 405).

12 *Ibid.*, t. III, p. 202 (l. 209).

"have been done away by Isis and Nephthys. Unȧs is in heaven, Unȧs is in heaven, in the form of air, in the form of air; he perisheth not, neither doth anything which is in him perish.[1] He is firmly stablished in heaven, and he taketh his pure seat in the bows of the bark of Rā. Those who row Rā up into the heavens row him also, and those who row Rā beneath the horizon row him also."[2] The life which the deceased leads is said to be generally that of him "who entereth into the west of the sky, and who cometh forth from the east thereof."[3] In brief, the condition of the blessed is summed up in the following extract from the Pyramid of Pepi I:—[4]

"**1.** Hail, thou Pepi, **2.** thou hast come, thou art a Spirit-soul, and thou hast gotten might like the god, **3.** behold thou art enthroned, Osiris. Thy Heart-soul is with thee in thee, **4.** thy vital strength is behind thee. Thy *Urrt* Crown is upon thy head, **5.** thy headdress is upon thy shoulders, thy face is before thee, and those who sing songs of joy are upon **6.** both sides of thee; those who follow in the train of God are behind thee, and the Spirit-bodies are upon each side of thee. **7.** They cry out, The god cometh, the god cometh, Pepi hath come upon the throne of Osiris. The Spirit-soul who **8.** dwelleth in Netȧt, the Power that dwelleth in Teni, hath come. Isis speaketh unto thee, Nephthys holdeth converse with thee, and the **9.** Spirit-souls come unto thee bowing their backs, they smell the earth at thy feet, by reason of thy slaughter, O Pepi, **10.** in the towns of Saa. Thou comest forth to thy mother Nut, and she graspeth thy arm, and she maketh a way for thee **11.** through the sky to the place where Rā abideth. Thou hast opened the gates of the sky, thou hast opened the doors of the celestial deep; thou hast found **12.** Rā and he protecteth thee, he hath taken thee by thy hand, he hath led thee into the two halves of **13.** heaven, and he hath placed thee on the throne

[1] *Recueil de Travaux*, t. IV, p. 51 (ll. 447 f.).

[2] *Ibid.*, t. V, p. 53 (l. 340).

[3] *Ibid.*, t. 8, p. 104 (l. 665).

[4] *Ibid.*, t. V, p. 159 (ll. 1–21).

" of Osiris. Hail, O Pepi! The Eye of Horus came to
" hold converse with thee; **14.** thy soul which is among the
" gods cometh unto thee; thy power which dwelleth among
" the Spirit-souls cometh unto thee. As a son fighteth for
" his father, and as Horus fought for Osiris, **15.** even so
" doth Horus deliver Pepi from the hand of his enemies.
" Stand up, avenged, endowed with all things like unto
" a god, and equipped with **16.** the Form of Osiris upon
" the throne of Khent-Ȧmenti. Thou doest that which he
" doeth among the imperishable Spirit-souls; **17.** thy son
" standeth upon thy throne being provided with thy Form,
" and it doeth that which thou doest in the presence of
" Him that is the First among the Living, by the command
" of Rā, the great god. **18.** He reapeth the wheat, he
" cutteth the barley, and he giveth it unto thee. Hail, Pepi!
" He that hath given unto thee life and all serenity for ever
" is Rā. **19.** Thou speakest to thy body, thou hast received
" the Form of God, and thou hast become magnified
" thereby before the gods who are at the head of the Lake.
" Hail, Pepi, thy Heart-soul standeth **20.** among the gods
" and among the Spirit-souls, and the fear of thee striketh
" into their hearts. Hail, Pepi! Stand up, Pepi, on thy
" throne at the head of the **21.** living, thy slaughter [striketh
" terror] into their hearts. Thy name liveth upon earth,
" thy name shall flourish upon earth, thou shalt neither
" perish nor be destroyed for ever and for ever."

Side by side however, with the passages which speak of the material and spiritual enjoyments of the deceased, we have others which seem to imply that the Egyptians believed in a corporeal existence,[1] or at least in the capacity for corporeal enjoyment, in the future state. This belief

[1] Compare "O flesh of Tetȧ, rot not, decay not, stink not." *Recueil de Travaux*, t. V, p. 55 (l. 347). "Pepi goeth forth with his flesh"; *ibid.*, t. V, p. 185 (l. 169). "thy bones shall not be destroyed, and thy flesh shall not perish"; *ibid.*, p. 55 (l. 353).

may have rested upon the view that the life in the next world was but a continuation of the life upon earth, which it resembled closely, or it may have been due to the survival of semi-savage gross ideas incorporated into the religious texts of the Egyptians. However this may be, it is quite certain that in the Vth dynasty the deceased king Unȧs eats with his mouth, and exercises other natural functions of the body, and gratifies his passions.[1] But the most remarkable passage in this connection is one in the pyramid of Unȧs. Here all creation is represented as being in terror when they see the deceased king rise up as a soul in the form of a god who devours "his fathers and mothers"; he feeds upon men and also upon gods. He hunts the gods in the fields and snares them; and when they are tied up

[1] Compare the following passages:—

(a)

Recueil de Travaux, t. IV, p. 76 (ll. 628, 629).

(b)

Ibid., t. V, p. 37 (l. 277).

(c)

Ibid., t. III, p. 197 (ll. 182 f.).

(d)

Ibid., t. V, p. 40 (l. 286), and see M. Maspero's note on the same page.

for slaughter he cuts their throats and disembowels them. He roasts and eats the best of them, but the old gods and goddesses are used for fuel. By eating them he imbibes both their magical powers, and their Spirit-souls. He becomes the "Great Power, the Power "of Powers, and the god of all the great gods who exist in "visible forms,"[1] and he is at the head of all the *sāḥu*, or Spirit-bodies in heaven. He carries off the hearts of the gods, and devours the wisdom of every god; therefore the duration of his life is everlasting and he lives to all eternity, for the Heart-souls of the gods and their Spirit-souls are in him. The whole passage reads:—[2]

"**496.** The skies lower, the stars tremble, **497.** the "Archers quake, the **498.** bones of Åkeru-gods tremble, "and those who are with them are struck dumb when they "see **499.** Unȧs rising up as a soul, in the form of the god "who liveth upon his fathers and who maketh to be his "food his **500.** mothers. Unȧs is the lord of wisdom, "and **501.** his mother knoweth not his name. The "adoration of Unȧs is in heaven, he hath become mighty "in the horizon **502.** like unto Temu, the father that gave "him birth, and after Temu gave him birth **503.** Unȧs "became stronger than his father. The Doubles of Unȧs "are behind him, the sole of his foot is beneath his feet, "his gods are over him, his uraei are [seated] **504.** upon "his brow, the serpent guides of Unȧs are in front of him, "and the spirit of the flame looketh upon [his] soul. The "**505.** powers of Unȧs protect him; Unȧs is a bull in "heaven, he directeth his steps where he will, he liveth "upon the form which **506.** each god taketh upon himself, "and he eateth the flesh of those who come to fill their "bellies with the magical charms in the Lake of Fire. "Unȧs is **507.** equipped with power against the Spirit-souls

1 . Pyramid of Tetȧ, l. 327; *Recueil de Travaux*, t. V, p. 50.

2 See Maspero, *Ibid.*, t. IV, p. 59, t. V, p. 50; and Sethe, *Pyramidentexte*, Bd. I, p. 205.

" thereof, and he riseth up in the form of the mighty one, " the lord of those who dwell in power (?). Unȧs hath " taken his seat with his side turned towards Ḳeb. " **508.** Unȧs hath weighed his words with the hidden god (?) " who hath no name, on the day of hacking in pieces the " firstborn. Unȧs is the lord of offerings, the untier of the " knot, and he himself maketh abundant the offerings of " meat and drink. **509.** Unȧs devoureth men and liveth " upon the gods, he is the lord of envoys, whom he sendeth " forth on his missions. 'He who cutteth off hairy scalps,' " who dwelleth in the fields, tieth the gods with ropes; " **510.** Tcheser-tep keepeth guard over them for Unȧs and " driveth them unto him; and the Cord-master hath bound " them for slaughter. Khonsu the slayer of the wicked " cutteth their throats **511.** and draweth out their intestines, " for it is he whom Unȧs sendeth to slaughter; and Shesmu " cutteth them in pieces and boileth their members in his " blazing caldrons of the night. **512.** Unȧs eateth their " magical powers, and he swalloweth their Spirit-souls; the " great ones among them serve for his meal at daybreak, the " lesser serve for his meal at eventide, and the least among " them serve for his meal in the night. **513.** The old gods " and the old goddesses become fuel for his furnace. The " mighty ones in heaven light the fire under the caldrons " where are heaped up the thighs of the firstborn; and he " that maketh those who live **514.** in heaven to go about for " Unȧs lighteth the fire under the caldrons with the thighs " of their women; he goeth round about the Two Heavens " in their entirety, and he goeth round about the two banks " of the Celestial Nile. Unȧs is the Great Power, the " Power of Powers, **515.** and Unȧs is the Chief of the gods " in visible forms. Whatever he findeth upon his path he " eateth forthwith, and the magical might of Unȧs is before " that of all the **516.** Spirit-bodies who dwell in the horizon. " Unȧs is the firstborn of the firstborn gods. Unȧs is " surrounded by thousands, and oblations are made unto " him by hundreds; he is made manifest as the Great " Power by Saḥ (Orion) **517.** the father of the gods. " Unȧs repeateth his rising in heaven and he is crowned " lord of the horizon. He hath reckoned up the bandlets " and the arm-rings, he hath taken possession of the hearts " of the gods. **518.** Unȧs hath eaten the Red Crown, and

" he hath swallowed the White Crown; the food of Unȧs " is the intestines, and his meat is hearts and their words of " power. **519.** Behold, Unȧs eateth of that which the Red " Crown sendeth forth, he increaseth, and the words of " power of the gods are in his belly; **520.** his attributes are " not removed from him. Unȧs hath eaten the whole of " the knowledge of every god, and the period of his life is " eternity, and the duration of his existence is **521.** ever-" lastingness in the form of one who doeth what he wisheth, " and doth not do what he hateth, and he abideth in the " horizon for ever and ever and ever. The Soul of the " gods is in Unȧs, their Spirit-souls are with **522.** Unȧs, " and the offerings made unto him are more than those " which are made unto the gods. The fire of Unȧs **523.** is " in their bones, for their soul is with Unȧs, and their " shades are with those who belong unto them. **524.** Unȧs " hath been with the two hidden (?) Kha (?) gods who are " without power (?) . . . . **525.**; the seat of the " heart of Unȧs is among those who live upon this earth " for ever and ever and ever."

The notion that, by eating the flesh, or particularly by drinking the blood, of another living being, a man absorbs his nature or life into his own, is one which appears among primitive peoples in many forms. It lies at the root of the wide-spread practice of drinking the fresh blood of enemies—a practice which was familiar to certain tribes of the Arabs before Muḥammad, and which tradition still ascribes to the wild race of Caḥṭân—and also of the habit practised by many savage huntsmen of eating some part (*e.g.*, the liver) of dangerous carnivora, in order that the courage of the animal may pass into them. The flesh and blood of brave men also are, among semi-savage or savage tribes, eaten and drunk to inspire courage. But the idea of hunting, killing, roasting and eating the gods as described above is not apparently common among ancient nations; the main object of the dead king in doing this was to secure the eternal life which was the peculiar attribute of the gods.[1] The text of the passage describing the cannibalism of Unȧs is as follows:—

[1] Cannibalism among the Egyptians is discussed at length in my *Osiris and the Egyptian Resurrection*, 2 vols. London, 1910.

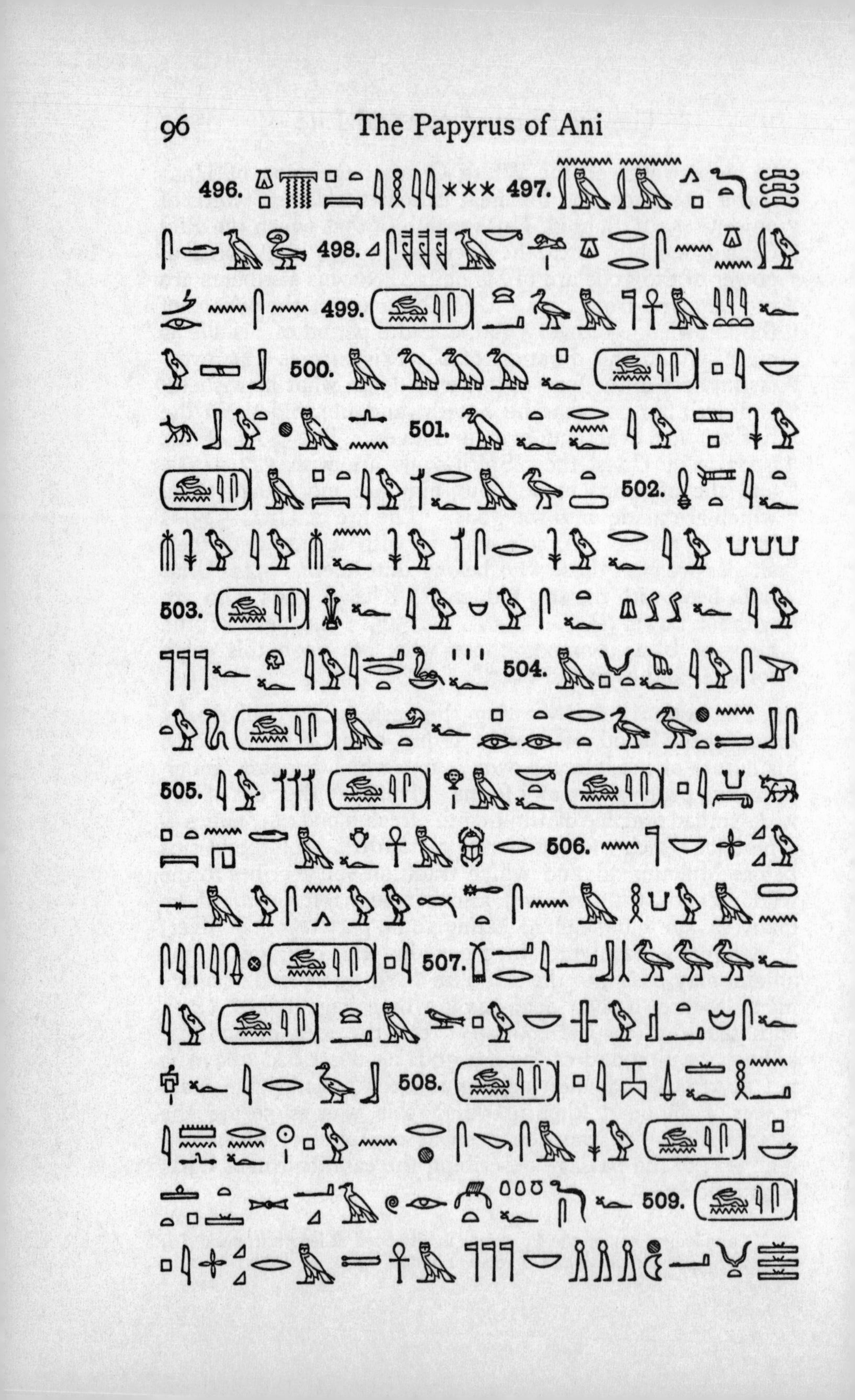

496. 497.

498.

499.

500.

501.

502.

503.

504.

505.

506.

507.

508.

509.

510.

511.

(var.)

512.

513.

514.

515.

516.

517.

518.

519.

520.

521.

522.

523.

524.

525.

EGYPTIAN IDEAS ABOUT GOD AND THE "GODS"

To the great and supreme Power which made the heavens, the gods, the earth, the sea, the sky, men and women, birds, animals and creeping things, all that is and all that is yet to come into being, the Egyptians gave the name of *neter* [hieroglyphs], or *nether* [hieroglyphs], a word which survives in Coptic under the form *nuti* ⲛⲟⲩϯ. This word has been translated "god-like," "holy," "divine," "sacred," "power," "strength," "force," "strong," "fortify," "mighty," "protect," but it is quite impossible to be certain that any word which we may use represents the meaning of *neter*, because no one knows exactly what idea the ancient Egyptians attached to the word. The truth is that the exact meaning of *neter* was lost at a very early period of Egyptian history, and even the Coptic does not help us to recover it. It has been asserted that the meaning of *neter* is "strong," but this is clearly a derived and not an original meaning. The late Dr. Brugsch defined *neter* to mean "the active power which produces and creates things in "regular recurrence; which bestows new life upon them, "and gives back to them their youthful vigour,"[1] and he adds that the innate conception of the word completely covers the original meaning of the Greek φύσις and the Latin *natura*. Such views about the meaning of *neter* may well have been held by the cultured and philosophical Greek, but their abstract character puts them out of the range of the mind of the native Egyptian, which was incapable naturally of formulating ideas of this kind. The difficulty that surrounds the meaning of *neter* is further increased by the manner in which the Egyptians used the word, for in texts of all periods it is used for God, and also for any being who was thought to possess some divine attribute or characteristic. Thus the great cosmic powers, and the

[1] Die thätige Kraft, welche in periodischer Wiederkehr die Dinge erzeugt und erschafft, ihren neues Leben verleiht und die Jugendfrische zurück giebt. *Religion und Mythologie*, p. 93.

beings who although held to be "divine" were yet finite and mortal, and were endowed by the Egyptians with love, hatred, and passions of every sort and kind, were called *neteru*, [hieroglyphs], or [hieroglyphs], or [hieroglyphs], or [hieroglyphs], or [hieroglyphs], or [hieroglyphs], or [hieroglyphs], and the word is translated "gods" by Egyptologists. The following extracts illustrate the use of the word *neter*. To King Unȧs it is said in his Pyramid Text (l. 209):—

1. "Thou art by the side of god." [hieroglyphs].

To King Tetȧ it is said in his Pyramid Text (ll. 231, 232).

2. "He weigheth words, behold, god he heareth the "words," [hieroglyphs]

3. "God hath called Tetȧ," [hieroglyphs] (l. 223).

In the Pyramid Text of Pepi I we have:—

4. "Thou hast received the form of god, thou art "great therewith before the gods at the head of the "Lake of Horus," [hieroglyphs] (l. 19).

4. "Hail, Osiris Pepi. These thy libations are "presented unto thee, libations to thee before Horus "in thy name of 'Comer forth from the cool water' "(or, from the Cataract). Incense is presented unto "thee, for thou art god. Thy mother Nut hath set "thee to be god to thine enemy in thy name of god," [hieroglyphs] (ll. 31, 32).

5. "This Pepi adoreth god," [hieroglyphs] (l. 185).

6. "This Pepi is then god, the son of god," (l. 574).

7. The officer Netchemȧb says,[1] "I never defrauded "anyone in respect of his property, making him to "complain of me because of it to the god of my town," , and again he says, "Never did "I let any man be afraid of one who was stronger than "himself, [thereby] causing him to complain [of me] "because of it to god,"

In the first six of these examples it is possible to say that the god referred to in them is: 1. God. 2. The local town-god, or tribal-god. 3. Osiris. 4. Rā; but whichever explanation be accepted, it is quite clear that the writers of these texts had in their minds a Being who stood to them for God. In the seventh example the writer emphasizes the difference which he felt existed between the town-god and god. Matters that related to his material possessions could be dealt with by the town-god, but the intangible terror which the feudal lord of the day could make to sink into the mind of the serf was a matter which only the Supreme Being, by whatever name He was called at that time, could put right.

We may now quote a series of examples from the Prisse Papyrus, which contain moral precepts attributed to Kaqemna, who flourished in the reign of Seneferu, a king of the IVth dynasty, and to Ptaḥ-ḥetep, who flourished in the reign of Ȧssȧ, a king of the Vth dynasty.[2]

[1] Sethe, *Urkunden*, I, 28.

[2] For the hieratic text see Prisse d'Avennes, *Facsimilé d'un papyrus Égyptien en caractères hiératiques*, Paris, 1847; M. Jéquier, *Le Papyrus Prisse*, Paris, 1911; Maspero, *Recueil*, XXXI, pp. 146 ff.; Budge, *Hieratic Papyri*, London, 1910, No. V; Heath, *Proverbs of Aphobis*, London, Longman Brown & Co. [no date]; Chabas, *Rev. Arch.*, 1st series, tom. XV; Lauth, *Sitzungsberichte der Kgl. Bayer. Akad.*, 1869, 1870; Virey, *Les Maximes de Ptaḥ-ḥotep*, Paris, 1887; Griffith, *P.S.B.A.*, Vol. XIII, pp. 67–76.

1. Not known are the things of the work of god. (Plate II, l. 2.)

2. Do not cause terror in men; [it is] opposition [to] god. (Plate IV, l. 8.)

3. The eating of bread is under the dispensation of god. (Plate VII, l. 2.)

4. If thou ploughest crops (?) in a field, hath given it god. (Plate VII, l. 5.)

5. If thou wouldst be a wise man beget thou a son pleasing to god. (Plate VII, l. 11.)

6. Satisfy thy dependants by thy deeds, it is the act of the favoured ones of god. (Plate XI, l. 1.)

7. "If having been of no account, thou hast become great; "and, if having been poor, thou hast become rich, when "thou art governor of the city, be not hard-hearted because "of thy advancement, because thou art the governor "of the provisions of god," (Plate XIII, l. 8.)

8. Beloved of god is obedience; disobedience is an abomination to god. (Plate XVI, l. 7.)

9. Verily a son good is of the giving of god. (Plate XIV, l. 6.)

The following extracts from the Maxims of Ani or Khensu-ḥetep[1] are also very instructive; these Maxims were compiled not later than about 1000 B.C., but it is very probable that many of them are as old as the Ancient Empire:—

1. "The god is for magnifying his name,"

2. "The house of God, an abomination to it is much "speaking. Pray thou with a loving heart, all its words "being hidden. He will do thy business. He will hear "what thou sayest, [and] will receive thy offerings,"

3. "Thy god giveth existence,"

4. "The god judgeth the truth,"

[1] See Mariette, *Papyrus Égyptien*, Cairo; de Rougé, *Comptes Rendus*, Paris, 1871, pp. 340–350; Maspero, *Journal de Paris*, 15 Mars, 1871; Chabas, *L'Égyptologie*, Chalons, 1876–1878; Amélineau, *Morale Égyptienne*, Paris, 1892.

5. "[In] offering to thy god guard against the things
" which are abominations to him. Consider with thine eye
" his dispensations. Devote thyself to the adoration of his
" name. He giveth souls (or will, or strength) to millions
" of forms. He magnifieth him that magnifieth him. The
" god of this earth is Shu, the chief of the horizon. His
" similitudes are upon the earth, and to these incense and
" offerings are given daily,"

6. "I gave thee to thy mother who carried thee as she
" carried thee, and without any help from me she carried
" thee—a heavy burden. When after thy months [in the
" womb] thou wast born, she put herself under the yoke,
" for three years her breasts were in thy mouth. . . . . .
" When thou wast sent to school to be taught, day by day
" unfailingly she came to thy teacher, bringing bread and
" beer for thee from her house. Now that thou hast
" become a young man, and art married, and hast a house,
" watch well thy child, and bring him up as thy mother
" brought thee up. Make it not necessary for her (*i.e.*, thy
" mother) to suffer, lest if she lift up her hands to God He
" will hearken unto her [complaints and punish thee],"

7. "Give thyself to the god, guard thou thyself well for the god daily, and let to-morrow be as to-day" (*i.e.*, do not be strict one day and lax the next),

The following extract from Chapter CLIV of the Theban Recension of the Book of the Dead throws much light upon one of the views which the Egyptians held as to the mortal nature of the "gods": "Preserve me, O Temu, "as thou dost thyself from such decay as that which thou "workest on every god, every goddess, all animals, and all "creeping things. [Each] passeth away when his soul hath "gone forth after his death; he perisheth after he hath "passed away,"

As a result of their studies of Egyptian texts many of the earlier Egyptologists, *e.g.*, Champollion-Figeac, de Rougé, Pierret and Brugsch, came to the conclusion that the dwellers in the Nile Valley, from the earliest times, believed in the existence of one God, nameless, incomprehensible, and eternal. They believed that *neter* might in many places refer to God, and that the plural *neteru*, "gods," only indicated a class, or classes, of celestial beings who possessed some attribute which is usually associated with the Deity. In 1860 de Rougé wrote: "The unity of "a supreme and self-existent being, his eternity, his "almightiness, and external reproduction thereby as "God; the attributing of the creation of the world and

" of all living beings to this Supreme God; the immortality " of the soul, completed by the dogma of punishment and " rewards; such is the sublime and persistent base which, " notwithstanding all deviations and all mythological " embellishments, must secure for the beliefs of the ancient " Egyptians a most honourable place among the nations of " antiquity."[1] Nine years later he developed this view, and discussed "the difficulties of reconciling the belief in the " unity of God with the polytheism which existed in Egypt " from the earliest times," and he repeated his conviction that the Egyptians believed in a self-existent God who was One Being, who had created man, and who had endowed him with an immortal soul. (La Croyance à l'Unité du Dieu suprême, à ses attributs de Créateur et de Législateur de l'homme qu'il a doué d'une âme immortelle.)[2] In fact, de Rougé amplified what Champollion-Figeac (relying upon his brother's information) wrote in 1839: "The " Egyptian religion is a pure monotheism, which mani- " fested itself externally by a symbolic polytheism" (*Égypte*, Paris, 1839, p. 245). M. Pierret adopted the view that the texts show us that the Egyptians believed in One infinite and eternal God who was without a second, and he repeats Champollion's dictum.[3] But the greatest supporter of the monotheistic theory was Dr. Brugsch, who in his *Religion und Mythologie* (Leipzig, 1885–1888) collected a series of striking passages from the texts. From these the following are selected :—

God is One and only, and none other existeth with Him.—God is the One, the One who hath made all things. —God is a spirit, a hidden spirit, the spirit of spirits, the great spirit of the Egyptians, the divine spirit.—God is from the beginning, and He hath been from the beginning. He hath existed from of old, and was when nothing else had being, He existed when nothing else existed, and what existeth He created after He had come into being. He is the Father of beginnings.—God is the eternal One, He is eternal and infinite, and endureth for ever and aye.—God is

[1] *Études sur le Rituel Funéraire des Anciens Égyptiens* (in *Rev. Arch.*, Paris, 1860, p. 72).

[2] *Conférence sur la Religion des Anciens Égyptiens* (in *Annales de Philosophie Chrétienne*, 5ième Série, t. XX, Paris, 1869, pp. 325-337).

[3] *Le Panthéon Égyptien*, Paris, 1881, p. 4.

hidden and no man knoweth His form. No man hath been able to seek out His likeness; He is hidden to gods and men, and He is a mystery unto His creatures. No man knoweth how to know Him.—His name remaineth hidden; His name is a mystery unto His children. His names are innumerable, they are manifold, and none knoweth their number.—God is Truth, He liveth by Truth, He feedeth thereon, He is the King of Truth, and He hath established the earth thereupon.—God is life, and through Him only man liveth. He giveth life to man, He breatheth the breath of life into his nostrils.—God is father and mother, the father of fathers and the mother of mothers. He begetteth, but was never begotten; He produceth, but was never produced; He begat Himself and produced Himself. He createth, but was never created. He is the maker of His own form, and the fashioner of His own body.—God Himself is existence, He endureth without increase or diminution, He multiplieth Himself millions of times, He is manifold in forms and in members.—God hath made the universe, and He hath created all that therein is. He is the Creator of what is in this world, and of what was, and of what is, and of what shall be. He is the creator of the heavens, and the earth, and of the deep, and of the water, and of the mountains. God hath stretched out the heavens and founded the earth.—What His heart (*i.e.*, mind) conceived straightway came to pass. When He hath spoken it cometh to pass and endureth for ever.—God is the father of the Gods. He fashioneth man and formeth the gods.—God is merciful unto those who reverence Him, and He heareth him that calleth upon Him. God knoweth him that acknowledgeth Him. He rewardeth him that serveth Him, and He protecteth him that followteh Him.[1]

The above extracts were compiled by Brugsch from many texts, and they are not all of the same date, but several Hymns are extant in which all the ideas expressed above are embodied, and from one of these we quote the following:—

[1] Brugsch, *Religion*, pp. 96–99. The whole Chapter on the Egyptian conception of God should be read with Maspero's review of the book in *La Myth. Égyptienne* (*Études de Mythologie*, t. II, pp. 189 ff.).

"A Hymn to Åmen-Rā, the Bull in Heliopolis, "president of all the gods, beautiful god, beloved one, the "giver of life and heat to the young cattle. Hail to "thee, Amen-Rā, Lord of the thrones of the Two Lands, "Governor in the Åpts (Karnak), Kamutef, the prince of "his fields, he of the long strides, Governor of the Land "of the South, Lord of the Matchaiu (Nubians), Prince of "Punt, lord of the heavens, eldest son of the earth, lord of "things which exist, stablisher of things, stablisher of all "things, One in his times among the gods. Beautiful "Bull of the Nine gods, President of all the gods, Lord of "Truth (or Law), father of the gods, maker of men; "creator of beasts, lord of things which exist, creator of "the staff of life (wheat?), maker of the green herb "which nourisheth the cattle. The Form made by "Ptaḥ, the beautiful Child, the beloved one. The gods "adore him, the maker of things which are below, and of "things which are above. He shineth on Egypt as "he saileth over the sky in peace. King of the South and "North, Rā, whose word is truth, the Governor of the "world, the mighty one of valour, the lord of terror, the "chief who made the world as he made himself. His "forms are more numerous than those of any god. The "gods rejoice in his bounties, and they praise him as the "god of the horizon, as the god who riseth in the horizon of "fire. The gods love the smell of him when he, the eldest-"born of the dew, cometh from Punt, when he traverseth "the land of the Matchaiu, the Beautiful Face coming from "the Land of the god (*i.e.*, the South-Eastern Sûdân). "The gods cast themselves down at his feet when they "recognize His Majesty, their Lord, the lord of fear, "the mighty one of victory, the mighty of Will, the lord of "crowns, who maketh offerings to flourish, and createth "the divine food.

"Adorations be to thee, O Maker of the gods, who "hast stretched out the heavens and founded the earth! "The untiring Watcher Menu-Åmen, lord of eternity, "maker of the everlastingness, lord of adorations, "Governor of the Åpts . . . . lord of rays, creator of "light. The gods acclaim him, and he stretcheth out his "hand to him that loveth him. His flame casteth down "his enemies, his Eye overthroweth the rebels, it driveth "its spear into the sky and maketh the serpent Nȧk to "vomit what it hath swallowed.

"Hail to thee, Rā, Lord of Truth, whose shrine is "hidden, thou Master of the gods, thou god Kheperȧ in "thy boat; at the going forth of thy word the gods sprang "into being. Hail, Ȧtem, maker of mortals. However "many be their forms he nourisheth them, he maketh "the colour of one to be different from the other. He "heareth the prayer of the oppressed one, he is kind "of heart to him that calleth upon him, he delivereth "the timid man from the oppressor, he judgeth between "the mighty and the weak. He is the Lord of "Knowledge, and Wisdom is the utterance of his mouth. "At his will the Nile appeareth, when the greatly-"beloved Lord of the palm-tree cometh he maketh "mortals to live. He furthereth every work, he worketh "in heaven, he produceth the beneficent light; the gods "rejoice in his beautiful deeds, and their hearts live when "they see him ...... His name is hidden from his "children in his name 'Ȧmen' .... Beloved art "thou as thou passest through Egypt. When thou "risest thou sendest forth light from thy beautiful Eyes "(*i.e.*, Sun and Moon). The dead of olden times (*pāt*) "rejoice when thou shinest. When thou shinest in thy "full strength the cattle languish. Beloved art thou when "thou art in the northern sky, pleasant art thou when thou "art in the southern sky. Thy beauties seize and carry "away all hearts, the love of thee maketh the arms to "drop, thy beautiful deeds make the hands to tremble, all "hearts melt at the sight of thee, O Form, ONE, creator "of all things, O ONE, ONLY, maker of things which "are. Men came forth from his eyes, the gods sprang into "being at the utterance of his mouth. He maketh the "green herb whereon the cattle live, and the staff of life "(wheat, or barley) whereon men live. He maketh the "fish to live in the rivers, and the feathered fowl in "the sky. He giveth life to that which is in the egg, "he maketh birds of all kinds to live, and the reptiles "which crawl and spring. He maketh the rats (or mice) "in their holes to live, and the birds which are on every "green twig. Hail to thee, O thou maker of all these "things, thou ONLY ONE. In his mightiness he taketh "many forms. He watcheth over all people as they "sleep. He careth for the welfare of his animal creation. "O Åmen, thou stablisher of all things, O Åtmu, O "Ḥeru-Khuti, all people adore thee, saying, 'Praise be to "thee because thou dwellest among us, [we pay] homage "to thee because thou hast created us.' All creatures "cry out to thee 'Hail,' and all lands praise thee. From "the highest heights of heaven to the uttermost parts "of the earth and to the lowest depths of the sea thou "art praised. The gods bow down before Thy Majesty "and exalt the souls of their Creator. They rejoice "when they meet their begetter, and they say unto thee, "'Come in peace! (*i.e.*, Welcome!) O father of the fathers "of all the gods, who hast spread out the sky, who hast "founded the earth, who hast made the things which "are, who hast created the things which shall be, thou "Prince, thou Life, thou Health, thou Strength, the "First among the gods. We adore thy Souls, for thou "didst make us. Thou didst make us. Thou hast given "birth to us, and we ascribe praise unto thee because "thou dwellest among us.'

"Hail to thee, maker of all things, Lord of Truth, "father of the gods, maker of man, creator of animals, "lord of grain, who makest the beasts on the hills to "live. Hail, Bull Åmen, Beautiful Face! Thou art "beloved in the Åpts, thou art the mighty one who "art crowned in thy shrine, thou art doubly crowned "in Heliopolis, [where] thou didst judge between Horus "and Set in the Great Hall. Thou art the Head of the "Great Company of the gods, the ONLY ONE, who hast "no second, the Head of the Åpts. Thou art the god "Åni, Head of the Company of thy gods, living on Truth "(or, by Law) Ḥeru-Khuti of the East! Thou hast at "thy Will created the mountains, and the silver, and the "gold, and the real lapis-lazuli [therein]. Incense and "fresh myrrh are ṣet before thy nose, O Beautiful Face, "as thou comest from the land of the Matchaiu (Nubians). "O Åmen-Rā, Lord of the thrones of the Two Lands, "Head of the Åpts, thou Åni, Head of thy shrine, King "ONE, among the gods. Thy names are myriad, they "cannot be told. Thou risest in the east and thou settest "in the west, and dost overthrow thy enemies when thou "art born daily. Thoth exalteth thy two Eyes (the Sun and Moon), and maketh thee to dwell in splendour. The gods rejoice in thy beauties, which those who are in thy train exalt. Thou art the lord of the Sektet Boat and of the Āṭet Boat, which travel over the sky with thee in peace. Thy sailors rejoice when they see Nȧk overthrown, his limbs stabbed with the knife, the fire devouring him, his accursed soul beaten out of his accursed body, and his feet cut off. The gods rejoice, Rā is satisfied, and Ȧnu (Heliopolis) is glad that the enemies of Ȧtem are overthrown; the heart of the goddess Nebt-Ānkh rejoiceth because the enemies of her lord are destroyed."[1]

Another very interesting collection of the attributes of Ȧmen-Rā is found in one of the funerary papyri which were written for the Princess Nesi-Khensu, at the beginning of the tenth century before Christ.[2] It forms the introductory paragraph of a very remarkable agreement concluded between the princess and the god, who undertook to grant certain favours to her in the Other World in return for the zeal and devotion which she had shown in her faithful service of the god. The text reads: "This holy god, the lord of all the gods, Ȧmen-Rā; the lord of the Throne of the Two Lands, the governor of Ȧpt; the holy soul who came into being in the beginning; the great god who liveth upon Truth; the First God of primeval time, [hieroglyphs], who produced the Ancient Gods, [hieroglyphs], the being through whom every [other] god hath existence; the One One [hieroglyphs] who hath made everything which hath come into existence since primeval time when the world was created; the being whose birth is hidden, whose evolutions are manifold, whose growth is incomprehensible; the holy form, beloved, terrible, and mighty in his risings; the lord of space (?), the Power, Khepera who createth every evolution of his existence,

[1] For the text see Mariette, *Les Papyrus Égyptiens du Musée de Boulaq*, Plates 11–13, and see the edition by Grébaut, *Hymne à Amon-Rā*, Paris, 1875.

[2] See Maspero, *Les Momies Royales de Deir al-Baḥarî*, pp. 594 f.

except whom at the beginning none other existed; who at the dawn of primeval time was Åtmu, the prince of light and splendour; who having made himself [made] all men to live; who saileth over the celestial regions and faileth not; whose ordinances are permanent at dawn to-morrow; who though an aged being showeth in the form of one that is young; who leadeth the uttermost parts of eternity, going round about the celestial regions, and journeying through the Ṭuat to illumine the Two Lands which he hath created; the god who acteth as God, who fashioned himself, who made the heavens and the earth by his will (or, thought); the greatest of the great, the mightiest of the mighty, the Prince who is mightier than the gods, the young Bull with horns ready to gore; the Protector of the Two Lands in his mighty name of 'Everlasting One who cometh and possesseth his might'; who bringeth the remotest limit of eternity; the god-prince who hath been prince from the time that he came into being; the conqueror of the Two Lands through his might; the terrible one of the double Divine Face; the divine aged one, the divine form who dwelleth in the forms of all the gods; the Lion-god with the awesome eye, the sovereign who sendeth forth the two Eyes (the sun and moon), the lord of flame opposing his enemies; the god Nu, the prince who advanceth at his hour to vivify that which cometh forth from his potter's wheel; the disk of the Moon-god who openeth a way both in heaven and upon earth for the beautiful form; the beneficent god, the untiring one, vigorous of heart in rising and in setting; from whose divine eyes men and women came forth, at the utterance of whose mouth the gods came into being, and food is created, and celestial food is made, and all things [are made] which come into being; traverser of eternity, the aged one who reneweth his youth; who possesseth myriads of pairs of eyes and innumerable pairs of ears, whose light is the guide of the god of millions of years; the lord of life, who giveth unto whom he pleaseth the circuit of the earth along with the seat of his divine face; who setteth out upon his journey and suffereth no mishap by the way, whose work none can destroy; the lord beloved, whose name is sweet and beloved, unto whom mankind make supplication at dawn; the mighty one of victory, the mighty one of two-fold strength; the lord who inspireth fear, the young Bull who maketh an end of the hostile ones, the mighty one who doeth battle with his foes, through whose divine plans the earth came into being; the Soul who giveth light from his two Eyes; the god Baiti, who createth the divine transformations; the holy one who cannot be comprehended, the king who maketh kings to rule, who girdeth up the earth in its courses; the god to whose souls the gods and goddesses pay homage by reason of the greatness of the terror which he inspireth; since he hath gone before that which followeth shall endure; the creator of the world by his secret counsels; god Kheperȧ, incomprehensible, who is the most hidden of the gods, whose deputy is the solar disk; the one incomprehensible, who hideth himself from that which cometh forth from him; the flame which sendeth forth rays of light with mighty splendour; who is seen in form and observed at his appearance, yet cannot be understood; to whom at dawn men make supplications; whose risings are like crystal among the company of the gods, who art beloved of every god; who is hidden in the North wind which Nut bringeth forward; who maketh decrees for millions of millions of years, whose ordinances stand fast and are not destroyed, whose utterances are gracious, whose statutes fail not in his appointed season; who giveth duration of life and doubleth the years of those unto whom he hath a favour, who graciously protecteth him whom he hath set in his heart; who hath formed eternity and everlastingness; the king of the South and of the North, Ȧmen-Rā, the king of the gods, the lord of heaven, and of the earth, and of the Ṭuat, and of the two mountains; in whose form the earth began to exist, the mighty one, who is pre-eminent among all the gods of the Great First Company of the gods."

After reading the above extracts it is impossible not to conclude that the ideas of the ancient Egyptians about God were of a very exalted character, and it is clear that they made in their minds a sharp distinction between God and the "gods." Several passages in the Theban Recension of the Book of the Dead prove that under the XVIIIth dynasty, about 1600 B.C., they believed that there was a time when the god Tem existed by himself, and that it was he who, by a series of efforts of his mind, created the heavens and the earth, and gods and men, and every creature which has life. It was believed that he was self-created and self-existent, and that he was One Only, , and the texts, as will be seen later on, state clearly that there was none with him, and that he was quite alone when he arrived at the decision to create the heavens and the earth, and gods and men. The gods proceeded from his body, and men from the words of his mouth. Here, then, we have One God who was self-created, self-existent, and almighty, who created the universe. According to the LXXVIIIth Chapter of the Book of the Dead, and the other Chapters of Transformations, he possessed a dual-soul, *i.e.*, a KHU and a BA, and the element in which these lived was thought to be the great mass of Celestial Waters which the Egyptians called Nu, . The first act of creation was the sending forth from Nu of the ball of the sun, *i.e.*, the creation of light. Temu evolved the thought in Nu, and when the thought was expressed in a word, or words, the sun appeared as the result. Every succeeding act of creation represented a thought of Temu and its expression in words, which probably took the form of commands. The God of the Sun was, under the second half of the period of the Ancient Empire, called Rā, but it is very probable that Rā was identified with Temu at an early date, and that to the creature was paid the worship due to the Creator. The material sun, or the body of the sun, was worshipped as the source of all heat, and light, and life by many Egyptians, especially under the political influence of the priests of Rā at Heliopolis, which began first to assume great importance towards the close of the IVth dynasty; but at all times there must have existed those whose minds were able to separate the body of the sun from its spirit and soul, which were the direct emanations of Temu.

The greater number of the Egyptians, like the peoples of Africa in later times, were well content to admit the existence of a great, almighty God who created the universe and all in it, but they seem to have thought, also like modern African peoples, that he was too great and too remote to concern himself with the affairs of man, and that he had committed the management of this world, and of all in it, to a series of "gods," and spirits, good and evil, whom it was necessary for them to worship or propitiate as the case might be. It is the existence of these "gods" and spirits that has caused modern investigators to describe the Egyptian religion as polytheistic, and even pantheistic, and to find the greatest difficulty in reconciling the polytheistic phase of it with the monotheistic. And it was this difficulty which made the eminent theologian Tiele declare that the religion of Egypt was from the beginning polytheistic, but that it developed in two opposite directions; in the one direction gods were multiplied by the addition of local gods, and in the other direction the Egyptians drew nearer and nearer to monotheism.[1] The truth of the matter seems to me to be that the Egyptian religion never wholly lost the monotheistic element which was in it. It existed in the earliest times, and it frequently appears in the early religious texts. It is often observed in the hymns and texts which represent the teachings of bodies of priests who emphasize the greatness and importance of the "gods" which they served, and it was never entirely eliminated. In the hymns written under the XVIIIth dynasty the monotheistic element became exceedingly prominent, and, even before the religious troubles which brought about the downfall of the dynasty began, men worshipped the god who was One Only with a sincerity and whole-heartedness hitherto unknown. It cannot, of course, be rightly claimed that the monotheism of this period was identical with that which has been evolved by modern Christian nations, but it was very similar, in my opinion, to the monotheism of the Hebrews. In fact, the word NETER, 𓊹𓀭, is used in Egyptian religious literature in much the same way as EL, אֵל, is used in the Hebrew Scriptures, and also as אֱלוֹהַּ and its plural אֱלֹהִים.

The difficulty which many students of the Egyptian Religion have found in their attempts to reconcile the monotheistic and polytheistic elements in it is due chiefly to the priests of the various "gods" of Egypt. The priests of Heliopolis asserted that the Sun-god Rā was the greatest of all the gods, and that all the other "gods" of his

[1] See *Geschiedenis van den Godsdienst in de Oudheid*, Amsterdam, 1893, p. 25; and Lieblein, *Egyptian Religion*, Leipzig, 1884, p. 10.

company were forms of him. These "forms" of Rā were Shu, Tefnut, Ḳeb, Nut, Osiris, Isis, Set, and Nephthys. Now Shu and Tefnut were Sûdânî deities, the original seat of whose worship was Buḳem, , a country in the Eastern Sûdân, and they were introduced into Egypt in very early times with the worship of the Sûdânî Cow-goddess Hathor.[1] Ḳeb is a very old Earth-god, on whose back all the trees and vegetation in the world grew, yet the priests of Ȧnu make him a form of Rā. At the time when they were stating in their writings that Osiris was subordinate to Rā, the worship of Osiris was predominant throughout Egypt, from Memphis to Northern Nubia.

In like manner the priests of Ptaḥ of Memphis claimed that it was their god Ptaḥ who was the creator of the heavens and the earth, and that the other great gods were merely forms of him. They were well aware that Tem, Temu, or Ȧtem, had been regarded as the creator of the gods and the world and men from time out of mind in Egypt. Yet they attributed to Ptaḥ powers greater than his. Their method of procedure was artificial and is readily explained. They first identified Ptaḥ with old gods like Tatenn and Tem, and made him a member of their companies of gods; when this had been done they invented stories to prove that his power was greater than that of his colleagues, and that he was the greatest of all the gods of the old companies. Finally, they placed him at the head of a company of gods which consisted of forms of himself. The best proof of these statements is found in Prof. Erman's paper entitled *Ein Denkmal memphitischer Theologie*,[2] which contains a discussion on the contents of a text found on a basalt slab presented to the British Museum by the Earl Spencer in 1805.[3] This text is much mutilated, but

[1] See Dr. H. Junker's important paper *Der Auszug der Hathor-Tefnut aus Nubien* (in *Abhand. der Königl. Preuss. Akad.*, Berlin, 1911).

[2] Published in the *Sitzungsberichte der Königl. Preuss. Akad.*, Berlin, 1911.

[3] See *Guide to the Egyptian Galleries*, p. 220 (No. 797). It was first published by Sharpe, *Egyptian Inscriptions*, I, Plates 36–38; next by Messrs. Bryant and Read, in *P.S.B.A.*, 1901, pp. 160 ff.; and a facsimile was published by Mr. Breasted in *A.Z.*, Bd. XXXIX, pp. 39 ff., with a sketch of its contents.

enough of it remains to show that it contains a statement of Memphite theology as it was understood by some priest, who flourished probably under the Ancient Empire. The actual copy which we possess was made in the reign of Shabaka, from an older copy on papyrus, which was worm-eaten. This document states that Ptaḥ made Tem and his gods, and that he was the arbiter of life and death. Everything on the earth came into existence through him, and everything which is existed before it came into being in the mind of Ptaḥ, who was the heart and tongue of the company of the gods. Thus, at the very same time, we have within twenty miles of each other one body of priests at Ȧnu asserting that their god Rā was the creator of the heavens and the earth, and another body of priests at Memphis declaring the same thing of their god Ptaḥ. And if we had all the religious literature of Egypt at this period we should no doubt find that the priests of Ḥensu (Herakleopolis), and of Khemenu (Hermopolis), and of Ȧbṭu (Abydos), and of Uast (Thebes), and of Beḥuṭet (Edfû), and of Suȧn (Syene), were claiming the absolute sovereignty of the gods for Ḥerushefit, Thoth, Osiris, Ȧmen, Horus, and Khemenu respectively.

The religious texts of all periods contain evidence that the Egyptians were always occupied in trying to puzzle out the riddle of creation, and we are fortunate in possessing a papyrus which contains a more or less connected theory about the origin of God and the gods, and of the heavens and the earth. This papyrus was written for a priest called Nesi-Menu, and is dated on the first day of the fourth month of the twelfth year of Pharaoh Alexander, the son of Alexander, *i.e.*, 311 B.C.[1] The story of the Creation is entitled "The Book of knowing how Rā came into being," [hieroglyphs], and is told by the god Nebertcher [hieroglyphs], the Everlasting God of the Universe. Where and how this god existed is not said, but it is clear that he was supposed to have created himself and to be self-existent. The desire to create the heavens

[1] The hieratic text is published in facsimile, with a hieroglyphic text and English translation, in my *Egyptian Hieratic Papyri in the British Museum*, London, 1910.

and the earth arose in his heart, or mind, and he assumed the form of the god Kheperà, who from first to last was regarded as a form of Nu, or the Creator, *par excellence.* At this time nothing existed except the vast mass of Celestial Waters which the Egyptians called Nu, , and in this existed the germs of all living things that subsequently took form in heaven and on earth, but they existed in a state of inertness and helplessness. When Kheperà rose out of this watery mass, he found himself in an empty space, and he had nothing to stand upon. Kheperà came into being by pronouncing his own name, and when he wanted a place whereon to stand, he first conceived the similitude of that standing place in his mind, and when he had given it a name, and uttered that name, the standing place at once came into being. This process of thinking out the existence of things is expressed in Egyptian by words which mean literally "laying the foundation in the heart," *i.e.*, in the mind. Kheperà also possessed a BA or Heart-soul, which assisted him in depicting in his mind the image of the world which was to be. And he was also assisted in this work by *maāt*, *i.e.*, law, order, truth, etc., who acted the part of Wisdom as described in the Book of Proverbs, chapter viii, verses 22 ff.

Kheperà next created the first triad of gods. He had union with his shadow, and so begot offspring, who proceeded from his body under the forms of Shu, *i.e.*, air and dryness, and Tefnut, water and moisture. Shu and Tefnut were next united, and their offspring were Ḳeb the Earth-god, and Nut, the Sky-goddess. Ḳeb and Nut were united, and the offspring of their embraces were Osiris, Horus, Set, Isis and Nephthys. Of these, Osiris, , is "the essence of the primeval matter" of which Ḳheperà himself was formed. Thus Osiris was of the same substance as the Great God who created the world, and was a re-incarnation of his great-grandfather, a truly African belief. This portion of the text helps to explain the views held about Osiris as the great Ancestor-god, who when on earth was the great benefactor of the Egyptians, and who, after his murder and resurrection, became the saviour of their souls.

In continuing his narrative Neb-er-tcher refers to some calamity which befell his Eye, *i.e.*, the Sun, and extinguished its light. It is possible that eclipse or storm is here referred to, but from the context it seems that the god is referring to the coming on of the darkness of night. For he goes on to say that he made a second Eye, *i.e.*, the moon, to which he gave some of the splendour of his first Eye. He then assigned to it a place in his face, from which it ruled over the earth, having special power in respect of the production of trees, plants, vegetables, herbs, etc. The next paragraph deals with the creation of man, who sprang, not from the earth, but directly from the body of the god Kheperȧ, or Neb-er-tcher. He joined his members together, and then wept tears upon them, and men and women came into being from the tears which fell from his eyes. The creation of quadrupeds is not specially mentioned, but the god says that he created creeping things, and quadrupeds are probably meant to be included among them. Men and women and all other living creatures which were made by the god then reproduced their species, each creature in its own way, and so the earth became filled with their descendants.

Basing his statements contained in a number of texts composed or copied at different periods, the late Dr. Brugsch formulated the following account of the origin of the gods : In the beginning there existed neither heaven nor earth, and nothing existed except the boundless mass of primeval water which was shrouded in darkness, and which contained within itself the germs and beginnings, male and female, of everything which was to be in the future world. The divine primeval spirit, which formed an essential part of the primeval matter, felt within itself the desire to begin the work of Creation, and its word woke to life the world, the form and shape of which it had already depicted within itself. The first act of creation began with the formation of an egg out of the primeval water, from which emerged Rā, the immediate cause of all life upon the earth. The almighty power of the divine spirit embodied itself in its most brilliant form in the rising sun. When the inert mass of primeval matter felt the desire of the primeval spirit to begin the work of creation, it began to move, and the creatures which were to constitute the future world were formed according to the divine intelligence *Maāt*. Under the influence of Thoth, or that form of the divine intelligence which created the world by a word, eight elements, four male and four female, arose out of the primeval Nu, which possessed the properties of the male and female. These eight elements were called Nu and Nut, Ḥeḥ and Ḥeḥet, Kek and Keket, and Nen and Nenet; collectively they were called "Khemenu," or the "Eight," and they were considered as primeval fathers and mothers. They appear in two forms: 1. As apes, four male and four female, who stand in adoration of the sun when he rises, and greet him with songs and hymns of praise. 2. As human beings, four having the heads of frogs, and four the heads of serpents. The birth of light from the waters, and of fire from the moist mass of primeval matter, and of Rā from Nu, formed the starting point of all mythological speculations, conjectures, and theories of the Egyptian priests. The light of the sun gave birth to itself out of chaos, and the conception of the future world was depicted in Thoth the divine intelligence; when Thoth gave the word, what he commanded at once took place by means of Ptaḥ and Khnemu, the visible representatives who turned Thoth's command into deed. Khnemu made the egg of the sun, and Ptaḥ gave to the god of light a finished body. The first company of the gods consisted of Shu, Ṭefnut, Ḳeb, Nut, Osiris, Isis, Set, Nephthys, Horus, and their governor Tem, or Ȧtmu.

The reader has now before him the main points of the evidence concerning the Egyptians' notions about God, and the cosmic powers and their phases, and the anthropomorphic creations with which they peopled the Other World, all of which have been derived from the native literature of ancient Egypt. The different interpretations which different Egyptologists have placed upon the facts demonstrate the difficulty of the subject. Speaking generally, the interpreters may be divided into two classes: (1) Those who regard the Egyptian religion as the product of half-savage men, and think that it is nothing but a mixture of crude, and often disgusting, nature cults and superstitions of the most stupid and childish character. (2) Those who admit the savage origins of many of the beliefs which the natural conservatism of the Egyptians preserved carefully, but who think they are able to trace a steady development in the religion until it reached a point at which it possessed true ideas about God and many of the spiritual conceptions which are on a par with those of the Hebrews and Arabs, and many Oriental Christian peoples. The mind of the Egyptian was incapable of abstract thought in the modern sense of the word, and in every subject he sought for concrete facts, which could be expressed in definite statements. From first to last the texts proclaim the unalterable belief of the Egyptian in the resurrection and in the immortality of the soul that was to be enjoyed in a transformed Spirit-body, in the Kingdom of Osiris, the god who had come upon the earth "to set right in the place of wrong." None but the souls of the just could enter that kingdom, and no liar and worker of deceit could hope to pass the searching trial in the Judgment Hall and be declared innocent on the day of the "weighing of words." Being finite, the Egyptian failed to comprehend the infinite and eternal God, but the God-man Osiris was ever present in his mind, as the tombs of all periods testify, and the Egyptian who sang the hymns and prayed the prayers given in the Book of the Dead was unlikely to allow his spiritual needs to be satisfied by a belief in "gods" who ate and drank, loved and hated, waged war, and grew old and died. And here we may give a rendering of the ancient Legend of Rā and Isis, which will illustrate the stories which the Egyptians told of their gods. The papyrus containing the story is preserved in Turin,[1] and versions of the story have been published in English, French, and German.[2] The Legend runs:—

THE CHAPTER OF THE DIVINE GOD, WHO CREATED HIMSELF, WHO MADE THE HEAVENS AND THE EARTH, AND THE BREATH OF LIFE, AND FIRE, AND THE GODS, AND MEN, AND BEASTS, AND CATTLE, AND REPTILES, AND FEATHERED FOWL, AND THE FISH; WHO IS THE KING OF MEN AND GODS, THE ONE FORM, TO WHOM PERIODS OF ONE

[1] See Pleyte and Rossi, *Papyrus de Turin*, Plates 31, 77, 131, 138.

[2] See Lefébure, *A.Z.*, 1883, pp. 27 ff.; Wiedemann, *Die Religion*, p. 29; Budge, *First Steps in Egyptian*, pp. 241 ff.; and for summaries of it see Erman, *Aegypten*, p. 359, and Maspero, *Les Origines*, pp. 162–164.

HUNDRED AND TWENTY YEARS ARE AS SINGLE YEARS, WHOSE MULTITUDINOUS NAMES ARE UNKNOWABLE, FOR [EVEN] THE GODS KNOW THEM NOT.

" Behold, the goddess Isis lived in the form of a " woman, who had the knowledge of words of power. Her " heart turned away in disgust from the millions of men, " and she chose for herself the millions of the gods, but she " esteemed more highly the millions of the spirits. Was it " not possible to become even as was Rā in heaven and " upon earth, and to make herself mistress of the earth " and a mighty goddess by means of the knowledge of the " Name of the holy god ? Thus did she meditate in her " heart.

" Behold, Rā entered [heaven] each day at the head of " his mariners, stablishing himself upon the double throne " of the two horizons. Now the divine one had " become old, he dribbled at the mouth, and he let his " emissions go forth from him upon the earth, and his " spittle fell upon the ground. This Isis kneaded with " dust in her hand, and she fashioned it in the form of a " sacred serpent with dart-like fangs, so that none might " be able to escape alive from it, and she placed it on the " path whereon the great god was about to travel, " according to his desire, round about the Two Lands (*i.e.*, " Egypt). Then the holy god rose up in the tabernacle of " the gods in the Great House (*i.e.*, the sky), Life, Strength, " Health [be to him]! among those who were in his train, " and [as] he journeyed on his way according to his custom " daily, the holy serpent drove his fangs into him. The " living fire [began] to depart from the god's body, and the " reptile destroyed the dweller among the cedars. Then " the mighty god opened his mouth, and the cry of His " Majesty, Life, Strength, Health [be to him]! rang " through the heavens. The Company of the gods said, " 'What is it?' and the gods of Rā said, 'What is the " matter?' Now the god found [no words] wherewith to " answer concerning himself, for his jaws shut, his lips " trembled, and the poison conquered all his members, just " as Ḥāpi (*i.e.*, the Nile) conquereth all the land through " which he floweth.

" Then the great god made firm his heart, and he cried " out to the gods who were in his following saying : 'Come

" ye unto me, O ye who have sprung from my members, ye " gods who have proceeded from me, for I wish to tell you " what hath happened. I have been stung by some deadly " thing, of which my heart hath no knowledge, and which " I have neither seen with my eyes nor made with my " hand. I have no knowledge whatsoever of that which " hath done this thing to me. Never before have I felt " pain like unto this, and no pain can be worse than this. " I am a Prince, and the Son of a Prince, I am a divine " emanation, I was produced by a god. I am a Great One, " and the son of a Great One, and my father determined " for me my name. My names are multitudinous, my " forms are manifold, and my being existeth in every god. " I am invoked as Thoth and Ḥeru-Ḥekenu. My father " and my mother uttered my name, and they hid it in my " body when I was born, so that none of those who would " use against me words of power might succeed in making " their enchantments to have dominion over me. I was " coming forth from my tabernacle to look upon that " which I had made, and was making my way through the " Two Lands (*i.e.*, Egypt), which I made, when I was " stung, but by what I know not. Can it be fire? Can " it be water? My heart is full of burning fire, my limbs " are shivering, and in my members are shooting pains. " Let there come to me my children the gods, who possess " words of power, whose mouths are skilled in uttering " them, and whose powers reach to the very heavens.'

" Then his children came unto him, and every god was " there uttering cries of lamentation. And Isis came with " her words of power, and in her mouth was the breath of " life. Now the words which she stringeth together " destroy diseases, and they make to live those whose " throats are stopped up (*i.e.*, the dead) and she said, " 'What is this, O divine father? What is the matter? " Hath a serpent shot his venom into thee? Hath " anything which thou hast fashioned [dared] to lift up his " head against thee? Verily, it shall be overcome by " effective words of power, and I will drive it away before " thy light.' The holy god opened his mouth and said, " 'I was coming along the road, and was passing through " my country of Egypt, for I wished to look upon what I " had made, when lo! I was bitten by a serpent. Can it "be fire? Can it be water? I am colder than water. "I am hotter than fire. All my members sweat, my body "quaketh, mine eye faileth me, I cannot look at the "heavens. Water exudeth from my face, as in the time "of the Inundation.'

"Then Isis said unto Rā, 'O my divine father, tell me "thy name, for he who is able to pronounce his name shall "live.' [And Rā said], 'I am the maker of the heavens "and the earth. I have knit together the mountains, and "I have created everything which existeth upon them. "I am the maker of the waters. I have made Meḥturt to "come into being. I made Ka-en-mut-f, and I have "created the joys of love. I am the maker of heaven. "I have made to be hidden the two gods of the horizon. "I have placed the soul of the gods in them. I am the "Being who openeth his eyes and the light cometh; I am "the Being who shutteth his eyes and darkness cometh. "I am he who commandeth, and the waters of the Nile "flow forth. I am he whose name the gods know not. "I am the maker of the hours and the creator of the days. "I inaugurate festivals. I make the waterflood. I am "the creator of the fire of life through which the products "of the workshops come into being. I am Kheperȧ in "the morning, Rā at mid-day, and Temu in the evening.' "Nevertheless the poison was not turned aside from its "course, and the pain of the great god was not relieved.

"Then Isis said unto Rā: 'Among the words which thou "hast said unto me there is no mention of thy name. Declare "thou to me thy name, and the poison shall leave thee, for "he who declareth his name shall live.' Meanwhile the "poison burned like blazing fire, and the heat thereof was "stronger than that of a fire that burneth brightly. Then "the Majesty of Rā said: 'I will permit Isis to search me, "and my name shall come forth from my body and go "into hers.' Then the divine one hid himself from the "gods, and the throne in the Boat of Millions of Years was "empty. And when the time came for the heart [of the "god] to come forth, Isis said unto her son Horus: 'The "great god bindeth himself by an oath to give his two "Eyes' (*i.e.*, the sun and moon). Thus was the great "god made to yield up his name. Then Isis, the great lady "of words of power, said: 'Flow poison, come out of Rā.

"Let the Eye of Horus come forth from the god and "shine (?) outside his mouth. I work, I make the poison "to fall on the ground, for the venom is conquered. Verily "the name of the great god hath been taken away from "him. Rā shall live, and the poison shall die; if the "poison liveth then Rā shall die. Similarly so-and-so "[if he hath been poisoned and these words be said over "him] shall live, and the poison shall die.' These were "the words which Isis spake, the great lady, the Queen of "the gods, and she had knowledge of Rā's own name."

RUBRIC: The above words shall be said over an image of Temu, and an image of Ḥeru-Ḥekenu, and an image of Isis, and an image of Horus.

APPENDIX

LIST OF THE GODS WHOSE NAMES WERE RECITED BY THE DECEASED TO PERFECT HIS SPIRIT-SOUL

The following names form an important section of the Theban Recension of the Book of the Dead, and the recital of them, either by the father or son of the deceased, was obligatory during every festival of Ȧment. The recital of them made the deceased a companion of the gods, and made him dear to the heart of Rā, and conferred upon him the power to leave the Ṭuat and to re-enter it at will. The list presumably gives the names of all the gods who were officially recognised by the priests of Osiris. The last section of it, which gives the names of all the great towns in which the Cult of Osiris flourished, is interesting as proving that under the XVIIIth dynasty the recognition of Osiris as the great Ancestor-god of the whole of Egypt was complete. The list is taken from the Papyrus of Nu (Brit. Mus. No. 10477, Sheet 15):—

1. Osiris Khenti Ȧmenti
2. Rā-Ḥeru-Khuti
3. Nu

4. Maāt

5. Boat of Rā

6. Tem

7. Great Company of the Gods.[1]

8. Little Company of the Gods

9. Horus, lord of the Urrt Crown

10. Shu

11. Tefnut

12. Ḳeb

13. Nut

14. Isis

15. Nephthys

16. Ḥetkau-Nebtertcher[2]

17. Shenȧt-pet-uthest-neter

18. Ȧuḳert-khentt-ȧsts

19. Khebit-sāḥt-neter

[1] Perhaps we are to read *pestchet neteru*, "the nine gods," and not *paut neteru*.

[2] The Seven Cows of Chapter CXLVIII.

20. Urmertus-ṭesher-sheni

21. Khnemtemānkh-ȧnuit

22. Sekhmet-rens-em-ābuts

23. The Bull of the Seven Cows

24. Sekhem Nefer [1]

25. Nekhen-semu-taui

26. Khu-ḥerȧb-ḥet-āshemu

27. Khenti-ḥerȧb-ḥet-ṭesheru

28. Ḳestȧ (or Mestȧ) [2]

29. Ḥepi

30. Ṭuamutef

31. Qebḥsenuf

32. The Southern Ȧtert (Upper Egypt).

33. The Northern Ȧtert (Lower Egypt).

34. The Sektet Boat

[1] The Four Rudders of heaven of Chapter CXLVIII.
[2] The Four Sons of Horus.

35. The Āṭet Boat
36. Thoth
37. Gods of the South
38. Gods of the North
39. Gods of the West
40. Gods of the East
41. Gods of the Thigh (Great Bear)
42. Gods of offerings
43. The Great House
44. The House of Fire
45. The Gods of the Åats
46. The Gods of the Horizon
47. The Gods of the Fields
48. The Gods of Grain (?)
49. The Gods of Fire
50. The Roads of the South
51. The Roads of the North
52. The Roads of the East
53. The Roads of the West
54. The Gates of the Ṭuat-gods

55. The Pylons of the Ṭuat-gods

56. The Hidden Doors

57. The Hidden Gates

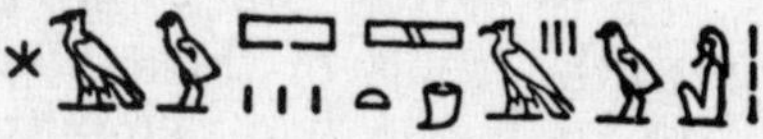

58. The Keepers of the Doors

59. The Gates of the Ṭuat-gods

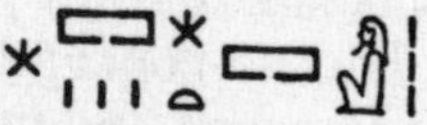

60. The Hidden Faces

61. Guards of the Roads

62. The Keepers . . . . .

63. The Keepers of the Cemeteries (?)

64. The Fire-gods

65. The Altar-gods

66. The Opener-gods, who extinguish fire and flame in Ȧment

THE ABODE OF THE BLESSED

In primitive times the Egyptians believed that after death the souls of those who had spoken the truth upon earth, and who had committed no act of fraud, deceit, or double-dealing, made their way by some means or other to a heaven, and took up their abode with the gods. Where this heaven was situated they had no idea, and of what it was like they had no conception, but they formulated vague views about the unseen and unknown home of their beloved, and some of these have been preserved in the religious texts of the later Egyptians which have come down to us. About one thing they had no doubt at all, namely, that the spirits of the dead left this earth. Primitive man assumed naturally that they went up into the sky, and from thence to some place beyond it. What the sky was exactly he did not know, but in the earliest times he seems to have thought that it was formed of a very large flat slab of a kind of stone or metal called *bàa*, which formed a ceiling for the earth, and more or less corresponded with it in general shape. Now such a slab must have something to rest on, so it was believed that it rested on two mountains, one in the east and the other in the west. The eastern mountain was called Bakha, and the western mountain Manu. How this slab was represented pictorially in early times cannot be said, but in the oldest hieroglyphic texts known, the sky is indicated by the hieroglyph 𓇯, which seems to be intended for a picture of the slab, very slightly vaulted, with a projection at each end of it by which it rested on the mountains of Bakha and Manu. Another early view was that the slab of the sky rested on four pillars, which in later texts are represented by [hieroglyph], and when the inventors of the hieroglyphic system of writing wanted a determinative to indicate a rainstorm or a hailstorm, with thunder and lightning, they used the sign [hieroglyph], *i.e.*, the sky falling down, and the four pillars projecting through it. The four pillars of the sky in still later times represented the Four Cardinal Points, and the pillars were thought to be kept in position by "the four gods who stood by them."[1] These four gods were the "Children of Horus" , who were called Åmset , Ḥap , Ṭuamutef , and Qebḥsenuf . Each god ruled over one quarter of the world. The reader of the Book of the Dead will find that in religious literature generally they appear chiefly as the guardians of the intestines of the dead, which were mummified separately and placed in jars commonly called "Canopic." Before we pass on to other early theories about the sky we may note that the sun was supposed to emerge from a hole in one end of the slab of the sky, and to pass under it, lighting this world as it passed, and to disappear in a hole at the other end of the slab. The stars were thought to be lamps which hung from the slab, as the hieroglyph shows . When the moon waned it was thought that a bit of it was eaten away by the fiend of darkness, and when it disappeared altogether, it was believed that it had been swallowed by him.

Another very early view was that the sky was the body of a gigantic woman, and that it was supported by her two legs and her two arms , which were the four pillars of heaven. The body of this Sky-woman was sometimes studded with stars ★★★★★. The sun was born each morning, and passed along her body towards her mouth, into which it disappeared in the evening to be re-born the following morning. The night-sky was supposed to be another woman, and the moon was born, and having passed along her body disappeared into her mouth. The Sky-women are well illustrated in the annexed illustration (p. 132), which is reproduced from Lanzone, *Mitologia*, tav. 155. Here we have: 1. A woman whose body is decorated with two winged disks, which probably represent the morning and evening sun; she has a Sûdânî crown of plumes on her head, and wears armlets and bracelets. 2. A smaller woman, whose body is decorated with small disks; on her hands stands a god whose head touches the hands of the larger woman. Between the front of the one woman and

[1] , *Recueil de Travaux*, V, p. 27 (l. 233).

the back of the other are a large winged disk, and some indeterminate object, winged. Round about them are stars. By the shoulders of the smaller woman is the goddess Nephthys, holding in her hands one of the two boats in which the sun sailed across the sky, and by the

thighs stands the goddess Isis holding the other boat. 3. A god lying on the ground with his arms stretched out along it, and holding a disk in each hand. His body is bent round to form a kind of circle, and his feet rest on the ground. The space enclosed is thought to represent the region where the dead live.

In an interesting scene on a coffin in the British Museum (No. 6670, First Egyptian Room) we find the night-sky depicted in the form of a woman with her arms stretched out at full length above her head. On her body rest two yellow disks, which symbolize the moon, and a red disk, which is intended for the sun. The view that the sky was a woman was very popular among the Egyptians down to a comparatively late period, and the religious texts are full of allusions to the birth of the deceased on the thighs of a Sky-woman.

Another view represented the sky in the form of a gigantic cow, her body forming the sky, and her four legs the pillars of the same. Her legs were held in position by eight gods, two to each leg, and her body was kept in its place by a god who held it up with his upraised arms,  . This cow gave birth to the sun, which was then likened to a calf, and the deceased when re-born in the sky was compared to a sucking calf. According to another very old belief the sky was the face of a man, and the sun and the moon were his two eyes; the sun was his right eye  , and the moon his left  . When a storm came, and thunder-clouds concealed the sun, it was thought that the king of darkness had done some injury to the right eye, and caused it to shed tears (*i.e.*, rain). During an eclipse the right eye was supposed to be temporarily disabled. The moon was supposed to suffer in a similar manner. Yet another view held in primitive times was that the sky was a vast meadow over which a huge beetle crawled, pushing the disk of the sun before him. This beetle was the Sky-god, and, arguing from the example of the beetle (*Scarabaeus sacer*) which was observed to roll along with its hind legs a ball that was believed to contain its eggs, the Early Egyptians thought that the ball of the Sky-god contained his egg, and that the sun was his offspring. Thanks, however, to the investigations of the eminent entomologist, Monsieur J. H. Fabre, we now know that the ball which the *Scarabaeus sacer* rolls along contains not its eggs, but dung that is to serve as food for its egg, which it lays in a carefully prepared place.

Later still, the Egyptians came to the conclusion that the sky was nothing but a vast layer of water, and then their difficulties in explaining how the sun, moon, and stars travelled across it disappeared, for they were quite certain in their minds that the celestial bodies traversed the sky in boats. The sun possessed two boats called "Mantchet" and "Semktet," and the moon, planets and principal stars each possessed a boat. What these boats were made of they never stopped to inquire, and they seem to have been content to think that the Boats of Rā were made of some substance which could not be consumed. From the annexed interesting illustration (p. 134), which is reproduced from the marble sarcophagus of Seti I, we see that about 1350 B.C. the Egyptians still believed that the sun rose out of the Celestial Waters each morning in a boat. This boat is being lifted out of the water by the god Nu,  , and is supported by the hands of his upstretched arms, which, as the text says,

"Come forth from the waters, and bear up this god." In the boat we see the monster beetle already mentioned pushing the solar disk upwards and into the hands of the goddess Nut, *i.e.*, the Sky-goddess "who receives Rā," . On the right of the beetle are the goddess

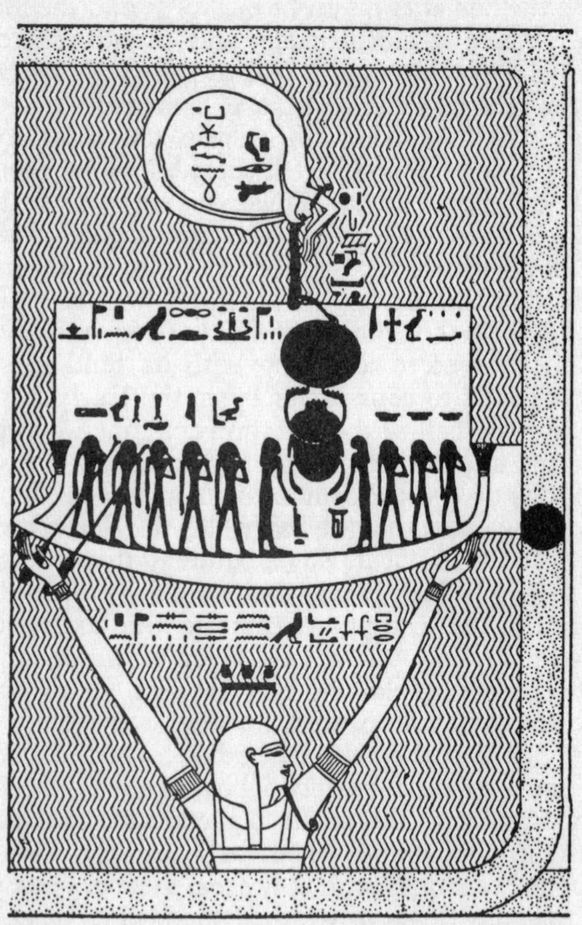

Nephthys, , and three gods, and on the left are Isis, , Ȧst, or Set, Ḳeb, the Earth-god, , Ȧ, *i.e.*, Thoth, , Ḥeka, the god who utters words of power, Ḥu, , and Sa, . The legend above reads: "This god rests in the Ānṭ (=Māntcheṭ) Boat with the gods who are with him."

In the upper part of the illustration, *i.e.*, in a remote place among the Celestial Waters, we see the body of a man bent round backwards in such a way as to form a circle, and the toes touching the back of the head. This god is, the text tells us, Osiris, and it is his body which forms the circle of the Ṭuat. But what is the Ṭuat, and what is the meaning of the name? Ṭuat is the name which the Egyptians gave in primitive times to the region to which the dead departed after they had left this earth, and the word has been translated by "Other World," "Hades," "Underworld," "Hell," the "place of departed spirits," and the like. The exact meaning of the word is unknown, and it seems to have been lost in very early times. No English word or words will convey the idea which those who first used the word "Ṭuat" applied to it, and it must not be translated by "Underworld," or "Hell," or "Sheol," or "Jehannum," for each of these words has a special and limited meaning. On the other hand, the Ṭuat possessed all the characteristics which we associate with these words, for it was "unseen," and dark and gloomy, and there were pits of fire in it, and it formed the home of hellish monsters, and of the damned. Speaking generally, we may say that "Other World" is a fairly accurate rendering of "Ṭuat." The oldest form of the name is Ṭat, , which is found in the Pyramid Texts. The chief god of the Ṭuat, or the personification of the place, was "Ṭuaut," , and the gods of it were the "Ṭuatiu," . Later forms of the name are , , , , and .

The early Egyptians thought that Egypt was the world, and that it was surrounded by a chain of lofty mountains, like the Gebel Ḳâf of the Arabs, which was pierced in two places, one in the east and the other in the west. In the evening the sun passed through the western hole, and travelling, not under the earth, but on the same plane and outside the chain of mountains, it came round to the eastern hole in the mountains, through which it entered to begin the new day above the earth. Outside the chain of mountains, but quite close to them, was situated the Ṭuat, and it ran parallel with them. On the outer side of the Ṭuat was another chain of mountains, and a river ran between them. We may say, then, that the Ṭuat closely resembled that part of the Valley of the Nile which constitutes Egypt, and that it was to all intents and purposes circular in form. Now as the Ṭuat lay on the other side of the chain of mountains which surrounded Egypt, and was therefore deprived of the light of the sun and moon which illumined its skies, it was shrouded in the gloom and darkness of night, and was therefore a place of gloom and terror. At each end of the Ṭuat was a space which was neither wholly darkness, nor wholly light, the eastern end being partially lighted by the rising sun, and the western end by the setting sun. Where these partially lighted spaces ended "thick darkness," or "solid darkness," *i.e.*, the "outer darkness," began.

The part of the Ṭuat that was close to Egypt was a terrible place, which much resembled the African "bush." Parts of it were desert, and parts of it were forest, and parts of it were "scrub" land, and there were no "roads" through any part of it. Tracks there were, just as there are in the forests of the Sûdân, but it was hopeless for the disembodied soul to attempt to find its way by means of them, unless guided by some friendly being who knew the "ways" of that awful region. Everywhere there was thick darkness. All the region of the Ṭuat was inhabited, but the beings who dwelt there were hostile to all new-comers, and they could only be placated by gifts, or made subservient to the souls of the dead on their way to the kingdom of Osiris, by the use of spells, or words of power. The way was barred, too, by frightful monsters which lived on the souls of the dead, and at one place or another the deceased was obliged to cross streams which were fed by the river in the Ṭuat, and even the river itself. In one part of this terrible region was situated a district called "Sekhet Ḥetepet, *i.e.*, the "Field of Offerings," or the Elysian Fields, and within this was a sub-district called "Sekhet Ȧaru," *i.e.*, the "Field of Reeds"; in the latter lived the god Osiris and his court. In primitive times his kingdom was very small, but gradually it grew, and at length absorbed the whole of the Ṭuat. He ruled the inhabitants thereof much as an earthly king ruled men, and from first to last there seem to have been in his kingdom nobles, chiefs, and serfs, just as there were in Egypt.

The desire of every good man in Egypt was to go to the Kingdom of Osiris, the "Lord of Souls," and, as we learn from the "Book of the Two Ways," or the "Two Ways of the Blessed Dead,"[1] he might go there by water or by land. The difficulties which beset him if he went by land have already been indicated, and if he attempted to go there by water the difficulties which he would have to encounter were no less serious. The Egyptians thought that the Nile which flowed through Egypt was connected with the river in the Ṭuat, but to reach the latter the deceased would have to pass through the two holes in the First Cataract from which the Nile rose, and then he would have to sail over streams of fire and of boiling water before he arrived in port. The banks of these streams were filled with hostile beings which sought to bar his progress, and lucky indeed was that soul which triumphed over all obstacles, and reached the City of God.

The Theban Recension of the Book of the Dead contains several Chapters dealing with the Kingdom of Osiris, and from these the following facts are derived. The CXLIVth Chapter states that there were seven halls or mansions in Sekhet Åaru, all of which had to be passed through by the deceased before he could see the god. Each door of each Ārit, or hall, was under the care of three gods; the first was the doorkeeper, the second kept a look-out and acted as watchman, and the third questioned the traveller who arrived, and reported his arrival and name to Osiris or his officers. Unless the traveller could tell each god his name, he was not permitted to enter the Ārit guarded by the three gods. The names of the gods of the Seven Ārits (Papyrus of Nu) were:—

Ārit I.	Doorkeeper,	Sekheṭ-ḥer-āshtåru;	Watcher,	Smeṭu;	Herald,	Hukheru.
Ārit II.	"	Ṭunḥåt;	"	Seqeṭḥer;	"	Sabes.
Ārit III.	"	Unemḥuatentpeḥuif;	"	Resḥer;	"	Uāau.
Ārit IV.	"	Khesefḥerāshtkheru;	"	Resåb;	"	Neteqaḥer-khesefaṭu.
Ārit V.	"	Ānkhemfentu;	"	Ashebu;	"	Tebḥer-kehaat.
Ārit VI.	"	Åkentaukhakheru;	"	Ånḥer;	"	Meṭesḥer-årishe.
Ārit VII.	"	Meṭessen;	"	Āakheru;	"	Khesefḥer-khemiu.

[1] See the version published by Schack-Schackenburg, *Das Buch von den Zwei Wegen des Seligen Toten* (Leipzig, 1903), from a coffin at Berlin.

From another Chapter in the same Papyrus (CXLVI) we learn that the Secret Gates of the House of Osiris in Sekhet Åaru were ten in number, and the names of the Gates and of their keepers were :—

GATE I. NEBT-SEṬAU-QAT-SEBT-ḤERT-NEBT-KHEBKHEBT-SERT-MEṬU-KHESFET-NESHNIU-NEḤMET-ĀUAI-EN-I-UAU.
Gatekeeper. NERI.

GATE II. NEBT-PET-ḤENT-TAUI-NESBIT-NEBT-TEMEMU-TENT-BU-NEBU.
Gatekeeper. MES-PEḤ or MES-PTAḤ.

GATE III. NEBT-KHAUT-ĀAT-ĀABET-SENETCHMET-NETER-NEB-ÅMS-HRU-KHENT-ER-ÅBṬU.
Gatekeeper. ERṬĀTSEBANQA.

GATE IV. SEKHMET-ṬESU-ḤENT-TAUI-ḤETCHET-KHEFTI-NU-URṬ-ÅB-ÅRIT-SARU-SHUT-EM-ÅU.
Gatekeeper. NEKAU.

GATE V. KHET-NEBT-REKḤU-RESHT-TEBḤET-ṬĀTU-NES-ÅN-ĀQ-ERES-UN-ṬEP-F.
Gatekeeper. ḤENTIREQU.

GATE VI. NEBT-SENKET-ĀAT-HEMHEMET-AN-REKHTU-QAS-ER-USEKH-S-ÅN-QEMTU-QEṬ-S-EM-SHAĀ-ÅU-ḤEFAU-ḤER-S-ÅN-REKH-TENNU-MES-ENTHU-KHER-ḤĀT-URṬU-ÅB.
Gatekeeper. SMAMTI.

GATE VII. AḲḲIT-ḤEBSET-BAḲ-ÅAKHEBIT-MERT-SEḤAP-KHAT.
Gatekeeper. ÅKENTI.

GATE VIII. REKḤET-BESU-ĀKHMET-TCHAFU-SEPṬ-PĀU-KHAT-ṬET-SMAM-AN-NETCHNETCH-ÅTET-SESH-ḤER-SEN-SENT-NÅH-S.
Gatekeeper. KHUTCHETF.

GATE IX. ÅMT-ḤĀT-NEBT-USER-HERT-ÅB-MESTET-NEB-S-KHET-SHĀĀ- . . . . . -EM-SHEN-S-SATU-EM-UATCHET-SHEMĀ-THESET-BES-ḤEBSET-BAḲ-FEQAT-NEB-S-RĀ-NEB.
Gatekeeper. TCHESEF.

GATE X. QAT-KHERU-NEHESET-ṬENÅTU-SEBḤET-ER-QA-EN-KHERU-S-NERT-NEBT-SHEFSHEFT-ÅN-ṬERN-S-NETET-EM-KHENNU-S.
Gatekeeper. SEKHENUR.

Some papyri add four, or six, or eleven other Gates to the above series of ten, but though they give their names in full they do not supply the names of their keepers. The original number of the Gates appears to have been ten. It will be noted that the name of each Gate consists of an address to it, in which many honorific titles occur, and that the name is really a many-worded spell.

From another Chapter (CXLIX) we learn that Sekhet Åaru was divided into Fifteen Åats, or Regions, each of which was presided over by a god. The FIRST ÅAT was called "Åmentet," and the dwellers therein lived on the offerings which were made to them; the god who ruled it was Menuqeṭ. The SECOND ÅAT was called "Sekhet Åaru," and the walls which surrounded it were made of the material which forms the sky (*båa*). Its god was Rā Ḥeru-Khuti, and the inhabitants thereof were Spirit-souls who were nine cubits high. The wheat and the barley which grew there were five and seven cubits high respectively. This Åat seems to have been the centre of the Kingdom of Osiris. The THIRD ÅAT was called the Åat of the Spirit-souls, and was a place of blazing fire; it was ruled over by Rā or Osiris. The FOURTH ÅAT was called "Ṭui-qaui-āaui," and its extent was 300 measures by 230 measures. Its ruler was the monster serpent "Sati-ṭemui," which was seventy cubits long, and which lived by slaughtering the Spirit-souls and the dead who were in the Ṭuat. There was another serpent in this Åat called "Akriu," and it appears to have been an enemy of Rā. The FIFTH ÅAT was inhabited by Spirit-souls whose thighs were seven cubits long; they lived upon the shadows of the helpless and weak. They owed fealty to Osiris, for the deceased adjured them in the name of Osiris, the Great Spirit-soul, to let him pass over their roads. The SIXTH ÅAT was called "Amḥet," and was ruled by a god in the form of a worm called "Sekher Āṭ." It was a place sacred to the gods, but was a region of mystery to the Spirit-souls, and was unsuitable for the dead. The SEVENTH ÅAT was called Åses, and was situated in a remote place, full of fire. The lord of this Åat was a serpent, with a back seven cubiṭs long. It was gifted with the evil eye, and it first fascinated Spirit-souls and then destroyed them. It had a mortal enemy in the Lynx-goddess Mafṭet, which bit off its head. No soul wished to meet it, or to come in its way, and only the words of power which a soul possessed enabled it to escape death through its venom. The EIGHTH ÅAT. This Åat was called "Haḥetep," and it was under the rule of a god called "Qa-haḥetep," , and it appears to have contained an underground canal which was connected with this earth; at one part of it was a sort of well, and the noise made by the waters as they entered it, and their roar as they rushed out was greatly terrifying. One creature was able to pass over this region, namely the Ennur bird, with which the deceased identified himself. In this Åat he was obliged to make offerings to the "lords of offerings," otherwise the fiends would carry him off to the block where the sacrifices to the gods were slaughtered. The NINTH ÅAT was called "Åksi," and not even the gods knew exactly where it was. It was ruled over by the "holy god who dwelt in his egg," and who terrified both gods and Spirit-souls; no one could enter or leave the region without this god's consent. At the entrance to the Åat was a mighty fire, the heat, fumes, and vapours of which destroyed the nostrils and mouths of any who tried to pass through it; only the god of the Åat could breathe its air with impunity, or those who formed his bodyguard. The souls who wished to pass through this Åat without being consumed were obliged to make obeisance to the god, and then to obtain permission to become one of his bodyguard. The TENTH ÅAT was likewise a region of terror, and it was ruled over by a god who carried a butcher's knife in each hand, and bore a serpent on his head. Among the Serpent-gods who lived here were the awful beings Nāu and Neḥebkau, and they fed upon the Spirit-souls and the shadows of the dead. The deceased was obliged to make offerings to these gods, to burn myrrh, and to slaughter animals, and even so he could not pass through the Åat unharmed unless Isis and Nephthys were his companions. The ELEVENTH ÅAT was in Khert-Neter, and its chief town was called "Åtu." Its ruler had the form of a jackal-headed man, and he was armed with two slaughtering-knives. The Åat was situated among hills, or on a hill with terraces. The deceased who wished to pass through this Åat armed himself with the knife wherewith Horus mutilated Set, and against this weapon no other weapon could prevail. Even so, the deceased was obliged to declare that he was Rā, and that his strength was due to the Eye of Horus. It will be remembered that when Osiris had been mummified, and when his body was still without life, Horus brought his Eye, which he had taken out of the possession of Set, and gave it to his father to eat. Osiris swallowed the Eye, and immediately he became a living being. The deceased also took the form of the Smen goose, the cackling of which pleased the gods, and he rose like a god, being filled with the divine food of the Field of Offerings. Then was he able to set up a ladder, and to climb up by its means to the place where the gods and the imperishable stars were, and his speech became like that of the beings who dwell in the star Sepṭ (the Dog-star, or Sothis). The TWELFTH ÅAT was close to Rasta, and its chief town was called "Unt." It also was a place full of fire, and the souls of the dead were unable to approach it by reason of the uraei which attacked all comers. The THIRTEENTH ÅAT. This Åat was also a region of fire, and the streams which flowed through it were of boiling water. It was a place which caused the Spirit-souls great trouble, for though they wished to drink and quench their thirst they were unable to do so, because of the fear with which the fire inspired them. The god who presided over the region was a hippopotamus, which we see represented with one forefoot resting on a beetle. His name appears to be Ḥebṭ-re-f, and he was the symbol of the celestial river of which the Nile was the continuation on earth. The deceased could only gain power over the waters of this region by the help of this god, whose chief place of abode in it was called "Uārt-ent-mu" [hieroglyphs]. The FOURTEENTH ÅAT is called "Kherāḥa," and it appears to have been a region through which a great canal flowed, and to have contained many lakes. The name suggests that the Åat was the celestial equivalent of the region which lay between the Nile and the ancient city of Heliopolis. There appears to be in the text that describes this Åat an allusion to a great canal which was fed directly from the Nile, and flowed through the whole district until at length it reached the great canal which flowed into the Bitter Lakes. The modern equivalent of the canal of Kher-āḥa was the great Khalig Canal, at the mouth of which the famous ceremony of "cutting the dam" was performed annually. Somewhere near the mouth a bride was offered to the Nile-god annually. The allusion to the Serpent-god who guarded the two caverns at Elephantine, through which the Nile-god poured his waters into Egypt, and to the town of Ṭeṭu (Busiris) proves that we are here dealing with one of the principal domains of Osiris.

In the great papyri of the Book of the Dead, according to the Theban Recension, we find detailed pictures of the Field of Offerings and the Field of Reeds, wherein the followers of Osiris hoped to enjoy a life of everlasting bliss. As these regions have been described in connection with the Vignette of Chapter CX (see Vol I, pp. 107 ff.), and a translation of the text of the Chapter has also been given in the Second Volume, there is no need to discuss them further here.

In addition to the Chapters already mentioned, there are other sources of information about the Ṭuat or Other World of the Egyptians, and of these the principal works are the "BOOK OF HIM THAT IS IN THE ṬUAT," and the "Book of Gates."[1] The Book Åm Ṭuat, or Åmi Ṭuat, describes the journey which the Sun-god makes through the Ṭuat, after he has set upon this world. As the Sun-god approaches the ante-chamber or vestibule of the Ṭuat in the west, the gods who are in charge of his boat steer directly for the entrance to the Ṭuat. The Sun-god takes the form of a man-headed ram, and stands within a shrine, in other words, he takes the form of Osiris, so that he may pass safely through the Kingdom of the dead, which is ruled by Osiris. In this form the Sun-god is called ÅF RĀ, "flesh of Rā," *i.e.*, the dead body of Osiris. As he approaches, the Ape-gods and the other gods and goddesses sing praises to him, and serpents belch forth fire, which provides the light that enables his Pilot-gods to steer his boat. The doors which bar the way are thrown open by the gods, and Åf Rā proceeds on his way

[1] See my editions of the *Book Åm Ṭuat*, the *Book of Gates*, and the *Egyptian Heaven and Hell*, London, 1905.

over the waters of the river of the Ṭuat. The light from the boat wakes the dead who are there to life, and the air which Åf Rā carries with him enables them to live again for an hour. Every being that ministers to the god, and every creature in this section of the Tuat receive meat and drink by the command of Åf Rā. The dead whom he finds here are souls who for some cause or other have failed to find their way to the realm of Osiris, and they are only saved from utter destruction by the light, air, and food which they receive from Åf Rā. When the god reaches the entrance to the Second Section of the Ṭuat, the goddess of the Hour and the other gods of the section leave him, and return to their places to await his arrival on the following night.

The SECOND SECTION of the Ṭuat is called "Urnes" [hieroglyphs], as is also the river which flows through it. It lay to the north of the ante-chamber already described, and was situated in the domain of Osiris Khenti Åmenti, which included the territory of Abydos. The Boat of Åf Rā is now accompanied by the boats of Osiris and his attendant gods, and when it arrives in Urnes the god addresses the inhabitants of the district, who are called "Baiu Ṭuatiu," or "Souls of the Ṭuat," and orders them to receive from him food, light, and air in return for their labours which they have performed on his behalf. Åf Rā destroys the serpents Ḥau and Neḥa-ḥer, and the gods lead him into the Field of the Grain-gods [hieroglyphs], where for a time he rests. Here Åf Rā held converse with the Souls of Urnes, and he received the prayers of the living on behalf of the dead, and noted the offerings which were made by them. The pictures of this section of the Ṭuat and the descriptive texts were believed to possess special efficacy, and copies of them are tolerably numerous; they benefited the souls of the dead, and protected the bodies of those who had them made on earth. In Urnes only the followers of Osiris and Rā were to be found.

The THIRD SECTION of the Ṭuat is called "Net-nebuākheperaut," and is a continuation of the Kingdom of Osiris; in it is the House of the Ṭeṭ, wherein Osiris himself dwells. The Boat of Åf Rā is escorted over the waters of the river Net-Àsàr by a number of boats which are specially created by Osiris, and arrives at the head of the stream on which the throne of Osiris is placed. Here the god sits surrounded by his followers who are described as "Baiu Shetaiu," or "hidden souls." The banks of the stream are lined with gods who have been told off by Osiris to minister to the wants of Af Rā and to make his boat to travel in safety through the region. The duties of the servants of Osiris in this section may be thus described: **1.** They protect Nu, the god of the great celestial ocean from which rose the river which on earth was known as "Ḥap," or the Nile, from the attacks of the legion of devils called "Sebà." These devils were the active servants of Set, the god of chaos, darkness, and destruction, and they endeavoured to prevent the Nile from rising at its appointed time, and tried by every means in their power to fetter its waters during its annual inundation. At times Sebà succeeded in arresting the inundation, and then Egypt was attacked by famine. **2.** They hack souls in pieces, they imprison the shadows of the dead. They carry out the death sentence on those who are doomed to be destroyed in a place of fire, and they make and maintain the fires by which such beings are to be consumed. The "souls" and "shadows" here referred to must belong to the dead who have reached this place, but who through sin committed upon earth, and through the lack of offerings made to them upon earth, have failed to find nourishment and have perished in consequence. With them, too, are joined the souls which have been condemned in the Judgment by Osiris, and the souls of those who have rebelled against Rā. The execution and the burning of the damned take place soon after midnight each day, and thus the Kingdom of Osiris is cleared of the wicked, and the Boat of Àf Rā can pursue its course unhindered by them. In return for these services the gods receive daily rations from their god, and they rejoice so greatly in his light, that as soon as he leaves their region in darkness, they begin to weep and lament, and to sigh for his return on the following day.

From the Kingdom of Osiris the Boat of Af Rā passes northwards to the FOURTH SECTION of the Ṭuat, or the realm of Seker [hieroglyphs], an ancient Death-god, who is probably far older than Osiris, and whose territory lay a little to the south of Memphis. Here serious difficulties awaited Åf Rā, for there was no river in Ra-stau, the kingdom of Seker, and his boat was therefore useless. Here the half-light of the Kingdom of Osiris was exchanged for the blackest darkness, and the fertile fields and the streams of the Field of Offerings were exchanged for rocks, and mountains, and deserts, filled with winged serpents, and serpents with two or three heads, and monsters of most terrifying aspect. Åf Rā is, however, bound to traverse these on his way northward, and compelled by his words of power the gods of Ra-stau take him out of his own boat, and lead him by way of subterranean corridors and galleries in the rock through, or rather above, the awful Kingdom of Death. The vehicle in which he travels is no longer a boat, but is the body of a serpent, which glides easily through the passages of the rock. Very few gods attend him on his journey, but among them are Thoth, Horus, and the servants of Ånpu. Each passage has several doors in it, and everywhere are servants of Seker in the form of monster serpents which, apparently unwillingly, assist Åf Rā on his way. At no part of the journey does Åf Rā meet Seker, and the dead Sun-god takes care to avoid that portion of Ra-stau where Death sits in majesty, with deadly serpents and monsters about him. The sanctuary of Seker, as we see from the pictures of the Fifth Section of the Ṭuat, is enclosed by a wall of sand. This god is in the form of a man but has a hawk's head and a pair of wings, which emerge from the back of a two-headed serpent. The shrine of Seker is pyramidal in form, and is filled with the blackest darkness. As Åf Rā passes it, the Beetle of Kheperȧ enters his boat, and the revivification of the dead Sun-god begins. This part of Ra-stau is called Åmḥet [hieroglyphs], and here is situated the stream of fire, or boiling water, in which were burned, or boiled, those who had incurred the displeasure of Seker. A company of the gods and a goddess presided over this place, and it was their duty to carry out the executions decreed by the gods. Each god was provided with a block of slaughter, on which he hacked the dead to pieces, and this done he cast the pieces into the fire which he produced from his own body; the goddess lived partly on the blood of the dead, and partly on rations decreed to her by the gods. We may note in passing, that no provision for the beatified existed in the kingdom of Seker, and it seems as if the priests of this ancient god assumed that with his death a man came to an end eternally.

Meanwhile the Boat of Åf Rā moves on, assisted by the gods of the dead of Seker, and at length it reaches the waters which existed on the northern boundary of his kingdom. Here the god leaves his serpent-boat, and re-enters his river-boat, which by some means has been transported to the entrance of the SIXTH SECTION of the Ṭuat. The Sixth Section of the Ṭuat lies to the north of the realm of Seker, and Åfu Rā traverses it in a boat. It is called Metchet-mu-nebt-Ṭuat, and contains the abodes of the dead kings of Egypt and of the Khu, or Spirit-souls. As Åfu Rā passed through it he saluted all the dwellers there and besought them to slay Āapep for him; in return for their services he decreed them offerings in abundance. In the pictures of this section, we see Åfu Rā lying on the back of the five-headed serpent Āsh-ḥeru, which has its body bent over him to protect him. On the head of the god is the Beetle of Kheperȧ, symbol of resurrection. At this point in his journey, Åfu Rā begins to travel towards the east, and to direct his course to the Mountain of the Sunrise, *i.e.*, Bakhau . Hitherto, he has been travelling from south to north. All the gods of this section assist Åfu Rā on his way, and the monster serpent Unem-Khu devours the shadows of the dead and the spirits of the enemies of the Sun-god. Among them are the Four Sons of Horus, who spring into being from the back of Unem-Khu as soon as they hear the voice of Åf Rā, and the Four Forms of Osiris, and the Nine Serpents, which represent the gods Tathenn, Temu, Kheperȧ, Shu, Ḳeb, Åsȧr (Osiris), Horus, Åfu, and Ḥetepui.

The SEVENTH SECTION of the Ṭuat is called "Thepḥet-shetat," or the "Hidden Region," and it is a continuation of the "secret road of Åmenti," on which Åfu Rā began to travel in the Sixth Section. The face of Åfu Rā is now turned in the other direction, and his crew is strengthened by the addition of Isis and Ser, or Semsu. His boat has now to travel through a region of swamps and shallows, and the path of the god is obstructed by the serpent Āapep or Neḥa-ḥer, which lies on a sand-bank 450 cubits long. The goddess Serqet and the god Ḥerthesuf drive their knives through his body, and fetter his tail and head, and so the boat of Åfu Rā moves onward. He passes the tombs of the Form of Tem, the Form of Kheperȧ, the Form of Rā, and the Form of Osiris, and he sees on the posts of the tombs the heads of those who were buried in the foundations when these tombs were built. These heads appear when they hear the voice of Åfu Rā, and they disappear as soon as he has passed. The boat of Åfu Rā is helped onward by the twelve gods and twelve goddesses of the Hours, and it passes the monster crocodile Ābshe-am-Ṭuat, which lies over the tomb of Osiris. Further on is Åfu Åsȧr seated on a throne watching the destruction of his enemies through decapitation by the Lynx-goddess Mafṭet; numbers of them are bound in chains held in the hands of the god Ånku.

When Åfu Rā enters the Eighth Section of the Ṭuat, which is called "Ṭebat-neterus," he is towed by a company of gods. He sees the Four Forms of Tathenn, which are preceded by the bodyguard of Rā, and he passes a series of Circles wherein dwell gods. Those on the right are Ḥetepetnebs, Ḥetemet Khemiu, Ḥapsemus, Seḥertbaius, and Āatsetekau; the door's name is Ṭesȧmen-mitemshetaf. The Circles on the left are Sesheta, Ṭuat, Åsneteru, Åakebi, and Nebtsemunifu; the door's name is Ṭeskhaibituṭuatiu. As Åfu Rā passes, he addresses words to the gods of the Circles, and the doors fly open, and they reply to the god with sounds like the mewing of male cats, the hum of the living, the cry of the hawk, the screams of waterfowl in their nests, the hum of bees, the noise of weeping, the sounds made by bulls, and shrieks of terror.

The boat of Åfu Rā moves through the Ninth Section of the Ṭuat, which is called "Bestȧruānkhet-kheperu," without the aid of towing or rowing gods.

The god is in the form of the serpent Meḥen, and he is accompanied by twelve Sailor-gods, who sing to him, and scatter water with their paddles on the beings who line the banks. The path of the god is lighted by twelve uraei, who pour out fire from their mouths, and at the end of the section Åfu Rā passes the field-labourers, who cultivate the fields of Osiris under the direction of Horus, Governor of the Lake of the Ṭuat, and the Twelve Taskmasters of Osiris (the Tchatchau), and the twelve goddesses, who weave the linen garments which are required in the section.

The TENTH and ELEVENTH SECTIONS of the Ṭuat are called "Metchetqatutchebu" and "Reenqerrtåptkhatu," and form part of the kingdom of the Sun-god of Ånu, or Heliopolis, and a part of the Eastern Delta. The beings who dwell in the Tenth Section have two duties to perform: 1. to slay the enemies of Åfu Rā and to destroy their bodies, and 2. to help in the reconstruction of the disk of the sun, which was to appear in the sky of this world that day. The boat of Åfu Rā now passes over a series of lakes, which seem to represent the lagoons of the Eastern Delta, in which we see a number of forms of men, in the various attitudes which human bodies assume as they are drowning. As Åfu Rā passes over these lagoons, Horus addresses the men drowned in them and assures them that "their members shall not perish, nor their flesh decay," but he makes no promise to bring them up, and to give them a renewed existence on dry land. This section contains many magical serpents, as well as gods and goddesses, and the mystic sceptre, and they all help Åfu Rā onward in his course.

The boat of Åfu Rā makes its way through the Eleventh Section, lighted by a disk of light, encircled by a serpent, which rests on the prow; this disk is called "Pesṭu." The tow-rope of the boat is formed of the body of the serpent Meḥen. Åfu Rā first passes the Red and White Crowns, and then arrives in the territory of the town of Saïs, where the god meets the Four Forms of the goddess Neith. Åfu Rā next passes the two-headed god Āperḥernebtchet, who wears two crowns, and the mystical forms of the body and soul of

Temu, and the body and soul of the Star-god Sheṭu. The region to the left of the god is one of fire, and in it, but quite close to the boat, stands Horus, who is working magic with the snake-headed boomerang which he holds in his hand. Before him is the serpent called "Set-ḥeḥ," *i.e.*, the "eternal Set." Horus is superintending the destruction of the bodies, souls, shadows, and heads of the enemies of Rā, which is being effected in the pits of fire before him. The fire in the pits is supplied from the bodies of the goddesses who are in charge of them. In the first pit, the victims are immersed in the fiery depths head downwards. When Åfu Rā arrives at the last of the pits, his journey through the Ṭuat proper is ended, and it only remains for him to pass through the ante-chamber to the east of it, in order to arrive at the sky of this world. In his journey he has traversed the Ṭuat of Thebes, the Ṭuat of Osiris of Abydos, the Ṭuat of Seker of Memphis, the Ṭuat of Neith of Sais, the Ṭuat of Bast of Bubastis, and the Ṭuat of Tem of Ånu, or Heliopolis, and he has followed a course which first went from south to north, then to the east, and finally towards the Mountain of the Sunrise. Åfu Rā has now reached the "uttermost limit of thick darkness," and arrives at the TWELFTH SECTION of the Other World, which is called "Kheperkekiukhāumestu." This section contains the great mass of Celestial Waters called Nu, and the goddess Nut, who is here the personification of the god of the morning. We see Åfu Rā in his boat as before, and in front of it is the Beetle of Kheperå, under whose form the new sun is to be born. Before the boat is the great serpent Ānkh-neteru, and twelve *åmkhiu*-gods, taking hold of the tow-line, enter this serpent at the tail, and, drawing the god in his boat through the body of the serpent, bring him out at his mouth. During his passage through the serpent Åfu Rā is transformed into Kheperå, and the *åmkhiu*-gods are also transformed, and emerge with him from the serpent, and minister to him all the day. Åfu Rā, in the form of Kheperå, is now towed into the sky by twelve goddesses, who lead him to Shu, the god of the atmosphere and sky of this world. Shu receives Kheperå, and places him in the opening in the semicircular wall which forms the end of this section, and people on this earth see him in the form of a disk of light. Åfu Rā, in the form of a disk of light, has no further use for his mummified form in which he traversed the Ṭuat, and we see it cast aside, and lying against the rounded end of the Ṭuat. As the disk appears in the sky, the newly-born god of day is acclaimed by gods and goddesses, who destroy any and every enemy who appears in the presence of the god, and sing hymns to him. It was assumed that the souls who travelled with Åfu Rā through the Ṭuat underwent the same transformations as he did, and were re-born on earth with him.

We may now consider the other Guide to the Ṭuat which was much used by the followers of Osiris under the XVIIIth and XIXth dynasties. This Guide may be called the "Book of Gates," because the most important features of the Ṭuat according to this work were the Gates and their guardians. In the FIRST SECTION, *i.e.*, the Western Vestibule, the Sun-god of night is seen in the form of a beetle within a disk, which is surrounded by a serpent with voluminous folds; he rests in his boat and is accompanied by the gods Sa and Ḥeka, *i.e.*, the personifications of knowledge and the word of power. The section is called "Set Åmentet" [hieroglyphs], and its guardian gods are Set and Ṭeṭ. On each side of the boat are twelve gods, one group being "gods of the mountain," and the other, "gods of the mountain of the Hidden Land." The "gods of the mountain" are the offspring of Rā himself, and they came into being from his eye.

The SECOND SECTION of the Ṭuat is guarded by the serpent SASET [hieroglyphs], and when the Sun-god of night enters it he takes the form of a ram-headed man; the Serpent-goddess Meḥen envelops his shrine, and his boat is towed by four gods, who are the gods of the four quarters of the earth. The work which Åfu Rā does in this Section of Åmenti is to "weigh words and deeds," to judge between the great and little gods, "to assign thrones to the spirits, "and to banish the damned to the place which is set apart "for them, and to destroy their bodies." From this text it is clear that a judgment of the dead took place in Åmenti, and that it was independent of the Judgment of Osiris. The gods who assist at the judgment of Åfu Rā live on the spirits of the offerings which are made to them upon earth, and those who made these offerings acquired merit before the god. The beings in this section are divided into two classes, the good and the wicked, the former being ranged to the right of the god, and the latter on his left. The good are divided into two classes, the Ḥeteptiu and the Maātiu. The former made offerings to Rā regularly when they were upon earth, and they praised him, and they recited curses upon Āapep the Arch-enemy of Rā; in return for these acts of piety Rā decrees that offerings shall be made to them in perpetuity, and that their souls shall never be destroyed. The Maātiu are so called because they were speakers of the truth upon earth, and because they were not in the habit of committing acts of fraud and deceit. Moreover, they had had no intercourse with the *neterit*, a word which seems to mean "contemptible gods," *i.e.*, gods which were disapproved of by Rā. As a reward for their veracity and orthodoxy they lived upon *maāt* food, *i.e.*, truth, and thus they became truth personified. They had access to an abundant supply of cold water, but if any sinful soul attempted to drink this water it turned into "fire water," *i.e.*, boiling water, and the soul was scalded. The wicked who stand to the left of Åfu Rā have their arms tied at the elbows behind their backs, and that they are suffering great agony is evident from their bowed backs; four of the wicked lie dead near their companions. These beings are charged with blasphemy against Rā, with having cursed him, and with having uttered abuse of Khuti, the Sun-god on the horizon; besides this they thrust aside the right. These "Stau," or apostates, were condemned to fetters for an indefinite period, and then their bodies were to be cut to pieces and their souls annihilated. The texts which describe this section of the Ṭuat prove beyond all doubt that those who were righteous upon earth received good gifts and eternal life in the Ṭuat, and that the wicked were punished with tortures and destruction. The making of propitiatory sacrifices and offerings is distinctly encouraged, and the texts prove that such were of great value both to the dwellers in the Ṭuat and to their kinsfolk upon earth.

The Third Section of the Ṭuat is approached through a gate called "Sepṭt-Uauau" [hieroglyphs], *i.e.*, "provided with flames," which is guarded by the serpent Aqbi [hieroglyphs]. Åfu Rā passes through this gate unharmed, for at the word of Sa the flames turned aside, and the warders withdrew their opposition. Åfu Rā next passes through the "Boat of the Earth," which is in the form of a long tunnel with a bull's head at each end of it. It is supported by eight gods, and guarded by seven gods who sit upon it, and it was the abode of the Earth-god [hieroglyphs]. Åfu Rā next passes the twelve shrines of the holy gods, and at his word their doors fly open, and they salute him; in return for this Åfu Rā gives them food and air, and when he has passed the doors close again, and the gods inside lament and bewail his departure. A little further on are twelve gods who are partially immersed in the Lake of Boiling Water, the stench of which is so strong that birds betake themselves to flight as soon as they see this Lake. The description of this Lake given in the text recalls the words of Diodorus Siculus (II, 48; XIX, 48) about the ἀσφαλτῖτις λίμην, and suggests that the writer had in mind the hot sulphur springs which exist in some parts of the Sûdân, or the hot springs of the Oasis of Khârgah. The quaint costume of the gods suggest that they were foreigners. Before each god is a *kemtet* plant, which was used in making beer, and Åfu Rā decrees to him a regular supply of bread and vegetables. Three serpents now attempt to block the way of Åfu Rā. The first of these, Āapep, collapses as the result of the utterance of a word of power by Temu, and lies spell-bound. The Tchatchau gods smash his head, and make gashes in his body. The serpents Sebȧ and Åf are attacked by the gods Nebu-khert, and they likewise are spell-bound, and reduced to helplessness. All these gods live upon the same food as Rā, but they also partake of the spirits of the offerings which are made to Khenti Åmenti, a very ancient god of the dead who was worshipped at Abydos. As Åfu Rā leaves this Section the Tchatchau and the other gods lament, and return to its entrance to await the arrival of the god on the following night. In this

Section we find no place for the dead or for the souls of human beings.

The Fourth Section of the Ṭuat is protected by a Gate which is called "Nebtstchefau", and is guarded by the serpent Tchetbi. As Åfu Rā enters it he sees the sepulchres of the gods who form the bodyguard of Osiris, and comes to the twelve Hour-goddesses, who are divided into two groups, six in each group, by the monster serpent Ḥerrt, which spawns twelve serpents. Åfu Rā orders the gods who tow his boat to take him to the habitations of the god Åres, or Sȧr, and on his arrival there he raises up to life the "broken souls," and apportions them meat and drink. On the right of Åfu Rā are the twelve gods who carry their Kau, or Doubles, which they offer to the god. Åfu Rā next passes the Lake of Life, and the Lake of the Living Uraei. Round the former stand twelve jackal-headed gods who invite the god to bathe in it, and say that its waters are too holy for any soul of the dead to approach. From the latter the uraei drive away every soul which attempts to approach it, and the words which they utter are so terrible that they destroy the shadows of the dead which have succeeded in getting near it. Further on Åfu Rā passes the shrine of Khenti Åmenti, who appears in mummy form, wears the White Crown, and stands on a serpent. Two companies of gods stand by the shrine, and Ḥeru-ur, one of the oldest gods of Egypt, addresses Khenti Åmenti as "Osiris," and declares that all spirits, both the good and the bad, hold him in awe. Åfu Rā does not address Osiris, and apparently he takes no notice of the gods who praise him, but he calls upon Horus to avenge him on those who conspire against him, and to cast them to the "Master of the Lords of the furnaces" that he may have them destroyed. The furnaces, or fire-pits, are four in number, and into these the enemies of Åfu Rā are hurled and destroyed. Who these enemies are is not clear, but that they have incurred the displeasure of Åfu Rā is certain.

The Fifth Section of the Ṭuat is called "Årit", and Åfu Rā is admitted through its gate by a Serpent-god called "Teka-ḥer" or "Fiery-face." The god is towed as before, and he first meets the nine gods Kheru-Ennutchi, and a group of gods who represent the "souls of men who dwell in the Ṭuat," and who are under the control of the god Ḥeriqenbetef. Åfu Rā next meets a company of gods who represent the souls of those "who were speakers of the truth upon earth, and who magnified Rā." As a reward they are given habitations of peace with Rā, praises are sung to their souls, they shall eat meat in the Field of Reeds (Sekhet Åaru), and offerings shall be made to them always upon earth, even as to Ḥetep, the Lord of the Field of Offerings (Sekhet Ḥetepet). From these statements it is clear that the souls of those who had led a life of truth and integrity upon earth enjoyed existence with the gods in the Field of Offerings, in a place specially set apart for the spirits and souls of the righteous. The importance of offerings is once again insisted on, and it is certain that the religion of the Egyptians was, in the main, one of sacrifices and offerings.

To the right of Åfu Rā are the twelve "gods who sing praises in the Ṭuat," and the twelve "gods who hold the measuring cord," and the four Ḥenbiu gods who are the overseers of the celestial domains. The first of these groups of gods enjoy their position in the Ṭuat because they praised Rā morning and evening, and because they "satisfied" him; and they partake of the food of the god. The gods with the measuring tape measure out the allotments for the blessed, and no soul takes possession of his allotment unless he has proved himself to have been a speaker of the truth upon earth. The ground which is cultivated by the blessed is kept in a fertile state by the Ḥenbiu gods, who from time to time dress it with "sand." To the left of the god are seen representatives of the four great nations of men into which the Egyptians divided mankind, namely Men (*i.e.*, Egyptians), Negroes, Libyans, and Asiatics; the Egyptians and the Libyans are said to have sprung from the eye of Rā. It is to be noted that the members of each nation or people live together in the Ṭuat. Near these are the gods who administer the Kingdom of Osiris of Abydos. First come the "holders of time in Ȧmenti," who hold in their hand the serpent Meteriu, and it is their duty to measure the period of the life of souls in that region, and to act as timekeepers generally for those who have to perform work for Osiris. Next come the Tchatchau, *i.e.*, "chiefs," or taskmasters, who have the lists of the men in the celestial corvée, and keep a record of the work which they do. They are impartial overseers, and they see that the commands of Osiris are carried out to the letter, and that no soul is made to do more than his share of the work of the Ṭuat. As men were rewarded or punished in the Ṭuat according to their deeds upon earth, and as these timekeepers and taskmasters rewarded or punished souls according to the entries in their registers, they may be regarded as the recording angels of the Kingdom of Osiris. The man who was a field-labourer in this world could hardly expect to be anything else in the next, but at least he would work there for a just and impartial Judge.

The Sixth Section of the Ṭuat is guarded by a gate called Nebtāḥā, and its warder is the Serpent-god Setem-Ȧritf, *i.e.*, "Fire in his eye." In or near this gate was situated the Judgment Hall of Osiris, and we see Osiris in it seated upon a chair of state placed upon the top of a platform with steps. The god, who is here called Sar, , is in mummy form, and wears the double crown, , and holds ☥ and in his hands. Before him is a Balance, the pillar of which is in the form of a human mummy. On each of the nine steps of the throne stands a god. Above these is a boat in which an ape is standing beating a pig called the "Eater of the Arm." In front of the boat is another ape, and above, in the corner, stands Anubis. This version of the Judgment Scene is quite different from that found in the papyri, as a glance at the Papyrus of Ani (Plates III and IV) will show. The boat of Ȧfu Rā is towed through this Section as before, and the god passes a series of jackal-headed sceptres to each of which two of the enemies of Osiris are tied. Ȧfu Rā, as he moves on, has on his right twelve Maātiu gods, and twelve Ḥeteptiu gods, who represent the souls of those "whose Kau, or Doubles, have "been washed clean, whose iniquities have been done away, "and who were declared speakers of the truth at the "Judgment." Twelve other gods are engaged in the cultivation of wheat, which is here called the "body and members of Sar," , and the beings who ate this wheat ate the body of their god.[1] Wheat was the "plant of truth," and Osiris was Truth, and the eaters of the divine wheat became truth, even as he was.

The SEVENTH SECTION of the Ṭuat is guarded by a gate which is called "Pesṭit," and its warder is the serpent-god ĀKHANÂRIT . Here are found a number of gods whose arms and hands are hidden, and who represent "invisible beings whom the dead are able to see." These must be followers of Rā, for Åfu Rā promises them that they shall be with him in Ḥet-Benben, *i.e.*, the House of the Benben Stone in Ånu (Heliopolis), wherein the spirit of the Sun-god was supposed to dwell on certain occasions. Next come gods armed with clubs having forked ends; these are the Kheru-Metauḥ, whose duty it was to maim and destroy the serpent Sebå. This monster is seen near them, and from out of his body twelve human heads emerge when Åfu Rā appears. Beyond is a group of Star-gods, who hold the rope which fetters Qān, or Āqen, or Nāq, a god whose functions are not known exactly. Close by, on the back of the serpent Nehep, lie twelve mummies, who represent "those who are asleep in the body of Osiris"; these are in the hands of Ṭuati, the god of the Ṭuat. As Åfu Rā passes these, Ṭuati addresses the mummies and bids them cast aside their bandages, and throw off their wigs, and collect their bones and flesh, and open their eyes, and rise up from their state of inertness, and take possession of their estates in Sekhet Nebt Ḥetepet. Further on is a pool of boiling water, or a lake of fire, and the heat which arises from the serpent in it is so fierce that the gods and souls of the earth dare not approach the pool. The duty of the gods who sit round about it is to provide warmth for the Governor of Åuḳert, *i.e.*, for the Governor of the Ṭuat of Heliopolis. After a time these gods receive

[1] Prof. Wiedemann has collected a number of important facts on this subject in his valuable paper "OSIRIS VÉGÉTANT."

their bodies and souls from the serpent Nehep, and then they proceed to the Field of Reeds.

When Åfu Rā enters the EIGHTH SECTION of the Ṭuat, which is guarded by a gate called Bekhkhi, [hieroglyphs], the warder of which is the Serpent-god SETḤER, [hieroglyphs], or "Fiery Face," he passes into the western part of the Ṭuat of Ånu, or Heliopolis. His boat is towed into a very long lake, or a series of lakes, or lagoons, which must represent the lakes in the Delta, or a part of the Mediterranean Sea; the god who is in charge of these waters is Nu. In the water itself we see four groups of men performing evolutions in the waters. These are addressed by the gods who are towing Åfu Rā, and are ordered by them to "praise the soul of Rā which is in heaven, and his body which is on the earth." Next the god of the waters, Nu, calls upon the men in the waters to worship Rā, and promises them that they shall breathe air through their nostrils, and enjoy peace in their waters. Offerings shall be made on earth to their souls, which shall never die, and they shall be fed like Rā, whose body is on earth, and whose soul is in heaven. The men in the water must assuredly represent those who have been drowned in the Nile, or in the Lakes of the Delta, or in the sea. Apparently the Egyptian theologians did not know how to arrange for the bodies of those who were drowned being rejoined by their souls, so they decided that they must be content to remain separated from their souls, even as Rā is separated from his soul. Further on are the Tchatchau, or chiefs, or "taskmasters," who have been already mentioned, and a group of souls, each of whom stands with a loaf of bread and some *sekemu* vegetables before it. These souls represent the great company of those who have been permitted to take up their abode by the Lake of Fire called Serser, in the very centre of which stood the throne of Osiris, and who are fed daily by the order of Osiris. They receive a fixed daily ration, the quantity of which never varies, in fact their "daily bread." This ration was given by the Tchatchau, or by gods under their direction, and every soul received its portion without any addition or diminution. In passing through the Ṭuat, Åfu Rā confirms this ration to the souls who are the faithful servants of Osiris. Further on is a company of the enemies of Osiris, who stand with their arms tied together at the elbows behind their backs in a most painful attitude. Before these, and facing them, is the monster serpent Khati, which belches fire on them, whilst the seven gods who stand on his back aid the work of their destruction. The offences with which they are charged is contempt of secret things (*i.e.*, the mysteries), insult offered to the sacred object called *sekem*, and the profanation of the mysteries of the Ṭuat, and the punishment which Horus the Aged inflicts upon them is mutilation and burning of their bodies, and annihilation of their souls.

The NINTH SECTION of the Ṭuat is guarded by the gate called "Āat-shefsheft," the warder of which is the Serpent-god ĀBTA. The pictures which illustrate this Section represent the performance of the ceremonies that were carried out in it with the view of making Åfu Rā to finish his journey in the Ṭuat successfully. The boat of the god is towed as before by four gods, but the way of the god is blocked by the serpent Āapep and the crocodile Seshsesh, or Sessi. To destroy them seems to be impossible, but they may be rendered impotent by means of spells cast on them by Åfu Rā. Against them go forth gods possessing words of power, and the Saiu Ape-gods, and the Sait goddesses: the second and the third of these groups work magic against the monsters by tying knots in ropes, and muttering spells over them as they work. Having taken up their positions all these shake out the nets which they hold in their hands, and recite their incantations, and Āapep and Sessi are rendered powerless. Between the monsters and the groups of gods already described is the prostrate figure of a god called Åai, who is grasping with both hands the end of a rope, which is held by three men armed with harpoons. Åai has on his head a small disk, and two objects which resemble the ears of an ass. He may be a form of the Sun-god, for the ass is one of the types of the god, or he may represent a victim which had been placed there to tempt the crocodile from his place. Next Åfu Rā approaches the serpent Khepri, who has a head and a pair of human legs at each end of his body, and under him passes a rope which is hauled by the Eight Powers on the one side, and by the Souls of Åmenti, and the Followers of Thoth, Horus, and Rā on the other. The other gods in this Section, namely Horus in his boat, the two-headed god Horus-Set, *i.e.*, Day and Night, the gods who raise the Crowns of the South and the North, are all engaged in performing ceremonies connected with the reconstitution of Åfu Rā as the Day-Sun of this world. At the end of the section are: 1. The serpent Shemti, with four heads at each end of his body. 2. The serpent Båta, with a head at each end of his body. 3. The serpent Ṭepi, with four human heads and bodies at each end of his body. 4. Ṭepi's warder, Åbeth. Against all these go forth two gods, each armed with a net.

In the TENTH SECTION of the Ṭuat, which is guarded by the gate "Tcheserit," the warder of which is the Serpent-god SETHU, Åfu Rā is towed by four gods as before. All opposition to his progress has been overcome, and the gods of this Section have nothing to do except to assist in the further reconstitution of the god. Unti, with two stars, lights up the Ṭuat, four fire-gods supply light and fire, three star-gods bring the face of the disk of the sun of this earth, Semi acts as guide, Besi supplies the materials for the sun's fires, Ānkhi determines the duration of the day, four goddesses address words of welcome to the god, and Meḥen, bearing the double bow of Horus-Set, leads Åfu Rā towards the east. On his right are the imperishable stars, and the goddesses who tow the boat of Åfu Rā at dawn, and the Eye of Rā, which takes its place in the face already mentioned, and several other gods of the Ṭuat. On his left lies the serpent Āapep, and about his neck is a chain which is grasped by the Setfiu gods, and the Tchaṭiu gods, and the colossal hand of Åmen-khat. Attached to the chain are the five small chains of Ḳeb and the Four Sons of Horus, and by another chain lies the goddess Serq. The Åntiu gods and the Ḥenātiu gods armed with knives and sticks with curled ends also attack Āapep, and, as the monster is now utterly subdued, Åfu Rā continues his course without further hindrance from him.

The ELEVENTH SECTION of the Ṭuat is guarded by a gate called "Shetatbesu", the warder of which is the Serpent-god ÅMNETUF [hieroglyphs]. Once more Āapep appears, but he is in fetters, and the gods of the Section stand ready to attack him with knives if necessary. Next come four Ape-gods, each holding a large hand, and their duty is to stand near the Sun-god, two on this side and two on that, and hold up the disk in the sky, and sing hymns to it. The gods who stand on the right of Åfu Rā place crowns on the head of the Sun-god, and give names to all his forms, and drive away Set, and sing hymns to the new Sun-god. Those on the left carry disks for him, and open the Gate of Åkert to him, and bear stars, and, like the "morning stars" in Job xxxviii, 7, sing hymns to him when he is received into the arms of the Sky-god Nu.

The TWELFTH SECTION of the Ṭuat is guarded by a gate called "Ṭesert-baiu" [hieroglyphs], the warders of which are the Serpent-gods SEBI [hieroglyphs] and RERI [hieroglyphs]. This gate is different from all the rest, for no companies of gods guard it, and, though flames of fire sweep round about it to keep away enemies, its chief protectors are the Serpent-gods and the standards of Kheperå and Temu. Just before Åfu Rā reaches this part of the Ṭuat he transforms himself into the Beetle of Kheperå, which has the solar disk in front of it, and so emerges from the eastern end of the Ṭuat into the vestibule which is the immediate entrance to the sky of this world. When the ball of the sun comes to the celestial ocean it is placed by the gods of the dawn in the Māntchet Boat, and it begins its journey across the sky. Thus Åfu Rā has completed his journey through the Ṭuat, has triumphed over all dangers therein, has passed judgment on his enemies, and bestowed rewards on his friends, and as Rā in the eastern sky he begins to dispense heat, and light, and life to the inhabitants of this world. All the souls who have accompanied him in his boat live again, and they look down from it upon their old homes and friends. They live with Rā, eat of his food, are arrayed in apparel like his, and partake of his nature.

For the beings in the Ṭuat who were not provided for by Osiris, existence must have been very sad, for they were obliged to live in darkness and misery, except for the brief space of time each night when Áfu Rā passed through the Ṭuat. In fact, the Ṭuat was a place of darkness, hunger, thirst, and suffering for many souls. The Egyptians did not believe in purgatory or everlasting punishment; the souls in the Ṭuat lived just so long as their friends and relatives on earth made the prescribed funerary offerings in their tombs upon earth, and no longer, then they died the "second death." The enemies of Rā and Osiris, that is to say, the wicked, were slaughtered daily and their bodies consumed by fire, but each day brought its own supply of these, and thus the avenging gods were kept busy daily, and the fire-pits were filled with victims daily. There is no evidence in the texts that the Egyptians thought that the burning of the same victims could go on for ever.

THE GODS OF THE BOOK OF THE DEAD

Tem, or **Átmu** is, according to Egyptian tradition, the oldest of the gods, and he is called the "divine god," the "self-created," the "maker of the gods," the "creator of men," "who stretched out the heavens," "who illumineth the Ṭuat with his Eyes" (*i.e.*, the sun and moon). He existed when

not was sky, not was earth, not were men,

not were born the gods, not was death.[1]

In what form he existed is not stated, but he created for himself, as a place wherein to dwell, the great mass of Celestial Waters to which the Egyptians gave the name of Nu. In these, for a time, he lived quite alone, and then, in a series of efforts of thought, he created

[1] Pyramid Text of Pepi I, l. 664.

the heavens and the celestial bodies in them, and the gods, and the earth, and men and women, animals, birds, and creeping things, in his own mind. These thoughts or ideas of creation were translated into words by Thoth, or the intelligence or mind of Temu, and when he uttered these words all creation came into being. The great College of the Priests of Ȧnu, or Heliopolis, made Temu the head of their Company of the Gods, and so far back as the IVth dynasty they made Rā, the god of the sun, to usurp his place, and his powers, and his attributes. In their system of theology, so far as it can be learned from the Pyramid Texts, Temu was made to be a form of the Sun-god in the evening or early night, and in this character he generally appears in the later Recensions of the Book of the Dead. It is interesting to note that Temu is always depicted in the form of a man or king, and he wears the Crowns of the South and the North; like all other gods he carries in his hands the sceptre and the symbol of "life". Many of the attributes of Temu were absorbed by the god Kheperȧ, who was also a great Creation-god and a form of the Sun-god. In late times, the Egyptians formulated the existence of a female counterpart of Temu called **Temt** or **Temit**. In an interesting passage in Chapter CLIV of the Theban Recension, the name of Temu is coupled with that of Osiris as being gods whose flesh never saw corruption. On the part played by Tem in the creation of the great eternal Soul-spirit, or the Light-spirit, which is the source from which all the Spirit-souls of men are descended, see Chapter LXXVIII.

Nu, , is the name given to the vast mass of water which existed in primeval times, and was situated presumably in the sky; it formed the material part of the great god Tem, or Ȧtmu, who was the creator of the universe and of gods and men. In this mass, which was believed to be of fathomless depth and of boundless extent, were the germs of all life, and of all kinds of life, and for this reason the god who was the personification of the water, *i.e.*, Nu, was called the "Father of the Gods," and the "producer of the Great Company of the Gods," [hieroglyphs]. The watery mass of Nu was the prototype of the great World-Ocean which later ancient nations believed to surround the whole world. Out from Nu came the river which flowed through the Ṭuat, or Other World, and divided its valley into two parts, making it to resemble Egypt. From Nu also came the waters which appeared in the two famous caverns in the First Cataract, and which, flowing from their mouths, formed the river Nile. The waters of Nu formed the dwelling place of Tem, and out of them came the sun, which was the result of one of Tem's earliest acts of creation. The early inhabitants of Egypt thought that the sun sailed over the waters of Nu in two magical boats, called Māntchet, or Māṭet, or Āṭet, and Semktet, or Sektet, respectively; in the former the sun set out in the morning on his journey, which he finished in the latter. A very ancient tradition in Egypt asserted that Nu was the head of a divine company, which consisted of four gods and four goddesses. These were :—

Nu, [hieroglyphs]. **Nut,** [hieroglyphs].

Ḥeḥu, [hieroglyphs]. **Ḥeḥut,** [hieroglyphs].

Kekui, [hieroglyphs]. **Kekuit,** [hieroglyphs].

Ḳerḥ, [hieroglyphs]. **Ḳerḥet,** [hieroglyphs].

The gods of these pairs were depicted in human form, with the heads of frogs, and the goddesses in the forms of women, with serpents' heads. Nu was the primeval water itself, Ḥeḥu personified its vast and endless extent, Kekui the darkness which brooded over the water, and Ḳerḥ its inert and motionless character. Very little is known about the three last-named gods and their female counterparts, for they belong to a system of cosmogony which was superseded by other systems in which the Sun-god Rā played the most prominent part. The goddess **Nut**, who was in the earliest times a Water-goddess, was depicted under the New Empire in the form of a woman, and also in the form of a cow.

Rā, [hieroglyphs], is the name which was given to the Sun-god by the early Egyptians, but the meaning of the word and its origin are unknown. Rā, according to dynastic tradition, was the first being created by Tem out of the Celestial Waters of Nu, and he was regarded as the visible emblem of God, and as the great god of this world, and to him sacrifices and offerings were made daily. The seat of Rā-worship was, under the Ancient Empire, situated at Ȧnu, or Heliopolis, a large city which lay a few miles to the east of the site occupied by modern Cairo. This city was, from the earliest times, the terminus of the great caravan road between Syria and Egypt, and was densely populated with inhabitants of many nationalities. Several kinds of gods must have been worshipped there, among them being many who were favourites of the caravan men and merchants who came from Asia, but the greatest of them all was Rā. These facts show that the bulk of the people who flocked to Ȧnu were worshippers of Rā, for the temple of the Sun-god was maintained by the offerings of the faithful, and the importance of the temple proves that the devotees of the Sun-god were very numerous and very well-to-do. The worship of the sun was common enough at all periods among the tribes of Syria and the Delta, but there is no evidence to show that it was as common among the inhabitants of Upper Egypt, or of any part of the Upper Nile Valley. Among the bulk of Africans the moon was, and still is, the favourite object of worship, and not the sun. As I have given the proofs of this statement in my *Osiris and the Egyptian Resurrection*, they need not be repeated here. The importance of Rā-worship in Lower Egypt under the Ancient Empire was due entirely to the political influence of the priests, which was used very skilfully. The first king of the Vth dynasty was Userkaf, who was a priest of Rā, and it seems that he succeeded in wresting the supreme power from the successors of the great kings Khufu, Khāfrā, and Menkaurā. Whether this be so or not matters little, but it is almost certain that he was the first king of Egypt who added the title "Son of Rā," [hieroglyphs], to his other titles, and who gave himself an additional name as son of Rā. The priests of Rā at that early period claimed to have in their bodies the veritable blood of Rā, and they asserted that their high priests were the offspring of Rā by human mothers. And of the existence of this dogma under the Ancient Empire we have traditional proof in the Westcar Papyrus, where we read that Userkaf and his two immediate successors, Saḥurā and Kakaȧ, were the sons of the god Rā by Ruṭ-ṭeṭt, the wife of a priest of the god Rā of the town of Sakhabu, [hieroglyphs]. The three boys were assisted into the world by the goddesses Isis, Nephthys, Meskhenet and Ḥeqet, and by the god Khnemu, and their future greatness was prophesied at the time of their birth. The belief that Rā came down from heaven and was united to a mortal woman, and that every king of Egypt was the offspring of such a union, persisted throughout the country for about three thousand years. Ḥātshepsut decorated the walls of her temple at Dêr al-Baḥarī with scenes which illustrate the principal events connected with her conception and birth, and prove conclusively that she believed herself to be of the seed of Ȧmen. A part of the temple of Ȧmen-ḥetep III at Luxor was decorated with a series of reliefs which prove that this king believed himself to be Ȧmen-Rā incarnate, and there is no doubt that every king of Egypt, including even kings of Egypt of Nubian origin, held the same belief. Popular tradition, as represented by the Pseudo Callisthenes, declared that Alexander the Great was an incarnation of Ȧmen, who took the form of the last native king of Egypt, Nekhtnebf, and seduced Olympias, the wife of Philip, king of Macedon. And the story of the journey of Alexander the Great to the temple of Ȧmen in the Oasis of Sîwâh, in order to be acknowledged by the god as his son is too well known to need mention.[1]

The form in which Rā was worshipped in the large Sun-temples which were built by some of the kings of the Vth dynasty was that of a stone. The stone had the shape of a massive, truncated obelisk, with a pyramid above it, and it stood on a strong masonry base. The spirit of the Sun-god was supposed to enter the stone at certain periods, and on these occasions human sacrifices

[1] A statement about the languages into which this story has been translated, and an account of its wanderings will be found in my *History of Alexander the Great*, Cambridge, 1890.

were offered to it. The victims were probably prisoners of war who had been captured alive, and foreigners, and when these failed, the priests must have drawn upon the native population, as priests have done in Africa from time immemorial.

Rā sailed over the sky in two boats; his morning boat was called "Māntchet," or Māṭet, or Āṭet, and his evening boat "Semktet." His course was guided by *Maāt*, the personification of law, order, unfailing regularity, etc. After he set in the west in the evening he entered the Ṭuat under a different form, and by the help of the gods who were there, and by the power which he possessed in his own person, he passed through that region successfully, and appeared in the sky of this world the next morning in his usual form. As he passed through the Ṭuat he gave air, and light, and food to those who, for some reason or other had been doomed to dwell there. Two fishes swam before the boat of Rā, and acted as pilots and warned him of coming danger; these were called "Abṭu", and "Ant", respectively. Each morning as he was about to enter the sky, and just before he left the Ṭuat, he engaged in battle with the great Devil called "Āapep", which, aided by a group of powerful monster serpents, attempted to bar his progress, and make his reappearance in this world impossible. All Āapep's attacks failed, because Rā first cast spells on him, and when he was incapable of motion, the supporters of the Sun-god bound him in chains, then hacked him to pieces, which were finally consumed by the flames of Rā. The priests of Rā told this story of their god, but it is far older than the period when Rā's fame was great, and the two great protagonists in the daily fight between Light and Darkness were Ḥeru-ur and Set. Under the Vth dynasty the priests of Rā made a vigorous attempt to combat the spread of the cult of the Man-god Osiris, which had spread all over the Delta from Busiris, the northern centre of the cult, and all over Upper Egypt from Abydos, the southern centre. Before the end of the VIth dynasty the priests of Osiris prevailed, and Rā was relegated to an inferior position, and the greatest of his attributes were ascribed to Osiris. What the exact cause of the contest was cannot be said, but it is quite certain that there was something in the doctrines of the priests of Rā, or in the worship that was the practical expression of them, which was contrary to the instincts of the Egyptians as a nation. Heliopolis always contained a mixed population, and it is probable that the doctrines of the priests of Rā were tainted with Asiatic beliefs which were an abomination to the indigenous population of Egypt. There was, of course, a very important element of native Egyptian belief associated with the cult of Rā, and that explains the reception of sun-worship in Upper Egypt during the Middle and New Empires. Still, we see that from the XIIth dynasty onwards the cult of Ȧmen was predominant in Upper Egypt, and that the local god of Thebes absorbed all the attributes of Rā, which his priests had transferred to him from Tem. Under the XIXth and XXth dynasties seventy-five forms of Rā were distinguished, and the Addresses to these formed a sort of Litany of Rā which was said or sung during the services in the temples, and copies of them were painted on the walls of the tombs of several kings, *e.g.*, those of Seti I, Seti II, Rameses IV.[1]

Khepra̓ [hieroglyphs], [hieroglyphs], is a very ancient god whom religious tradition associated with the creation of the world and of all things in it. He is usually called KHEPRȦ KHEPER TCHESEF, *i.e.*, Khepra̓, the self-produced, [hieroglyphs], and his principal type and symbol was a beetle. He is usually represented in human form with a beetle upon his head, but sometimes a beetle takes the place of the human head. In the Chapter on Egyptian Ideas of God, we have already described the part which he took in the creation of the world. There can be little doubt that the cult of the beetle is far older than that of Rā of Heliopolis, and when we find the priests of Rā identifying their god with Khepera̓, we must understand that it is only another example of their method of grafting new beliefs on the cult of the old indigenous gods of their country. The cult of the beetle was general in Egypt and the Sûdân, and

[1] See Naville, *La Litanie du Soleil*, Leipzig, 1875.

many of the ideas which the inhabitants of the Nile Valley held concerning it still survive in those countries. The particular beetle which the Egyptians chose as the symbol of their god Kheperȧ belongs to the family called *Scarabaeidae* (Coprophagi) of which the SCARABAEUS SACER is the type. These insects form a very numerous group of dung-feeding Lamellicorns, of which, however, the majority live in tropical countries; they are usually black, but many are adorned with bright metallic colours. They fly during the hottest part of the day, and it was this peculiarity which probably caused the primitive Egyptians to associate them with the sun. Thus, as far back as the Vth or VIth dynasty, it is said in the text of King Unȧs: "This Unȧs flieth like "a goose (or duck), he alighteth like the beetle; he flieth "like a goose (or duck), he alighteth like the beetle upon "the empty throne in thy Boat, O Rā," (ll. 476, 477).

The beetle which was the symbol of Kheperȧ was the subject of many curious theories among ancient classical writers. Aelian,[1] Porphyry[2] and Horapollo[3] thought that beetles were all males, and that as there were no females among them they were all self-produced. This view arose from the fact that to the ordinary observer the male and female are very much alike and because the male and female each take part in rolling along the ball which is so frequently seen with them. The female digs a hole in the ground in which she deposits one egg. Whilst she is doing this the male goes about and collects a quantity of dung, which he rolls over and over again until it becomes a tolerably compact ball, from one to two inches in diameter. This he rolls along to the hole in which the female has deposited her egg, and, sometimes alone and sometimes helped by the female, he pushes the ball into the hole on

[1] *De Nat. Animalium*, X, 15.
[2] *De Abstinentia*, IV, 9.
[3] Ed. Leemans, p. 11.

top of the egg, where it remains until the young beetle is hatched out, when the ball serves for its food. It was formerly thought that the ball of dung contained many eggs, which were mixed up together with the dung on which the larvae were to feed, but it has been proved by entomologists that the female of the *Scarabaeus sacer* only lays one egg at a time. This fact was probably known to the ancients, for Horapollo says that the scarab denotes an "only-begotten," μονογενής. Be this as it may, the ball of the sun, which was the immediate cause of life to the world, was supposed to be rolled across the sky by a gigantic beetle, KHEPRER [hieroglyphs], who was at a very early period identified with Kheperȧ, the Creator and the Father of the gods [hieroglyphs]. The Egyptians believed that the beetle was an incarnation of Kheperȧ, and imagined some resemblance between the ball of food for the larva which it rolled over the ground and the ball of the sun, which was the visible expression of the life of Kheperȧ, and was rolled across the sky by him. They thought that if they made figures of the beetle of Kheperȧ, and wore them, they would attract the power of the god to them, and secure his protection for their bodies, both when living and when dead. The scarab was associated with burial as far back as the IVth dynasty, according to one tradition, and another tradition shows that it was placed on the bodies of the dead as an amulet under the Ist dynasty. See the text of Chapter XXXB and the translations of it and the Rubrics to Chapter LXIV.

Ptaḥ [hieroglyphs], or Ptaḥ, Lord of Life, [hieroglyphs], was one of the oldest and greatest gods of Memphis, and local tradition asserted that he was the creator of the universe; his worship, in one form or another, goes back to the beginning of the Dynastic Period. He was identified with Temu and Rā and was called "the very great god who existed in primeval time," [hieroglyphs]; the "father of fathers," [hieroglyphs], *i.e.*, the great-great-grandfather of the gods; "the father of beginnings (?), the creator of the egg of the sun and moon," "the lord of

"Maāt, the king of the two lands, the god of the beautiful "face, who created his own image, who fashioned his own "body, the Disk of heaven, who illumineth Egypt with the "fire of his two eyes," etc. He was the great celestial worker in metals, and the chief smelter, caster, and sculptor to the gods. He was the master architect of the world, and he made the design for every part of the framework of the world. He fashioned the bodies of men in this world, and also the new bodies into which souls entered in the Ṭuat. His name was joined to that of several gods with whom at first sight it seems that he could have had little in common, *e.g.*, Ptaḥ-Åsår (Ptaḥ-Osiris), Ptaḥ-Ḥāpi (Ptaḥ-Nile), Ptaḥ-Nu, Ptaḥ-Seker, Ptaḥ-Seker-Åsår, Ptaḥ-Seker-Tem, Ptaḥ-Taten, etc., which shows that his priests made him to usurp the functions and attributes of many older gods. The Theban Recension of the Book of the Dead states that Ptaḥ performed the operation of "Opening the Mouth" on the gods, with a metal instrument which he had made, that is to say, he raised them up from inertness and gave them life; and every follower of Osiris believed that Ptaḥ would do the same for him. Ptaḥ is depicted in the form of a bearded man with a bald head and swathed in mummy bandages, from which through an opening in front of him his hands project. From the back of his neck hangs the *menåt* 𓈙, a symbol of physical well-being and sexual intercourse, and he holds in his hands the emblems of "content" 𓌀, "life" 𓋹, and "stability" 𓊽. He stands upon the symbol of *maāt* 𓌶. Ptaḥ was the chief member of the great triad of Memphis, his female counterpart and son being called **Sekhmet** and **Nefer-Tem,** *i.e.*, Young Tem, respectively.

Ptaḥ-Nu, 𓊪𓏏𓎛𓀭 𓌀𓈖𓀭 and **Ptaḥ-Ḥāp** 𓊪𓏏𓎛𓀭 𓎛𓂝𓊪 𓈗𓀭 have no special representations in the reliefs, for they are merely forms of the Celestial Waters and the Nile.

Ptaḥ-Seker 𓊪𓏏𓎛 𓊃𓎡𓂋𓀭 represents the union of Ptaḥ with **Seker,** the oldest and greatest god of that portion of the Ṭuat which was set apart for the inhabitants of the nome of Memphis. Seker was originally a personification of inert matter, motionless and dead, and he sat enthroned in a region of utter blackness and night; in later times he became the Death-god of Memphis. He is depicted, like Ptaḥ, in the form of a mummy, but he sometimes has a hawk's head; he holds the same sceptres, etc., and he is called "the greatest god who was in the beginning, and dwelleth in the darkness". In the XVIIth Chapter of the Book of the Dead the deceased prays to be delivered from "the great god "who carrieth away the soul, and eateth hearts, and "feedeth upon filth, the guardian of the darkness, the "dweller in the Seker Boat." In reply to the question "Who is this?" the answer is given, "It is Suti (or Seti), or Smamur, the Soul of Ḳeb." This makes it quite certain that Seker was Darkness and Death personified. The **Seker Boat,** which is seen in the Vignettes of Chapter LXXIV (see Plate XVIII), contained a coffer in which was placed the emblem of Seker. On the day of the festival this boat, which rested on a sledge with runners, was drawn round the sanctuary at sunrise by the priests of the god. This ceremony was performed under the direction of the high priest, whose official title was Ur-kherp-ḥem, *i.e.*, the "great chief of the hammer," a fitting title for the high-priest of the Blacksmith-god Ptaḥ. The name given to the boat itself was **Ḥenu**, and it is represented on objects which date from the Ist dynasty.

Ptaḥ-Seker-Àsȧr is a triune god, to whom belonged all the attributes of Seker, the god of death, and of Osiris, the god of the resurrection, and of Ptaḥ, the Creator. Originally, as Death-gods, Seker and Osiris had many attributes in common, and the fusion of the two gods was the result of the triumph of Osiris over all the gods of death over all Egypt. Seker represented death absolute and final, but Osiris represented the death which was merely a temporary phase or state through which the righteous had to pass introductory to a renewed life obtained by resurrection, in the Kingdom of Osiris. The union of Ptaḥ with Seker and Osiris symbolized the addition of creative power to death, which manifested itself in providing the new bodies in which the souls of the righteous were to live. Ptaḥ-Seker-Åsår has to all intents and purposes the form of Osiris, but Egyptian artists delighted to depict him as a squat pigmy, with a large bald head and thick limbs, with a beetle on the top of his head, and a lock of hair on the right side of it. He thus possessed all the virile power of Menu, and the creative power of Kheperȧ, and the youth and vigour of Harpokrates. The union of Ptaḥ with Seker and Osiris may also be the result of an attempt made by the priests of Memphis to make those gods subordinate to Ptaḥ, just as the priests of Thebes under the New Empire tried to make Osiris subordinate to Åmen.

Ptaḥ-Tatenn [hieroglyphs] is depicted in the form of a god in mummy form with a pair of horns, and a disk, and a pair of plumes on his head, and the ordinary symbols of rule [hieroglyphs] in his hands. Tatenn was a very ancient god, and his attributes were those of a creative god, and resembled those ascribed to Ptaḥ. The following extract from a hymn,[1] written about 1200 B.C., illustrates the view of the Egyptians about this god. "The winds come forth "from thy nostrils, and the celestial water from thy mouth, "and the staff of life (*i.e.*, wheat, barley, dhura, etc.) "springeth from thy back. Thou makest the earth to bring "forth fruit so that gods and men may have abundance, "and cattle like unto the Cow-goddess Meḥurt are seen "in thy fields. When thou art at rest the darkness cometh, "and when thou openest thy two eyes, light is produced ". . . . . . . Thou art the great god who didst stretch "out the heavens, who makest thy Disk to revolve in the "body of Nut, and to enter therein in thy name of Rā; "thou art the fashioner of gods and men, and of everything "which existeth, thou art the maker of all countries and "lands, and of the Great Green [Sea] in thy name of "'Kheper-ta,' [hieroglyphs]; thou dost bring the Nile out "from his cavern, thou makest the staff of life to flourish, "thou makest the grain to come forth therefrom in thy "name of Nu the Aged, thou makest the celestial deep to

[1] For the hieratic text see Lepsius, *Denkmäler*, Abth. VI, Bl. 118.

"bring forth, thou makest water to appear on the mountains "to give life to men and women." Among the titles of this god are:—

1. BABE, who art born daily, [hieroglyphs].

2. AGED ONE, dweller in the eternal borders, [hieroglyphs].

3. EXALTED BEING, the unapproachable one, [hieroglyphs].

4. HIDDEN ONE, his form cannot be known, [hieroglyphs].

Khnemu, [hieroglyphs], was the first member of the great triad of the First Cataract, which was worshipped in a temple on the Island of Elephantine; the second and third members were **Sati** and **Ānqet**, [hieroglyphs], [hieroglyphs], respectively. The cult of this god is very ancient, and we find his name preserved by the Gnostics, two or three centuries after Christ. The animal in which Khnemu became incarnate was the ram, with flat horns projecting at right angles to his head; this ram disappears from the monuments before the period of the XIIth dynasty. Khnemu is usually depicted as a ram-headed man, seated or standing, who holds in his hands the symbols of "serenity" and "life." He wears the White Crown, to which are attached a pair of horns, a pair of plumes, and a disk. He possessed many attributes, and from the earliest times, whether as a Water-god, or a Sun-god, he was regarded as one of the creators of the universe. His name Khnemu seems to be connected with words which mean "to build," "to fashion," "to put together," and he "united" the sun and moon at various seasons of the year, and built up the gods, and men, and the year. He made the cosmic egg which contained the sun, and he fashioned man on a potter's wheel. Khnemu was the god *par excellence* of the First Cataract, and his principal sanctuaries were at Philae and Elephantine. In very early times he was merely the local Water-god of the Cataract region, and it is possible that he was the personification of the Nile-flood; but later he was regarded as the Nile-god of all Egypt, and the attributes of many creator-gods were bestowed upon him. Thus he was "the father in the beginning," ; "the Maker of "things which are, Creator of things which shall be, Source "of the lands, Father of fathers, Mother of mothers," ; "Father of the fathers of the gods and goddesses, lord of "things created in himself, maker of heaven, and earth, and "the Ṭuat, and water, and the mountains," ; "supporter of the sky upon its four pillars, raised up of the same in the firmament (?)" . Khnemu united within himself the souls of the gods Rā, Shu, Ḳeb, and Osiris, and in this aspect he is represented in pictures with four rams' heads upon a human body; these, according to Brugsch, represented fire, air, earth, and water. A legend, which is cut on a rock on the Island of Sâḥal in the First Cataract, states that a great famine which lasted seven years came upon Egypt in the reign of Tcheser, a king of the IIIrd dynasty. This famine was due to the neglect of Khnemu by the Egyptians, and to the niggardliness of the offerings which they made to him. When the country was well-nigh ruined, the king went to the temple of Khnemu at Elephantine, and suitable offerings having been made, the god appeared to him, and proclaimed himself to be the Nile, and promised to restore the Inundation provided that the king restored his worship and endowed his temples suitably. When these things were done, Khnemu made the Nile to flow forth from his two caverns (Qerti,), and prosperity was restored to Egypt. The Egyptians distinguished, in the late period, seven forms of Khnemu: 1. Khnemu, the modeller; 2. Khnemu, Governor of Egypt; 3. Khnemu, the weaver (?); 4. Khnemu, Governor of the House of Life; 5. Khnemu, Lord of the Land of Life; 6. Khnemu, Governor of the pleasures of the Ānkhet Chamber; 7. Khnemu, the Lord.

Shu, the second member of the company of the gods of Ȧnu, was the firstborn son of Rā, Rā-Temu, or Tum, by the goddess Hathor, the sky, and was the twin brother of Tefnut. He typified the light, and dryness, and dry objects. He lifted up the sky, Nut, from the earth, Ḳeb, and placed it upon the steps which were in Khemenu. He is usually depicted in the form of a man, who wears upon his head a feather, or feathers, and holds in his hand the sceptre. At other times he appears in the form of a man with upraised arms; on his head he has the emblem, and he is often accompanied by, the four pillars of heaven, *i.e.*, the cardinal points. Among the many *faïence* amulets which are found in tombs are two that have reference to Shu: the little models of steps typify the steps upon which Shu rested the sky in Khemenu; and the crouching figure of a god supporting the sun's disk symbolizes his act of raising the sun's disk into the space between sky and earth at the time when he separated Nut from Ḳeb. He may be compared to the Atlas of classical writers. From an inscription published by Brugsch in his *Dict. Géog.*, p. 211, and in his *Thesaurus*, p. 500, we see plainly that Shu and Tefnut were gods of Sûdânî or Nubian origin, and that their worship was introduced into the Island of Senmut, in the First Cataract, from the South. The description of the advent of these gods is not only depicted on the walls of the temple of Philae, but also on many other temples of the Graeco-Roman Period. The texts recording the legend of the advent of the gods have been collected and published by Dr. H. Junker, in *Der Auszug der Hathor-Tefnut aus Nubien* (Abhandl. der Königl. Preuss. Akad. Berlin, 1911).

Tefnut, the third member of the company of the gods of Ȧnu, was the daughter of Rā, Rā-Temu, or Temu, and twin sister of Shu; she represented in one form moisture, and in another aspect she seems to personify the power of sunlight. She is depicted in the form of a woman, usually with the head of a lioness surmounted by a disk or uraeus, or both; in *faïence*, however, the twin brother and sister have the head of a lion and the head of a lioness respectively. The original home of Tefnut was the Nubian deserts, through which she roamed, drenched in the blood of her enemies, whose flesh she tore off their bodies and ate, and whose blood she drank. Fire flew out of her eyes, and she breathed fire from her mouth. In the Pyramid Texts the two gods play a curious part, Shu being supposed to carry away hunger from the deceased, and Tefnut his thirst.[1]

Ḳeb, the fourth member of the company of the gods of Ȧnu, was the son of Shu, husband of Nut, and by her father of Osiris, Isis, Set, and Nephthys. Originally he was the god of the earth, and is called both the "father of the gods", and the "*erpā* (*i.e.*, the tribal, hereditary head) of the gods." He is depicted in human form, sometimes with a crown upon his head and the sceptre in his right hand; and sometimes he has upon his head a goose, which bird was one of his incarnations. In many places he is called the "great cackler", and he was supposed to have laid the egg from which the world sprang. Already in the Pyramid Texts he has become a god of the dead by virtue of representing the earth wherein the deceased was laid.

Ȧsȧr or **Ser**, the sixth member of the company of the gods of Ȧnu, was, according to Heliopolitan tradition, the son of Ḳeb and Nut, and the husband of his sister Isis, the father of "Horus, the son of Isis," and the brother of Set and Nephthys. The version by Plutarch of his sufferings and death has been already described (see pp. 53 ff.). Whatever may have been the foundation of the legend, it is pretty certain that his character as a god of the dead was

1 . *Recueil de Travaux*, t. V, p. 10 (l. 61).

well defined long before the versions of the Pyramid Texts known to us were written, and the only important change which took place in the views of the Egyptians concerning him in later days was the ascription to him of the attributes which in the early dynasties were regarded as belonging only to Rā or to Rā-Temu. Originally Osiris was the personification of the Nile-flood, and among his attributes was that of a destroying god; he may also be said to have represented the sun after he had set, and as such was the emblem of the motionless dead; later texts identify him with the moon. The Egyptians asserted that he was the father of the gods who had given him birth, and, as he was the god both of Yesterday, *i.e.*, the Past, and of To-day, *i.e.*, the Present, he became the type of eternal existence and the symbol of immortality; as such he usurped not only the attributes of Rā, but those of every other god, and at length he became both the god of the dead and the god of the living. As judge of the dead he was believed to exercise functions similar to those attributed to God. Alone among all the many gods of Egypt, Osiris was chosen as the type of what the deceased hoped to become when, his body having been mummified in the prescribed way and ceremonies proper to the occasion having been performed and the prayers said, his glorified body should enter into the presence of Osiris in heaven; to him as the "lord of truth" and the "lord of eternity," by which titles as judge of the dead he was commonly addressed, the deceased appealed to make his flesh to germinate and to save his body from decay.[1] The various forms in which Osiris is depicted are too numerous to be described here,[2] but he is usually represented in the form of a mummy wearing the White Crown and holding in his hands the emblems of sovereignty and power and serenity. A very complete series of illustrations of the forms of Osiris is

[1] Compare

See Chapter CLIV of the Theban Recension.

[2] For the Iconography of Osiris see Budge, *Osiris and the Egyptian Resurrection*, Vol. I, p. 24.

given by Lanzone in his *Dizionario*, tavv. 258–299. The ceremonies connected with the celebration of the events of the sufferings, the death, and the resurrection of Osiris occupied a very prominent part in the religious observances of the Egyptians, and in the month of Choiak a representation of them took place in various temples in Egypt; the text of a minute description of the ceremonies performed at this miracle-play has been published by M. Loret in *Recueil de Travaux*, tom. III, pp. 43 ff., and in a subsequent volume. A perusal of this work explains the signification of many of the ceremonies connected with the burial of the dead, the use of amulets, and certain parts of the funeral ritual; and the work in this form being of a late date proves that the doctrine of immortality, gained through the god who was "lord of the heavens and of the earth, of the "underworld and of the waters, of the mountains, and of "all which the sun goeth round in his course,"[1] had remained practically unchanged for at least four thousand years of its existence. For the early history of Osiris see the chapter entitled "The Legend of Osiris."

Ȧst or **Set** [hieroglyphs], the seventh member of the company of the gods of Ȧnu, was the wife of Osiris and the mother of Horus; her woes have been described both by Egyptian and Greek writers.[2] Her commonest names are "the great "goddess, the divine mother, the mistress of words of power "or enchantments"; in later times she is called the "mother of the gods," and the "living one." She is usually depicted in the form of a woman, with a headdress in the shape of a seat [hieroglyph], the value of the hieroglyph for which forms her name. The animal in which she sometimes became incarnate was the cow, hence she sometimes wears upon her head the horns of that animal accompanied by plumes and feathers. In one aspect she is identified with the goddess Selk or Serq, and she then has upon her head a

[1] [hieroglyphs].

[2] Chabas, *Un Hymne à Osiris* (in *Revue Archéologique*, t. XIV, pp. 65 ff.); Horrack, *Les Lamentations d'Isis et de Nephthys*, Paris, 1866; *The Festival Songs of Isis and Nephthys* (in *Archaeologia*, Vol. LII, London, 1891); Golénischeff, *Die Metternichstele*, Leipzig, 1877; Plutarch, *De Iside et Osiride*, etc.

scorpion, the emblem of that goddess; in another aspect she is united to the star Sothis, and then a star ★ is added to her crown. She is, however, most commonly represented as the mother suckling her child Horus, and figures of her in this aspect, in bronze and *faïence*, exist in thousands. As a nature-goddess she is seen standing in the Boat of the Sun, and she was probably the deity of the dawn.

Ḥeru or **Horus** , the Sun-god, was originally a totally distinct god from Horus, the son of Osiris and Isis, but in very early times it seems that the two gods were confounded, and that the attributes of the one were ascribed to the other; the fight which Horus the Sun-god waged against night and darkness was also at a very early period identified with the combat between Horus, the son of Isis, and her brother Set. The visible emblem of the Sun-god was at a very early date the hawk , which was probably the first living thing worshipped by the early Egyptians; already in the Pyramid Texts the hawk on a standard is used indiscriminately with to represent the word "god." The principal forms of Horus the Sun-god, which probably represent the sun at various periods of the day and night, are:—Ḥeru-ur (Ἀρωήρις), "Horus the Great"; Ḥeru-p-khart , "Horus the Child"; Ḥeru-merti , "Horus of the two eyes," *i.e.*, of the sun and moon;[1] Ḥeru-nub , "the golden Horus"; Ḥeru-khent-khat ; Ḥeru-khent-ȧn-ȧriti (?) , "Horus dwelling in blindness"; Ḥeru-khuti , "Horus of the two horizons,"[2] Harmakhis, the type

[1] A very interesting figure of this god represents him holding his eyes in his hands; see Lanzone, *Dizionario*, p. 618.

[2] *I.e.*, Horus between the mountains of Bekhatet and Manu, the most easterly and westerly points of the sun's course, and the places where he rose and set.

of which on earth was the Sphinx; Ḥeru-sma-taui [hieroglyphs], "Horus the uniter of the North and South"; Ḥeru-ḥekenu [hieroglyphs], "Horus of Ḥeken"; and Ḥeru-beḥuṭet [hieroglyphs], "Horus of Beḥuṭet."[1] The cippi of Horus, which became so common at a late period in Egypt, seem to unite the idea of the physical and moral conceptions of Horus the Sun-god and of Horus the son of Osiris and Isis.

Horus, the son of Osiris and Isis, [hieroglyphs], appears in Egyptian texts usually as Ḥeru-p-khart [hieroglyphs], or "Horus the Child," who afterwards became the "avenger of his father Osiris," and occupied his throne, as we are told in many places in the Book of the Dead. In the Pyramid Texts the deceased is identified with Ḥeru-p-khart, and a reference is made to the fact that the god is always represented with a finger in his mouth.[2] The curious legend which Plutarch relates concerning Harpokrates and the cause of his lameness[3] is probably based upon the passage in the history of Osiris and Isis given in a Hymn to Osiris of the XVIIIth dynasty.[4]

Set [hieroglyphs] or Sutekh [hieroglyphs], Gr. Σήτ, the eighth member of the company of the gods of Ȧnu, was the son of Ḳeb and Nut, and the husband of his sister Nephthys. The worship of this god is exceedingly old, and in the Pyramid Texts we find that he is often mentioned with Horus and the other gods of the Heliopolitan company

[1] For figures of these various forms of Horus, see Lanzone, *op. cit.*, tavv. 214 ff.

[2] [hieroglyphs]. *Recueil de Travaux*, t. V, p. 44 (l. 301).

[3] Τὴν δ' Ἶσιν μετὰ τὴν τελευτὴν ἐξ Ὀσίριδος συγγενομένου, τεκεῖν ἠλιτόμηνον καὶ ἀσθενῆ τοῖς κάτωθεν γυίοις τὸν Ἁρποκράτην. *De Iside et Osiride*, § xix.

[4] [hieroglyphs]. Ledrain, *Monuments Égyptiens*, Pl. XXV, ll. 2, 3.

in terms of reverence. He was also believed to perform friendly offices for the deceased, and to be a god of the Sekhet-Åaru, or abode of the blessed dead. He was the king of the South as Horus was the king of the North, and the power of each was equal. He is usually depicted in human form with the head of an animal which has not yet been identified ; in later times the head of the ass was confounded with it, but the figures of the god in bronze which are preserved in the British Museum and elsewhere prove beyond a doubt that the head of Set is that of an animal unknown to us. The Set animal is not the *okapi*, as some Egyptologists think ; the opinion of naturalists has settled this question. In the early dynasties Set was a beneficent god, and one whose favour was sought after by the living and by the dead, and so late as the XIXth dynasty kings delighted to call themselves "beloved of Set." After the cult of Osiris was firmly established, and this god was the "great god" of all Egypt, it became the fashion to regard Set as the origin of all evil, and his statues and images were so effectually destroyed that only a few which escaped by accident have come down to us.[1] Originally Set, or Sut, represented darkness and night, and perhaps the desert, and was the opposite of Horus;[2] that Horus and Set were opposite aspects or forms of the same god is proved by the figure given by Lanzone (*Dizionario*, tav. 37, No. 2), where we see the head of Set and the head of Horus upon one body. The natural opposition of light (Horus) and darkness (Set) was at an early period confounded with the battle which took place between Horus, the son of Isis, and Set, wherein Isis intervened, and it seems that the moral idea of the battle of right against wrong[3] became attached to the latter combat, which was undertaken by Horus to avenge his father's murder by Set.

[1] See the two bronze figures of the god in the British Museum (Fourth Egyptian Room, Nos. 18191, 22897).

[2] In the Pyramid of Unås, l. 190, they are called the or "two combatants"; and see Pyramid of Tetå, l. 69, where we have the spelling .

[3] On the personification of evil by Set, see Wiedemann, *Die Religion*, p. 117.

Nebt-ḥet, or Nephthys [hieroglyphs], the last member of the company of the gods of Ȧnu, was the daughter of Ḳeb and Nut, the sister of Osiris and Isis, and the sister and wife of Set. When the sun rose at the creation out of the primeval waters Nephthys occupied a place in his boat with Isis and other deities; as a nature-goddess she either represents the day before sunrise or after sunset, but no portion of the night. She is depicted in the form of a woman, having upon her head the hieroglyphs, the values of which form her name, "lady of the house" [hieroglyph]. A legend preserved by Plutarch[1] makes her the mother of Ȧnpu, or Anubis, by Osiris. In Egyptian texts Ȧnpu is called the son of Rā.[2] In religious texts Nephthys is made to be the companion of Isis in all her troubles, and her grief for her brother's death is as great as that of his wife.

Ȧnpu, or Anubis, [hieroglyphs], the son of Osiris or Rā, sometimes by Isis and sometimes by Nephthys, seems to represent as a nature-god either the darkest part of the night or the earliest dawn. He is depicted either in human form with a dog's head, or as a dog.[3] In the legend of Osiris and Isis, Anubis played a prominent part in connexion with the finding of the dead body of Osiris; one tradition asserts that he only found it with the help of dogs. In papyri we see him standing as a guard and protector of the deceased lying upon the bier; in the Judgment Scene he is found as the guard of the balance, the pointer of which he watches with great diligence. He was the "Embalmer" *par excellence*, and as such was the god of the chamber of embalmment, and eventually he presided over the whole of the "funeral mountain." He is always regarded in the Book of the Dead as the messenger of Osiris, but in the older text he was the chief envoy of Rā, who sent him to embalm the body of Osiris.

Up-uat, the [hieroglyphs] of the Pyramid Text,[4] or "Opener of the ways," was depicted in the form of a wolf,

[1] *De Iside et Osiride*, § 14.

[2] See Lanzone, *op. cit.*, p. 65.

[3] In pictures the animal which symbolizes Anubis often resembles a jackal as much as a dog.

[4] Pyramid of Unȧs, l. 187.

but Anubis and Up-uat are often confounded in funerary scenes. On sepulchral stelae and other monuments two dog-like animals are frequently depicted; one of these represents Anubis, and the other Up-uat, and they probably have some connexion with the northern and southern parts of the funereal world. According to a legend described by Professor Maspero the god Anubis led the souls of the dead to the Elysian Fields in the Great Oasis.[1]

Among the primeval gods are two, **Ḥu** [hieroglyphs], and **Sȧa** [hieroglyphs], who are seen in the Boat of the Sun at the creation. They are the children of Temu, or Temu-Rā, but the exact part which they play as nature-gods has not yet, it seems, been satisfactorily made out. They seem to be personifications of two of the senses. The first mention of them in the Pyramid Texts records their subjugation by the deceased,[2] but in the Theban Book of the Dead they appear among the company of the gods who are present when the soul of the deceased is being weighed in the balance.

Teḥuti, or **Thoth**, [hieroglyph], represented the divine intelligence, which at creation uttered the words that when spoken turned into the objects of the material world. He was self-produced, and was the great god of the earth, air, sea, and sky; and he united in himself the attributes of many gods. He was the scribe of the gods, and, as such, he was regarded as the inventor of all the arts and sciences known to the Egyptians; some of his titles are "lord of writing," "master of papyrus," "maker of the palette and the ink-jar," "the mighty speaker," "the sweet-tongued"; and the words and compositions which he recited on behalf of the deceased preserved the latter from the influence of hostile powers and made him invincible in the Other World. He was the god of right and truth, wherein he lived, and whereby he established the world and all that is in it. As the chronologer of heaven and earth, he became the god of

[1] See *Le Nom antique de la Grande-Oasis* (in *Journal Asiatique*, IXe Série, tom. I, pp. 233–40).

[2] [hieroglyphs]. Pyramid of Unȧs, l. 439.

the moon; and as the reckoner of time, he obtained his name *Teḥuti, i.e.*, "the measurer"; in these capacities he had the power to grant life for millions of years to the deceased. When the great combat took place between Horus and Set, or between Horus, the son of Isis, and Set, Thoth was present as judge, and in the struggle between the two gods he gave to Isis the cow's head in the place of her own, which had been cut off by Horus in his rage at her interference; having reference to this fact he is called Up-reḥui [hieroglyphs], "The judge of the two Men, or Fighters." One of the Egyptian names for the ibis was [hieroglyphs] *Tekh*, and the similarity of the sound of this word to that of Teḥu, the name of the moon as a measurer of time, probably led the Egyptians to depict the god in the form of an ibis, notwithstanding the fact that the dog-headed ape was generally considered to be the animal sacred to him. It has been thought that there were two gods called Thoth, one being a form of Shu; but the attributes belonging to each have not yet been satisfactorily defined. In the monuments and papyri Thoth appears in the form of a man with the head of an ibis, which is sometimes surmounted by the crown [hieroglyph], or [hieroglyph], or [hieroglyph], or by disk and horns [hieroglyph], or [hieroglyph], and he holds in his left hand the sceptre [hieroglyph], and in the right [hieroglyph]; sometimes he is depicted holding his ink-jar [hieroglyph] and the crescent moon [hieroglyph], and sometimes he appears in the form of an ape holding a palette full of writing-reeds.[1] Thoth is mentioned in the Pyramid Texts[2] as the brother of Osiris, but whether he is the same Thoth who is called the "Lord of Khemenu" and the "Scribe of the gods" is doubtful.

Maāt [hieroglyphs], the female counterpart of Thoth, was, according to Heliopolitan tradition, the daughter of Rā, and a very ancient goddess; she seems to have assisted Ptaḥ and Khnemu in carrying out rightly the work of creation ordered by Thoth. There is no one word which will exactly describe the Egyptian conception

[1] See Lanzone, *op. cit.*, tav. 304, No. 1.
[2] Pyramid of Unȧs, l. 236.

of Maāt both from a physical and from a moral point of view; but the fundamental idea of the word is "straight," and from the Egyptian texts it is clear that *maāt* meant right, true, truth, real, genuine, upright, righteous, just, steadfast, unalterable, etc. Thus already in the Prisse Papyrus it is said: "Great is *maāt*, the "mighty and unalterable, and it hath never been broken "since the time of Osiris,"[1] and Ptaḥ-ḥetep counsels his listener to "make *maāt*, or right and truth, to flourish."[2] The just, upright, and straight man is *maāt* [hieroglyphs], and in a book of moral precepts it is said, "God will judge the right (*maā*)"[3] [hieroglyphs].[4] Maāt, the goddess of the unalterable laws of heaven, and the daughter of Rā, is depicted in female form, with the feather [hieroglyph], emblematic of *maāt*, on her head, or with the feather alone for a head, and the sceptre [hieroglyph] in one hand, and [hieroglyph] in the other.[5] In the Judgment Scene two Maāt goddesses appear; one probably is the personification of physical law and the other of moral rectitude; or one may have presided over Upper Egypt, and the other over Lower Egypt.

Ḥet-ḥeru, or **Hathor** [hieroglyph], the "house of Horus," was the goddess of the sky wherein Horus the Sun-god rose and set. Subsequently a great number of goddesses of the same name were developed from her, and these were identified with Isis, Neith, Iusāset, and many other goddesses whose attributes they absorbed. A group of seven Hathors is also mentioned, and these appear to have partaken of the nature of good fairies.

[1] Page 17, l. 5, [hieroglyphs].

[2] Page 18, l. 1, [hieroglyphs].

[3] Amélineau, *La Morale*, p. 138.

[4] The various meanings of *maāt* are illustrated by abundant passages from Egyptian texts by Brugsch, *Wörterbuch* (Suppl.), p. 329.

[5] See Lanzone, *op. cit.*, tav. 109.

In one form Hathor was the goddess of love, beauty, happiness; and the Greeks identified her with their own Aphrodite. She is often depicted in the form of a woman having disk and horns upon her head, and at times she has the head of a lion surmounted by a uraeus. Often she has the form of a cow—the animal sacred to her—and in this form she appears as the goddess of the tomb or Ta-Tchertet, and she provides meat and drink for the deceased.[1] As a Cow-goddess she is probably of Sûdânî origin.

Meḥt-urt [hieroglyphs] is the personification of that part of the sky wherein the sun rises, and also of that part of it in which he takes his daily course; she is depicted in the form of a cow, along the body of which the two barks of the sun are seen sailing. Already in the Pyramid Texts we find the attribute of judge ascribed to Meḥ-urt,[2] and down to a very late date the judgment of the deceased in the hall of Double Maāt in the presence of Thoth and the other gods was believed to take place in the abode of Meḥ-urt,[3] *i.e.*, in the sky.

Net, or **Neith,** [hieroglyphs], or [hieroglyph], "the divine mother, the lady of heaven, the mistress of the gods," was one of the most ancient deities of Egypt, and in the Pyramid Texts she appears as the mother of Sebek.[4] The centre of her cult was at Saïs in the Delta. Like Meḥ-urt she personifies the place in the sky where the sun rises. In one form she was the goddess of the loom and shuttle, and also of the chase; in this aspect she was identified by the Greeks with Artemis. She is depicted in the form of a woman, having upon her head the shuttle [hieroglyph] or arrows [hieroglyph], or she wears the crown [hieroglyph] and holds arrows [hieroglyph], a bow [hieroglyph], and a sceptre in her left hand; she also

[1] A good set of illustrations of this goddess will be found in Lanzone, *op. cit.*, tav. 314 f.

[2] [hieroglyphs]. *Recueil de Travaux*, t. IV, p. 48 (l. 427).

[3] Pleyte, *Chapitres supplémentaires du Livre des Morts* (Chapp. 162, 162,* 163), p. 26.

[4] *Recueil de Travaux*, t. IV, p. 76 (l. 627).

appears in the form of a cow.[1] The goddess Neith was believed to be self-produced, and an ancient Saïte tradition made her to be the mother of Rā, the Sun-god.

Sekhmet [hieroglyphs], was in Memphis the wife of Ptaḥ, and the mother of **Nefer-Temu** and of **I-em-ḥetep.** She was the personification of the burning heat of the sun, and as such was the destroyer of the enemies of Rā and Osiris. When Rā determined to punish mankind with death, because they scoffed at him, he sent Sekhmet, his "eye," to perform the work of vengeance; illustrative of this aspect of her is a figure wherein she is depicted with the sun's eye for a head.[2] Usually she has the head of a lion surmounted by the sun's disk, round which is a uraeus; and she generally holds a sceptre [hieroglyph], but sometimes a knife.

Bast [hieroglyphs], according to one legend, was the mother of Nefer-Temu. She was the personification of the gentle and fructifying heat of the sun, as opposed to that personified by Sekhmet. The cat was sacred to Bast, and the goddess is usually depicted cat-headed. The most famous seat of her worship was the city of Bubastis, the modern Tell Bastah, near Zaḳâzîḳ, in the Delta.

Nefer-Temu [hieroglyphs], was the son either of Sekhmet or Bast, and he personified some form of the morning sun. He is usually depicted in the form of a man, with a cluster of lotus flowers upon his head, but sometimes he has the head of a lion; in the little *faïence* figures of him, which are so common, he stands upon the back of a lion.[3] He no doubt represents the Sun-god in the legend which made him to burst forth from a lotus, for in the pyramid of Unȧs the king is said to:

[hieroglyphs]

χāā	*em*	*Nefer-Temu*	*em*	*seššen*	*er*	*šert*	*Rā*
"Rise	like	Nefer-Temu	from	the lotus (lily)	to	the nostrils of	Rā,"

and to "come forth on the horizon every day."[4]

[1] See Lanzone, *op. cit.*, tav. 177.
[2] *Ibid.*, *op. cit.*, tav. 364.
[3] *Ibid.*, *op. cit.*, tav. 147.
[4] *Recueil de Travaux*, t. IV, p. 45 (l. 394).

Neḥeb-ka [hieroglyphs], is the name of a goddess who is usually represented with the head of a serpent, and with whom the deceased identifies himself.

Sebȧk [hieroglyphs], a form of Horus the Sun-god, must be distinguished from Sebȧk, the companion of Set, the opponent of Osiris; of each of these gods the crocodile was the sacred animal, and for this reason probably the gods themselves were confounded. Sebȧk-Rā, the lord of Ombos, is usually depicted in human form with the head of a crocodile, surmounted by [hieroglyph], [hieroglyph], or [hieroglyph], or [hieroglyph].[1]

Menu [hieroglyphs],[2] or **Ȧmsi** [hieroglyphs], is one of the most ancient gods of Egypt. He personified the power of generation, or the reproductive force of nature; he was the "father of his own mother," and was identified with "Horus the mighty," or with Horus the avenger of his father Un-nefer or Osiris. The Greeks identified him with the god Pan, and called the chief city where his worship was celebrated Khemmis,[3] after one of his names. He is depicted usually in the form of a man standing upon [hieroglyph]; and he has upon his head the plumes, [hieroglyph], and holds the flail, [hieroglyph], in his right hand, which is raised above his shoulder.[4]

Neb-er-tcher [hieroglyphs], a name which signifies "lord to the uttermost limit," *i.e.*, "lord of the universe"; this name was subsequently given to Osiris. Some have thought that it was given to Osiris after the completed re-construction of his body, which had been hacked to pieces by Set.

Un-nefer [hieroglyphs], a name of Osiris in his capacity of god and judge of the dead in the Underworld. The name probably means "good being."

Ȧsṭennu [hieroglyphs], a name given to one of the associates of the god Thoth, and to Thoth himself.

[1] Lanzone, *op. cit.*, tav. 353.

[2] Also read Khem.

[3] In Egyptian the town is called Apu [hieroglyphs].

[4] Lanzone, *op. cit.*, tav. 332.

Mert-seḳert, "the lover of silence," is a name of Isis or Hathor as goddess of the Underworld. The centre of her cult was a portion of Western Thebes. She is sometimes depicted in the form of a woman, having a disk and horns upon her head.[1]

Serq or **Selk**, is a form of the goddess Isis. She is usually depicted in the form of a woman, with a scorpion upon her head; occasionally she appears as a scorpion with a woman's head, surmounted by disk and horns.[2]

Ta-urt, the Thoueris of the Greeks, was identified as the wife of Set or Typhon; she is also known under the names Ȧpt and Sheput. Her common titles are "mistress of the gods," , and "bearer of the gods". She is depicted in the form of a hippopotamus standing on her hind legs, with distended paunch and hanging breasts, and one of her forefeet rests upon , the symbol of magical power, which probably represents a part of the organs of generation of the goddess; sometimes she has the head of a woman, but she always wears the disk, horns, and plumes .

Uatchit, was a form of Hathor, and was identified with the appearance of the sky in the north when the sun rose. She is either depicted in the form of a woman, having upon her head the Crown of the North and a sceptre , round which a serpent is twined, or as a winged uraeus wearing the Crown of the North. She was the principal goddess of the town of Buto, in the Delta.

Nekhebit, was a very ancient goddess, the centre of whose cult was the town of Nekheb in Upper Egypt, the Eileithyiaspolis of the Greeks, and the modern Al-Kâb. She was the tutelary deity of Upper Egypt in

[1] See Lanzone, tav. 124.

[2] *Ibid.*, *op. cit.*, tav. 362.

very early dynastic times. She appears in the form of a woman, either with the vulture headdress, or with the head of a vulture, and sometimes as a vulture. Nekhebit and Uatchit divided between them the sovereignty of all Egypt.

Beb, Bebti, Baba, or **Babu,** , , , or , mentioned three times in the Book of the Dead, is the "firstborn son of Osiris," and seems to be one of the gods of generation.

Ḥāpi , perhaps originally **Ḥepr,** is the name of the great god of the Nile who was worshipped in Egypt under two forms, *i.e.*, "Ḥāpi of the South," , and "Ḥāpi of the North," ; the papyrus was the emblem of the former, and the lotus of the latter. From the earliest times the Nile was regarded by the Egyptians as the source of all the prosperity of Egypt, and it was honoured as being the type of the life-giving waters, out of the midst of which sprang the gods and all created things. In turn it was identified with all the gods of Egypt, new or old, and its influence was so great upon the minds of the Egyptians that from the earliest days they depicted to themselves a material heaven wherein the Isles of the Blest were laved by the waters of a Celestial Nile; the Nile of Egypt was only a continuation of the Nile of heaven. Others again lived in imagination on the banks of the heavenly Nile, whereon they built cities; and it seems as if the Egyptians never succeeded in conceiving a heaven without a Nile and canals. The Nile is depicted in the form of a man, who wears upon his head a clump of papyrus or lotus flowers; his breasts are androgynous, indicating fertility. Lanzone reproduces an interesting scene[1] in which the South and North Nile gods are tying a papyrus and a lotus stalk around the emblem of union , to indicate the unity of Upper and Lower Egypt, and this emblem is found cut upon the thrones of the kings of Egypt to indicate their sovereignty over the regions traversed by the

[1] *Dizionario*, tav. 198.

South and North Niles. It has already been said that Ḥāpi was identified with all the gods in turn, and it follows as a matter of course that the attributes of each were ascribed to him; in one respect, however, he is different from them all, for of him it is written :—

He cannot be sculptured in stone; in the images on which men place

crowns and uraei he is not made manifest; service cannot be rendered

nor offerings made to him; not can he be drawn in his form of mystery;

not is known the place where he is; not is he found in the

painted shrine.[1]

Here the scribe gave to the Nile the attributes of the great and unknown God its Maker.

In the Pyramid Texts we find a group of four gods with whom the deceased is closely connected in the Other World; these are the four "Sons of Horus", whose names are given in the following order :—**Ḥep**, **Ṭuamutef**, **Ȧmset**, and **Qebḥsenuf**.[2] The deceased is called their "father."[3] His two arms were identified with Ḥep and

[1] For the hieratic text from which this extract is taken see Birch, *Select Papyri*, Plates 20 ff. and 134 ff.; see also Maspero, *Hymne au Nil, publié et traduit d'après les deux textes du Musée Britannique*, Paris, 1868, 4to. See also Prof. Maspero's new edition published in Cairo, 4to, 1912 (*Bibliothèque d'Étude*, tom. V).

[2] Pyramid of Unȧs, l. 219; Pyramid of Tetȧ, ll. 60, 286; Pyramid of Pepi I, ll. 444, 593, etc.

[3] Pyramid of Pepi I, l. 593.

Ṭuamutef, and his two legs with Åmset and Qebḥsenuf;[1] and when he entered into the Sekhet-Åaru they accompanied him as guides, and went in with him two on each side.[2] They took away all hunger and thirst from him,[3] they gave him life in heaven and protected it when given,[4] and they brought to him from the Lake of Khemta the boat of the eye of Khnemu.[5] In one passage they are called the "four *Khu's* of Horus" [hieroglyphs],[6] and originally they represented the Four Horus gods, who held up the four pillars which supported the sky, [hieroglyphs], or their father Horus. Each was supposed to be lord of one of the quarters of the world, and finally became the god of one of the cardinal points. Ḥep represented the north, Ṭuamutef the east, Åmset the south, and Qebḥsenuf the west. The Egyptians were in the habit of embalming the intestines of the body separately, and they placed them in four jars, each of which was under the protection of one of the children of Horus, *i.e.*, under the care of one of the gods of the four quarters of the earth. The god of the north protected the small viscera, the god of the east the heart and lungs, the god of the south the stomach and large intestines, and the god of the west the liver and gall-bladder. With these four gods four goddesses were associated, viz., Nephthys, Neith, Isis, and Selk or Serq.

Connected with the god Horus are a number of mythological beings called **Ḥeru shemsu**[7] [hieroglyphs], who appear already in the pyramid of Unȧs in connection with Horus and Set in the ceremony of purifying and "opening the mouth"; and in the pyramid of Pepi I it is they who wash the king and who recite for him the

[1] *Recueil de Travaux*, t. III, p. 905 (ll. 219 f.).
[2] *Ibid.*, t. VII, p. 150 (ll. 261–63).
[3] *Ibid.*, t. V, p. 10 (ll. 59 ff.).
[4] [hieroglyphs]. *Ibid.*, t. VIII, p. 91 (l. 593).
[5] *Ibid.*, t. VII, p. 167 (l. 444).
[6] *Ibid.*, t. VII, p. 150 (l. 261).
[7] *Ibid.*, t. III, p. 182 (l. 17).

"Chapter of those who come forth," and the "[Chapter of] those who ascend."[1]

In the Judgment Scene in the Book of the Dead, grouped round the pan of the balance, which contains the heart of the deceased (see Plate III), are three beings in human form, who bear the names **Shai, Renenet,** and **Meskhenet.**

Shai [hieroglyphs], is the personification of Fate, and **Renenet** [hieroglyphs], of Fortune; these names are usually found coupled. Shai and Renenet are said to be in the hands of Thoth, the divine intelligence of the gods; and Rameses II boasts that he himself is "lord of Shai and creator of Renenet."[2] Shai was originally the deity who "fated" what should happen to a man, and Renenet, as may be seen from the Pyramid Texts,[3] was the goddess of plenty, good fortune, and the like; subsequently no distinction was made between these deities and the abstract ideas which they represented. In the Papyrus of Ani, Shai stands by himself near the pillar of the Balance, and Renenet is accompanied by **Meskhenet,** who acted as midwife and presided over the birth-chamber. In the story of the birth of the three sons of Rā, as related in the Westcar Papyrus, we find the goddess Meskhenet [hieroglyphs] mentioned with Isis, Nephthys, Heqet, and the god Khnemu as assisting at the birth of children. Disguised in human forms, the four goddesses go to the house of Rā-user, and, because they have a knowledge of the art of midwifery, they are admitted to the chamber where the children are to be born; Isis stands before the woman, Nephthys behind her, and Ḥeqet accelerates the birth. When the child is born Meskhenet comes and looking upon him says: "A king; he shall rule throughout

[1] [hieroglyphs], etc. *Recueil de Travaux*, t. VII, p. 170 (l. 463).

[2] See Maspero, *Romans et Poésies du Papyrus Harris*, No. 500, Paris, 1879, p. 27.

[3] Pyramid of Unås, l. 564.

"this land. May Khnemu give health and strength to his "body."[1]

The god **Amen** [hieroglyphs], his wife Mut [hieroglyphs], and their son Khensu [hieroglyphs] have nothing whatever to do with the Book of the Dead; but Åmen, the first member of this great Theban triad, must be mentioned in connection with the other gods, because he was usually identified with one or more of them. The name Åmen means the "hidden," and seems to refer to the mysterious and unknown power that causes conception in women and animals; one of his symbols is the belly of a pregnant woman. Åmen is a very ancient god, and is mentioned with Åment in the Pyramid Texts, but his cult did not assume any great importance at Thebes until the XIIth dynasty, when a large temple was built in his honour at Karnak. From that time until the close of the XVIIth dynasty, Åmen was the chief god of Thebes and nothing more. When, however, the last kings of the XVIIth dynasty had succeeded in expelling the Hyksos and had delivered the country from the yoke of the foreigner, their god assumed an importance hitherto unknown, and his priests endeavoured to make his worship the first in the land. But Åmen was never regarded throughout the entire country as its chief god, although his votaries called him the King of the gods. Speaking generally, in the time of the XVIIIth dynasty and onwards the god was the personification of the mysterious creating and sustaining power of the universe, which in a material form was typified by the sun. His name was changed to Åmen-Rā, and little by little all the attributes of the old gods of Egypt were ascribed to him, and the titles which among western nations are given to God were added to those powers which Åmen had usurped. The following extracts from a fine hymn[2] illustrate the views of the priesthood of Åmen-Rā concerning their god:—

[1] [hieroglyphs]. Erman, *Die Märchen des Papyrus Westcar*, Berlin, 1890, Bl. 10, ll. 13, 14.

[2] See Grébaut, *Hymne a Ammon-Rā*, Paris, 1874; and Wiedemann, *Die Religion*, pp. 64 ff.

"Adoration to thee, O Ȧmen-Rā, the Bull in Ȧnu "(Heliopolis), the ruler of all the gods, the beautiful "and beloved god who givest life to all. Hail to thee, "O Ȧmen-Rā, lord of the Throne of Egypt, thou dweller "in Thebes, thou Bull of thy mother that livest in thy "field, that extendest thy journeys in the land of the south, "thou lord of those who dwell in the west, thou governor "of Punt, thou king of heaven and sovereign of the "earth, thou lord of things that exist, thou stablisher "of creation, thou supporter of the universe. Thou "art one in thine attributes among the gods, thou beautiful "Bull of the company of the gods, thou chief of all the "gods, lord of *Maāt*, father of the gods, creator of men, "maker of beasts and cattle, lord of all that existeth, "maker of the staff of life, creator of the herbs which "give life to beasts and cattle .... Thou art the "creator of things celestial and terrestial, thou illuminest "the universe .... The gods cast themselves at thy "feet when they perceive thee .... Hymns of praise "be to thee, O Father of the gods, who hast spread out "the heavens and laid down the earth ..... thou "master of eternity and of everlastingness. ... Hail to "thee, O Rā, lord of *Maāt*, thou who art hidden in thy "shrine, lord of the gods. Thou art Kheperȧ in thy bark, "and when thou sendest forth the word the gods come "into being. Thou art Temu, the maker of beings which "have reason, and however many be their forms, thou "givest them life, and thou dost distinguish the shape and "stature of each from his neighbour. Thou hearest the "prayer of the afflicted, and thou art gracious unto him "that crieth unto thee; thou deliverest the feeble one from "the oppressor, and thou judgest between the strong and "the weak .... The Nile riseth at thy will ... Thou "Only Form, the maker of all that is, One Only, the "creator of all that shall be. Mankind hath come forth "from thine eyes, the gods have come into being from thy "mouth, thou makest the herbs for the use of beasts and "cattle, and the staff of life for the need of man. Thou "givest life to the fish of the stream and to the fowl of the "air, and breath unto the germ in the egg; thou givest "life unto the grasshopper, and thou makest to live the "wild fowl and things that creep and things that fly and "everything that belongeth thereunto. Thou providest "food for the rats in their holes and for the birds that sit "among the branches . . . . thou One, thou Only One "whose arms are many. All men and all creatures adore "thee, and praises come unto thee from the height of "heaven, from earth's widest space, and from the deepest "depths of the sea . . . . thou One, thou Only One who "hast no second . . . . . whose names are manifold and "innumerable."

We have seen above that among other titles the god Åmen was called the "One One", but the addition of the words "who hast no second" is remarkable as showing that the Egyptians had already conceived the existence of a god who had no like or equal, which they hesitated not to proclaim side by side with their descriptions of his manifestations. Looking at the Egyptian words in their simple meaning, it is pretty certain that when the Egyptians declared that their god was One and that he had no second, they had the same ideas as the Jews and Muḥammadans when they proclaimed their God to be "One"[1] and alone. It has been urged that the Egyptians never advanced to pure monotheism because they never succeeded in freeing themselves from the belief in the existence of other gods, but when they say that a god has "no second," even though they mention other "gods," it is quite evident that, like the Jews, they conceived him to be an entirely different being from the beings which, for the want of a better word, or because these possessed superhuman attributes, they named "gods."

The gods above enumerated represent the powers who were the guides and protectors and givers of life and happiness to the deceased in the new life, but from the earliest times it is clear that the Egyptians imagined the existence of other powers who offered opposition to the dead, and who are called in many places his "enemies." Like so many of the ancient gods, these powers were

[1] אֶחָד, Deut. vi, 4. Cp. כִּי יְהוָה הוּא הָאֱלֹהִים אֵין עוֹד מִלְּבַדּוֹ, Deut. iv, 35; and וְאֵין עוֹד זוּלָתִי אֵין אֱלֹהִים, Isaiah xlv, 5.

originally certain forces of nature, which were believed to be opposed to those that were regarded as beneficent to man, as for example darkness to light, and night to day; with darkness and night were also associated the powers which contributed in any way to obscure the light of the sun or to prevent his shining. But since the deceased was identified with Osiris and Rā, and their accompanying gods, the enemies of the one became the enemies of the other, and the welfare of the one was the welfare of the other. When the Egyptians personified the beneficent powers of nature, that is say, their gods, they conceived them in their own images; but when they personified the destroying powers, or opposing powers, they gave to them the shapes of noxious animals and reptiles, such as snakes and scorpions. As time went on, the moral ideas of good and right were attributed to the former, and evil and wickedness to the latter. The first personifications of Day and Night, or Light and Darkness, were Horus and Set, and in the combat—the prototype of the subsequent legends of Marduk and Tiamat, Bel and the Dragon, St. George and the Dragon, and many others—which took place between them, Horus was always the victor.

Now, though the deceased was identified with Osiris or Rā, the victory that Horus gained over Set only benefited the spiritual body which dwelt in heaven, and did not preserve the natural body which lay in the tomb. The principal enemy of the natural body was the worm, and from the earliest times it seems that a huge worm or serpent was chosen by the Egyptians as the type of the powers which were hostile to the dead and also of the foe against whom the Sun-god fought. Already in the Pyramid of Unȧs a long section of the text contains nothing but formulae, the recital of which was intended to protect the deceased from various kinds of snakes and worms.[1] These are exceedingly ancient, indeed they may safely be said to form one of the oldest parts of the funeral literature of the Egyptians, and we find from the later editions of the Book of the Dead and certain Coptic works that the dread of the serpent as the emblem of physical and

[1] Maspero, *Recueil de Travaux*, t. III, p. 220.

moral evil existed among the Egyptians in all generations, and that, as will be seen later, the belief in a limbo filled with snakes swayed their minds long after they had been converted to Christianity.

The charms against serpents in the Pyramid Texts of the Vth and VIth dynasties have their equivalents in the XXXIst and XXXIIIrd Chapters of the Book of the Dead, which are found on coffins of the XIth and XIIth dynasties;[1] and in the XVIIIth dynasty we find vignettes in which the deceased is depicted in the act of spearing a crocodile[2] and of slaughtering serpents.[3] In the Theban and Saïte Recensions are several small chapters[4] the recital of which drove away reptiles: and of these the most important is the XXXIXth[5] Chapter, which preserved the deceased from the attack of the great serpent Āapef or Āapep [hieroglyphs] or [hieroglyphs], who is depicted with knives stuck in his folds [hieroglyph].[6] In the period of the later dynasties a service was performed daily in the temple of Åmen-Rā at Thebes to deliver the Sun-god from the assault of this fiend, and on each occasion it was accompanied by a ceremony in which a waxen figure of Āapep was burnt in the fire; as the wax melted, so the power of Āapep was destroyed.[7] Another name of Āapep was Nȧk [hieroglyphs], who was pierced by the lance of the Eye of Horus and made to vomit what he had swallowed.[8]

The Judgment Scene in the Theban Recension of the Book of the Dead reveals the belief in the existence of a tri-formed monster, part crocodile, part lion, and part hippopotamus, whom the Egyptians called Ām-mit

[1] Goodwin, *Aeg. Zeitschrift*, 1866, p. 54; see also Lepsius, *Aelteste Texte*, Bl. 35, ll. 1 ff.

[2] Naville, *Todtenbuch*, Bd. I, Bl. 44.

[3] *Ibid.*, Bd. I, Bl. 46.

[4] *I.e.*, Chapters 32, 34, 35, 36, 37, 38, etc.

[5] For the text see Naville, *Todtenbuch*, Bd. I, Bl. 53; and Lepsius, *Todtenbuch*, Bl. 18.

[6] See Lanzone, *Dizionario*, p. 121.

[7] The service for the *Overthrowing of Āpepi* is printed in *Archaeologia*, Vol. LII, pp. 393–608.

[8] [hieroglyphs] Grébaut, *Hymne*, p. 10.

[hieroglyphs], *i.e.*, "the Eater of the Dead," and who lived in Amenta; her place is by the side of the scales wherein the heart is weighed, and it is clear that such hearts as failed to balance the feather of Maāt were devoured by her. In one papyrus she is depicted crouching by the side of a lake.[1] Other types of evil were the insect Āpshai [hieroglyphs],[2] confounded in later times with the tortoise[3] [hieroglyphs], which dies as Rā lives;[4] the crocodile Sebåk, which afterwards became identified with Rā; the hippopotamus, the ass, etc.

The Pyramid Texts afford scanty information about the fiends and devils with which the later Egyptians peopled certain parts of the Ṭuat, wherein the night sun pursued his course, and where the souls of the dead dwelt; for this we must turn to the composition entitled the "Book of him that is in the Ṭuat," several copies of which have come down to us inscribed upon tombs, coffins, and papyri of the XVIIIth and following dynasties. The Ṭuat was divided into twelve parts, corresponding to the twelve hours of the night; and this Book professed to afford to the deceased the means whereby he might pass through them successfully. In one of these divisions, which was under the rule of the god Seker, the entrance was guarded by a serpent on four legs with a human head, and within were a serpent with three heads, scorpions,[5] vipers, and winged monsters of terrifying aspect; a vast desert place was their abode, and seemingly the darkness was so thick there that it might be felt. In other divisions we find serpents spitting fire, lions, crocodile-headed gods, a serpent that devours the dead, a huge crocodile, and many other reptiles of divers shapes and forms.

From the descriptions which accompany the scenes, it is evident that the Ṭuat was regarded by the Egyptians of the XVIIIth dynasty from a moral as well as from

1 See Chapter CXXV.
2 Naville, *Todtenbuch*, Bd. I, Bl. 49.
3 Lepsius, *Todtenbuch*, Bl. 17.
4 [hieroglyphs]. Naville, *Todtenbuch*, Bd. I, Bl. 184.
5 See Maspero, *Les Hypogées Royaux de Thèbes*, p. 76.

a physical point of view.[1] Āapep, the emblem of evil, was here punished and overcome, and here dwelt the souls of the wicked and the righteous, who received their punishments or rewards, meted out to them by the decree of Rā and his company of gods. The chief instruments of punishment employed by the gods were fire and beasts which devoured the souls and bodies of the enemies of Rā; and we may see from the literature of the Copts, or Egyptians who had embraced Christianity, how long the belief in a hell of fire and torturing fiends survived. Thus in the Life of Abba Shenuti,[2] a man is told that the "executioners of Amenti will not show compassion upon thy wretched soul,"[3] and in the history of Pisentios, a Bishop of Coptos in the seventh century of our era, we have a series of details which reflect the Ṭuat of the ancient Egyptians in a remarkable manner. The bishop having taken up his abode in a tomb filled with mummies, causes one of them to tell his history.[4] After saying that his parents were Greeks who worshipped Poseidon, he states that when he was dying, already the avenging angels came about him with iron knives and goads as sharp as spears, which they thrust into his sides, while they gnashed their teeth at him; when he opened his eyes, he saw death in all its manifold forms round about him; and at that moment angels without mercy (ⲛⲓⲁⲅⲅⲉⲗⲟⲥ ⲛ̄ ⲁⲑⲛⲁⲓ) came and dragged his wretched soul from his body, and tying it to the form of a black horse they bore it away to Amenta (ⲉⲙⲉⲛⲧ =). Next, he was delivered over to merciless tormentors, who tortured him in a place where there were multitudes of savage beasts; and, when he had been cast into the place of outer darkness, he saw a ditch more than two hundred feet deep filled with reptiles, each of which had seven heads, and all their bodies were covered as it were with scorpions. Here also were serpents, the very

[1] See Lefébure, *Book of Hades* (*Records of the Past*, Vol. X, p. 84).

[2] See Amélineau, *Monuments pour servir à l'Histoire de l'Égypte Chrétienne*, p. 167.

[3] ⲙⲛ ⲥⲉⲛⲁϯⲁⲥⲟ ⲉⲧⲉⲕⲯⲩⲭⲏ ⲛ̄ⲧⲁⲗⲁⲓⲡⲱⲣⲟⲥ ⲛ̄ϫⲉ ⲛⲓⲇⲏⲙⲱⲣⲓⲥⲧⲏⲥ ⲛⲧⲉ ⲁⲙⲉⲛϯ.

[4] See Amélineau, *Étude sur le Christianisme en Égypte au Septième Siècle*, Paris, 1887, p. 147.

sight of which terrified the beholder, and to one of them which had teeth like iron stakes was the wretched man given to be devoured; for five days in each week the serpent crushed him with his teeth, but on the Saturday and Sunday there was respite. Another picture of the torments of Hades is given in the Martyrdom of Macarius of Antioch, wherein the Saint, having restored to life a man who had been dead six hours, learned that when he was about to die he was surrounded by fiends, ϩⲁⲛⲇⲏⲕⲁⲛⲟⲥ, some of whom had the faces of dragons, ⲛ̀ϩⲟ ⲛ̀ⲇⲣⲁⲕⲱⲛ, others of lions, ⲛ̀ϩⲟ ⲛ ⲙ̀ ⲙⲱⲟⲩⲓ, others of crocodiles, ⲛ̀ϩⲟ ⲛⲉⲙⲥⲁϩ, and others of bears, ⲛ̀ϩⲟ ⲛ̀ⲗⲁⲃⲟⲓ. They tore his soul from his body with great violence, and they fled with it over a mighty river of fire, in which they plunged it to a depth of four hundred cubits; then they took it out and set it before the Judge of Truth, ⲙ̀ ⲡⲓⲕⲣⲓⲧⲏⲥ ⲙ̀ ⲙⲏⲓ. After hearing the sentence of the Judge the fiends took it to a place of outer darkness where no light came, and they cast it into the cold where there was gnashing of teeth. There it beheld a snake which never slept, ϥⲉⲛⲧ ⲛ̀ ⲁⲧ ⲉⲛⲕⲟⲧ, with a head like that of a crocodile, and which was surrounded by reptiles which cast souls before it to be devoured, ⲉⲣⲉ ⲛⲓϭⲁⲧϥⲓ ⲧⲏⲣⲟⲩ ϧⲁⲧⲟⲧϥ ⲉⲩⲥⲓϯ ⲛ̀ ⲛⲓⲯⲩⲭⲏ ϩⲓⲧϩⲏ ⲙ̀ⲙⲟϥ; when the snake's mouth was full it allowed the other reptiles to eat, and though they rent the soul in pieces it did not die. After this the soul was carried into Åmenta for ever, ⲁ̀ⲙⲉⲛϯ ϣⲁ ⲉ̀ⲛⲉϩ.[1] The martyr Macarius suffered in the reign of Diocletian, and the MS. from which the above extract is taken was copied in the year of the Martyrs 634 = A.D. 918. Thus, the old heathen ideas of the Egyptian Ṭuat were applied to the construction of the Coptic Hell.

[1] See Hyvernat, *Les Actes des Martyrs de l'Égypte*, Paris, 1886, pp. 56, 57.

THE PRINCIPAL GEOGRAPHICAL AND MYTHOLOGICAL PLACES IN THE BOOK OF THE DEAD

Ȧbṭu [hieroglyphs], the Abydos of the Greeks (Strabo, XVII, i, 42), and the ⲉⲃⲱⲧ of the Copts, was the capital of the eighth nome of Upper Egypt. It was the seat of the worship of Osiris in Upper Egypt, and the god was believed to have been buried there. For many centuries its priests boasted the possession of the head of Osiris, and the great annual miracle-play, in which the sufferings, death, and resurrection of Osiris were acted, drew thousands of people to the festival from every part of Egypt. Local tradition made the sun to end its daily course at Abydos, and to enter into the Ṭuat at this place through a "gap" in the mountains called in Egyptian *peq*, [hieroglyphs].[1] These mountains lay near to the town; and in the XIIth dynasty it was believed that the souls of the dead made their way into the Other World by the valley which led through them to the Great Oasis, where some placed the Elysian Fields.[2] Under the New Empire the tomb of King Khent at Abydos was identified by local tradition as the tomb of Osiris, and it became the object of pilgrimages from every part of Egypt. Under the XXIInd dynasty the cult of Osiris declined, and the town never regained the importance which it had enjoyed under the XVIIIth dynasty.

Ȧmenta or **Ȧmentet,** [hieroglyphs], or [hieroglyphs], was originally the place where the sun set, but subsequently the name was applied to all the cemeteries which were built in the stony plateaus and mountains on the western bank of the Nile. Some believe that Ȧmenta was, at first, the name of a small district, without either funereal or mythological signification. The Christian Egyptians, or Copts, used the word Amenti to translate the Greek word Hades, to which

[1] See Brugsch, *Dict. Géog.*, p. 227.
[2] See Maspero, *Études de Mythologie*, t. I, p. 345

they attributed all the ideas which their heathen ancestors had associated with the Åmenta of the Book of the Dead.

Ånu [hieroglyphs], the Heliopolis of the Greeks (Herodotus, II, 3, 7, 8, 9, 59, 93; Strabo, XVII, i, 27 ff.), was the capital of the thirteenth nome of Lower Egypt. The Hebrews called it On (Genesis xli, 45, 50; xlvi, 20), Aven (Ezekiel xxx, 17), and Bêth-Shemesh (Jeremiah xliii, 13); this last name is an exact translation of the Egyptian [hieroglyphs] *per Rā*, "house of the sun," which was also a designation of Ånu. The Copts have preserved the oldest name of the city under the form ⲱⲛ. A Coptic bishop of this place was present at the Council of Ephesus. The city of Ånu seems to have become associated with the worship of the sun in prehistoric times. Already in the Vth dynasty its priesthood had succeeded in gaining supremacy for their religious views and beliefs throughout Egypt, and from first to last it maintained its position as the chief seat of the cult of Rā. The body of the Aged One, a name of Osiris, reposed in Ånu, and there dwelt the Eye of Osiris. The deceased made his way to Ånu, where souls were joined unto bodies in thousands, and where the blessed dead lived on celestial food for ever.

Ån-rutf, or **Naårutf** [hieroglyphs], [hieroglyphs], was a section of the Ṭuat of Herakleopolis; the meaning of the name is "the place where nothing groweth."

Ån-ṭes (?) [hieroglyphs], an unknown locality where [hieroglyph], the tower of a Light-god (?), was adored.

Åpu [hieroglyphs], the Panopolis of the Greeks (Πανῶν πόλις, Strabo, XVII, i, 41), was the metropolis of the ninth nome of Upper Egypt, and the seat of the worship of the god [hieroglyphs], whose name is variously read Åmsi, Khem, and Menu. In ancient days it was famous as the centre for stone cutting and linen weaving, and the latter industry still survives among the modern Coptic population, who, following their ancestors, call their city ϣⲙⲓⲛ, which the Arabs have rendered by Akhmîm.

Åḳert, a common name for the abode of the dead.

Bast, more fully Pa-Bast, or Per-Bast, the Bubastis of the Greek writers (Herodotus, II, 59, 137, 156, 166; Strabo, XVII, i, 27), the metropolis of the eighteenth nome of Lower Egypt, and the seat of the worship of Bast, a goddess who was identified with the soul of Isis, *ba en Ast*. The city is mentioned in the Bible under the form פִּי בֶסֶת (Ezekiel xxx, 17), Pi-beseth, which the Copts have preserved in their name for the city, ⲡⲟⲩⲃⲁⲥⲧⲓ; the Arabs call the place Tell Basṭah تل بسطة.

Ḥet-benbent, the name given to many sun-shrines in Egypt and the Sûdân, and also to one of the places in the Other World where the deceased dwelt.

Ḥet-Ptaḥ-ka, the sacred name of the city of Memphis, the metropolis of the first nome of Lower Egypt; it means the "House of the *ka* of Ptaḥ," and was probably in use in the period of the Ist dynasty. Other names for Memphis were, Åneb-ḥetchet, "the city of the white wall"; Men-nefer; and Khā-nefert.

Kam-ur, a name given to the district of the fourth and fifth nomes of Upper Egypt.

Khemenu, , *i.e.*, the city of the eight great cosmic gods, the Hermopolis of the Greek writers (Ἑρμοπολιτικη φυλακή, Strabo, XVII, I, 41), was the metropolis of the fifteenth nome of Upper Egypt. The old Egyptian name for the city is preserved in its Coptic and Arabic names, ϣⲙⲟⲩⲛ and Eshmûnên.

Kher-āḥa, a very ancient city which was situated on the right bank of the Nile, a little to the south of Ånu, near the site of which the "Babylon of Egypt" (ⲃⲁⲃⲩⲗⲱⲛ ⲛ̄ⲧⲉ ⲭⲏⲙⲓ, the Βαβυλών, φρούριον ἐρυμνόν of Strabo, XVII, i, 30) was built.

Manu [hieroglyphs] or [hieroglyphs], is the name given to the region where the sun sets, which was believed to be exactly opposite to the district of Bekha, [hieroglyphs], where he rose in the east; Manu is a synonym of west, just as Bekha is a synonym of east.[1]

Nekhen [hieroglyphs], or [hieroglyphs], the name of the shrine of the goddess Nekhebet, which is supposed to have been near to Nekheb, the capital of the third nome of Upper Egypt and the Eileithyiaspolis of the Greeks.

Neter-khertet, or **Khert Neter,** [hieroglyphs] or [hieroglyphs], a common name for the abode of the dead; it means the "divine subterranean place."

Pe [hieroglyphs], a district of the town of Per-Uatchet, [hieroglyphs], the Buto of the Greeks (Βοῦτος, Strabo, XVII, i, 18), which was situated in the Delta.

Per-Åsår [hieroglyphs], "House of Osiris," the Busiris of the Greek writers. It was situated in the Delta, and was the centre of the cult of Osiris in Lower Egypt.

Punt [hieroglyphs], the tropical district which lay to the south and east of Egypt, and which included, in later times, a part of the Arabian peninsula and the eastern coast of Africa along and south of Somaliland.

Ra-stau [hieroglyphs] or [hieroglyphs], a name given to the passages in the tomb which lead from this to the Other World; originally it designated the cemetery of Ṣaḳḳârah only, and its god was Seker, later Seker-Åsår.

Sa [hieroglyphs], the Saïs of the Greeks (Σάϊς, Strabo, XVII, i, 23), the metropolis of the fifth nome of Lower Egypt, and the seat of the worship of the goddess Neith.

[1] See Brugsch, *Dict. Géog.*, pp. 199, 260; Maspero, *Études de Mythologie*, t. I, p. 332; and *Aeg. Zeitschrift*, 1864, pp. 73–76.

Sekhem , or , the Letopolis of the Greeks, and capital of the Letopolites nome (Strabo, XVII, i, 30); it was the seat of the worship of Ḥeru-ur , "Horus the elder," and one of the most important religious centres in Egypt.

Sekhet-Ȧanru , *i.e.*, "Field of the Reeds," was a name originally given to the islands in the Delta, or to the Oases, where the souls of the dead were supposed to live. Here was the abode of the god Osiris, who bestowed estates in it upon those who had been his followers, and here the beatified dead led a new existence and regaled themselves upon food of every kind, which was given to them in abundance. According to the vignette of the CXth Chapter of the Book of the Dead, the Sekhet-Ȧanru is the third division of the Sekhet-ḥetepu, or "Fields of Peace," which have been compared with the Elysian Fields of the Greeks.

Set Ȧmentet , *i.e.*, "the mountain of the Underworld," a common name of the cemetery, which was usually situated in the mountains or desert on the western bank of the Nile.

Suten-ḥenen , more correctly **Ḥensu,** the metropolis of the twentieth nome of Upper Egypt, called by the Greeks Herakleopolis Magna (Strabo, XVII, i, 35). The Hebrews mention the city Hanes (חָנֵס, Isaiah xxx, 4) as the representative of Upper Egypt, and in Coptic times it was still of considerable size and importance; the Copts and Arabs have preserved the ancient name of the city under the forms ϩⲛⲏⲥ and اهناس, *Ahnas*.

Tanenet , a district sacred to the gods Osiris and Ptaḥ; it was probably situated near Memphis.

Ta-tchesert , *i.e.*, the Holy Land, a common name for the Other World.

Ṭep [hieroglyphs], a district of the town Per-Uatchet [hieroglyphs], the Buto of the Greeks (Strabo, XVII, i, 18), which was situated in the Delta.

Teṭu-t [hieroglyphs], a name given both to the metropolis [1] of the ninth nome and to the metropolis [2] of the sixteenth nome of Lower Egypt.

Ṭuat [hieroglyphs], a common name for the Other World.

FUNERAL CEREMONIES

In illustration of the ceremonies that accompanied the burial of the dead the reader will find extracts from different texts printed in the description of Plate V. To these may be added an extract from the great Liturgy of Funerary Offerings which was in vogue in the Vth and VIth dynasties, and which commemorated the ceremonies that were performed for the god Osiris. It is to be noticed how closely the deceased is identified with Osiris, the type of incorruptibility. Osiris takes upon himself "all that is hateful" in the dead: that is, he accepts the burden of his sins; and the dead is purified by the typical sprinkling of water.

Throughout the ceremony, the Eye of Horus,[3] which is represented by various substances, plays a prominent part, for it is that which gave life to the heart of Osiris, and it revivified the dead also. That portion of the ceremony which was believed to procure the unlocking of the jaws and the opening of the mouth of the deceased, or of the statue which sometimes represented him, was performed after the purification by water and incense had been effected;

[1] *I.e.*, [hieroglyphs], Pa-Åsår, or Per-Åsår, the Busiris of the Greeks.

[2] *I.e.*, [hieroglyphs], Ba-neb-Ṭeṭt, the Mendes of the Greeks.

[3] On the Eyes of Horus, see Lefébure, *Le Mythe Osirien—Les Yeux d'Horus*, Paris, 1874; and Grébaut, *Les deux yeux du Disque Solaire* (*Recueil de Travaux*, t. I, pp. 72, 87, 112–131).

and hereby was he enabled to partake of the meat and drink offerings, whereof the friends and relatives also partook, in order that they might cement and seal their mystic union with the dead and with the god with whom he was identified.

Certain formulae were directed to be repeated four times: a direction which takes us back to the time when the Egyptians first divided the world into four parts, each corresponding to one of the four pillars which held up the sky, that is to say, to one of the four cardinal points, East, South, West, and North, presided over by a Horus-god. The deceased sought to obtain the assistance of each of the Horus-gods, and to have the right to roam about in his district; hence the formula was repeated four times. Originally four animals or four geese were sacrificed, one to each god, but subsequently East and North, and West and South, were paired, and two bulls (or birds) only were sacrificed, one of which was called the Bull of the North,[1] and the other the Bull of the South. The custom of four-fold repetition continued to the Ptolemaïc times and even later. The priest whose official title was *kher ḥeb*, [hieroglyphs], recited the prayers in the Ṭuat Chamber [hieroglyphs] of the tomb, and the *sem* or *setem* priest [hieroglyphs], presented the prescribed offerings.[2]

I. Osiris, everything that is hateful of X[3] hath been carried away for thee;

Here sprinkle water.

that evil which was spoken in his name Thoth hath advanced and carried it to Osiris. I have brought the evil which was spoken in the name of X, and I have placed it in the palm of thy hand.

[1] This subject has been lucidly discussed by Maspero, *Recueil de Travaux*, t. XII, pp. 78, 79.

[2] For the text and translations, see Schiaparelli, *Il Libro dei Funerali*, Rome, 1881–90; Maspero, *Recueil de Travaux*, t. III, pp. 179 ff.; Sethe, *Pyramidentexte*, Vol. I; Budge, *Liturgy of Funerary Offerings*, London, 1909; Dümichen, *Der Grabpalast*, Leipzig, 1884, 1885.

[3] X = the deceased.

Recite four times.

The fluid of life shall not be destroyed in thee, and thou shalt not be destroyed in it.

Let him that advanceth advance with his KA.
Horus advanceth with his KA.
Set advanceth with his KA.
Thoth advanceth with his KA.

Recite four times and burn incense.

Sep advanceth with his KA.
Osiris advanceth with his KA.
Khent-åriti advanceth with his KA.

Thy Ṭeṭ 𓊽 (backbone) shall advance with thy KA.

Hail, X The arm of thy KA is before thee.
Hail, X The arm of thy KA is behind thee.
Hail, X The leg of thy KA is before thee.
Hail, X The leg of thy KA is behind thee.

Osiris, I have given unto thee the Eye of Horus, and thy face is filled therewith, and the perfume of the Eye of Horus is to thee.

This libation is for thee, Osiris, this libation is for thee, Osiris X, coming forth

Here pour out from a vessel water in which two grains of incense have been dissolved.

before thy son, coming forth before Horus. I have come. I have brought unto thee the Eye of Horus, that thy heart may be refreshed thereby. I have brought it unto thee [under] thy sandals, and I have presented unto thee the efflux which cometh forth from thee. There shall be no stoppage to thy heart with it,

Recite four times.

and there shall be a coming forth to thee [of offerings] through the word which is spoken, there shall be a coming forth to thee [of offerings] through the word which is spoken.

II. [Cleansing by] Semmån! [Cleansing by] Semmån!

Open thy mouth, O X,

Here offer five grains of Nekheb incense from the city of Nekheb.

and taste thereof in the halls of the god. Semmȧn is an emission of Horus. Semmȧn is an emission of Set. Semmȧn is the stablisher of the heart of the two Horus gods.

Recite four times.

III. Thou art cleansed with natron, and art like unto the Followers of Horus. Thou art purified with natron, and Horus is purified with natron, thou art purified with natron, and Set is purified with natron.

Here offer five grains of natron of the North from Shetpet.

IV. Thou art purified with natron, and Thoth is purified with natron. Thou art purified with natron, and Sep is purified with natron. Thou art purified with natron and thou art established among them (*i.e.*, the gods). Thy mouth is like the mouth of a sucking calf on the day of its birth.

V. Thou art purified with natron, and Horus is purified with natron. Thou art purified with natron, and Set is purified with natron. Thou art purified with natron,

Here offer one grain of natron.

and Thoth is purified with natron. Thou art purified with natron, and Sep is purified with natron. Thou art purified with natron, and thy Ka is purified with natron.

Thou art purified with natron [**Recite four times**], O thou who art established among thy brethren the gods. Thy head is purified for thee with natron, and thy bones have been thoroughly cleansed for thee, and thou art filled with that which belongeth to thee. Osiris, I have given unto thee the Eye of Horus, and thy face is filled therewith, and the odour thereof [is spread abroad].

VI. Osiris X, thy two jaw-bones which were separated have been established.

Here present the Peseshkef .

VII. Osiris X, the two gods (Horus and Set) have opened for thee thy mouth.

Here present the two iron instruments ⁊⁊ of the South and North.

VIII. Osiris X, the Eye of Horus hath been presented unto thee, and with it the god passeth; I have brought it unto thee, place it in thy mouth.

Here offer cheese of the South and cheese of the North.

IX. Osiris X, the nipple cakes of Osiris are presented unto thee, the nipple of the breast of Horus, thou takest into thy mouth;

Here offer a small vessel of milk.

and the nipple of the breast of thy sister Isis; the emission from thy mother hast thou taken possession of for thy mouth.

Here offer a jug of whey.

X. This libation is for thee, Osiris; this libation is for thee, Osiris X,

Here offer clean cold water of the North.

coming forth before thy son, coming forth before Horus. I have come, and I have brought unto thee the Eye of Horus, that thy heart may be refreshed therewith. I have brought it and [set] it under thy sandals. I have presented unto thee that which floweth from thee. There shall be no stoppage to thy heart whilst it is with thee, [**Recite four times**] and there shall be a coming forth to thee [of offerings] through the word which is spoken.

XI. [That which cometh forth] from the two Eyes of Horus, the White and the Black, thou hast seized, and when [these emissions] are in front of thee they illumine thy face.

Here offer two jugs of wine, one black and one white.

XII. Day hath made an offering unto thee in the sky; the South and the North have caused an offering to be made unto thee. NIGHT hath made an offering unto thee in the sky; the North and the South have caused an offering to be made unto thee. An offering hath been made unto thee, thou seest the offering, thou hearest thereof. There is an offering before thee, and an offering behind thee; there is an offering with thee.

Here offer a cake for the journey.

XIII. Osiris X, the white teeth of Horus are presented unto thee so that they may fill thy mouth.

Here offer five bunches of onions, and recite four times THE KING GIVETH AN OFFERING TO THE KA OF X.

XIV. Osiris X, the Eye of Horus is presented unto thee, the bread which thou eatest.

Here offer the Uṭen cake.

XV. Osiris X, the Eye of Horus is presented unto thee. It hath been snatched from the hand of Set, and thou hast taken possession of it

Here offer a white jug containing two measures of wine.

for thy mouth, and thou hast opened thy mouth therewith.

XVI. Osiris X, thy mouth is opened by that which floweth from thee.

Here offer a black jug containing two measures of wine.

XVII. Osiris X, there hath been presented unto thee that which was pressed out from thee, that which hath come forth from thee.

Here offer a black jug containing one measure of beer.

XVIIA. O Rā, may every kind of adoration which is made to thee in heaven be made to X, and may everything offered to thee be offered to the KA of X, and may every offering made to him be, at the same time, made to thee.

Here offer the holy table of offerings.

XVIII. [Osiris] X, the Eye of Horus is presented unto thee for thee to taste.

Here offer a Ṭept cake.

XIX. The darkness becometh dense, and more dense.

Here offer an Aḥ cake.

XX. [Osiris] X, the Eye of Horus is presented unto thee to embrace thee.

Here offer a breast.

XXI. [Osiris] X, the Eye of Osiris, which was delivered from Set, and was rescued for thee, is presented unto thee, and thou dost open thy mouth with it.

Here offer a white vessel containing one measure of wine.

XXII. [Osiris] X, what was pressed out and came forth from Osiris is presented unto thee.

Here offer a black vessel containing one measure of beer.

XXIII. [Osiris] X, the Eye of Horus, which was rescued for thee, is presented unto thee; there is no iron therein, it belongeth unto thee.

Here offer an iron vessel containing one measure of beer.

XXIV. [Osiris] X, the Eye of Horus is presented unto thee, that thou mayest be filled therewith.

Here offer a vessel containing one measure of beer.

XXV. Osiris X, I have filled thine eye with *metchet* oil.

Recite four times, and present Seth-ḥeb unguent.

XXVI. Osiris X, what hath been pressed out of thy face is presented unto thee.

Here offer Ḥeken unguent.

XXVII. Osiris X, the Eye of Horus is presented unto thee, and Set is weakened thereby.

Here offer a jar of bitumen.

XXVIII. Osiris X, the Eye of Horus is presented unto thee, that it may unite with thee.

Here offer a jar of Neshmen unguent.

XXIX. Osiris X, the Eye of Horus is presented unto thee, that the gods may be brought unto thee.

Here offer a jar of Tuatu unguent.

XXX. O ye Oils, ye Oils, which are on the forehead of Horus [**Say three times**], set yourselves on the forehead of X, and make him to smell sweet through you.

Here offer cedar oil of the finest quality.

Let him become a Khu (Spirit) through you. Give him power over his body, and let him open his eyes; let all the Spirits see him, and let them all hear his name.

XXXI. Behold, Osiris X, the Eye of Horus is brought to thee, it hath been seized on thy behalf that it may be before thee.

Here offer the finest Libyan oil (Theḥenu).

XXXII. Osiris X, with the Eye of Horus thine eyes are painted, that they may be healthy in thy face.

Recite four times, and offer a bag of copper eye-paint, and one bag of stibium eye-paint.

XXXIII. Watch in peace, Tȧat watcheth in peace, she watcheth

Here offer two swathings.

in peace. The Eye of Horus in Ṭep (Buto) is in peace. The Eye of Horus in the temple of Neith [in Saïs] is in peace. Receive thou the milk-white, bleached swathings of the goddess Urā. O swathings, make Egypt to submit to X even as it doth to Horus, make Egypt to fear X even as it feareth Set. Be ye before X as god. Open a way for him at the head of the Spirits, let him stand at their head. Come forward, O Ȧnpu Khenti Amenti, forward, to the Osiris X.

Let him advance, let him advance with his KA, for Horus advanceth with his KA, and Set advanceth with his KA.

Here burn incense.

As Thoth advanceth with his KA, and Sep with his KA, and Osiris with his KA, and Khenti-ȧriti with his KA, so shall thy Ṭeṭ 𓊽 advance with thy KA.

XXXIV. Thoth hath returned bringing the Eye of Horus, and he hath appeared therewith;

Here offer a table of offerings.

he hath given the Eye of Horus, and he is content therewith.

Here one shall enter with the Royal offering.

XXXV. Osiris X, the Eye of Horus is presented unto thee, and he is content.

Here present the Royal offering twice.

XXXVI. Osiris X, the Eye of Horus is presented unto thee, and he is content.

Here present two tables of offerings in the Usekh Hall.

Here say: THOU HAST MADE IT TO BE UNDER THEE.

Here shall the assistants sit down by the royal offerings.

XXXVII. Osiris X, the Eye of Horus is presented unto thee, it approacheth thy mouth.

Here present a cake and a breadcake.

XXXVIII. Osiris X, the Eye of Horus is presented unto thee, protecting . . . . . .

Here offer one Tut cake.

The above extract will give the reader an idea of the general character of the Liturgy of Funerary Offerings. The priest presented a very large number of offerings, one at a time, and as he did so he pronounced a formula in which there was either some obscure allusion to the object which he was about to present, or some play upon words. Besides the offerings already enumerated there were given: a Reth̤u cake, a vessel of Tchesert drink, a vessel of Khenem beer, a cake and a vessel of drink, a Shebu cake, a *sut* joint, two vases of water, cakes of Beṭ incense, a Tun cake, a Shens cake, two Ḥeth cakes, two Neḥrȧ cakes, four Tept cakes, four Peten cakes, four Shes cakes, four Amta cakes, four Khenfu cakes, Ḥebent cakes, white flour, Ȧtet cakes, Pat cakes, a haunch of beef, a breast of an animal, two ribs of beef, roasted flesh, a liver, a Nenshem joint, a Ḥā joint, a forequarter joint, a Re goose, a Therp goose, a Set goose, a Ser goose, a swallow (or dove), a Sȧf cake, two Shȧt cakes, Nepat grain, Mest grain, Khenemes beer or wine, Sekhpet grain, Pekh grain, baskets of figs, Northern wine, White wine, Pelusium wine, Ḥetem wine, Senu (Syene) wine, Ḥebnent wine, Ȧsht fruit, Babat fruit, mulberries, Tenbes cakes, fruits of all kinds, flowers of all kinds, vegetables of all kinds, etc. Certain articles of dress were also given, and we see clearly that the object of the Liturgy was to supply the deceased with everything which was considered to be necessary for his well-being when he was alive. The Pyramid Texts and the *maṣṭabah* tombs prove that this Liturgy was in use about 3800 B.C., and the papyri of the Roman Period supply copies of the text which show that it remained unchanged in form in the second century of our era. Nothing proves more clearly than this fact that one of the fundamentals of the Egyptian Religion was the belief in the efficacy of sacrifices and offerings.

THE PAPYRUS OF ANI, ITS DATE AND CONTENTS

The Papyrus of Ani ( ) was found at Thebes, and was acquired by me for the Trustees of the British Museum in 1888. It measures 78 feet by 1 foot 3 inches, is mounted under glass in thirty-seven sheets, and bears the number 10470. It is the finest and the longest of all the painted papyri inscribed with the Theban Recension of the Book of the Dead. The Papyrus of Nebseni (No. 9900) measures 77 feet 7½ inches by 13 inches; the Papyrus of Nu measures 65 feet 3½ inches by 1 foot 1½ inches (No. 10477); the Papyrus of Hunefer (No. 9901) measures 18 feet 10 inches by 1 foot 3⅝ inches; the Papyrus of Qenna (at Leyden) is about 50 feet long, and the Dublin Papyrus published by Naville (D 9 of his *Todtenbuch*) is 24 feet 9 inches long. The Papyrus of Ani is made of six distinct lengths of papyrus that vary from 5 feet 7 inches to 26 feet 9 inches in length. The material is composed of three layers of papyrus supplied by plants that measured in the stalks about 4½ inches in diameter. The several lengths have been joined together with great neatness, and the repairs and insertions (see Plates XXV, XXVI) have been dexterously executed. When brought to England the papyrus was of a very light colour, similar to that of the Papyrus of Hunefer (No. 9901), but after it was unrolled it became darker, the whites, yellows, blues, and greens lost their intense vividness, and certain parts of the sections contracted.

The papyrus contains a large selection of Chapters of the Theban Recension of the Book of the Dead, nearly all of which are accompanied by Vignettes; text and Vignettes have at top and bottom a border of two colours, red and yellow, or yellow and orange. At the beginning and end of the papyrus spaces of 6 and 11 inches respectively were left blank; these spaces were allowed so that in unrolling the papyrus the opening Vignette might not be damaged, and that in rolling it up the last Vignette might not be damaged. The inscribed portion is to all intents and purposes complete, and the loss of the few characters that were damaged in unrolling (see Plates I, XV, XXIV) does not interrupt the text. More than one scribe seems to have been employed in copying it, but the uniformity of the execution of the Vignettes suggests that they are all the work of one man. Ani, as we know from his papyrus, was a "veritable scribe," that is to say, his title of scribe was not honorary, and it is probable that some of the Chapters were copied by his own hand. The titles of the Chapters, rubrics, catchwords, etc., are written in red, but the text generally is in black. In some instances the artist who painted the Vignettes has occupied so much space that the scribe has been obliged to crowd the text (*e.g.*, in Plate XI), and at times he has been obliged to write it on the border (see Plates XIV, XVII). These facts suggest that the Vignettes were drawn and painted before the text was written.

The different sections of the papyrus were not all originally written for Ani, for in several places his name has been added by a later hand. *e.g.*, in Plates XV, XVI, XVIII, XXII, XXV, XXVIII, and XXXVI. As, however, such additions do not occur in the first section, which measures 16 feet 4 inches in length, it must be concluded that this section was written expressly for him, and that the others were some of those ready-written copies in which blank spaces were left for the insertion of the names of the deceased persons for whom they were purchased. The scribe who filled in Ani's name in those spaces wrote hurriedly, for in Plate XV he left himself no space to write the word "Osiris" in the phrase, "Ani, whose word is truth before Osiris," . In Plate XVII he has written the name twice; in Plate XVIII he has omitted the determinative ; in Plate XX he wrote instead of ; in Plate XXX he wrote twice, probably with a view of filling up the line; in Plate XXXIV the writing of the name is crooked, and the determinative is omitted; and in Plates XII and XXII the scribe has in two places forgotten to write the name altogether. It seems tolerably clear that all the sections of the papyrus were written about the same time. The variations in the depth of the space occupied by the text, and the difference in the colours of the border lines prove that the best scribes did not bind themselves by any very strict rule of uniformity in such matters. The text contains many serious errors. By some extraordinary oversight it includes two copies of the XVIIIth Chapter, one with a most unusual introduction, and the other without any introduction at all. In the one the gods are grouped so as to be near the sections of the text referring to them, and in the other the gods are all seated in one row. A large section of Chapter XVII, one of the most important of the whole Book, has been omitted, and it seems as though the scribe did not notice the omission! The texts relating to the gods of the mummy chamber contain so many mistakes that portions of them are wholly untranslatable. Mistakes in spelling and slips of the pen are very common. Such omissions and mistakes, however, occur in papyri older than that of Ani, for in the Papyrus of Nebseni (Brit. Mus. No. 9900), which was written at Memphis early in the XVIIIth dynasty, of Chapters L, LVI, LXIV, and CLXXX two copies, of Chapters C and CVI three copies, and of Chapter XVII two extracts, are given in different parts of the papyrus.

The Papyrus of Ani is undated, and it is impossible to collect from it any exact data whereby it might be assigned to the reign of any particular king. An examination of the papyri of the Theban Period preserved in the British Museum shows that two distinct classes of Book of the Dead papyri existed in the XVIIIth dynasty. In the first, both text and Vignettes are traced in black outline, as in the Papyrus of Nebseni, the rubrics, catchwords, etc., alone being in red colour; in the second, the text only is in black, the rubric, titles, catchwords, etc., are in red colour, and the Vignettes are beautifully painted in a number of bright colours. To the latter class the Papyrus of Ani belongs, but, if the text and Vignettes be compared with those found in any other early Theban papyri, it will be seen that it occupies an independent position in all respects. Though agreeing in the main with the papyri of the XVIIIth dynasty in respect of textual readings, the Papyrus of Ani has peculiarities of spelling, etc., which are not found in any of them. The handwriting of the first section, at least, suggests the best period of the XVIIIth dynasty; but as the scribe forms some of the hieroglyphs in a way peculiarly his own, the palaeographic evidence on this point is not decisive. That the papyrus belongs to the period that produced such documents as the Papyrus of Neb-qeṭ (ed. Devéria, Paris, 1872), and the Papyrus of Qenna (ed. Leemans, Leyden, 1882), *i.e.*, to some period of the XVIIIth dynasty, is tolerably certain; and it is impossible not to assume that it is older than the Papyrus of Hunefer, which was written during the reign of Seti I. For, though belonging to the same class of highly decorated papyri, the execution of the Vignettes is finer and more careful, and the free, bold forms of the hieroglyphs in the better written sections more closely resemble those of the texts inscribed in stone under the greatest kings of the XVIIIth dynasty. The "Lord of the Two Lands," *i.e.*, the king of Upper and Lower Egypt, mentioned in Plate IV, is probably one of the last kings of the XVIIIth dynasty, and accordingly we may place the period of the Papyrus of Ani between 1450 B.C. and 1400 B.C.

Of the birth and parentage of Ani we know nothing, but it is most probable that his family was undistinguished, and that he owed his high official position, under the king's favour, to his ability and tact. His titles are :—

1. , "veritable royal scribe," *i.e.*, he was a "royal scribe," who really worked at his profession, and not one who enjoyed the honorary rank of "royal scribe," a title which was often bestowed by the king on officials of high birth and rank.

2. , "scribe, reckoner (or, assessor) of the divine offerings of all the gods." By this title it seems that we must understand that Ani was registrar-in-chief of the offerings that were made by the devout to all the gods of Thebes. It is probable that it also fell to his duty to assess the amounts of produce, grain,

cattle, etc., which the various priesthoods of Egypt demanded from wealthy Egyptians as obligatory contributions to the revenues of their gods.

3. , "overseer of the granaries of the Lords of Abydos." The offerings of grain, dhura, wheat, etc., were delivered by their givers to the temple granaries, or probably to a single granary which served as a general storehouse for the grain that was the property of the various gods. This granary was very large, and the management of it must have demanded great knowledge and ability on the part of its manager.

4. , "scribe of the divine offerings of the Lords of Thebes." If the wealth possessed by the temples of Thebes under the XVIIIth dynasty be considered for a moment, it will at once be clear that this office of Ani was one of very great importance, and one demanding not only the highest ability, but the highest integrity on the part of the holder.

Tutu, , the wife of Ani, is called "lady of the house," , and *shemāt en Ȧmen*, , *i.e.*, "singing woman of Ȧmen." The first title shows that Tutu was Ani's chief wife, if he had more than one wife, and the second that she was one of the ladies of good family who were officially attached to the service of Ȧmen-Rā, the king of the gods, at Thebes. She attended in the temple, and was one of the ladies of the choir who sang hymns to Ȧmen and portions of the Liturgy. She is usually represented carrying a sistrum, which she rattled as she sang in the choruses. The wires of the sistrum made a peculiar sound which was believed to be efficacious in driving away fiends from the sanctuary. Thus, though Ani was a lay scribe, his wife was a priestess, and it is probable that he owed some of the offices which he enjoyed to her influence.

The contents of the Papyrus of Ani may be divided into two parts :—

Part I contains : A Hymn to Rā, introductory to the Judgment Scene (Plate I), a Hymn to Osiris, also introductory to the Judgment Scene (Plate II) ; the former has two Vignettes, the first being on Plate I and the second on

Plate II. The second Vignette represents the Sunrise in the physical world, and the resurrection of Osiris and also of the deceased, who is identified with Osiris and is called "the Osiris," in the Other World. This Vignette is commonly known as Chapter XVI, and, as it immediately follows the Hymn to Rā, it shows that the scribe regarded this introductory hymn as a form of Chapter XV. Following the hymns comes the great Judgment Scene, which is supposed to take place in the Hall of Maāti, or the Hall of the Two Truth-goddesses, at the end of which Osiris sits enthroned within his shrine. The weighing of the heart of Ani is depicted in Plate III, and the presentation of Ani to Osiris by Horus, the son of Isis, after he has been declared to be a speaker of the truth by Thoth and the Gods of Ȧnu, on Plate IV. The Judgment Scene in the Papyrus of Ani is more fully represented and better described than in any other papyrus containing the Theban Recension. Usually the Introductory Section opens with a Vignette of Osiris and a short address or hymn to the god, but here the Hymn to Rā precedes everything. This fact suggests that at the close of the XVIIIth dynasty, under the influence of the priests of Ȧmen, the Sun-god began to invade the domains of Osiris, and to assert his sovereignty over Night and Dead-land as well as over Day and the Land of the Living.

Part II contains a long series of Chapters of the Theban Recension of the Book of the Dead, which appear in the following order:—

I, with Vignette, Plates V and VI; XXII, Plate VI; Rubric of LXXII, Plate VI; XVII, with a long series of Vignettes, Plates VII–X; CXLVII, the Seven Ȧrits, with Vignettes, Plates XI and XII; CXLVI, the Ten Pylons, with Vignettes, Plates XI and XII; XVIII, Introductions, with Vignettes, Plate XII; XVIII, with Vignettes, Plates XIII and XIV; XXIII, with Vignette, Plate XV; XXIV, Plate XV; XXVI, with Vignette, Plate XV; XXXB, Plates III and XV; LXI, with Vignette, Plate XV; LIV, with Vignette, Plate XV; XXIX, with Vignette, Plate XV; XXVII, with Vignette, Plates XV and XVI; LVIII, with Vignette, Plate XVI; LIX, with Vignette, Plate XVI; XLIV, with Vignette, Plate XVI; XLV, with Vignette, Plate XVI; XLVI, with Vignette, Plate XVI;

L, with Vignette, Plate XVI; XCIII, with Vignette, Plate XVII; XCIIIA, with Vignette, Plate XVII; XLIII, Plate XVII; LXXXIX, with Vignette, Plate XVII; XCI, with Vignette, Plate XVII; XCII, with Vignette, Plate XVII; LXXIV, with Vignette, Plate XVIII; VIII, with Vignette, Plate XVIII; II, with Vignette, Plate XVIII; IX, with Vignette, Plate XVIII; CXXXII, with Vignette, Plate XVIII; X or XLVIII, with Vignette, Plate XVIII; XV, with three Vignettes, Plates XVIII–XXI; CXXXIII, with two Vignettes, Plates XXI and XXII; CXXXIV, with Vignette, Plate XXII; Vignette of the Ladder, Plate XXII; XVIII *bis*, with Vignettes, Plates XXIII and XXIV; CXXIV, with Vignette, Plate XXIV; LXXXVI, with Vignette, Plate XXV; LXXVII, with Vignette, Plate XXV; LXXVIII, with Vignette, Plates XXV and XXVI; LXXXVII, with Vignette, Plate XXVII; LXXXVIII, with Vignette, Plate XXVII; LXXXII, with Vignette, Plate XXVII; LXXXV, with Vignette, Plate XXVII; LXXXIII, with Vignette, Plate XXVII; LXXXIV, with Vignette, Plate XXVIII; LXXXIA, with Vignette, Plate XXVIII; LXXX, with Vignette, Plate XXVIII; CLXXV, with Vignette, Plate XXIX; CXXV, Introduction, with two Vignettes, Plates XXIX and XXX; CXXV, The Negative Confession, with four Vignettes, Plates XXXI and XXXII; XLII, with Vignette, Plate XXXII: Rubric to XLII or CXXV, with Vignette, Plate XXXII; CLV, with Vignette, Plate XXXIII; CLVI, with Vignette, Plate XXXIII; XXIXB, with Vignette, Plate XXXIII; CLXVI, with Vignette, Plate XXXIII; CLI, with a complete series of Vignettes, Plates XXXIII and XXXIV; CX, portions only, with Vignettes, Plates XXXIV and XXXV; CXLVIII, with Vignettes, Plates XXXV and XXXVI; CLXXXV, with Vignette, Plate XXXVI; CLXXXVI, with Vignette, Plate XXXVII. The titles of these Chapters, arranged according to the numeration introduced by Lepsius in his *Todtenbuch*, are as follows:—

CHAPTER I. "Here begin the Chapters of Coming "Forth by Day, and of the songs of praise and glorifying, "and of coming forth from and of going into the glorious "Khert-Neter in the Beautiful Åmenti. It shall be recited "on the day of the burial; going in after coming forth."

See Plates V and VI. The papyri belonging to the early part of the XVIIIth dynasty call this Chapter "The "Chapter of entering into the presence of the Tchatchau "Chiefs of Osiris," . The large numbers of the men attending the bier and of the weeping women are peculiar to the Ani Papyrus.

Chapter II. "The Chapter of Coming Forth by Day and of living after death." See Plate XVIII.

Chapter VI. In the Papyrus of Ani, this Chapter is included in Chapter CLI. See Plate XXXII. In the Papyrus of Nebseni (Brit. Mus. No. 9900) the Chapter stands by itself, and is entitled, "The Chapter of making the Ushabti figure to perform work for a man in Khert-Neter," .

Chapter VIII. "The Chapter of making a way through Åmenti, and of coming forth by day." See Plate XVIII. This composition is sometimes incorporated with another Chapter.

Chapter IX. "The Chapter of Coming Forth by Day, having passed through the Åmḥet chamber." See Plate XVIII. The Vignette in the Papyrus of Ani is similar to that which stands at the head of Chapters VIII and IX in other papyri of this period.

Chapter X, or Chapter XLVIII. "Another Chapter "to be said by a man who cometh forth by day against his "enemies in Khert-Neter." See Plate XVIII.

Chapter XV. 1. "A Hymn of Praise to Rā when he riseth in the eastern sky." See Plate I. This version of the Chapter is peculiar to the Papyrus of Ani.

Chapter XV. 2. "A Hymn of Praise to Osiris Un-Nefer, the great god who dwelleth in Abydos." See Plate II. Osiris is in this hymn regarded as one of the two forms of Rā, and is therefore included in this Chapter.

Chapter XV. 3. "A Hymn of Praise to Rā when he "riseth in the eastern sky, and when he setteth in the land "of life." See Plates XVIII–XXI.

Chapter XVI. Owing to the numbering of the Chapters by Lepsius this consists of a Vignette only, which, as has been already said, belongs to Chapter XV, or to that part of it which refers to the rising sun. It may be noted in passing that the Papyrus of Ani, like many ancient papyri of the Book of the Dead, contains no Vignette of the Sunset. See Plate II.

CHAPTER XVII. "Here begin the praises and "glorifyings of coming out from and of going into the "glorious Khert-Neter in the Beautiful Ȧmenti, of coming "forth by day in all the transformations which it may please "the deceased to assume, of playing at draughts, and of "sitting in the Seṭ chamber, and of coming forth as a "living heart-soul." See Plates VII–X. This is one of the oldest and most important Chapters of the Theban Recension, and in the form here given contains the dogmas about God and the creation of the sun, moon, stars, and earth, and about Osiris, and the gods and goddesses who were associated with him, as formulated by the priesthood of Rā at Heliopolis. The variant readings may represent the views of the priesthood of Thebes. A large section of the text is, quite unaccountably, omitted by the scribe, and the missing lines have been supplied from the Papyrus of Nebseni.

CHAPTER XVIII. This is without a title in the Papyrus of Ani, a fact which suggests that the Chapter was regarded by the Theban scribes as the continuation of Chapter XVII. A few papyri give it a title, viz., "The Chapter of entering into the presence of the Tchatchau Chiefs." The Papyrus of Ani contains two copies of this Chapter. In the first the gods of the towns are grouped in a series of Vignettes, each of which stands near the Section which it illustrates. This copy is preceded by an Introduction, which is peculiar to the Papyrus of Ani. The Ȧnmutef and Samerefpriests are seen introducing Ani to the gods, with appropriate speeches, and the addresses of Ani are given. See Plates XII–XIV. In the second copy the gods are not separated into groups, but are arranged in a row above the text; a few of the gods mentioned in the text are omitted in this copy. See Plates XXIII and XXIV.

CHAPTER XXII. "The Chapter of giving a mouth to the Osiris Ani, the scribe and registrary of all the gods." See Plate VI. This Chapter is without Vignette in the Papyrus of Ani, and it is remarkable that it follows Chapter I. Perhaps the concluding passage of Chapter I, which deals with offerings, suggested that the text that would provide

Ani with a mouth to eat the same should follow immediately.

Chapter XXIII. "The Chapter of opening the mouth of the Osiris, the scribe Ani"; this is a kind of supplement to the preceding Chapter. See Plate XV.

Chapter XXV. "The Chapter of bringing words of power unto the Osiris Ani in Khert-Neter." See Plate XV. As in other ancient Theban papyri this Chapter is without Vignette in the Papyrus of Ani.

Chapter XXVI. "The Chapter of giving a heart unto the Osiris Ani in Khert-Neter." See Plate XV. The Vignette to this Chapter in the Papyrus of Ani is probably unique.

Chapter XXVII. "The Chapter of not letting the heart of a man be snatched away from him in Khert-Neter." See Plate XV. The Vignette to this Chapter in the Papyrus of Ani is uncommon.

Chapter XXIX. "The Chapter of not letting the heart of a man be snatched away from him in Khert-Neter." See Plate XV. No other copy of this Chapter is at present known.

Chapter XXIXb. "The Chapter of a heart of carnelian." See Plate XXXIII.

Chapter XXXb. "The Chapter of not letting the heart of a man be driven away from him in Khert-Neter." See Plate XV. An imperfect duplicate copy is also given in the Judgment Scene. See Plate III.

Chapter XLII. Only a portion of the Chapter is given, and that in tabular form, and without title. See Plate XXXII. In the older papyri the title of the Chapter is "The Chapter of repulsing slaughter in Ḥensu" (the Herakleopolis of the Greeks).

Chapter XLIII. "The Chapter of not letting the head of a man be cut off from his body in Khert-Neter." See Plate XVII. As in other Theban papyri this Chapter is without Vignette in the Papyrus of Ani.

Chapter XLIV. "The Chapter of not dying a second time in Khert-Neter." See Plate XVI. Chapter CLXXV has the same title. The Vignette is peculiar to the Papyrus of Ani.

CHAPTER XLV. "The Chapter of not suffering corruption in Khert-Neter." See Plate XVI. Among Theban papyri the Vignette is peculiar to the Papyrus of Ani.

CHAPTER XLVI. "The Chapter of not perishing, and of becoming alive in Khert-Neter." See Plate XVI. Among Theban papyri the Vignette is peculiar to the Papyrus of Ani.

CHAPTER XLVIII. "Another Chapter of one who cometh forth by day against his foes in Khert-Neter." See Plate XVIII. Among Theban papyri the Vignette is peculiar to the Papyrus of Ani. The text of this Chapter agrees rather with the second version in the Papyrus of Nebseni than with that of Brit. Mus. No. 9964. As the Papyrus of Ani is of Theban origin this was to be expected.

CHAPTER LIV. "The Chapter of providing air in Khert-Neter." See Plate XV. Another copy of this Chapter published by Naville (*op. cit.*, *Einleitung*, p. 134) is without Vignette.

CHAPTER LVIII. "The Chapter of breathing the air, and of having power over the water in Khert-Neter." See Plate XVI. Copies of this Chapter are very rare.

CHAPTER LIX. "The Chapter of breathing the air, and of having power over the water in Khert-Neter." See Plate XVI. Copies of this Chapter are very rare.

CHAPTER LXI. "The Chapter of not letting the soul of a man be taken away from him in Khert-Neter." See Plate XV. The Vignette is similar to that found in the Papyrus of Sutimes.

CHAPTER LXXII—Rubric. See Plate VI.

CHAPTER LXXIV. "The Chapter of walking with the legs and of coming forth upon the earth." See Plate XVIII.

CHAPTER LXXVII. "The Chapter of making the transformation into a golden hawk." See Plate XXV.

CHAPTER LXXVIII. "The Chapter of making the transformation into the hawk that is divine." See Plates XXV and XXVI.

CHAPTER LXXX. "The Chapter of making the trans-"formation into the god who produceth light to illumine "the darkness." See Plate XXVIII.

Chapter LXXXIa. "The Chapter of making the transformation into the lotus (or lily)." See Plate XXVIII. The pool of water in the Vignette is uncommon.

Chapter LXXXII. "The Chapter of making the transformation into the god Ptaḥ." See Plate XXVII. As in other papyri of the same period this Chapter has a Vignette.

Chapter LXXXIII. "The Chapter of making the transformation into the Benu bird (phoenix?)." See Plate XXVII. This Chapter lacks the addition that is found in the Papyrus of Sutimes; several other papyri also lack the addition.

Chapter LXXXIV. "The Chapter of making the transformation into a heron." See Plate XXVI.

Chapter LXXXV. "The Chapter of making the transformation into the soul of Temu." See Plate XXVII. The Vignette of this Chapter is similar to that of the Papyrus of Tura, surnamed Nefer-uben-f, of the XVIIIth dynasty.

Chapter LXXXVI. "The Chapter of making the transformation into the swallow." See Plate XXV.

Chapter LXXXVII. "The Chapter of making the "transformation into the serpent Sa-ta (*i.e.*, Son of the "Earth)." See Plate XXVII.

Chapter LXXXVIII. "The Chapter of making the transformation into a crocodile." See Plate XXVII.

Chapter LXXXIX. "The Chapter of causing the soul to be united to its body in Khert-Neter." See Plate XVII. The two standards for censers, which stand one at the head and one at the foot of the bier, are peculiar to the Papyrus of Ani.

Chapter XCI. "The Chapter of not letting the soul of a man be kept captive in Khert-Neter." See Plate XVII.

Chapter XCII. "The Chapter of opening the tomb "to the soul and the shadow, of coming forth by day, and "of getting power over the legs." See Plate XVII. The Vignette of this Chapter is unusual and of great interest, for in it Ani's soul accompanies his shadow.

Chapter XCIII. "The Chapter of not letting a man travel to the East in Khert-Neter." See Plate XVII. The arrangement of the Vignette of this Chapter is peculiar to the Papyrus of Ani.

Chapter XCIIIa. "Another Chapter." See Plate XVII.

Chapter CX. "Here begin the Chapters of the "Sekhet-Ḥetepet, and the Chapters of Coming Forth by "Day, and of going into and coming forth from Khert-"Neter, and of arriving in the Sekhet-Åaru, and of being "in peace in the great city wherein are fresh breezes." See Plate XXXIV. Many of the details of the Vignette are peculiar to the Papyrus of Ani, and the text of the Chapter given only contains a few of its opening lines.

Chapter CXXIV. "The Chapter of going into the presence of the Tchatchau Chiefs of Osiris." See Plate XXIV. One god is wanting in the Vignette.

Chapter CXXV, Part i. "The Chapter of entering into the Hall of Maāti; a Hymn to Osiris." See Plate XXX. The text of this part as found in the Papyrus of Ani is not met with elsewhere.

Chapter CXXV, Part ii. The "Negative Confession" [without title]. The Vignette possesses four sub-Vignettes, which are peculiar to the Papyrus of Ani. See Plate XXXI.

Chapter CXXV. [Omitted in the Papyrus of Ani.]

Chapter CXXXII. "The Chapter of making a man to return to see again upon the earth." See Plate XVIII.

Chapter CXXXIII. ["A Chapter] to be said on the [first] day of the moon." See Plate XXI.

Chapter CXXXIII—Rubric. See Plate XXII.

Chapter CXXXIV. "A Hymn of praise to Rā on the [first] day of the month wherein he saileth in the boat." See Plate XXII.

Chapter CXLVI. "The Chapter of the Pylons in the House of Osiris that is in Sekhet-Åaru." See Plates XI and XII.

Chapter CXLVII. ["A Chapter which is to be said when Ani cometh to the Ārits."] See Plates XI and XII.

Chapter CXLVIII. ["The Chapter of providing Ani with food." Without title in the Papyrus of Ani.]

Chapter CLI. A series of texts containing the speeches which are made by the gods, goddesses, and amulet-spirits who protect the mummy of Ani on its bier and in the mummy chamber. See Plates XXXIII and XXXIV. Some of these texts are so corrupt as to be in places unintelligible. Many of the details of the Vignettes are incorrect, and the artist appears not to have understood the general plan of the Vignette which he copied.

CHAPTER CLV. "The Chapter of a Ṭeṭ of gold." See Plate XXXIII.

CHAPTER CLVI. "The Chapter of a Tet of carnelian." See Plate XXXIII.

CHAPTER CLXVI. "The Chapter of the headrest which is to be placed under the head of Ani." See Plate XXXIII.

CHAPTER CLXXV. "The Chapter of not dying a second time." See Plate XXIX. This Chapter is incomplete, and breaks off in the middle of a sentence. It is, however, most valuable, for only one other copy of it is known. This second copy is found in a papyrus at Leyden, but, as the beginnings and ends of a large number of lines are wanting, it is impossible to make a connected translation from it.

CHAPTER CLXXXV. "A Hymn of Praise to Osiris Khenti Åmenti Un-Nefer, the dweller in Åbṭu." See Plate XXXVI.

CHAPTER CLXXXVI. [A Hymn of Praise to Hathor in her character of goddess of the Beautiful Åmenti.] See Plate XXXVII.

THE PAPYRUS OF ANI

DESCRIPTION OF THE PLATES

PLATE I

Vignette: The scribe Ani [hieroglyphs], standing with his hands raised in adoration before a table of offerings consisting of haunches of beef [hieroglyph], loaves of bread and cakes [hieroglyph], [hieroglyph], [hieroglyph], [hieroglyph], [hieroglyph], [hieroglyph], vases of wine [hieroglyph], oil [hieroglyph], fruits, vegetables, lilies [hieroglyph], [hieroglyph], and other flowers. He wears a close-fitting tunic covered with a white and saffron-coloured garment, which reaches to his ankles; from the shoulders hang long fringes. On his head is a wig that reaches his shoulders, about his neck hangs a necklace, and he wears bracelets and armlets. He stands barefooted in the presence of his god, and he is supposed to be in a state of ceremonial purity. Behind him stands his wife, "The Osiris, the lady of the house, the singing woman of Åmen," [hieroglyphs], who was called Tutu [hieroglyphs]. (For the name see Plate XIX.) This description of Tutu shows that she was probably dead when the papyrus was written, and her title "lady of the house" indicates that she was either Ani's sole wife, or that she was the chief of his wives. Tutu wears a long plain linen garment that reaches to her feet, and her long, wavy black hair flows down from her head over her shoulders. A cluster of lilies, or lotus, lies above her hair, with their blossoms projecting over her forehead. Above is a small object, made probably of reeds or light wood, which contains a ball of scented unguent; this melted by degrees and ran down over the head and shoulders, diffusing a sweet odour, and affording Tutu pleasure. She wears bracelets and armlets. In her right hand she grasps a bunch of flowers and a sistrum, and in her left are a vine-branch and a *menȧt*. The *menȧt* was an object that was sometimes offered to the gods with the sistrum. It was presented to guests at a feast by their host, and was regularly carried by priestesses at religious festivals. It was sometimes hung round the neck, and sometimes carried in the left hand. It was believed to convey to the holder virility and strength, and was originally an emblem of sexual pleasure. See the paper by Lefébure, "Le Menȧt, et le Nom de l'eunuque," in *Proc. Soc. Bibl. Arch.*, 1891, pp. 333–349. Many very fine examples of the *menȧt* may be seen in the British Museum, *e.g.*, Nos. 17166, 13950, 8172, 8173, 20607, 18109, etc. Tutu carries the sistrum and *menȧt* as symbols of her position at Thebes as "singing woman" of Ȧmen-Rā, the King of the Gods. She shook the sistrum during the services in the sanctuary, and the rattling noise made by the wires drove away the evil spirits who wished to obstruct the service of the god. She carried the *menȧt* as a symbol of her allegiance to Ȧmen-Rā, the god of virility, generation, and conception.

Fig. 1.

Fig. 2.

Text: A version of Chapter XV. In the older papyri the opening section is always a hymn to Osiris, the King and Judge of the dead, but at the close of the

Fig. 3.

XVIIIth dynasty, when the power of Rā, or Åmen-Rā, was paramount at Thebes, a hymn to Rā was given the place of honour in hieroglyphic papyri, which always begin at the left-hand end of the rolls. The subject of the hymn is the glory of Rā, who is identified with Kheperȧ, Tatun, and other great cosmic gods. The defeat of Āapep, the great adversary of Rā, is commemorated in boastful terms, and the overthrow of all the fiends of the Evil One is frequently referred to. The commonest form of the monster Āapep is a crocodile (Fig. 1), which crouched by the path of the sun at dawn ready to swallow up the solar disk. Next we see him in the form of a huge speckled python (Fig. 2), then as an ordinary serpent (Fig. 3), and finally as a huge serpent of many folds biting the neck of the Ass, which represents the Sun-god (Fig. 4).

Fig. 4.

PLATE II

Vignette: A scene representing the sunrise. Here we see the disk of the sun ⊙, resting on the top of the loop of the symbol of "life" ☥, and supported by two human arms and hands. The *ānkh* ☥, rests upon the top of the Ṭeṭ 𓊽, which rests upon a reed mat. The Ṭeṭ represents Osiris, who was, in one aspect, the dead sun of yesterday, and from it proceeds the power of "life," which sends forth the solar disk on its course. On the upper part of the Ṭeṭ are the two *utchats* 𓂀𓄤𓂀, or Eyes of the Sun and Moon, with 𓄤, the symbol of "good," between them. On each side of the solar disk are three apes, with their paws raised in adoration of the great luminary. These sing to the sun in the form of the Spirits of the Dawn whilst he is rising, but as soon as he has risen they turn into apes. On the left of the Ṭeṭ is the goddess Isis [hieroglyphs], and on the right the goddess Nebt-ḥet, or Nephthys; each goddess kneels on the emblem of "gold," and each has her hands raised in adoration of the Sun-god. Over all is stretched the vault of the sky [hieroglyph]. This Vignette belongs, properly speaking, to the Hymn to Rā on Plate I, which Ani was intended to say as the sun rose.

Fig. 1 is the Vignette of the Sunrise as it is found in the Papyrus of Hunefer. Here the sun appears in the well-known form of a hawk, with the solar disk encircled by a serpent upon his head. The apes that adore him are seven in number, and are called "*Ȧmhetet-Rā*" [hieroglyphs]. Below the hawk stands the Ṭeṭ of Osiris, which is here provided with a pair of human arms and hands holding the symbols of sovereignty, a crook [hieroglyph], and a flail [hieroglyph]. On each side of the Ṭeṭ stands a goddess, that on the left of it being Isis, and that on the right Nephthys. The legends read: "I am thy sister Isis," "I am thy sister Nephthys."

FIG. 1.

Text: A Hymn to Osiris. This is a short composition that merely enumerates the titles of Osiris, and refers to him in his character of the everlasting ruler of heaven and giver of life to men. The **Vignette** is practically a repetition of that on Plate I.

PLATE III

Vignette: Scene of the Weighing of the Heart of the deceased in the Judgment Hall of Osiris. Ani and his wife Tutu enter the Hall of Maāti, wherein the heart [hieroglyph], emblematic of the conscience, is to be weighed in the Balance against the ostrich feather, emblematic of "law," "truth," etc. Above, twelve gods, each holding a sceptre [hieroglyph], are seated upon thrones before a table of offerings of fruit, flowers, etc. Their names are :—

1. [hieroglyphs] ḤERU-KHUTI (Harmakhis), the great god in his boat.
2. [hieroglyphs] TEMU, the father of the gods of Ȧnu.
3. [hieroglyphs] SHU, god of the light and air.
4. [hieroglyphs] TEFNUT, the lady of heaven.
5. [hieroglyphs] ḲEB, the Earth-god.
6. [hieroglyphs] NUT, the Sky-goddess.
7. [hieroglyphs] ȦST (Isis), wife and sister of Osiris.
8. [hieroglyphs] NEBT-ḤET, Nephthys, sister of Osiris.
9. [hieroglyphs] HORUS, the great god, son of Osiris.
10. [hieroglyphs] ḤET-ḤERT (Hathor), lady of Ȧmentet.
11. [hieroglyphs] ḤU, god of taste.
12. [hieroglyphs] SA, god of feeling.

The Balance is set in the middle of the Hall. Upon the beam sits the dog-headed ape [hieroglyph], the associate of Thoth, the "Lord of Khemenu, the just judge," [hieroglyphs]. The god Anubis, jackal-headed, examines the "tongue" or pointer of the Balance, the suspending bracket of which is in the form of an ostrich feather, emblematic of truth. On the left of the Balance, facing Anubis, stands the god SHAI [hieroglyphs], who represents Ani's guardian angel, or his luck, fate, or destiny, and above it, resting on a small sepulchral building, is a rectangular object, like a slab or box, with a human head. This is probably the box that held Ani's navel string,[1] [hieroglyphs]. Behind these stand the goddesses MESKHENET [hieroglyphs], and Rennt [hieroglyphs], the former presided over the birth of Ani, and the latter acted as his wet-nurse, or foster mother. Behind the [hieroglyphs] is the soul of Ani, in the form of a human-headed bird standing on a sepulchral building called "Serekh" [hieroglyphs]. On the right of the Balance, behind Anubis, stands Thoth, the self-created, self-existent personification of the mind of God, and the inventor of writing, letters, mathematics, astronomy, and the arts. He stands here as the "Scribe of the gods," and holds a reed pen, and a palette containing black and red inks, with which to record the result of the weighing of the heart. Behind Thoth stands the monster "ĀMĀM" [hieroglyphs], *i.e.*, the "Devourer," or as it is sometimes called, "ĀMMIT," [hieroglyphs], *i.e.*, the "Eater of the dead." Some contemporary papyri afford very interesting variants of this scene. Thus in Fig. 1 the Judgment takes place in a Hall, in the presence of the Maāti-goddesses only, and the heart is weighed against a figure of the goddess of Truth herself. The Ape of Thoth sits by the side of the Balance, and not on the pillar of it. In Fig. 2 the actual weighing is performed by the goddess Maāt, whilst

FIG. 1.

FIG. 2.

[1] The preservation of the navel string in Egypt and Uganda is described in my *Osiris and the Egyptian Resurrection*, Vol. II, p. 95.

the monster Āmām sits at her feet. The Ape of Thoth sits on the left, and wears on his head the disk of the moon and lunar horns. The head of the pillar of the Balance is in the form of that of Anubis. In Fig. 3 the Ape of Thoth is seated on the pillar of the Balance, and it is Horus who takes the place of Anubis, and holds the tongue of the Balance. In the lower register of this Vignette we see Anubis leading the deceased into the presence of Osiris, and presenting the heart of the deceased to the god. The two Apes seated by Osiris represent Thoth and Åsṭes.

FIG. 3.

The Eater of the Dead is also called the "Devourer of Åmenta." It is a female monster with the fore-part of a crocodile, the hind-quarters of a hippopotamus, and the body of a lion . It usually sits near the Balance, but in one Vignette (Fig. 4) it is seen crouching by the Lake of Fire in the Other World.

When Ani enters the Hall of Maāti to witness the weighing of his heart, he recites an address to his heart and a prayer, which together form Chapter XXXB of the Book of the Dead. He prays that no false witness may be borne against him, and that no evidence may be produced of a hostile character. He prays that the Tchatchau , or Great Chiefs of Osiris, may not oppose him, and that the Shenit Chiefs of the court of Osiris may not blacken his character, or, as the text says, "make his name to stink" in the nostrils of the god Osiris. He prays also that no lies may be told about him, and that his heart may

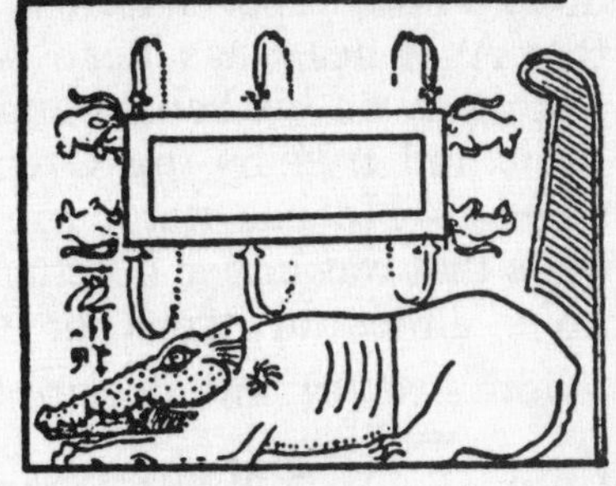

FIG. 4.

not be separated from him. This pathetic prayer is one of the oldest parts of the Book of the Dead, and a tradition preserved in the Rubric of Chapter LXIV, as found in the Papyrus of Nu, asserts that it is as old as the reign of Menkaurā, a king of the IVth dynasty, who flourished about 3700 B.C. It was used regularly down to the end of the Ptolemaïc Period, *i.e.*, to the time of the reign of Cleopatra, about 30 B.C., and so we see that the prayer was current among all classes of Egyptians for at least 3500 years. It must be one of the oldest prayers in the world.

The heart, having been placed in one of the pans of the Balance, is weighed against the ostrich feather, emblematic of Truth. Ani's guardian angel (Shai), and his Heart-soul (Ba), and his navel string are all present ready to bear their testimony on behalf of their lord; and the goddess who acted as midwife to his mother when he was born, and the goddess who presided over his nursing, are prepared to testify to his integrity. Anubis examines the pointer of the Balance, and the Ape of Thoth reports to Thoth that the weighing has been carried out fairly and impartially. From the Vignette we see that the beam of the Balance is exactly horizontal, and that the heart and the feather of Maāt exactly counterbalance each other; in other words, the heart is neither too light nor too heavy, and thus the demands of the Law of Osiris are satisfied. This being done Thoth reports formally to the Company of the Gods that Ani's heart has been weighed, that his soul has borne testimony on his behalf, and that his heart has been found right and true by the Great Balance. Therefore Ani is sinless. He has not purloined any of the property of the gods that was under his charge officially, and he has harmed none either by word or deed. The gods then accept Thoth's report, and declare that Ani is a man true and right, and they declare that he has neither sinned against them nor done harm to them in any way. They next order that he shall not be given over to the Eater of the dead, and that he shall be endowed with an estate in Sekhet-ḥetepet, with an adequate supply of offerings, and with the right to enter into the presence of Osiris. The texts that supply these facts make it clear that the fundamental demands of the Law from a man were that he should: 1. Speak the truth. 2. Do no harm to any man by word or deed. 3. Observe strict honesty in dealing with the property of others, whether it belonged to the gods or to men. 4. Commit no sin against the gods, and do nothing to belittle their dignity or destroy sacrosanct property. From many other texts, and from inscriptions of all periods, it is clear that what Osiris abominated above all other things were lying, prevarication, deceit, and insincerity. To him the speaker of crooked words must necessarily be a doer of crooked deeds, and the proof of this fact is the words *maāt kheru*, "whose word is truth," which it was the proud hope of every Egyptian to have applied to him by Thoth, by the gods, and by Osiris himself, the God of Truth. These words are added immediately after the name of the deceased on papyri, stelae, and other sepulchral monuments, and they mean nothing more nor less than that the professions of right-dealing and truth-speaking made by the deceased have been tested by the officers of the Judgment Hall of Osiris, and that he has been found to be one whose word is truth, that is to say, a truth-speaker. See the remarks made in the Chapter on the Legend of Osiris in the Introduction.

PLATE IV

Vignette: In accordance with the decree of the gods, Ani, whom they have found right and true, is brought into the presence of Osiris. On the left the hawk-headed god Horus, the son of Isis, wearing the Double Crown of the South and the North, takes Ani by the hand and leads him forward towards "Osiris, the Lord of Eternity," , who is enthroned on the right within a shrine in the form of a funeral chest. The god wears the *Atef* crown with plumes; a *menāt* (see above p. 232) hangs from the back of his neck; and he holds in his hands the crook , the sceptre , and the flail , emblems of sovereignty and dominion. His body is either painted with ochres of various colours, or is tattooed. On the side of his throne are painted the doors of a tomb, which proves that he is sitting upon a sepulchral chest or coffer that is intended to represent a tomb. I have shown elsewhere[1] that this throne probably contained the genitals, the navel string, and perhaps the lower jawbone of the god. Behind Osiris stand Nephthys on his right hand and Isis on his left. Facing him and standing on a lotus flower are the Four Sons of Horus, who were identified with the gods of the cardinal points. The first, Ḳestȧ (Mestȧ), has the head of a man; the second, Ḥāpi, the head of an ape; the third, Ṭuamutef, the head of a jackal; and the fourth, Qebḥsenuf, the head of a hawk. Suspended near the lotus is the hide of an animal from which the head has been cut off; in the Papyrus of Ani the hide is that of a pied cow, or bull, but in some papyri, *e.g.*, the Greenfield Papyrus, the animal is clearly of the lynx class. In the Papyrus of Ani the hide is that

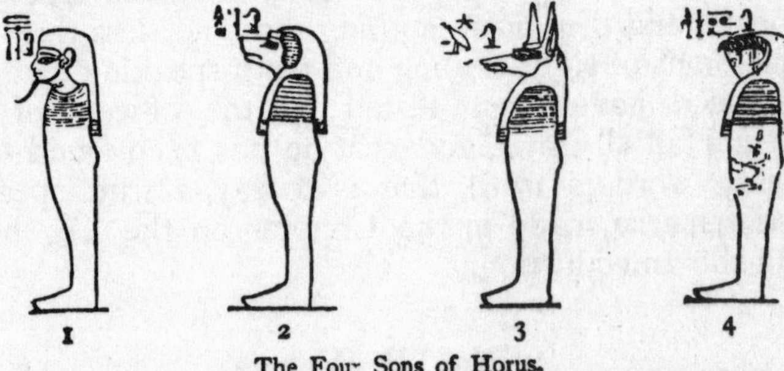

The Four Sons of Horus.

of the bull slaughtered during the solemn ceremonies that were performed when Osiris was laid in his tomb. The slaughter of this bull symbolized the slaughter of Set, and its skin the skin of Set. Tradition declared that when Isis and Horus had reunited the members of the body of Osiris that Set had scattered, and wished to revivify the reconstituted body, they wrapped it up in the skin of the cow or bull which had been slain for the funeral sacrifice. This skin thus symbolized the human placenta, and when Osiris was enveloped in it he received "new life," and his exit therefore was regarded as his "new birth," *i.e.*, "re-birth." The skin was called "Meskhent" , or , *i.e.*, "birthplace," but later the name was given to the tomb in general, and even to the whole of

[1] *Osiris and the Egyptian Resurrection*, Vol. II, pp. 93 ff.

a tomb region, or necropolis.[1] The roof of the shrine is supported by pillars with lotus capitals, and is surmounted by a figure of Horus-Sepṭ, or Horus-Seker, and rows of uraei.

In the centre Ani kneels before the god upon a reed mat, raising his right hand in adoration, and holding in his left the *kherp* sceptre, emblematic of his high official position upon earth. He wears a wig, which appears to be whitened, but the whiteness is probably intended to represent the shining grease flowing from the conical object on the top of his wig. This object has already been described (see p. 231). Round his neck is a deep collar of precious stones. Near him stands a table of offerings, of meat, fruit, flowers, etc., and in the compartments above are a number of vessels for wine, beer, oil, unguents, etc., together with bread, cakes, geese, wreaths, and single flowers.

In some papyri the shrine of Osiris is in the form of a pylon, and it usually rests upon a pedestal made in the form of, *i.e.*, the object which symbolizes Truth (*maāt*), or upon a reed mat. In a very interesting Vignette in the Papyrus of Hunefer (see Fig. 1) the throne of the god is set either upon or by the side of a lake of water, from which springs a lotus flower bearing upon it the Four Sons of Horus. In the papyri of the XXth and XXIst dynasties the god Osiris wears a different kind of crown, and instead of the *Atef* crown, we see on his head that of Ptaḥ-Seker-Āsȧr, a triune god of the resurrection.

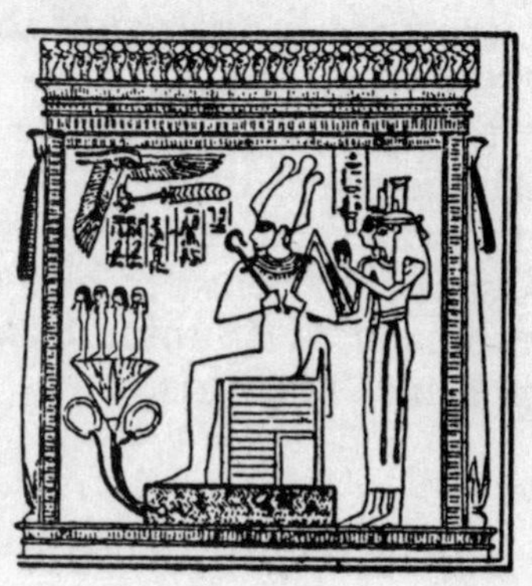

FIG. 1.

On the left of the Plate is the address which Horus, the son of Isis, makes to Osiris when he presents Ani to his father. He declares to Osiris that the weighing of the heart of Ani, which the gods ordered Thoth to do, has taken

[1] See Moret, *Mystères Égyptiens*, p. 29; Junker, *Die Stundenwachen*, pp. 51 ff.

place, and that the heart has been found to be "right"; further, it has been pronounced that Ani has not committed sin against any god or any goddess. Therefore Horus entreats Osiris to grant cakes and ale to Ani, to admit him into his presence, and to include him among those deified human beings who are known as the "Followers of Horus." On the right of the Plate we see Ani kneeling as he addresses Osiris and says: "O Lord of Åmentet, I am in thy presence. "There is no sin in me. I have not lied wittingly. I have "not done aught with a false heart." From this we see that the only merit which Ani claimed before Osiris was that he had neither spoken lies, nor acted lies. To him, and to Osiris also, to tell the truth and to act honestly was the utmost that a man could do to prepare himself for a life in the Kingdom of Osiris. Therefore Ani continues his prayer and says: "Grant thou that I may be like unto those "favoured ones who are round about thee, I, the Osiris, "the greatly praised of the Beautiful God,[1] and beloved of "the Lord of the Two Lands.[2] I, the real royal scribe, "loving him, Ani, whose word is truth before Osiris." It will be noted that Ani does not ask for sepulchral offerings, or for an estate in the Kingdom of Osiris; all he asks is that Osiris will consider him worthy to be introduced into the company of truthful Spirit-souls who live always in the presence of Osiris.

PLATE V

Vignettes: The funeral procession to the tomb: running the whole length of Plates V and VI. In the centre of Plate V the mummy of Ani is seen lying in a funerary coffer or shrine mounted on a boat provided with runners, which is drawn by oxen. At the head and foot of the coffer are masses of flowers and branches of trees. In the fore-part of the boat is a painted wooden figure of the goddess Nephthys, and in the stern is a similar figure of Isis. Just behind Isis are the two posts to which are fastened steering oars, or paddles. By the side of the mummy kneels Ani's wife Tutu, with her left hand raised

[1] 𓊹𓄤 A title of the king of Egypt who was reigning when the Papyrus of Ani was written.

[2] *I.e.*, "Lord of Upper and Lower Egypt."

to her forehead in an attitude of lamentation. Her arms and shoulders are bare, and she wears a single garment fastened about her waist. In front of the boat is the SEM priest, arrayed in white linen garments, over which he wears a leopard skin. The leopard was always associated with the Land of the Dead, and the skin of the animal was supposed to bestow upon its wearer special powers in dealing with the souls of the dead. In his right hand the SEM priest holds a libation vase, from which he sprinkles on the bier water in which natron, or some compound of salt or soda, has been mixed, and so renders the resting-place of the mummy ceremonially pure. In his left hand he holds over the fore-part of the boat a censer containing burning incense, and, as he sprinkles the water on the boat, and causes the incense to burn by moving about the censer, he recites on behalf of the deceased sections of the text which forms Chapter I of the Theban Recension of the Book of the Dead. The prayers which he recites for Ani entered into the smoke of the incense, and were carried by it up to heaven and into the ears of Osiris and the other gods who presided over the souls of the dead, and the Egyptians always believed that prayers so wafted to heaven were duly considered and answered by the gods. The bier is followed by eight men who lament the death of Ani, and one of these has his hair whitened. Behind these come four men who wear white tunics and haul by means of a rope a funerary chest, made in the form of a pylon, which rests upon runners. At each end of the coffer are small branches, and above it is a figure of the Jackal-god Anubis. The side of the coffer is decorated with figures of the Ṭeṭ and Tet, which symbolize the *sacrum* bone of Osiris and the uterus of Isis, and drew to the coffer the power of the great Ancestor god Osiris, and the virtue of the blood and magical spells and words of power of the great Ancestress goddess Isis. The coffer contained four vases, each of which held an important internal organ of Ani mummified, and was under the divine protection of one of the Four Sons of Horus. In the rear are two men, who have their hands raised and are reciting the praises of, or prayers for, the deceased.

In the upper register are: 1. A servant who carries in his right hand the staff of Ani and two pots containing myrrh and unguents. 2. A servant carrying on his head Ani's couch or bed, the modern "Angarêb," with a frame of ebony, and a rope-work mat on which to lie; that it was a very heavy piece of furniture is proved by the bent knees of the man who is carrying it. 3. A servant bearing on his shoulders the heavy ebony chair in which Ani used to sit. 4. A servant carrying articles connected with Ani's profession as a scribe, namely, his palette [hieroglyph], with the traces of the red and black ink still upon it, and the reed pens projecting from the cavity made in it for them, the scribe's wrist rest, and a box containing materials used by the scribe, water-jar, etc., and another small box [hieroglyph]. It was assumed that Ani would require all the objects in the Ṭuat, or Khert-Neter, *i.e.*, the Other World, and they were therefore being carried to his tomb in Western Thebes. Meanwhile, the funerary coffer, or bier, is being hauled along by two pairs of oxen, which are guided by four of Ani's slaves. The ropes are fastened round the horns of the animals, just as they are in some places in the Sûdân at the present day. The oxen were intended to be offered up as sacrifices during the elaborate funerary ceremonies that were performed either at the door of the tomb, or in the great Ṭuat Chamber inside it, wherein the transmutation of the offerings into food suitable for the gods and spirits was effected. The oxen were four in number, so that one might be slaughtered for each of the Four Quarters of the World.

Text: Chapter I. Here begin the Chapters of Coming Forth by Day.

PLATE VI

Vignette: The funeral procession continued up to the tomb. In the centre is a group of professional wailing-women, who are seen beating their breasts and pulling out their hair. These are followed by attendants or slaves carrying on yokes boxes of flowers, vases of unguents, etc. In front of the women are a cow and her calf, chairs made of painted wood with bunches of flowers, etc., upon them, and an attendant, with shaven head, carrying the fore-leg of an ox, which has been newly slaughtered. To the right of the Plate is seen a group of priests who are performing on the mummy of Ani the ceremony of "Opening the Mouth." Ani's mummy is standing on a reed mat, and is provided with its festal decorations, head-covering, lotuses or lilies, beard, etc. At its feet kneels Tutu lamenting the departure of her husband. Behind the mummy stands Anubis, the god of embalming, embracing it with his arms. Behind Anubis is the tomb, painted white. It consists of a small low, rectangular building, which in many respects resembles a maṣṭabah tomb of the Ancient Empire, surmounted by a pyramidal structure. About half way up the pyramidal portion is a small opening or niche, which was specially made to form a resting-place for the Heart-soul of Ani, whenever it wished to visit the mummy in the chamber below the tomb, or whenever it wished to alight and enjoy the sight of familiar people and things. In the accompanying cut we see the soul descending the pit of the tomb to the mummy chamber in order to carry air to the mummy.

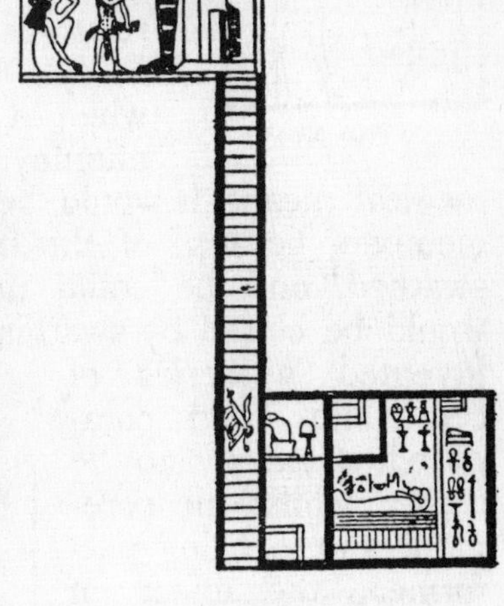

A table piled with the usual offerings is in front of Ani's mummy, and standing there before it we see the SEM priest, dressed as before, and sprinkling with water and censing the mummy, and another man, who may be Ani's son or an assistant priest who bore the title SA-MER-F, *i.e.*, "his loving son." This last-named holds a remarkable instrument called "Ur ḥeka" (Fig. 1), a name which means "great one of spells," or "great one of words of power." Behind or beside these priests on the ground

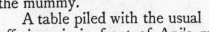

FIG. 1.

in a row lie the other instruments which are employed in performing the ceremony of "Opening the Mouth" of Ani. These are the meskhet, the box for holding unguents, the boxes for purification, the *nemes* bandlet, the libation vases, the ostrich feather, and the three instruments called *Seb-ur*, *Temānu*, and *Pesh-en-kef*. The KHER-ḤEB priest stands behind them reciting the various sections of the service from a papyrus. The ceremony of "Opening the Mouth" is very ancient, and probably dates from the end of the Neolithic Period in Egypt. It was performed on the gods after they were created, and was ever after performed on all dead men whose relatives could afford to pay for the ceremony. The Egyptians foresaw that when a man had been made into a mummy, if life were restored to him by magical means, it would be impossible for him to move his members because of the bandages with which they were swathed, and he could not breathe because his mouth would be closed by swathings also. The priests therefore invented a series of ceremonies, and composed a liturgy to be recited whilst the ceremonies were being performed, the effect of which would be to remove the swathings from the body, and to permit it to open the mouth and nostrils, and to breathe, eat, drink, think, and walk. The KHER-ḤEB priest touched the mouth with the series of instruments mentioned above, and so opened it, and then performed a number of ceremonies in which all the other objects played symbolic but very important

FIG. 2.

FIG. 3.

parts. Sometimes the "Guardian of the balance" opened the mouth of the deceased (Fig. 2). In the Appendix which follows the description of this Plate several of these ceremonies are described, and the outline drawings illustrate the way in which they were performed. In some papyri the ceremony of opening the mouth is clearly shown, as will be seen from the accompanying tracing (Fig. 3). One priest uses the *Ur-ḥeka* and the *Seb-ur* on the mummy, another presents pots of unguent for lubricating the lips, and the KHER-ḤEB purifies the place where the ceremonies are being performed by sprinkling natron water, and burning incense. By the side of the tomb is a large stele with a rounded top which, it seems, the Ba-soul of the deceased was supposed to occupy at times. On the top of it is a scene in which the deceased Hunefer is represented adoring Osiris. Below is the following text:—

This text opens with the words SUTEN ṬĀ ḤETEP, meaning "the king hath given an offering." This formula is very ancient, and was cut on stelae and tombs under the Ancient Empire, when no man was allowed to build a tomb, or have one built, except by royal consent, and when the king did actually send a contribution in kind to the funerary offerings. The intense conservatism of the Egyptians made them preface their funerary inscriptions by the formula SUTEN ṬĀ ḤETEP many centuries after the king had ceased to give gifts personally to the dead. There is no reason for doubting that every king gave gifts for the funerary ceremonies performed for priests and officials who were well known and liked by him, but it was manifestly impossible for the king to contribute to the funeral of every man buried in a tomb throughout the length and breadth of Egypt. The remaining part of the inscription reads: "Osiris, Khenti Amentet, Lord of "Eternity, Creator everlasting, Lord "to whom praisings are made, First "of his Company of Gods; hail, Ȧnpu, "dweller in the mummy chamber, great "god, governor of the divine house; "may they grant to the KA of the Osiris, "him who is praised (or, favoured) of "his god, Hunefer, [the power] to go in "and to come forth from Khert-Neter, "and to follow in the train of Osiris "during all his festivals of the New "Year, and to receive offerings of cakes, "and to appear in his presence."

FIG. I.

APPENDIX

DESCRIPTION OF THE CEREMONIES OF OPENING THE MOUTH

The ceremonies[1] which took place at the door of the tomb in an Egyptian funeral are of considerable interest. The priest called KHER-ḤEB, holding the SEM priest by the arm, gives directions for the slaughter of "a bull of the South." The slaughterer, standing on the bull, cuts off a fore-leg (Fig. I) and takes out the heart. A woman, called the *Tcheràu ur*, who personifies Isis, then whispers in the deceased's ear: "Behold, thy lips are set in order for thee, so that thy mouth may be opened." Next, an

[1] The following description of them is based upon the chapters on this subject in Dümichen, *Der Grabpalast des Patuamenap*, Part II, Plates I ff., pp. 3 ff.

antelope[1] and a duck[2] are brought by order of the KHER-ḤEB, and their heads are cut off.[3] The KHER-ḤEB then addresses the SEM priest: "I have seized them for thee, "I have brought unto thee thine enemies. His hands "bring his head [as] his gift. I have slain them for thee, "O Tmu; let not his enemies rise up against this god." The slaughterer then presents the thigh to the KHER-ḤEB, and the heart to an official whose title was SMER, and all three then "place the thigh and the heart upon the ground before this god" (*i.e.*, Osiris). The KHER-ḤEB then says to the deceased, represented by his mummy or statue: "I "have brought unto thee the thigh (Fig. 2) "as the Eye of Horus. I have brought "unto thee the heart; let there be no rising "up against this god. I have brought "unto thee the antelope, his head is cut off; I have brought "unto thee the duck, his head is cut off." Here the sacrifice ends.

FIG. 2.

The next part of the ceremony, *i.e.*, "the opening of the mouth and eyes," is performed by the SEM priest, who addresses the deceased: "I have "come to embrace thee, I am thy "son Horus, I have pressed thy "mouth; I am thy son, I love thee. "His mother beats her breast and "weeps for him, and those who are "in chains with him (*i.e.*, Isis and "Nephthys) beat their breasts. Thy "mouth was closed, but I have set in order for thee thy

FIG. 3.

1 *āri.*

2 *smennu.*

3 The slaughter of the antelope and duck typified the destruction of the enemies of the deceased; for, when Horus destroyed the enemies of his father Osiris, "he cut off their heads [which took] the form of ducks in "the sky, making them to fall headlong to the ground in the form of "antelopes, and into the water in the form of fishes." For the text, see Schiaparelli, *Il Libro dei Funerali degli Antichi Egiziani* (in *Atti della R. Accademia dei Lincei*; Rome, 1883 and 1890), p. 94; Naville, *Todtenbuch*, chap. 134.

"mouth[1] and thy teeth." The KHER-ḤEB next calls on the SEM priest four times: "O SEM, take the *Seb-ur*[2] (Fig. 3) and open the mouth and the eyes"; and while the SEM priest is performing the ceremony the KHER-ḤEB continues: "Thy "mouth was closed, but I have set in "order for thee thy mouth and thy teeth. "I open for thee thy mouth, I open for "thee thy two eyes, I have opened for "thee thy mouth with the instrument of "Anubis. I have opened thy mouth "with the instrument of Anubis, with "the iron tool with which the mouths "of the gods were opened. Horus, open "the mouth, Horus, open the mouth. "Horus hath opened the mouth of the "dead, as he whilom opened the mouth of "Osiris, with the iron which came forth from Set, with the "iron tool (Fig. 4) with which he opened the mouths of the "gods. He hath opened thy mouth with it. The dead "shall walk and shall speak, and his body shall [be] with "the Great Company of the Gods in the Great House of the "Aged one in Ȧnu, and he shall receive there the *ureret* "crown from Horus, the lord of "mankind." The KHER-ḤEB next says: "Let the ȦMI-KHENT priest "(Fig. 5) stand behind him (*i.e.*, the "deceased), and say, 'My father, my "father,' four times." The eldest son of the deceased then stands behind the deceased, and in his name the KHER-ḤEB says: "His mother beateth "her breast and weepeth for him, "and those who are in chains with "him also beat their breasts." Another priest, called ȦM-KHENT-ḤERU, takes up the same position and says: "Isis goeth unto Horus, who em-

FIG. 4.

FIG. 5.

[1] See Schiaparelli, *Il Libro dei Funerali degli Antichi Egiziani*; Maspero, *Le Rituel du Sacrifice Funéraire* (in *Revue de l'Histoire des Religions*, 1887, pp. 159 ff.).

[2] For a complete list of these instruments, see Schiaparelli, *Il Libro dei Funerali degli Antichi Egiziani*, p. 109.

braceth his father." A priestly official belonging to the *mesenti* class then goes behind the deceased, and the SEM, SMER and KHER-ḤEB priests stand in front, and the SEM priest and the KHER-ḤEB, personifying Horus and Sut, respectively cry: "I am Horus, I am Sut; I will not let "thee illumine the "head of my father." The SEM priest then leaves the KA-chapel and returns, leading in the SA-MER-F, *i.e.*, "the son who loveth him"; whereupon the KHER-ḤEB says: "O "SEM, let the SA-"MER-F come into the tomb in order that he may see the "god." The SEM priest holding him by the arm then leads forward the SA-MER-F, who addresses the deceased: "I have come; I have brought unto thee thy son who "loveth thee; he shall open for thee thy mouth and "thine eyes." (Fig. 6.) A tomb-official, *Ȧm-ȧs*, then takes up his position behind the deceased, and the SA-MER-F and the KHER-ḤEB stand in front; the KHER-ḤEB repeating four times: "The SA-MER-F openeth the mouth "and the two eyes of the deceased, first with a needle[1] of "iron, then with a rod of *smu* metal"; the *Am-ȧs* addressing the deceased: "Behold the SA-MER-F"; and the KHER-ḤEB saying, in the name of the SA-MER-F: "I have pressed for thee "thy mouth, even as thy father "pressed it in the name of Seker. "Hail, Horus hath pressed thy "mouth for thee, he hath opened "thine eyes for thee; Horus hath "opened thy mouth for thee, he "hath opened for thee thine eyes: "they are firmly stablished. Thy "mouth was closed; I have or-"dered thy mouth and thy teeth for thee in their true "order. Thou hast [again] opened thy mouth; Horus

FIG. 6.

FIG. 7.

1 [hieroglyphs] *ṭeṭṭef.*

"hath opened thy mouth. I have stablished thy mouth "firmly. Horus hath opened for thee thy mouth, Horus "hath opened for thee thy two eyes."

FIG. 8.

The KHER-ḤEB then speaks on behalf of the SEM priest: "Thy mouth was "closed up. I have ordered aright for "thee thy mouth and thy teeth. Thy "mouth is firmly stablished. Thy mouth "was tightly closed. His mouth is "firmly stablished, and [his] two eyes "are firmly stablished." The SEM priest next presents to the deceased (Fig. 7) a cone-shaped offering △,[1] and at the same time the KHER-ḤEB says: "Open the mouth and the two "eyes, open the mouth and "the two eyes. Thou hadst "tightly closed thy mouth, "thou hast [again] opened "thy two eyes." Then the KHER-ḤEB says on behalf of the SMER (Fig. 8) priest who stands behind the deceased: "One cometh unto thee for thy purification." Next the SA-MER-F comes forward with four boxes (Fig. 9) in his hands, and the KHER-ḤEB says: "O SA-MER-F, take the four boxes "of purification, press the mouth "and the two eyes, and open the "mouth and the two eyes with "each of them four times, and "say, 'Thy mouth and thy two "eyes are firmly stablished, and "they are restored aright,' and "say also, 'I have firmly pressed "thy mouth, I have opened thy "mouth, I have opened thy two "eyes by means of the four boxes of purification.'" The SEM priest then approaches the deceased (Fig. 10) with the

FIG. 9.

FIG. 10.

[1] A large collection of such offerings is exhibited in the Third Egyptian Room.

instrument 𓌻,[1] and the KHER-ḤEB at the same time says: "O SEM priest, lay the *pesh-en-kef* upon his mouth, and "say, 'I have stablished for thee thy two jaw-bones in "thy face which was divided into two parts.'" The SEM priest next makes an offering of grapes (Fig. 11), the KHER-ḤEB saying: "O SEM priest, place the "grapes upon his mouth and say, "'He bringeth to thee the eye of "Horus, he graspeth it; do thou "also grasp it.'" After an ostrich feather has been offered (Fig. 12) by the SEM priest, and a number of the ceremonies described above have been repeated, and other animals slaughtered, the KHER-ḤEB addresses the SEM priest, and says: "Take the instrument *Ṭun-ṭeṭ*[2] (thrice) and open the mouth and the eyes" (four times). He then continues: "O SEM priest, take the iron instrument of "Anubis, *Ṭun-ṭeṭ* (thrice). Open the mouth and the two "eyes (four times), and say, 'I open "for thee thy mouth with the iron "instrument of Anubis with which he "opened the mouths of the gods. "Horus openeth the mouth, Horus "openeth the mouth, Horus openeth "the mouth with the iron which cometh "forth from Set, wherewith he hath "opened the mouth of Osiris. With "the iron tool (*meskhet*) wherewith he "opened the mouths of the gods doth "he open the mouth. He [the deceased] shall go in and "he shall speak [again], and his body shall dwell with the "Company of the Great Gods in Ȧnu, wherein he hath "received the *ureret* crown from Horus, lord of men. Hail, "Horus opened thy mouth and thy two eyes with the "instrument *Seb-ur* or *Temān*,[3] with the instrument *Ṭun-ṭeṭ*

FIG. 11.

FIG. 12.

[1] It is called *Pesh-en-kef* [hieroglyphs]. See Dümichen, *Der Grabpalast des Patuamenap*, Part I, pp. 18, 19.

[2] [hieroglyphs].

[3] [hieroglyphs].

"of the Opener of the Roads (*i.e.*, Anubis) wherewith he "opened the mouth of all the gods of the North. Horus "the Great[1] cometh to embrace thee. I, thy son who "loveth thee, have opened thy mouth and thy two eyes. "His mother beateth her breast in grief while she embraceth "him, and the two sisters (*i.e.*, Isis "and Nephthys), who are one, "strike themselves in grief. All "the gods open thy mouth according to the book of the service.'" The KHER-ḤEB next instructs the SEM priest to clothe the mummy or statue of the deceased with the *nemes*[2] band or fillet (Fig. 13), and to say: "Lo! the *nemes* fillet, the "*nemes* fillet, which cometh as the "light, which cometh as the light; it cometh as the eye "of Horus, the brilliant; it cometh forth from Nekheb. "The gods were bound therewith; bound round is thy "face with it in its name of *Ḥetch* (*i.e.*, light, or brilliance), "coming forth from Nekheb. All that could do harm "to thee upon earth is destroyed." The SEM priest, holding a vase of ointment in his left hand, and smearing the mouth with his fore-finger (Fig. 14), says: "I have anointed thy face "with ointment, I have anointed "thine eyes. I have painted thine "eye with *uatch* and with *mestchem*. "May no ill-luck happen through "the dethronement of his two eyes "in his body, even as no evil fortune came to Horus through the "overthrow of his eye in his body. "Thy two eyes are decked there-"with in its name of *Uatch*, which maketh thee to give forth "fragrance, in its name of Sweet-smelling." A number of scented unguents and perfumes are brought forward, and at the presentation of each a short sentence is recited by the

FIG. 13.

FIG. 14.

[1] Ḥeru-ur, the Haroeris of the Greeks.

[2] [hieroglyphs].

KHER-ḤEB, having reference to the final triumph of the deceased in the Underworld and to the help which the great gods will render to him.

Text: [CHAPTER I.] HERE BEGIN THE CHAPTERS OF COMING FORTH BY DAY, AND THE SONGS OF PRAISE AND GLORIFYING, AND OF COMING FORTH FROM AND OF GOING INTO THE GLORIOUS KHERT-NETER IN THE BEAUTIFUL ÅMENTET.

This is the opening Chapter of the Theban Recension of the Book of the Dead, and its object is clear. It was to be recited on the day of the funeral, and if this were done by the KHER-ḤEB priest it would give the deceased power to leave the Other World whensoever he pleased, and to return to this world, and to resume his place in the Other World when he was tired of this one. The words "coming forth by day" have formed the subject of many discussions by Egyptologists, and they have been translated in many ways, *e.g.*, "Coming forth from [or, as] the day" (Birch); "The departure from the day" (Birch); "Sortir du jour" (Devéria and Naville); "Sortie de la journée" (Pierret); "Ausgang bei Tage" (Brugsch). The true meaning seems to me to be "Coming forth by (or into) the day." All the events described in the Book of the Dead take place in the Other World, and what the dead man craved for above everything else was to come back into the light of day of this world. He longed to have the power to leave Khert-Neter, or Åmentet, *i.e.*, the Other World, whensoever he wished, and to return to it whensoever he wished. There was no other place for him to go to except this earth, or the sky above it, and as he firmly believed that the Other World was a place of semi-darkness, as compared with this earth when the sun was shining in the sky, he longed to have the power to come back to earth and bask in the sunshine, or in the glorious light of the full moon. Every Egyptian knew that only the gods possessed naturally the power to leave the Other World at will, and he therefore strove with all his might to find the means whereby he might identify himself with them or become absorbed in them. In this Chapter the priest declared that the deceased was the Sun-god, and Thoth, and a Tchatcha chief, and the kinsman of Osiris and Horus, and Ṭeṭ, and the SEM priest, and that he had assisted Horus in performing the ceremonies which had resulted in the resurrection of Osiris. As Osiris confounded his enemies, so the deceased has confounded his enemies ; as Thoth proved the words of Osiris to be true, so also does he prove that the words of Ani are truth. Ani also claims to have performed the priestly duties of the SEM priest and of Ptaḥ, and to have ploughed the earth in Ḥensu (Herakleopolis), and to have worked into it the blood of his slaughtered enemies, just as did Horus for his father Osiris. Having performed all these meritorious acts and been declared innocent in the Judgment, he demands admission into the presence of Osiris, and the right to hear and see what the gods hear and see, and to stand up and sit down as they do.

It was not, however, easy to reach the House of Osiris, for it was situated far away from this earth, on the remote side of Dead-land. A soul might easily lose its way in trying to cross that awful country, or it might be molested and driven back by hostile souls, or by those souls who could never hope to win through to the kingdom of Osiris. The only certain means of traversing Dead-land in safety was to obtain the services of some benevolent god, or gods, who knew the roads, and could act therefore as trustworthy guides to the souls who wished to reach the Elysian Fields. Hence we find Ani praying to the "openers of the ways," or divine guides, to lead him to the House of Osiris, and to protect him from the evil actions of those who might attempt to turn him out of his path, and make him to lose his way "in the bush." Such "guides" were the servants of Osiris, and they would only conduct the souls of the loyal followers of Osiris to their lord, and it was necessary for souls to convince them that they really were followers of Osiris by reciting the words of power of the Book of the Dead, or by producing authorized amulets. When this had been done the guides led the souls of the beatified through Dead-land, and helped them to pass through the fortresses of Osiris in safety until they entered the presence of the god.

According to a supplementary text, which is known as the "Chapter of making the *Sāḥu* to enter into Khert-Neter on the day of the funeral," the road between this world and the next was infested with snakes, "which lived "upon the bodies of men and women and fed upon their "blood." In the recently discovered Papyrus of Iuȧa these snakes are said to be nine in number, and their names are as follow:—

1. Nārti-ānkh-em-sen-f.
2. Ḥer-f-em-qeb-f.
3. Ānkh-em-fentu.
4. Sām-em-qesu.
5. Hahutiȧmsau (?)
6. Shept-temesu.
7. Unem-sāḥu.
8. Sām-em-snef.
9. Ānkh-em-betu-mitu.[1]

PLATE VII

The Vignettes which run along the tops of Plates VII–X all illustrate the XVIIth Chapter of the Theban Recension, the text of which is written below them.

Vignettes: 1. Ani and his wife Tutu seated in a bower or chamber, which appears to be made of mats, stiffened and supported by poles. Ani is seated on a chair with a back, and is engaged in moving a piece on a chequer-board with his right hand; in his left he holds an object made of linen, the use and signification of which are unknown. Tutu is seated a little behind her husband on a stool, which is provided with a cushion; the feet of both husband and wife rest on footstools made of matting, or perhaps on leather-covered cushions. In the Papyrus of Hunefer

[1] See Budge, *The Chapters of Coming Forth by Day*, Vol. I, Plate LXXXVIII, London, 1909.

(Fig. 1) we see one figure of the deceased seated in the *seḥ* chamber, and two outside it, with the emblem of Ȧmentet and symbols of bread and beer between them. One of the two outside figures is going into the *seḥ* chamber and the other is leaving it. In the Papyrus of Mut-em-uȧa the queen (Fig. 2) is seated before a table with a box of unguent on it, and she is playing a game on a draught board. Her Heart-soul stands outside, and is adoring the two Horus-gods, or the gods of the rising and setting sun.

FIG. 1.

2. The Heart-souls of Ani and Tutu, in the form of human-headed hawks, standing upon the roof of their tomb; before each is a pot in which incense is burning. Above the head of Ani is the legend [hieroglyphs], "the Ba-soul of the Osiris" [Ani].

3. A light table, or altar, with a pillared stand, on which rests a vase with a spout [hieroglyph], probably containing wine. On the table are two lotuses or lilies. These objects probably represent the offerings which were made to Ani and Tutu by their kinsfolk upon earth.

FIG. 2.

4. Two lions seated back to back and supporting the horizon [hieroglyph], over which extends the sky [hieroglyph]. The lion on the right is called SEF [hieroglyphs], *i.e.*, "Yesterday," and that on the left ṬUAU [hieroglyphs], *i.e.*, "To-day" (to illustrate ll. 13–16).

5. The Benu bird [hieroglyphs], with a libation vase and lotus resting on an altar before him. The Benu bird is

usually thought to be identical with the phoenix of the Greeks, who considered that bird to have been self-produced. The Benu is at once a symbol of Rā and of Osiris.

6. The mummy of Ani lying on a bier within a funerary coffer or shrine, to the ends of which are attached coloured streamers; the bier rests on the roof of a long, low sepulchral building that is probably intended to represent Ani's tomb. At the head and foot of the bier is a vulture, that at the head representing Nephthys, and that at the foot Isis; these birds are the two goddesses in the character of "nursing mothers," TCHERTI. Beneath the bier are two vases of unguents, Ani's palette, the box containing implements used in writing and painting, and two wooden or stone vessels painted in imitation of variegated glass. Examples of such vases are to be seen in the Fourth Egyptian Room of the British Museum, Nos. 4875, 4877, 4879, etc. In some papyri (see annexed cut) the Heart-soul of the deceased is seen hovering over the mummy in the form of a human-headed hawk, bearing in its claws the emblem of the sun's orbit (*shen*), which symbolizes eternity. The older and more correct form of the *shen* is, but here it is shortened, and resembles a signet ring.

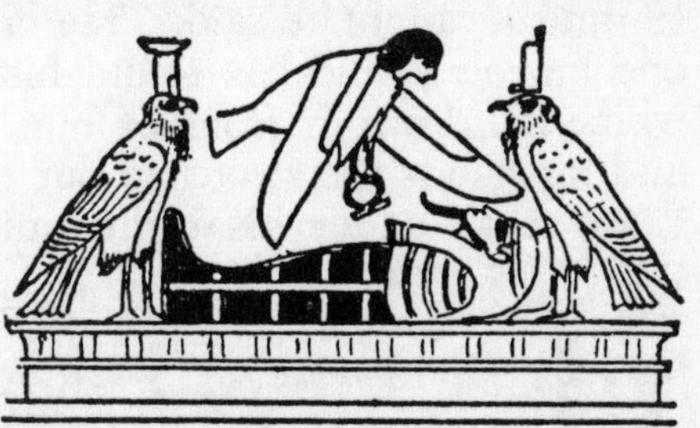

7. From other papyri we see that after the Vignette of Ani's mummy we ought to find in our papyrus a Vignette representing the two Uraei-goddesses who are referred to in ll. 33–36 of the text. They are here supplied from the Papyrus of Hunefer, in which the legends tell us that one uraeus represents the goddess of the South, Nekhebit, and the other the goddess of the North, Uatchit.

PLATE VIII

8. The figure of a god, painted dark blue, or cobalt, and marked with wavy lines to indicate his nature as a Water-god. He wears the long characteristic African beard, and has a somewhat pendulous stomach. His androgynous nature is indicated by his left breast, which is that of a woman. On his head is the symbol for "year," and in his right hand he holds a similar symbol; he is called "Ḥeḥ-en-renput" [hieroglyphs], and he may be a primitive Egyptian or Nilotic Year-god. His left hand is extended over an oval within which is the Eye of Horus [hieroglyph] (to illustrate l. 46).

9. The god "whose name is Uatch-t-urȧ" [hieroglyphs], *i.e.*, the god of the Great Green, or the god of the Sea, whether of the Red Sea or of the Mediterranean cannot be said. He is painted red, wears armlets and bracelets, and has round his waist a girdle, the ends of which fall down in front of him. His arms are extended, and his hands are stretched out over two rectangular lakes [hieroglyph]; that under his right hand is called *She-en-ḥesmen*, [hieroglyphs], *i.e.*, "Lake of Natron," and that under his left, *She-en-maāt*, [hieroglyphs], *i.e.*, "Lake of Salt." This god seems to be of androgynous nature also, for his left breast, like that of the god in Vignette 8, is that of a woman (to illustrate ll. 47–50).

10. A doorway in the form of a pylon, with palm-leaf cornice, and two leaves which are shut and bolted; its name is *Rasta*, or *Rastau* [hieroglyphs], which means the "door of the corridors in the mountain." This Vignette illustrates ll. 51 ff., from which we learn that it is the south gate of Anruṭef, a district of Herakleopolis, and the northern gate of the Land of the Dead. The name was given originally to a gate in the kingdom of Seker, the god of Death, which lay to the south of Memphis. In any case it is the gate which all souls must pass through on leaving this world to enter the Ṭuaṭ, or Other World, and a picture of it is given here so that souls may gain an idea of what it was like.

11. A funerary building, painted white, with a palm-leaf cornice. The door is unlike that of Rasta. Above is the Right Eye of Rā, which is supposed to rise up out of the building. This building probably represents the door through which the sun emerges at sunrise, when he starts on his journey across the heavens (to illustrate l. 73).

12. A very ancient Sky-goddess called "Meḥurt ȧrit Rā" [hieroglyphs], *i.e.*, "Meḥurt, the daughter of Rā." Her face is yellow and her body red. She has a deep collar, or halter, round her neck, to which is fastened a *menȧt*, emblem of virility, fecundity, and female sexuality, which lies along her back (Fig. 1). Above her back is a flail. She lies along the top of a low building, which rests on a mat. In the Papyrus of Hunefer (Fig. 2) we see the god Thoth kneeling before her and presenting to her the Eye of Rā, or the Sun. The allusion here is to the ancient legend in which it is said that Set carried away the sun from the sky and attempted to destroy it. Thoth set out in quest of the sun, overtook Set, and having inflicted great injury upon him, took the sun and carried it back and placed it in the sky, in its proper place (to illustrate ll. 75–79).

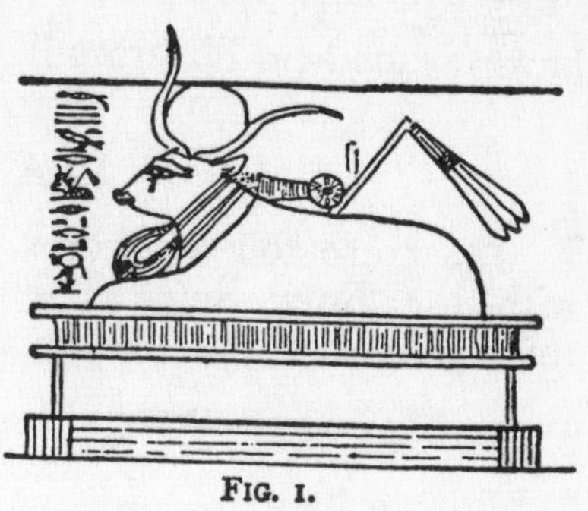
Fig. 1.

Fig. 2.

13. A funeral chest or coffer which represents the burial ground or the great cemetery of Abydos [hieroglyphs]. The supports and domed cover of the coffer are painted green and red, and the side is black. On this are traced in outline the figures of the Four Sons of Horus, Ḳestȧ (Mestȧ) and Ḥāpi facing Ṭuamutef and Qebḥsenuf. Above the cover rise the head of a man, presumably that of Ani, and his forearms and hands, in each of which he grasps the symbol of "life" ☥. It was at Abydos that Osiris arose from

the dead, and it is suggested by this Vignette that Ani will rise there also. This coffer is supposed to contain the internal organs of the deceased, which are under the protection of the Four Sons of Horus. On the left of the coffer stand two of the Sons of Horus, Ḳestȧ (Mestȧ) [hieroglyphs], man-headed, and Ḥāpi, or Ḥepi [hieroglyphs], ape-headed; on the right stand the other two, namely Ṭuamutef [hieroglyphs], jackal-headed, and Qebḥsenuf [hieroglyphs], hawk-headed (to illustrate ll. 82 and 83).

PLATE IX

14. Here follow figures of three gods, who, together with the Four Sons of Horus, form the Seven Spirits referred to in l. 99. These are:—

1. MAA-ȦTEF [hieroglyphs], man-headed and seated on a mat.
2. KHERI-BEQ-F [hieroglyphs], man-headed and seated on a mat.
3. ḤERU-KHENTI-ȦRI-TI [hieroglyphs], hawk-headed and seated on a mat.

15. The god Ȧnpu (Anubis) [hieroglyphs], jackal-headed and seated on a mat.

16. A group of Seven Gods, who, according to some authorities, formed the Seven Spirits, and, according to others, the Seven Gods who watched over the Tomb of Osiris. Their names are:—

1. [hieroglyphs] NETCHEḤ-NETCHEḤ, man-headed.
2. [hieroglyphs] ÀAQEṬQEṬ, snake-headed.
3. [hieroglyphs] KHENTI-HEH-F, man-headed.
4. [hieroglyphs] ȦMMI-UNNUT-F, snake-headed.
5. [hieroglyphs] ṬESHER-ȦRITI (?), man-headed.

6. [hieroglyphs] BES-MAA-EM-ḲERḤ, man-headed.

7. [hieroglyphs] ÅN-EM-HRU, man-headed.

These figures illustrate ll. 99–106 of the text.

17. A sepulchral building, with a palm-leaf cornice, having at each end of it a *ṭeṭ* [hieroglyph], *i.e.*, a figure which was in later times identified with the *sacrum* bone of Osiris, mounted on a stand. On the top of the building stand the hawk of Rā, with the solar disk on his head, and a human-headed hawk wearing the White Crown, and representing the Heart-soul of Osiris. The souls of Rā thus meet in Ṭeṭu, and are united to form one god. The *ṭeṭ* was in very primitive times the symbol of a god to which human sacrifices were offered, and the ground in front of it was "watered" with the blood of human beings. The victims were sometimes foreigners, and sometimes warriors who had been taken prisoner alive. The centre of the cult of the *ṭeṭ* was the town in Lower Egypt, which was in Pharaonic times known as Ṭeṭu, or Busiris. By some means or other the cult of Osiris was established at Ṭeṭu, and little by little it supplanted that of the *ṭeṭ*, and Osiris absorbed many of the attributes of the god Ṭeṭ. In the Vignette we see the hawk of Rā face to face with the Heart-soul of Osiris, and the text says that when the Heart-soul of Osiris goes to Ṭeṭu he finds the Heart-soul of Rā there, indicating that the cult of Rā was established in Ṭeṭu as was also the cult of Osiris. This Vignette then symbolizes the fusion of the cults of the gods Ṭeṭ, Rā, and Osiris, and is of very rare occurrence. It illustrates lines 111 and 112.

PLATE X

18. A large Cat, holding a knife [hieroglyph] in his right forepaw, cutting into a huge python, the head of which it holds firmly on the ground with the other forepaw. The python's tongue is projecting from its mouth. The Cat is Rā, and the python is the symbol of Set, the arch-enemy of

Rā. Behind the Cat is the famous Acacia Tree, which flourished in very early times in Ȧnu, *i.e.*, On, or Heliopolis.

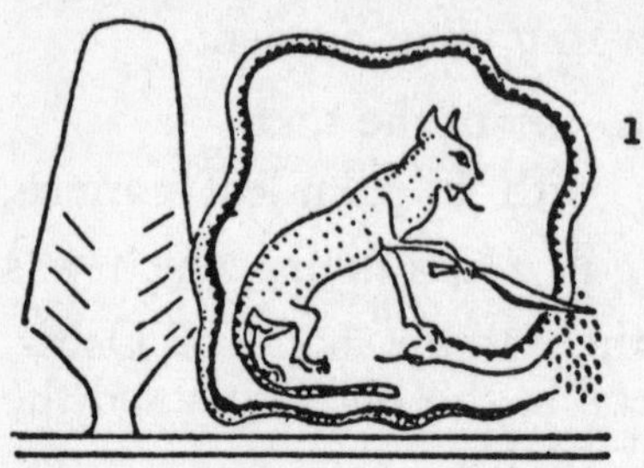
[1]

The slaying of the python by the Cat is symbolic of the famous slaughter of the foes of Rā, or Osiris, which took place at Heliopolis, either in the Predynastic Period or in early dynastic times. The appearance of the Acacia Tree here suggests that a tree-cult once existed at Heliopolis.

19. Three seated gods, two man-headed and the third hawk-headed; each holds a large knife. They probably represent the gods Sau, Horus of Sekhem, and Nefer-Tem.

20. The god Kheperȧ, in the form of a beetle-headed man, seated in his boat. Behind him is the symbol of "servant" , or "bodyguard." The tops of the steering poles and posts are in the form of the head of the hawk of Horus. In the bows of the boat are a libation jar on a stand and a lotus. Over the prow of the boat hangs a reed mat, or a mass of reeds, on which the look-out god usually takes his place. In this case the stand is occupied by a swallow. In front of the boat kneel Ani and his wife, with their hands raised in adoration of the god. The solar character of the boat is indicated by the *utchat* , which is painted on its side.

21. Two seated dog-headed apes, with their forepaws raised in adoration of the Eye of Rā ; before each is a five-rayed star. These apes represent Isis and Nephthys.

22. Tem , the god of the setting sun, seated within his disk in the Sektet Boat; the god wears the Crown of the South and North , and his face is towards the right hand. In the bows of the boat is the sign . In front of the boat are a lotus and a libation vase on a stand.

23. The god Reḥu in the form of a lion lying on a long low building. Over his back are bent some large plants,

[1] This form of the Vignette is taken from a papyrus in Dublin.

round the stalk of one of which is coiled a uraeus. Behind these is 𓋔, the symbol of Uatchet, the Lady of Flame.

Text: [CHAPTER XVII.] HERE BEGIN THE PRAISES AND GLORIFYINGS OF COMING FORTH FROM AND OF GOING INTO THE GLORIOUS KHERT-NETER, WHICH IS IN THE BEAUTIFUL AMENTET, AND OF COMING FORTH BY DAY IN ALL THE FORMS OF EXISTENCE WHICH IT MAY PLEASE THE DECEASED TO TAKE, OF PLAYING AT DRAUGHTS AS HE SITTETH IN THE SEḤ CHAMBER, AND OF APPEARING AS A LIVING SOUL.

This Chapter is most difficult to understand, but its importance from a mythological point of view cannot be over-estimated. Why it is included in the Book of the Dead at all is impossible to say, but as it is found in all the great papyri it must have been regarded as a most precious document by the theologians of Egypt. Its subject matter is the creation of the world and the origin of the gods, and the views set forth in it represent the special doctrines taught by the priesthood of Heliopolis. The oldest copies of it date from the XIth dynasty, and a complete copy is found in the Turin Papyrus, which may be assigned to the XXVIth dynasty, or a little later; therefore it is clear that the Chapter was in use for about two thousand years. It is the only ancient Egyptian exegetical work known. Speaking generally, the Chapter consists of a series of statements, each of which is followed by a demand for an explanation of what has been stated. Thus in the Papyrus of Nebseni we have: "I am Tem when he existed alone "in Nu; Rā in his risings, in his beginning, ruling what he "had made." These words are followed by the demand, "Explain it," *i.e.*, What does this mean? or To whom does this refer? Then comes the explanation: "This is Rā in "his beginning, [when he was] ruling what he had made. "In the beginning was Rā, rising on the throne of "sovereignty [over] what he had made. When the pillars "of Shu (*i.e.*, of heaven) did not exist, he was on the high "ground (or hill) in Khemenu (Hermopolis). Behold, "there were given to him the inert ones in Khemenu." Or again,

"I am the Great God who created himself."

Explain this.

"The Great God who created himself is Nu, the father "of the gods.

"There is, however, another reading which says that "the Great God who created himself is Rā, who created "the Nine Gods (or, the Company of the Gods) out of his "own names."

Explain this.

"It is Rā who made his own names into his members, and these became the gods who are in his following."

The author of the Chapter begins by mentioning Tem, a very ancient god of Heliopolis, and then refers to the time when Tem existed by himself in Nu [hieroglyphs]. But Nu was also a god, and we know from the hieroglyphs which form his name that he was the personification of the primeval Celestial Waters; therefore there was something in existence before Tem, and that something was the primeval waters. According to the Egyptian theologian, everything that exists had its origin in these waters. Now the author of the Chapter wished to prove that the Sun-god Rā, the greatest of the Heliopolitan gods from the IVth dynasty onwards, was directly descended from Nu, the Celestial Waters, and he therefore identified him at once with Tem. Since, however, some might think that the sky was older than the Sun-god Rā, he goes on to affirm that Rā was on the high ground in Khemenu (*i.e.*, Hermopolis, the city of Thoth) before the supports of the sky (Shu) were created; meaning that Rā existed before there was any sky at all. And when he says that Rā was ruling what he had made he intends us to understand that Rā made everything that exists. It was a common belief at Heliopolis when the Pyramid Texts were written (Vth and VIth dynasties) that the immediate descendants of Tem were Shu, Tefnut, Ḳeb, Nut, Osiris, Isis, Set, Nephthys, and Horus (or Anubis); Rā, in fact, was not mentioned in the group. The only way out of the difficulty was to identify Rā with Tem, and this was the course adopted by the author of the Chapter. With reference to the "inert ones, or children of revolt" [hieroglyphs], the questions, "Who were they?" and "What were they?" arise naturally. When the Celestial Water-god wished to create Tem, he found that all the forces of inertness were arrayed against him;

stillness disliked movement, darkness abhorred light, cold was an enemy to heat, and lifelessness to life. The creation of Tem destroyed all these forces, and they were utterly vanquished when the sun rose for the first time. When Rā was identified with Tem he became their master. They were delivered over to Rā in Khemenu, the city of Thoth, who composed the spells which Rā used in effecting their subjection. This allusion to Thoth suggests that the XVIIth Chapter of the Book of the Dead must be regarded as one of the books which Clement of Alexandria calls "Hermetic," *i.e.*, composed by Thoth.

The next subject discussed is the statement "I am the Great God who created himself." The obvious answer to the question "Who is this?" is "Nu, the father of the gods." But then the author adds another reading, which says that the self-created god is Rā, and that he created the Nine Gods out of his own names, *i.e.*, that each of the great names of Rā became a god. This explanation is, however, difficult to understand, and further information is demanded. The answer then given is that the names of Rā became the members of his body, and that these became the gods who follow in his train.

In other sections of the XVIIth Chapter explanations of words are given which show that they had special mythological significations. Thus in the phrase "I am Yesterday; I know To-day," Yesterday is explained to mean Osiris, and To-day Rā; and Eternity is the day, and Everlastingness the night. Allusions to ancient legends of the gods are also common; in line 25 it is said that Rā had union with his own body by means of his phallus; in ll. 61–64 the gods Ḥu and Saa are said to have come into being from the drops of blood which fell from Rā when he cut off his phallus; in l. 67 we read of the fight between Set and Horus, when the former threw filth in the face of Horus, and the latter destroyed the genital organs of Set; in l. 72 mention is made of the bringing back of the Eye of Rā by Thoth; in l. 19 (Nebseni) the great fight in Ȧnu, when the foes of the great god Neb-er-tcher were destroyed, is referred to; in l. 22 the great battle which took place between the gods and the Mesu Beṭesh, or rebels, is mentioned; and a little further on we read of the burning of the damned, the destruction of the wicked, and the slaughter of souls.

The section of the XVIIth Chapter that is omitted in the Papyrus of Ani is naturally without illustrative Vignettes, and we cannot therefore know the forms of Ȧnāf and of Shesmu, the headsman of Osiris, and the similitude of the dread god Mātchet also is not depicted. All must regret, too, the want of Vignettes referring to the god who watched by the Bend in the Lake of Fire, and the heart of Osiris, and the Mesqet chamber, wherein the deceased was re-born. The frequent prayers found throughout the Chapter prove that Ani was a firm believer in the doctrines enunciated in it, and that the chamber of torture in the Other World, wherein were merciless gods with "cruel fingers," which sliced up the bodies of the dead and shredded their flesh, and a bloodthirsty executioner who slaughtered always, were to him very real things indeed. Notwithstanding the many difficulties that beset the modern student of this Chapter, due partly to the perplexing character of the subject matter and partly to the mistakes and omissions in the text, its general meaning is clear, and it is easy to see that a knowledge of its contents was held to be absolutely indispensable to that soul who hoped to reach the Kingdom of Osiris and to live with the god who alone could sustain it, who was the only destroyer of wrong and the Guide to the paths of Eternity. It was not Nu, the father of the gods, or Tem, or Rā, who had the power to bestow everlasting life, but Osiris, and Osiris only.

PLATES XI AND XII

The Egyptians believed that the country forming the Kingdom of Osiris was divided into districts, or parts, the boundary of each of which was marked by a fortress or stronghold, which was held by a group of servants of the god. They also thought that these forts were used by the souls of the dead on their journey to the "City of God," much as modern travellers in the Sûdân, or Persia, or Mesopotamia, use the "khans" or inns, or halting-places, which supply the weary wayfarer with shelter and food, and enable him to enjoy some days of rest in security. At one time these forts, or strongholds, or "gates," were thought to be seven in number, and at other times the Egyptians believed their number was ten, or fourteen, or sixteen, or even twenty-one. The seven forts that formed a chain across Dead-land were called "Ārits," a word which is often translated "Mansions," or "Halls." Each Ārit was provided with a doorkeeper, a watcher, or official who kept a good look out to announce the arrival of a traveller, and a herald, who interviewed the visitor and enquired his name, and reported it to his companions. This arrangement is identical with that which has been common in all parts of Africa from time immemorial in respect of the forts that are built at the entrances to towns and villages. In the case of the Seven Ārits no soul could hope to gain admission to anyone of them unless it was able to state the names of the doorkeeper and watcher and herald, and to repeat a formula which would convince them of its good faith. The writer of the Book of the Dead composed a Chapter in which the names of all the officials of the Ārits were given, as well as the seven formulae that secured for those who knew them admission into the Ārits. In Plates XI and XII we see Ani and his wife Tutu approaching the Ārits, and pictures of the gods who guarded them.

Vignette 1. The First Ārit. The cornice of the door of the First Ārit is ornamented with symbols of life 𓋹, stability 𓊽, and power 𓌀. At the entrance sit three gods, the first having the head of a hare, the second the head of a serpent, and the third the head of a crocodile. The first holds a whisk, made probably of the tail of some animal, and each of the others a knife.

Text: [Chapter CXLVII.]
The name of the Doorkeeper is Sekhetḥerāsh-tāru.
The name of the Watcher is Metiheh.
The name of the Herald is Hakheru.
These are followed by the formula that Ani recites.

Vignette 2. The Second Ārit. This Ārit is guarded by three gods: the first has the head of a lion, the second the head of a man, and the third the head of a dog. Each holds a knife.

Text: The name of the Doorkeeper is Unḥāt.
The name of the Watcher is Seqeṭḥer.
The name of the Herald is Useṭ.
These are followed by the formula that Ani recites.

Vignette 3. THE THIRD ĀRIT. This Ārit is guarded by three gods: the first has the head of a jackal, the second the head of a dog, and the third the head of a serpent. The first holds a whisk, and each of the others a knife.

Text: The name of the Doorkeeper is Unemḥau-auentpeḥui.
The name of the Watcher is Seresḥer.
The name of the Herald is Āa.

These are followed by the formula that Ani recites.

Vignette 4. THE FOURTH ĀRIT. This Ārit is guarded by three gods: the first has the head of a man, the second the head of a hawk, and the third the head of a lion. The first holds a whisk, and each of the others a knife.

Text: The name of the Doorkeeper is Khesefḥerāsht-kheru.
The name of the Watcher is Serestepu.
The name of the Herald is Khesefaṭ.

These are followed by the formula that Ani recites.

Vignette 5. THE FIFTH ĀRIT. This Ārit is guarded by three gods: the first has the head of a hawk, the second the head of a man, and the third the head of a serpent. The first holds a whisk, and each of the others a knife.

Text: The name of the Doorkeeper is Ānkhfemfent.
The name of the Watcher is Shabu.
The name of the Herald is Ṭebḥerkehakheft.

These are followed by the formula that Ani recites. In it the deceased says: "I have brought unto thee thy jaw-"bones in Rasta, I have brought unto thee thy backbone "in Ȧnu, gathering together all thy members there." The word "jawbones," *ārti*, has been understood by some to mean the upper and the lower jaw, but this is not the case, for it indicates the right and left sides of the lower jaw only. The Arab physicians in Egypt thought that the lower jaw consisted of two parts, which were joined at the chin, and the ancient Egyptians probably thought the same. The mention here of the bringing of the "jawbones" is most interesting, for it shows that at one time in Egypt the lower jaw and the backbone were carefully preserved so that they might be re-used in the reconstitution of the body. On the preservation of the jawbone in Uganda and the bearing of the custom on primitive Egyptian religious beliefs see my *Osiris and the Egyptian Resurrection*, Vol. II, pp. 91 ff. The association in the text of the "jawbones" with Osiris is a valuable proof of the identity of beliefs in the Sûdân and Egypt.

Vignette 6. THE SIXTH ĀRIT. This Ārit is guarded by three gods: the first has the head of a jackal, and the second the head of a crocodile, and the third the head of a dog. The first holds a whisk, and each of the others a knife.

Text: The name of the Doorkeeper is Åtektaukehaq-kheru.
The name of the Watcher is Ånḥer.
The name of the Herald is Aṭesḥer.

These are followed by the formula that Ani recites.

Vignette 7. THE SEVENTH ĀRIT. This Ārit is guarded by three gods: the first has the head of a hare, the second the head of a lion, and the third the head of a man. The first and second each hold a knife, and the third a whisk.

Text: The name of the doorkeeper is Sekhemme-tenusen.
The name of the Watcher is Āamaākheru.
The name of the Herald is Khesefkhemi.

These are followed by the formula that Ani recites.

The CXLVIth Chapter of the Book of the Dead also deals with the Seven Ārits; that is, the Vignette consists of the pictures of seven doors, and the text that accompanies each picture contains merely three names. Of these names one appears to be that of the door, and the other two are the names of the officers of the door who are depicted below the text. The guardian gods are sometimes all human-headed, and at others all animal-headed; in one papyrus (Naville, *Todtenbuch*, Bl. CLIV, IK) Set appears as one of the guardians. In the Papyrus of Bakou (Brocklehurst Papyrus) the CXLIVth Chapter is entitled the "Chapter of entering in", and it is prefaced by a short prayer in which the doorkeepers are entreated to "make a way to him so that he may pass through you, for he is Nu," and "to open the hidden habitations." In the CXLVIIth Chapter the text of a prayer is added to the Vignette of each Ārit, which in some papyri consists of a door by which only one god is seated.

It has already been said that the fortresses in Dead-land were sometimes believed to be ten, or fourteen, or sixteen, or even twenty-one, in number; the Papyrus of Ani makes them to be ten, and calls them "Sebkhet," or "Pylons." In Plates XI and XII we see Ani and his wife Tutu advancing to the Ten Pylons, with their hands raised in adoration. Each Pylon is guarded by a ministering god or goddess, seated on a mat. As the deceased arrived at each Pylon he made to it a short address, which to all intents and purposes formed the name of the Pylon and of the deity inside it. Thus, when he came to the First Pylon he said: "I have made the way. I know you. I know thy "name. I know the name of thy warder. NEBT-SEṬAU-QAT-"SEBT-HERT-NEBT-KHEBKHEB-SERT-MEṬU-KHESFET-NESHNI-"NEHMET-UAI-EN-I is thy name." This name translated means: "Lady of tremblings, [surrounded by] lofty walls, "the chieftainess, lady of destruction, the disposer of the "words that drive away storms and deliver from destruction "him that travelleth along the way."

Vignette 1. THE FIRST PYLON. In this Pylon is seated a vulture-headed goddess wearing a disk on her head, and holding a whisk. Above the Pylon is a row of [hieroglyphs], which presumably represent spears or a protecting wall.

Text: [CHAPTER CXLVI.] An address to the goddess, and the name of the warder of the Pylon—NERUIT.

Vignette 2. THE SECOND PYLON. In this Pylon is seated a lion-headed goddess, holding a whisk, and on its roof lies a monster speckled serpent.

Text: An address to the goddess, and the name of the warder of the Pylon—MES-PTAḤ.

Vignette 3. THE THIRD PYLON. In this Pylon is seated a man-headed deity, holding a whisk, and above it are the two Eyes of heaven, the Sun and the Moon, with the emblems of eternity, water, and a vase between them [hieroglyphs].

Text: An address to the deity of the Pylon, and the name of its warder—SEBAQ.

Vignette 4. THE FOURTH PYLON. In this Pylon is seated a hornless, cow-headed goddess, holding a whisk, and above it is a cornice formed of uraei with solar disks on their heads 𓆗𓆗𓆗.

Text: An address to the goddess, and the name of the warder of the Pylon—NEḲAU.

Vignette 5. THE FIFTH PYLON. In this Pylon is seated a hippopotamus-goddess. Her forefeet rest upon the symbol of an organ of her body, and between them she holds a large knife. Above the roof of the Pylon are the symbols of "heat" and the "strength of youth," or perhaps "fecundity" [hieroglyphs].

Text: An address to the goddess, and the name of the warder of the Pylon—ḤENTET-ĀRQIU.

Vignette 6. THE SIXTH PYLON. In this Pylon is seated a squat dwarf, who holds in his right hand a whisk and in his left a large knife. On the roof lies a monster speckled serpent. The size of this serpent cannot be comprehended, and it is said to have been born in the presence of the Still-Heart, *i.e.*, Osiris.

Text: An address to the god, and the name of the warder of the Pylon—SEMȦTI.

Vignette 7. THE SEVENTH PYLON. In this Pylon is seated a ram-headed god, holding a whisk. On the roof is a row of [hieroglyphs].

Text: An address to the god, and the name of the warder of the Pylon—SȦKTIF.

Vignette 8. THE EIGHTH PYLON. In this Pylon is the hawk of Horus standing on a sepulchral building called *serekh* [hieroglyphs]; he wears the double crown of the South and the North [hieroglyph], and has a whisk before him and an *utchat* 𓂀, behind him. On the roof of the shrine are two human-headed hawks, emblems of the Souls of Rā and Osiris, and two emblems of "life" [hieroglyphs].

Text: An address to the god, and the name of the warder of the Pylon—KHUTCHETEF.

Vignette 9. THE NINTH PYLON. In this Pylon is seated a lion-headed deity with a disk on his head, and holding a whisk. Above the shrine is a series of uraei.

Text: An address to the deity, and the name of the warder of the shrine—ÅRISUTCHESEF.

Vignette 10. THE TENTH PYLON. In this shrine is seated a ram-headed deity wearing the *Atef* Crown, and holding a whisk. On the roof of the Pylon are two serpents.

Text: An address to the deity, and the name of the warder of the Pylon—SEKHENUR. The texts of the 11th–21st Pylons are wanting in the Papyrus of Ani. In the Papyrus of Thena (Naville, *op. cit.*, Bl. CLXIIIF), fourteen Vignettes are given, and each is quite different from any of the Vignettes in the Papyrus of Ani. The doors are decorated with a variety of strange designs, *e.g.*, the eleventh door has on it the solar disk floating on water, the third is decorated with and, the sixth with four uraei on a standard, etc.; and many of the doors are surmounted by bulls' heads, lions' heads, etc. In the Turin Papyrus the first ten Pylons are surmounted by serpents, the eleventh by two cats, the twelfth by a serpent, the thirteenth by figures of the two Nile-gods, the fourteenth by a bull's head and a serpent, and the fifteenth by a row of.

PLATES XII (continued) and XIII

INTRODUCTION TO CHAPTER XVIII

Vignette 1. The Osiris Ani standing with his hands raised in adoration of the series of gods who preside over the great cities of Egypt; behind him stands his wife Tutu, holding a sistrum in her right hand and the green head of some plant in her left.

Text: A prayer of Ani to Khent Åmentet Un-Nefer in Abydos. He declares that his heart holds truth, that there is no sin in his body, that he has not told lies or acted deceitfully.

Vignette 2. A door surmounted by ostrich feathers and uraei wearing disks [hieroglyphs]. Before it stands the Ånmutef [hieroglyphs] priest, wearing the lock of hair [hieroglyph], symbolic of youth, on the right side of his head. His dress consists of a short white linen loin cloth and a leopard skin, his arms coming through holes in the skin where the fore-legs of the leopard had been. His left hand clasps the skin of the right hind leg of the animal.

Text: An address to the Tchatchau Chiefs of heaven, earth, and Khert-Neter. The Ånmutef priest presents Ani who, he says, is not obnoxious to any of the gods, and claims admission for him among the Chiefs.

Vignette 3. Ani and Tutu as in Vignette 1.

Text: Ani's prayer to the King of Khert-Neter and Governor of Åḳert.

Vignette 4. A door surmounted by a figure of Anubis [hieroglyph] and an *utchat*. Before it stands the SA-MER-F [hieroglyphs], dressed like the Ånmutef priest.

Text: An address by the SA-MER-F priest to the Tchatchau of Ra-stau. He presents Ani and demands an estate for him in Sekhet Ḥetepet, with cakes and air, and asks that his rations may be like those of the Followers of Horus. This Introduction is found in no papyrus save that of Ani. Usually Chapter XVIII is regarded as a continuation of Chapter XVII, and it is very rarely accompanied by Vignettes, other than those containing figures of the gods only. In the Papyrus Busca (Naville, *op. cit.*, Bd. I, Bl. XXXI) we see the deceased ploughing and sowing, and he and his wife are dragging along the shrine of Seker mounted on a sledge.

Vignette 1. The five Chiefs of Ånu (Heliopolis): (1) Temu, wearing the Crowns of the South and North and a *menàt*. (2) The Sûdânî god Shu, with a black face, wearing a low crown made of feathers, with a sort of streamer, which falls down behind his back. (3) The Lioness-goddess Tefnut, also of Sûdânî origin, wearing on her head the solar disk. (4) The god Osiris, wearing the *Atef* Crown and a *menȧt*. His face is green, which seems to suggest old age, and he has the usual pointed and curved African beard. (5) The god Thoth, ibis-headed.

Text: [CHAPTER XVIII.] Without title. The opening sẹction of this Chapter is unaccountably omitted in the Papyrus of Ani, and a version of it is supplied in my translation from the Papyrus of Nebseni.

Vignette 2. The gods and goddesses of Ṭeṭu (Busiris): (1) The god Osiris, as before. (2) The goddess Isis, with ⌷ on her head. (3) The goddess Nephthys with the hieroglyph for her name on her head ⌷. (4) The god Horus, son of Isis, hawk-headed.

Text: Section relating to setting up the *ṭeṭ* in Ṭeṭu.

Vignette 3. The gods of Sekhem (Letopolis): (1) Osiris, as before. (2) Horus, wearing the Crowns of the South and the North. (3 and 4) The two Eyes of Rā, each on a pylon. (5) The god Thoth.

Text: Section relating to the "Things of the Night Festival" in Sekhem.

Vignette 4. The gods of Pe-Ṭep (Buto in the Delta): (1) Horus, as in the second Vignette. (2) Isis, as before. (3) Ḳestȧ (Mestȧ), a son of Horus, man-headed. (4) Ḥāpi (Ḥep), a son of Horus, ape-headed.

Text: Section relating to the setting up of the canopied throne for Horus after the overthrow of Set and his fiends by the followers of Horus.

Vignette 5. The gods who are in Taiu-Rekhti: (1) Osiris, as before. (2) Isis, as before. (3) Anubis, jackal-headed. (4) A bearded god. (5) The god Thoth, with a crescent moon, having the full moon inside it, on his head.

Text: Section referring to the lamentation of Isis for Osiris.

PLATE XIV

Vignette 6. The gods who are in Abydos: (1) Osiris, as before. (2) Isis, as before. (3) Anubis, as before. (4) The *ṭeṭ* with the Two Eyes of Rā [hieroglyphs].

Text: Section referring to the judgment of the dead and the infliction of punishment upon those who are condemned to destruction in the judgment.

Vignette 7. The gods who preside over the judgment of the dead: (1) Thoth, as before. (2) Osiris, as before. (3) Anubis, as before. (4) A bearded god, Åsṭen [hieroglyphs], the associate of Thoth.

Text: Section relating to the condemnation of Set and his fiends, and to the carrying out of their sentence of doom.

Vignette 8. The three gods who presided over the ploughing up of the earth in Ṭeṭu, and the mingling of the blood of the rebels with the earth.

Text: Section referring to the slaughter of the followers of Set, and the pouring out of their blood on the earth before the gods, and the digging of the blood into the ground. This section shows that a great slaughter of the enemies of Osiris took place at Ṭeṭu, as well as at Ḥensu (Herakleopolis), and it is clear that the sacrifices made there were offered up to the *ṭeṭ*, the symbol of a god who was worshipped at Busiris in predynastic times.

Vignette 9. The great gods of Ånruṭef, a district of Ḥensu in Upper Egypt: (1) Rā, hawk-headed, and wearing the solar disk on his head. (2) Osiris, as before. (3) Shu, the Sûdânî god from Baqem, with a green face, and wearing a crown of feathers, from which a sort of streamer falls down behind. (4) Beba, the first-born son of Osiris, dog-headed. The forms of the name of the god last mentioned are Beb [hieroglyphs], Baba [hieroglyphs], [hieroglyphs], and Ababi [hieroglyphs].

Text: Section relating to the deposit of the relics of Osiris, the thigh, the leg. and the heel at Ånruṭef, the place where nothing grows.

Vignette 10. The gods of Rasta: (1) Horus, hawk-headed, and wearing the Crowns of the South and the North. (2) The god Osiris, wearing the *Atef* Crown. (3) Isis, wearing the symbol of a Sûdânî goddess on her head instead of 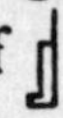 . (4) A god who is unnamed. We may note, in passing, the omission of two of the Sons of Horus, Ṭuamutef and Qebḥsenuf, from the Vignettes.

Text: Section referring to the satisfaction of heart of Osiris, and to the existence of peace in the east and west.

The XVIIIth Chapter contains ten addresses by the deceased to Thoth, who is prayed to make his word truth before his enemies, just as Thoth made the word of Osiris truth before his enemies. In each address reference is made to one of the very critical events which took place in the history of Osiris. It will be noted that none of the great cosmic gods took part in these occurrences.

The **Rubric** states that the recital of the Chapter shall cause the deceased to come forth by day, to escape every fire in the Other World, and to take any and every form he pleases, and shall purify him from all uncleanness, and free him from all the disabilities that cling to him upon earth.

PLATE XV

Vignette: A seated statue of Ani the scribe. Facing it is a figure of the *Sem* priest  , who is clad in linen garments over which he has put a leopard's skin. He holds in his hand the wooden instrument "*urḥeka*" 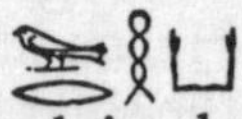 , *i.e.*, "the mighty one of spells," which has one end in the form of a ram's head. In front of the statue is a small box containing unguents and colours, the instruments *Sebur*,  , and *Ṭunā* 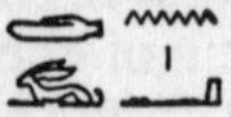 , and the *Pesh-en-kef*  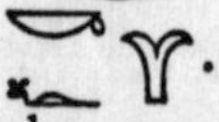 . The priest touches the mouth, the nose, and the eyes of the statue with these instruments, and thereby performs the great and solemn ceremony of *Un-ra*  , or "Opening the mouth." These ceremonies gave to the deceased in the Other World the power to eat, drink, think, talk, and move about at pleasure. As the priest performed each ceremony he recited a formula that had the effect of restoring to the deceased some power or faculty of which the death of his body had deprived him. The ceremony of "Opening the mouth" is very ancient, and was certainly performed on the statues of the dead in the earliest dynasties. Tradition asserts that Ptaḥ unbandaged the gods, and that Shu opened their mouths with an iron knife, and that the words that were recited whilst these gods were opening the mouths of the gods were composed by Thoth, the great magician of Rā, whose intelligence, or mind, he was. The series of ceremonies which were performed when the mouth of a king was opened, and the formulae which were recited are given in a handy form in my edition *The Opening of the Mouth*, 2 vols.: London, 1909.

Text: [CHAPTER XXIII.] THE CHAPTER OF OPENING THE MOUTH OF THE OSIRIS ANI. The text states that it is Set who keeps the mouth of Ani closed by bandages, and says that Tem shall cast them away. Ani identifies himself with the Sun-goddess Sekhmet, and with Saḥit, a powerful Star-goddess and wife of Orion the Giant, and he calls upon all the gods to do away with the ill-effects of any spell which any ill-disposed being shall cast upon him.

Vignette: [Wanting in the Theban Recension.]

Text: [CHAPTER XXIV.] THE CHAPTER OF BRINGING WORDS OF POWER, OR SPELLS, TO THE OSIRIS ANI IN KHERT-NETER. In this Chapter Ani identifies himself with Tem-Kheperȧ, who composed the words of power that Thoth pronounced, which resulted in the creation of the heavens and the earth. In the character of this god Ani could pronounce words, the effect of which would be to give him everything that he desired. Now, the Egyptians thought that words were concrete things, and that it was possible to steal from a man his words of power, or the spells wherewith he had been provided; and whereas we should say that we had forgotten a formula, the Egyptian would say that it had been stolen from him. The object of this Chapter was to give a man in Khert-Neter the ability to make his words of power, supposing they had gone away, or been carried away from him, to return to him, no matter how far away they had been carried. When the Chapter was recited by Ani, his spells would return to him more swiftly than greyhounds can run, and quicker than the light. Its recital, too, would obtain for him the help of "him that brought the ferry-boat of Rā," , *i.e.*, of the god Ḥerfḥaf , who ferried the souls of the righteous over to the Island of Fire, wherein Osiris reigned. The word of power which Ani wanted to possess was that the utterance of which would enable him to recreate himself. Closely connected with this Chapter is the XXVth, a rendering of which is given in the Appendix. The recital of this Chapter enabled a man to recall to memory his name, if by any chance he forgot it, and also the name of any and every god whom he might happen to meet. As we have already seen, the deceased was called upon to declare the names of the guardians of the Ārits and Pylons in the land of Osiris, and, if he were unable to remember these names, he would assuredly not be admitted into them. The nameless soul in the Other World could not be presented to the Great God, and, as his name could not appear in the list of the names of those who were to receive their rations from the table of the god, he would perish. The name of a man was an integral part of his being, and to steal it from him was to ensure his destruction. No greater harm could be done to the deceased than the erasing of his name from his statues, stelae, or tomb, for the destruction of his name was equivalent to the destruction of his individuality.

Vignette: The scribe Ani standing upright and arrayed in white. His right hand is laid on his breast, over his heart, and with his left he touches a necklace, which presumably he is receiving from the god Anubis. The necklace is composed of several rows of beads and to it is attached a pectoral in the form of a pylon, made of faïence, and inlaid with a figure of the Boat of Rā, with the solar disk[1] resting in it. Anubis is jackal-headed, and he holds

[1] Or perhaps a scarab; see the specimens exhibited in the Fourth Egyptian Room in the British Museum.

a sceptre in the right hand, and a symbol of "life" ☥, in the left.

Text: [Chapter XXVI.] The Chapter of giving a heart to the Osiris Ani in Khert-Neter. The object of this Chapter was the restoration of the heart of the deceased to him. In primitive times the internal organs were removed from the body after death and destroyed, but when mummification of the bodies of the wealthy became general, the heart, lungs, gall-bladder, etc., were mummified separately. As it was Anubis who presided over the mummification of the dead, and who had therefore authority over the hearts of the dead, it was necessary to invoke his goodwill, and to persuade him to return to the deceased his heart in Khert-Neter. In the Vignettes to this Chapter we see the god returning to the deceased his heart, or giving to him a necklace with a pectoral containing a stone scarab on which were written the magical words of the most important of the Chapters of the Heart (XXXB). The heart was the home of the Ba-soul, on which the Ka, or Double, depended for existence. The destruction of the heart involved the annihilation of the Ba-soul and the Ka; and it was the Ba-soul which partook of the offerings made to the dead. In the Chapter Ani says clearly: "If I have "no heart I cannot eat of the cakes of Osiris, and I cannot "sail up and down the Nile to Abydos and Ṭeṭu (Busiris)." With the restoration of his heart Ani gained the power to use his mind and understanding, to use his hands and legs, and to do whatever his Ka called upon him to do, and to revisit this earth at pleasure.

Vignette: [Wanting in the Papyrus of Ani.] In the Papyrus of Nebseni the Vignette to this Chapter shows us the heart of the deceased being weighed against himself by an ape in the presence of Osiris (see illustration). In other papyri the deceased is seen addressing his heart, which rests on a standard, or the Vignette is simply a heart, or a heart-pectoral.

Text: [CHAPTER XXXB.] THE CHAPTER OF NOT LETTING THE HEART OF THE OSIRIS ANI BE DRIVEN AWAY FROM HIM IN KHERT-NETER. This Chapter is one of the most important of the Chapters of the Book of the Dead, and it is unquestionably one of the oldest. It is found on coffins of the XIth dynasty, and in all great papyri which have not been mutilated, and upon hundreds of hard green stone scarabs. Egyptian traditions assign to it great antiquity, one of them declaring it was "found" cut upon the pedestal of a statue of Thoth in the reign of Ḥesepti (Semti), a king of the Ist dynasty; and another assuring us that it was "found" by Prince Ḥeruṭāṭāf, the son of Khufu (Cheops). The older tradition states that it was the work of Thoth himself. The copy of the Chapter given in this Plate is, like that found in the Judgment Scene (Plate III), incomplete, but the reader will find the missing words supplied in the hieroglyphic text. The contents of the Chapter have already been discussed in the description of the Judgment, and nothing further need therefore be said here.

Vignette: The scribe Ani arrayed in white apparel, hugging closely to his body his Ba-soul, which is in the form of a man-headed hawk.

Text: [CHAPTER LXI.] THE CHAPTER OF NOT LETTING THE BA-SOUL OF A MAN BE SNATCHED AWAY FROM HIM IN KHERT-NETER. The title of this Chapter is easy to understand, for a belief has always been common in many parts of Africa that a man's soul can be bewitched out of him, and that if an enemy succeeds in stealing the soul, the man whose soul has been stolen will die. But the connection of the title with the contents of the Chapter is not so evident, for the deceased says that he came forth from the primeval waters, *aḳab* [hieroglyphs], and he prays that he may have abundance of water, and have the mastery over streams of water. In the Papyrus of Nefer-uben-f this Chapter forms part of a much longer composition, which comprises Chapters LX, LXI, and LXII, and which has for its Vignette the picture of a man washing out his mouth by the side of a lake or stream. In the Saïte Recension the Chapter has a Vignette with the figure of a man holding in one hand a sail. The contents of Chapter LXI certainly refer to the drinking of water in Khert-Neter, and we can only conclude that the present title of it is the result of some mistake or misunderstanding of its words.

Vignette: The scribe Ani, arrayed in white apparel, holding in his left hand a sail, symbolic of air or breath.

Text: [CHAPTER LIV.] THE CHAPTER OF GIVING AIR TO THE SCRIBE ANI IN KHERT-NETER. Ani identifies himself with the Egg of the Great Cackler, that is to say, with the egg of the Sun, which was laid by the great god Ḳeb. As the embryo inside the shell obtains air and grows to maturity, so the embryo of Ani's spirit-body breathes, and lives and grows inside the tomb, which takes the place of the shell of the Egg. Ani also identifies himself with the god *Utchā-aābt*, of whom little is known. The "dweller in his nest," and "the babe," are, of course, himself. In Chapters LV and LVI, which are translated in the Appendix, he identifies himself with the "jackal of jackals", and with Shu, the god of the air, and he addresses Tem, the god of the north wind, and beseeches him to give him the breath which is in his nostrils.

Vignette: The scribe Ani, arrayed in white apparel, holding in his right hand an unidentified object and in his left a staff.

Text: [CHAPTER XXIX.] THE CHAPTER OF NOT LETTING THE HEART OF A MAN BE TAKEN AWAY FROM HIM IN KHERT-NETER. This Chapter is extant in three forms, and the principal object of all three was to prevent Ani's heart from being bewitched away from him. In Chapter XXIXA the deceased identifies himself with the "Lord of hearts, the slayer of the heart," and with Horus, "the dweller in hearts." In Chapter XXIXB he declares that he is Benu, the soul of Rā, and the Guide of the gods of the Ṭuat. With the help of this Chapter Ani could prevent the messenger of any god from stealing his heart, but he might steal the hearts of others.

PLATE XVI

Vignette: The scribe Ani, arrayed in white apparel, standing with both hands raised in the attitude of prayer to his heart, which is resting on a stand. Facing him, seated on the cubit of *maāt*, are four bearded gods, who represent the Four Sons of Horus, Ḳestȧ (Mestȧ), Ḥāpi, Ṭuamutef, and Qebḥsenuf.

Text: [CHAPTER XXVII.] THE CHAPTER OF NOT LETTING THE HEART OF A MAN BE TAKEN FROM HIM IN KHERT-NETER. This Chapter is an address to the gods who steal hearts, and crush them, and who reward a man according to the deeds of his heart. Ani calls on them not to touch his heart, because it belongs to the god of many names (Tem, or Rā, or Thoth). Ani declares that his heart is made new, that he has power over it, that it and his members obey him, and that it shall never leave his body. In the Appendix translations are given of the supplementary Chapters XXVIII, XXIXA, and XXXA. The first part of Chapter XXXA resembles that of a part of Chapter XXXB, but the ending is different, and the Sons of Horus are entreated by the deceased to intercede for him with Rā, and to cause the terrible goddess Neḥebka to do him no harm. The Vignette of Chapter XXVIII is of interest, for we see in it a monster in human form with a shaggy mane and whiskers round his face and a tail; and his general appearance suggests that he was intended to represent a gorilla, or chimpanzee, though of course these animals have no tails. It is probable that the artist drew the monster, of which he must have heard by reports that filtered down the Nile from the Southern Sûdân, and added a tail because he thought he ought to have one.

Vignette: The scribe Ani and his wife Tutu standing up to their knees in a canal or arm of the Nile, scooping up water into their mouths with their right hands. Ani holds in his left hand a sail, symbolic of air or wind, and Tutu holds in her left hand a fan. By the side of the water two young palms and a large mature palm are growing, and from the leafy crown of the large palm hang two clusters of ripe dates.

Text: [Chapter LVIII.] The Chapter of breathing the air, and of having dominion over the water in Khert-Neter. About the meanings of the Vignette and of the title of this Chapter there is no room for doubt; they refer to the drinking of water and to the breathing of air by Ani in the Other World. The text of the Chapter seems to indicate that Ani wishes to enter into a certain part of the Other World, in the company of the Merti goddesses. Some god, name unknown, asks him who he is, what is his name, and where he is going. Ani refers to a boat which he has, and repeats the magical names of it and its parts. The Chapter ends with a prayer for cakes, bread, ale, and flesh, of which he wishes to partake in the temple of Ȧnpu. This Chapter is not found in other papyri containing the Theban Recension, and its title in the Papyrus of Ani must have been given to it by mistake.

Vignette: The scribe Ani, arrayed in white apparel, kneeling in adoration under the branches of a large fine sycamore tree, which is growing by the side of a lake of water . Almost hidden in the branches is the figure of the goddess Nut, who is giving to Ani a table of food with one hand, and a vessel of pure water with the other. The tree appears to be the sycamore fig-tree, and to be laden with fruit. This Vignette suggests that at one time tree-worship was common in Egypt, as it is in certain other parts of Africa at the present day.

Text: [Chapter LIX.] The Chapter of snuffing the air, and of having power over the water in Khert-Neter. Ani's petition for the water and air which are in Nut, *i.e.*, the Sky, of which goddess the sycamore was the symbol. Ani again identifies himself with the Egg of the Great Cackler, with the life in which his own life is bound up.

Vignette: The scribe Ani, arrayed in white apparel, seated upon a chair of state with a high back. In his right hand he holds the *Kherp* sceptre, symbolic of his authority, and in the other his staff of office. Before him is a table. In the Turin Papyrus the deceased stands before a sepulchral shrine.

Text: [Chapter XLIV.] The Chapter of not dying a second time in Khert-Neter. The Egyptians believed that the KAU, or Doubles of the dead, lived on the souls of the offerings that were made regularly in the tombs wherein their bodies were laid, and that if for any reason an interruption in the supply of food took place, the KAU suffered hunger and thirst. The KAU might wander about and prolong their existence by eating offal in the desert, and by drinking dirty water, but unless the supply of offerings was renewed they starved to death. Moreover, it was possible, they also thought, that the KAU might suffer death a second time through the displeasure of the Tchatchau chiefs and the Sheniu officials who administered the Kingdom of Osiris. This Chapter was written to enable the deceased to identify himself with the never-setting, or imperishable, stars, and with Rā and Horus, who were immortal. He who was crowned "King of the Gods" could not die a second time.

Vignette: The mummy of the Osiris Ani being embraced by Anubis, the god of the embalmment chamber and master of medical knowledge.

Text: [CHAPTER XLV.] THE CHAPTER OF NOT ROTTING IN KHERT-NETER. The object of this Chapter is quite clear, namely, to prevent the mummy of the deceased from rotting away through the effects of improper or unskilful mummification. Ani wished to be mummified by Anubis, who carried out the mummification of Osiris whilst Isis recited spells that had been composed for her by Thoth. Anubis embalmed Osiris with such skill that the flesh of the god never decayed, or crumbled away, or fell into dust, and the medicaments and swathings which he employed in the work were of the finest quality, and possessed preservative properties in the highest degree. The recital of this Chapter provided the deceased with the services of Anubis. Chapters CLXXV and CLXXVI bear the same title, and were written with the same object as this Chapter.

Vignette: A doorway, presumably the doorway of the tomb. By one jamb stands the Heart-soul of Ani in the form of a man-headed hawk, and by the other a Benu bird, which symbolized the soul of Rā.

Text: [CHAPTER XLVI.] THE CHAPTER OF NOT PERISHING, AND OF BECOMING ALIVE IN KHERT-NETER. The object of this Chapter was to enable the spiritual members of Ani to emerge from his body and from his tomb, and to join the Ḥenmemet spirits [hieroglyphs], or [hieroglyphs], one of the oldest orders of spirits, who dwelt in heaven. It is possible that the Benu bird may here symbolize the Spirit-soul of Ani, which, unlike the Heart-soul, could never be destroyed or die. The Heart-soul, as we have seen, might in certain circumstances suffer the second death. The Benu bird as the incarnation of the Soul of the Sun-god imparted some of its character of immortality to the mortal soul of Ani.

Vignette: The scribe Ani, arrayed in white linen garments, walking away from the block of slaughter in Khert-Neter, which somewhat resembles a guillotine. Those who were to be slaughtered placed their necks between the two upright posts, and the huge knife descending upon them cut off their heads.

Text: [Chapter LA.] The Chapter of not entering into the chamber of the block of execution. This text states that the vertebrae of the neck that join Ani's head to his body were knitted together in heaven for him by Rā in primeval times. This being so, it is impossible for any hostile god to separate the vertebrae of his neck, or to remove his head from his body. Curiously enough, it is also said that Set knitted together the vertebrae of Ani's neck, just as Rā did. Now Set succeeded in hacking off the head of Osiris, and, as he might cut off Ani's head also, Ani relies on the recital of this Chapter to give his body strength to resist any possible attack of Set. The beheading of the wicked was performed nightly in the torture chambers of the Other World under the direction of Shesmu [hieroglyphs], the terrible executioner of Osiris. The recital of this Chapter also secured for Ani immunity from the passing upon him of the sentence of beheading by Osiris.

PLATE XVII

Vignette: Ani, arrayed in white linen garments, standing with his hands raised in entreaty or prayer to three gods, each of whom holds a sceptre [hieroglyph] in his right hand and the symbol of "life" in his left. In a Vignette published by Naville, a figure of the Tet, or symbol of the uterus of Isis, is seen grasping the left arm of the deceased with a pair of human arms and hands.

Text: [Chapter XCIII.] The Chapter of not letting a man be transported to the East in Khert-Neter. The meaning of the text of this Chapter is comparatively plain. It opens with an address to the Phallus of Rā, and continues with a prayer in which Ani begs that he may not be carried by force to the East, or be made to take part in the festivals that are held there. The Kingdom of Osiris, we know, was situated to the west of the Nile, and it is possible that the only object of the recital of this Chapter was to prevent Ani from being set on the wrong road, and from arriving at the place of slaughter instead of the realms of joy of Osiris. On the other hand, it seems that there must be some meaning in the Chapter which we have not grasped, and the mention of the phallus of Rā and the Vignette of the genital organs of Isis seem to suggest that the East was a place of abomination to the Egyptians, because sexual orgies of an irregular character were carried on there.

Vignette: The scribe Ani, arrayed in white linen apparel, standing and addressing a god, who has his face turned round behind him, and who is seated in a boat; Ani grasps his palette in his left hand. This is the god Ḥerfḥaf, who was the celestial Ferryman, and who ferried over the souls of the righteous to the Island of Fire where Osiris reigned. None but the just could enter his boat, and his face was turned round in order that he might see what was going on behind his back, and prevent improperly qualified souls from making use of his boat. In the Turin Papyrus there is a table of offerings in the boat, and in front of the boat itself is the symbol of the East. It is not clear why Ani is grasping his palette, and in the Turin Papyrus the deceased has both hands empty.

Text: [Chapter XCIIIa.] Another Chapter. In other papyri these two Chapters form one, and the Turin Papyrus suggests that it should properly only have one Vignette, namely, that in which Ḥerfḥaf appears.

Vignette: The scribe Ani addressing three gods. The Turin Papyrus proves that the Vignette which is described above under Chapter XCIII really belongs to Chapter XLIII, and that either the artist who illustrated the Papyrus of Ani painted it in the wrong place, or the scribe misplaced the text.

Text: [CHAPTER XLIII.] THE CHAPTER OF NOT LETTING THE HEAD OF A MAN BE CUT OFF HIM IN KHERT-NETER. In this Chapter Ani identifies himself with the Great One and the Son of Fire, to whom his head was given after it had been cut off. Since the head of Osiris was cut off, Ani could not expect to avoid a similar fate, but the head of Osiris was not taken away from him, and Ani prays that his head may never be carried away, for he is Osiris himself. It is now well known that in primitive times in Egypt the bodies of the dead were dismembered before burial, probably as the result of religious beliefs. This is clear from passages like the following, wherein we read that the gods :—

Give to thee thy head,

Present to thee thy bones,

Collect thy members,

Bring to thee thy heart in thy body,[1]

As the practice of embalming grew and spread in Egypt in early dynastic times, as the result of the growth of the cult of Osiris, the custom of dismembering the body gradually fell into disuse, and at length the only portions of the body which were removed from it during the process of embalming were the viscera, and these were mummified separately. At the time when the Papyrus of Ani was written there was little chance of the head being severed from the mummy wilfully, nevertheless Ani had the Chapter included in his papyrus, wishing to run no risk of dismemberment, accidental or otherwise.

[1] Pyramid of Pepi I, l. 110.

Vignette: The mummy of Ani lying on its bier, with a stand containing burning incense at the head and at the foot of it. Above the mummy hovers his Heart-soul in the form of a man-headed hawk, holding in his claws *shen* Ω, the symbol of the sun's course and of eternity. This the soul is presenting to its body with the view of making it everlasting.

Text: [CHAPTER LXXXIX.] THE CHAPTER OF CAUSING THE HEART-SOUL TO BE UNITED TO ITS BODY IN KHERT-NETER. By the recital of this very important Chapter Ani hoped to gain possession of his Heart-soul (Ba) and of his Spirit-soul (Khu), and to effect the union of the former with its material body *khat* [hieroglyphs], and the union of the latter with its Spirit-body *sāḥ* [hieroglyphs]. Heart-soul and body would then exist eternally upon the earth, and the Spirit-soul and its ethereal and indestructible envelope would have their being among the gods. The **Rubric** of the Chapter orders that an amulet in the form of a Heart-soul made of gold and inlaid with precious stones shall be tied to the neck of the mummy. If this were done it was believed that the gods would compel Ani's Heart-soul to visit its body regularly, and so prevent it from decaying, and that both Heart-soul and body would be able to visit during the seasons of festivals the city of Ȧnu, where Heart-souls were united to their bodies by thousands. In the Turin Papyrus it is expressly stated that the presence of such an amulet on the body would prevent it from decaying, and would prevent the Heart-soul from leaving it.

Vignette: The Heart-soul of the scribe Ani, in the form of a man-headed bird, standing in front of the door of his tomb. The papyri afford many variants of the Vignette of this most interesting Chapter. In the Papyrus of Khari (Fig. 1) we see the deceased standing before his tomb, of which he has opened the door [hieroglyph], and his Heart-soul in the form of a man-headed hawk flying out to meet him. In the Papyrus of Ȧmenḥetep

FIG. 1.

(Fig. 2) we see the deceased actually opening the door of a shrine resting on the cubit of *maāt* ▭, and behind him stands his Heart-soul with the symbol of "life" above it. The third variant (Fig. 3), from the Papyrus of Nefer-uben-f, is very interesting. The building here represented is not a tomb, but an ordinary house, above which shines the noon-day sun. Walking away from the house is a figure of the deceased coloured black, and above his head hovers his Heart-soul. The black figure is the KA, or Double of the deceased, which as we have seen is always intimately connected with the Heart-soul. The KA died if the Heart-soul died, for it depended for its existence on the Heart-soul, which maintained itself on the offerings that were made in the tomb. The connection between the Heart-soul and the KA was so close that if the former were imprisoned in the tomb, the latter suffered imprisonment also.

FIG. 2.

FIG. 3.

Text: [CHAPTER XCI.] THE CHAPTER OF NOT LETTING THE SOUL OF A MAN BE SHUT UP IN KHERT-NETER. This Chapter is an address to the Soul-god, *i.e.*, Osiris, who is entreated to make a path for the dual-soul of Ani. Ani rejoices in the fact that he is an "equipped Spirit-soul" [hieroglyphs], which means, presumably, that his dual-soul is complete now that he is master of his Heart-soul, or now, as we read in the Papyrus of Nu, that his Spirit-soul, and Heart-soul, and KA, or Double, are re-united. The **Rubric** states that the Spirit-soul that possesses a knowledge of this Chapter shall not be stopped at any door in Khert-Neter, and that it shall go in and out of every part of this region millions of times.

Vignettes: (1) Ani standing by the door of his tomb; (2) Ani walking out of the tomb, with his Heart-soul hovering above his head.

Text: [CHAPTER XCII.] THE CHAPTER OF OPENING THE TOMB TO THE HEART-SOUL AND THE SHADOW, AND OF COMING FORTH BY DAY, AND OF HAVING POWER OVER THE LEGS. The recital of this Chapter procured for Ani the power to leave the tomb on the "day of souls," *i.e.*, All Souls' Day, and to see Rā seated in his boat, and to behold the Great God on the day when souls were "counted up" (or inspected, or judged), and to sit down among the Chiefs in the Other World. A soul that possessed a knowledge of this Chapter had no need to fear the opposition of the fiends who fetter the members of Spirit-souls, and shut in Spirit-souls, and who wished to do harm to it.

PLATE XVIII

Vignette: The boat containing the shrine, or ark, of the god Seker, or Death personified, resting upon its sledge; before it kneels the Osiris Ani, with both hands grasping a part of the boat.

Text: [CHAPTER LXXIV.] THE CHAPTER OF LIFTING UP THE FEET (*i.e.*, OF WALKING), AND OF COMING FORTH UPON THE EARTH. This Chapter contains a petition to Seker, who had the power to stand on his feet in Khert-Neter, for strength to walk. Ani identifies himself with the god who illumines the great constellation of the Thigh, *i.e.*, the Great Bear in the northern sky. The Thigh was in the older mythology associated with Set, who, it will be remembered, was wounded in the thigh by Horus because he had swallowed the crescent moon one evening when wandering about the sky. The lack of power to walk which characterized the dead body was associated by the Egyptians with the evil influence of Set. This could only be overcome by the power of the god of light, *i.e.*, the Eye of Horus, and, when Ani had identified himself with this god, the power to stand on his feet and walk was assured to him.

Vignette: The Osiris Ani standing before the Mountain of Amenti, by which are placed a vessel of drink and a loaf of bread.

Text: [CHAPTER VIII.] THE CHAPTER OF PASSING THROUGH AMENTI, AND OF [COMING FORTH BY DAY]. In this Chapter Ani claims the power to pass through Ȧmenti because he is Osiris, and because he has delivered the Eye of Horus, that is to say, he has secured for himself the attributes and strength of Thoth. Ani also identifies himself with the Moon-god, who was a form of Osiris and the symbol and type of new birth, or resurrection. This Chapter is important as showing that Osiris was certainly regarded as the god of the moon under the XVIIIth dynasty, and that the death of the body was compared to the period of the month during which the moon was invisible. As surely as the moon reappeared in the sky, so surely would Ani appear in heaven; and his course through Ȧmenti would be as triumphant as that of the moon through the heavens.

Vignette: [Wanting in the Papyrus of Ani.]

Text: [CHAPTER II.] THE CHAPTER OF COMING FORTH BY DAY, AND OF LIVING AFTER DEATH. This Chapter is an address to the One who makes his presence visible by shining from the moon. Among modern African nations he is called the "spirit of the moon." Ani appeals to him as the great symbol of the resurrection, and as the being who revivified himself, and who has gathered about him the spirits who share his nature and his attributes. The favour of the god of the moon enabled Ani to make his way successfully through the Other World to the realm of Osiris, and this Chapter is one of the oldest and most important spells in the Book of the Dead.

Vignette: A Ram-god, symbolic of the Soul-god of Ṭeṭu, standing upon a sepulchral building, which rests on a mat. He has on his head a high crown with plumes, which, together with a disk, rests upon a pair of long horizontal horns. This ram is identical in form with the ram that was the incarnation of Khnemu, the great god of the First Cataract. Before him is a stand with offerings upon it, and in front of him is Ani, arrayed in white apparel, with his hands raised in adoration.

Text: [CHAPTER IX.] THE CHAPTER OF COMING FORTH BY DAY HAVING PASSED THROUGH ȦMḤET. The recital of this Chapter by Ani gave him power to pass through the awful chamber of Ȧmḥet in the kingdom of

Seker, the god of Death, and to traverse every path in Dead-land successfully, and to emerge before Osiris sound and well. Ani cries out in triumph: "I have stabbed (or, cut out, this heart of Suti", which is only a figurative way of saying: "I have slain death." In the land of Death Suti, *i.e.*, Set, ruled supreme, and every soul who entered unprovided with the knowledge of the words of this Chapter suffered death, final and absolute. But Ani has traversed his domain, and slain the heart of Set by means of these words, and he confidently calls upon the gods and the Spirit-souls in the kingdom of the Soul-god to make a path for him among them, as the beings have done in Dead-land.

Vignette: The scribe Ani, arrayed in white apparel, and holding in his right hand a symbol of his office and in the other a long staff such as was carried by high officials, standing before the door of a house.

Text: [CHAPTER CXXXII.] THE CHAPTER OF MAKING A MAN TO RETURN TO SEE HIS HOUSE UPON EARTH. The recital of this Chapter enabled Ani to revisit his house upon the earth. By means of it he identified himself with the Lion-god and with the Eye of Horus, and was enabled thereby to transform himself into its light, and to come upon the earth and to look upon his old home. In the Vignette to the Chapter in the Brocklehurst Papyrus we see the Heart-soul of the deceased hovering above the house, close to which is a tree. One papyrus (Naville, *op. cit.*, Bd. I, Bl. 145) adds the apparently irrelevant words: "Behold, I have advanced, I have not been found light in "the Balance, which is rid of my case" .

Vignette: The scribe Ani, arrayed in white apparel, spearing a serpent.

Text: [CHAPTER X OR XLVIII.] THE CHAPTER OF A MAN COMING FORTH BY DAY AGAINST HIS FOES IN KHERT-NETER. By the recital of this Chapter Ani obtained the protection of the Great Spirit-soul, *i.e.*, Osiris, and the use of his words of power; these enabled him to eat with his mouth, and to masticate his food with his jaws. The appositeness of the latter remark is not evident. In the Papyrus of Iuȧu (ed. Naville, Plate XI) the deceased is seen driving a spear into the neck of an enemy in human form, who is kneeling before him, and who has his arms tied at the elbows behind his back. It is possible that we have here a reminiscence of the old cannibalistic custom of eating an enemy, and the allusion to the mouth and jaws seems to support this view.

PLATE XIX

Vignette: The Boat of Rā resting on the sky ⲉ. The god is hawk-headed, and has the solar disk on his head. On the mat hanging over the prow of the boat is seated a figure of Harpokrates, and before him stands Ani, with his hands raised in adoration of the god.

Text: [CHAPTER XV.] A HYMN OF PRAISE TO RĀ WHEN HE RISETH UPON THE HORIZON, AND WHEN HE SETTETH IN THE [LAND OF] LIFE. This Section of the Book of the Dead contains hymns to the Sun-god, some of which were sung in the morning and some in the evening. The subjects of all these hymns are: (1) The strength, greatness, and glory of the Sun-god, and the joy with which he traversed the heavens in his morning and evening boats. (2) The homage which is paid to him on earth, and the reverent worship accorded to him by the gods. (3) The overthrow of Āapep, the Arch-fiend, and of all the devils who aid him in his attempt to obstruct the rising of Rā in the sky. (4) The attributes of the Sun-god, and the things which he has created.

Vignette: The scribe Ani, arrayed in white apparel, with his hands raised in adoration of the god; behind him stands his wife, "the Osiris, the lady of the house, the singing-woman of Ȧmen, Tutu." She is dressed as before, and holds in her hands the symbols of her office.

Text: A short hymn to Osiris, the everlasting Lord, Un-Nefer-Ḥeru-Khuti, who is Ptaḥ-Seker-Tem in Ȧnu, and the creator of the gods of Memphis, and the Guide of the gods in heaven, and who is here addressed as the god who raises up the dead to look upon him, and who bestows upon them the air that they breathe. This is followed by a Litany containing nine short sections, after each of which were repeated a petition by Ani for power to continue his journey in the Other World in safety, and a declaration that his words were true, that he had not told lies knowingly nor committed any fraudulent or deceitful act. This Litany in the form in which it here appears is found in no other Theban papyrus of the period.

PLATE XX

Vignette: Osiris, in the form of a mummy standing in a shrine, with Isis. He wears the Crown of the South, and holds in his hands , symbols of sovereignty and dominion. Isis embraces the body of the god with her right arm.

Text: [CHAPTER XV.] A HYMN OF PRAISE TO RĀ WHEN HE RISETH IN THE EASTERN PART OF HEAVEN. This interesting composition contains a series of addresses to the Sun-god among which are several short personal prayers that are put into the mouth of Ani himself. It is important to note that Ani wishes to appear in the sky with the Sun-god when he rises in the morning, and to sail with him in the Āntchet and Sektet Boats, and to enter with him into the night-sky when he sets upon this world. Thus Ani becomes a worshipper of Rā, and a devout votary of the Sun-god, and it seems as if he will be content with nothing less than living in the absolute presence of the god himself. The light of Rā is to draw him forth from the tomb, and to renew the life of all his members, and Ani beseeches the god to raise him to life again, because, he says: "I am one "of those who worshipped thee when thou livedst upon the "earth." It is difficult at first sight to reconcile his adherence to the cult of Rā with his belief in Osiris, and to understand how he could live in the Boat of Rā all day and yet be a loyal servant of Osiris carrying out the behests of that god, at the same time. The true explanation of the matter is that Rā and Osiris are only two forms of one god. Rā was the form which that god assumed during the day-time, and Osiris was the form which he took during the hours of the night. The sun was the habitation of this god during the day, and the moon was his dwelling place during the night.

The second section of the Hymn contains meditations upon the greatness and majesty of the god of the sky. Having once entered upon his course he follows it by a law that cannot be altered. As he passes over the sky with irresistible force every face watches the symbol of the god who makes himself visible to all men at dawn and at even. The strength of his light and the variety of its colours can neither be told nor described. The god who is invisible by day because of the dazzling splendour in which he is enshrined is One, and one only, and it is only through his own will and word that he becomes the Prince of Heaven. The speed of the Sun-god made the author of the hymn to marvel, for in one moment the god travels a distance which it would take a man millions of years to accomplish; and by his journeying the hours of the night as well as those of the day are numbered. Equally worthy of wonder is the daily birth of Rā, whose members are fashioned and whose body is born into the sky without any pain arising in the being of his creator.

PLATE XXI

[CHAPTER XV—*continued.*] The great god, the begetter and maker of Rā, is the creator of eternity, and is mightier than the gods; to him Ani gives his heart unhesitatingly. Moreover, this god is almighty, for he is able to overthrow all the powers of evil and to stablish his throne, despite the powers of wickedness and darkness; and he can destroy all sin. Therefore to him Ani appeals to make his word truth in Khert-Neter, and to make him sinless therein. Only by his help can Ani hope to obtain a place with the vassals of the Spirit-souls of Rā, and to live among the souls in the Land of Holiness; unless the Sun-god makes to prosper his journey he can never hope to arrive safely in Sekhet-Åaru. The two paragraphs at the end of the hymn suggest that the Sun-god is speaking to Ani, for the text reads: "Thou shalt appeär in heaven, "thou shalt traverse the sky, thou shalt be side by side "with the gods of the stars," and he is assured that he shall have a place in the Boat of the Sun, and shall see the Two

Fishes, the Åbṭu and the Ånt, performing their evolutions by the prow of the Boat, and shall behold Thoth and Maāt directing the Boat, and Horus acting as its steersman. And he shall be with the gods who welcome Rā.

Vignette: Rā, hawk-headed, with the solar disk upon his head and the symbol of "life" upon his knees, seated on *maāt* in one of the Boats of Rā which rests upon heaven; before him in the boat stands Ani with his hands raised in adoration. On the mat that falls over the prow of the boat a swallow is perched.

Text: [Chapter CXXXIII.] The title of this Chapter is wanting, and the only note at the beginning of the text is to the effect that the Chapter is to be recited on the "day of the moon," *i.e.*, on the first day of the New Moon. In other papyri it is called the "Book of making perfect the "Spirit-soul in Khert-Neter in the presence of the Great "Company of the Gods." The text refers to the strength and soundness of the body of Rā, and to his triumphant journey towards Åmenti, to which he comes in a re-constituted body daily. The recital of this Chapter renewed the members and life of Ani as those of Rā were renewed, and secured for him a welcome from the gods similar to that accorded to Rā himself. Moreover, it prevented him from remaining inert in the earth, and gave him the power to hear and to see everything said and done in Khert-Neter. Above all, it transformed the flesh of Ani into the divine flesh of Rā, and when he seated himself in the Boat of Rā the gods believed that they were looking upon Rā himself.

PLATE XXII

Vignette to the Rubric: The god Rā, hawk-headed, with the solar disk upon his head and the symbol of "life" ☥, upon his knees, seated on *maāt* in one of the Boats of Rā which rests on heaven. The paddles, which are fastened to hawk-headed supports, have curved handles in the form of the uraei of Isis and Nephthys, and the Boat is protected by an *utchat* amulet on the port bow. In front of the Boat is a "heaven of stars."

Rubric: The recital of the above Chapter would compel the gods to mistake Ani for Rā, provided that the directions given in the Rubric were obeyed: "Make a " model of the boat of Rā seven cubits long, put in it " figures of the gods and a figure of Rā, and paint a " representation of the starry sky, and purify the same " with natron [water] and incense. Then make a figure " of Ani and set him in the boat with the other figures, " and the dead shall prostrate themselves before him, and " the gods see in him a god like unto themselves. The " ceremonies connected with this Chapter must be per- " formed with great secrecy, and no woman may be " present; no one, in fact, except the father or the son of " him that performeth them."

Vignette: The god Rā, hawk-headed, with the solar disk upon his head and the symbol of life on his knees, seated on the emblem of "truth" 𓌷, in a long boat, which rests upon heaven. On the port bow is the amulet of the *utchat*, and in the boat itself is a huge disk, presumably that of Rā. In the older papyri, *e.g.*, the Papyrus of Nebseni, this Boat of Rā is filled with the figures of the gods Shu, Tefnut, Ḳeb, Nut, Osiris, Isis, Horus, and Hathor, and perched on the prow is the hawk of Horus, wearing the White Crown and holding a whip. In the Turin Papyrus the Boat contains the hawk of Horus and nine gods, and behind them is the huge disk. In the Nebseni Papyrus the deceased stands in adoration outside the Boat, but in the Turin Papyrus he stands in the Boat itself.

Text: [Chapter CXXXIV.] A Hymn of Praise to Rā on the day of the month wherein he saileth in the Boat. This title shows that the Chapter was intended at one time to be recited on the first day of the New Moon, but in several old papyri it is entitled "Another Chapter of making perfect the Spirit-soul." The object of the recital of the Chapter was to destroy the enemies of Rā and of the deceased. In the opening lines is a very interesting allusion to the Legend of Horus, who in later days was identified specially as the Solar-god of the town of Beḥuṭet, or Edfu, in Upper Egypt. It will be remembered that in very early times, when Horus had inflicted several defeats on the enemies of his father Rā, large numbers of these enemies succeeded in escaping, and, by means of magic, in taking the forms of birds, animals, and reptiles, *i.e.*, crocodiles, etc. Horus, however, penetrated their disguises, and pursued them relentlessly, and slew them. This same Horus is seen in the Boat of Rā in the Vignette, and the recital of this Chapter by Ani secured for him the protection of the god. According to the **Rubric** the words of the Chapter were to be said over a plaque, on which were painted figures of Horus and the gods already mentioned, and a figure of the deceased, seated in a boat, or over a model of the Boat of Rā in which figures of the gods were placed; if this were done the deceased would be able to travel with the Sun-god everywhere.

Vignette: A ladder.

Text: In the Papyrus of Ani there is no text given with the Vignette of the Ladder, and in the Theban Recension of the Book of the Dead there is no Chapter of the Ladder, although there are several allusions to the Ladder. Thus in Chapter XCVIII, the deceased Nu says: "The god Shu hath made me to stand up, the Light-"god hath made me vigorous by the two sides of the "LADDER, and the imperishable stars make me to advance "and lead me away from slaughter." In Chapter CXLIX (Aat XI) he says: "I rise up like Rā. I am strong like the "Eye of Horus. My heart, once brought low, is now "made strong. I am a spirit in heaven, and mighty upon "the earth. I fly like a hawk, I cackle like the *Smen* goose, "and I alight by the Lake of the Thigh. I stand up and "sit down by it. I rise up like a god, I eat food in the "Field of Offerings, I advance to the realm of the Star-"gods. The doors of Maāt are opened to me, and the "doors of the sky are unbolted before me. I set up a "LADDER to heaven [to ascend to the gods], and I am a "divine being among them." And in Chapter CLIIIA (lines 34, 35) it says: "The Osiris Nu, whose word is truth, "appeareth upon the LADDER that Rā hath made for him, "and Horus and Suti hold him tightly by the arm [as he "ascendeth it]."

The belief in the Ladder as a means of reaching heaven is very old, and a tradition existed among the Egyptians which stated that Osiris himself was obliged to ascend into heaven by a Ladder. Rā stood on one side of it and Horus on the other, and they lifted Osiris up the Ladder step by step.[1] Among the texts cut on the walls of the Pyramid of Pepi I (l. 192 f.) we find a version of the Chapter of the Ladder, which reads: "Homage to thee, "O divine Ladder! Homage to thee, O Ladder of Set! "Stand thou upright, O divine Ladder. Stand thou "upright, O Ladder of Set. Stand thou upright, O Ladder "of Horus, whereby Osiris appeared in heaven when he "used the words of power of Rā . . . . . Pepi is thy son, "Pepi is Horus. Thou hast begotten Pepi even as thou "hast begotten the god who is the Lord of the Ladder. "Give thou unto Pepi the Ladder of the god [Horus], give "thou unto him the Ladder of the god Set, whereby Pepi "shall appear in heaven, when he hath made use of the "words of power of Rā. Hail, thou god of the KAU "(Doubles) who advance when the Eye of Horus soareth "upon the wings of Thoth on the eastern side of the Ladder "of the god. Hail, ye who desire that your bodies shall "go into heaven. Pepi is the Eye of Horus, and whenso-"ever the Eye of Horus directeth itself to any place where "he is Pepi goeth by its side. Hail, brethren of the gods, "rejoice ye, for Pepi journeyeth among you. The brethren "of the gods shall be glad when they meet Pepi, even as "Horus is glad when he meeteth his Eye, which he placed "before his father Ḳeb. Every god and every Spirit-soul "reach out their hands to Pepi when he appeareth in "heaven from the Ladder. Pepi needeth not to plough "or to collect offerings, and he needeth not to go to the "Hall in Ȧnu (Heliopolis), or to the Ṭuat Chamber in "Ȧnu; for that which he seeth and that which he heareth "shall feed him and nourish him when he appeareth in "heaven from the Ladder. Pepi standeth up like the "uraeus on the forehead of Rā, and every god and every "goddess stretch out the hand to Pepi on the Ladder. "Pepi hath collected his bones, and gathered together his "flesh, and he hath gone speedily into heaven by means of "the two fingers of the god of the Ladder."

According to the text of Pepi II (ll. 975 ff.) the sides of the Ladder were cut into shape by an adze wielded by the god Sashsa, the rungs were made of the sinews of Ḳasut, the Bull of the Sky, and they were fastened to the

[1] Text of Unȧs, l. 579.

sides of the Ladder by thongs cut from the hide of the god Utes, the son of Ḥesat. Elsewhere we read[1] that the Ladder was carried by Khensu, Ȧaḥes, Ṭeṭun, and Sepṭ, who set up the Ladder for Pepi, and who made it to stand firmly. The gods mentioned in the last extract are gods of the South, or Sûdânî gods, a fact which suggests that the legend of the Ladder reaching from earth to heaven is of Sûdânî origin. When Osiris ascended the Ladder " he was " covered with the covering of Horus, he wore the apparel " of Thoth, Isis went before him, Nephthys followed behind " him, Upuatu opened out the way (*i.e.*, cleared a path) for " him, Shu bore him up, the Souls of Ȧnu drew him up " the steps, one by one, and the goddess Nut gave him her " hands" (Pepi I, l. 256). In primitive times it was customary to place models of the Ladder of Osiris in the tombs, so that the souls of the dead might have the means whereby they could ascend to heaven, provided that they were properly equipped with an adequate knowledge of the name of the Ladder, and of the words of power that were necessary to make it to raise itself up and to stand firm. In later times, when the custom had fallen into disuse, the scribes seem to have painted figures of the Ladder on coffins and papyri, but whether with or without the text of the Chapter of the Ladder cannot be said. The Ladder in the Papyrus of Ani is a very interesting proof of the survival of the belief in the efficacy of a picture of the Ladder in the Theban Period.

PLATE XXIII

Vignette : The scribe Ani, arrayed in white apparel, kneeling upon one knee, and with his hand raised in adoration of the gods of :—

1. Ȧnu (Heliopolis), Temu, Shu, and Tefnut.
2. Ṭeṭu (Busiris), Osiris, Isis, Nephthys, and Ḥeru-netch-tef-f.
3. Sekhem (Letopolis), Ḥeru-khenti-en-ȧriti, and Thoth.
4. Pe-Ṭep (Buto), Horus, Isis, Ḳestȧ (Mestȧ), and Ḥapi.
5. Taiu-Rekhti, Isis, Horus, and Ḳestȧ (Mestȧ).
6. Ȧbṭu (Abydos), Osiris, Isis, and Upuatu.
7. The Judgment of the Dead, Thoth.

[1] Pepi I, l. 200 = Pepi II, l. 936.

PLATE XXIV

7. The Judgment of the Dead—*continued.* A man-headed god and a jackal-headed god.
8. The ploughing of the earth, three man-headed gods.
9. Neruṭef, Rā, Shu and Tefnut (?), and Beba.
10. Rasta, Horus, Isis (?), a god with a short beard.

The above are the gods of the great towns of Egypt which are enumerated in Chapter XVIII, arranged in a row; they have already been given in groups in Plates XIII and XIV. The artist has omitted some of the gods given in the earlier copy of the Chapter, and has modified the forms of some so much that they cannot be identified. The text says that the gods of Nerutef are Rā, Osiris, Shu, and Beba, but the artist has painted figures of Rā, Shu with a goddess, and Beba, thus omitting Osiris, and inserting a goddess who must be Tefnut.

Text: [Chapter XVIII.] Without title in the Papyrus of Ani. The **Rubric** is given on Plate XXIV, and shows that the object of the Chapter was to make the deceased to come forth by day, after death, whensoever he pleased. It enabled him to walk about on earth, to make his escape from any fire which might break out on his path, and to prevent him from being assailed by any evil circumstance incidental to his condition for ever and for ever.

Vignette: The scribe Ani and his wife Tutu, both arrayed in white linen apparel, standing before three gods, who are seated on a mat, which is spread on the roof of a low sepulchral building. The other papyri of the period of the Papyrus of Ani have four gods in their Vignette to this Chapter; sometimes they are in mummy forms with the heads of men, and sometimes they have the characteristic heads of the Four Sons of Horus.

Text: [Chapter CXXIV.] The Chapter of entering into the presence of the Tchatchau chiefs of Osiris. In this Chapter Ani says that he has built himself a house in Ṭeṭu, the city of Osiris, and that his vassals have ploughed his fields, or it may be that he has ploughed the earth, digging into it the blood of his vassals whom he has sacrificed to the Ṭeṭ, a god who was worshipped in Ṭeṭu in very early times, before the great growth of the cult of Osiris that took place there under the rule of the dynasties. Ani next refers to the purity of the food which he has eaten; filth is an abomination to him, and he will not eat it, or touch it, or even walk upon it. His food is the food of Rā, and it is brought to him by the Boats of Rā, the Āntchet and the Sektet. His position among the gods is a very strong one, and he threatens any god who may wish to attack him that, in the event of his so doing, he shall be judged by the "ancestors of the years," or the gods of the year, and that Osiris shall devour him when he comes forth from Abydos. He shall also be judged by the "ancestors of Rā," and by the great Spirit-soul, or Light-god. Here clearly we have an allusion to the ancient gods of the year who were worshipped in Egypt before Osiris or Rā was known. And Ani has the power to hold converse with the disk and with the solar gods. He sits side by side with Osiris, who speaks to him in the language of the gods, and Ani replies in the speech of men. Ani absorbs the attributes of all the gods of Ȧnu, Ṭeṭu, Ḥensu, Ȧbṭu, Ȧpu, and Senu, and becomes the great Sāḥu of heaven, the counterpart of Osiris, and the overlord of every god and goddess in Khert-Neter. It must be noted that the gods Ḳestȧ, Ḥāpi, Ṭuamutef, and Qebḥsenuf, who presided over the safety of his mummified intestines, also became his judges, a fact that suggests the existence of a belief that the testimony of the internal organs of a man might be given by them for or against him in the Judgment Hall of Osiris, before Osiris and his Forty-two Assessors.

PLATE XXV

With this Plate begins the series of very important Chapters of the Book of the Dead that are known as the "Chapters of making the Transformations." The object of the formulae of which they are composed was to enable the deceased to take any form he pleased, and to make himself to appear in any guise so long as it assisted him in making his way through Dead-land into the Kingdom of Osiris.

Vignette: A swallow perched on a conical object painted in stripes, red and green. What this object is cannot be said, but it is probably meant to represent the alighting place of the swallow that carried the news of the death of Horus and the grief of Isis to the gods.

Text: [CHAPTER LXXXVI.] THE CHAPTER OF MAKING THE TRANSFORMATION INTO THE SWALLOW. By the recital of this Chapter Ani transformed himself into the swallow, which was an incarnation of Serqet, the Scorpion-goddess, the daughter of Rā and of Isis. The swallow was a harbinger of glad tidings, and was, and still is, welcomed everywhere in Egypt and the Sûdân. The glad tidings that Ani proclaims is that Horus sits on the throne of his father Osiris, and that he is the Captain of the Boat of Rā, and that Set is bound fast, and is a helpless prisoner in the fetters which Ani had prepared for him. Ani proclaims his innocence and his purity of soul and body, and claims the right to enter in among the gods because he is holy, as they are holy. All roads are known to him, and no door is closed to him, and as the swallow flies about everywhere in the sunshine, so does he travel about over Sekhet Åaru. Since Isis took the form of a swallow, and raised up Osiris to life, Ani on taking the form of a swallow is able to restore to life his dead body that is lying in the earth. The soul that knew not this Chapter was doomed to remain in Dead-land.

Vignette: A golden hawk, holding a flail or whip 𓋭, standing upon the symbol of gold 𓋞.

Text: [CHAPTER LXXVII.] THE CHAPTER OF MAKING THE TRANSFORMATION INTO A HAWK OF GOLD. The recital of this Chapter enabled Ani to take the form of the golden hawk, with pinions that were four cubits from tip to tip, and plumage in colour like the precious *uatch* stone that is found in the South. The object of taking this form was to obtain the means of flying from this earth up into the sky, and so into the Āntchet and Sektet Boats of the Sun-god. In the form of a hawk he could fly up among the gods and take his seat with them, and he could visit the Field of Offerings and refresh himself on celestial food at will. Once there he could transform himself into a Spirit-soul, and live with the Spirit-souls of Osiris and Rā. The celestial Grain-god Neprȧ would supply him with food, and Rā would listen to his words as to those of the Benu bird, into which the soul of the Sun-god transformed itself. The early Egyptians believed that the souls of the just passed from earth to heaven on the wings of the ibis of Thoth, but the later

Egyptians preferred to travel thither by taking the form of the hawk of gold.

Vignette: A green hawk, holding a whip, and standing upon the roof of the sepulchral building called *serekh*.

Text: [CHAPTER LXXVIII, ll. 1–16.] THE CHAPTER OF MAKING THE TRANSFORMATION INTO THE GOD-HAWK. This Chapter is at once the longest of all the Chapters of Transformations and the most important. The object of the recital of the Chapter was not only to enable the deceased to take the form of any hawk, but to incorporate himself in that very hawk in which Horus, the son of Osiris and Isis, who was begotten by Osiris when dead, and who was conceived and brought forth by Isis from his father's seed, appeared on earth. Ani, and every worshipper of Osiris, wished to become soul of the soul of Horus, heart of the heart of Horus, and flesh of the flesh of Horus. The attainment of this desire made Ani to be the son of Osiris and Isis, and the son of the Sun-god Rā, his being was therefore merged in that of the "Great God," and he became almighty and everlasting, and the recipient of the homage which "the gods" paid to their Overlord. He became the Great Spirit-soul wherein all Spirit-souls lived, and the Great Sāḥu, or Spirit-body, wherein all Sāḥu lived. With this exalted and divine relationship Ani was not fain to be content. The Egyptians imagined a time very far back when the "gods" did not exist, and when neither Osiris nor Rā had come into being. There was no heaven and no earth, no sun, no moon, no stars, no death, and no men and women; and what existed was the great mass of Celestial Waters wherein dwelt the great, almighty, invisible, unknowable God, whom the Egyptians called Tem or Temu. At some period unknown to gods and men this Tem created

PLATE XXVI

[CHAPTER LXXVIII—*continued.*]

a Spirit-soul and caused it to live in a creation of light [hieroglyphs]. Now this Spirit-soul proceeded from the "eye of the Lord One" [hieroglyphs], and it was the essence of Tem and his very being, and it was the source from which sprang the Light-god, whose visible emblem was the sun, or the god Rā. With this primeval Spirit-soul, the emanation of God, Ani declares his identity, and he asserts boldly his direct descent from God, adding: "When as yet Isis had not given birth to Horus, I had "sprouted and flourished, and I was the greatest of all the "Spirit-souls who had come into being with the Spirit-"souls, and I was older than they." Horus [the Elder] provided this primeval Spirit-soul with a Spirit body, leaving his own soul inside it, and in later times it dwelt in Horus, the son of Isis, and reigned jointly with Osiris in the Ṭuat. Thus, the recital of this Chapter was believed to make the deceased to become a part of the being and substance and essence of God, and a fellow-god with Osiris, Horus, and Rā, and the equal and companion of the kings of Egypt in the Ṭuat.

PLATE XXVII

Vignette: The serpent Sata, with human legs and feet.

Text: [Chapter LXXXVII.] The Chapter of making the transformation into the serpent Sata (*i.e.*, the Son of the Earth). The recital of this Chapter enabled Ani to acquire the power of the serpent Sata to cast its old skin, and to appear in a new one. It is impossible to identify the particular serpent typified by Sata, but there must have been some physical characteristic in the creature which caused it to be associated with new birth and a rejuvenated body. As the text refers to the number of its years we may assume that Sata was one of the longest-lived serpents.

Vignette: A huge crocodile lying upon a pylon or doorway.

Text: [Chapter LXXXVIII.] The Chapter of making the transformation into a crocodile. In this Chapter Ani identifies himself with the Lord who was worshipped in Sekhem, a town in the Letopolite nome of Lower Egypt, and with the Great Fish, who lived in Kamur, a town in the Athribite nome in Lower Egypt, thus acquiring the power of striking terror that has always been associated with the crocodile. The object of his taking the form of the crocodile was to enable him to traverse the Nile, or any stream, without danger to himself. The crocodile has always been worshipped in Egypt and the Sûdân, and as late as the reign of Muḥammad 'Âlî a sacred crocodile was kept in a tank at Kharṭûm and venerated by the people there. On the Blue Nile until quite recently the natives believed that by means of magic men could be transformed into crocodiles, and so have the power of crossing the Nile at will. At the present day the genitals of the crocodile find ready purchasers, who cut them up into small pieces and sell them as an aphrodisiac. In very early times the crocodile was considered to be a form of the Sun-god.

Vignette: The god Ptaḥ standing in a shrine. He is in mummy form, and holds a sceptre in his hands, and stands upon the cubit of Maāt; from his neck hangs the *menàt*, symbolic of virility and sexual pleasure. Before the shrine is a stand with offerings upon it.

Text: [CHAPTER LXXXII.] THE CHAPTER OF MAKING THE TRANSFORMATION INTO THE GOD PTAḤ. This god was originally a master blacksmith, but divine honours were paid to him after his death, and eventually he was regarded as one of the great cosmic gods, who executed the commands of Thoth when he decreed the making of the heavens and the earth. The recital of this Chapter secured for Ani the strength of Ptaḥ and an abundance of offerings, and enabled him to identifiy himself with Temu and Rā. He became thereby the Bull of the Gods of Ȧnu, his strength increased moment by moment, and his loins were made strong to endure for millions of years.

Vignette: A Ram, symbolic of the Soul-god of Ṭeṭu, *i.e.*, Busiris.

Text: [CHAPTER LXXXV.] THE CHAPTER OF MAKING THE TRANSFORMATION INTO THE SOUL OF TEMU. This Chapter formed a most powerful spell, the object of which was to transform Ani into the Soul-god of Nu, or the heavens; its contents resemble those of a part of the LXXVIIIth Chapter. The Soul-god who was symbolized by a ram was the counterpart of the primeval Soul which Temu, the Father of all the Gods, placed in Rā the Sun-god, and which came into being under the name of

"Kheperȧ." Since Ani abominates sin and lives in Truth, he has the power to take the form of the Great Soul and to become an emanation of the Light-god.

Vignette: A Benu bird.

Text: [Chapter LXXXIII.] The Chapter of making the transformation into the Benu bird. The Benu bird, which was at a later period identified with the phoenix, was supposed to be self-produced, and was therefore a type of the god Kheperȧ, a god who was self-produced and self-begotten. By the recital of this Chapter Ani was able to declare that the germs of every god were in him, and that he was Yesterday, *i.e.*, Osiris, and that he was Khensu, the Moon-god, who was irresistible. The allusion to the Tortoise is not quite clear, but seems to mean that Ani is clothed with a garment which is as durable as is the shell of the Tortoise, or Turtle. The **Rubric,** which is found in some papyri, informs us that a knowledge of this Chapter will provide the deceased with the food which Osiris eats, will enable him to take any form he pleases, to travel over the earth with Rā, to see this god daily, and to be free from the influence of every evil thing for ever.

PLATE XXVIII

Vignette: A heron.

Text: [Chapter LXXXIV.] The Chapter of making the transformation into a heron. Owing to our lack of knowledge of the views that the Egyptians held concerning the bird figured in the Vignette, it is impossible to say exactly what the recital of this Chapter was supposed to effect, and what benefit would accrue to Ani from taking the form of a heron. The text suggests that it would give him power over the animals that were brought for sacrifice, in other words, that he would be able to supply himself with food. It also asserts that Ani has rendered service to the dweller in Hermopolis, *i.e.*, Thoth, that he has set the gods in their places, that he knows Nut, the Sky-goddess, and Tatun, a very ancient Earth-god, and the "Red Goddess" (Tesherṭt), and Ḥeka, the great god of spells and incantations. As Ani proclaims his truthfulness, and his daily progress towards Truth, it is clear that he could never hope to take the form of the heron unless he was sinless in word and in deed. The concluding lines of this Chapter as found in the Papyrus of Ani did not really belong to it, for they form the last part of Chapter LXXXVI, which the scribe appears to have copied here because there was no room for it in its proper place.

Vignette: A human head springing from a lotus flower growing in a pool of water.

Text: [Chapter LXXXIa.] The Chapter of making the transformation into a lotus flower. The lotus, or lily, was believed to be the favourite flower of Rā, and to be the product of an emanation of that god. The flower here referred to is, however, the celestial lotus, from the calyx of which the rising sun, or Harpokrates, rose day by day. Thus the idea of resurrection was associated with the lotus, and when Ani wished to have the power to transform himself into the lotus, it was in order that he might be able to give new birth to his body, and to emerge into heaven daily like the Sun-god. In the second version of this Chapter the lotus is said to be the symbol of Nefer-Tem, *i.e.*, Young Tem, who was the son of Ptaḥ and the goddess Sekhmet. Chapter LXXXII gave Ani the power to transform himself into Ptaḥ, one of the great creator-gods, and the knowledge of Chapter LXXXI enabled him to become the son of Ptaḥ. The first version of this Chapter helped him to take the form of Horus, but Horus and Nefer-Tem were only juvenile forms of one and the same god, *i.e.*, the rising sun. In the older form of the Vignette as given in the Papyrus of Nebseni, we have a lotus in full flower, but no human head, and the text proves that the lotus was growing in the "field of Rā," and not in a lake or pool of water. In many papyri the Vignette is the same in both versions.

Vignette: A seated, bearded god, with the solar disk on his head.

Text: [Chapter LXXX.] The Chapter of making the transformation into the god who giveth light in the darkness. The Land of the Dead contained many dark places through which Ani would have to travel before he emerged into the light of the Kingdom of Osiris, and many souls were lost therein, and fell a prey to the fiends of darkness who lay in wait there for the worshippers of Osiris. To avoid this possibility Ani found it necessary to take the form of the god who produced light from his own person, for by this means he would be able to lighten the dark places, and to travel through them in safety. The words of this Chapter enabled him to identify himself with "the girdle of Nu," from which came the light which lightened heaven. He became the personification of Horus, the god of Light, and of Set, the god of Darkness, and could therefore emit light or remain in darkness at pleasure; in other words, he was master of the darkness. He had the power to establish the light of the moon on the day of the full moon, to hold Set in equilibrium, *i.e.*, not to allow him to filch away any part of the *utchat*, or Eye of the Moon, and to equip Thoth in his struggle with Set, when he should pursue Set, and make him to restore the Eye, which he stole month by month and swallowed. The recital of this Chapter enabled Ani to merge himself in the substance of the Moon-god, *i.e.*, Osiris, just as the recital of Chapter LXVIII enabled him to merge his body and dual-soul into those of Temu, the primeval god, the creator of the universe, and Father of the Gods.

PLATE XXIX

Vignette: The scribe Ani and his wife Tutu standing with their hands raised in adoration before the god Thoth, who in the form of an ibis-headed man is seated upon a sepulchral building, holding the symbol of "life" ☥ upon his knees.

Text: [CHAPTER CLXXV.] THE CHAPTER OF NOT DYING A SECOND TIME. This Chapter is of very great interest, but is full of difficulties, chiefly because the text is incomplete at the end; there is a second copy of it in a Leyden papyrus, but it is very much mutilated. According to the text of Ani the deceased is troubled by the actions of the Children of Nut, who have brought confusion into everything. Not being able to understand this disorder he applies to Thoth for an explanation of it, believing that this god, as the secretary of Osiris, will know all his master's secrets. There is, however, no explanation forthcoming. Next Ani finds himself in a place of unfathomable depth, darker than the darkest night, and where there is neither water nor air. Why he is there or where the place is is not clear. After this we have allusions to Horus, and the dweller in the Lake of Fire, and the Boat of Millions of Years, etc., but it is impossible to fit them together in a connected fashion with the prayers of Ani, who is supposed to be in doubt about the continuity of his existence in the Other World. Again he applies to Thoth, and asks him how long he has to live. Thoth's answer is both definite and satisfactory, for he replies: "Thou shalt live for millions of years, a life of millions of years." The rest of the Chapter refers to the succession of Horus to the throne of Osiris, the departure of Set, the felicity of Ani in the Other World, the destruction of his foes, etc. According to M. Naville, who bases his views upon a minute study of the Chapter as found in the Leyden papyrus, this composition contains the remains of a Herakleopolitan legend of the Flood. Tem is supposed to tell Ani that he is about to destroy everything that he has made by the Flood which he will bring upon the earth. Everything shall be destroyed except himself (Tem) and Osiris, and a very small serpent which no god shall be able to see. After the Flood Osiris shall establish his kingdom in the Island of Fire, and after his departure his son Horus shall sit upon his throne. If this view be correct this Chapter throws considerable light upon the mental attitude of Ani, who ventured to suggest by it that Thoth would regard him with such favour and confidence, that he, the god who was the personification of the mind of God, would reveal to him the purpose of the Creator, and make known to him his design to destroy man and beast by a Flood. It is interesting also to note that Ani could imagine Thoth promising to him a life of "millions of years," and believe that he alone among men would survive the death and destruction that the Flood would bring upon the earth.

PLATES XXIX AND XXX

Vignettes: I. The scribe Ani, arrayed in white linen apparel, standing with both hands raised in adoration of the god Osiris. In front of him are altar stands and tables loaded with offerings of every kind, which he is presenting to Osiris; behind him stands his wife Tutu, holding a sistrum, a *menåt*, and flowers in her hands.

2. The god Osiris, bearded and wearing the White Crown, standing inside a funerary chest or coffer, the roof of which is surmounted by a head of the hawk that represents Seker, the god of Death, and uraei. This chest is symbolic of the kingdom of Seker. Osiris is in mummy form, and his body is decorated with a sort of scale-work design, which was probably painted on his swathings in colours. From the back of his neck hangs a *menåt*, and he holds two sceptres and a whip in his hands, which emerge from his swathings, and he stands upon the cubit of *maāt*. The face and hands and wrists of Osiris are painted green to indicate that Osiris is old. Out of the point of the cubit grows a lotus flower in full bloom, on which stand figures of the Four Sons of Horus, viz., Ḳestå (Mestå), Ḥāpi, Ṭuamutef, and Qebḥsenuf. Behind Osiris stands Isis, whose right arm is embracing him; she wears , the hieroglyph for her name, upon her head, and carries in her left hand the symbol of "life" ☥. The chest in which the two gods stand rests upon, or is a continuation of the sepulchral, pylon-shaped building, which represents the tomb of Osiris.

Text: [Chapter CXXV. Introduction, or Part I.] The Chapter of entering into the Hall of Maāti. This Chapter is one of the most interesting and remarkable in the Book of the Dead, and it well illustrates the lofty moral and spiritual conceptions of the Egyptians under the XVIIIth dynasty. The ideas that it embodies are as old as dynastic civilization, but the form in which they are here presented is probably not older than the XIth dynasty. The deceased is supposed to be standing before the doors of the Hall of Judgment, which are guarded by Anubis, and to him he describes the various acts of piety which he has performed, his object being to see the great gods and to feed with them on their celestial food. He has visited Ṭeṭu (Busiris) and Åbṭu (Abydos), and has taken part in the ceremonies performed there, and he has seen the gods of Kamur and Neruṭef. Anubis is satisfied that Ani knows the towns and the roads in Khert-Neter, and the smell of him is to Anubis as that of one of the gods. Before he permits Ani to enter into the Hall of Judgment he must be certain that Ani knows the magical names of these doors, and he questions him on the subject. When Ani has told their names Anubis says: "Pass on, for thou knowest [the names]." The Introduction (Part I of this Chapter in the Papyrus of Ani) is quite different from that found in the other papyri of the period, and is far more suitable to Parts II and III than the usual Introduction. In the Papyrus of Nebseni and the Papyrus of Nu the deceased states that he knows the name of Osiris, and the names of the Forty-two Judges who sit with him in judgment, and he then goes on to enumerate the sins and moral offences which he has not committed: in short, he declares that he has not sinned against God or man. In Part II, which is commonly known as the Negative Confession, the deceased addresses each of the Forty-two gods by name, and then makes to him a categorical denial that he has committed such and such a sin. Thus in the papyri generally the subject matter of Parts I and II is the same, only in Part II the deceased states the names of the Forty-two gods of whom in Part I he professes to know the names.

PLATES XXXI AND XXXII

Vignette: The Hall of Maāti, or the Judgment Hall of Osiris, in which Ani has to address severally the Forty-two gods who are seated in a row down the centre of the Hall. At each end is a door : that on the right is called *Neb-maāt-ḥeri-tep-reṭui-f* , and that on the left *Neb-peḥti-thes-menment* . Over the centre of the roof, which is crowned with a series of feathers of *maāt* and uraei arranged alternately, is a seated deity with arms and hands extended, the right over the Eye of Horus , and the left over a pool of water . He is painted blue, and symbolizes the primeval Water-god, who was the creator of the heavens and the earth. He is discussed fully in connection with a similar Vignette that is found above a part of Chapter XVII (see page 260). On the right, at the end of the Hall (see Plate XXXII), are **four small Vignettes**, in which are depicted:

1. The two Maāti goddesses, or two goddesses of Truth, who probably represent Isis and Nephthys. Each wears a heavy headdress, tied round with a ribbon, and above it is an ostrich feather, the phonetic value of which is the name of the goddess—Maāt. Round her neck is a collar, and she wears a long light tunic reaching to her ankles. On each wrist is a bracelet, and she holds a sceptre in her right hand and the symbol of "life" in her left.

2. The Osiris Ani, standing with both hands raised in adoration before Osiris, who is seated on a throne or chair of state; he is in mummy form, is painted white, and wears the *Atef* Crown and a collar. In his hands he holds the usual sceptre and whip. Before the god is an altar-stand with a libation jar and lotus upon it.

3. The heart of Ani being weighed in the Balance against the symbol of Truth . Anubis examines the pointer, and Ām-mit, the Devourer of the dead, is seated by the side of the Balance ready to eat up the heart if it should happen to be "light in the scales."

4. The god Thoth, ibis-headed, seated on a sepulchral building, and engaged in painting the feather symbolic of Truth. The exact significance of this Vignette is not clear.

The Forty-two gods have different faces and heads: Nos. 1–5, 7, 8, 10, 11, 13–20, 22–25, 27–34, 36, 37, 41 and 42, have the heads of men, No. 6 has the head of a lion, No. 9 the head of a crocodile, No. 12 has a human head turned behind him, Nos. 21, 38–40 have snakes' heads, No. 26 has a hawk's head, and No. 35 has the head of a hippopotamus. In the Papyrus of Nebseni each of the Forty-two gods is in the form of a mummy and has upon his head. In the Papyrus of Ȧnhai the gods have the forms of men, but many have heads of animals, four have serpent forms, and one has the form of a child . Very few of the names of these gods are found in the ordinary lists of gods, and as a rule the name of each describes his function or occupation, or some personal characteristic. Thus we have: Usekh-nemmȧt "He of the long stride"; Fenṭi, "He of the nose"; Unem-khaibitu, "Eater of shadows"; Neḥa-ḥāu, "Stinking body"; Seṭ-qesu, "Bone-crusher"; Ḥetch-ȧbeḥu, "He of the white teeth"; Unem-snef, "Eater of blood"; Ḥerfḥaf, "He whose face is turned behind him"; etc.

Text: [CHAPTER CXXV. THE NEGATIVE CONFESSION, OR PART II.] This composition contains a series of forty-two addresses to the Judges or Assessors, who sit with Osiris in the Hall of Maāti. Ani addresses each god by his name, and mentions the name of the place where his shrine is, and says, "I have not committed" such and such a sin, *e.g.*, "Hail, Crusher of bones, who comest forth from Ḥensu, I have not uttered falsehood."

[The **Vignette** and **Text** of Part III of Chapter CXXV and the **Rubric** are wanting in the Papyrus of Ani. A translation of the "Address which the righteous heart maketh" to the gods in the Hall of Maāti, and of the Rubric made from the Papyrus of Nu will be found in the Appendix to Chapter CXXV.]

PLATE XXXII—(*continued*)

Vignettes: **1.** A bearded man-god, Nu.
" **2.** Rā, hawk-headed, with the solar disk on his head.
" **3.** Hathor, in the form of a woman, with disk and horns on her head.
" **4.** The Wolf-god, Up-uatu, on a standard.
" **5.** The Jackal-god, Ȧnpu, seated.
" **6.** A scorpion holding *shen* and .
" **7.** The goddess Isis, woman-headed.
" **8.** The Ram-god, Ba-neb-Ṭeṭ.
" **9.** The goddess Uatchit, serpent-headed.
" **10.** The goddess Mert, with a cluster of plants on her head, standing upon the symbol of gold.
" **11.** The goddess Neith, in the form of a woman, with a vase on her head.
" **12.** The god Set, in the form of a bearded man.
" **13.** A god in the form of a bearded man.
" **14.** A god in the form of a bearded man.

Vignettes: 15. The goddess Sekhmet, in the form of a woman having the head of a lioness with the solar disk on her head.

„ **16.** An *utchat*, or Eye of Horus, resting on a sepulchral building.

„ **17.** The Man-god Osiris, seated, and wearing the *Ȧtef* Crown.

„ **18.** The goddess Nut, in the form of a woman, with a vase on her head.

„ **19.** A bearded god in mummy form, with a *menȧt* at the back of his neck, holding a sceptre 𓋹 and standing on *maāt*.

„ **20.** A five-rayed star, symbolic of Sāḥu, or Orion.

„ **21.** Three "living uraei."

The forms of the Vignette of this Chapter vary in the other papyri. Thus in the Papyrus of Nefer-uben-f the deceased is seen touching his mouth with the tip of a finger of his left hand; in the Papyrus of Sutimes the deceased is lassoing the top of a *ṭeṭ* pillar (?); and in a papyrus in the British Museum (No. 9950), he is adjuring a serpent, which seems to be taking to flight. In the Papyrus of Ȧmen-ḥetep in Cairo the Vignette contains the figures of eighteen gods.

Text: [CHAPTER XLII. THE CHAPTER OF REPULSING THE SLAUGHTERING KNIVES IN ḤENSU. This title is wanting in the Papyrus of Ani.] The object of this Chapter was to enable the deceased to escape from the slaughter that took place in Ḥensu, and presumably from decapitation and dismemberment. It seems as though the deceased feared that he might be mistaken for an enemy of Osiris and be slain accidentally. The only way to avoid this was to place each member of the body under the protection of a god or goddess, and to identify it with him or her. In the Pyramid Text of Pepi I the composition that in later times became Chapter XLII was metrical in character, and seems to have been chanted or sung with a sort of refrain (see the Appendix to the Chapter). In the Theban Recension the refrain has been dropped, and the various lines relating to the deification of the members have been grouped together, and form a middle section in the Chapter. In the Papyrus of Ani, and in the later papyri down to the Ptolemaïc and Roman Periods, this section is arranged in tabular form, and illustrated with Vignettes. It was very highly prized by the followers of Osiris in all periods, for it was believed to make the deceased "a god, and the son of a god," and to cause him to merge his being in the "Only One, who proceedeth from an Only One." The concluding portion of the Chapter as found in the Pyramid Texts is totally different from that of Chapter XLII in the Theban Recension.

PLATE XXXIII

Vignette: A Lake of Fire or of boiling water, from the four sides of which fire or boiling steam rises. At each corner a dog-headed ape is seated.

Text: A Rubric which, after referring to the state of physical comfort in which Ani shall live in the Other World, and to the abundant supply of offerings that shall be made to him, goes on to order that a picture of a table of offerings be drawn upon a clean plaque, which shall be buried in a field whereon no swine have trodden. If in addition to this picture the text be written upon the plaque, his children's children shall flourish upon earth, and he himself shall live with the Followers of Osiris and with the Kings of Egypt, and he shall sit at meat with the gods.

In the Papyrus of Nebseni we find the Vignette placed among the text of the Third Part of Chapter CXXV, of which it seems to be an integral part; on the other hand, there is no reference to a lake of fire in the text, nor to the Four Holy Apes. As regards the Rubric it is found at the end of Chapter CXXV (see Naville, *op. cit.*, Bd. I, Bl. 139), and it is then clearly to be considered a part of Chapter CXXV. Thus there seems to be good reason for assuming that both the Vignette and the Rubric in the Papyrus of Ani belong to Chapter CXXV, although the Chapter of the Deification (or Assimilation) of members is inserted between them and the Negative Confession. Some scribes, however, place the Vignette with a different text, and treat them as a separate Chapter, namely, Chapter CXXVI This is the case in a papyrus in the British Museum

(No. 9913=Naville *Ab*) where we have the Address to the Four Holy Apes written in the upper part of the papyrus, and the Vignette with figures of the Four Apes and the Eight Uraei in the lower. In the Turin Papyrus the Vignette stands above the text of Chapter CXXVI (Address to the Apes), and a figure of the deceased is seen praying to the Apes. If we regard these instances as conclusive we must assign the Rubric in the Papyrus of Ani to Chapter CXXV, and assume that the Vignette is really that of Chapter CXXVI, and that the scribe has omitted the text of the Chapter.

Vignette: The amulet of the . Various theories have been enunciated about the *ṭeṭ*. It has been described as the roof-tree of a house, the four bars representing four branches that stretch out from the trunk, one to the south, one to the north, one to the west, and one to the east. Some have said that it represents a mason's table, and others have called it the "key of the Nile," but the most probable explanation of all is that it represents some part of the body of Osiris. Many peoples and tribes in Africa have been in the habit of preserving carefully a bone belonging to the body of some great or beloved ancestor, and there can be little doubt that the is a conventional representation of a part of the backbone of Osiris, namely, the *sacrum* bone, which, on account of its proximity to the sperm bag, was regarded as the most important member of his body. The oldest forms of this bone are and . Now if we set this sign upon a stand we have , which was modified later into . In the period when the Theban Recension of the Book of the Dead was made, the may have represented the whole of the backbone of Osiris, for it is said "thy backbone is to thee, O Still-heart, thy neck vertebrae are to thee, O Still-heart!" It will be noted that the determinative of the word for "backbone," *pesṭ* , is , which could easily be, when set upright, [hieroglyph], confused with 𓊽. The *ṭeṭ* bone or bones came to be regarded as a very powerful amulet at a very early period, and under the Middle and New Empires models of it were made of gold, glass, faïence, and sometimes of *lapis lazuli*, and of wood, painted black. Large wooden models of the *ṭeṭ* are often found in the wooden hands that lie on the breasts of anthropoid coffins, and under the later dynasties large figures of the *ṭeṭ* were painted on the bottoms of coffins, either inside or out. These are sometimes between five and six feet long. A fine collection of *ṭeṭ* amulets is exhibited in the Fourth Egyptian Room in the British Museum.

Text: [Chapter CLV.] The Chapter of the Ṭeṭ of Gold. This Chapter was a mighty spell that enabled the deceased to rise up, and, because he was provided with his backbone and his neck vertebrae, to stand in his place on his feet; in other words it effected his resurrection. In the miracle plays that were performed annually at Abydos and other towns in Egypt the "setting upright the *ṭeṭ*" and placing the head of Osiris upon it was the most important scene, and it indicated that the body of the god had been reconstituted, and that he had risen from the dead. It is interesting to note that the *ṭeṭ* referred to in the Chapter is made of gold. This metal was believed to possess great and peculiar properties, because the blood of the Sun-god was made of gold.

Vignette: The amulet Tet, which has been commonly called a "buckle" or "tie," but there is no doubt that this figure really represents the uterus of Isis with the adjacent organs. That it was supposed to possess very great power is proved by the large number of models of it which are found in all important Egyptian collections. It is usually made of red or reddish stone, red glass, red porphyry, etc., and large models of it made of painted wood are found in the wooden hands that lie on the breasts of anthropoid coffins. Thus the deceased went into the Other World bearing in his hands symbols of the principal generative organs of Osiris and Isis, the great Ancestor-god and Ancestress-goddess of Egypt.

Text: [Chapter CLVI.] The Chapter of a Tet of carnelian. The object of the recital of this Chapter is clear. It brought to Ani the protection that was to be derived from the blood, and magical knowledge, and utterances, and words of power of Isis, and kept away from him every being or thing that was an abomination to him. When a carnelian model of the TET was on his neck, especially if the words of this Chapter were cut upon it, it was as if the very life-blood of Isis were present there, and his resurrection was assured.

Vignette: A human heart.

Text: [CHAPTER XXIXB.] THE CHAPTER OF A HEART OF CARNELIAN. This is one of the three versions of this Chapter, of which two have already been described. By the recital of this Chapter Ani identified himself with the Benu bird, which was the incarnate form of the heart of Rā, *i.e.*, he became the heart of the Sun-god. He could then perform the labours of Rā, and direct the gods, who were forms of him. Since their Heart-souls came forth on earth to carry out the orders of their Doubles, Ani sees no reason why his Heart-soul should not come forth to do the will of his Double. This Chapter well illustrates the relationship that existed between the physical heart, which was the seat of the Heart-soul, and the Ka, or Double, which directed the desires and inclinations of the Heart-soul.

Vignette: An African pillow, or head-rest.

Text: [CHAPTER CLXVI.] THE CHAPTER OF THE PILLOW, WHICH IS TO BE PLACED UNDER THE HEAD OF THE OSIRIS ANI TO WARD OFF EVIL FROM THE DEAD BODY OF THE OSIRIS. The recital of this Chapter caused the head of Ani to be lifted up, not only off the earth but into the horizon, and, according to the fuller version of the Chapter that is found in the Papyrus of Nebseni, it secured for him the services of Ptaḥ, the Master-craftsman who built up his body anew, and also of Horus, the son of Hathor, and of the Fire-goddess Nesert. The last-named goddess would supply his body with heat, and Horus would prevent his head from being cut off during the slaughters that took place from time to time in Khert-Neter. Since Ani had power to lift up his head in that region, it followed as a matter of course that all his enemies were destroyed.

PLATES XXXIII (*continued*) AND XXXIV

Vignette: A general view of the mummy-chamber showing the figures of the gods and the amulets that protected Ani's mummy. In the centre of the chamber stands the bier, with a canopy, on which the mummy lies, and beneath it are the vases that hold Ani's mummified internal organs ; only three vases are shown instead of four. By the left side of the mummy stands Anubis, who is resting his hands upon it in an attitude of protection. At the head of the bier kneels Nephthys, and at the foot Isis ; each goddess is leaning forward with her hands resting on Ω, the symbol of "eternity." In a space at each of the two top corners is a figure of the Heart-soul of Ani in the form of a man-headed hawk standing on a funerary building, or his tomb. At each of the four corners of the inner rectangle stands a bearded god in mummified form ; these represent the Four Sons of Horus, Ḳestȧ (Mestȧ), Ḥāpi, Ṭuamutef, and Qebḥsenuf, and they stand there to protect the internal organs of Ani, which are in the four jars. Now, we know from Chapter CXXXVII, which treats of the "four blazing torches" (for the full text and translation see Vol. II, Appendix at end), that an amulet was placed in a cavity of each of the walls of the tomb to protect the mummy from any enemies that might approach that wall to do harm to the mummy. Thus a *ṭeṭ* of crystal was placed in the West wall, a figure of Anubis in the East wall, a *shabti* figure in the South wall, and a reed, to represent a palm, in the North wall. Each of these objects was placed upright in a brick made of crude mud, and then set in a cavity, which was walled up. In the Vignette in the Papyrus of Ani we see the *ṭeṭ* at the top of the plate and the figure of Anubis at the bottom ; on the right hand is a pot of burning incense [hieroglyph], which here represents the reed, and in the bottom left-hand corner is the *shabti* figure, standing below a second pot of burning incense. As to this being the *shabti* there is no doubt, for close by it is written the text of Chapter VI, which was commonly cut upon *ushabtiu* figures. Thus, the artist made a mistake, and put in two pots of burning incense instead of one, and moved the *shabti* from its proper place. Having made this blunder he committed another for the sake of giving the Vignette a symmetrical appearance, and placed another *shabti* figure in the right-hand bottom corner. And the scribe added a text in which this figure is said to be a "perfect Heart-soul."

Text: [Chapter CLI. Without title.] The text of this Chapter consists of a series of addresses to the mummy, which are supposed to be spoken by the gods and the amulets. Thus we have: (1) Address of Nephthys; (2) Address of Isis; (3–6) Addresses by the Four Sons of Horus; (7–11) Addresses by the *Ṭeṭ*, Anubis, the two reeds with burning incense, and the *Shabti* figure; (12) Speech by the "Perfect Heart-soul"; (13, 14) Short forms of praises by the two Heart-souls. In the twelve addresses enumerated above the gods and amulets assure Ani that they are there ready to protect his body, and to drive away from it any devils that may wish to destroy it, or to do it harm. In the Second Egyptian Room of the British Museum is exhibited a set of the four amulets, which were taken from the four walls of a tomb, and are very much like those represented in the Vignette of this Chapter as given in the Papyrus of Ani.

Vignette 1: Ani and his wife standing before a table of offerings.

PLATES XXXIV (*continued*) AND XXXV

Vignette 2: The Sekhet-Ḥetepet, *i.e.*, "Field of Offerings," or the Elysian Fields of the Egyptians. It is supposed to be in the sky somewhere, but the idea of this place was suggested by some very fertile spot, either in the Southern Sûdân or in the Delta. The following scenes are represented:—

I. First Register: 1. Thoth, the scribe of the gods, holding his reed and palette, introducing Ani into the Sekhet-Ḥetepet, according to the decree of the Great Company of the Gods who sat in judgment on him at the weighing of his heart.

2. Ani, dressed in white apparel, as upon earth, standing before three gods to whom he presents a libation vessel, or a pot of incense; the first god has the head of a hare, the second that of a serpent, and the third that of a bull. With the exception of the last, these three gods have the forms of those which guard the First Ārit of the Kingdom of Osiris. See Chapter CXLVII.

3. Ani seated in a boat, which is protected by the *utchat* and contains a table of offerings; he appears to be taking this to the god at the end of the register. The boat is similar in form to that in which Rā travels.

4. Ani, with one arm extended as if in the act of addressing a god.

5. The hawk of Horus standing on the *serekh*.

6. A god in mummy form standing upright; before him is an altar-stand on which are a libation vessel and a lotus flower. This god may be an ancestor of Ani, his father or grandfather.

7. Three ovals, which represent lakes. These have no names in this Vignette, but in the Papyrus of Nebseni they are called Urti, Ḥetep, and Qetqet. Originally they appear to have been small islands. The two short lines of hieroglyphs read "Living in Sekhet-Ḥetepet [with] air in the nose."

II. Second Register: 1. Ani reaping wheat, with the words "the Osiris reapeth."

2. Three oxen treading out the corn on a circular piece of ground with a raised edge to prevent the grain from being scattered. Ani is urging round the oxen with cries and the flourishing of a whip.

3. Ani standing with both hands raised in adoration.

4. A bird on a perch, symbol of "abundance," or the Nile-god.

5. Ani, holding the *kherp* sceptre, symbolic of his high rank, kneeling before two large heaps of grain, either dhura and wheat, or dhura and barley. The words seem to indicate that the grain is the food of the *Kau* and *Khu*, *i.e.*, of the Doubles and Spirit-souls.

6. Three ovals, which represent three lakes; in the Papyrus of Nebseni the lakes are four in number, and they are called Nebtaui, Uakha, Kha, and Ḥetep.

III. Third Register. Ani ploughing with a yoke of oxen in Sekhet-Åanru , a division of Sekhet-Ḥetepet. The hieroglyphic text reads "Mouth of the canal (?), a stream [one thousand "cubits] wide. Its length cannot be stated. No fishes of "any kind live in it, there are no worms (*i.e.*, serpents) "in it" .

IV. Fourth Register: 1. Two bifurcations of the streams whereby two islands are formed. The upper island is the "Birth-place of the god of the city Qenqen," according to the Papyrus of Nebseni; on the lower is a flight of steps and the legend .[1]

2. A boat, each end of which terminates in the head and neck of a serpent, lying at the end of a short canal. In the centre of it is a flight of steps, and it has eight oars, four of which were used in propelling it in one direction, and four in the opposite direction. By the side of it are the words "the god therein is Unn-Nefer" , and the name of a part of a canal "Åshet" . A boat, in which is a flight of steps, floating on one of the streams of the region; in the Turin Papyrus it is said to be "the boat wherein Rā Ḥeru-Khuti sails in Sekhet-Ḥetepet."[2] Above is written the word *tchefau* , *i.e.*, divine food.

[1] Var. and .

[2] .

3. At the other end of this Register are the words: , *i.e.*, "the place of the Spirit-"souls, who are seven cubits high. The wheat (or dhura) "is three cubits high [and] the Spirit-bodies reap it."

Text: [CHAPTER CX.] HERE BEGIN THE CHAPTERS OF SEKHET-ḤETEPET, AND THE CHAPTERS OF COMING FORTH BY DAY, AND OF GOING INTO AND OF COMING FORTH FROM KHERT-NETER, AND OF ARRIVING IN SEKHET-ÅARU, AND OF LIVING IN THE GREAT CITY WHEREIN IS FRESH AIR. In the older papyri Chapter CX is very long, and it contains a number of repetitions. The object of the Chapter was to provide the deceased with an estate in the Kingdom of Osiris, wherein he would live under conditions closely resembling those under which he lived when upon earth. The recital of the Chapter would enable him to obtain food and drink in abundance, to plough, sow, and reap there, to marry, to sail about in a boat on the canals, and to live a life wholly unaffected by any personal disabilities, or by any of the troubles that formed the necessary concomitants of the life upon earth. Having placated Horus and Set, the "Two Fighters," he would never be overcome by any of the minor fiends who acknowledged Set to be their overlord, and having triumphed over death, and put away all the defects and the sins which appertained to his material body, he felt confident that he would enjoy the happiness and the bliss of life everlasting. This Chapter is quite different from the CXth Chapter in the Papyrus of Nebseni, and only the opening words of the second paragraph resemble any part of the text of the older papyrus. It is probable that the artist did not leave space sufficient for this long Chapter, and that the scribe had only room to write down a series of short sentences by which he strove to give the general sense of the ancient proposition.

PLATES XXXV (*continued*) AND XXXVI

Vignette: The Osiris Ani, arrayed in white linen apparel, with his hands raised in adoration, presenting the two libation vases and the two lotus flowers, which are placed on stands, to the god Seker-Osiris. This god is in mummy form, he has the head of a hawk, with the solar disk upon it, he holds in his hands the sceptre , and he stands upon the cubit of *maāt*. In some papyri he is called "Osiris, lord of Ṭeṭu," and in the Turin Papyrus he is addressed as "Osiris, Lord of Eternity, King, Lord of Everlastingness, Great God, Governor of Åkerti," , and is accompanied by the goddess Åmentet-Nefert, or "Beautiful Åmenti."

Text: [CHAPTER CXLVIII.] THE CHAPTER OF PROVIDING THE DECEASED WITH FOOD IN KHERT-NETER. In the older versions of this Chapter the deceased addresses the god who shines from his disk, and says that he knows his name and the names of the seven kine and their bull. Then follows a petition to the kine and their bull for cakes and ale, and glory in Khert-Neter, and to be allowed to be in their train, and to be born on their thighs; and this is followed by the names of the seven kine and their bull. In this papyrus Osiris, the Lord of Maāt, the ONE, the Lord of Eternity and Creator of Everlastingness, is addressed by Ani who says that he has made offerings to the seven kine and their bull. The names of these are not given in the Papyrus of Ani, but they will be found in the Notes to the Chapter CXLVIII, edited from another papyrus

Vignette: The seven kine, each one couchant before a table of offerings, and each with a disk between her horns, and a *menăt* lying on her back near the neck. Below them is the bull with a table of offerings before him.

Text: An address to the seven kine and their bull.

Vignette: The four rudders or steering oars of the Boat of Rā, each belonging to one of the four quarters of heaven. In the Turin Papyrus each rudder has an *utchat* behind it.

Text: Four addresses, one to each of the four steering oars of heaven.

Vignette: Four triads of gods, each triad with a libation vase and a lotus on a stand before him. From the Vignette in the Turin Papyrus it is clear that these four triads represent four gods only, namely, the Four Sons of Horus, who appear there in their characteristic forms.

Text: An address to the Father-gods and Mother-goddesses, who dwell in heaven and in Khert-Neter, and who are entreated to deliver the deceased from every evil thing that can be done unto him by men, and by gods, and by the Spirit-souls, and by the dead. Only the opening part of this address is given in the Papyrus of Ani.

This Chapter is one of the most important in the Book of the Dead, for it was written with the object of providing the deceased with animal food and milk in the Other World. One fact in connection with it must be remembered. The god addressed is Osiris, or one of his forms, and Osiris was himself the Bull of Åmenti; the food therefore that Osiris is asked to give is himself. Now the seven kine are only incarnations of Isis, Hathor, and other goddesses, and the milk with which the kine supply the deceased is the milk of these goddesses; he therefore drinks the divine milk whereon the gods themselves live. Viewed from another aspect the kine and the bull supplied the celestial meat and milk upon which Rā the Sun-god lived, and the **Rubric** states distinctly that if this Chapter be recited at sunrise on behalf of the deceased, its effect will be to ensure to him a perpetual supply of food in abundance. That a very great mystery was associated with this Chapter is proved by the Rubric to it given in the Papyrus of Nu, where it is ordered that this "Book of Un-Nefer" be not recited by a man in the presence of anyone except himself. In the Turin Papyrus (ed. Lepsius, Bl. LXIX) the Chapter is said to be a "very great and real mystery" [hieroglyphs], that no other (*i.e.*, outsider) is ever to know it, [hieroglyphs], that it is to be repeated to no one [hieroglyphs], that no eye is to see it, and no ear to hear it [hieroglyphs], and that none of the dwellers in the Delta is to know it [hieroglyphs]. The man that taught the

Chapter to him that recites it may be present at the recital, as well as the reciter's dearest friend [hieroglyphs] (ll. 6 and 7).

Vignettes: The scribe Ani and his wife standing before a table of offerings, with hands raised in adoration of the god Seker-Osiris.

Text: [Chapter CLXXXV.] A Hymn of praise to Osiris Khenti Åmenti. In this hymn Ani praises the Lord of Lords and King of Kings, the Prince and God of Gods, and prays that Osiris will grant him a seat with the followers of the god, and will permit his Ka to have authority in the Ṭuat over all who are there, and to go in and come out at will.

PLATE XXXVII

Vignette: The god Seker-Osiris, in mummy form, standing in a funerary coffer, the roof of which is surmounted by a hawk and uraei. He wears the White Crown, with two plumes attached, and holds in his hands a whip [hieroglyph] and two sceptres [hieroglyphs]. He is called "Sekri Osiris, Lord of the Shetait shrine, great god, Lord of Khert-Neter" [hieroglyphs].

Vignette: 1. The Hippopotamus-goddess Ta-urt standing upon the roof of a sepulchral building. On her head is a pair of horns with a disk between them, and she holds in her right fore-foot a whisk (?), and in her left, which rests upon [hieroglyph] the symbol of the magical fluid of life, the symbol of "life," [hieroglyph]. Before her are two altar-stands on which rest many offerings, cakes, joints of meat, fruit, vegetables, flowers, etc.

Vignette: 2. The tomb of Ani in the mountain of Western Thebes. The tomb is a rectangular building with a cornice surmounted by a pyramid, in one side of which is the niche in which Ani's Heart-soul rested when it returned from the Other World to visit his body in the tomb.

Similar niches may still be seen in the pyramids at Meröe, and in front of one at least is a ledge on which the soul may alight. In front of the tomb is a small portico, the roof of which is supported by a pillar with a papyrus capital. From a small pool or lake close to the tomb spring a number of large flowering plants. From the mountain itself projects the head of the Cow-goddess Hathor in her character of goddess of Åmenti. Between her horns are a disk and two plumes.

Text: [Chapter CLXXXVI. Without title.] The text of the Chapter is incomplete and lacks the prayers that are found in other papyri; only a few of the titles of Hathor are enumerated. With these words and the accompanying Vignettes the Papyrus of Ani comes to an end.

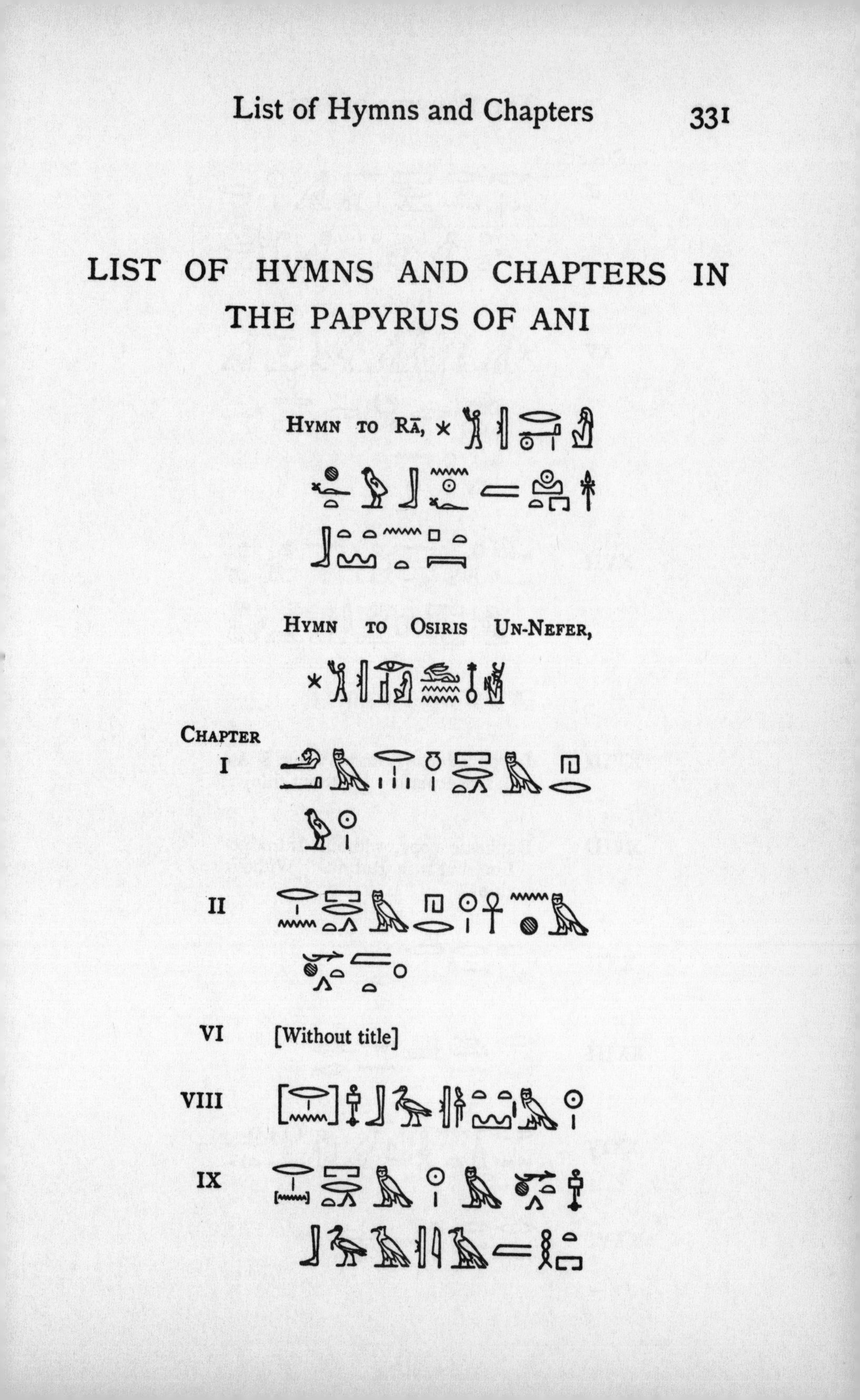

LIST OF HYMNS AND CHAPTERS IN THE PAPYRUS OF ANI

HYMN TO RĀ,

HYMN TO OSIRIS UN-NEFER,

CHAPTER

I

II

VI [Without title]

VIII

IX

CHAPTER

X

XV

XVII

[A large section omitted.]

XVIII Introductions (A and B), text §§ A–J, and Rubric. [Without title]

XVIII Duplicate copy, without Introduction, but with Rubric. [Without title]

XXII

XXIII

XXIV

XXVI

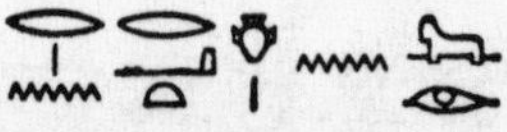

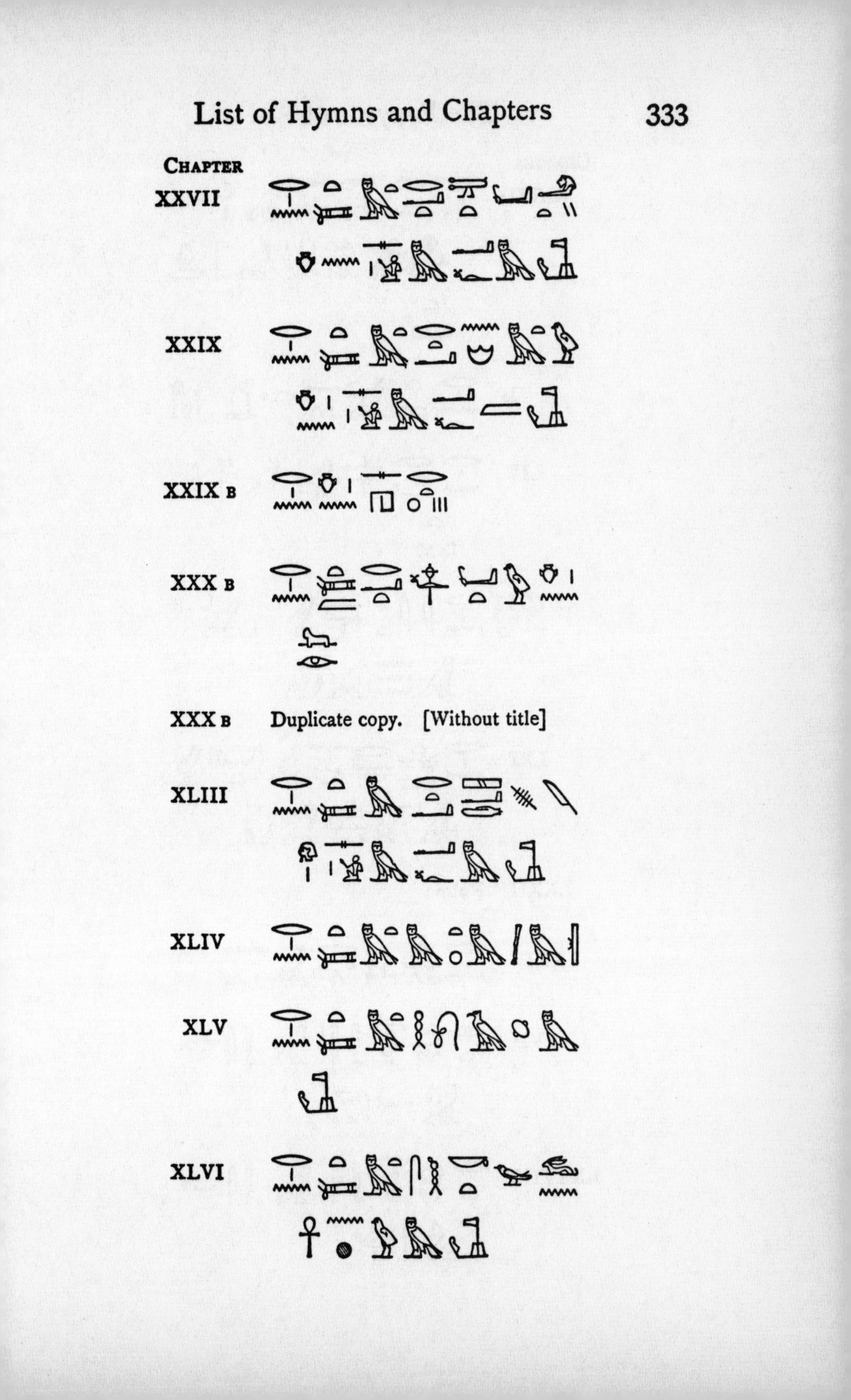

CHAPTER

XXVII

XXIX

XXIX B

XXX B

XXX B Duplicate copy. [Without title]

XLIII

XLIV

XLV

XLVI

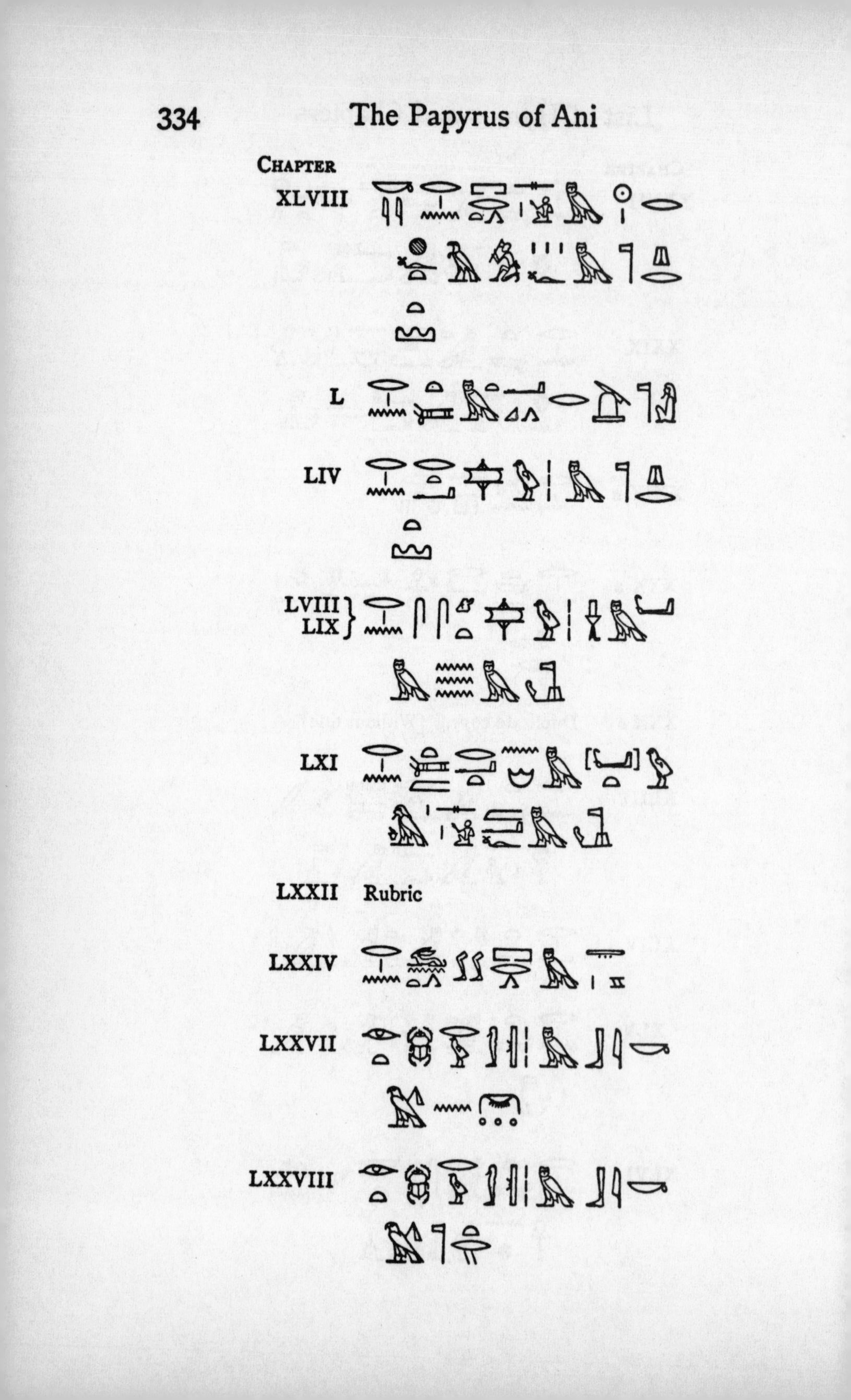

CHAPTER

XLVIII

L

LIV

LVIII
LIX

LXI

LXXII Rubric

LXXIV

LXXVII

LXXVIII

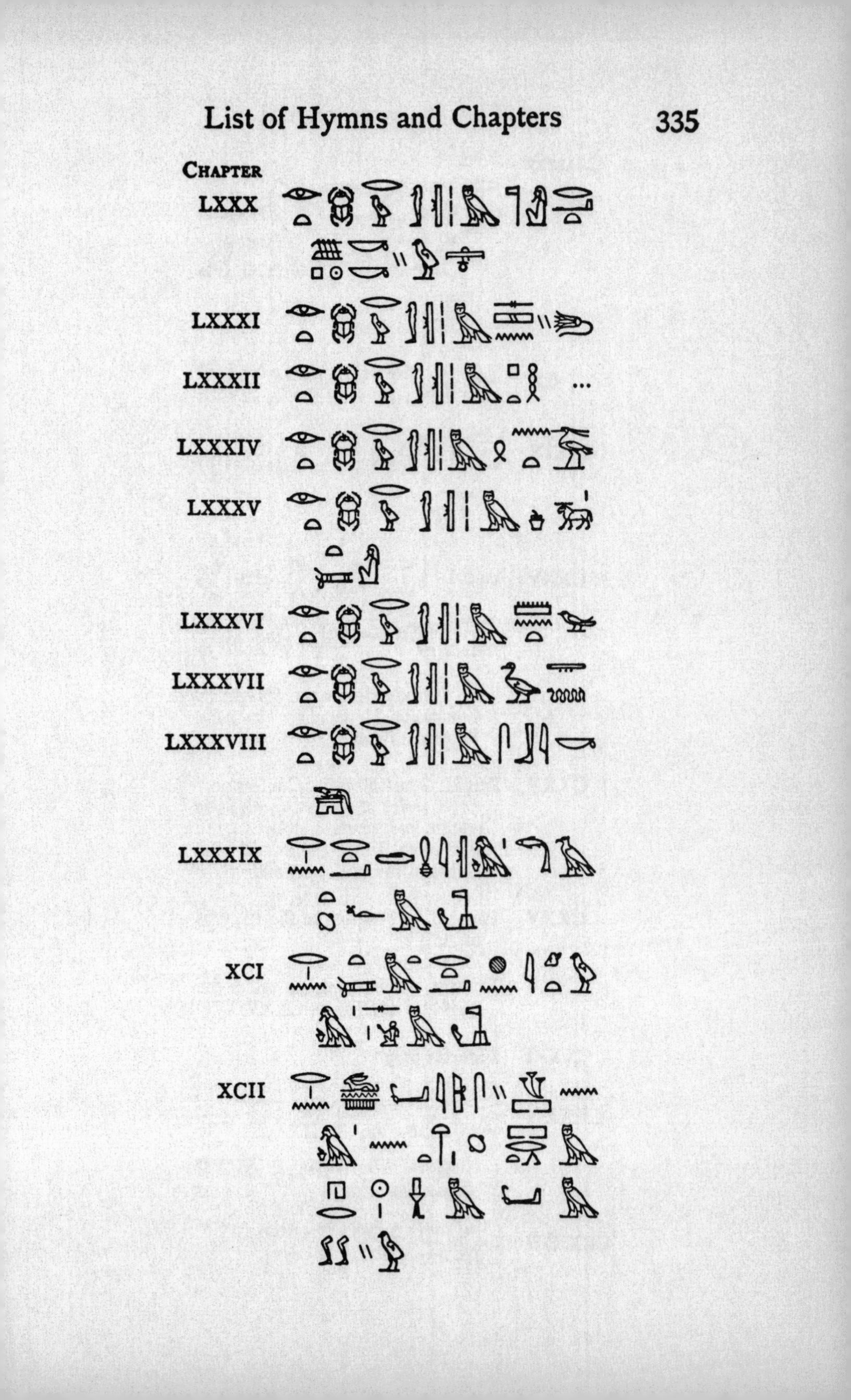

CHAPTER

LXXX

LXXXI

LXXXII ...

LXXXIV

LXXXV

LXXXVI

LXXXVII

LXXXVIII

LXXXIX

XCI

XCII

CHAPTER	
XCIII	
CX	
CXXIV	
CXXV	Part I. An Introduction to the "Negative Confession" peculiar to the Papyrus of Ani
CXXV	Part II. The "Negative Confession," *i.e.*, a series of Forty-two negative statements made by Ani to the Forty-two Judges, who sat with Osiris in the Hall of Maāti
CXXV	Part III. [Wanting in the Papyrus of Ani]
CXXV	RUBRIC. This is placed under the Vignette of Chapter CXXVI
CXXVI	Vignette only
CXXXII	
CXXXIII	

CHAPTER

CXXXIII RUBRIC

CXXXIV

CXLVIII Of the giving of food to the Spirit-soul in Khert-Neter, and of delivering him from all evil things. [Without title in the Papyrus of Ani]

CLI The plan of the Mummy-chamber. [Without title in the Papyrus of Ani]

CLV

CLVI

CLXVI

CLXXV

CLXXXV

CLXXXVI [Without title in the Papyrus of Ani]

THE PAPYRUS OF ANI

A HYMN TO RĀ THE SUN-GOD

[CHAPTER XV]

PLATE I

1\. A Hymn of Praise to Rā when He Riseth in the Eastern Part of Heaven: Behold, the Osiris[1] Ani, the scribe of the holy offerings of all the gods, **2.** saith: Homage to thee, O thou who hast come as Kheperȧ,[2] Kheperȧ the creator of the gods. Thou art seated on thy throne (or, thou art crowned), thou risest up in the sky,

[1] In funerary texts the name of the deceased is usually preceded by the name of Osiris, and the deceased is throughout the texts of all periods always identified with Osiris. Since the formulae which were recited over the dead body of Osiris, and the ceremonies which were performed over it, caused Osiris to be revivified and to rise from the dead, the Egyptians believed that a repetition of both formulae and ceremonies would certainly be followed by the resurrection of any person on whose behalf the all-powerful words were recited and the ceremonies performed. In calling the deceased "Osiris" the priest imparted to his dead body some of the powers of the god Osiris, and so made his resurrection assured.

[2] Kheperȧ was self-produced, and he was the creator of the world and of all on it. He was the father of the gods, and men and women sprang from the tears that fell from his eyes upon his members, and so became sources of life. His name in its simplest form seems to mean "he who existeth," "he who is," but in later times the verb derived from it means "to evolve," "to develop." The oldest symbol of Kheperȧ is the beetle, and the earliest conception of Kheperȧ was that he existed in the form of a gigantic beetle, which rolled the ball of the sun across the sky. The ball of the sun was regarded as the source of all life, and was compared to the ball of excrementitious matter which the *Scarabaeus sacer*

3. illumining thy mother [Nut], thou art seated on thy throne as the king of the gods. [Thy] mother Nut[1] stretcheth out her hands, and performeth an act of homage to thee. 4. The domain of Manu[2] receiveth thee with satisfaction. The goddess Maāt[3] embraceth thee at the two seasons of the day (*i.e.*, at morn and at eve). May Rā

---

collects, and rolls along to the place where its larva is so that it may feed upon it. See Lanzone, *Dizionario*, pp. 927 ff.; Brugsch, *Religion*, p. 245; Budge, *Gods of the Egyptians*, Vol. I, pp. 308–321; and Budge, *Archaeologia*, Vol. LII, pp. 541 ff. The cult of the Beetle-god came into Egypt from the Sûdân, and after the spread of sun-worship in the north of Egypt and the priests of Rā, the Sun-god, had become all powerful, Kheperȧ was made to be a phase of the Sun-god, who was declared to be "Kheperȧ in the morning, Rā at mid-day, and Temu in the evening." Subsequently he was identified with the Horus gods.

[1] Nut was the female form of Nu, the god of the mass of water which was believed to have existed in primeval times, and she represented the sky, or rather the waters which were in the firmament. She was the mother of Rā, the Sun-god, in one aspect, and his daughter in another. She appears in the form of a woman bearing on her head a vase, which is her symbol as the Mother-Womb that produced all things. Heliopolitan theology made her to be the daughter of Shu and Tefnut, the wife of Ḳeb, and the mother of Osiris, Isis, Set, Nephthys, and Horus, or Anubis, all of whom she brought forth at a birth.

[2] Manu is a name for the west, and for the whole of the region where the sun sets, just as Bakha is a name for the east, and for the whole region where the sun rises. The Mount of Manu was the hilly district of Western Thebes where such large numbers of rock-hewn tombs are found.

[3] Maāt is the personification of righteousness, truth, and justice, and she stood as the type of absolute regularity and order, and of moral rectitude. She was the daughter of Rā, the Sun-god, and the female counterpart of Thoth, whom she assisted in carrying out the work of creation which had been conceived in the mind of Kheperȧ. From a moral point of view her chief duty was to assist at the judgment of the souls of the dead, and in many papyri she is seen leading the deceased into the Hall of Judgment. She appears in the form of a woman, and her symbol is the ostrich feather, which she wears on her head. Her attributes were shared by several goddesses, and especially by Isis and Nephthys, who are called the "Two Maāti Goddesses," *i.e.*, the two Truth-goddesses.

give glory, and power, and truth-speaking,[1] **5.** and the appearance as a living soul[2] so that he may gaze upon Ḥeru-khuti,[3] to the Ka[4] of the Osiris the Scribe Ani, who speaketh truth before Osiris, **6.** and who saith : Hail,

[1] The words *maā kheru* have formed the subject of many discussions by Egyptologists, *e.g.*, Naville, *Litanie du Soleil*, p. 74, and Devéria in *Recueil de Travaux*, tom. 1, pp. 10 ff. The words mean literally "true of speech," and have nothing whatever to do with the meanings "triumphant," "justified," "blessed," etc., which have been associated with them. This is evident when we consider what the object of the Judgment was. The deceased was believed to be, like Osiris, the subject of a series of infamous accusations which were made against him by Set, whose desire was to obtain the damnation of his soul. In answer to these the deceased made a series of forty-two statements, each to one of the Forty-two Assessors in the Judgment Hall, in which he swore that he had not committed certain sins. The Company of the Gods and Thoth, the advocate of the deceased, then tried these statements, in order to discover whether the deceased had told the truth or not. When they found that the deceased *had* spoken the truth, Thoth declared him to be "true of speech," *i.e.*, innocent of the offences which were imputed to him by Set, or as we should say "not guilty," or "acquitted."

[2] The opposite of the dead, or damned, soul which was condemned to remain for ever in Dead-land.

[3] *I.e.*, "Horus of the two horizons," the Harmakhis of the Greeks. The words "two horizons" refer to Bakhet and Manu, the most easterly and westerly points of the sun's course, and the regions wherein he rose and set. As the god of the noon-day sun he is called "Rā Ḥeru-khuti," and as the god of the setting sun "Temu Ḥeru-khuti." The Sphinx at Gîzah was dedicated to him as the god of the rising sun, that is to say, this is the tradition which was current about that monument under the XVIIIth dynasty, and perhaps very much earlier.

[4] The Ka was an abstract individuality or spiritual thing which came into being when the body to which it belonged was born. It was wholly independent and distinct from the physical body, but its abode was the body, whose actions it was supposed to direct, and guide, and keep watch over, and it lived in the body until the body died. It was, in short, the "double" of the body. It was represented by the sign ⊔, *i.e.*, two human arms extended at right angles to the breast as if ready to embrace someone. The Ka did not die with the body, but it is somewhat uncertain if it was thought to be immortal. The body was placed in a tomb, and the Ka could visit it if it pleased, but it was usual to provide for the Ka a statue in which it might at all times dwell. The Ka lived upon the

O all ye gods of the House of the Soul,[1] who weigh heaven and earth in a balance, and who give celestial food[2] [to the dead]. Hail, Tatun,[3] [who art] One,[4] **7.** thou creator of mortals [and] of the Companies of the Gods of the South and of the North, of the West and of the East, ascribe ye praise to Rā,[5] the lord of heaven, **8.** the KING,[6] Life, Strength, and Health [be to him], the maker of the gods. Give ye thanks unto him in his beneficent form which is enthroned in the Āṭett Boat[7]; **9.** beings celestial praise

---

offerings which were made to the dead, and if these failed it left its statue and wandered about in the desert, and ate the offal which it found there. If it could find no food of any kind it died of starvation. The true meaning of the sign for "double," , was discovered by Nestor L'Hôte, and many years later, was re-discovered by Maspero (see *Étude sur quelques peintures*, pp. 191 ff.), by Birch, *Mémoire sur une patère Égyptienne*, Paris, 1858, and by Renouf (see *Trans. Soc. Bibl. Arch.*, VI, pp. 494 ff.).

[1] A name probably of one of the sanctuaries of Osiris, either at Heliopolis, or Busiris, or Mendes. The word *Ba*, here rendered "soul," also means "ram," in which animal a form of Osiris became incarnate.

[2] *Tchefau* is the name of the food on which the gods lived, and may be compared to the ambrosia and nectar on which the gods lived on Olympus.

[3] Or Taten, or Tathenen, or Tenen. He was a very ancient god of the earth, and the priests of Heliopolis identified him with Ḳeb , a later Earth-god, and the husband of Nut, the Sky-goddess. Tatun was associated with Ptaḥ in the creation of gods and men, and he is said to have been the creator of the sun and moon.

[4] *I.e.*, he possessed the quality of oneness in common with Temu, of whom he was an important form.

[5] About the time of the IVth dynasty Rā became the head of all the gods of Egypt, and the king of Egypt was officially described on all documents as his son.

[6] ÅTI, one of the very ancient Egyptian words for "king"; its exact meaning is unknown. As Rā once reigned over Egypt in human form the words "Life, strength, and health be to him," are here added.

[7] The boat in which he started on his journey across the sky in the morning; the old form of the word is "Māntchet."

10.

thee, beings terrestrial praise thee.[1] Thoth[2] and the goddess Maāt mark out thy course for thee day by day and every day. Thine enemy the Serpent[3] hath been given over **10.** to the fire. The Serpent-fiend Sebȧu[4] hath fallen headlong, his forelegs are bound in chains, and his hind legs hath Rā carried away from him. The

[1] *I.e.*, the gods and their followers who live in heaven and on the earth.

[2] He was self-created, and self-existent, and he was the personification of the mind, wisdom, and knowledge of the great god who created the universe. He was also the heart of Rā. He was the Word, the pronunciation of which resulted in the creation of the world, and he invented letters, writing, arithmetic, astronomy, and all the arts and sciences. He was the "lord of Law," the "maker of Law," and the "begetter of Law." He acted as the advocate of Osiris when the god was tried, at the instance of Set (the Devil), by the gods in the Divine Court at Heliopolis, and he proved the truthfulness of Osiris, and showed that he was innocent of the charges made against him by Set, and secured the acquittal of Osiris. He presided at the weighing of the hearts of the dead before Osiris, and composed the formulae which enabled souls to find their way through Dead-land in peace and safety. When Horus and Set were fighting to the death for mastery, Thoth appeared and acted the part of arbitrator, and arranged the conditions under which each god consented to live peacefully ever after. As a mathematician Thoth computed times and seasons, and ordained laws for the heavenly bodies, and so effected the ordering and well-being of the world which his utterance had caused to come into being. According to an ancient legend Set attacked the eye of the sun, and injured it very seriously; and, finding the new moon in the sky one evening as he was wandering about the heavens, he swallowed it. Thoth attacked Set, and cut off one of his limbs, and healed the eye of the sun, thus restoring its light to the world, and then he treated Set in such a way that he vomited forth the crescent moon, which Thoth at once restored to the night-sky. Thoth also acted as secretary to Osiris, and kept the registers in his kingdom in which the acts of men were written down.

[3] The enemy of Rā was a huge serpent, which took up its place each morning in the darkest portion of the sky, and waited there in order to swallow up the sun when it appeared at dawn. Rā cast a spell on the serpent which rendered it powerless, and his heat scorched its body and destroyed it.

[4] An enemy of Rā who often took the form of a crocodile.

Sons of **11.** Revolt[1] shall never more rise up. The House of the Aged One[2] keepeth festival, and the voices of those who make merry are in the Great Place.[3] **12.** The gods rejoice when they see Rā crowned upon his throne, and when his beams flood the world with light. The majesty **13.** of this holy (or, august) god setteth out on his journey, and he goeth onwards until he reacheth the land of Manu; the earth becometh light at his birth each day; he proceedeth until he reacheth the place where he was yesterday. **14.** O be thou at peace with me. Let me gaze upon thy beauties. Let me journey above the earth. Let me smite the Ass.[4] Let me slit asunder the

[1] The *mesu beṭshet*, or "children of rebellion," or "sons of impotent revolt," were the fiends and inferior devils who carried out the commands of Set, Sebȧ, and the other great devils whose principal occupation consisted of making attempts to destroy the Sun-god. In later times they became powers of evil from a moral point of view.

[2] A name of the temple of Rā at Heliopolis, wherein the god was worshipped under the form of Temu.

[3] A name of the chief sanctuary of Rā in many towns, *e.g.*, Thebes and Heliopolis.

[4] The text should probably be corrected to, "Let me smite the Eater of the Ass," the allusion being to the monster serpent which is seen biting the neck of an ass in the Vignette of Chapter XL. The ass is a well-known symbol of the Sun-god because of his generative powers, and "Ass" is one of the names of the Sun-god. It is hardly possible for the ass to be an associate of Set, and therefore some correction of the text is necessary.

15. Serpent-fiend Sebȧu. Let me destroy Āapep[1] at the moment of his greatest power. Let me behold the Abṭu Fish at his season, and the Ȧnt Fish[2] **16.** with the Ȧnt Boat as it piloteth it in its lake. Let me behold Horus[3] when he is in charge of the rudder [of the Boat of Rā], with Thoth and the goddess Maāt on each side of him. Let me lay hold of the tow-rope of the **17.** Sektet Boat,[4] and the rope at the stern of the Māṭett Boat. Let Rā grant to me a view of the Disk (*i.e.*, the sun), and a sight of Ȧḥ (*i.e.*, the moon) unfailingly each day.[5] **18.** Let my Ba-soul[6] come forth to walk about hither and thither

[1] Āapep is the monster serpent of many folds and of most malignant characteristics which attacked the Sun-god daily, and one of his commonest abodes was the black thunder-cloud. His great ally was the monster Shesshes, which had the body of a crocodile, the tail of which terminated in a serpent. Each morning Rā cast a spell on Āapep, and he was seized by the gods, and a long chain tied to his head, and in this state was hacked in pieces which were consumed by the fires of Rā. These scenes are depicted in my *Book of Gates*, pp. 241, 268 ff.

[2] The Abṭu and Ȧnt were two mythological fishes which swam immediately in front of the Boat of Rā, to give warning to the god on the look-out place whenever any water-devil or fiend approached to do to it, or to the god himself, any harm.

[3] Horus directed the course of the boat under the direction of Thoth and Maāt, who "set the course" of the god each day.

[4] The Sektet Boat was the boat in which Rā made his journey during the latter part of the day. The deceased wished to have power over the rope which connected the two boats, the Māṭett leading and the Sektet following.

[5] The deceased expected to be in a region where the moon was visible every day.

[6] The Ba-soul inhabited the KA, or Double.

20. 21.

22. 23. 24.

25. 26.

27. 28.

19. and whithersoever it pleaseth. **20.** Let my name be called out, **21.** let it be found inscribed on the tablet[1] **22.** which recordeth the names of those who are to receive offerings. **23.** Let meals from the sepulchral offerings be given to me in the presence [of Osiris], as to those who are in the following of **24.** Horus.[2] Let there be prepared for me **25.** a seat in the Boat of the Sun on the day whereon the **26.** god saileth.[3] Let me be received **27.** in the presence of Osiris in the Land (or, Island) **28.** of Truth-speaking —the KA of Osiris Ani.

[1] This assumes the existence in heaven of a list containing the names of those who formed the household of Osiris, and who were fed daily by the god.

[2] The "Followers of Horus" are probably the beings, or "blacksmiths," who were the companions in predynastic times of the Horus god-king who then reigned upon earth. In later times they were represented by the Four Sons of Horus, Mestȧ (or Ḳestȧ), Ḥāp, Ṭuamutef, and Qebḥsenuf.

[3] *I.e.*, the deceased prays that a seat may be reserved for him in the Boat of Rā on the day when he departs from this world, so that his soul may set out from Thebes in it under the protection of the god, and so arrive in due course at Abydos, near which were the Kingdom of Osiris and the Islands of the Blessed.

[4] The reading is probably "island." The island referred to was that on which, according to Chapter CLXXV, Osiris lived. The god who worked the ferry-boat to it would transport thither no one who was not a speaker of the truth, and the island itself repelled any untruthful person who succeeded in getting near it.

APPENDIX TO CHAPTER XV

HYMN TO RĀ, THE SUN-GOD

[From the Papyrus of Nekht (Brit. Mus. No. 10471, Sheet 21)]

NEKHT, THE CAPTAIN OF SOLDIERS, THE ROYAL SCRIBE, SINGETH A HYMN OF PRAISE TO RĀ, and saith :—Homage to thee, O thou glorious Being, thou who art dowered [with all sovereignty]. O Tem-Ḥeru-Khuti (Tem-Harmakhis), when thou risest in the horizon of heaven a cry of joy goeth forth to thee from all people. O thou beautiful Being, thou dost renew thyself in thy season in the form of the Disk, within thy mother Hathor. Therefore in every place every heart swelleth with joy at thy rising for ever. The regions of the South and the North come to thee with homage, and send forth acclamations at thy rising on the horizon of heaven, and thou illuminest the Two Lands (*i.e.*, Upper and Lower Egypt) with rays of turquoise-[coloured] light. O Rā, who art Ḥeru-Khuti, the divine man-child, the heir of eternity, self-begotten and self-born, king of the earth, prince of the Ṭuat (*i.e.*, the Other World), governor of Åuḳert,[1] thou didst come from the Water-god, thou didst spring from the Sky-god Nu, who doth cherish thee and order thy members. O thou god of life, thou lord of love, all men live when thou shinest; thou art crowned king of the gods. The goddess Nut embraceth thee, and the goddess Mut enfoldeth thee at all seasons. Those who are in thy following sing unto thee with joy, and they bow down their foreheads to the earth when they meet thee, the lord of heaven, the lord of the earth, the King of Truth, the lord of eternity, the prince of everlastingness, thou sovereign of all the gods, thou god of life, thou creator of eternity, thou maker of heaven wherein thou art firmly stablished.

The Company of the Gods rejoice at thy rising, the earth is glad when it beholdeth thy rays; the people who have been long dead come forth with cries of joy to behold thy beauties every day. Thou goest forth each day over heaven and earth, and thou art made strong each day by thy mother Nut. Thou passest over the heights of heaven,

[1] A name of the Other World of Heliopolis.

thy heart swelleth with joy; and the Lake of Testes (?) (*i.e.*, the Great Oasis) is content thereat. The Serpent-fiend hath fallen, his arms are hewn off, the Knife hath severed his joints. Rā liveth by Maāt (*i.e.*, Law), the beautiful! The Sektet Boat advanceth and cometh into port. The South and the North, and the West and the East, turn to praise thee. O thou First, Great God (PAUTA), who didst come into being of thine own accord, Isis and Nephthys salute thee, they sing unto thee songs of joy at thy rising in the boat, they stretch out their hands unto thee. The Souls of the East follow thee, and the Souls of the West praise thee. Thou art the Ruler of all the gods. Thou in thy shrine hast joy, for the Serpent-fiend Nȧk hath been judged by the fire, and thy heart shall rejoice for ever. Thy mother Nut is esteemed by thy father Nu.

HYMN TO OSIRIS UN-NEFER

PLATE II

1.

2.

1. A Hymn of Praise to Osiris Un-Nefer,[1] the great god who dwelleth in Abṭu,[2] the king of eternity, the lord of everlastingness, who traverseth millions of years in his existence. Thou[3] art the eldest son of the **2.** womb of Nut.[4] Thou wast begotten by Ḳeb,[5] the Erpāt.[6] Thou

[1] A title of Osiris meaning the "Beneficent Existence." Originally Un-Nefer was probably an independent god, but the priests of Osiris transferred his special attributes, whatever they were, to Osiris. A most curious form of Un-Nefer is sculptured on a relief at Abydos (see *Abydos*, ed. Mariette, I, 40). On a high pylon-shaped pedestal is a kneeling human figure, on the neck of which stand a and , which form the head of the figure.

[2] Abydos in Upper Egypt, the principal seat in the South of the cult of Osiris. At Neṭát, close to Abydos, Osiris was slain by Set, and his body was taken to Abydos, where it was embalmed and revivified by Isis, Thoth, Horus, and his Four Sons. The tomb of Osiris was at Abydos, as also were the famous well, and stairs, and grove, and it was believed that an entrance to the Other World was situated near the temple. The offerings carried down into the Uārt corridor below ground were supposed to be transmitted directly to the beatified who lived in the kingdom of Osiris.

[3] A change from the third to the second person, so characteristic of Oriental poems in general and of the Hebrew Psalms.

[4] The Mother-goddess who brought forth Osiris, Isis, Set, Nephthys, and Horus (or, Anubis) at a birth.

[5] Ḳeb was the Earth-god, and the husband of Nut, the Sky-goddess: in primeval times these deities were locked in a perpetual embrace, but at the command of Thoth, who uttered the thought of the Creator, Shu separated them and raised Nut up from the body of Ḳeb. Light and air were then made to exist in the space between them, and this event was the first act of the Creation. Each evening as the sun set and the light left the earth, Nut descended and was rejoined to Ḳeb, her husband, until the following morning; as the sun rose she resumed her position above the earth. By the nightly embraces the generations of living things on the earth were continued.

[6] A very old title which seems to mean something like "hereditary chief of the tribe"; he was the great ancestor of the Osiris cycle of gods.

art the lord of the Urrt Crown.[1] Thou art he whose White Crown[2] is lofty. Thou art the KING (Åti) of gods [and] men. 3. Thou hast gained possession of the sceptre of rule, , and the whip, , and the rank and dignity of thy divine fathers. Thy heart is expanded with joy, O thou who art in the kingdom of the dead.[3] Thy son Horus is firmly placed on thy throne. 4. Thou hast ascended thy throne as the Lord of Ṭeṭu,[4] and as the Ḥeq[5] who dwelleth in Abydos. Thou makest the Two Lands[6] to flourish through 5. Truth-speaking, in the presence of him who is the Lord to the Uttermost Limit.[7] Thou drawest on that

[1] The Urrt Crown was a very old symbol of sovereignty, and the word probably belongs to predynastic times.

[2] The White Crown resembles the crowns worn by chiefs of some of the tribes of Central Africa at the present day.

[3] Originally this kingdom was at Abydos, but in later times its limits were extended until it included all the western bank of the Nile of Egypt, where the dead were usually buried; this was commonly called "Åmentet," which means both "the West," and the "Hidden Land."

[4] *I.e.*, the famous town of Busiris in the Delta, which at one time seems to have included Mendes. Busiris was the centre of the cult of Osiris in the North, and was to the Delta what Abydos was to Upper Egypt. Abydos maintained its importance because the head of Osiris was buried there, and the dead were brought there from all parts of Egypt so that they might be buried near it.

[5] A very old word for "Governor" or "Ruler."

[6] *I.e.*, Upper and Lower Egypt, the South and the North.

[7] Neb-er-tcher, or the Lord of the Universe. The name has also been explained to mean "lord of wholeness," and to be a title of Osiris when his scattered limbs had been collected and rejoined by Thoth, Horus, Isis, and the other gods who effected his resurrection.

6. 7. 8. 9.

which hath not yet come into being* in thy name of 6. "Ta-ḥer-sta-nef."[1] Thou governest the Two Lands by Maāt in thy name of "Seker."[2] Thy power is wide-spread, 7. thou art he of whom the fear is great in thy name of "Usȧr"[3] (or "Ȧsȧr"). Thy existence endureth for an infinite number of double *ḥenti*[4] periods in thy name of "Un-Nefer."[5]

8. Homage to thee, King of Kings, and Lord of Lords, and Prince of Princes. Thou hast ruled the Two Lands from the womb of the goddess Nut.[6] Thou hast governed the 9. Lands of Ȧḳert.[7] Thy members are of silver-

[1] A name meaning something like "he leadeth the earth"; there is a play here on the word *sta*.

[2] There is a play here on the words *sek* and *Seker*, a very ancient god, the lord of the Other World of Memphis. Seker appears to have been a personification of death, and in late times many of his attributes were absorbed by Osiris.

[3] There is a play here on the words *user* "power," and *Ȧsȧr* "Osiris." This seems to indicate that at Thebes, under the XVIIIth dynasty, this god's name was pronounced "Usȧr," and not "Ȧsȧr" or "Sar."

[4] The ḤEN period = 60 years, the double period, 120 years. Men reckon their existence by years, but each year of the existence of Osiris is equal to 120 years.

[5] There is a play on the words *unt* "existence," and the first part of the name of the god "Un-Nefer." Un-Nefer is often written inside a cartouche thus: , , and .

[6] *I.e.*, he was predestined to rule Egypt before he was born.

[7] Strictly speaking, Aḳert is the name of the region to which the dead from Heliopolis and Kher-āḥa departed, but in later times it indicated the Other World in general. This region was situated between the modern Maṭarîyah and Fusṭâṭ.

gold,[1] thy head is of lapis-lazuli, and the crown of thy head is of turquoise. Thou art Ȧn[2] of millions of years. **10.** Thy body is all pervading,[3] O Beautiful Face in Ta-tchesert.[4] Grant thou to me glory in heaven, and power upon earth, and truth-speaking in the Divine Underworld, and [the power to] sail down the river[5] **11.** to Ṭeṭu[6] in the form of a living Ba-soul, **12.** and [the power to] sail up the river **13.** to Ȧbydos in the form of a Benu[7] bird, and [the power to] pass in through and to pass out from, **14.** without obstruction,

[1] *I.e.*, the gold which is mixed with a large quantity of silver. We are not to imagine Osiris as a being with a silver-gold body, and a face of lapis-lazuli, and a skull of turquoise, but a being whose body was of the *colour* of silver-gold, whose face had the colour of lapis-lazuli, and whose skull was green in colour. The natural object here referred to as the symbol of Osiris was the moon.

[2] Ȧn, or Ȧni, was an ancient form of the Sun-god and Moon-god who is said to be the president of the Company of the Gods . Ȧni is also said to be a form of the Eye of Horus, and as such has a place in the Māṭet Boat of the rising sun.

[3] *I.e.*, the body of Osiris is the world.

[4] The land of holiness, the sacred land, a name of the Other World, or the kingdom of Osiris.

[5] The Egyptians thought that the souls of the blessed spent a great deal of their time in going about visiting the shrines of Osiris and those of all the great gods. Thus the living enjoyed communion with many of them at every great shrine during the celebration of every great festival.

[6] Busiris and Abydos were famous shrines, and pilgrims flocked thither from all parts of Egypt, just as the Muslims flock to Mecca, and the Shiahs to Karbala, and Christians to Jerusalem.

[7] A bird which was commonly thought to be chosen as a dwelling place by a beatified soul. It was probably the original of the phoenix of the Greeks, who associated with that bird ideas of renewed life and resurrection.

the **15.** doors[1] of the lords of the Ṭuat. Let there be given unto me **16.** bread-cakes in the House of Refreshing,[2] **17.** and sepulchral offerings of cakes and ale, and propitiatory offerings in Ȧnu,[3] and a **18.** permanent homestead[4] in Sekhet-Ȧaru,[5] **19.** with wheat and barley therein —to the Double of **20.** the Osiris, the scribe Ani.

[1] The lords of the Ṭuat, or Other World, were grouped together in that region in sections called "Ārits," which were seven in number. The door, or gate, or entrance of each was guarded by a Watcher, and a Herald, and a Porter. The first of these reported the coming of a soul, the second repeated its name to Osiris, and the third admitted it, if ordered to do so. According to another view the divisions of the Ṭuat were *ten* in number, and at each end of the series there was a vestibule. The door or gate of each was guarded by a Watcher and a Porter. Under the XVIIIth dynasty there were thought to be *twenty-one* doors in the Other World. And on arrival at the door or gate of each division, the soul that wished for admission was obliged to give the necessary passwords, which were the names of the officers of the gate and of the gate itself. If it forgot one or other of these, admission was refused to it, and it was "turned back" and obliged to remain where it was, in a sort of limbo. The names of the Ārits, and the Sebkhut, or Pylons, and their officers are given in Chapters CXLIV–CXLVII of the Book of the Dead.

[2] Or, House of Coolness, a name of a chamber in the tomb, and of a part of the Other World.

[3] This shows that Ani, though an inhabitant of Thebes, wished to visit Heliopolis after his death, and to partake of the spiritual food of the gods and beatified souls who dwelt there.

[4] The size of this estate, or homestead, varied according to the merit of the deceased, and its position depended on the favour of Osiris. Each estate was carefully measured by the celestial land surveyors, and Osiris took precautions to prevent mistakes in the measurements. Osiris in fact "settled" his servants in his kingdom, and gave them a supply of seed corn to begin their labours with.

[5] A name meaning something like "Field of Reeds." This region formed the dwelling place of the beatified, who passed their lives there in cultivating the *maāt* plant, which was their food, and which formed the body of Osiris. The land was very fertile, and was intersected by numerous canals. One portion of it contained the "birthplace of the gods," and another section of it was called "Sekhet-ḥetept," or the "Field of Offerings." A picture of the region forms the Vignette of Chapter CX of the Book of the Dead, and its various divisions (Ȧats) are described in Chapter CXLIX.

THE CHAPTERS OF COMING FORTH BY DAY

[CHAPTER I]

PLATES V and VI

I. Here begin the Chapters of Coming Forth[1] by Day, and the songs of praising[2] and glorifying which are to be recited 2. for "coming forth" and for entering into Khert-Neter,[3] and the spells which are to be said in Beautiful Amentet.[4] They shall be recited on the 3. day of the funeral, entering in after coming forth.

[1] *I.e.*, the Chapters which make the soul of a man to leave his body, and make its appearance by day, or in the day; they are popularly known as the "Book of the Dead." The title "Pert-em-hru" has been translated and explained in various ways, *e.g.*, "Coming forth from [or as] the Day" (Birch), "The departure from the Day" (Birch), "Sortir du jour" (Naville, Devéria), "Sortie de la journée" (Pierret), "Ausgang bei Tage" (Brugsch), etc.

[2] The title of this Chapter mentions three kinds of compositions, , , and , which indicate the commemorative praisings, and the forms of words which were recited during the performance of ceremonies, and spells or words of power, respectively. The object of all these was to secure the life and safety of the departed soul, and to enable it to move about freely, and to return to the earth at pleasure.

[3] That portion of the Other World (literally Under World) which was under the rule of Osiris, the god of the dead.

[4] The "beautiful hidden land"; it was unlucky to apply any but honorific titles to the kingdom of the dead.

The Osiris Ani, the Osiris the 4. scribe Ani saith:—Homage to thee, O Bull of Åmentet,[1] Thoth the 5. king of eternity is with me. I am the great god by the side of the divine boat, 6. I have fought for thee, I am one of those gods, those divine chiefs, who proved the truth-speaking 7. of Osiris before his enemies on the day of the weighing of words. 8. I am thy kinsman Osiris. I am [one of] those gods who were 9. the children of the goddess Nut, who hacked in pieces the enemies of Osiris, 10. and who bound in fetters the legion of Sebåu devils on his behalf. I am thy kinsman Horus,[2] 11. I have fought on thy behalf, I have come to thee for thy name's sake. I am Thoth[3] who proved the truth of the words of

[1] The Bull is Osiris, who was Lord of the Field of Reeds, just as the bull on earth is the lord of his herd, or as the Egyptians said, "lord of his field."

[2] The identity of Ani with the god Osiris is assumed so completely that Horus is ready to regard him as his father, and to do for him all that he did for Osiris.

[3] Thoth, the Advocate of Osiris, who defended Osiris against the accusations of Set, and proved that Osiris was a speaker of the truth, and Set a liar.

12. Osiris before his enemies (*or* enemy) on the day of the weighing of words[1] **13.** in the great House of the Prince,[2] who dwelleth in Ȧnu. I am Ṭeṭi,[3] the son of Ṭeṭi. **14.** My mother conceived me in Ṭeṭu, and gave birth to me in **15.** Ṭeṭu.[4] I am with the mourners [and with] the women who tear out their hair and make lament for **16.** Osiris in Taui-Rekhti,[5] proving true the words of Osiris before his enemies. **17.** Rā commanded Thoth to prove true the words of Osiris before his enemies; what was commanded

[1] *I.e.*, the famous trial of Osiris before all the gods in Heliopolis. The gods wished to make Osiris "Lord of heaven," and Set, to prevent this, made a series of terrible charges against him. Osiris was proved to be innocent, and Thoth at the bidding of the gods caused Set to be fettered and dragged into the judgment hall, and made Osiris to stand upon his back as a mark of his triumph.

[2] Or, "House of the Very Aged One," *i.e.*, Rā, the Sun-god. The temple here referred to must have been in existence in pre-dynastic times.

[3] The name of a very ancient god whose worship was merged into that of Osiris. The symbol of the god was the sacrum bone, which was placed on a pedestal, and so took the form, which was, during the whole of the Dynastic Period in Egypt, regarded as the backbone of Osiris. The "setting up" of this *ṭeṭ* formed one of the principal scenes in the miracle play of Osiris. The cult of the *ṭeṭ* originated in the Sûdân.

[4] The town of Busiris in the Delta, which was in very early times a centre of the cult of the.

[5] The exact site of this town is unknown.

18. [for Osiris], let that be done for me by Thoth. I am with Horus on the day of dressing **19.** Teshtesh.[1] I open the hidden water-springs for the ablutions of Urṭ-àb.[2] **20.** I unbolt the door of the Shetait Shrine[3] in Ra-stau.[4] I am with Horus **21.** as the protector (or defender) of the left shoulder of Osiris, the dweller in Sekhem.[5] **22.** I enter in among and I come forth from the Flame-gods on the day of the destruction of **23.** the Sebàu fiends in Sekhem.[6]

[1] Teshtesh is the name of the figure which represented Osiris during the great annual festivals of the god. The "dressing" of this figure refers to the performance of the ceremonies of arraying the god in his sacred attire, and the setting of a crown on his head and sceptres in his hands.

[2] The "god whose heart is at rest," a euphemistic name for the dead body of Osiris.

[3] The name of the most holy shrine of Seker, the Death-god.

[4] Ra-stau is the name given to the entrance to the corridors which led down to the Kingdom of Seker at or quite near to the modern region of Ṣaḳḳârah.

[5] The town of Letopolis in the Delta. In this town was preserved as a most holy relic the left shoulder of Osiris. The "lifting up of the shoulder" of Osiris was the most important of the many ceremonies which were performed at Sekhem during the miracle plays which were acted in connection with the great festivals of Osiris. The gods who presided over the "night offerings" at Sekhem were Thoth and Ḥeru-khenti-ȧn-ȧriti (?). Sekhem lay about twenty-five miles to the north of Memphis.

[6] The allusion is to the great fight which took place at Sekhem between the followers of Osiris or of Horus, and those of Set; the followers of Set were conquered, and many of them slain, and those who were captured alive were slain and their blood poured out before the god of the conquerors.

I am with Horus on the day[s] of **24.** the festivals of Osiris, at the making of offerings and oblations, namely, on the festival which is celebrated on the sixth day of the month, and on the day of the Ṭenȧt[1] festival in **25.** Ȧnu. I am the UĀB priest (*i.e.*, libationer) in Ṭeṭu, Rera (?),[2] the dweller in Per-Ȧsȧr.[3] **26.** I exalt him that is upon the high place of the country.[4] I look upon the hidden things (*i.e.*, the mysteries) in Ra-stau.[5] **27.** I recite the words of the liturgy of the festival of the Soul-god[6] in Ṭeṭu. I am the SEM priest,[7] **28.** and [perform] his duties. I am the UR-

[1] This festival was celebrated on the seventh day of the month, and the Ṭenȧ basket, or bowl, containing some special object, was presented with great ceremony and reverence to the god.

[2] I cannot explain this reading.

[3] "The House of Osiris" *par excellence*, or Busiris in the Delta.

[4] The text is probably corrupt here. The allusion is to the god who sat upon the top of the steps, or stairs, *qait* at Abydos, *i.e.*, Osiris.

[5] The mysteries here referred to are the ceremonies which were performed in the sanctuary of Seker, the god of death, at Ṣaḳḳȧrah. These were performed between midnight and dawn, and they were believed to cause the Sun-god of night, or the dead Day-sun, to be re-born and to rise on the world. With him arose to life the souls of the dead who had been loyal servants of the god upon earth. These ceremonies are illustrated and described in the book "Ȧm Ṭuat."

[6] One of the forms of Osiris of Ṭeṭu was a ram ; as the word for "soul" and "ram" is *ba*, we may translate either Ram-god or Soul-god.

[7] The SEM or SETEM priest performed many important ceremonies in the ritual connected with the service for "Opening the Mouth" of the

KHERP-ḤEM[1] priest on the day of placing the Ḥenu[2] Boat of Seker 29. upon its divine sledge.[3] I have taken in my hand the digging tool 30. on the day of digging up the earth[4] in Ḥensu.[5]

Hail, O ye who make perfect souls 31. to enter into the House of Osiris, make ye the well-instructed soul of the Osiris 32. the scribe Ani, whose word is true, to enter in and to be with you in the House of Osiris. Let him hear even as ye hear; let him have sight 33. even as ye have

---

deceased, *i.e.*, in bringing about his resurrection. He was the chief assistant of the KHER-ḤEB, or chief officiating priest, and was supposed to possess supernatural powers. He read the liturgy, and directed generally the performance of the ceremonies.

[1] *I.e.*, the "great master of the hammer," or the "chief blacksmith." This was the title of the high priest of Ptaḥ, the man-god of Memphis, who when upon earth had been a worker in metals.

[2] Ḥenu was the name of one of the boats of Seker, which contained a shrine of the god. During the night it rested in a certain place in the sanctuary, but at dawn it was placed with great ceremony upon a sledge, which was then drawn round the sanctuary, the course of the sledge representing the supposed course of the sun round the earth. A picture of the Ḥenu Boat forms the Vignette of Chapter LXXIV.

[3] *M'khait* is a common word for "scales," "balance."

[4] In very early times human and other sacrifices were offered up before the great god, and their blood was poured out on the ground at the feet of the figure of the god, and was worked into the earth with a tool of some kind. The modern equivalent of this ceremony is the annual "watering" (with blood) of the graves of the kings of Dahomey.

[5] A town in Upper Egypt called Herakleopolis Magna by the Greeks, Khânês by the Hebrews, ϩⲛⲏⲥ by the Copts, and Ahnâs by the Arabs.

sight; let him stand up even as ye stand up; let him take his seat 34. even as ye take your seats.

Hail, O ye who give cakes and ale to perfect souls in the House of 35. Osiris, give ye cakes and ale twice each day (*i.e.*, in the morning and in the evening) to the soul of the Osiris Ani, 36. whose word is true before the gods, the Lords of Abydos, and whose word is true with you.

Hail, O ye who open up the way, 37. who act as guides to the roads [in the Other World] to perfect souls in the House 38. of Osiris, open ye up for him the way, and act ye as guides to the roads 39. to the soul of the Osiris, the scribe, the registrary of all the offerings made to the gods, Ani, 40. [whose word is true] with you. May he enter the House of Osiris with boldness, and may he come forth therefrom in peace (*i.e.*, satisfied). May there be no 41. opposition made to him, and may he not be sent back [therefrom]. May he enter in under favour[1] [of Osiris],

[1] Perhaps, "may he enter in with the approbation of his heart."

and may he come forth 42. gratified [at the acceptance of] his true words.[1] May his commands be performed in the House of Osiris, may his words 43. travel with you,[2] may he be glorious as ye are. May he be not found to be light in the Balance, 44. may the Balance dispose of his case.[3]

In the Turin Papyrus (ed. Lepsius) this Chapter ends with the following :—

16. Permit thou not me to be judged according to the mouths of the multitude. May my soul lift itself up before 17. [Osiris], having been found to have been pure when on earth. May I come into thy presence, O Lord of the gods; may I arrive at the Nome of Maāti (Truth); may I rise up on my seat like a god endowed with life; may I give forth light like the Company of the Gods who dwell in heaven; may I become 18. like one of you; may I lift up

[1] Or, "gratified by his acquittal," or "pleased that he was able to prove his innocence."

[2] *I.e.*, may his orders run, or have currency, with yours.

[3] *I.e.*, let the fact that his soul outweighs the feather of Truth prove his innocence. It is possible to translate: "He hath not been found to rise up there, the Balance is empty of his case."

my footsteps in the town of Kher-Āḥa[1]; may I look upon the Sekṭet[2] Boat of the god, Sȧaḥ,[3] the holy one, as it passeth across the sky; may I not be repulsed; may I look upon the Lords of the Ṭuat,[4] **19.** or, according to another reading, the Company of the Gods; may I smell the savour of the divine food of the Company of the Gods; may I sit down with them; may my name be proclaimed for offerings by the KHER-ḤEB[5] priest at the sacrificial table; may I hear the petitions which are made when offerings are presented; may I draw nigh unto the **20.** Neshem

[1] A town on the right or east bank of the Nile which lay between Heliopolis and the river. All the remains of it which were above ground have disappeared, and its exact site is unknown; it seems, however, to have stood upon the ground now occupied by Fusṭâṭ, or Old Cairo. Kher-āḥa was a very old town even in ancient times, and it seems to have decayed as the great neighbouring town of Heliopolis grew in importance.

[2] The Boat of the setting sun. The old form of the name is Semkett.

[3] Presumably here the god Orion.

[4] Ṭuat is a very old name for the Other World, and its meaning is unknown. At first it was the name of the region which was ruled over by Osiris, but at a later period the name was applied to all the kingdoms of the dead on the west bank of the Nile, and later still to the Land of the Dead in general.

[5] Literally, "he with the book." This funerary official was the greatest of all the priests, for he kept the rolls inscribed with magical formulae, and he could not only read the services, but could pronounce the sentences in such a way as to produce the effect desired by the deceased and his friends. His modern equivalent among Sûdânî tribes is the "medicine-man," or "witch-doctor," or "rain-maker."

21. 22. RUBRIC :

Boat[1]; and may neither my Heart-soul nor its lord be repulsed.

Homage to thee, O Chief of Åmentet, thou god Osiris, who dwellest in the town of Nifu-ur.[2] Grant thou that I may arrive in peace in Åmentet. May **21.** the Lords of Ta-Tchesert[3] receive me, and may they say unto me: "Hail, hail; welcome, welcome!" May they make ready for me a seat by the side of the President[4] of the Chiefs; may the Nursing-goddesses[5] receive me at the seasons, and may I come forth into the **22.** presence of Un-Nefer true of word. May I be a Follower of Horus in Ra-stau,[6] and of Osiris in Ṭeṭu[7]; and may I perform all the transformations which my heart may desire to make in every place wherein my Double (KA) wisheth to be.

[1] Many gods were associated with a Neshem Boat, but the boat here referred to is that which was specially sacred to Osiris. In it some important events connected with the resurrection of Osiris took place, and the deceased prayed to be admitted to this boat in order that his own resurrection might be certain.

[2] The capital of the nome of Abṭu, or Abydos, in Upper Egypt. This town was the centre of the cult of Osiris in the South, and tradition associated it with the winds which assisted in resuscitating Osiris.

[3] *I.e.*, the Holy Land, a name of the Other World in general, and of the realm of Osiris in particular.

[4] The President is of course Osiris, and the Chiefs are the TCHATCHAU, or the principal councillors of his kingdom, who regulated the conditions under which the subjects of Osiris lived, and superintended the performance of the commands of the god.

[5] *I.e.*, Isis and Nephthys.

[6] A part of the Other World of Memphis.

[7] Busiris.

RUBRIC: If this text be known [by the deceased] upon earth **23.** or if he causeth it to be done in writing upon [his] coffin, then will he be able to come forth on any day he pleaseth, and to enter into his habitation unrepulsed. Cakes and ale and joints of **24.** meat from those which are on the altar of Rā shall be given unto him, and his homestead shall be among the fields of the Field of Reeds (Sekhet-Åaru), and wheat and barley shall be given unto him therein, and he shall flourish there even as he flourished upon earth.

APPENDIX TO CHAPTER I

CHAPTER Ib

[From the Papyrus of Nekhtu-Åmen, ed. Naville, I, 5]

1. The Chapter of making the Sāḥu to enter the Ṭuat on the day of the funeral, **2.** when the following words are to be said: Homage to thee, O thou who dwellest in the Holy Hill (Set-Tchesert) of Åmentet! **3.** The Osiris, the royal scribe, Nekhtu-Åmen, whose word is true, knoweth thee, **4.** he knoweth thy name. Deliver thou him from the worms **5.** which are in Ra-stau, which live upon the bodies of men and women, and **6.** feed upon their blood, for Osiris, the favoured servant of the god of his city, **7.** the royal scribe Nekhtu-Åmen, knoweth you, and he knoweth your names. Let the order for his protection be the first command of Osiris, the Lord to the

Uttermost Limit, 8. who keepeth his body hidden. May he give him release from the Terrible One who dwelleth at the Bend of the River of Åmentet, and may he decree the acts that will 9. make him to rise up. Let him pass on to him whose throne is placed within the darkness, who giveth light in Ra-stau. 10. O thou Lord of Light, come thou and swallow up the worms which are in Åmentet. Let the Great God who dwelleth in Ṭeṭu (Busiris), 11. and who is himself unseen, hear his prayers, and let those who cause afflictions hold him in fear as he cometh forth 12. with the sentence of their doom to the Divine Block. I the Osiris, the royal scribe, Nekhtu-Åmen, come, bearing the decree 13. of Neb-er-tcher, and I am the Horus who taketh possession of his throne for him. His father, the lord of all those who are in 14. the Boat of his Father Horus, hath ascribed praise unto him. He cometh bearing tidings . . . . . . let him see 15. the town of Ånu (Heliopolis). Their chief shall stand on the earth before him, the scribes shall magnify him at the doors of their assemblies, 16. and they shall swathe him with swathings in Ånu. He hath led heaven captive, and he hath seized the earth in his grasp. Neither the heavens nor the earth 17. can be taken away from him, for, behold, he is Rā, the firstborn of the gods. His mother shall nurse him, and shall give him her breast 18. on the horizon.

RUBRIC: The words of this Chapter shall be said after [the deceased] is laid to rest in Åmentet; by means of them the region Tenn-ṭ shall be contented with her lord. And the Osiris, the royal scribe, Nekhtu-Åmen, whose word is truth, shall come forth, 19. and he shall embark in the Boat of Rā, and [his] body upon its bier shall be counted up, and he shall be established in the Ṭuat.

CHAPTER XXII

The Chapter of giving a mouth to the scribe Ani in Khert-Neter

PLATE VI

1. Chapter XXII. The Chapter of giving a mouth to 2. the Osiris Ani, the scribe, and teller of the offerings which are made to all the gods, whose word is true, who saith:—3. I rise up out of the Egg in the Hidden Land. May my mouth be given unto 4. me that I may speak therewith in the presence of the Great God, the Lord of the 5. Ṭuat. Let not my hand and my arm be repulsed in the presence of the Chiefs (*Tchatchau*) of any god. I am Osiris, the Lord of Ra-stau. 6. May I, the Osiris, the scribe Ani, whose word is true, have my portion with him who is 7. on the top of the Steps (*i.e.*, Osiris). According to the desire of my heart I have come forth from the Island of Nesersert, and 8. I have extinguished the fire.[1]

[1] The XXIInd Chapter usually ends here. In the Saïte Recension the XXIst and the XXIInd Chapters are quite distinct, and each has its own title, while a single Vignette stands over both.

CHAPTER XXI

The Chapter of giving a mouth to Ani

PLATE VI

[The Chapter of giving a mouth to the Osiris, the scribe Ani, who saith]:—**1.** Homage to thee, O thou lord of brightness, Governor of the Temple, Prince of the night and of the thick darkness. **2.** I have come unto thee. I am shining (or, glorious), I am pure. My hands are about thee, **3.** thou hast thy lot with thy ancestors. Give thou unto me my mouth that I may speak **4.** with it. I guide my heart at its season of flame and of night.

RUBRIC OF CHAPTER LXXII

Rubric [Chapter LXXII.] **1.** If this Chapter be known by the Osiris the scribe Ani, upon earth, [or if it be done] in writing upon [his] coffin, he shall come forth by day **2.** in every form which he pleaseth, and he shall enter into [his] abode, and shall not be repulsed. **3.** And

cakes, and ale, and joints of meat [from those which are on] the altar of Osiris shall be given unto him; and he shall enter 4. in peace into Sekhet-Åaru, conformably to the decree of the Dweller in Busiris. 5. Wheat and barley (dhura) shall be given unto him therein, and he shall flourish there just as he did 6. upon earth; and he shall do whatsoever it pleaseth him to do, even as do the Company of the Gods who are in 7. the Ṭuat, regularly and continually, for millions of times.

APPENDIX

The text of Chapter LXXII is not given in the Papyrus of Ani. The following rendering of it is made from the text of the Nebseni Papyrus (Sheet 3), which gives as its Vignette the figure of a man holding a symbol of office in his right hand and a staff in his left. The Egyptian text is given in my *Chapters of Coming Forth by Day*, Vol. II.

CHAPTER LXXII

1. The Chapter of Coming Forth by Day and of opening up a way through the Ameḥet:— [hieroglyphs].

Behold, the scribe Nebseni, whose word is truth, saith:— Homage to you, O ye Lords of Kau, ye who are without 2. sin, and who live for the endless and infinite æons of time which make up eternity. I have opened up a way for myself to you. I have become a spirit 3. in my forms, I have gotten the mastery over my words of magical power, and I am adjudged a spirit; **4.** therefore deliver ye me from the Crocodile [which liveth in] this Country of Truth (or, Law). Grant ye to me my mouth that I may speak therewith, **5.** and cause ye that sepulchral offerings shall be made unto me in your presence, for I know you, and I know your **6.** names, and I know also the name of the mighty god before whose face ye set your celestial food. His name is "Tekem" [hieroglyphs]. **7.** [When] he openeth up his path on the eastern horizon of heaven, [when] he alighteth towards the western horizon of heaven, **8.** may he carry me along with him, and may I be safe and sound. Let not the Mesqet[1] make an end of me, let not the Fiend (Sebåu [hieroglyphs]) gain the mastery over me, let me not be driven away from the doors of the Other World, **9.** let not **10.** your doors be shut in my face, for my cakes are in the city of Pe, and my ale is in **11.** the city of Ṭep. And there, in the celestial mansions of heaven which my divine father Tem hath stablished, let my hands lay hold **12.** upon the wheat and the barley, which shall be given unto me therein in abundant measure, and may the son of my own body make ready for me my food therein. And grant ye unto me when I am there sepulchral meals, and incense, and unguents, and all the pure and **13.** beautiful things whereon the god liveth, in very deed for ever, in all the **14.** transformations which it pleaseth me [to perform], and grant unto me the power to float down and to sail up the stream in the Field of Reeds (Sekhet-Åaru), [and may I reach Sekhet-ḥetepet (or, the Field of Offerings)]. I am the twin Lion-gods (*i.e.*, Shu and Tefnut).

[1] Either a chamber in which the deceased was supposed to pass through the skin of a bull, or the actual bull-skin.

TEXTS RELATING TO THE WEIGHING OF THE HEART OF ANI

PLATES III AND IV

I. The names of the Gods of the Great Company :—

II. The Prayer of Ani. [Chapter XXX b] :—

I. The names of the Gods of the Great Company :—**1.** Rā Harmakhis, the Great God in his boat. **2.** Temu. **3.** Shu. **4.** Tefnut. **5.** Ḳeb. **6.** Nut, the Lady of Heaven. **7.** Isis. **8.** Nephthys. **9.** Horus, the Great God. **10.** Hathor, Lady of Amentet. **11.** Ḥu. **12.** Sa.

II. The Prayer of Ani. [Chapter XXXb] :—My heart, my mother; my heart, my mother! My heart whereby I came into being! May nought stand up to oppose me at [my] judgment, may there be no opposition to me in the presence of the Chiefs (Tchatchau); may there be no parting of thee from me in the presence of him that keepeth the Balance! Thou art my Ka, which dwelleth in my body; the god Khnemu who knitteth together and strengtheneth my limbs. Mayest thou come forth into the

[1]

III. The Speech of Thoth :—

place of happiness whither we go. May the Sheniu officials, who make the conditions of the lives of men, not cause my name to stink, and may no lies be spoken against me in the presence of the God. [Let it be satisfactory unto us, and let the Listener god be favourable unto us, and let there be joy of heart (to us) at the weighing of words. Let not that which is false be uttered against me before the Great God, the Lord of Åmentet. Verily, how great shalt thou be when thou risest in triumph.][2]

III. The Speech of Thoth :—Thoth, the judge of right and truth of the Great Company of the Gods who are in the presence of Osiris, saith : Hear ye this judgment. The heart of Osiris hath in very truth been weighed, and his Heart-soul hath borne testimony on his behalf ; his heart hath been found right by the trial in the Great Balance. There hath not been found any wickedness in him ; he hath not wasted (or stolen) the offerings which have been made in the temples ; he hath not committed any evil act ; and

[1] In other papyri this Chapter ends differently :—

[2] The words within [ ] are added from the Papyrus of Nebseni (Sheet 4).

IV. Legend over Anubis:—

[Variant from the Papyrus of Ȧnhai (Brit. Mus. No. 10472)

V. The Speech of the Gods:—

he hath not set his mouth in motion with words of evil whilst he was upon earth.

IV. Speech of the Dweller in the Embalmment Chamber (*i.e.*, Anubis):—Pay good heed, O righteous Judge to the Balance to support [the testimony] thereof. Variant: Pay good heed (or, turn thy face) to the weighing in the Balance of the heart of the Osiris, the singing-woman of Ȧmen, Ȧnhai, whose word is truth, and place thou her heart in the seat of truth in the presence of the Great God.

V. The Speech of the Gods:—The Great Company of the Gods say to Thoth who dwelleth in Khemenu (Hermopolis): That which cometh forth from thy mouth shall be declared true. The Osiris the scribe Ani, whose word is true, is holy and righteous. He hath not committed any sin, and he hath done no evil against us. The devourer Ām-mit shall not be permitted to prevail over him. Meat

VI. The Speech of Horus, son of Isis:—

VII. The Speech of Ani:—

offerings and admittance into the presence of the god Osiris shall be granted unto him, together with an abiding habitation in the Field of Offerings (Sekhet-ḥetepet),[1] as unto the Followers of Horus.[2]

VI. The Speech of Horus to Osiris in introducing Ani to him:—**1.** Horus, the son of Isis, saith: I have come to thee, O Un-Nefer, and I have brought unto thee the Osiris Ani. His heart is righteous, **2.** and it hath come forth from the Balance; it hath not sinned against any god or any goddess. Thoth hath weighed it according to the decree pronounced **3.** unto him by the Company of the Gods, and it is most true and righteous. Grant thou that cakes and ale may be given unto him, and let him appear in the presence of the god Osiris, **4.** and let him be like unto the Followers of Horus for ever and ever.

VII. The Speech of Ani:—**1.** And the Osiris Ani **2.** saith: Behold, I am in thy presence, O Lord of **3.** Åmentet. There is no sin in my **4.** body. I have not

[1] A picture of this region will be found on Plate XXXII, and a description of it in Chapter CX.

[2] These were a number of beings who formed the body-guard of Horus the Elder. The name "Shemsu Ḥeru" was also given to the great king Horus who conquered Egypt, and later still to the body-guard of Horus, the son of Isis, who vanquished Set, the murderer of Osiris.

VIII. Description of the Beast :

spoken that which is not true 5. knowingly, nor have I done anything with a false heart. Grant thou that I may be like unto those favoured ones who are in thy following, 6. and that I may be an Osiris greatly favoured of the beautiful god, and beloved of the Lord of the Two Lands (*i.e.*, the king of Egypt), I who am a veritable royal scribe who loveth thee, Ani, whose word is true before the god Osiris.

VIII. Description of the beast Ām-mit :—Her fore-part is like that of a crocodile, the middle of her body is like that of a lion, her hind quarters are like those of a hippopotamus.

CHAPTER OF PRAISES AND GLORIFYINGS, AND OF COMING FORTH BY DAY

[CHAPTER XVII]

PLATES VII–X

1. HERE BEGIN THE PRAISES AND GLORIFYINGS OF COMING OUT FROM AND OF GOING INTO THE GLORIOUS KHERT-NETER, WHICH IS IN THE BEAUTIFUL AMENTET, OF COMING FORTH 2. BY DAY IN ALL THE FORMS OF EXISTENCE WHICH IT MAY PLEASE THE DECEASED TO TAKE, OF PLAYING AT DRAUGHTS, OF SITTING IN THE SEḤ HALL, AND OF APPEARING 3. AS A LIVING SOUL:

The Osiris the scribe Ani saith 4. after he hath arrived in his haven of rest—now it is good for [a man] to recite [this work whilst he is] upon earth, for then all the words of 5. Tem come to pass—

"I am the god Tem in rising. I am the Only One:

"I came into existence in **6.** Nu. I am Rā who rose in "the beginning, the ruler of this [creation]." **7.**

Who is this?[1]

"It is Rā, when at the beginning he rose in **8.** the "city of Ḥensu (Herakleopolis), crowned like a king "for his coronation. The Pillars[2] of the god Shu[3] were "not as yet created, when he was **9.** upon the steps of him "that dwelleth in Khemenu.

"I am the Great God who created himself, even Nu, "**10.** who made his names to become the Company of the "Gods as gods."

Who is **11.** this?

"It is Rā, the creator of the names of his limbs, which "came into being **12.** in the form of the gods who are in "the train of Rā.

"I am he who cannot be repulsed among the gods." **13.**

[1] Literally "explain it."

[2] The four pillars which supported the sky; the places where they were set marked the four cardinal points.

[3] The first-born son of Rā by the goddess Hathor; he typified light and the atmosphere, and supported the sky [Nut] in the daytime, and he it was who lifted it upon the steps [steps hieroglyph] which were in Khemenu (Hermopolis), in Upper Egypt.

Who is this?

"It is Temu, the dweller in his disk, but others say
"that **14.** it is Rā when he riseth in the eastern horizon
"of the sky.

"I am Yesterday, I know **15.** To-day."

Who is this?

"Yesterday is Osiris, **16.** and To-day is Rā, when he
"shall destroy the enemies of Neb-er-tcher (*i.e.*, the lord to
"the uttermost limit), **17.** and when he shall establish as
"prince and ruler his son **18.** Horus.

"Others, however, say that To-day is Rā, on the day
"when we commemorate the festival of **19.** the meeting of
"the dead Osiris with his father Rā, and when the battle
"of the **20.** gods was fought, in which Osiris, the Lord of
"Åmentet, was the leader."

What is this? **21.**

"It is Åmentet, [that is to say] the creation of the souls of
"the gods when Osiris was leader in Set-Åmentet. **22.**

" Others, however, say that it is the Ȧmentet which Rā " hath given unto me; when any god cometh he must rise " up and **23.** fight for it.

" I know the god who dwelleth therein." **24.**

Who is this?

" It is Osiris. Others, however, say that his name is " Rā, and that the god who dwelleth in Ȧmentet is the " **25.** phallus of Rā, wherewith he had union with himself.

" I am the Benu bird **26.** which is in Ȧnu " (Heliopolis). I am the keeper of the volume of the book " (*i.e.*, the Register, or the Tablet of Destiny) of the things " which have been made, and of the things which shall be " made."

Who is this? **27.**

" It is Osiris.

" Others, however, say that it is the dead body of Osiris, " and yet others say that **28.** it is the excrement of Osiris. " The things which have been made, and the things which " shall be made [refer to] the dead body of Osiris. Others " again say that **29.** the things which have been made " are Eternity, and the things which shall be made are

" Everlastingness, and that Eternity is the Day, and " Everlastingness the **30.** Night.

" I am the god Menu in his coming forth ; may his two " plumes **31.** be set on my head for me."

Who is this ?

" Menu is Horus, the Advocate (or, Avenger) **32.** of " his father [Osiris], and his coming forth means his birth. " The two plumes **33.** on his head are Isis and Nephthys, " when these goddesses go forth and set themselves thereon, " **34.** and when they act as his protectors, and when they " provide that which his head **35.** lacketh.

" Others, however, say that the two plumes are the " two exceedingly large uraei which are upon the head of " their father **36.** Tem, and there are yet others who say " that the two plumes which are upon the head of Menu " are his two eyes.

" The Osiris **37.** the scribe Ani, whose word is true, " the registrar of all the offerings which are made to the " gods, riseth up and cometh into **38.** his city."

What (or, where) is this [city]?

" It is the horizon of his father Tem. **39.**

" I have made an end of my shortcomings, and I have " put away my faults."

What is **40.** this?

" It is the cutting of the navel string[1] of the body of the " Osiris the scribe Ani, **41.** whose word is true before all " the gods, and all his faults are driven out."

What is this? **42.**

" It is the purification [of Osiris] on the day of his " birth. **43.**

" I am purified in my great double nest which is in " Ḥensu (Herakleopolis) **44.** on the day of the offerings of " the followers of the Great God who dwelleth **45.** therein."

What is the "great double nest"?

" The name of one nest is 'Millions of years,' and " 'Great Green [Sea]' **46.** is the name of the other, that is " to say 'Lake of Natron' and 'Lake of Salt.'

[1] *I.e.*, the umbilical cord.

" 47. Others, however, say the name of the one is 'Guide
" of Millions of Years,' and that 'Great Green Lake' 48.
" is the name of the other. Yet others say that 'Begetter
" of Millions of Years' is the name of one, and 'Great
" Green Lake' 49 is the name of the other. Now, as
" concerning the Great God who dwelleth therein, it is Rā
" 50. himself.

" I pass over the way, I know the head of the Island of
" Maāti."[1] 51.

What is this?

" It is Ra-stau, that is to say, it is the gate to the 52.
" South of Neruṭef, and it is the Northern Gate of the
" Domain (or, Tomb of the god).

" Now, as concerning the 53. Island of Maāti it is
" Abṭu (Abydos).

" Others, however, say that it is the way by which
" Father Tem 54. travelleth when he goeth forth to Sekhet-

[1] Or, perhaps, the Lake of Maāti.

" Åaru, 55. [the place] which produceth the food and " sustenance of the gods who are [in] their shrines.

" 56. Now the Gate Tchesert is the Gate of the Pillars " of Shu, 57. that is to say, the Northern Gate of the Ṭuat.

" Others, however, say that the Gate of Tchesert is the " two leaves of the door 58. through which the god Tem " passeth when he goeth forth to the eastern horizon of the " sky. 59.

" O ye gods who are in the presence [of Osiris], grant " to me your arms, for I am the god who 60. shall come " into being among you."

Who are these gods?

" They are the drops of blood 61. which came forth " from the phallus of Rā when he went forth to perform his " own 62. mutilation. These drops of blood sprang into " being under the forms of the gods Ḥu and Sa, who are in " the 63. bodyguard of Rā, and who accompany 64. the " god Tem daily and every day.

" I, Osiris the scribe Ani, whose word is truth, 65. have " filled for thee the *utchat* (*i.e.*, the Eye of Rā, or of Horus), " when it had suffered extinction 66. on the day of the " combat of the Two Fighters (*i.e.*, Horus and Set)."

What was this combat? 67.

" It was the combat which took place on the day when " Horus fought with Set, 68. during which Set threw filth " in the face of Horus, and Horus crushed the genitals 69. " of Set. The filling of the *utchat* [1] Thoth performed with " his own fingers.

" I remove the 70. thunder-cloud from the sky when " there is a storm with thunder and lightning therein."

What is this?

" This storm was the raging of Rā at the thunder-cloud " which [Set] sent forth 72. against the Right Eye of Rā

[1] *I.e.*, the restoration of the light to the Eye of Horus, and the reconstruction of the Eye after it was destroyed or swallowed by Set. Thoth made Set disgorge it, and brought it back, and replaced it in the face of Rā, or Horus, *i.e.*, in the sky.

" (*i.e.*, the sun). Thoth removed the thunder-cloud from " the Eye of Rā, and brought back the Eye **73.** living, " healthy, sound, and with no defect in it to its owner.

" Others, however, say that the thunder-cloud is caused " by sickness in the Eye of Rā, which **74.** weepeth for its " companion Eye (*i.e.*, the Moon); at this time Thoth " cleanseth the Right Eye of Rā. **75.**

" I behold Rā who was born yesterday from the thighs " of **76.** the goddess Meḥurt; his strength is my strength, " and my strength is his strength."

Who is this? **77.**

" Meḥurt is the great Celestial Water, but others say that " Meḥurt is the image (or, similitude) **78.** of the Eye of Rā " at dawn at his birth daily.

" [Others, however, say that] **79.** Meḥurt is the *utchat* " of Rā.

" Now Osiris **80.** the scribe Ani, whose word is truth, " is a very great one among the gods who are in the " following of **81.** Horus; they say that he is the prince " who loveth his lord."

Who are the 82. gods who are in the train of Horus?
" [They are] Ḳestȧ, Ḥāpi, Ṭuamutef, and Qebḥsenuf.
" 83. Homage to you, O ye lords of right and truth, ye
" sovereign princes (Tchatcha) who [stand] round about
" Osiris, who do away utterly 84. sins and offences, and
" who are in the following of the goddess Ḥetepsekhus,
" 85. grant ye that I may come unto you. Destroy ye all
" the faults which 86. are within me, even as ye did for the
" Seven Spirits 87. who are among the followers of their
" lord Sepa.[1] Ȧnpu (Anubis) appointed to them 88. their
" places on the day [when he said unto them], 'Come ye
" hither.'"

Who 89. are the "lords of right and truth"?
" The lords of right and truth are Thoth and 90. Ȧsṭes,
" the Lord of Ȧmentet.

[1] A name of Osiris.

"The Tchatcha round about Osiris are Ḳestȧ, **91.** Ḥāpi, "Ṭuamutef, and Qebḥsenuf, and they are also **92.** round "about the Constellation of the Thigh (*i.e.*, the Great Bear), "in the northern sky.

"Those who do away utterly **93.** sins and offences, and "who are in the following of the goddess Ḥetepsekhus, "**94.** are the god Sebek and his associates who dwell in the "water.

"The goddess Ḥetepsekhus is the Eye of **95.** Rā.

"Others, however, say that it is the flame which "accompanieth Osiris to burn up the **96.** souls of his "enemies.

"As concerning all the faults which are in **97.** Osiris, "the registrar of the offerings which are made unto all the "gods, Ani, whose word is truth, [these are all the offences "which he hath committed against the Lords of Eternity] "since he came forth from **98.** his mother's womb.

"As concerning the Seven Spirits **99.** who are Ḳestȧ, "Ḥāpi, Ṭuamutef, Qebḥsenuf, **100.** Maa-ȧtef, Kheribeqef,

" and Ḥeru-khenti-en-ȧriti (?), **101.** these did Anubis appoint
" to be protectors of the dead body of Osiris.

" Others, however, say that he set them **102.** round
" about the holy place (or, sanctuary) of Osiris.

" Others say that the Seven Spirits [which were
" appointed by Anubis] were **103.** Netcheḥ-netcheḥ,
" Aatqeṭqeṭ, Nerṭānef-besef-khenti-hehf, **104.** Āq-ḥer-ȧmi-
" unnut-f, Ṭesher-ȧriti-ȧmi- **105.** Ḥet-ȧnes, Ubes-ḥer-per-
" em-khetkhet, and **106.** Maaem-ḳerḥ-ȧnnef-em-hru.

" The chief of the Tchatcha (or, sovereign princes)
" **107.** who is in Naȧruṭef is Horus, the Advocate (or,
" Avenger) of his father.

" As concerning the **108.** day wherein [Anubis said to
" the Seven Spirits], 'Come ye hither,' [the allusion
" here] is to the words 'Come ye **109.** hither,' which Rā
" spake unto Osiris."

Verily may these same words be said unto me in Amentet.[1]

" I am the Divine Soul which dwelleth in the Divine " Twin-gods." **110.**

Who is this Divine Soul?

" It is Osiris. [When] he goeth into Ṭeṭu (Busiris), " **111.** and findeth there the Soul of Rā, the one god " embraceth the **112.** other, and two Divine Souls spring " into being within the Divine Twin-Gods."

[The following passage is taken from the Papyrus of Nebseni (Brit. Mus. No. 9900), Sheet 14, ll. 16 ff.]

16. " As concerning the Divine Twin-gods they are " Ḥeru-netch-ḥer-tefef **17.** and Ḥeru-khent-en-Ȧriti (*i.e.*, " Horus the Advocate (or, Avenger) of his father [Osiris], " and Horus the sightless).

" Others say that the double Divine Soul which dwelleth " in the Divine Twin-gods is the Soul of Rā and the Soul " of Osiris, and yet others say that it is the **18.** Soul which

[1] Clearly the expression of a pious wish which Ani interpolates into the Egyptian Catechism.

" dwelleth in Shu, [and] the Soul which dwelleth in Tefnut, " and that these two Souls form the double Divine Soul " which dwelleth in Ṭeṭu (Busiris).

" I am the Cat which fought near the Persea Tree " **19.** in Ȧnu (Heliopolis) on the night when the foes of " Neb-er-tcher were destroyed."

Who is this Cat?

" This male Cat is Rā **20.** himself, and he was called " 'Mȧu' because of the speech of the god Sa, who said " concerning him: 'He is like (*mȧu*) unto that which he " hath made'; therefore did the name of Rā become " 'Mȧu.'[1]

" Others, however, say that the male Cat is the god " **21.** Shu, who made over the possessions of Ḳeb[2] to " Osiris.

" As concerning the fight which took place near the " Persea Tree in Ȧnu, [these words have reference to the " slaughter] of the children of rebellion, when **22.** righteous " retribution was meted out to them for [the evil] which " they had done.

[1] Here we have a very ancient pun on the words *mȧu* " cat," and *mȧu* " like."

[2] The Earth-god, whose throne was inherited by Osiris, by Horus, son of Osiris, and then by the first earthly king of Egypt.

"As concerning the 'night of the battle,' [these words
"refer to] the invasion of the eastern portion of the heaven
"by the children of rebellion, whereupon a great battle
"arose in heaven and in all the earth.

"O thou who art in thine egg **23.** (*i.e.*, Rā), who
"showest from thy Disk, who risest on thy horizon, and
"dost shine with golden beams in the height of heaven,
"like unto whom there is none among the gods, who sailest
"above the Pillars **24.** of Shu, who sendest forth blasts of
"fire from thy mouth, [who illuminest the Two Lands
"(*i.e.*, Upper and Lower Egypt) with thy splendour,
"deliver] thou Nebseni, the lord of fealty [to Osiris], from
"the god **25.** whose form is hidden (*i.e.*, is invisible), and
"whose eyebrows are like unto the two arms of the
"Balance on the night when the sentences of doom are
"promulgated."

Who is this invisible god?

"It is Ȧn-ā-f (*i.e.*, he who bringeth his arm). **26.**

"As concerning 'the night when the sentences of doom

" are promulgated,' it is the night of the burning of the " damned, and of the overthrow of the wicked at the Block, " **27.** and of the slaughter of souls."

Who is this [slaughterer of souls]?

" It is Shesmu, the headsman of Osiris.

" [Concerning the invisible god] some say that he is " Āapep when he riseth up with a head bearing upon it [the " feather of] Maāt (*i.e.*, Truth). **28.** But others say that he " is Horus when he riseth up with two heads, whereon " one beareth [the feather of] Maāt, and the other [the " symbol of] wickedness. He bestoweth wickedness on " him that worketh wickedness, and right and truth upon " him that followeth righteousness and truth.

" **29.** Others say that he is Ḥeru-ur (*i.e.*, the Old Horus), " who dwelleth in Sekhem (Letopolis); others say that " he is Thoth; others say that he is Nefer-Tem; and " others say that he is Sepṭ who doth bring to nought the " acts of the **30.** foes of Nebertcher.

" Deliver thou the scribe Nebseni, whose word is truth, " **31.** from the Watchers, who carry murderous knives, who "possess cruel fingers, and who would slay those who are "in the following of 32. Osiris."

May these Watchers never gain the mastery over me, and may I never fall under their knives!

Who are these Watchers?

"They are Anubis and Horus, [the latter being] in the "form of Horus the sightless. 33. Others, however, say that "they are the Tchatcha (or, sovereign princes of Osiris), "who bring to nought the operations of their knives; and "others say that they are the chiefs of the Sheniu "chamber.[1]

"May 34. their knives never gain the mastery over me. "May I never fall under the knives wherewith they inflict "cruel tortures. For 35. I know their names, and I know "the being, Mātchet, who is among them in the House of "Osiris. He shooteth forth rays of light from his eye,

[1] First, the council-chamber in which the Sheniu officials held their deliberations, and secondly, a hall in which punishments were inflicted.

" being himself invisible, and 36. he goeth round about " heaven robed in the flames which come from his mouth, " commanding Ḥāpi, but remaining invisible himself. May " I be strong on earth before Rā, may I arrive safely 37. in " the presence of Osiris. O ye who preside over your " altars, let not your offerings to me be wanting, for I am " one of those who follow after Nebertcher, according to the " writings 38. of Kheperȧ. Let me fly like a hawk, let " me cackle like a goose, let me slay always like the serpent-" goddess Neḥeb-ka."

Who are those who preside over their altars? 39.

" Those who preside over their altars are the similitude " of the Eye of Rā, and the similitude of the Eye of Horus.

" O Rā-Tem, 40. thou Lord of the Great House [in " Ȧnu], thou Sovereign (life, strength, health [be to thee]) of " all the gods, deliver thou the scribe Nebseni, whose word " is truth, from the god whose face 41. is like unto that of " a greyhound, whose brows are like those of a man, who " feedeth upon the dead, who watcheth at the Bend of the

" Lake 42. of Fire, who devoureth the bodies of the dead, " and swalloweth hearts, and who voideth filth, but who " himself remaineth unseen."

Who is this greyhound-faced god? 43.

" His name is 'Everlasting Devourer,' and he liveth in " the Domain [of Fire] (or, in the Lake of Unt).

" As concerning the Domain of Fire, it is that Åat " which is in Naårutef, and is near 44. the Sheniu chamber. " The sinner who walketh over this place falleth down " among the knives [of the Watchers].

" Others, however, say that the name of this god is " 'Māṭes,' 45. and that he keepeth watch over the door of " Åmentet; others say that his name is 'Beba,' and that he " keepeth watch over the Bend [of the stream] of Åmentet, " and yet others say that his name is 'Ḥerisepef.'

" Hail, Lord of Terror, Chief of the Lands of the South " and North, thou Lord of the Desert, 46. who dost keep " prepared the block of slaughter, and who dost feed on the " intestines [of men]!"

Who is this Lord of Terror?

" It is the Keeper of the Bend [ot the stream] of " Åmentet." **47.**

Who is this Keeper?

" It is the Heart of Osiris, which is the devourer of all " slaughtered things.

" The Urrt Crown hath been given unto him, with " gladness of heart, as Lord of Ḥensu (Herakleopolis)."

Who **48.** is this?

" He to whom the Urrt Crown hath been given with " gladness of heart as Lord of Ḥensu is Osiris. He was " bidden to rule among the gods on the day of the union " of earth [with earth] **49.** in the presence of Nebertcher."

Who is this?

" He who was bidden to rule among the gods is the " son of Isis (*i.e.*, Horus), who was appointed to rule in the " room of his father **50.** Osiris.

" As concerning [the words] 'day of the union of earth " with earth,' they have reference to the union of earth with " earth in the coffin of Osiris, the Soul that liveth in Ḥensu, " the giver of meat and drink, the destroyer of wrong, and " the guide to the everlasting paths."

Who is this?
" It is Rā himself."

[The conclusion of this Chapter is found in the Papyrus of Ani (Sheet 10).]

" [Deliver thou the Osiris the scribe Ani, whose word is " truth] **113.** from the great god who carrieth away souls, " who eateth hearts, who feedeth upon **114.** offal, who " keepeth watch in the darkness, who dwelleth in the Seker " Boat; those who live in sin **115.** fear him."

Who is this?

" It is Suti, but others say that it is Smamur, **116.** the " soul of Ḳeb.

" Hail, Kheperȧ in thy boat, the two Companies of the " Gods are in thy body. Deliver thou the Osiris **117.** the " scribe Ani, whose word is truth, from the Watchers who " pass sentences of doom, who have been appointed by the " god Nebertcher **118.** to protect him, and to fasten the

119.

120.

121.

122.

123.

124.

125.

" fetters on his foes, and who slaughter in the **119.** torture " chambers; there is no escape from their fingers. May " they never stab me with their knives, **120.** may I never " fall helpless into their chambers of torture. **121.** I have " never done the things which the gods hate. I am he who " is pure in the Mesqet chamber. **122.** And saffron cakes " have been brought unto him in Tannt."

Who is this? **123.**

" It is Kheperȧ in his boat; it is Rā himself.

" As concerning the Watchers who pass **124.** sentences " of doom, they are the Apes Isis and Nephthys.

" As concerning the things which the gods hate, they " are acts of deceit (or, fraud) **125.** and lying. He who " passeth through the place of purification within the Mesqet " chamber is Ȧnpu (Anubis), who is hȧrd by the coffer (or,

" casket) 126. which containeth the inward parts of Osiris. " He to whom saffron cakes have been brought in 127. in " Tannt is Osiris.

" Others, however, say that the saffron cakes 128. in " Tannt represent heaven and earth, and others say that " they represent Shu, the strengthener of the Two Lands " (*i.e.*, Upper and Lower Egypt) 129. in Ḥensu; and " others say that they represent the Eye of Horus, and that " Tannt 130. is the burial-place of Osiris.

" Tem hath builded thy house, and the double Lion-god " hath laid the foundations of thy habitation. 131. Lo! " medicaments have been brought. Horus purifieth Set " and Set strengtheneth, and Set purifieth and Horus " strengtheneth. 132.

" The Osiris the scribe Ani, whose word is truth before " Osiris, hath come into this land, and he hath taken " possession thereof with his two feet. He is Tem, and he " is in the city.

" 133. Turn thou back, O Reḥu, whose mouth shineth,
" whose head moveth, turn thou back before his strength."
" Another reading is, 'Turn thou back from him who
" keepeth 134. watch, and is himself unseen.' Let the
" Osiris Ani be safely guarded. He is Isis, and he is found
" 135. with her hair spread over him; it is shaken out over
" his brow. He was conceived by Isis, and engendered
" 136. by Nephthys, and they have cut away from him the
" things which should be cut from him.

" Fear followeth after thee, terror is about 137. thine
" arms. Thou hast been embraced for millions of years by
" arms; mortals go round about thee. Thou smitest down
" the mediators 138. of thy foes, and thou seizest the arms
" of the powers of darkness. Thy two sisters (*i.e.*, Isis and
" Nephthys) are given to thee for thy delight. 139. Thou
" hast created that which is in Kher-āḥa, and that which is
" in Ȧnu (Heliopolis). Every god feareth thee, for thou
" art exceedingly great and terrible; thou [avengest] every

" **140.** god on the man who curseth him, and thou shootest
" arrows at him. Thou livest according to thy will. Thou
" art Uatchet, the Lady of Flame, evil befalleth **141.** those
" who set themselves up against thee."

What is this?

" ' Hidden in form, given of **142.** Menḥu,' is the name
" of the tomb. ' He who seeth what is on his hand' is the
" name of Qerȧu, or, as others say, it is **143.** the name of
" the Block.

" Now, he whose mouth shineth and whose head
" moveth is the phallus of Osiris, but others say it is [the
" phallus] of **144.** Rā. ' Thou spreadest thy hair, and
" I shake it out over his brow' is said concerning Isis, who
" hideth in her hair, **145.** and draweth it round about her.

" Uatchet, the Lady of Flames, is the Eye of Rā."

CHAPTER CXLVII

THE SEVEN ĀRITS

PLATES XI, XII

The First Ārit.

I. **1.** The name of the Doorkeeper is Sekheṭ-ḥer-āsht-āru. The name of the **2.** Watcher is Smetti. The name of the Herald is Hakheru.

The Osiris Ani, **3.** whose word is truth, shall say when he cometh unto the First Arit: "I am the mighty one who createth his own light. **4.** I have come unto thee, O Osiris, and, purified from that which defileth thee, I adore thee. Lead on. **5.** Name not the name of Ra-stau to me. Homage to thee, O Osiris, in thy might and in thy strength **6.** in Ra-stau. Rise up and conquer, O Osiris, in Ȧbṭu (Abydos). Thou goest round about heaven, thou sailest in the presence of Rā, **7.** thou lookest upon all the beings who have knowledge. Hail, Rā, thou who goest

8. 9. 10. 11.
12. 13. 14. 15. 16.
17.

II. 1. 2. 3.
4. 5.
6.
7.
8.

round about in the sky, I say, O Osiris in truth, that I am the Sāḥu (*i.e.*, the Spirit-body) **8.** of the god, and I beseech thee **9.** not to let me be driven away, **10.** nor to be cast **11.** upon the wall **12.** of blazing fire. **13.** Let the way be opened in **14.** Ra-stau, **15.** let the pain **16.** of the Osiris be relieved, **17.** embrace that which the Balance hath weighed, let a path be made for the Osiris in the Great Valley, and let the Osiris have light to guide him on his way."

The Second Ārit.

II. **1.** The name of the **2.** Doorkeeper is Unḥāt. **3.** The name of the Watcher is Seqṭ-ḥer. **4.** The name of the Herald is **5.** Usṭ.

6. The Osiris Ani, whose word is truth, shall say [when he cometh to this Ārit]: "He sitteth to carry out his heart's desire, and he weigheth **7.** words (*i.e.*, he acteth as judge) as the Second (*i.e.*, deputy) of Thoth. The strength which protecteth Thoth humbleth the hidden Maāti gods, **8.** who feed upon Maāt[1] during the years of their lives. I offer up

[1] The maāt plant, *i.e.*, corn, wheat.

my offerings **9.** [to him] at the moment when he maketh his way (*i.e.*, travelleth on). I advance, and I enter on the path. O grant thou that I may continue to advance, and that I may attain to the sight of Rā, and of those who offer up [their] offerings."

The Third Ārit.

III. **1.** The name of the **2.** Doorkeeper is Unem-ḥauatu- **3.** ent-peḥui. The name **4.** of the Watcher is Seres- **5.** ḥer. The name of the Herald is Āa.

The Osiris the scribe Ani, whose word is truth, shall say [when he cometh to this Ārit]: "I am he who is hidden **6.** in the great deep.[1] I am the Judge of the Reḥui,[2] I have come and I have done away the offensive thing which was upon Osiris. I tie firmly the place on which he standeth, **7.** coming forth from the Urt.[3] I have stablished things (*i.e.*, offerings) in Àbṭu (Abydos), I have opened up a way through Ra-stau, and I have relieved **8.**

[1] *I.e.*, Temu, or Kheperà, who in primeval times dwelt alone in the Celestial Waters.

[2] These were Horus and Set, and their Judge was Thoth.

[3] A crown or a goddess.

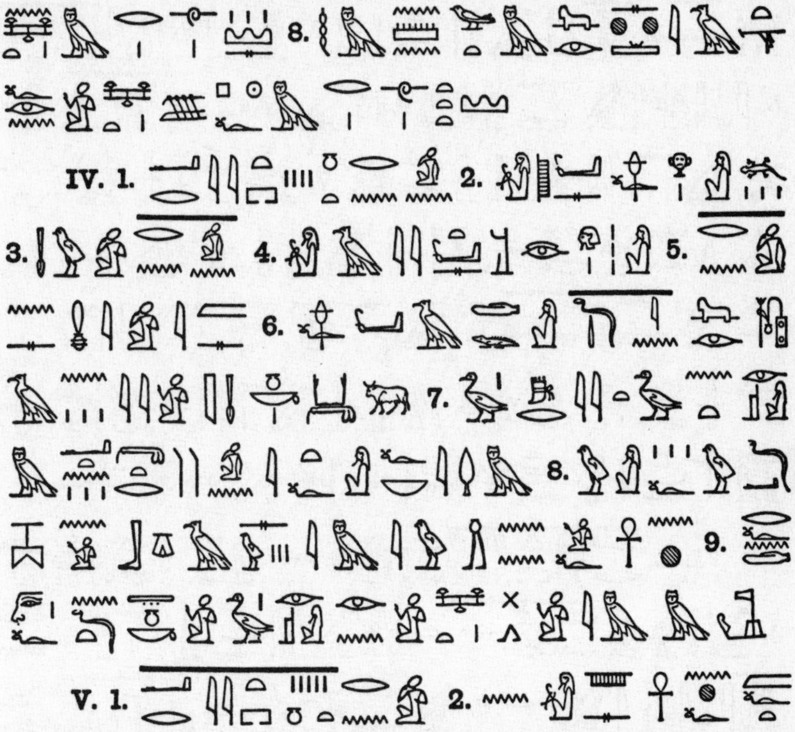

the pain which was in Osiris. I have balanced the place whereon he standeth, and I have made a path for him ; he shineth brilliantly in Ra-stau."

The Fourth Ārit.

IV. **1.** The name of the **2.** Doorkeeper is Khesef-ḥer-āsht- **3.** kheru. The name of **4.** the Watcher is Seres-tepu. **5.** The name of the Herald is **6.** Khesef-aṭ.

The Osiris the scribe Ani, whose word is truth, shall say [when he cometh to this Ārit]: "I am the Bull, **7.** the son of the ancestress of Osiris. O grant ye that his father, the Lord of his god-like **8.** companions, may bear witness on his behalf. I have weighed the guilty in judgment. I have brought unto **9.** his nostrils the life which is ever lasting. I am the son of Osiris, I have accomplished the journey, I have advanced in Khert-Neter."

The Fifth Ārit.

V. **1.** The name **2.** of the Doorkeeper is Ānkhf-emfent. 3. The name of the Watcher is 4. Shabu. The name 5. of the Herald is Ṭeb-ḥer-k 6. ha-kheft.

The Osiris the scribe Ani, whose word is truth, shall say [when he cometh to this Ārit]: "I have brought unto thee the 7. jawbone in Ra-stau. I have brought unto thee thy backbone in Ȧnu (Heliopolis). I have gathered together his manifold members 8. therein. I have driven back Āapep for thee. I have spit upon the wounds [in his body]. I have made myself a path among you. I am 9. the Aged One among the gods. I have made offerings to Osiris. I have defended him with the word of truth. I have gathered together his bones, and have collected all his members."

The Sixth Ārit.

VI. 1. The name 2. of the Doorkeeper is Ȧtek-tau-kehaq- 3. kheru. The name of the 4. Watcher is Ȧn-ḥer. 5. The name of the Herald is 6. Aṭes-ḥer-[ari]-she.

The Osiris the scribe Ani, whose word is truth, shall say [when he cometh to this Ārit]: "I have come **7.** daily, I have come daily. I have made myself a way. I have advanced over that which was created by Ȧnpu (Anubis). I am the Lord of the Urrt Crown. **8.** I am the possessor [of the knowledge of] the words of magical power, I am the Avenger according to law, I have avenged [the injury to] his Eye. I have defended **9.** Osiris. I have accomplished my journey. The Osiris Ani advanceth with you with the word which is truth."

The Seventh Ārit.

VII. **1.** The name **2.** of the Doorkeeper is Sekhmet-em-ṭesu-sen. **3.** The name of the **4.** Watcher is Āa-maā-kheru. **5.** The name of the Herald is Khesef-khemi.

The Osiris the scribe Ani, whose word is truth, **6.** shall say [when he cometh to this Ārit]: "I have come unto thee, O Osiris, being purified from foul emissions (or, emanations). Thou goest round about heaven, thou seest Rā, thou seest the beings who have knowledge. **7.** [Hail], thou One!

8.

RUBRIC: [1]

Behold, thou art in the Sektet Boat which traverseth the heavens. I speak what I will to his Sāḥu (Spirit-body). **8.** He is strong, and cometh into being even [as] he spake. Thou meetest him face to face. Prepare thou for me all the ways which are good [and which lead] to thee."

RUBRIC: If [these] words be recited by the spirit (*i.e.*, the deceased) when he shall come to the Seven Ārits, and as he entereth the doors, he shall neither be turned back nor repulsed before Osiris, and he shall be made to have his being among the blessed spirits, and to have dominion among the ancestral followers of Osiris. If these things be done for any spirit he shall have his being in that place like a lord of eternity in one body with Osiris, and at no place shall any being contend against (or, resist) him.

[1] See Naville, *Todtenbuch*, II, p. 376.

CHAPTER CXLVI

THE PYLONS OF THE HOUSE OF OSIRIS

PLATE XI

I. The following shall be said when one cometh to the First Pylon. The Osiris the scribe Ani, whose word is truth, saith: "Lady of tremblings (or, terror), high-walled, "the sovereign lady, the lady of destruction, who uttereth "the words which drive back the destroyers, who delivereth "from destruction him that cometh." The name of her Doorkeeper is Neruit.

II. The following shall be said when one cometh to the Second Pylon. The Osiris the scribe Ani, whose word is truth, saith: "Lady of heaven, Mistress of the Two Lands "(*i.e.*, Egypt), devourer by fire, Lady of mortals, who art "infinitely greater than any human being." The name of her Doorkeeper is Mes-Ptah.

III. The following shall be said when one cometh to the THIRD PYLON. The Osiris the scribe Ani, whose word is truth, saith: "Lady of the altar, the mighty lady to "whom offerings are made, greatly beloved one of every "god sailing up the river to Abydos." The name of her Doorkeeper is SEBQA.

IV. The following shall be said when one cometh to the FOURTH PYLON. The Osiris the scribe Ani, whose word is truth, saith: "Prevailer with knives, Mistress of the Two "Lands (*i.e.*, Egypt), destroyer of the enemies of the Still-"Heart (*i.e.*, Osiris), who decreeth the release of those who "suffer through evil hap." The name of her Doorkeeper is NEḲAU.

V. The following shall be said when one cometh to the FIFTH PYLON. The Osiris the scribe Ani, whose word is truth, saith: "Flame, Lady of fire (?), absorbing (or, "inhaling) the entreaties which are made to her, who "permitteth not to approach her the rebel (?)" The name of her Doorkeeper is ḤENTI-REQIU.

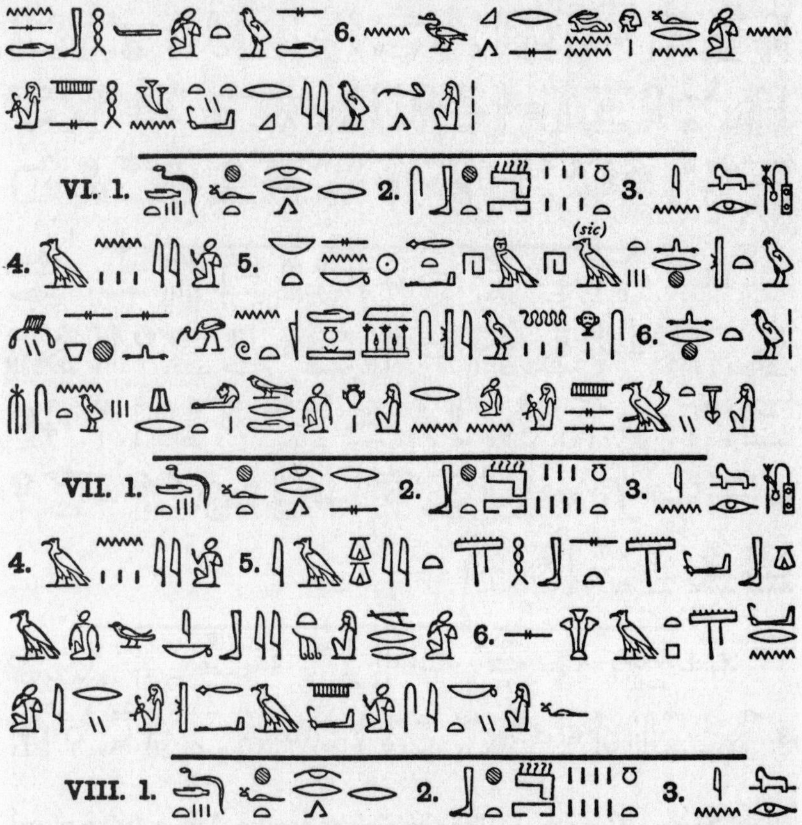

VI. The following shall be said when one cometh to the SIXTH PYLON. The Osiris the scribe Ani, whose word is truth, saith: "Lady of light, who roareth mightily, whose "breadth cannot be comprehended. Her like hath not "been found since the beginning. There are serpents over "her which are unknown. They were brought forth before "the Still-Heart." The name of her Doorkeeper is SEMATI.

VII. The following shall be said when one cometh to the SEVENTH PYLON. The Osiris the scribe Ani, whose word is truth, saith: "Garment which envelopeth the "helpless one, which weepeth for and loveth that which it "covereth." The name of her Doorkeeper is SÁKTIF.

VIII. The following shall be said when one cometh to

the Eighth Pylon. The Osiris the scribe Ani, whose word is truth, saith: "Blazing fire, unquenchable, with far-"reaching tongues of flame, irresistible slaughterer, which "one may not pass through fear of its deadly attack." The name of her Doorkeeper is Khutchetef.

IX. The following shall be said when one cometh to the Ninth Pylon. The Osiris the scribe Ani, whose word is truth, saith: "Chieftainess, lady of strength, who giveth "quiet of heart to the offspring of her lord. Her girth (?) "is three hundred and fifty *khet*, and she is clothed with "green feldspar of the South. She bindeth up the divine "form and clotheth the helpless one. Devourer, lady of all "men (?)." The name of her Doorkeeper is Ȧrisutchesef.

X. The following shall be said when one cometh to the Tenth Pylon. The Osiris the scribe Ani, whose word is truth, saith: "Goddess of the loud voice, who maketh her "suppliants to mourn, the awful one who terrifieth, who

The texts relating to Pylons XI–XIV are taken from the Papyrus of Nu, Sheet 25.

"herself remaineth unterrified within." The name of her Doorkeeper is SEKHENUR.

XI. Nu, the steward of the keeper of the seal, saith when he cometh to the ELEVENTH PYLON of Osiris: "I have made my way, I know you, and I know thy "name, and I know the name of her who is within thee: "She who slayeth always, consumer of the fiends by fire, "mistress of every pylon, the lady who is acclaimed on the "day of darkness" is thy name. She inspecteth the swathing of the helpless one.

XII. The Osiris Nu, the steward of the keeper of the seal, saith when he cometh to the TWELFTH PYLON of Osiris: "I have made my way, I know you, and I know

50.

51.

XIII. 52.

53.

54.

55.

XIV. 56.

57.

" thy name, and I know the name of her who is within thee : " Invoker of thy Two Lands, destroyer of those who come " to thee by fire, lady of spirits, obeyer of the word of thy " Lord " is thy name. She inspecteth the swathing of the helpless one.

XIII. The Osiris Nu, the steward of the keeper of the seal, saith when he cometh to the THIRTEENTH PYLON of Osiris : " I have made my way, I know you and I know thy " name, and I know the name of her who is within thee : " Osiris foldeth his arms about her, and maketh Ḥāpi (the " Nile-god), to emit splendour out of his hidden places " is thy name. She inspecteth the swathing of the helpless one.

XIV. The Osiris Nu, the steward of the keeper of the seal, saith when he cometh to the FOURTEENTH PYLON of Osiris : "I have made my way, I know thee, and I know thy

The texts relating to Pylons XV–XXI are taken from the Papyrus of Ḥeru-em-khebit (Naville, *Todtenbuch*, I, Bl. 161 f.).

" name, and I know the name of her who is within thee. " Lady of might, who trampleth on the Red Demons, who " keepeth the festival of Haȧker on the day of the hearing " of faults" is thy name. She inspecteth the swathing of the helpless one.

XV. THE FIFTEENTH PYLON. The Osiris Ḥeru-em-khebit, whose word is truth, shall say when he cometh to this pylon : " Fiend, red of hair and eyes, who appeareth " by night, and doth fetter the fiend in his lair. Let her " hands be given to the Still-Heart in his hour, let her " advance and go forward" is thy name. She inspecteth the swathing of the helpless one.

XVI. THE SIXTEENTH PYLON. The Osiris Ḥeru-em-khebit, whose word is truth, shall say when he cometh to

43. 44. 45.

XVII. 46.

XVIII. 47. 48. 49.

50.

this pylon: "Terrible one, lady of the rain-storm, destroyer "of the souls of men, devourer of the bodies of men, "orderer, producer, and maker of slaughter" is thy name. She inspecteth the swathing of the helpless one.

XVII. THE SEVENTEENTH PYLON. The Osiris Ḥeru-em-khebit, whose word is truth, shall say when he cometh to this pylon: "Hewer-in-pieces in blood, Àḥibit, lady of hair" is thy name. She inspecteth the swathing of the helpless one.

XVIII. THE EIGHTEENTH PYLON. The Osiris Ḥeru-em-khebit, whose word is truth, shall say when he cometh to this pylon: "Fire-lover, pure one, lover of slaughterings, "cutter off of heads, devoted one, lady of the Great House, "slaughterer of fiends at eventide" is thy name. She inspecteth the swathing of the helpless one.

XIX. THE NINETEENTH PYLON. The Osiris Ḥeru-em-khebit, whose word is truth, shall say when he cometh to this pylon: "Light-giver for life, blazing all the day, "lady of strength [and of] the writings of the god Thoth "himself" is thy name. She inspecteth the swathings of the White House.

XX. THE TWENTIETH PYLON. The Osiris Ḥeru-em-khebit, whose word is truth, shall say when he cometh to this pylon: "Dweller in the cavern of her lord, her name "is Clother, hider of her creations, conqueror of hearts, "swallower [of them]" is thy name. She inspecteth the swathings of the White House.

XXI. THE TWENTY-FIRST PYLON. The Osiris Ḥeru-em-khebit, whose word is truth, shall say when he cometh to this pylon: "Knife which cutteth when [its name] is

59.

In the Turin Papyrus (ed. Lepsius, Bl. 64) the text referring to the twenty-first Pylon reads:

71. 72.

73.

74.

uttered, slayer of those who approach thy flame" is thy name. She possesseth hidden plans.

71. THE OSIRIS AUFĀNKH, WHOSE WORD IS TRUTH, SAITH: Hail, saith Horus, O Twenty-first pylon of the Still-Heart! I have made the way. I know thee. I know thy name. 72. I know the name of the goddess who guardeth thee. "Sword that smiteth at the utterance of its "own name, stinking face, overthrower of him that "approacheth her flame" is thy name. Thou keepest the hidden things of the avenger of the god, thou guardest them. ĀMĀM 73. is his name. He maketh the *āsh* trees (cedars) not to grow, and the *shenu* trees (acacias) not to blossom, and preventeth copper from being found in the mountain. The TCHATCHA (*i.e.*, Chiefs) of this Pylon are Seven Gods. Tchen, or Ānthch (Āṭ), is the name of 74.

the one at the door. Ḥetepmes is the name of another there. Messep is the name of another there. Utchara is the name of another there. Upuatu is the name of another there. Beq is the name of another there. Ȧnp (Anubis) is the name of another there.

75. I have made the way. I am Menu-Ḥeru, the avenger of his father, the heir of his father Un-Nefer. I have come. I have given (offerings) to my father Osiris. I have overthrown all his enemies. I have come daily with the word of truth, the lord of fealty, **76.** in the house of my father Tem, the Lord of Ȧnu, I, the Osiris Ȧuf-ānkh, whose word is truth in the southern heaven. I have done what is right for him that made the right, I have celebrated the Haker festival to the lord thereof. I have acted as the leader of the festivals. I have given cakes to the Lords of the Altar. **77.** I have been the leader of the propitiatory offerings, cakes, ale, oxen, and geese, to my father Osiris Un-Nefer. I am the protector of the Ba-soul, I have made the *Benu* bird to appear [by my] words. I have come daily into the house of the god to make offerings of incense. **78.** I have come with the *shenti* tunic. I have set the Neshem Boat afloat on the water. I have made the word of Osiris Khenti Åmenti to be truth before his enemies. I have carried away in a boat all his enemies to the slaughter-house of the East, and they shall never escape from the wardship of the god Ḳeb **79.** who dwelleth therein. I have made the Kefaiu gods of Rā to stand up, I have made his word to be truth. I have come as a scribe. I have explained [the writings]. I have made the god to have power over his legs. I have come into the house of him that is upon his mountain (*i.e.*, Anubis). I have seen the Chief of the Seḥ hall. **80.** I have entered into Ra-stau. I have made myself invisible. I have found for myself the boundary. I have approached Neruṭef. I have clothed the naked. **81.** I have sailed up the river to Abydos. I have performed

82. 83. 84. 85. 86.

the ceremonies of Ḥu and Sa. I have entered the house of Åsṭes. I have made supplication to the **82.** Khati gods and to Sekhmet in the temple of Net (Neith), or the Aged Ones. I have entered Ra-stau. I have made myself invisible. I have found the frontier. I have approached **83.** Neruṭef. I have clothed the naked. I have sailed up the river to Abydos. I have performed the ceremonies of Ḥu and Sa. I have received. I have risen like **84.** a king crowned. I fill my seat on the throne in the place of my father, the God Who was at the beginning. I have praised the Meskhen of Ta-tchesert. My mouth is full of (?) **85.** Maāt (Truth). I have overwhelmed the Akhekhau serpents. I have come into the Great House with [my] body in a flourishing condition. I have caused myself to travel in the Boat of Ḥai (?). The myrrh unguent of . . . . . **86.** is in the hair of men (*Rekhit*). I have entered into the House of Åsṭes. I have approached with worship the two Khati gods and Sekhmet, who are in the temple 87. of the Aged One [in Ȧnu, *i.e.*, Heliopolis].

[And the god Osiris saith:] "Thou hast come, thou "shalt be a favoured one in Ṭeṭu (Busiris), O Osiris Ȧuf-"ānkh, whose word is truth, the son of the lady Shert-en-"Menu, whose word is truth."

CHAPTER XVIII

INTRODUCTION

PLATE XII

I. THE SPEECH OF THE PRIEST ȦNMUTEF. **1.** I have come unto you, O ye great Tchatcha Chiefs who dwell in heaven, and upon earth, **2.** and in Khert-Neter, and I have brought unto you the Osiris Ani. He hath not committed any act which is an abomination before all the gods. Grant ye that he may live with you every day.

3. The Osiris the scribe Ani adoreth Osiris, Lord of Rasta, and the Great Company of the Gods who live in Khert-Neter. **4.** He saith: "Homage to thee, Khenti "Ȧmenti, Un-Nefer, who dwellest in Abṭu (Abydos). "I come to thee. My heart holdeth Truth. There is no

" 5. sin in my body. I have not told a lie wittingly, I have
" not acted in a double manner. Grant thou to me cakes,
" 6. let me appear in the presence (*i.e.*, thy presence), at the
" altar of the Lords of Truth, let me go in and come forth
" from Khert-Neter [at will], let not my Heart-soul be driven
" away [from me]; and grant me a sight of the Disk (*i.e.*,
" the Sun) and the beholding of the 7. Moon for ever and
" ever."

II. The Speech of the Priest Sameref. 1. I have come unto you, O ye Tchatcha Chiefs who dwell in Rasta, and I have brought unto you the Osiris 2. Ani, grant ye unto him cakes, and water, and air, and a homestead in Sekhet-ḥetep as to the followers of Horus.

3. The Osiris the scribe Ani, whose word is truth, adoreth Osiris, the Lord of everlastingness, and the Tchatcha Chiefs, the Lords of Rasta. 4. He saith: " Homage to thee, O King of Khert-Neter, thou Governor " of Ȧkert! I have come unto thee. I know thy plans (?),

"5. I am equipped with the forms which thou takest in the "Ṭuat. Give thou to me a place in Khert-Neter, near the "Lords of Truth. 6. May my homestead be lasting in "Sekhet-ḥetep, may I receive cakes in thy presence."

CHAPTER XVIII

PLATES XIII, XIV

1. Hail, Thoth, who madest to be true the word of 2. Osiris against his enemies, make thou the word of the scribe Nebseni to be true against his enemies, even as thou didst make the word of Osiris to be true against his enemies, in the presence of the 3. Tchatcha Chiefs who are with Rā and Osiris in Ȧnu (Heliopolis), on the night of the "things of the night,"[2] and the night of battle,[3] 4. and

[1] This section is added from the Papyrus of Nebseni, Sheet 15.

[2] The "things of the night" means the rebellion or attack which was made either by the disaffected inhabitants of heaven, or by men upon earth. This rebellion took place in the last hours of the night, before the dawn.

[3] This battle was between Osiris and Set, and it took place at dawn, on the right bank of the Nile, close to Heliopolis.

of the fettering of the Sebȧu fiends,[1] and the day of the destruction of the enemies[2] of Neb-er-tcher.[3]

A. **1.** Now the great Tchatcha Chiefs in Ȧnu are Tem, Shu, Tefnut, [Osiris and Thoth]. **2.** Now the "fettering of the Sebȧu fiends" signifieth the destruction of the Smaiu fiends of Set, when **3.** he wrought iniquity a second time.

Hail, Thoth, who didst make the word of Osiris to be true against his enemies, make thou the word of the Osiris Ani to be true **4.** against his enemies, with the great Tchatcha Chiefs who are in Ṭeṭu, on the night of setting up the Ṭeṭ in Ṭeṭu (Busiris).[4]

[1] The Sebȧu were the forces of the rebels, large numbers of whom were slain, but clearly very many of them were made prisoners, and were taken in chains to the temple in Heliopolis.

[2] The "day of the destruction" means the day of the slaughter of the captives, who were offered up as sacrifices to Neb-er-tcher, *i.e.*, the "god to the uttermost limit." They were slain before the symbol of the god in the large courtyard, and their blood poured out on its base.

[3] The original battle referred to in this paragraph certainly seems to have taken place between human followers of Osiris and Set, but the religious texts contain allusions to a battle between the gods which must have taken place in heaven. The cause of this was the revolt of Set against the authority of Horus the Elder, or his predecessor.

[4] The setting up of the Ṭeṭ,  , was one of the most important ceremonies of the Annual Festival of Osiris which took place in all the great shrines of the god. It symbolized the final act of the reconstruction of Osiris, and his resurrection.

B. 1. Now the great Tchatcha Chiefs who are in Ṭeṭu are Osiris, Isis, Nephthys, and Horus the avenger of his father. Now the "setting up of 2. the Ṭeṭ in Ṭeṭu" signifieth [the raising up of] the shoulder of Horus, the Governor of Sekhem (Letopolis). They (*i.e.*, these gods) are round about Osiris in the band [and] the bandages (?).

3. Hail, Thoth, who didst make the word of Osiris to be true against his enemies, make thou the word of the Osiris Ani to be true against his enemies, with 4. the great Tchatcha Chiefs who are in Sekhem, on the night of the "things of the night" in Sekhem.[1]

C. 1. Now the great Tchatcha Chiefs who are in Sekhem are Ḥeru-khenti-en-ȧriti (?) and Thoth who is with the Tchatcha Chiefs of Neruṭef. 2. Now the night of the

[1] Thus it seems that a fight took place between Osiris and Set at Letopolis.

"things of the night festival" signifieth the dawn on the sarcophagus of Osiris.

Hail, Thoth, who didst make the word of Osiris to be true 3. against his enemies, make thou the word of the Osiris the scribe Ani to be true against his enemies, with the great Tchatcha Chiefs who are in the double town Pe-Ṭep, 4. on the night of setting up the "Senti"[1] of Horus, and of establishing him in the inheritance of the possessions of his father Osiris.

D. 1. Now the great Tchatcha Chiefs who are in Pe-Ṭep[2] are Horus, Isis, Ḳestȧ (Mestȧ) and Ḥapi. Now the "setting up of the 'Senti' of 2. Horus" hath reference to the words which Set spake to his followers, saying: "Set up the Senti."[3]

[1] A kind of canopy with two pillars, in which the coronation of the king took place.

[2] Pe-Ṭep were the two halves of the town of Per-Uatchet, the metropolis of the XIXth Nome of Lower Egypt.

[3] Thus it is clear that Set claimed the crown of Egypt, and ordered the ceremonial canopy or tent to be made ready for his coronation. Set was defeated, and the text shows that it was Horus who was crowned king of all Egypt.

Hail, Thoth, who didst make the word of Osiris to be true against his 3. enemies, make thou the word of the Osiris the scribe Ani to be true, in peace, against his enemies, with the great Tchatcha Chiefs who are in the Lands of the Rekhti (Taiu-Rekhti), 4. in the night when Isis lay down, and kept watch to make lamentation for her brother Osiris.

E. 1. Now the great Tchatcha Chiefs who are in Taiu-Rekhti are Isis, Horus, Ḳestȧ (Mestȧ) [Ȧnpu and Thoth].

Hail, Thoth, who didst make the word of Osiris true 2. against his enemies, make thou the word of the Osiris the scribe Ani, whose word is truth, in peace, to be true against his enemies, with the great 3. Tchatcha Chiefs who are in Abṭu, on the night of the god Haker, when the dead are separated, and the 4. spirits are judged, and when the procession taketh place in Teni.[1]

[1] The capital of the VIIIth Nome of Upper Egypt. It lay near Abydos, and its site is probably marked by Kôm as-Sulṭân. It is the ⲐⲒⲤ of Coptic writers.

F. 1. Now the great Tchatcha Chiefs who are in Abṭu (Abydos) are Osiris, Isis, and Up-uat.

Hail, Thoth, who didst make the word of Osiris to be true 2. against his enemies, make thou the word of the Osiris, the scribe and assessor of the sacred offerings which are made to all the gods, Ani, to be true 3. against his enemies, with the Tchatcha Chiefs who examine the dead on the night 4. of making the inspection (or, counting) of those who are to be annihilated.

G. 1. Now the great Tchatcha Chiefs who are present at the examination of the dead are Thoth, Osiris, Ȧnpu and Ȧsṭen (read Ȧsṭes). 2. Now the inspection (or, counting) of those who are to be annihilated signifieth the shutting up of things from the souls of the sons of revolt.

3. Hail, Thoth, who didst make the word of Osiris true against his enemies, make thou the word of the Osiris the scribe Ani to be true against his enemies, with the 4. great Tchatcha Chiefs who are present at the digging up of the

earth [and mixing it] with their blood[1] (*i.e.*, the blood of the enemies of Osiris), and of making the word of Osiris to be true against his enemies.

H. 1. As concerning the Tchatcha Chiefs who are present at the digging up of the earth in Ṭeṭu: When the Smaiu fiends of Set came [there], having transformed themselves into 2. animals, these Tchatcha Chiefs slew them in the presence of the gods who were there, and they took their blood, and carried it to them. These things
3. were permitted at the examination [of the wicked] by those [gods] who dwelt in Ṭeṭu.

Hail, Thoth, who didst make the word of Osiris to be true against his enemies, make thou the word of the Osiris
4. [the scribe] Ani to be true against his enemies, with the

[1] The victims were slain before the Ṭeṭ, the symbol of Osiris, and their blood was dug into the earth, in the same way as at the present time in Dahomey, and other parts of Africa, the blood of the victims is dug into the ground immediately before the figures of the gods which are to be appeased. These "ploughing ceremonies" are described by Burton, Skertchley, and others.

great Tchatcha Chiefs who are in Neruṭef,[1] on the night of the "Hidden of Forms."[2]

I. **1.** Now the great Tchatcha Chiefs who are in Neruṭef are Rā, Osiris, Shu and Bebi.

Now, the night of the "Hidden **2.** of Forms" referreth to the placing on the sarcophagus [of Osiris] the arm, the heel(?), and the thigh of Osiris Un-Nefer.

Hail, Thoth, who didst make the word of **3.** Osiris true against his enemies, make thou the word of the Osiris, whose word is truth, to be true against his enemies, with the great Tchatcha Chiefs who are in **4.** Rasta, on the night when Ȧnpu lay with his arms on the things by Osiris, and when the word of Horus was made to be true against his enemies.

[1] A part of the temple of Osiris at Herakleopolis.

[2] A name of Osiris.

J. 1. The great Tchatcha Chiefs who are in Rasta are Horus, Osiris, and Isis. The heart of Osiris is happy, the heart of Horus 2. is glad, and the two halves of Egypt (Återti) are well satisfied thereat.

Hail, Thoth, who didst make the word of Osiris true against his enemies, make thou the word of the Osiris 3. the scribe Ani, the assessor of the holy offerings made to all the gods, to be true against his enemies, with the Ten great 4. Tchatcha Chiefs who are with Rā, and with Osiris, and with every god, and with every goddess, in the presence of the god Nebertcher. He hath destroyed his enemies, and 5. he hath destroyed every evil thing which appertained to him.

RUBRIC: If this Chapter be recited for, or over, the deceased, he shall come forth by day, purified after death, 6. according to the desire of his heart. Now, if this Chapter be recited over him, he shall progress over the earth, and he shall escape from every fire, and none of the evil things which appertain to him shall ever be round about him; never, a million times over, shall this be.

The XIXth and XXth Chapters are substantially repetitions of the XVIIIth, but each has a Rubric which is of interest. These rubrics read:

Chapter XIX. This Chapter shall be recited over the divine Chaplet which is laid on the face of the deceased, and thou shalt cast incense into the fire on his behalf. Thus shalt thou cause him to triumph over his enemies, dead or alive, and he shall be among the bodyguard of Osiris, and a hand shall be stretched out to him with meat and drink in the presence of the Great God. This Chapter shall be said by thee twice at dawn—now it is a never-failing charm—regularly and continually.

Chapter XX. If this Chapter be recited regularly and continually by a man who hath made himself pure by means of water in which natron hath been mixed, he shall come forth by day after he hath come into port (*i.e.*, is dead), and he shall perform all the transformations which his heart shall dictate, and he shall escape from the fire.

CHAPTER XXIII

THE CHAPTER OF OPENING THE MOUTH

PLATE XV

1. The Chapter of Opening the Mouth of the Osiris Ani. To be said:—The god Ptaḥ shall open my mouth, and the god of my town shall unfasten the swathings, the swathings which are over my mouth. **2.** Thereupon shall come Thoth, who is equipped with words of power in great abundance, and shall untie the fetters, even the fetters of the god Set which are over my mouth. **3.** And the god Tem shall cast them back at those who would fetter me with them, and cast them at him. Then shall the god Shu open my mouth, and make an opening into my mouth **4.** with the same iron implement wherewith he opened the mouth of the gods. I am the goddess Sekhmet, and I take my seat upon the place by the side of Åmt-ur (?) **5.** the great wind of heaven. I am the great Star-goddess Sȧaḥ,[1] who dwelleth among the Souls of Ånu (Heliopolis). Now as concerning every spell (or, magical incantation), and every word which shall be spoken against me, **6.** every god in the Divine Company shall set himself in opposition thereto.

[1] *I.e.*, the Orion-goddess.

CHAPTER XXIV

THE CHAPTER OF BRINGING SPELLS TO THE SCRIBE ANI

PLATE XV

1. The Chapter of bringing Words of Power (or, spells or incantations) to the Osiris Ani, who saith :— 2. I am Tem-Kheperȧ who produced himself on the thighs of his divine mother. Those who dwell in Nu[1] have been made wolves, and those who are among the Tchatcha Chiefs 3. have become hyenas. Behold, I will gather together to myself this charm from the person with whom it is, [and from the place] wherein it is, [and it shall come to me] quicker than a greyhound, and swifter than light. 4. Hail, thou who bringest the Ferry-Boat of Rā,[2] thou holdest thy course firmly and directly in the north wind as thou sailest up the river towards the Island of Fire which is in Khert-Neter. Behold, thou shalt gather together to

[1] *I.e.*, the Sky-god.

[2] The Being here referred to is "Ḥer-f-ḥa-f", *i.e.*, "the god with his face turned behind him." He was the possessor of a magical ferry-boat, and he ferried the souls of the righteous from Deadland to the Island of Truth.

thee 5. this charm from wheresoever it may be, and from whomsoever it may be with [and it shall come to me] quicker than a greyhound, and swifter than light. It (*i.e.*, the charm) made the transformations 6. of Mut (?); it fashioned the gods [or] kept them silent; by it Mut (?) gave the warmth [of life] to the gods. Behold, these words of power are mine, and they shall come unto me from wheresoever they may be, or with whomsoever they may be, 7. quicker than greyhounds and swifter than light, or, according to another reading, "swifter than shadows."

APPENDIX

The following Chapter is closely connected with the two preceding Chapters:—

CHAPTER XXV

THE CHAPTER WHICH MAKETH A MAN TO REMEMBER HIS NAME IN KHERT-NETER. [The deceased] saith:— Let my name be given to me in the Great House (Per-ur), and let me remember my name in the House of

Fire (Per Neser), on the night wherein the years are counted up, and the number of the months is told. I am dwelling (?) with the Divine One, I take my seat on the eastern side of the sky. If any god cometh after me, I shall be able to declare his name forthwith.[1]

CHAPTER XXVI

THE CHAPTER OF GIVING A HEART

PLATE XV

1. THE CHAPTER OF GIVING A HEART TO THE OSIRIS ANI **2.** IN KHERT-NETER. He saith:—Let my heart be with me in the House of Hearts. Let my heart-case[2] be with me in the House of heart-cases. Let my heart be with me, and let it rest in [me or] I shall not eat the cakes of Osiris on the eastern side of the Lake of Flowers, **3.** nor have a boat wherein to float down the river, nor a boat to sail up the river to thee, nor be able to embark in a boat

[1] Or, perhaps, "I shall be able to declare my name to him forthwith."
[2] The pericardium (?).

with thee. Let my mouth be to me **4.** that I may speak therewith. Let my legs be to me that I may walk therewith. Let my arms be to me that I may overthrow the foe therewith. Let the two doors of the sky be opened to me. **5.** May Ḳeb,[1] the Erpāt[2] of the gods, open his jaws to me. May he open my two eyes which are blinded by swathings. May he make me to lift up my **6.** legs in walking which are tied together. May Ȧnpu make my thighs to become vigorous. May **7.** the goddess Sekhmet raise me, and lift me up. Let me ascend into heaven, let that which I command be performed in Ḥet-ḳa-Ptaḥ.[3] I know how to use my heart. I am master of my heart-case. **8.** I am master of my hands and arms. I am master of my legs. I have the power to do that which my KA (*i.e.*, Double)

[1] The Earth-god.
[2] The hereditary chief of the gods.
[3] The "House of the KA of Ptaḥ," *i.e.*, Memphis.

desireth to do. **9.** My Heart-soul shall not be kept a prisoner in my body at the gates of Åmentet when I would go in in peace and come forth in peace.

The readings of several passages of this Chapter are different in the Papyrus of Nebseni, *e.g.*, Let me eat. Let me have my mouth to speak, my legs to walk. Let me have my arms to overthrow my enemies. Let be opened my mouth and my arms in the earth. May the Erpāt Ḳeb open my jaws for me. Let me rise up then. Let the goddess Sekhmet open to me. Let be done what I command in Ḥet-ka-Ptaḥ. I am master of my heart. I am master of my heart-case (or breast). I am master of my arms. I am master of my legs.

CHAPTER XXXB

THE CHAPTER OF NOT LETTING THE HEART OF ANI BE TAKEN FROM HIM

PLATE XV

1. The Chapter of not **2.** letting the heart of the Osiris, the assessor of the divine offerings of all the gods, Ani, whose word is truth before Osiris, be driven back from him in Khert-Neter. He saith:— My heart of my mother. My heart of my mother. **3.** My heart-case of my transformations. Let not any one stand up to bear testimony against me. Let no one drive me away from (or, among) the Tchatcha Chiefs. Let no one make thee to fall away from me in the presence of the Keeper of the Balance. Thou art my

4.

KA, the dweller in 4. my body, the god Khnemu who makest sound my members. Mayest thou appear in the place of happiness whither we go. Let not make my name to stink the Shenit Chiefs, who make men to be stable (?). [Let it be satisfactory unto us, and let the listening (?) be satisfactory unto us, and let there be joy of heart to us at the weighing of words. Let not lies be told against me before the Great God, the Lord of Åmentet. Verily, how great shalt thou be when thou risest up in triumph!]

APPENDIX TO CHAPTER XXXB.

[Naville, *Todtenbuch*, II, 99.]

RUBRIC I: 1. 2. 3.

RUBRIC I: 1. These words are to be said over a scarab of green stone encircled with a band of refined copper, and [having] a ring (or rim) of silver; 2. which shall be placed on the neck of the Khu (*i.e.*, the deceased), etc.

RUBRIC II [FROM THE PAPYRUS OF NU, SHEET 21]:

RUBRIC II: 1. If this Chapter be known [by the deceased] he shall be declared a speaker of the truth both upon earth and in Khert-Neter, and he shall be able to perform every act which a living human being can perform. 2. Now it is a great protection which hath been given by the god. This Chapter was found in the city of Khemenu (Hermopolis) upon the slab of *ba* (iron? alabaster?), which was inlaid with [letters of] 3. genuine lapis-lazuli, and was under the feet of [the statue] of the god, during the reign of His Majesty, the King of the South and North, Menkaurā (Mycerinus),[1] true of word, by Prince Ḥeruṭāṭaf,[2] who found it 4. during a journey which he made to inspect the temples. One Nekht (?) was with him who was diligent in making him to understand it (?), and he brought it 5. to the king as a wonderful object when he perceived that

[1] The builder of the Third Pyramid at Gîzah.

[2] He was the son of Khufu, the builder of the First Pyramid at Gîzah.

it was a thing of great mystery, [the like of] which had
never [before] been seen or looked upon. This Chapter
6. shall be recited by a man who is ceremonially clean and
pure, who hath not eaten the flesh of animals, or fish, and
who hath not had intercourse with women. And behold, thou
shalt make a scarab of green stone, with a rim 7. [plated]
with gold, which shall be placed above the heart (or, in the
breast) of a man, and it shall perform for him the "opening
of the mouth." And thou shalt anoint it with myrrh
unguent, and thou shalt recite over it the following words
of magical power. [Here follows the text of Chapter
XXXB.]

CHAPTER LXI

CHAPTER OF NOT LETTING THE HEART-SOUL BE CARRIED AWAY

PLATE XV

1. THE CHAPTER OF NOT LETTING THE HEART-SOUL OF
A MAN BE SNATCHED AWAY FROM HIM IN KHERT-NETER.
The Osiris the scribe Ani saith :—I, even I, am he 2. who

cometh forth from the Celestial Water (Aḳeb). He (*i.e.*, Aḳeb) produced abundance for me, and hath the mastery there (*i.e.*, in the sky ?) in the form of the River.

The above is a portion of a longer Chapter which is found in its fullest form in the Papyrus of Nefer-uben-f (Naville, *op. cit.*, I, Bl. 72). The text reads :—

THE CHAPTER OF DRINKING WATER IN KHERT-NETER. The *àm khent* priest, Nefer-uben-f, whose word is truth, saith :—1. I, even I, am he who cometh forth from 2. the god Ḳeb. The water-flood is given to him, he hath become the master thereof in the form of Ḥāpi. I, the *àm khent* Nefer-uben-f, open 3. the doors of heaven. Thoth hath opened to me the doors of Qebḥ (*i.e.*, the Celestial Waters. Lo, Ḥepi Ḥepi, the two sons (?) of the Sky, 4. mighty in splendour, grant ye that I may be master over the water, even as Set had dominion over his evil power (?) 5. on the day of the storming of the Two Lands (*i.e.*, Egypt). I pass by the Great Ones, arm to shoulder (?), even as they pass that Great God, the Spirit 6. who is equipped, whose name is unknown. I have passed by the Aged One (or the Great One) of the shoulder (?). I am Nefer-uben-f, whose word is truth. Hath opened to me the Celestial Water 7. Osiris. Hath opened to me the Celestial Water Thoth-Ḥāpi, the Lord of the horizon, in his name of "Thoth, cleaver of the earth." 8. I am master of the water, as Set is master of his weapon. I sail over the sky, I am Rā, I am Ru. I am Sma. I have eaten 9. the Thigh, I have seized the bone and flesh. I go round about the Lake of Sekhet-Ar. Hath been given to me eternity without limit. Behold, I am 10. the heir of eternity, to whom hath been given everlastingness.

Closely connected with the above Chapter are the two following Chapters from the Papyrus of Nu (Sheets 7 and 12.)

CHAPTER LXIIIA. 1. 2. 3. (var.) 4. 5.

CHAPTER LXIIIA. 1. THE CHAPTER OF DRINKING WATER AND OF NOT BEING BURNT UP 2. BY FIRE [IN KHERT-NETER]. Nu saith :—Hail, Bull of Åmentet! I am brought unto thee. I am the paddle of Rā 3. wherewith he transported the Aged Gods. Let me neither be burnt up nor destroyed by fire. I am Beb, the firstborn son of Osiris, to whom every god maketh 4. an offering in the temple of his Eye in Ånu. I am the divine Heir, the Mighty One, the Great One, the Resting One. I have made my name to flourish. 5. Deliverer, thou livest in me [every day].

CHAPTER LXIIIB. 1. 2.

CHAPTER LXIIIB. 1. THE CHAPTER OF NOT BEING BOILED IN FIRE. Nu saith :—I am the paddle which is equipped, 2. wherewith Rā transported the Aged Gods, which raised up the emissions of Osiris from the Lake of blazing fire, 3. and he was not burned. I sit down like the Light-god, and like Khnemu, the Governor of lions (?). Come, cut away 4. the fetters from him that passeth by the side of this path, and let me come forth therefrom.

CHAPTER LIV

THE CHAPTER OF GIVING AIR

PLATE XV

1. THE CHAPTER OF GIVING AIR IN KHERT-NETER. The Osiris Ani saith :—I am the Egg which dwelt in the Great Cackler. I keep ward over that great 2. place which Ḳeb hath proclaimed upon earth. I live; it liveth. I grow up, I live, I snuff the air. I am 3. Utchā-aāb. I go round about his egg [to protect it]. I have thwarted the moment of Set. 4. Hail, Sweet one of the Two Lands! Hail, dweller in the *tchefa* food! Hail, dweller in the lapis

lazuli (*i.e.*, the blue sky?)! Watch ye over him that is in his cradle (literally nest), the Babe when he cometh forth to you.

An older version of this Chapter is found in the Papyrus of Nu (Sheet 12), the text of which reads:—

CHAPTER LIV. 1. THE CHAPTER OF GIVING AIR 2. TO NU IN KHERT-NETER. He saith:—Hail, thou God Temu, grant thou unto me the sweet breath which dwelleth in thy nostrils! I am the Egg 3. which is in Ḳenḳen-ur (*i.e.*, the Great Cackler), and I watch and guard that mighty thing which hath come into being, wherewith the god Ḳeb hath opened the earth. I live; it liveth; 4. I grow, I live, I snuff the air. I am the god Utchā-aābet, and I go about his egg. I shine at the moment of 5. the mighty of strength, Suti. Hail, thou who makest sweet the time (?) of the two Lands! Hail, dweller among the celestial food.

Hail, dweller among the beings of blue (or, lapis lazuli), watch ye to protect him that is in **6.** his nest (*i.e.*, cradle), the Child who cometh forth to you.

Other Chapters, which were written with the same object as the preceding, are Chapters LV and LVI, which, in the Papyrus of Nu (Sheet 12) read thus:—

CHAPTER LV. **1.** **2.** **3.** [1]

CHAPTER LV. **1.** THE CHAPTER OF GIVING AIR IN KHERT-NETER. Nu saith:—**2.** I am the jackal of jackals. I am Shu. I draw air from the presence of the Light-god, from the uttermost limits of heaven, from the uttermost limits of **3.** earth, from the uttermost limits of the pinion of the Nebeḥ bird (ostrich?). May air be given unto this young divine Babe. [My mouth is open, I see with my eyes.]

CHAPTER LVI. **1.** **2.** **3.**

CHAPTER LVI. THE CHAPTER OF SNUFFING THE AIR **2.** WITH WATER IN KHERT-NETER. Hail, Tem. Grant thou unto me the sweet breath which dwelleth in thy nostrils. I am he who embraceth that great throne **3.** which is in the city of Unu (*i.e.*, Hermopolis). I keep watch over the

[1] Added from a papyrus at Leyden (Naville, *op. cit.*, Bd. II, p. 125).

Egg of Ḳenḳen-ur (*i.e.*, the Great Cackler). I grow and flourish [as] it groweth and flourisheth. 4. I live [as] it liveth. I snuff the air [as] it snuffeth the air (or, my breath is its breath).

CHAPTER XXIXA

CHAPTER OF NOT LETTING THE HEART BE SNATCHED AWAY

PLATE XV

1. THE CHAPTER OF NOT LETTING THE HEART OF A MAN BE SNATCHED AWAY FROM HIM IN KHERT-NETER. The Osiris Ani, whose word is truth, saith :—Get thee back, O messenger of every god! 2. Art thou come to [snatch away] my heart-case which liveth? My heart-case which liveth shall not be given unto thee. 3. [As] I advance, the gods hearken unto my propitiation [prayer] and they fall down on their faces [whilst] they are on their own land.

APPENDIX

Chapter XXIXb. 1.

Chapter XXIXb. 1. The Chapter of not allowing the heart . . . . to be carried away dead in Khert-Neter. [Nu, whose word is truth, saith]:—My heart is with me, 2. and it shall never come to pass that it be carried away. I am the Lord of Hearts, the slayer of the heart-case. 3. I live in truth, I have my being therein. I am Horus, the Dweller in Hearts, 4. [I am] in the Dweller in the body. I have life by my word, my heart hath being. My 5. heart-case shall not be snatched away from me, it shall not be wounded, it shall not be put in restraint [if] wounds are inflicted upon me. [If] one take possession of it 6. I shall have my being in the body of my father Ḳeb and in the body of my mother Nut. I have not done that which is held in abomination by 7. the gods. I shall not suffer defeat [for] my word is truth.

There is yet another version of this Chapter, which is known as Chapter XXIXc, and which was originally engraved on a heart made of carnelian; this carnelian heart became an amulet of great power, but its use does not appear to have been very general. The subject matter of the Chapter is quite different from that of Chapters XXIXa and XXIXb, for it deals directly with the soul of Rā and his Ka, or Double. The *sehert* stone, which is rendered "carnelian," was believed to be similar to the substance of which the disk of Rā was made, and to possess its qualities, which the wearer of the heart-amulet absorbed into his body. A copy of Chapter XXIXc is found in the Papyrus of Ani, Sheet 33, where the amulet ranks with the amulet of the pillow, the amulet of the Ṭeṭ, and the amulet of the Tet; as all these are of very great antiquity we may assume that the heart of carnelian was used as an amulet in very early times. The text and translation of the Chapter will be found with the contents of Plate XXXIII.

CHAPTER XXVII

THE CHAPTER OF NOT LETTING THE HEART-CASE BE TAKEN FROM A MAN

PLATES XV AND XVI

1.

Chapter XXVII. 1. The Chapter of not letting the heart-case of a man be taken away from him in Khert-Neter. The Osiris Ani saith:—Hail, ye who steal and crush heart-cases [and who make the heart of a man to go through its transformations according to his deeds: let not what he hath done harm him before you].[1] 2. Homage to you, O ye Lords of Eternity, ye

[1] Added from Naville's text.

masters of everlastingness, take ye not this heart of Osiris Ani **3.** into your fingers, and this heart-case, and cause ye not things of evil to spring up against it, because this heart belongeth to the **4.** Osiris Ani, and this heart-case belongeth to him of the great names (*i.e.*, Thoth), the mighty one, whose words are his members. He sendeth his heart to rule **5.** his body, and his heart is renewed before the gods. The heart of the Osiris Ani, whose word is truth, is to him; he hath gained the mastery over it. He hath not said what he hath done (?) He hath obtained power **6.** over his own members. His heart obeyeth him, he is the lord thereof, it is in his body, and it shall never fall away therefrom. I command thee to be obedient unto me in Khert-Neter. **7.** I, the Osiris Ani, whose word is truth, in peace; whose word is truth in the Beautiful Ȧmentet, by the Domain of Eternity.

The two following Chapters, which are not in the Papyrus of Ani, are important for understanding the beliefs of the Egyptians concerning the heart; they are found in the Papyrus of Nu, Sheet 5:—

CHAPTER XXVIII. 1.

CHAPTER XXVIII. 1. THE CHAPTER OF NOT LETTING THE HEART OF NU, WHOSE WORD IS TRUTH, BE CARRIED AWAY 2. FROM HIM IN KHERT-NETER. He saith:—Hail, thou Lion-god! I am Unb (*i.e.*, the Blossom). That which is an abomination to me is the block of slaughter of the god. Let not this my heart-case be carried away from me by 3. the Fighting Gods in Ȧnu (Heliopolis). Hail, thou who dost wind bandages round Osiris, and who hast seen Set. Hail, thou who returnest after smiting and destroying him before the mighty ones! 4. This my heart (*ȧb*) weepeth over itself before Osiris; it hath made supplication for me. I have given unto him and I have dedicated unto him the thoughts 5. of the heart in the House of the god (Usekh-ḥer),[1] have brought unto him sand[2] at the entry to Khemenu.[3] Let not this my heart-

[1] *I.e.*, the god of the broad face, a name of Rā.
[2] So, but read "cakes."
[3] The city of the Eight Gods, *i.e.*, Hermopolis Magna.

case be carried away from me. **6.** I make you to ascend his throne, to fetter (*i.e.*, tie together) heart-cases for him in Sekhet-ḥetep, [to live] years of strength away from things of all kinds which are abominations to him, **7.** to carry off food from among the things which are thine, and which are in thy grasp through thy strength. And this my heart-case is devoted to the decrees of the god Tem, who guideth me through the **8.** caverns of Suti, but let not this my heart, which hath performed its desire before the Tchatcha Chiefs who are in Khert-Neter, be given to him. When they find the leg and the swathings **9.** they bury them.

Chapter XXXa. 1.

Chapter XXXa. 1. The Chapter of not letting the heart of Nu, whose word is truth, be driven away from him in Khert-Neter. He saith:—2. My heart of my mother. My heart of my mother. My heart-case of my existence upon the earth. Let no one stand up against me when I bear testimony in the presence of the Lords of Things. 3. Let it not be said against me and of that which I have done "He hath committed acts which are opposed to what is right and true," and let not charges be brought up against me in the presence of the Great God, the Lord of Åmentet. Homage to thee, O my heart (*àb*). Homage 4. to thee, O my heart-case. Homage to you, O my reins. Homage to you, O ye gods, who are masters of [your] beards, and who are holy 5. by reason of your sceptres. Speak ye for me words of good import to Rā,[1] and make ye me to have favour in the sight of Neḥebkau.[2]

[1] This is the reading of many ancient papyri, including the Papyrus of Nebseni. We should expect to find here the name of Osiris instead of that of Rā, and it actually occurs in the Turin Papyrus (ed. Lepsius).

[2] Neḥebkau is the Fortieth Assessor, who sat in the Hall of Osiris, and assisted him in judging the dead. The passage in Chapter CXXV in which he is mentioned reads: "Hail, Neḥebkau, who comest forth from "[thy town], I have not made myself to use words of violence (or "arrogance),". The word *sethen* must have presented a difficulty to the scribes, for we find the following variants (Naville, *op. cit.*, II, 308): "I have not committed acts of fraud"; "I have not committed fraud in the seat of law (*i.e.*, the law-court"); "I have not done *seten* to another". The text of

6.

And behold, even though it 6. (*i.e.*, the heart) be united to the earth, in the mighty innermost part thereof, let me flourish (or remain) upon the earth, and let me not die in Åmentet, but become a spirit therein.

CHAPTER LVIII

THE CHAPTER OF BREATHING THE AIR

PLATE XVI

1. 2. 3.

CHAPTER LVIII. 1. THE CHAPTER OF BREATHING THE AIR AND OF HAVING POWER OVER WATER IN KHERT-NETER. The Osiris Ani saith:—Open to me! Who art thou? Whither goest thou? 2. What is thy name? I am one of you. Who are these with you? The two Merti goddesses (*i.e.*, Isis and Nephthys). Thou separatest head from head when [he] 3. entereth the divine Mesqen

---

the Turin Papyrus reads: "I have not made his plans, I have not done his fraud (?), I have not given a command." The Papyrus of Nu has an entirely different reading: which seems to mean something like: "I have not made great my possessions except by [my own] things," but the exact sense of the words is not clear.

4. 5. 6. 7.

RUBRIC.

(sic)

chamber. He causeth me to set out for the temple of the gods Ḳem-ḥeru. "Assembler of souls" 4. is the name of my ferry-boat. "Those who make the hair to bristle" is the name of the oars. "Sert" (*i.e.*, "Goad") is the name of the hold (?). 5. "Steering straight in the middle" is the name of the rudder; likewise, [the boat] is a type of my being borne onward 6. in the lake. Let there be given unto me vessels of milk, and cakes, and loaves of bread, and cups of drink, and flesh, 7. in the Temple of Ȧnpu.

RUBRIC: If the deceased knoweth this Chapter, he shall go into, after coming forth from Khert-Neter of [the Beautiful Ȧmentet].

CHAPTER LIX

CHAPTER OF SNUFFING THE AIR IN KHERT-NETER

PLATE XVI

1. 2. 3. 4.

1. THE CHAPTER OF SNUFFING THE AIR, AND OF HAVING POWER OVER THE WATER IN KHERT-NETER. The Osiris Ani saith :—Hail, thou Sycamore tree of the goddess Nut! Give me of the [water and of the] air 2. which is in thee. I embrace that throne which is in Unu,[1] and I keep guard over 3. the Egg of Neḳeḳ-ur.[2] It flourisheth, and I flourish[3]; it liveth and I live; 4. it snuffeth the air, and I snuff the air, I the Osiris Ani, whose word is truth, in [peace].

[1] The town of Hermopolis, the chief god of which was, as its name signifies, Thoth.

[2] Other forms of the name are  and  . This god is Ḳeb, the Earth-god. The Egg is the sun.

[3] The meaning is, "if the Egg flourisheth, then I shall flourish; if it liveth, I shall live; if it snuffeth the air, I shall snuff the air; if it doth not flourish, nor live, nor snuff the air, then I shall do none of these things and shall die.

CHAPTER XLIV

THE CHAPTER OF NOT DYING A SECOND TIME

PLATE XVI

CHAPTER XLIV. 1. THE CHAPTER OF NOT DYING A SECOND TIME IN KHERT-NETER. The Osiris Ani saith:—My hiding place is opened, my hiding place is opened. The Spirits fall headlong 2. in the darkness, but the Eye of Horus hath made me holy, and Upuati hath nursed me. I will hide 3. myself among you, O ye stars which are imperishable. My brow (?) is like the brow (?) of Rā. My face is open. 4. My heart-case is upon its throne, I know how to utter words. In very truth I am Rā himself. I am not a man of no account (or, ignorance). 5. I am not a man to whom violence can be done. Thy father liveth for thee, O son of Nut. I am thy son, O great one, I have seen 6. the hidden things which are thine. I am crowned upon my throne like the king of the gods. I shall not die a second time in Khert-Neter.

CHAPTER XLV

THE CHAPTER OF NOT ROTTING IN KHERT-NETER

PLATE XVI

1. 2. 3.

RUBRIC.

CHAPTER XLV. 1. THE CHAPTER OF NOT ROTTING IN KHERT-NETER. The Osiris Ani saith :—O thou who art motionless, O thou who art motionless, O thou whose **2.** members are motionless, like unto those of Osiris. Thy members shall not be motionless, they shall not rot (or stink), they shall not crumble away, they shall not fall into decay. **3.** My members shall be made [permanent] for me as if I were Osiris.

RUBRIC : If this Chapter be known by the deceased he shall never see corruption in Khert-Neter.

The above Chapter is a very brief exposition of the belief that the body can be prevented from decaying, which is treated at length in Chapter CLIV, and is reproduced here from the Papyrus of Nu (Sheet 18).

CHAPTER CLIV. 1. 2.

CHAPTER CLIV. **1.** The Chapter of not letting the body perish. The Osiris Nu saith :—**2.** Homage to thee, O my divine father Osiris! I come to embalm thee. Do thou embalm these my members, for I would not perish and come to an end 3. [but would be] even like unto my divine father Kheperȧ, the divine type of him that never saw corruption. Come then, strengthen my breath, O Lord of the winds, 4. who dost magnify these divine beings who are like unto thyself. Stablish me, stablish me, and fashion me strongly, O Lord of the funeral chest. Grant thou that I may enter into the land of everlastingness, according to that which was done for thee, 5. along with thy father Tem, whose body never saw corruption, and who himself never saw corruption. I have never done that which thou hatest, nay, I have acclaimed thee among those who love thy 6. KA (*i.e.*, Double). Let not my body become worms, but deliver thou me as thou didst deliver thyself. I pray thee, let me not fall into rottenness, as thou lettest 7. every god, and every goddess, and every animal, and every reptile, see corruption, when the soul hath gone out of them, after their death.

And when the soul hath departed, a man seeth corruption, and the bones 8. of his body crumble away and become stinking things, and the members decay one after the other, the bones crumble into a helpless mass, and the flesh turneth into foetid liquid. 9. Thus man becometh a brother unto the decay which cometh upon him, and he turneth into a myriad of worms, and he becometh nothing but worms, and an end is made of him, and he perisheth in the sight of the god of day (*i.e.*, Shu), even as do every god, and every goddess, 10. and every bird, and every fish, and every creeping worm, and every reptile, and every beast, and every thing whatsoever. Let [all the Spirits fall] on 11. their bellies [when] they recognize me, and behold, the fear of me shall terrify them; and thus also let it be with every being that hath died, whether it be animal, 12. or bird, or fish, or worm, or reptile. Let life [rise out of] death. Let not the decay caused by any reptile make an end [of me], and let not [enemies] come 13. against me in their various forms. Give thou me not over to the Slaughterer in his execution-chamber, who killeth 14. the members, and maketh them rot, being [himself] invisible, and who destroyeth the bodies of the dead, and liveth by carnage. Let me live, and perform his order; I will do what is 15. commanded by him. Give me not over to his fingers, let him not overcome me, for I am under thy command, O Lord of the Gods.

Homage to thee, O my divine father Osiris, thou livest with thy members. 16. Thou didst not decay, thou didst not become worms, thou didst not wither, thou didst not rot, thou didst not putrefy, thou didst not turn into worms. I am the god Kheperȧ, and my members shall have being everlastingly. 17. I shall not decay, I shall not rot, I shall not putrefy, I shall not turn into worms, and I shall not see corruption before the eye of the god Shu. I shall have my being, I shall have my being; **18.** I shall live, I shall live; I shall flourish, I shall flourish, I shall flourish, I shall wake up in peace, I shall not putrefy, my intestines shall not perish, I shall not suffer injury. **19.** My eye shall not decay. The form of my face shall not disappear. My ear shall not become deaf. My head shall not be separated from my neck. My tongue shall not be removed. My hair shall not **20.** be cut off. My eyebrows shall not be shaved away, and no evil defect shall assail me. My body shall be stablished. It shall neither become a ruin, **21.** nor be destroyed on this earth.

CHAPTER XLVI

THE CHAPTER OF NOT PERISHING

PLATE XVI

CHAPTER XLVI. **1.** THE CHAPTER OF NOT PERISHING AND OF BEING ALIVE IN KHERT-NETER. The Osiris Ani saith :—Hail **2.** ye children of the god Shu. The Ṭuat hath gained the mastery over his diadem. Among the Ḥamemet Spirits may I arise, even as did arise Osiris.

In the Turin Papyrus this Chapter has an alternative title, viz., . "The Chapter of not letting be diminished the hour of life in Khert-Neter." The Chapter itself reads in the Saïte Recension: "Hail, ye two children of Shu, hail, ye two children of Shu, [who came forth] from his body. The Ṭuat hath gained the mastery over his diadem. Among the Ḥamemet Spirits make me to lift up the hand, rising," . The two children of Shu are Ḳeb and Nut, who produced Osiris, Isis, Set, Nephthys, Horus and Anubis. Another version of this Chapter, besides that published by Naville, is found in the Papyrus of Nu (Sheet 16). The Chapter is ancient, and is probably of Southern origin, and the variants prove that the text presented difficulties to the Theban scribes. There is no copy of it in the Greenfield Papyrus.

CHAPTER L

THE CHAPTER OF NOT GOING TO THE BLOCK OF THE GOD

PLATE XVI

CHAPTER L. 1. THE CHAPTER OF NOT GOING IN TO THE BLOCK OF THE GOD. The Osiris Ani saith:—My head was fastened on my body in heaven, O Guardian of the Earth, by Rā. 2. [This] was granted [to me] on the day of my being stablished, when I rose up out of a state of weakness upon [my] two feet. On the day 3. of cutting off the hair Set and the Company of the Gods fastened my head to my neck, and it became as firm as it was 4. originally. Let nothing happen to shake it off again! Make ye me safe from the murderer of my father. I have tied together 5. the Two Earths. Nut hath fastened together the vertebrae of my neck, and [I] behold them as they were originally, and they are seen in the order wherein they were when as yet Maāt was not seen, and when the gods were not born in visible forms. 6. I am Penti. I am the heir of the great gods, I the Osiris the scribe Ani, whose word is truth.[1]

CHAPTER XCIII

THE CHAPTER OF NOT BEING TRANSPORTED TO THE EAST

PLATE XVII

CHAPTER XCIII. 1. THE CHAPTER OF NOT BEING TRANSPORTED TO THE EAST IN KHERT-NETER. The Osiris Ani saith :—Hail, Phallus 2. of Rā, which advanceth and beateth down opposition. Things which have been without motion (or inert) for millions of years have come into life through Bȧbȧ. I am stronger thereby 3. than the strong, and I have more power thereby than the mighty. Now, let me not be carried away in a boat, or be seized violently and taken to the East, to have the festivals of the Sebȧu

[1] Other ancient copies of this Chapter are found in the Papyrus of Nebseni (Sheet 12) and in the Papyrus of Nu (Sheet 19).

Devils celebrated on me. Let not deadly **4.** wounds be inflicted upon me, and let me not be gored (or butted) by horns. Thou shalt neither fall [nor] eat **5.** fish made by Tebun (?).[1]

Another Chapter.

Now, no evil thing of any kind whatsoever shall be done unto me by the Sebâu Devils. [I shall not be gored by] **6.** horns. Therefore the Phallus of Rā, [which is] the head of Osiris, shall not be swallowed up. Behold, **7.** I shall come into my fields and I shall cut the grain. The gods shall provide me with food. Thou shalt not then be gored, **8.** Rā-Kheperȧ. There shall not be then pus in the Eye of Tem, and it shall not **9.** be destroyed. Violence shall not be done unto me, and I shall not be carried away in [my] boat to the East to have the festivals of the Sebâu Devils celebrated on me **10.** in evil fashion. Cruel gashes

[1] The text seems to be corrupt here.

with knives shall not be inflicted upon me, and I shall not be carried away in [my] boat to the East. **11.** I the Osiris, the assessor of the holy offerings of all the gods, Ani, whose word is truth, whose word is truth, happily, the lord of fealty [to Osiris].

It is clear from the text printed above that this Chapter was full of difficulty, and that the ancient scribes did not understand many parts of it. It is evident also that two versions of it were current under the XVIIIth dynasty. The following version from Naville (*op. cit.*, I, Bl. 105) helps to settle some of the mistakes which the scribes made in copying the Chapter :—

CHAPTER XLIII

THE CHAPTER OF NOT LETTING THE HEAD BE CUT OFF

PLATE XVII

CHAPTER XLIII. 1. THE CHAPTER OF NOT LETTING THE HEAD OF A MAN BE CUT OFF FROM HIS BODY IN KHERT-NETER. The Osiris Ani saith:—2. I am a Great One, the son of a Great One. [I am] Fire, the son of Fire, to whom was 3. given his head after it had been cut off. The head of Osiris was not removed from his body, and the head of the Osiris 4. Ani shall not be removed from his body.[1] I have knitted myself together, I have made myself whole and complete.[2] I shall renew my youth. I am Osiris Himself, the Lord of Eternity.

CHAPTER LXXXIX

THE CHAPTER OF UNITING THE SOUL TO ITS BODY

PLATE XVII

1. [hieroglyphs] 2. [hieroglyphs] 3. [hieroglyphs] 4. [hieroglyphs]

CHAPTER LXXXIX. 1. THE CHAPTER OF MAKING THE SOUL TO BE JOINED TO ITS BODY IN KHERT-NETER. The Osiris Ani saith:—Hail, thou god Ȧniu! Hail, thou god Peḥreri, 2. who dwellest in thy hall, the Great God. Grant thou that my soul may come to me from any place wherein it may be. Even if it would tarry, let my soul be brought 3. unto me from any place wherein it may be. Thou findest the Eye of Horus standing by thee like unto those beings who resemble Osiris, who never lie down in death. Let not 4. the Osiris Ani, whose word is truth, lie down dead among those who

[1] The Turin Papyrus adds here [hieroglyphs].

[2] The Turin Papyrus adds [hieroglyphs], I shall be made new.

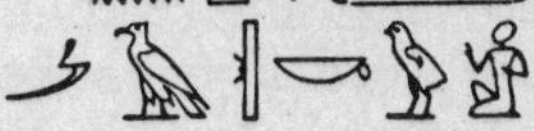

lie in Ȧnu, the land wherein [souls] are joined to their bodies in thousands. Let me have possession of my Ba-soul and of my Spirit-soul, and let my word be truth **5.** with it (*i.e.*, the Ba-soul) in every place wherein it may be. Observe then, O ye guardians of Heaven, my soul [wherever it may be]. Even if it would **6.** tarry, cause thou my Ba-soul to see my body. Thou shalt find the Eye of Horus standing by thee **7.** like [the Watchers].

Hail, ye gods who tow along the boat of the Lord of Millions of Years, who bring it over the **8.** sky of the Ṭuat, who make it to journey over Nent (Nut?), who make Ba-souls to enter into their Spirit-bodies, **9.** whose hands hold the steering poles and guide it straight, who grasp tightly your paddles, destroy ye the **10.** Enemy; thus shall the Boat rejoice, and the Great God shall travel on his way in peace. Moreover, grant ye that the Ba-soul of the Osiris Ani, **11.** whose word is truth before the gods, may come forth with your navel cords in the eastern part of the sky, and that it may follow Rā to the place where he was yesterday, and may set in peace, in peace in Åmentet. **12.** May it gaze upon its earthly body, may it take up its abode in its Spirit-body, may it neither perish nor be destroyed for ever and for ever.

RUBRIC: These words shall be said over a model of the Ba-soul made of gold, and inlaid with precious stones, which shall be placed on the breast of the Osiris.

CHAPTER XCI

THE CHAPTER OF NOT LETTING THE SOUL OF A MAN BE HELD CAPTIVE IN KHERT-NETER

PLATE XVII

CHAPTER XCI. **1.** THE CHAPTER OF NOT LETTING THE SOUL OF A MAN BE HELD CAPTIVE IN KHERT-NETER. The Osiris Ani saith:—Hail, thou who art exalted! Hail, thou who art adored! Hail, Mighty **2.** One of Souls, thou divine Soul who inspirest great dread, who dost set the fear of thyself in the gods, who are enthroned upon thy mighty seat. Make thou a path for the Spirit-soul **3.** and the

Ba-soul of the Osiris Ani. I am equipped with [words of power]. I am a Spirit-soul equipped with [words of power]. I have made my way to the place where are Rā and **4.** Hathor.

RUBRIC: If this Chapter be known by the deceased he shall be able to transform himself into a Spirit-soul who shall be equipped with [his soul and his shadow] in Khert-Neter, and he shall not be shut up inside any door in Åmentet, when he is coming forth upon the Earth, or when he is going back into [Khert-Neter.][1]

CHAPTER XCII

THE CHAPTER OF OPENING THE TOMB TO THE BA-SOUL AND SHADOW

PLATE XVII

CHAPTER XCII. **1.** THE CHAPTER OF OPENING THE TOMB TO THE BA-SOUL AND THE SHADOW, AND OF COMING FORTH BY DAY, AND OF HAVING MASTERY OVER THE TWO LEGS. The Osiris the scribe Ani, whose word is truth, saith:— **2.** The place which is closed is opened, the place which is shut (or sealed) is sealed. That which lieth down in the closed place is opened by (or, to) the Ba-soul which is in it. By the Eye of Horus I am delivered (?) Ornaments are

[1] In the Papyrus of Nu this Rubric is wanting.

3. stablished on the brow of Rā. My stride is made long. I lift up my two thighs [in walking]. I have journeyed over a long road. My limbs are 4. in a flourishing condition. I am Horus, the Avenger of his Father, and I bring the Urrt Crown [and set it on] its standard. The road of souls is opened. My twin soul 5. seeth the Great God in the Boat of Rā, on the day of souls. My soul is 6. in the front thereof with the counter of the years. Come, the Eye of Horus hath delivered for me my soul, my ornaments are 7. stablished on the brow of Rā. Light is on the faces of those who are in the members of Osiris. 8. Ye shall not hold captive my soul. Ye shall not keep in durance my shadow. The way is open to my soul 9. and to my shadow. It seeth the Great God in the shrine on the day of counting souls. It repeateth the words of 10. Osiris. Those whose seats are invisible, who fetter the members of Osiris, who fetter

Heart-souls and Spirit-souls, who set a seal **11.** upon the dead, and who would do evil to me, shall do no evil to me. Haste on the way to me (?). Thy heart **12.** is with thee. My Heart-soul and my Spirit-soul are equipped; they guide thee. I sit down at the head of the great ones **13.** who are chiefs of their abodes. The wardens of the members of Osiris shall not hold thee captive, though they keep ward over souls, and set a seal on **14.** the shadow which is dead. Heaven shall not shut thee in.

RUBRIC: If this Chapter be known by the deceased he shall come forth by day, and his soul shall not be kept captive.

The text of the above Chapter is corrupt in many places, and its general meaning can only be gained from a perusal of one of the older copies of the text; a translation of the Chapter as found in the Papyrus of Nebseni (Sheet 6) is therefore appended :—

That which was shut hath been opened [that is] the dead. That which was shut fast hath been opened by the command of the Eye of Horus, **3.** which hath delivered me. Established are the beauties on the forehead of Rā. My steps are long. My legs are lifted up. I have performed the journey, my members are mighty and **4.** are sound. I am Horus, the Avenger of his Father. I am he who bringeth along his father, and his mother, by means of his staff. The way shall be opened to him that hath **5.** power over his feet, and he shall see the Great God in the Boat of Rā, when souls are counted therein at the bows, and **6.** when the years also are counted up. Grant that the Eye of Horus, which maketh the adornments of splendour to be firm on the **7.** forehead of Rā, may deliver my soul for me, and let darkness cover your faces, O ye who would imprison Osiris. O keep not captive my soul. O keep not ward over **8.** my shadow, but let a way be opened for my soul and my shadow, and let them see the Great God in the shrine **9.** on the day of the counting of souls, and let them hold converse with Osiris, whose habitations are hidden, and those who guard the members of Osiris, and who **10.** keep ward over the Spirit-souls, and who hold captive the shadows of the dead, and who would work **11.** evil against me, so that they shall [not] work evil against me. A way shall be for thy Ka (*i.e.*, Double) with thee, and thy soul shall be prepared by those who keep ward over the members of Osiris, and who hold captive **12.** the shadows of the dead. Heaven shall not keep thee fast, the earth shall not hold thee captive. Thou shalt not live with the beings who slay, **13.** but thou shalt be master of thy legs, and thou shalt advance to thy body straightway in the earth, [and to] those who belong to the shrine of Osiris and guard his members.

CHAPTER LXXIV

THE CHAPTER OF LIFTING UP THE FEET AND OF APPEARING ON THE EARTH

PLATE XVIII

Chapter LXXIV. **1.** The Chapter of lifting up the feet, and of coming forth on the earth. The Osiris

Ani saith:—Perform thy work, O Seker,[1] perform thy work O Seker, O thou who dwellest in thy circle,[2] and who dwellest in my feet **2.** in Khert-Neter. I am he who sendeth forth light over the Thigh of heaven. I come forth in heaven. I sit down by the Light-god (Khu). **3.** O I am helpless. O I am helpless. I would walk. I am helpless. I am helpless in the regions of those who plunder in Khert-Neter, I the Osiris Ani, whose word is truth, in peace.

CHAPTER VIII

THE CHAPTER OF MAKING A WAY THROUGH ȦMENTET BY DAY

PLATE XVIII

CHAPTER VIII. **1.** THE CHAPTER OF FORCING A WAY INTO ȦMENTET [AND OF COMING FORTH] BY DAY. The Osiris Ani saith:—The town of Unu (Hermopolis) is opened.

[1] Or Sekri, *i.e.*, he who is shut up dead in his coffin or shrine. Seker, a very ancient god, was death personified, and his kingdom was situated under, or beyond, that part of the left bank of the Nile which lay a little to the south of Memphis. The name of this Death-god is probably preserved in the modern place-name of Ṣaḳḳârah. The attributes of Seker were ascribed to Osiris, who was in many respects the counterpart of the older god.

[2] The Egyptian Ṭuat was divided into a number of "circles," which were inhabited by different grades of Spirits.

My head **2.** is sealed up, Thoth. Perfect is the Eye of Horus. I have delivered the Eye of Horus which shineth with splendours on the brow of Rā, **3.** the Father of the gods, [I am] that self-same Osiris, [the dweller in] Åmentet. Osiris knoweth his day, and he knoweth that he shall live through his period of life ; I shall have my being with him. **4.** I am the Moon-god Åāḥ, the dweller among the gods. I shall not come to an end. Stand up therefore, O Horus, for thou art counted among the gods.

The following version (Naville, *op. cit.*, I, Bl. X) of the above Chapter explains many of the difficulties which are found in the text of the Papyrus of Ani :—

CHAPTERS VIII AND IX. 1.

CHAPTERS VIII AND IX. **1.** THE CHAPTER OF FORCING A WAY INTO THE ṬUAT. The Åm Khent priest Nefer-uben-f, whose word is truth, **2.** saith :—Hail, Soul, thou mighty one of terror. Behold, I have come unto thee. I see thee. I have forced a way through the Ṭuat. I see my father Osiris. I drive away **3.** the darkness. I love him. I have come. I see my father Osiris. He hath counted the heart of Set. [I] have made offerings for my father Osiris. I have opened 4. all the ways in heaven and on earth. I love him. I have come. I have become a Spirit-body and a Spirit-soul, who is equipped. Hail, every god and every Spirit-soul, I have made the ways. I am Thoth 5. . . . . .

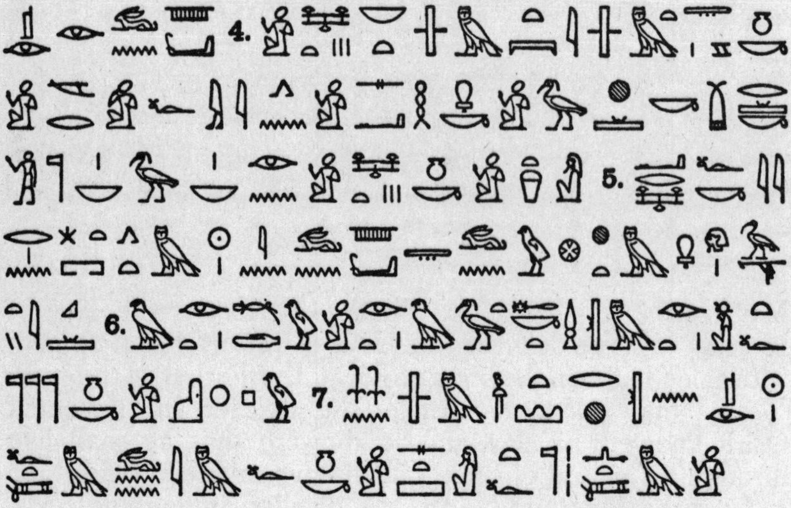

ANOTHER CHAPTER OF THE ṬUAT AND OF COMING FORTH BY DAY.

Open is the land of Unu. Shut is the head of Thoth. Perfect is 6. the Eye of Horus. I have delivered the Eye of Horus, the shining one, the ornament of the Eye of Rā, the Father of the Gods. I am that same Osiris who 7. dwelleth in Åmentet. Osiris knoweth his day, which cometh to an end. I am Set, the Father of the Gods. I shall never come to an end.

CHAPTER II

THE CHAPTER OF COMING FORTH BY DAY, AND OF LIVING AFTER DEATH

PLATE XVIII

CHAPTER II. **1.** THE CHAPTER OF COMING FORTH BY DAY AND OF LIVING AFTER DEATH. The Osiris Ani saith:—Hail, thou One, who shinest from the moon. **2.** Hail, thou One, who shinest from the moon. Grant that this Osiris Ani may come forth among thy multitudes who are at **3.** the portal. Let him be with the Light-God. Let the Ṭuat be opened to him. Behold, the Osiris **4.** Ani shall come forth by day to perform everything which he wisheth upon the earth among those who are living [thereon].

In the Papyrus of Åmen-neb in the British Museum (see Naville, *op. cit.*, I, Bl. 6) the above Chapter forms part of the composition which is commonly called Chapter III. The contents of this Chapter, translated from the Papyrus of Nu (Sheet 13), are as follows:—

2. Hail, thou god Tem, who comest forth from the Great Deep, who shinest gloriously under the form of the twin Lion-gods,[1] send forth with might thy words unto

[1] *I.e.*, Shu and Tefnut.

those who are in thy presence, 3. and let the Osiris Nu enter into their assembly. He hath performed the decree which hath been spoken to the mariners at eventide, 4. and the Osiris Nu, whose word is truth, shall live after his death, even as doth Rā every day. Behold, most certainly Rā was born 5. yesterday, and the Osiris Nu was born yesterday. And every god shall rejoice in the life of the Osiris Nu, even as they rejoice 6. in the life of Ptaḥ, when he appeareth from the Great House of the Aged One which is in Ȧnu (Heliopolis).

The text reads :

CHAPTER IX

THE CHAPTER OF COMING FORTH BY DAY AFTER PASSING THROUGH THE ÅAMḤET

PLATE XVIII

CHAPTER IX. 1. THE CHAPTER OF COMING FORTH BY DAY AFTER FORCING AN ENTRANCE THROUGH THE ÅAMḤET.[1] The Osiris Ani saith:—Hail, Soul, thou mighty one of terror! 2. Verily, I am here. I have come. I behold thee. I have passed through the Ṭuat. I have seen 3. Father Osiris. I have scattered the gloom of night. I am his beloved one. I have come, I have seen 4. my Father Osiris. I have stabbed the heart of Suti. I have made offerings to my Father Osiris. 5. I have opened every way in heaven and on the earth. I am the son who loveth his Fathers (*sic*) Osiris. 6. I am a Spirit-body. I am a Spirit-soul. I am equipped. Hail, every god and every Spirit-soul. I have made the way [to Osiris]. I the Osiris the scribe Ani, whose word is truth.

[1] A chamber in the domain of Seker, the god of Death.

CHAPTER CXXXII

THE CHAPTER OF MAKING A MAN TO RETURN TO LOOK UPON HIS HOUSE ON EARTH

PLATE XVIII

CHAPTER CXXXII. 1. THE CHAPTER OF MAKING A MAN TO RETURN TO LOOK UPON HIS HOUSE ON EARTH. The Osiris Ani saith :—I am the Lion-god 2. who cometh forth with long strides. I have shot arrows, and I have wounded my prey. I have shot arrows, and I have wounded my prey. I am the Eye of Horus, I traverse 3. the Eye of Horus at this season. I have arrived at the domains. Grant that the Osiris Ani may come in peace. [I have advanced, and behold, I have not been found light in weight, and the Balance is emptied of my case.]

The words within brackets are translated from a papyrus at Paris (Naville, *op. cit.*, Bl. 145), and the text of the passage reads :

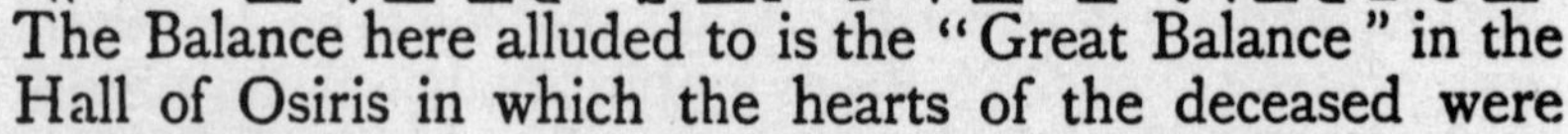

The Balance here alluded to is the "Great Balance" in the Hall of Osiris in which the hearts of the deceased were weighed in the presence of the god, but it is difficult to see the connection between the object with which this Chapter was written, and the words here added. In the Turin Papyrus they are wholly wanting.

CHAPTER X OR XLVIII[1]

ANOTHER CHAPTER OF A MAN COMING FORTH BY DAY AGAINST HIS ENEMIES IN KHERT-NETER

PLATE XVIII

1. ... 2. ... 3. ... 4. ...

CHAPTER X OR XLVIII. 1. ANOTHER CHAPTER OF THE COMING FORTH OF A MAN BY DAY AGAINST HIS ENEMIES IN KHERT-NETER. [The Osiris Ani saith :—] I have divided the heavens. I have 2. cleft the horizon. I have traversed the earth [following in] his footsteps. I have conquered the mighty Spirit-souls because 3. I am equipped for millions of years with words of power. I eat with my mouth. I evacuate with my body. 4. Behold, I am the God of the Ṭuat! Let these things be given unto me, the Osiris Ani, in perpetuity without fail or diminution.

The text of this Chapter in the Papyrus of Nebseni contains some interesting variants ; it reads :—

[1] The Chapter occurs twice in the Turin Papyrus.

The Eleventh Chapter has a title similar to that of Chapter X, but its contents are different; the Turin Papyrus contains two copies of it (Chapters XI and XLIX). The text as given in the Papyrus of Nu (Sheet 21) reads :—

Chapter XI or XLIX. **1.** The Chapter of coming forth against enemies in Khert-Neter. The Osiris Nu saith :—**2.** Hail, Ām-ā-f (*i.e.*, Eater of his arm), I have passed over (?) the road. I am Rā. I have come forth from the horizon against my enemies. I have not permitted him to escape **3.** from me. I have stretched out my hand like that of the Lord of the Urrt Crown. I have lifted up my feet even as the Uraei-goddesses lift themselves up. I have not permitted the enemy [to be saved] from me. **4.** As for mine enemy, he hath been given to me, and he shall not be delivered from me. I stand up like Horus. I sit down like Ptaḥ. I am strong like Thoth. **5.** I am mighty like Tem. I walk with my legs. I speak with my mouth. I chase my enemy. He hath been given unto me, and he shall not be delivered from me.

CHAPTER XV

A HYMN OF PRAISE [TO BE SUNG] TO RĀ WHEN HE RISETH ON THE HORIZON, [AND] WHEN HE SETTETH IN THE [LAND OF] LIFE

PLATE XIX

CHAPTER XV. **1.** A HYMN OF PRAISE TO RĀ WHEN HE RISETH UPON THE HORIZON, AND WHEN HE SETTETH IN THE LAND OF LIFE. Osiris the scribe Ani saith:—Homage to thee, **2.** O Rā, when thou risest as Tem-Ḥeru-Khuti. Thou art to be adored. Thy beauties are before mine eyes, [thy] **3.** radiance is upon my body. Thou goest forth to thy setting in the Sektet Boat with

[fair] winds, and thy heart is glad; **4.** the heart of the Māṭet Boat rejoiceth. Thou stridest over the heavens in peace, and all thy foes are cast down; the stars which never rest **5.** sing hymns of praise unto thee, and the stars which are imperishable glorify thee as thou **6.** sinkest to rest in the horizon of Manu, O thou who art beautiful at morn and at eve, O thou lord who livest, and art established, O my Lord!

Homage to thee, O thou who art Rā when thou risest, **7.** and who art Tem when thou settest in beauty. Thou risest and thou shinest on the back of thy mother [Nut], O thou who art crowned the king **8.** of the gods! Nut welcometh thee, and payeth homage unto thee, and Maāt, the everlasting and never-changing goddess, embraceth thee at noon and at eve. Thou stridest over the heavens, being glad at heart, and the Lake of Ṭesṭes,[1] **9.** is content. The Sebȧu-fiend hath fallen to the ground, his fore-legs and his hind-legs have been hacked off him, and the knife hath severed the joints of his back. Rā hath

[1] The Oases region in the Western Desert.

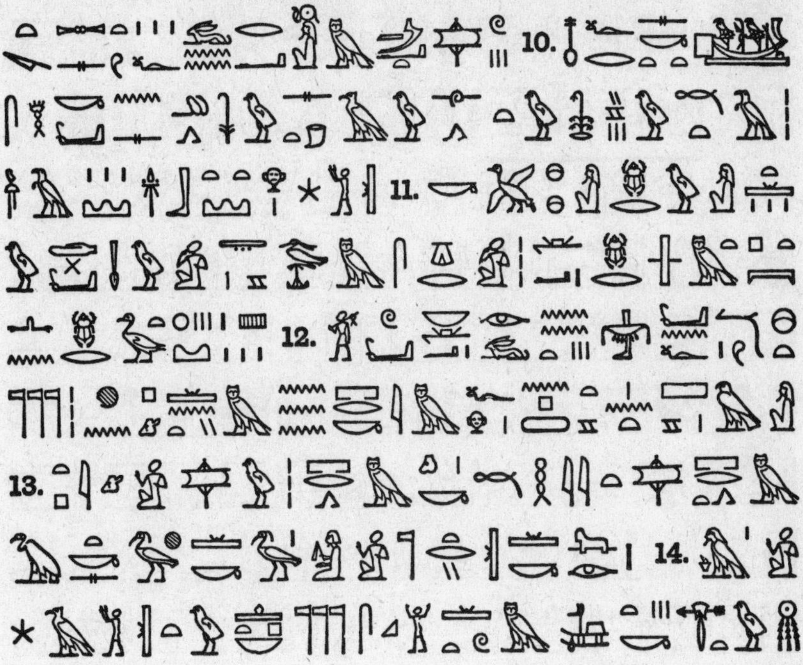

a fair wind, **10.** and the Sektet Boat setteth out on its journey, and saileth on until it cometh into port. The gods of the South, the gods of the North, the gods of the West, and the gods of the East praise **11.** thee, O thou Divine Substance, from whom all living things came into being. Thou didst send forth the word when the earth was submerged with silence, O thou Only One, who didst dwell in heaven before ever the earth and the mountains came into being. **12.** Hail, thou Runner, Lord, Only One, thou maker of the things that are, thou hast fashioned the tongue of the Company of the Gods, thou hast produced whatsoever cometh forth from the waters, thou springest up out of them above the submerged land of the Lake of Horus. **13.** Let me breathe the air which cometh forth from thy nostrils, and the north wind which cometh forth from thy mother Nut. Make thou my Spirit-soul to be glorious, O Osiris, **14.** make thou my Heart-soul to be divine. Thou art worshipped as thou settest, O Lord of the gods, thou art exalted by reason of thy wondrous works. Shine thou with thy rays of light upon my body day by day, **15.** upon me, Osiris the scribe, the assessor of the divine offerings of all the gods, the overseer of the granary of the Lords of Abydos, the real royal scribe who loveth thee, Ani, whose word is truth, in peace.

1. Praise be unto thee, O Osiris, the Lord of Eternity, Un-Nefer, Ḥeru-Khuti (Harmakhis), whose forms are manifold, whose attributes are majestic [Praise be unto thee], **2.** O thou who art Ptaḥ-Seker-Tem in Ȧnu (Heliopolis), thou Lord of the hidden shrine, thou Creator of the House of the Ka of Ptaḥ (Ḥet-ka-Ptaḥ = Memphis) and of the gods [therein], thou Guide of the Ṭuat, **3.** who art glorified when thou settest in Nu (*i.e.*, the Sky). Isis embraceth thee in peace, and she driveth away the fiends from the entrances **4.** of thy paths. Thou turnest thy face towards Ȧmentet, and thou makest the earth to shine as with refined copper. Those who have lain down in death rise up to see thee, they **5.** breathe the air, and they look upon thy face when the disk riseth on the horizon. Their hearts are at peace since they behold thee, O thou who art Eternity and Everlastingness.

Litany.

1. *Address.*—Homage to you, O ye gods of the Dekans in Ȧnu, and to you, O ye Ḥememet-spirits in Kher Āḥa, and to thee, O Unti,[1] who art the most glorious of all the gods who are hidden in Ȧnu,

Petition.—O grant thou unto me a path whereover I may pass in peace, for I am just and true; I have not spoken falsehood wittingly, nor have I done aught with deceit.

2. *Address.*—Homage to thee, O Ȧn[2] in Ȧntes(?), Ḥeru-khuti, who dost with long strides march across the heavens,

Petition.—O grant thou unto me a path whereover I may pass in peace, for I am just and true; I have not spoken falsehood wittingly, nor have I done aught with deceit.

3. *Address.*—Homage to thee, O Everlasting Soul, thou Soul who dwellest in Ṭeṭu (Busiris), Un-Nefer, the son of Nut, who art the Lord of Ȧḳert,

Petition.—O grant thou unto me a path whereover I may pass in peace, for I am just and true; I have not

[1] A god who is represented holding a star in each hand, and walking before a solar bark.

[2] A solar god of great antiquity, who was worshipped in Heliopolis.

4.

5.

6.

spoken falsehood wittingly, nor have I done aught with deceit.

4. *Address.*—Homage to thee in thy dominion over Ṭeṭu, upon whose brow the Urrt Crown is established, thou One who createst the strength to protect thyself, and who dwellest in peace,

Petition.—O grant thou unto me a path whereover I may pass in peace, for I am just and true; I have not spoken falsehood wittingly, nor have I done aught with deceit.

5. *Address.*—Homage to thee, O Lord of the Acacia Tree, whose Seker Boat is set upon its sledge, who turnest back the Fiend, the Evildoer, and dost cause the Eye of Rā (*utchat*) to rest upon its seat,

Petition.—O grant thou unto me a path whereover I may pass in peace, for I am just and true; I have not spoken falsehood wittingly, nor have I done aught with deceit.

6. *Address.*—Homage to thee, O thou who art mighty in thine hour, thou great and mighty Prince who dost dwell in Ȧnruṭef, thou Lord of Eternity and Creator of the Everlastingness, thou Lord of Ḥensu (Herakleopolis),

Petition.—O grant thou unto me a path whereover I may pass in peace, for I am just and true; I have not spoken falsehood wittingly, nor have I done aught with deceit.

7.

8.

9.

7. *Address.*—Homage to thee, O thou who restest upon Truth, thou Lord of Abṭu (Abydos), whose limbs form the substance of Ta-tchesert,[1] unto whom fraud and deceit are abominations,

Petition.—O grant thou unto me a path whereover I may pass in peace, for I am just and true; I have not spoken falsehood wittingly, nor have I done aught with deceit.

8. *Address.*—Homage to thee, O thou who dwellest in thy boat, who dost bring Ḥāpi (the Nile) forth from his cavern, whose body is the light, and who dwellest in Nekhen,[2]

Petition.—O grant thou unto me a path whereover I may pass in peace, for I am just and true; I have not spoken falsehood wittingly, nor have I done aught with deceit.

9. *Address.*—Homage to thee, O thou Creator of the gods, thou King of the South and North, Osiris, whose

[1] *I.e.*, the "Holy Land."

[2] A town in Upper Egypt, on part of the site of which stands the modern town of Al-Kâb. The chief deity of the place was the goddess Nekhebet, who was the protectress of the South *par excellence*. Her sanctuary was one of the oldest in Egypt. The Greeks called the town Eileithyiaspolis.

word is truth, who rulest the world by thy gracious goodness, thou Lord of the Âṭebui,[1]

Petition.[2]—O grant thou unto me a path whereover I may pass in peace, for I am just and true; I have not spoken falsehood wittingly, nor have I done aught with deceit.

In the Saïte Recension this Litany contains *ten* Addresses (ed. Lepsius, Bl. V), and the subject matter differs in many important particulars from that in the Litany of Ani. These Addresses read:—

1. Homage to thee, O thou who comest as Tem, who didst come into being to create the Company of the Gods.

2. Homage to thee, O thou who comest as the Soul of Souls, the Holy One in Âmentet.

3. Homage to thee, O President of the Gods, who illuminest the Ṭuat with thy beauties.

4. Homage to thee, O thou who comest as the Light-god, who travellest in thy Disk.

[1] A name given to the two series of corn lands which lay on the right and left banks of the Nile.

[2] This petition is written once only, but it was clearly intended to be repeated after each of the nine addresses. This is proved by the Saïte Recension where the words "Grant thou the sweet breath of the north wind," etc., are written in *two* places, and are intended to be said after each of the ten addresses above them.

5. Homage to thee, O thou greatest of all the gods, who art crowned King in heaven, Governor in the Ṭuat.

6. Homage to thee, O thou who makest a way through the Ṭuat, who dost lead the way through all doors.

7. Homage to thee, O thou who art among the gods, who dost weigh words (*i.e.*, judge actions) in Khert-Neter.

8. Homage to thee, O thou who dwellest in thy secret places, who dost fashion the Ṭuat with thy might (?).

9. Homage to thee, O great one, O mighty one, thine enemies have fallen in places where they were smitten.

10. Homage to thee, O thou who hast hacked the Sebȧu-fiends in pieces, and hast annihilated Āapep.

Grant thou the sweet breeze of the north wind to the Osiris Ȧuf-ānkh, whose word is truth.

CHAPTER XV

A HYMN OF PRAISE TO RĀ WHEN HE RISETH ON THE EASTERN HORIZON OF HEAVEN, AND TO THOSE WHO ARE IN HIS TRAIN

PLATES XX AND XXI

1. A Hymn of Praise to Rā when he riseth in the eastern part of heaven. **2.** Those who are in his following rejoice, and the Osiris, the scribe Ani, whose word is truth, saith :—Hail, thou Disk, thou lord of rays, **3.** who risest on the horizon day by day. Shine thou with thy beams of light upon the face of the Osiris Ani, whose word is truth, for he singeth hymns of praise to thee at **4.** dawn, and he maketh thee to sit at eventide [with words of adoration]. May the soul of the Osiris Ani, whose word is truth, come forth **5.** with thee into heaven! May he set out with thee in the Māṭet Boat [in the morning], may he come into port in the Sektet Boat [in the evening], and may he cleave his path among the stars **6.** of heaven which never rest.

The Osiris Ani, whose word is truth, being at peace [with his god], maketh adoration to his Lord, 7. the Lord of Eternity, and saith :—Homage to thee, O Ḥeru-khuti, who art the god Kheperȧ, the self-created. When thou risest on the 8. horizon and sheddest thy beams of light upon the Lands of the South and of the North, thou art beautiful, yea beautiful, and all the gods rejoice when they behold thee, 9. the king of heaven. The goddess, the Lady of the Hour,[1] is stablished upon thy head, her Uraei of the South and of the North are upon thy brow, 10. and she taketh up her place before thee. The god Thoth is stablished in the bows of thy boat to destroy utterly all thy foes. 11. Those who dwell in the Ṭuat come forth to meet thee, and they bow to the earth in homage as they come towards thee, to look upon thy 12. beautiful Form (or, Image). And I, Ani, have come into thy presence, so that I may be with thee, and may behold thy Disk every day. Let me not be kept

[1] Each hour of the night was under the protection of a goddess, and each goddess was responsible for the safety of the Boat of Rā for one hour, and she was called the "Lady of the Hour."

captive [by the tomb], and let me not be 13. turned back [on my way]. Let the members of my body be made new again when I contemplate thy beauties, even as are the members of all thy favoured ones, 14. because I am one of those who worshipped thee upon earth. Let me arrive in the Land of Eternity, let me enter into the 15. Land of Everlastingness. This, O my Lord, behold thou shalt ordain for me.

AND MOREOVER, THE OSIRIS ANI, WHOSE WORD IS TRUTH, IN PEACE, THE TRUTH-SPEAKER, SAITH:—16. Homage to thee, O thou who risest on thy horizon in the form of Rā, who restest upon Law, [which can neither be changed nor altered]. Thou passest over the sky, and every face, (*i.e.*, all mankind) watcheth thee 17. and thy course, for thou thyself art hidden from their gaze. Thou dost show thyself [to them] at dawn and at eventide each day. 18. The Sektet Boat, wherein Thy Majesty dwelleth, setteth forth on its journey with vigour. Thy beams [fall] upon all faces, thy light with its manifold colours is incomprehensible [to man], and thy brilliant 19. rays cannot be reported (or, told). The Lands of the Gods[1] see thee, they could write [concerning thee]; the Deserts of Punt[2] could count (or, estimate) **20.** thee. Thy creation is hidden. It is one by the opening of thy mouth. Thy form (?) is the head of Nu.[3] May he (*i.e.*, Ani) **21.** advance, even as thou dost advance, without cessation, even as Thy Majesty [ceaseth not to advance] even for a moment. With great strides **22.** thou dost in one little moment pass over limitless distances which would need millions and hundreds of thousands of years [for a man to pass over; this] thou doest, and then thou sinkest to rest. Thou bringest to an end **23.** the hours of the night, even as thou stridest (?) over them. Thou bringest them to an end by thine own ordinance, and dawn cometh on the earth. **24.** Thou settest thyself

[1] *I.e.*, the countries of the Eastern Sûdân and Arabia.

[2] The South-eastern Sûdân.

[3] This section of the hymn is very difficult to understand. The writer seems to mean that the work of creating the sun is a mystery, that it is, in fact, incomprehensible. The substance of the sun was, it seems, made living by means of the ceremony of "opening the mouth," which must have been performed by the god who made the sun. As this ceremony when performed on a dead body restored to it life, thought, and motion, so the same ceremony performed by Temu or Thoth made the sun to live, *i.e.*, to send out light and heat. The last words *kheperu tep Nu* may mean, "thy creations are (or, thy forms are) above Nu, or, on Nu."

before thy handiwork in the form of Rā, and thou rollest up on the horizon. **25.** . . . . Thou sendest forth light when thy form raiseth itself up, **26.** thou ordainest the increase of thy splendours (or, beauties). Thou mouldest thy limbs as thou advancest, thou bringest them forth, thou who wast never brought forth, in the form **27.** of Rā, who rolleth up into the height of heaven. Grant thou that I may reach the heaven of eternity, and the region where thy favoured ones dwell. May I unite with **28.** those holy and perfect Spirit-souls of Khert-Neter. May I come forth with them to behold thy beauties as thou rollest on **29.** at eventide, as thou journeyest to thy mother Nut (*i.e.*, the Night-sky), and dost place thyself at the right hand (*i.e.*, in the West). My two hands are raised to thee in praise and thanksgiving **30.** when thou settest in life (*i.e.*, as a living being, or in the Land of Life). Behold, thou art the Creator of Eternity (or Eternal Creator), who art adored when thou settest in Nu.[1] I have set thee in my heart, without **31.** wavering, O thou who art more divine than the gods.

[1] The Celestial Waters deified.

The Osiris Ani, whose word is truth, saith :—

Praise and thanksgiving be unto thee, O thou who rollest on 32. like unto gold, thou Illuminer of the Two Lands (*i.e.*, Egypt) on the day of thy birth. Thy mother brought thee forth on her hand, and thou didst light up with splendour the circle which is travelled over by the Disk. 33. O Great Light who rollest across Nu, thou dost raise (?) up the generations of men from the deep source of thy waters, and dost make to keep festivals all districts (or, lands) and cities, 34. and all habitations. Thou protectest [them] with thy beauties. Thy KA (*i.e.*, Double) riseth up with the celestial food *ḥu* and *tchefau*. O thou mightily victorious one, 35. thou Power of Powers, who makest strong thy throne against the sinful ones, whose risings on thy throne in the Sektet Boat are mighty, whose strength is widespread 36. in the Āṭett Boat, make thou the Osiris Ani to be glorious by virtue of his word, which is truth, in Khert-Neter. Grant thou that he may be in Āmentet

37. free from evil (or, sin), and let [his] offences be [set] behind thee. Grant thou that he may [live there] a devoted slave 38. of the Spirit-souls. Let him mingle among the Heart-souls who live in Ta-tchesert (the Holy Land). Let him travel about in the Sekhet-Åaru 39. (*i.e.*, the Field of Reeds, or the Elysian Fields), conformably to [thy] decree with joy of heart—him the Osiris Ani, whose word is truth.

[And the god maketh answer] :—

40. Thou shalt come forth into heaven, thou shalt sail over the sky, and thou shalt hold loving intercourse with the Star-gods. Praises shall be made 41. to thee in the Boat. Thy name shall be proclaimed in the Āṭett Boat. 42. Thou shalt look upon Rā within his shrine. Thou shalt make the Disk to set [with prayer] every day. Thou shalt see 43. the Ant Fish in his transformations in the depths of the waters of turquoise. Thou shalt see 44. the Åbṭu Fish in his time. It shall be that the Evil One shall fall when he

deviseth a plan to destroy thee, 45. and the joints of his neck and back shall be hacked asunder. Rā saileth with a fair wind, and the Sektet Boat progresseth 46. and cometh into port. The mariners of Rā rejoice, and the heart of the Lady of the Hour is glad, 47. for the enemy of her Lord hath been cast to the ground. Thou shalt behold Horus standing on the pilot's place in the Boat, and Thoth and Maāt shall stand one on each side of him. 48. All the gods shall rejoice when they behold Rā coming in peace 49. to make the hearts of the Spirit-souls to live, and the Osiris Ani, whose word is truth, the assessor of the holy offerings of the Lords of Thebes, shall be with them!

CHAPTER CXXXIII

[THE CHAPTER OF THE NEW MOON]

PLATE XXI

CHAPTER CXXXIII. 1. THE FOLLOWING IS TO BE RECITED ON THE DAY OF THE MONTH (*i.e.*, NEW MOON DAY). The Osiris the scribe Ani, whose word is truth, in peace, whose word is truth, saith :—Rā ascendeth his throne 2. on his horizon, and the Company of his Gods follow in his train. The God cometh forth from his hidden place, [and] *tchefau* food falleth (?) 3. from the eastern horizon of heaven at the word of Nut. They (*i.e.*, the gods) rejoice over the paths of Rā, the Great Ancestor 4. [as] he journeyeth round about. Therefore art thou exalted, O Rā, the dweller in thy Shrine. Thou swallowest the winds, thou drawest into thyself the north wind, 5. thou eatest up the flesh (?) of thy seat (?) on the day when thou breathest truth. Thou dividest [it among] the gods who are [thy] followers. 6. [Thy] Boat saileth on travelling among the Great Gods at thy word. Thou countest thy bones, thou gatherest together thy members, **7.** thou settest thy face towards Beautiful Åmentet, and thou comest there, being made new every day. Behold, thou art that Image of Gold, thou hast the **8.** unitings of the disks of the sky, thou hast quakings (or terrors), thou goest round about, and art made new each day. Hail! There is rejoicing **9.** in the horizon! The gods who dwell in the sky descend the ropes [of thy Boat] when they see **10.** the Osiris Ani, whose word is truth, they ascribe praise unto him as unto Rā. The Osiris Ani is a Great Chief. **11.** [He] seeketh the Urrt Crown. His provisions are apportioned to him—the Osiris Ani, whose word is truth. [His] fate is strong from the exalted body **12.** of the Åāmu gods, who are in the presence of Rā. The Osiris Ani, whose word is truth, is strong on the earth and in Khert-Neter. **13.** O Osiris Ani, whose word is truth, wake up (or keep watch), and be strong like unto Rā every day. The Osiris Ani, whose word is truth, shall not tarry, **14.** he shall not remain motionless in this land for ever. Right well shall he see with his two eyes, right well shall he hear with his two ears, the things which are true, the things which are true. **15.** The Osiris Ani, whose word is truth, is in Ȧnu (Heliopolis), the Osiris Ani, whose word is truth, is as Rā, and he is exalted by **16.** reason of [his] oars (or paddles) among the Followers of Nu. The Osiris Ani, whose word is truth, cannot tell what he hath seen **17.** [or] narrate [what he hath heard] in the House of the God of Mysteries. Hail! Let there be shouts of acclamation of the Osiris Ani, whose word is truth, **18.** the divine body of Rā in the Boat of Nu, who beareth propitiatory offerings for the KA of the god of that which he loveth. The Osiris **19.** Ani, whose word is truth, in peace, whose word is truth, is like Horus, the mighty one of transformations.

RUBRIC: 20. 21. 22. 23. 24. 25. 26.

RUBRIC: This Chapter is to be recited over a boat 20. seven cubits long, made of green stone (or faïence) of the Tchatchau. Make a heaven of stars, 21. and purify it and cleanse it with natron and incense. Make then a figure 22. of Rā upon a tablet of new stone in paint, and set it in the bows of 23. the boat. Then make a figure of the deceased whom thou wilt make perfect, [and place it] 24. in the boat. Make it to sail in the Boat of Rā, and 25. Rā himself shall look upon it. Do not these things in the presence of any one except thyself, 26. or thy father, or thy son. Then let them keep guard over their faces (*i.e.*, watch intently), and they shall see the deceased in Khert-Neter in the form of a messenger (or angel) of Rā.

CHAPTER CXXXIV

A HYMN TO RĀ FOR THE DAY OF THE NEW MOON

PLATE XXII

CHAPTER CXXXIV. 1. A HYMN TO RĀ [WHICH IS TO BE SUNG] ON THE DAY OF THE MONTH (*i.e.*, THE DAY OF THE NEW MOON) [WHEN] THE BOAT OF RĀ SAILETH. [The Osiris the scribe Ani, whose word is truth, saith :—] Homage to thee, O thou who dwellest in thy Boat. Thou rollest on, thou rollest on, 2. thou sendest forth light, thou sendest forth light. Thou decreest rejoicing for [every] man for millions of years unto those who love him. Thou givest [thy] face to the Ḥememet spirits, thou god Kheperȧ 3. who dwellest in thy Boat. Thou hast overthrown the Fiend Āapep. O ye Sons of Ḳeb, overthrow ye the enemies of the Osiris 4. Ani, whose word is truth, and the fiends of destruction who would destroy the Boat of Rā. Horus hath cut off 5. your heads in heaven. Ye who were in the forms of geese, your navel strings (?) are on the earth. The animals are set upon the earth . . . . .

in the form of fish.[1] Every male fiend 6. and every female fiend shall be destroyed by the Osiris Ani, whose word is truth. Whether the fiends descend from out of heaven, or whether they come forth 7. from the earth, or whether they advance on the waters, or whether they come from among the Star-gods, Thoth, [the son of Åner], 8. coming forth from Ånerti shall hack them to pieces. And the Osiris Ani shall make them silent and dumb. And behold ye, this god, the mighty one of slaughters, 9. the terror (or awe) of whom is most great, shall wash himself clean in your blood, and he shall bathe in your gore, and ye shall be destroyed 10. by the Osiris Ani in the Boat of his Lord Rā-Horus. 11. The heart of the Osiris Ani, whose word is truth, shall live. His mother Isis giveth birth to him,

[1] The allusion here is to the great fight which Horus fought on behalf of the Sun-god. He drove Set and his followers from place to place, and conquered them, but a number of them escaped, and took the form of birds, animals, reptiles, and fish, and attempted to destroy Horus and the boat in which he sailed over the river and canals of Egypt. Horus, however, snared and slew the birds in which the foes had made their dwellings, and the animals, and the creatures which were hostile to him in the waters.

and Nephthys nurseth him, 12. just as Isis gave birth to Horus, and Nephthys nursed him. [He] shall repulse the Smait fiends of Suti. They shall see 13. the Urrt Crown stablished upon his head, and they shall fall down upon their faces [and worship him]. Behold, O ye Spirit-souls, and men, 14. and gods, and ye dead, when ye see the Osiris Ani, whose word is truth, in the form of Horus, and the 15. favoured one of the Urrt Crown, fall ye down upon your faces. The word of the Osiris Ani is truth 16. before his enemies in heaven above, and on earth beneath, and before the Tchatchau Chiefs 17. of every god and of every goddess.

Rubric: This Chapter shall be recited over a large hawk standing upright with the White Crown upon his head, [and over figures of] Tem, 18. Shu, Tefnut, Ḳeb, Nut, Osiris, Isis, [Suti] and Nephthys. And they shall be painted in colour upon a 19. new tablet, which shall be placed in a boat, together with a figure of the deceased.

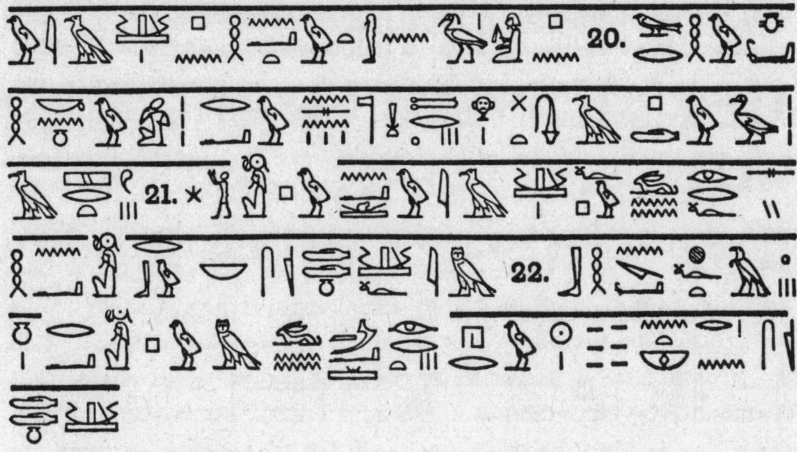

20. Anoint them with *ḥeken* oil, and offer unto them burning incense, and geese, and joints of meat roasted. 21. It is an act of praise to Rā as he journeyeth in his boat, and it will make a man to have his being with Rā, and to travel with him wheresoever he goeth, 22. and it will most certainly cause the enemies of Rā to be slain. And the Chapter of travelling shall be recited on the sixth day of the festival.

The Turin Papyrus contains another composition of a somewhat similar character, and a Rubric which is of interest in connection with the formulae which were recited on the day of the new moon; this composition forms Chapter CXXXV in the Saïte Recension, and reads :—

CHAPTER CXXXV. 1.

CHAPTER CXXXV. ANOTHER CHAPTER WHICH IS TO BE RECITED WHEN THE MOON RENEWETH ITSELF ON THE DAY OF THE MONTH [WHEREON IT DOETH THIS]. 1. Osiris unfettereth (or, as others say, openeth) the storm-cloud in the body of heaven, and is unfettered himself; Horus is made strong happily each day. He whose transformations are many hath had offerings made unto him at the moment, **2.** and he hath made an end of the storm which is in the face of the Osiris, Åuf-ānkh, whose word is truth. Verily, he cometh, and he is Rā in journeying, and he is the four celestial gods in the heavens above. The Osiris Åuf-ānkh, whose word is truth, cometh forth **3.** in his day, and he embarketh among the tackle of the boat.

RUBRIC: If this Chapter be known by the deceased he shall become a perfect Spirit-soul in Khert-Neter, and he shall not die a second time, and he shall eat his food side by side with Osiris. **4.** If this Chapter be known by the deceased upon earth, he shall become like unto Thoth, and he shall be adored by those who live. He shall not fall headlong at the moment of the intensity of the royal flame of the goddess Bast, and the Great Prince shall make him to advance happily.

CHAPTER XVIII[1]

PLATES XXIII AND XXIV

1. 2. 3. 4. 5. 6. 7. 8. 9. 10. 11. 12. 13.

[1] A duplicate copy, with an Introduction, is given on Plates XIII and XIV.

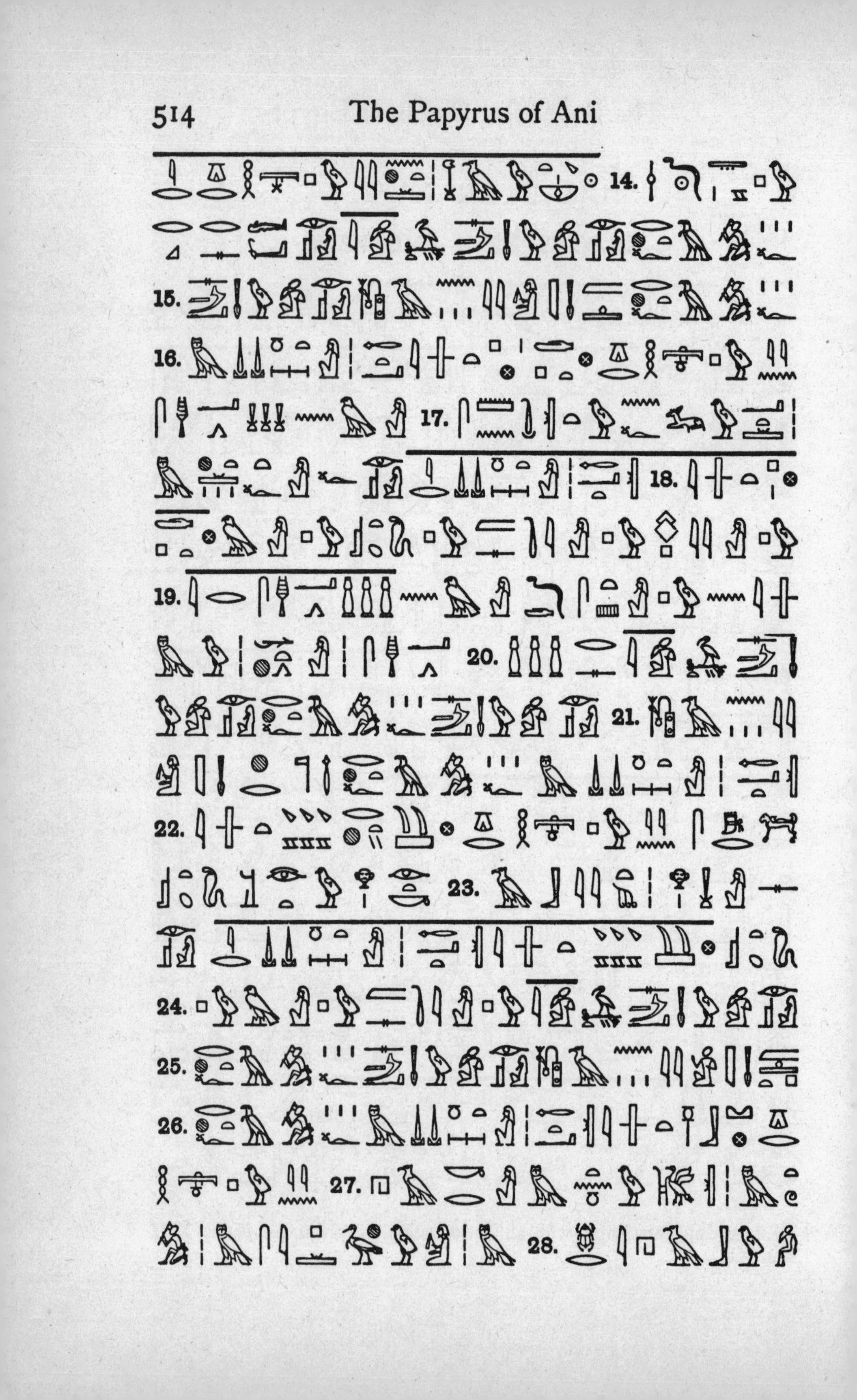

14.

15.

16.

17.

18.

19.

20.

21.

22.

23.

24.

25.

26.

27.

28.

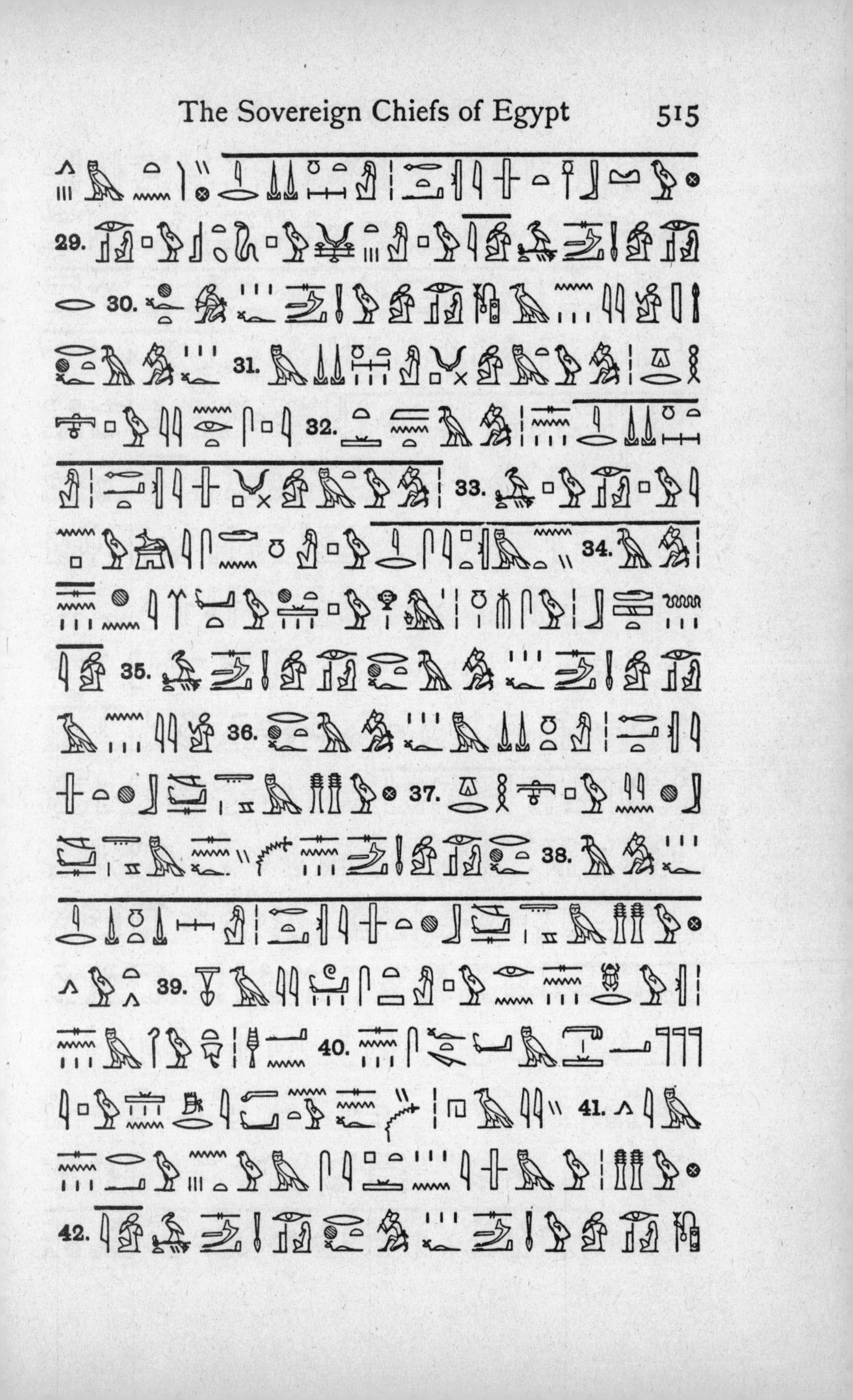

29.

30.

31.

32.

33.

34.

35.

36.

37.

38.

39.

40.

41.

42.

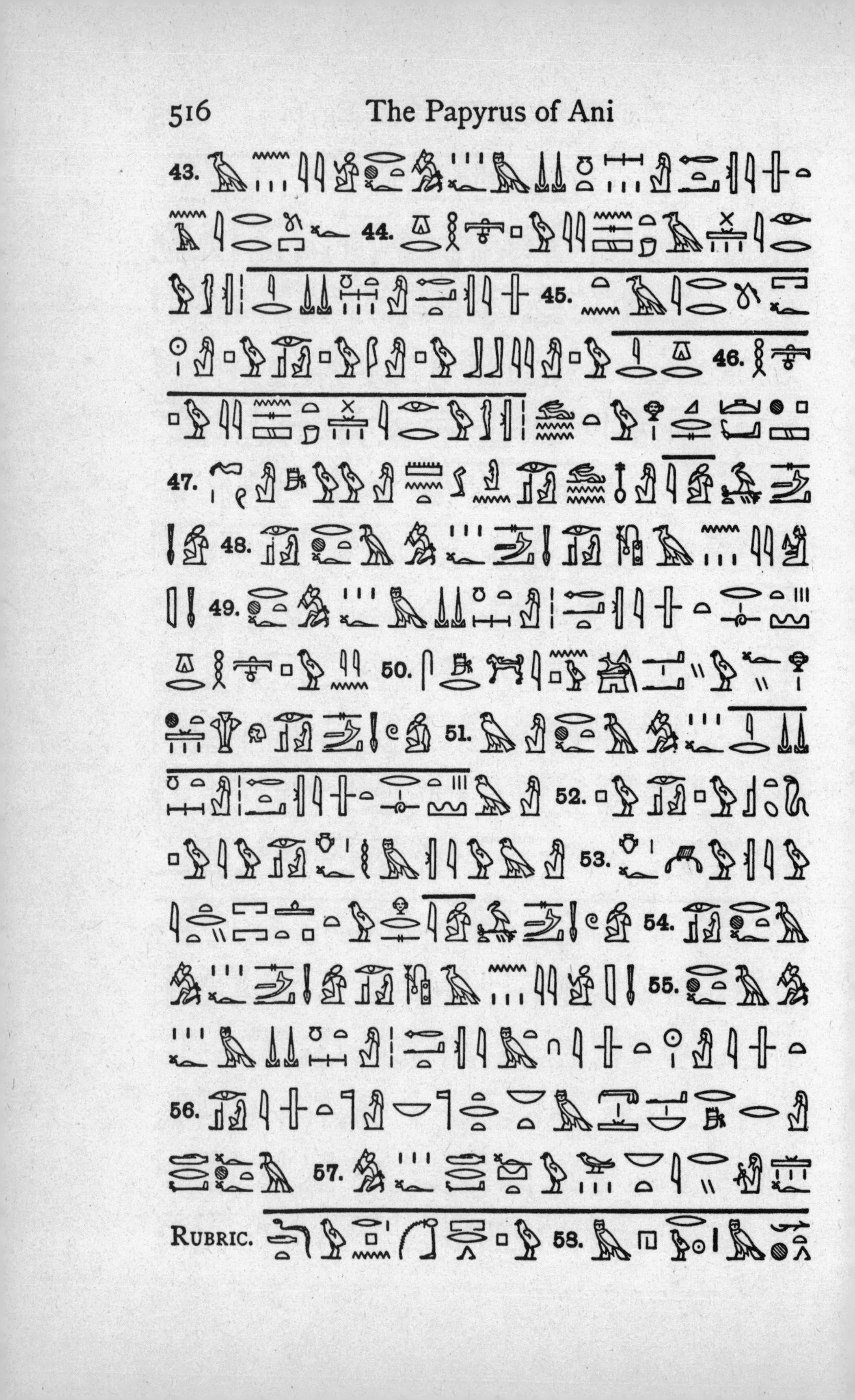

43.

44.

45.

46.

47.

48.

49.

50.

51.

52.

53.

54.

55.

56.

57.

Rubric. 58.

CHAPTER CXXIV

THE CHAPTER OF ADVANCING TO THE TCHATCHAU CHIEFS OF OSIRIS

PLATE XXIV

CHAPTER CXXIV. 1. THE CHAPTER OF ADVANCING TO THE TCHATCHAU CHIEFS OF OSIRIS. The Osiris Ani, whose word is truth, saith :—I have built a house for my Ba-soul 2. in the sanctuary in Ṭeṭu (Busiris). I sow seed in the town of Pe (Buto). I have ploughed the fields with

[1] The Rubric of this Chapter given in the Papyrus of Nebseni contains some interesting variants, and reads :—

my labourers. My palm tree 3. [standeth upright and is] like Menu[1] upon it. I abominate abominable things. I will not eat the things which are abominations unto me. What I abominate is filth: I will not eat it. 4. I shall not be destroyed by the offerings of propitiation and the sepulchral meals. I will not approach filth [to touch it] with my hands, I will not tread upon it with 5. my sandals. For my bread shall be made of the white barley (*dhura?*), and my ale shall be made from the red grain 6. of the god Ḥāpi (the Nile-god), which the Sektet Boat and the Āṭett Boat shall bring [unto me], and I will eat my food 7. under the leaves of the trees whose beautiful arms (*i.e.*, branches) I myself do know. 8. O what splendour shall the White Crown make for me which shall be lifted up on me by the Uraei-goddesses! 9. O Doorkeeper of Seḥetep-taui, bring thou to me that wherewith the cakes

[1] A god of generation and fertility. He is represented in the form of an upright mummy, ithyphallic, with plumes on his head, and one arm and hand raised upon a whip,

of propitiation are made. Grant thou to me that I may **10.** lift up the earth. May the Spirit-souls open to me [their] arms, and let the Company of the Gods hold their peace **11.** whilst the Ḥememet spirits hold converse with the Osiris Ani. May the hearts **12.** of the gods lead him in his exalted state into heaven among the gods who appear in visible forms. **13.** If any god, or any goddess, attack the Osiris Ani, whose word is truth, when he setteth out, the Ancestor of the year who liveth upon hearts **14.** [Osiris] shall eat him when he cometh forth from Abydos, and the Ancestors of Rā shall reckon with him, and the Ancestors of Light shall reckon with him. **15.** [He is] a god of splendour [arrayed in] the apparel of heaven, and he is among the Great Gods. Now the subsistence of the Osiris Ani, whose word is truth, **16.** is among the cakes and the ale which are made for your mouths. I enter in by the Disk, I come forth by the god Åḥui. I shall hold converse with the Followers **17.** of the Gods. I shall hold converse with the Disk. I shall hold converse with the Ḥememet-spirits. He shall set the terror of me in the thick **18.** darkness (*i.e.*, the outer darkness), in the inside of the goddess Meḥurt, by the side of his forehead. Behold, I shall be with Osiris, and my **19.** perfection shall be his perfection among the Great Gods. I shall speak unto him with the words of men, I shall listen, **20.** and he shall repeat to me the words of the gods. I, the Osiris Ani, whose word is truth, in peace, have come equipped. Thou makest to approach [thee] **21.** those who love thee. I am a Spirit-soul who is better equipped than any [other] Spirit-soul.[2]

[1] The Saïte Recension adds :

[2] In the Saïte Recension there is an allusion to the Spirit-bodies which are in Ȧnu (Heliopolis), Ṭeṭu (Busiris), Ḥensu (Herakleopolis), Abṭu (Abydos), Ȧpu (Panopolis) and Senu, a town near Panopolis. The Chapter ends with the words, "The Osiris Ȧuf-ānkh, the son of Sheret-"Menu, whose word is true, is triumphant before every god and every "goddess who are hidden in Khert-Neter."

CHAPTER LXXXVI

THE CHAPTER OF CHANGING INTO A SWALLOW

PLATE XXV

HERE BEGIN THE CHAPTERS OF MAKING TRANSFORMATIONS

CHAPTER LXXXVI. 1. THE CHAPTER OF MAKING THE TRANSFORMATION INTO A SWALLOW. 2. The Osiris Ani, whose word is truth, saith:—I am a swallow, [I am] a swallow. [I am] that Scorpion, 3. the daughter of Rā. Hail, O ye gods whose odour is sweet. Hail, O ye gods whose odour is sweet. Hail, Flame, who comest forth from 4. the horizon. Hail, thou who art in the city. I have brought the Warder of his corner there. Give me thy 5. two hands, and let me pass my time in the Island of Flame. I have advanced with a message, I have come having the report thereof [to make]. Open to me. 6. How shall I tell that which I have seen there? I am like Horus, the governor of the Boat, when the throne of his father was given unto him, and when Set, that son of

Nut, was [lying] under the fetters 7. which he had made for Osiris. He who is in Sekhem hath inspected me. I stretch out my arms over Osiris. I have advanced for the examination, 8. I have come to speak there. Let me pass on and deliver my message. I am he who goeth in, [I am] judged, [I] come forth magnified 9. at the Gate of Nebertcher. I am purified at the Great *Uārt*.[1] I have done away my wickednesses. 10. I have put away utterly my offences (or, sins). I have put away utterly all the taints of evil which appertained to me [upon the earth]. I have purified myself, 11. I have made myself to be like a god. Hail, O ye Doorkeepers, I have completed my journey. I am like unto you. I have come forth by day. I have advanced on my legs. I have gained the mastery over [my] footsteps. [Hail, ye] 12. Spirit-souls! I, even I, do know the hidden roads and the Gates of Sekhet Åaru.

[1] Probably the Uārt of Abydos, where the worshippers of Osiris placed their offerings for transmission to the kingdom of the god in Sekhet Åaru.

I live 13. there. Verily, I, even I, have come, I have overthrown my enemies upon the earth, although my body lieth a mummy in the tomb.

In several papyri this Chapter has a Rubric (Naville, *op. cit.*, II, Bl. 202) which reads: If this Chapter be known by the deceased, he shall enter in after he hath come forth by day. In the Saïte Recension the Rubric reads:—

If this Book be known by the deceased, he shall come forth by day from Khert-Neter, and he shall go in [again] after he hath come forth. If this Chapter be not known [by the deceased], he shall not go in again after he hath come forth [and he] shall not know [how] to come forth by day.

CHAPTER LXXVII

THE CHAPTER OF CHANGING INTO A HAWK OF GOLD

PLATE XXV

CHAPTER LXXVII. 1. [THE CHAPTER] OF MAKING THE TRANSFORMATION INTO A HAWK OF GOLD. The Osiris Ani saith:—2. I have risen up out of the *seshett* chamber, like the golden hawk 3. which cometh forth from his egg. I fly, I alight (or, flutter in the air) like a hawk with a back of 4. seven cubits, and the wings of which are like unto the mother-of-emerald of the South. I have come forth from the Sektet Boat, 5. and my heart hath been brought unto me from the mountain of the East. I have alighted on the Āṭet Boat, and there have been brought unto me those who dwelt in 6. their substance (?), and they bowed in homage before me. I have risen, I have gathered myself together 7. like a beautiful golden hawk, with the head of the Benu (phoenix ?), and Rā hath entered in [to hear my speech]. I have taken my seat among 8. the great gods, [the children of] Nut. I have settled myself, the Sekhet-ḥetepet (*i.e.*, the Field of Offerings) is before me. I eat therein, 9. I become a Spirit-soul therein, I am supplied with food in abundance therein, as much as I desire. The Grain-god (Nepra̓) hath given unto me food for my throat, and I am master over myself and over the attributes of my head.

CHAPTER LXXVIII

THE CHAPTER OF CHANGING INTO A DIVINE HAWK

PLATES XXV AND XXVI

CHAPTER LXXVIII. 1. [THE CHAPTER OF] MAKING THE TRANSFORMATION INTO A DIVINE HAWK. The Osiris Ani saith:—2. Hail, thou Great God, come thou to Ṭeṭu (Busiris). Make thou ready for me the ways, and let me go round [to visit] my 3. thrones. I have laboured. I have made myself perfect. O grant thou that I may be held in fear. 4. Create thou awe of me. Let the gods of the Ṭuat be afraid of me, and let them fight for me 5. in their halls. Permit not thou to come nigh unto me him that would attack me, or would injure me in the House of Darkness. 6. Cover over the helpless one, hide him. Let do likewise the gods who hearken unto the word [of truth], the Khep[r]iu gods 7. who are in the following of Osiris. Hold ye your peace then, O ye gods, whilst the God holdeth speech with me, he who listeneth to the truth. **8.** I speak unto him my words. Osiris, grant thou that that which cometh forth from thy mouth may circulate to me. Let me see thine own Form. **9.** Let thy Souls envelop me. Grant thou that I may come forth, and that I may be master of my legs, and let me live there like Nebertcher upon **10.** his throne. Let the gods of the Ṭuat hold me in fear, and let them fight for me in their halls. Grant thou that I may move forward with him and with **11.** the Āriu gods, and let me be firmly stablished on my pedestal like the Lord of Life. Let me be in the company of Isis, the goddess, and let [the gods] keep me safe **12.** from him that would do an injury unto me. Let none come to see the helpless one. May I advance, **13.** and may I come to the Ḥenti boundaries of the sky. Let me address words to Ḳeb, and let me make supplication to the god Ḥu 14. with Nebertcher. Let the gods of the Ṭuat be afraid of me, and let them fight for me in their halls. Let them see that thou hast 15. provided me with food for the festival. I am one of those Spirit-souls who dwell in the Light-god. I have made 16. my form in his Form, when he cometh to Ṭeṭu (Busiris). I am a Spirit-body among his 17. Spirit-bodies; he shall speak unto thee the things [which concern] me. Would that he would cause me to be held in fear! Would that he would create [in them] awe of me! Let the gods of the Ṭuat be afraid of me, 18. and let them fight for me [in their halls]. I, even I, am a Spirit-soul, a dweller in the Light-god, whose form hath been created 19. in divine flesh. I am one of those Spirit-souls who dwell in the Light-god, who were created 20. by Tem himself, and who exist in the blossoms (*i.e.*, eyelashes) of his Eye. He hath made to exist, he hath made glorious, and he hath magnified (or, made distinguished) their faces during their existence with him. **21.** Behold, he is Alone in Nu. They acclaim him when he cometh forth from the horizon, and the gods **22.** and the Spirit-souls who have come into being with him ascribe fear unto him.

I am one of the worms which have been created by the Eye of the Lord One. And behold, **23.** when as yet Isis had not given birth to Horus, I was flourishing, and I had waxed old, and had become pre-eminent **24.** among the Spirit-souls who had come into being with him. I rose up like a divine **25.** hawk, and Horus endowed me with a Spirit-body with his soul, so that [I] might take possession of the property of Osiris in the Ṭuat. He shall say to the twin Lion-gods **26.** for me, the Chief of the House of the Nemes Crown (or bandlet), the Dweller in his cavern :

Get thee back to the heights of heaven, for behold, inasmuch as thou 27. art a Spirit-body with the creations of Horus, the Nemes Crown shall not be to thee: [but] thou shalt have speech even to the uttermost limits 28. of the heavens. I, the warder, took possession of the property of Horus [which belonged] to Osiris in the Ṭuat, and Horus repeated to me 29. what his father Osiris had said unto him in the years [past], on the days of his burial. Give thou to me the Nemes Crown, say the twin Lion-gods 30. for me. Advance thou, come along the road of heaven, and look upon those who dwell in the uttermost limits of the horizon. The gods of the Ṭuat 31. shall hold thee in fear, and they shall fight for thee in their halls. The god Àuheṭ[1] belongeth to them (?). All the gods who guard the shrine of the Lord One 32. are smitten with terror at [my] words.

[1] Variants

Hail, saith the god who is exalted upon his coffer to me! He hath bound on the Nemes Crown, 33. [by] the decree of the twin Lion-gods. The god Åaheṭ hath made a way for me. I am exalted [on my coffer], the twin Lion-gods have bound the Nemes Crown on me 34. and my two locks (?) of hair are given unto me. He hath stablished for me my heart by his own flesh (?), and by his great, two-fold strength, and I shall not fall headlong 35. before Shu. I am Ḥetep, the Lord of the two Uraei-goddesses who are to be adored. I know the Light-god, 36. his winds are in my body. The Bull which striketh terror [into souls] shall not repulse me. I come daily into the House of the twin Lion-gods. 37. I come forth therefrom into the House of Isis. I look upon the holy things which are hidden. I am guided to 38. the holy things which are hidden. I see the being who is therein. I speak to the great ones of Shu, they repulse him that is wrathful in his hour. 39. I am

Horus who dwelleth in his divine Light. I am master of his crown (or tiara). I am master of **40.** his radiance. I advance towards the Ḥenti boundaries of heaven. Horus is upon his seat. Horus is upon his thrones. **41.** My face is like that of a divine hawk. I am one who is equipped [like] his lord. I shall come forth to Ṭeṭu (Busiris). I shall see Osiris. I shall live **42.** in his actual presence . . . . Nut. They shall see me. I shall see the gods [and] the Eye of Horus burning with fire before my eyes (?). **43.** They shall reach out their hands to me. I shall stand up. I shall be master of him that would subject me to restraint. They shall open the holy paths **44.** to me, they shall see my form, they shall listen to my words.

[Homage] to you, O ye gods of the Ṭuat, whose faces are turned back, whose **45.** powers advance, conduct ye me to the Star-gods which never rest. Prepare ye for me the holy ways to the Ḥemat house, and to your **46.** god, the Soul, who is the mighty one of terror (or awe). Horus hath commanded me to lift up your faces; do ye look upon **47.** me. I have risen up like a divine hawk. Horus hath made me to be a Spirit-body by means of his **48.** Soul, and to take possession of the things of Osiris in the Ṭuat. Make ye for me a path. I have travelled and I have arrived at those who are chiefs of their caverns (or, shrines), and who are guardians **49.** of the House of Osiris. I speak unto them his mighty deeds. I make them to know concerning his victories. He is ready [to butt with his] two horns at Set. They know **50.** him who hath taken possession of the god Ḥu, and who hath taken possession of the Powers of Tem.

Travel thou on thy way safely, cry out the gods **51.** of the Ṭuat to me. O ye who make your names pre-eminent, who are chiefs in your shrines, and who are guardians of the House of Osiris, grant, I pray you, **52.** that I may come to you. I have bound up and I have gathered together your Powers. I have directed the Powers of the ways, the wardens of the horizon, 53. and of the Ḥemat House of heaven. I have stablished their fortresses for Osiris. I have prepared the ways for him. I have performed the things which [he] hath commanded. I come forth 54. to Ṭeṭu (Busiris). I see Osiris. I speak to him concerning the matter of his Great Son, whom he loveth, and concerning [the smiting of] the heart of 55. Set. I look upon the lord who was helpless. How shall I make them to know the plans of the gods, and that which Horus did 56. without the knowledge of his father Osiris?

Hail, Lord, thou Soul, most awful and terrible, behold me. I have 57. come, I make thee to be exalted! I have forced a way through the Ṭuat. I have opened the roads which appertain 58. to heaven, and those which appertain to the earth, and no one hath opposed me therein. I have exalted thy face, O Lord of Eternity. [Exalted art thou on thy throne, O Osiris! Thou hast heard fair things, O Osiris! Thy strength is vigorous, O Osiris Thy head is fastened on thy body, O Osiris! Thy neck is made firm, O Osiris! Thy heart is glad, [O Osiris!]. Thy speech is made effective, O Osiris! Thy princes rejoice Thou art established the Bull in Åmentet. Thy son Horus hath ascended thy throne, and all life is with him. Millions of years minister unto him, and millions of years hold him in fear. The Company of the Gods are his servants, and they hold him in fear. The god Tem, the Governor, the only One among the gods, hath spoken, and his word passeth not away. Horus is both the divine food and the sacrifice. He made haste to gather together [the members of] his father. Horus is his deliverer. Horus is his deliverer. Horus hath sprung from the essence of his divine father and from his decay. He hath become the Governor of Egypt. The gods shall work for him, and they shall toil for him for millions of years. He shall make millions of years to live through his Eye, the only one of its lord, Nebertcher.]

The last section of this Chapter, which is enclosed within brackets, is given from the text found in the Papyrus of Nu, Sheet 14. Copies of the Chapter containing this section are few, and it seems as if the section was not originally included in the Chapter. The text of the section as found in the Turin Papyrus (Bl. XXX) is as follows:—

37. 38.

Exalted is thy throne, O Osiris. Thou hearest well, O Osiris. Thy strength flourisheth, O Osiris. I have fastened
37. thy head [on thy] body for thee. I have stablished thy throat, the throne of the joy of thy heart. Thy words are stable (?) Thy *shenit* princes are glad. Thou art stablished as the Bull of Åmentet. 38. Thy son Horus hath ascended

thy throne. All life is with him. Millions of years work for him. The Company of the Gods fear him. Tem, the One Power of the Gods, hath spoken, and what he hath said is not changed, Ḥetu Āabi. Horus hath stood up. **39.** I have gone about collecting his father. Horus hath delivered his father. Horus hath delivered [his mother]. My mother is Horus. My brother is Horus. My uncle is Horus. I have come. Horus followeth his father. **40.** . . . . there the dirt (?) of his head. The gods shall serve him. Millions of years . . . . . . in his Eye, the Only One of its Lord, Neb-er-tcher.

The text of the LXXVIIIth Chapter given by Naville is so very important for the right understanding of this very interesting Chapter that it is here reproduced in full :—

APPENDIX

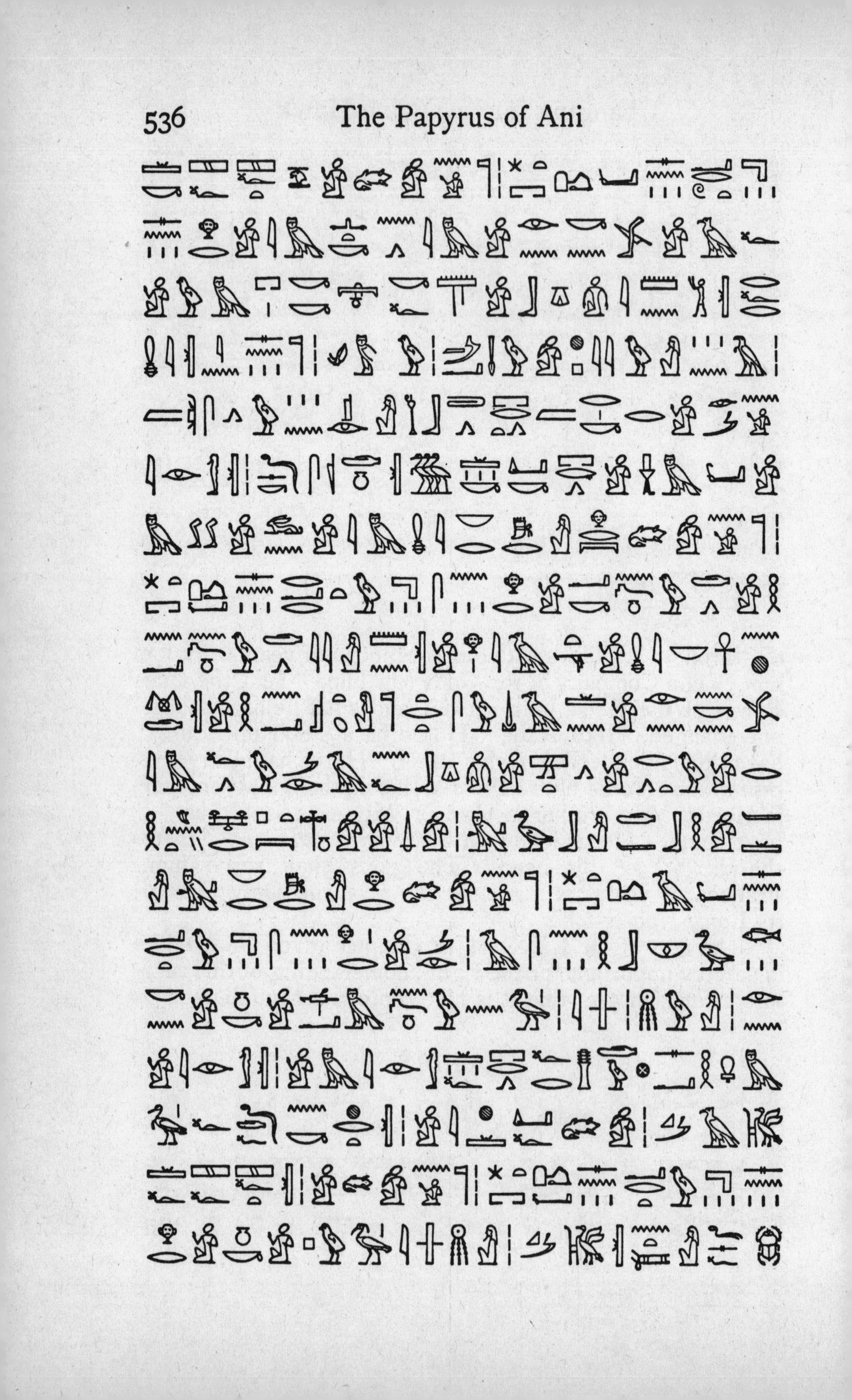

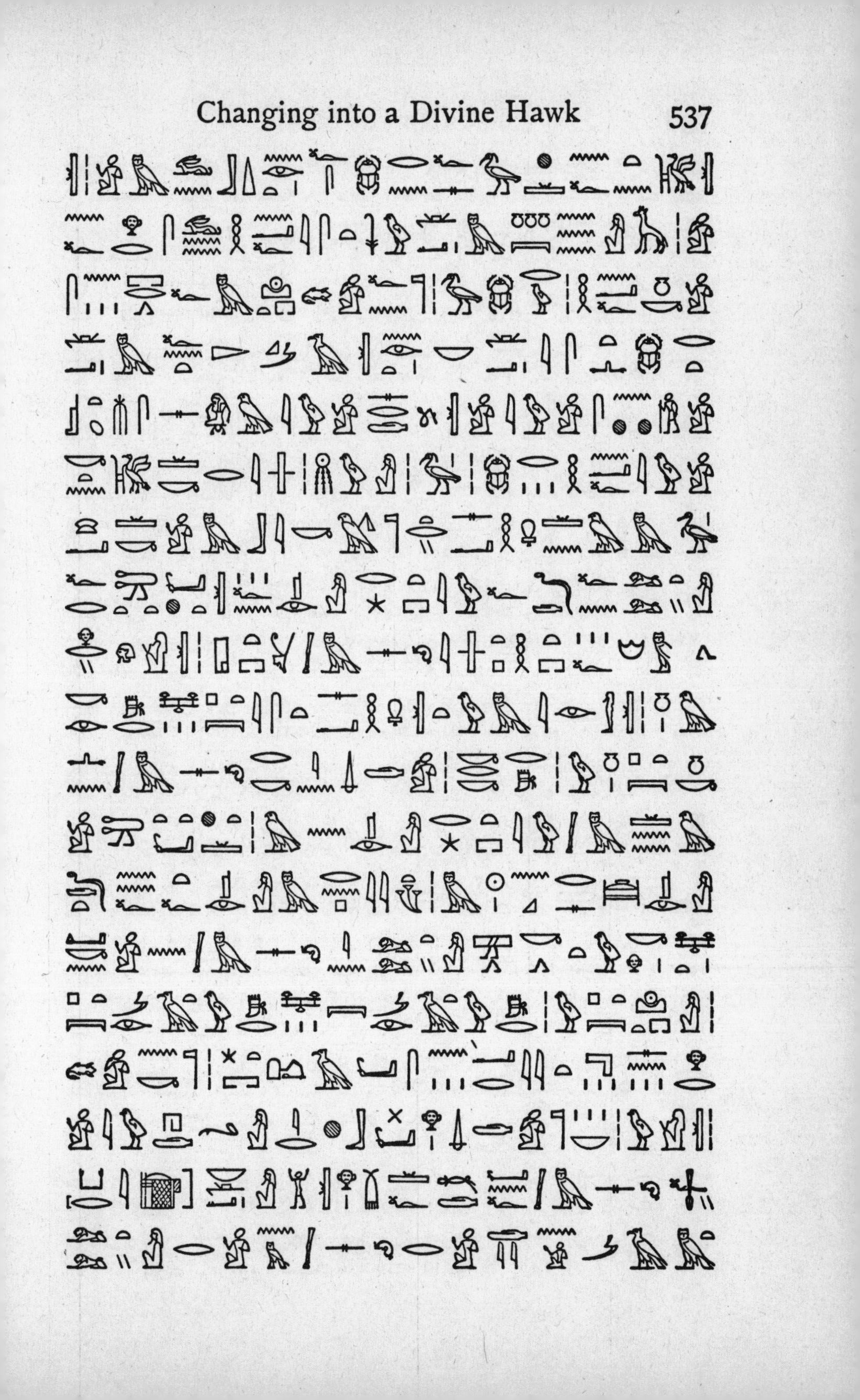

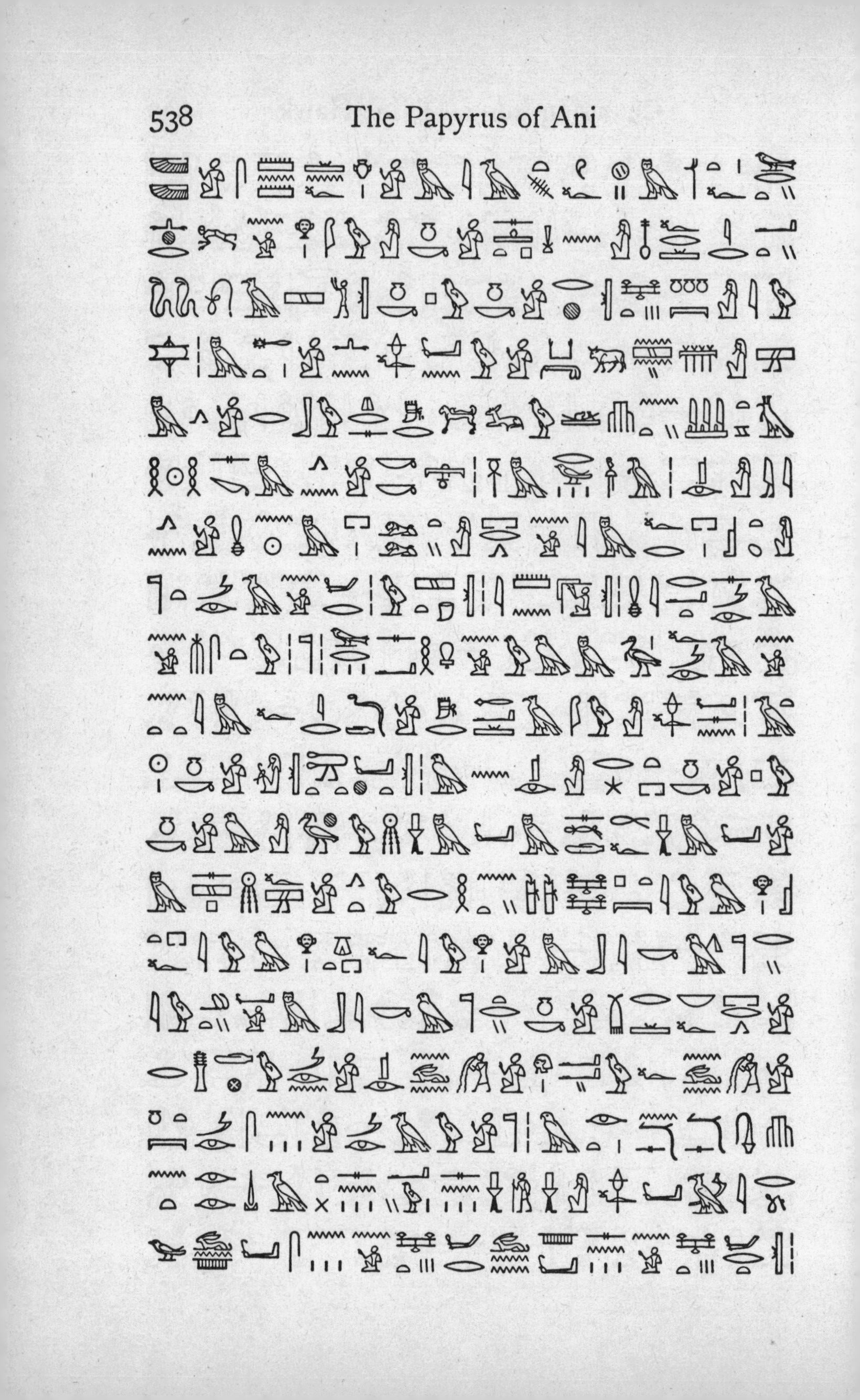

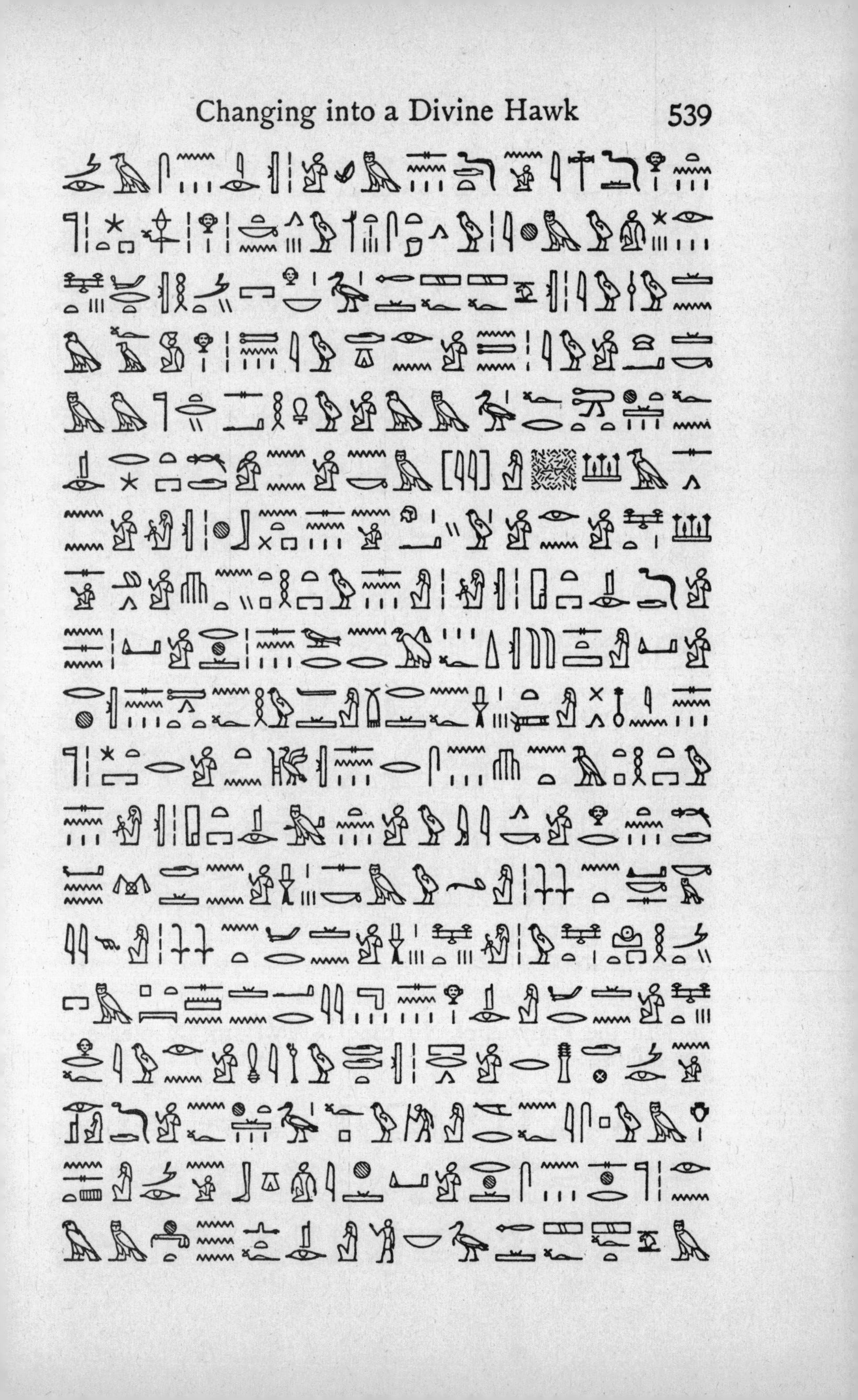

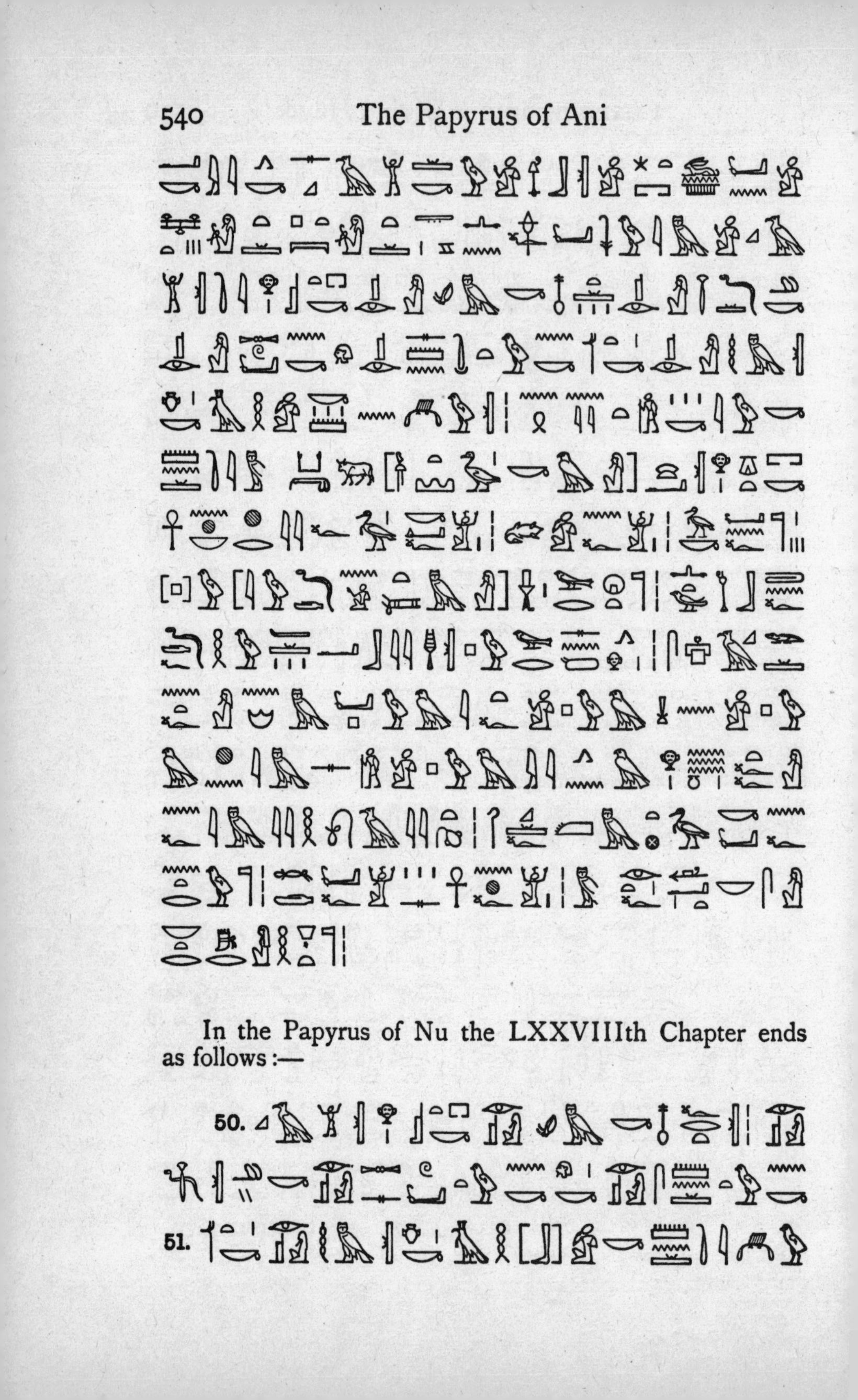

In the Papyrus of Nu the LXXVIIIth Chapter ends as follows:—

50.

51.

52. … 53. … 54. … 55. …

CHAPTER LXXIX

APPENDIX

THE CHAPTER OF CHANGING INTO THE PRINCE OF THE TCHATCHAU CHIEFS

CHAPTER LXXIX. 1. …. …. 2. …

CHAPTER LXXIX. 1. THE CHAPTER OF BEING TRANSFORMED INTO THE PRINCE OF THE TCHATCHAU CHIEFS. The Osiris Nu, whose word is truth, saith :—2. I am the god Tem, the maker of the sky, the creator of the things which are, who cometh forth from the earth, who made the seed of man to come into being, the Lord of things, who fashioned the gods, the Great God, who created himself, 3. the Lord of Life, who made to flourish the Two Companies of the Gods. Homage to you, O ye divine Lords of things, ye holy beings, whose seats are veiled! Homage to you, O ye Lords of Eternity, 4. whose forms are concealed, whose sanctuaries are mysteries, whose places of abode are not known! Homage to you, 5. O ye gods, who dwell in the Tenait (or, the Circle of Light)! Homage to you, O ye gods of the Circle of the country of the Cataracts! Homage to you, O ye gods who dwell in Amentet! 6. Homage to you, O ye gods who dwell within Nut! Grant ye to me that I may come before you, I am pure, I am 7. like a god. I am endowed with a Spirit-soul. I am strong. I am endowed with a Heart-soul. I bring unto you incense, and spice, and natron. I have done away with the chidings (?)

of your **8.** mouths. I have come, I have done away the evil which was in your hearts, and I have removed the offences which appertained to you [against me]. I bring to you **9.** deeds of well-doing, and I present before you truth. I know you. I know your names. I know **10.** your forms which are not known. I come into being among you. My coming is like unto that god who eateth men, **11.** and who feedeth upon the gods. I am strong before you even like that god who is exalted upon his pedestal, unto whom the gods come with rejoicing, and **12.** the goddesses make supplication when they see me. I have come unto you. I have ascended my throne like your Two Daughters (?). I have taken my seat in the horizon. **13.** I receive my offerings of propitiation upon my altars. I drink my fill of *seth* wine every evening. I come to those **14.** who are making rejoicings, and the gods who live in the horizon ascribe unto me praises, as the divine Spirit-body, the Lord of mortals. **15.** I am exalted like that holy god who dwelleth in the Great House. The gods rejoice greatly when they see my **16.** beautiful appearances from the body of the goddess Nut, and when the goddess Nut bringeth me forth.

CHAPTER LXXXVII

THE CHAPTER OF CHANGING INTO THE SERPENT SATA

PLATE XXVII

CHAPTER LXXXVII. **1.** [THE CHAPTER OF] MAKING THE TRANSFORMATION INTO THE SERPENT SATA. The Osiris Ani, whose word is truth, saith :—**2.** I am the serpent Sata whose years are infinite. I lie down dead. I am born daily. I am the serpent 3. Sa-en-ta, the dweller in the uttermost parts of the earth. I lie down in death. I am born, 4. I become new, I renew my youth every day.

Other papyri read:

CHAPTER LXXXVIII

THE CHAPTER OF CHANGING INTO THE CROCODILE-GOD

PLATE XXVII

CHAPTER LXXXVIII. 1. [THE CHAPTER OF] MAKING THE TRANSFORMATION INTO THE CROCODILE-GOD. The Osiris Ani, whose word is truth, saith:—2. I am the Crocodile-god (Sebȧk) who dwelleth amid his terrors. I am the Crocodile-god and I seize [my prey] like a ravening beast. 3. I am the great Fish which is in Kamui. I am the Lord to whom 4. bowings and prostrations are made in Sekhem (Letopolis). And the Osiris Ani is the lord to whom bowings and prostrations are made in Sekhem.

The Papyrus of Nebseni has some interesting variants, and its text of this Chapter reads: [1] Behold, I am the dweller in his terrors, I am the crocodile, his firstborn (?). I bring (prey) from a distance. I am the Fish of Horus, the Great One in Kamui. I am the lord of bowings in Sekhem.[2]

CHAPTER LXXXII

THE CHAPTER OF CHANGING INTO PTAḤ

PLATE XXVII

CHAPTER LXXXII. 1. THE CHAPTER OF MAKING THE TRANSFORMATION INTO PTAḤ. The Osiris Ani [whose word is truth, saith]:—I eat 2. bread. I drink ale. I gird

[1] The Turin Papyrus has . I am the Crocodile, when his soul cometh among his people.

[2] Var. In Sekhem of that great god whose form is hidden; in Ṭeṭu of Osiris, the Bull of Åmentet.

up my garments. I fly 3. like a hawk. I cackle like the Smen goose. I alight upon that 4. place hard by the Sepulchre on the festival of the Great God. That which is abominable, that which is abominable I will not eat. 5. [An abominable thing] is filth, I will not eat thereof. That which is an abomination unto my KA shall not enter my body. I will live upon that whereon 6. live the gods and the Spirit-souls. I shall live, and I shall be master of their cakes. I am master of them, and I shall eat them 7. under the trees of the dweller in the House of Hathor, my Lady. I will make an offering. My cakes are in Ṭeṭu (Busiris), my offerings are in 8. Ȧnu (Heliopolis). I gird about myself the robe which is woven for me by the goddess Tait. I shall stand up and sit down in whatsoever place it pleaseth me to do so. 9. My head is like unto that of Rā. I am gathered together (or, I am complete) like Tem.

Here offer the four cakes of Rā, and the offerings of the earth.[1]

[1] This is a rubrical direction.

I shall come forth. My tongue is **10.** like that of Ptaḥ, and my throat is like unto that of Hathor, and I remember the words of Tem, of my father, with my mouth. He forced **11.** the woman, the wife of Ḳeb, breaking the heads near him; therefore was the fear of him there. [His] praises are repeated with vigour. I am decreed to be **12.** the Heir, the lord of the earth of Ḳeb. I have union with women. Ḳeb hath refreshed me, and he hath caused me to ascend his throne. Those who dwell **13.** in Ȧnu (Heliopolis) bow their heads to me. I am [their] Bull, I am stronger than [the Lord] of the hour. I unite with women. I am master for millions of years.

CHAPTER LXXXV

THE CHAPTER OF TURNING INTO THE SOUL OF TEM

PLATE XXVII

CHAPTER LXXXV. 1. [THE CHAPTER OF] MAKING THE TRANSFORMATION INTO THE SOUL OF TEM. The Osiris Ani, whose word is truth, saith:—2. I shall not enter into the place of destruction, I shall not perish, I shall not know [decay]. I am 3. Rā, who came forth from Nu, the Soul of the God who created his own members. What I abominate is 4. sin; I will not look thereon. I cry not out against truth, nay, I live 5. therein. I am the god Ḥu, the imperishable god, in my name 6. of "Soul." I have created myself with Nu, in the name of 7. "Kheperȧ." I exist in them like Rā. I am the Lord of Light.

The above lines form only the opening section of the LXXXVth Chapter; the concluding portion, according to the text of the Papyrus of Nu, reads:—

That which is an abomination unto me is death; let me not go into the chamber of torture which is in the Ṭuat. I am the delight of the Khu of Osiris. I make to be content the heart[s] of **6.** those who dwell among the divine things which are beloved [by me]. They cause the fear of me [to abound], they create the awe of me **7.** to be in those divine beings who dwell in their own circles. Behold, I am exalted on my own standard, **8.** and upon my throne, and upon my seat which is assigned [to me]. I am the god Nu, and those who commit sin shall not destroy me. **9.** I am the firstborn of the primeval god, and my soul is the **10.** Souls of the Eternal Gods, and my body is Everlastingness. My created form is [that of] the god Eternity, the Lord of Years, **11.** and the Prince of Everlastingness. I am the Creator of the Darkness, who maketh his seat in the uttermost limits of the heavens, [which] I love.

12. I arrive at their boundaries. I advance upon my two legs. I direct my **13.** resting place (?). I sail over the sky. I fetter and destroy the hidden serpents **14.** which are about my footsteps [in going to] the Lord of the Two Arms. My soul is the Souls of the **15.** Eternal Gods, and my body is Everlastingness. I am the exalted one, the Lord of the Land of Tebu. **16.** I am the Child in the city: "Young man in the country" is my name. "Imperishable one" is my name. I am the Soul Creator of Nu. I make my habitation in **17.** Khert-Neter. My nest (or place of birth) is invisible, my egg is not broken. I have done away the evil which is in me. I shall see my Father, **18.** the Lord of the Evening. His body dwelleth in Ȧnu (Heliopolis). I am made to be the Light-god, a dweller in the Light-god, over the Western Domain of the *Hebt* bird (Thoth?).

CHAPTER LXXXIII

THE CHAPTER OF CHANGING INTO THE BENU BIRD

PLATE XXVII

CHAPTER LXXXIII. 1. [THE CHAPTER OF] MAKING THE TRANSFORMATION INTO 2. THE BENU BIRD. The Osiris, the scribe Ani, whose word is truth, saith:—I flew up out of primeval matter. I came 3. into being like the god Kheperȧ. I germinated (or, grew up) like the plants. I am concealed (or, hidden) like the tortoise (or, turtle) [in his shell]. I am the seed (?) of every 4. god. I am Yesterday of the Four [Quarters of the Earth, and] the Seven Uraei, who came into being in the Eastern land. [I am] the Great One (*i.e.*, Horus) who illumineth the Ḥememet spirits 5. with the light of his body. [I am] that god in respect of Set. [I am] Thoth who [stood] between them (*i.e.*, Horus and Set) as the 6. judge on behalf of the Governor of Sekhem (Letopolis) and the

7. [hieroglyphic text] 8. [hieroglyphic text]

RUBRIC: [hieroglyphic text][1]

Souls of Ȧnu (Heliopolis). [He was like] a stream between them. I have come. I rise up on my throne. I am endowed with a Khu (*i.e.*, Spirit-soul). **8.** I am mighty. I am endowed with godhood among the gods. I am Khensu, [the lord] of every kind of strength.

RUBRIC: [If] this Chapter [be known by the deceased], he shall come forth pure by day after his death, and he shall perform every transformation which his soul desireth to make. He shall be among the Followers of Un-Nefer (*i.e.*, Osiris), and he shall satisfy himself with the food of Osiris, and with sepulchral meals. He shall see the Disk [of the Sun], he shall be in good case upon earth before Rā, and his word shall be truth in the sight of Osiris, and no evil thing whatsoever shall have dominion over him for ever and ever.

1 From a papyrus in Paris (Naville, *op. cit.*, II, p. 185).

CHAPTER LXXXIV

THE CHAPTER OF CHANGING INTO A HERON

PLATE XXVIII

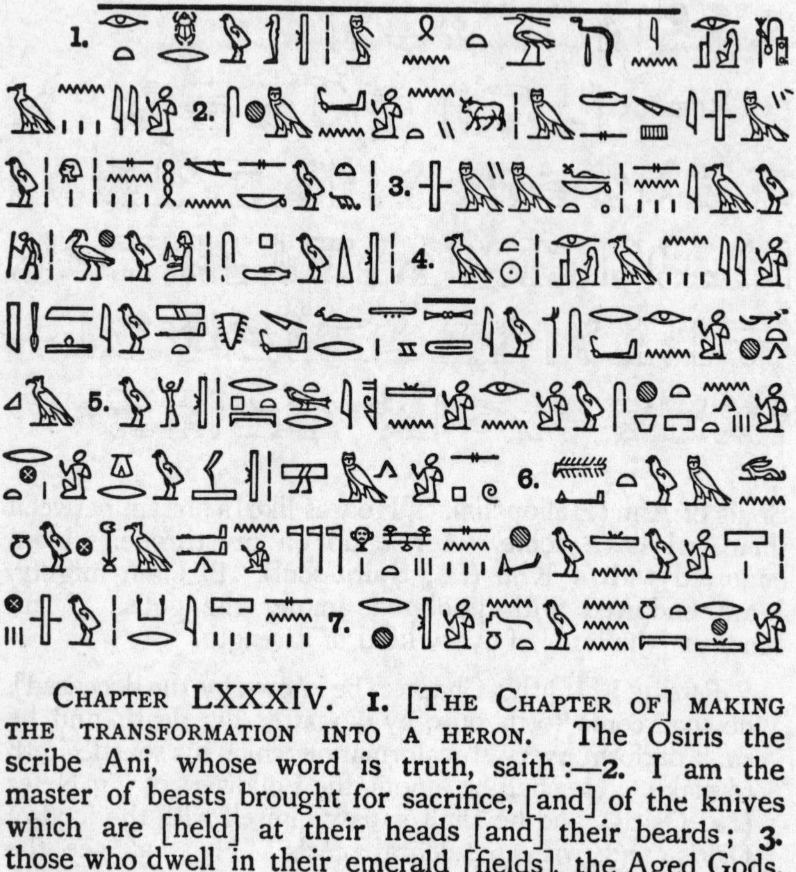

CHAPTER LXXXIV. 1. [THE CHAPTER OF] MAKING THE TRANSFORMATION INTO A HERON. The Osiris the scribe Ani, whose word is truth, saith:—2. I am the master of beasts brought for sacrifice, [and] of the knives which are [held] at their heads [and] their beards; 3. those who dwell in their emerald [fields], the Aged Gods, and the Spirit-souls, are ready at 4. the moment for the Osiris Ani, whose word is truth, in peace. He maketh slaughter on the earth, and I make slaughter on the earth. I am strong. I follow the 5. heights unto heaven. I have made myself pure. I walk with long strides to my city. I have become an owner of land there. I advance to Sepu. 6. . . . . . is given to me in Unu (Hermopolis). I have set the gods upon their roads. I have made splendid the houses and towns of those who are in their shrines. 7. I know the stream of Nut. I know Tatun.

I know Ṭeshert. I have brought along their horns. **8.** I know Ḥekạ. I have hearkened to his words. I am the Red Bull-calf which is marked with markings. The gods shall say when they hear **9.** [of me]: Uncover your faces. His coming is to me. There is light which ye know not. Times and seasons are in my body. **10.** I do not speak [lies] in the place of truth, daily. The truth is hidden on the eyebrows (?) [By] night [I] sail up the river to keep the feast **11.** of him that is dead, to embrace the Aged God, and to guard the earth, I the Osiris Ani, whose word is truth.

What follows of this Chapter as given in the Papyrus of Ani is really the end of Chapter LXXXV, which the scribe copied here either inadvertently, or for want of space in the

[1] Chapter LXXXIV ends here.

proper place. As a translation of the remaining lines has already been given from another papyrus of the XVIIIth dynasty, there is no need to add a second rendering here. The reader will note the variants in the text, and will make the necessary alterations in the translation. In the Saïte Recension the Chapter has a RUBRIC, which reads :—

RUBRIC :

If this Chapter be known [by the deceased], he will live like a perfect Spirit-soul in Khert-Neter; no evil thing whatsoever shall overthrow him.

CHAPTER LXXXIa

THE CHAPTER OF CHANGING INTO A LOTUS (OR, LILY)

PLATE XXVIII

Chapter LXXXIa. 1. [The Chapter of] making the transformation into the lotus (or, lily). The Osiris Ani, whose word is truth, saith :—I am 2. the holy lotus that cometh forth from the light which belongeth to the nostrils of Rā, and which belongeth to the 3. head of Hathor. I have made my way, and I seek after him, that is to say, Horus. I am the pure lotus that cometh forth from the field [of Rā].

APPENDIX

CHAPTER LXXXIb

(Naville, *op. cit.*, I, Bl. XCIII)

Chapter LXXXIb. 1. Chapter of making the transformation into a lotus. The Osiris, the lady of the house, Àui, whose word is truth, in peace, saith :—2. Hail, thou

Lotus, thou type of the god Nefer-Temu! I am the man who knoweth your names (?). 3. I know your names among the gods, the lords of Khert-Neter. I am one among you. 4. Grant ye that I may see the gods who are the Guides of the Ṭuat. Grant ye to me a seat in 5. Khert-Neter, near the Lords of Åmentet. Assign to me a habitation in the land of Tchesert. Receive ye me 6. in the presence of the Lords of Eternity. Let my soul come forth in whatsoever place it pleaseth. Let it not be rejected in the presence of the Great Company of the Gods.

The above version of Chapter LXXXIB is extant in one papyrus only, namely, that of Paqrer, a priest of Ptaḥ. To assign an exact date to this papyrus is difficult, but it is certainly not older than 950 B.C., and it may have been written as late as 700 B.C. The name Paqrer is not common, but it is found in the Dream of Tanut-Åmen,[1] l. 37, where it occurs under the form of. The determinative shows the meaning of the name, *i.e.*, "the frog" (compare the Coptic πκροүρ). The Paqrer of this inscription was the governor of the town of Sepṭ (Phacusa), in the Eastern Delta, and M. Naville has pointed

[1] See Budge, *Annals of Nubian Kings*, p. 85.

out (*Einleitung*, p. 95) that the Paqrer for whom the papyrus was written is twice called "King of the Two Lands" , *i.e.*, a royal title was applied to him. It may be that he and the enemy of Tanut-Ȧmen were one and the same person. It is interesting to note that in Chapter LXXXIB the name of the wife of Paqrer, the priest of Ptaḥ, is given.

CHAPTER LXXX

THE CHAPTER OF TURNING INTO THE GOD WHO LIGHTENETH THE DARKNESS

PLATE XXVIII

CHAPTER LXXX. [THE CHAPTER OF] **1.** MAKING THE TRANSFORMATION INTO THE GOD WHO LIGHTENETH THE DARKNESS. The Osiris the scribe Ani, whose word is truth, saith:—I am **2.** the girdle of the garment of the god Nu, which giveth light, and shineth, and belongeth to his breast, the illuminer of the darkness, the uniter of the two Reḥti deities, **3.** the dweller in my body, through the great spell of the words of my mouth. I rise up, but he who was coming after me hath fallen. **4.** He who was with him in the Valley of Ȧbṭu (Abydos) hath fallen. I rest. I remember **5.** him. The god Ḥu hath taken possession of me in my town. I found him **6.** there. I have carried away the darkness by my strength, I have filled the Eye [of Rā] when it was helpless, and when **7.** it came not on the festival of the fifteenth day. I have weighed Sut in the celestial houses against the Aged One who was with him. I have **8.** equipped Thoth in the House of the Moon-god, when the fifteenth day of the festival came not. I have taken possession of the Urrt Crown. Truth is in my body; **9.** turquoise and crystal are its months. My homestead is there among the lapis-lazuli, among the furrows thereof. I am **10.** Ḥem-Nu (?), the lightener of the darkness. I have come to lighten the darkness; it is light. I have lightened the darkness. **11.** I have overthrown the *āshmiu*-fiends. I have sung hymns to those who dwell in the darkness. I have made to stand up **12.** the weeping ones, whose faces were covered over; they were in a helpless state of misery. Look ye then upon me. I am Ḥem-Nu(?). I will not let you hear concerning it. [I have fought. I am Ḥem-Nu (?). I have lightened the darkness. I have come. I have made an end to the darkness which hath become light indeed.[1]]

CHAPTER CLXXV

THE CHAPTER OF NOT DYING A SECOND TIME

PLATE XXIX

1. 2. 3. 4.

Chapter CLXXV. 1. [The Chapter of] not dying a second time. The Osiris Ani, whose word is truth, saith:—2. Hail, Thoth! What is it that hath happened to the children of Nut? 3. They have waged war, they have upheld strife, they have done evil, 4. they have created the fiends, they have made slaughter, they have caused

[1] . Added from Naville, *op. cit.*, II, p. 176.

[1] Var. .

5. trouble; in truth, in all their doings the strong have worked against the weak. 6. Grant, O might of Thoth, that that which the god Tem hath decreed [may be done]! And thou regardest not evil, nor art thou 7. provoked to anger when they bring their years to confusion, and throng in and push in to disturb their months. For in all that they have done 8. unto thee they have worked iniquity in secret. I am thy writing-palette, O Thoth, and I have brought unto thee thine ink-jar. I am not 9. of those who work iniquity in their secret places; let not evil happen unto me.

The Osiris, the scribe Ani, 10. whose word is truth, saith:—Hail, Temu! What manner of land is this unto which I have come? It hath not water, it hath not air; it is depth unfathomable, 11. it is black as the blackest night, and men wander helplessly therein. In it a man cannot live in quietness of heart; nor may the longings of love be satisfied therein. **12.** But let the state of the Spirit-souls be given unto me instead of water and air, and the satisfying of the longings of love, and let quietness of heart be given unto me instead of cakes **13.** and ale. The god Tem hath decreed that I shall see thy face, and that I shall not suffer from the things which pain thee. May every god transmit unto thee **14.** his throne for millions of years. Thy throne hath descended unto thy son Horus, and the god Tem hath decreed that thy course shall be among the holy princes. **15.** In truth he shall rule from thy throne, and he shall be heir to the throne of the Dweller in the fiery Lake [Neserser]. In truth it hath been decreed that in me he shall see his likeness, and that my face **16.** shall look upon the face of the Lord Tem. How long then have I to live? It is decreed that thou shalt live for millions of years, a life of millions of years. **17.** Let it be granted to me to pass on to the holy princes, for indeed, I have done away all the evil which I committed, from the time when this earth came into being from Nu, 18. when it sprang from the watery abyss even as it was in the days of old. I am Fate (or Time) and Osiris, I have made my transformations into the likeness of divers 19. serpents. Man knoweth not, and the gods cannot behold the two-fold beauty which I have made for Osiris, the greatest of the gods. I have given unto him 20. the region of the dead. And, verily, his son Horus is seated upon the throne of the Dweller in the fiery Lake [of Neserser], as his heir. I have made him to have his throne 21. in the Boat of Millions of Years. Horus is stablished upon his throne [among his] kinsmen, and he hath all that is his with him. Verily, the Soul of Set, which 22. is greater than all the gods, hath departed. Let it be granted to me to bind his soul in fetters in the Boat of the God, 23. when I please, and let

24. 25. 26.

him hold the Body of the God in fear. O my father Osiris, thou hast done for me that which thy father Rā did for thee. Let me abide upon the earth permanently. **24.** Let me keep possession of my throne. Let my heir be strong. Let my tomb, and my friends who are upon the earth, flourish. **25.** Let my enemies be given over to destruction, and to the shackles of the goddess Serq. I am thy son. Rā is my father. **26.** On me likewise thou hast conferred life, strength, and health. Horus is established upon his tomb (*serekh*). Grant thou that the days of my life may come unto worship and honour.

From the fragmentary copy of this Chapter which M. Naville has published in his *Todtenbuch*, Bd. I, Bll. 198, 199, it is clear that the text given in the Papyrus of Ani forms only about one half of it, and that its contents refer to the establishment of the Kingdom of Osiris, and the succession to his throne of his son Horus, with whom the deceased is identified. It is well nigh impossible to make any connected sense of this fragmentary version, for the beginnings and ends of the lines of the texts are wanting almost throughout. Isolated fragments can be translated, *e.g.*, Horus, or the deceased, takes his place at the head of the vassals of Osiris;[1] shouts of joy ascend in Ḥensu (Herakleopolis), and gladness reigns in Neruṭef, the tomb

[1]

of Osiris in Herakleopolis;[1] he inherits the throne of Osiris, and rules Egypt with the approval of the gods;[2] the god Suti fears him;[3] all sorts and conditions of men and spirits, both living and dead, come before him, and bow down in homage before him; fear and awe of him are set in every being;[4] Set comes unto him with his head bent low to the ground;[5] his name shall endure for millions of millions of years;[6] he shall wear the mighty *Atef* Crown upon his head for millions, and hundreds of thousands, and tens of thousands, and thousands, and hundreds, and tens of years.[7] And, naturally, the very best kinds of offerings shall be made to him, and he shall be supplied with an abundance of fresh water, which shall be drawn from the river, and not from the little side streams which are fed by the large canals, or from the pools of standing water.

1

2

3

4

5

6

7

Finally, the deceased shall never cease from the earth, but like his divine namesake Rā he shall be there for a "million, million, million," or a "million billions of years"

The Chapter in the Leyden Papyrus of Rā, the scribe, is followed by the

RUBRIC:

"This Chapter shall be recited over a figure of Horus, "made of lapis-lazuli, which shall be placed on the neck "of the deceased. It is a protection upon earth, and it "will secure for the deceased the affection of men, gods, "and the Spirit-souls which are perfect. Moreover it "acteth as a spell in Khert-Neter, but it must be recited "by thee on behalf of the Osiris Rā, regularly and con-"tinually millions of times."

The whole of the above Chapter in its two versions has been specially treated by Prof. Naville in the *Proceedings of the Society of Biblical Archaeology*, Vol. XXVI, pp. 151 and 287 ff. The learned writer thinks that an allusion to a flood occurs in the text.

CHAPTER CXXV Introduction (A)

THE CHAPTER OF ENTERING THE HALL OF MAĀT

PLATE XXX

Chapter CXXV. Introduction (A). 1. [The Chapter of] entering into the Hall of Maāti to praise Osiris Khenti-Åmenti. The Osiris the scribe Ani, whose word is truth, saith :—2. I have come unto thee. I have drawn nigh to behold (*i.e.*, to experience) thy beauties (*i.e.*, thy beneficent goodness). My hands are [extended] in adoration of thy name of "Maāt" (*i.e.*, Truth). I have come. I have drawn nigh unto [the place where] the cedar-tree existeth not, 3. where the acacia tree doth not put forth shoots,[1] and where the ground produceth neither grass nor herbs. Now I have entered into the habitation which is hidden, and I hold converse 4. with Set. My protector[2] advanced to me, covered was his face (?) . . . . on the hidden things. 5. He entered into the house of

[1] Or, where the acacia tree cannot grow.

[2] A protecting ancestor?

Osiris, he saw the hidden things (mysteries) which were therein. The Tchatchau Chiefs of the Pylons were in the form of Spirits. The god **6.** Ȧnpu spake unto those about him (?) with the words of a man who cometh from Ta-merȧ,[1] saying, "He knoweth our roads [and] our towns (or, "villages). I am reconciled unto him. **7.** When I smell his "odour it is even as the odour of one of you." And I say unto him: I the Osiris Ani, whose word is truth, in peace, whose word is truth, **8.** have come. I have drawn nigh to behold the Great Gods. I would live upon the propitiatory offerings [made] to their Doubles. I would live on the borders [of the territory of] **9.** the Soul, the Lord of Ṭeṭu (Busiris). He shall make me to come forth in the form of a Benu bird, and to hold converse [with him]. I have been in the stream [to purify myself]. I have made offerings **10.** of incense. I betook myself to the Acacia Tree of the [divine] Children. I lived in Abu (Elephantine) in the House of the goddess Satet. **11.** I made to sink in the water the boat of the enemies. I sailed over the lake [in

[1] *I.e.*, in the Egyptian language.

the temple] in the Neshmet Boat. I have looked upon the Sāḥu (or Spirit-bodies) **12.** of Kamur.[1] I have been in Ṭeṭu (Busiris). I have held my peace. I have made the god to be master of his **13.** legs. I have been in the House of Tepṭuf (*i.e.*, Anubis). I have seen him, that is the Governor of the Hall of the God. I have entered into the House of Osiris **14.** and I have removed the head-coverings (wigs?) of him that is therein. I have entered into Rasta,[2] and I have seen the the Hidden One (or, Mystery) **15.** who is therein. I was hidden, [but] I found the boundary. I journeyed to Neruṭef,[3] and he who was **16.** therein covered me with a garment. I gave myrrh of women,[4] together with the *shenu* powder (?) of living folk. Verily he (*i.e.*, Osiris) **17.** told me the things which

[1] A town near Memphis.
[2] The Other World of Seker near Memphis.
[3] The site of the grave of Osiris in Herakleopolis.
[4] *I.e.*, the kind of myrrh used by women.

concerned himself. I said: Let thy weighing of me be even as we desire.

And the Majesty of Ȧnpu shall say unto me, **18.** "Knowest thou the name of this door, and canst thou tell it?" And the Osiris the scribe Ani, whose word is truth, in peace, whose word is truth, shall say, **19.** "Khersek-Shu" is the name **20.** of this door. And the Majesty of the god Ȧnpu shall say unto me, **21.** "Knowest thou the name of the upper leaf, **22.** and the name of the lower leaf?" [And the Osiris the scribe Ani] shall say: "Neb-Maāt **23.** -ḥeri-reṭiu-f" is the name of the upper leaf **24.** and "Neb-peḥti-thesu-menment" [is the name of the lower leaf. And the Majesty of the god Ȧnpu shall say], **25.** "Pass on, for thou **26.** hast knowledge, O Osiris the scribe, the assessor of **27.** the holy offerings of all the gods of Thebes **28.** Ani, whose word is truth, the lord of loyal service [to Osiris]."

APPENDIX

CHAPTER XXV INTRODUCTION (B)

[From the Papyrus of Nu (Brit. Mus. No. 10477, Sheet 22)]

1. [THE FOLLOWING][1] WORDS SHALL BE SAID BY THE STEWARD OF THE KEEPER OF THE SEAL, NU, WHOSE WORD IS TRUTH, WHEN HE COMETH FORTH TO THE HALL 2. OF MAĀTI, SO THAT HE MAY BE SEPARATED FROM EVERY SIN WHICH HE HATH COMMITTED, AND MAY BEHOLD THE FACES OF THE GODS. The Osiris Nu, whose word is truth, saith: 3. Homage to thee, O Great God, Lord of Maāti! I have come unto thee, O my Lord, and I have brought myself hither that I may 4. behold thy beauties.[2] I know thee, I know thy name, I know the names of the Forty-two Gods who live with thee 5. in this Hall of Maāti, who live by keeping ward over sinners, and who feed upon their blood 6. on the day when the consciences of men are reckoned up

[1] The words within [ ] are added from Naville, *Todtenbuch*, II, 334.
[2] *I.e.*, experience thy gracious acts.

in the presence of the god Un-Nefer. In truth thy name is "Reḥti-merti-nebti-Maāti."[1] In truth **7.** I have come unto thee, I have brought Maāti (Truth) to thee. I have done away sin for thee. I have not committed sins against men. I have not opposed my family and kinsfolk. **8.** I have not acted fraudulently (or, deceitfully) in the Seat of Truth.[2] I have not known men who were of no account.[3] I have not wrought evil. I have not made it to be the first [consideration daily that unnecessary] **9.** work should be done for me. I have not brought forward my name for dignities. I have not [attempted] to direct servants [I have not belittled God]. I have not defrauded the humble man of his property. I have not done what the gods **10.** abominate. I have not vilified a slave to his master.

[1] *I.e.*, the two women, the two eyes, the two ladies of Maāti.

[2] A name of the judgment hall, or of the law court. Therefore the meaning of this sentence is that the deceased did not commit perjury.

[3] *I.e.*, I have never been a friend of worthless or profligate men and wasters.

I have not inflicted pain. I have not caused anyone to go hungry. I have not made any man to weep. I have not committed murder. **11.** I have not given the order for murder to be committed. I have not caused calamities to befall men and women. I have not plundered the offerings in the temples. I have not defrauded the gods of their **12.** cake-offerings. I have not carried off the *fenkhu* cakes [offered to] the Spirits. I have not committed fornication (or, had intercourse with men). I have not masturbated [in the sanctuaries of the god of my city]. I have not diminished from the bushel. **13.** I have not filched [land from my neighbour's estate and] added it to my own acre. I have not encroached upon the fields [of others]. I have not added to the weights of the scales. I have not depressed the pointer of the **14.** balance. I have not carried away the milk from the mouths of children. I have not driven the cattle away from their pastures.

I have not snared **15.** the geese in the goose-pens of the gods. I have not caught fish with bait made of the bodies of the same kind of fish. I have not stopped water when it should flow. I have not made a cutting in a canal of **16.** running water. I have not extinguished a fire (or, lamp) when it should burn. I have not violated the times [of offering] the chosen meat offerings. I have not driven away **17.** the cattle on the estates of the gods. I have not turned back the god (or, God) at his appearances. I am pure. I am pure. I am pure. I am pure. My pure offerings are the pure offerings of **18.** that great Benu (phoenix?) which dwelleth in Ḥensu. For behold, I am the nose of Neb-nefu (*i.e.*, the lord of the air), who giveth sustenance unto all mankind, **19.** on the day of the filling of the Utchat [1] in Ȧnu, in the second month [2] of the season

[1] *I.e.*, the day of the full moon.

[2] The Coptic month Mekhir, the sixth month of the Egyptian year.

Pert,[1] on the last day of the month, [in the presence of the Lord of this earth].[2] I have seen the filling of the Utchat in Ånu, therefore let not **20.** calamity befall me in this land, or in this Hall of Maāti, because I know the names of the gods who are therein, [and who are the followers of the Great God].[3]

CHAPTER CXXV

THE NEGATIVE CONFESSION

PLATES XXXI AND XXXII

1. Hail, Usekh-nemmt, who comest forth from Ånu (Heliopolis), I have not committed sin.

2. Hail, Ḥept-khet, who comest forth from Kher-āḥa I have not committed robbery with violence.

3. Hail, Fenti, who comest forth from Khemenu (Hermopolis), I have not stolen.

[1] *I.e.*, the season of growing; it began in the middle of November, and ended in the middle of March.

[2] Added from the Papyrus of Nebseni.

[3] Added from the Papyrus of Ani.

4. Hail, Ām-khaibit, who comest forth from Qernet, I have not slain men and women.

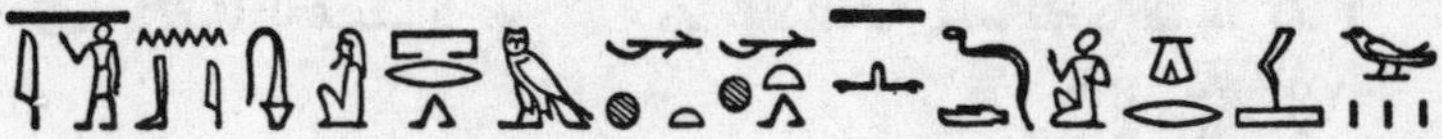

5. Hail, Neḥa-ḥer, who comest forth from Rasta, I have not stolen grain.

6. Hail, Ruruti, who comest forth from heaven, I have not purloined offerings.

7. Hail, Ȧrfi-em-khet, who comest forth from Saut (Asyûṭ), I have not stolen the property of God.

8. Hail, Nebȧ, who comest and goest, I have not uttered lies.

9. Hail, Seṭ-qesu, who comest forth from Ḥensu (Herakleopolis), I have not carried away food.

10. Hail, Utu-nesert, who comest forth from Ḥet-ka-Ptaḥ (Memphis), I have not uttered curses.

11. Hail, Qerrti, who comest forth from Åmentet, I have not committed adultery, I have not lain with men.

12. Hail, Ḥer-f-ḥa-f, who comest forth from thy cavern, I have made none to weep.

13. Hail, Basti, who comest forth from Bast (?) (Bubastis), I have not eaten the heart (*i.e.*, I have not grieved uselessly, or felt remorse).

14. Hail, Ta-reṭiu, who comest forth from the night, I have not attacked any man.

15. Hail, Unem-snef, who comest forth from the execution chamber, I am not a man of deceit.

16. Hail, Unem-besek, who comest forth from Mābit, I have not stolen cultivated land.

17. Hail, Neb-Maāt, who comest forth from Maāti, I have not been an eavesdropper.

18. Hail, Tenemiu, who comest forth from Bast, I have slandered [no man].

19. Hail, Serṭiu, who comest forth from Ȧnu (Heliopolis), I have not been angry without just cause (?)

20. Hail, Ṭuṭu, who comest forth from Ȧti (the Busirite Nome), I have not debauched the wife of [any] man.

21. Hail, Uamemti, who comest forth from the Khebt chamber, I have not debauched the wife of [any] man.

22. Hail, Maa-ȧntuf, who comest forth from Per-Menu (Panopolis), I have not polluted myself.

23 Hail, Ḥer-uru, who comest forth from Nehatu, I have terrorized none.

24. Hail, Khemiu, who comest forth from Kaui (?), I have not transgressed [the law].

25. Hail, Sheṭ-kheru, who comest forth from Urit, I have not been wroth.

26. Hail, Nekhenu, who comest forth from Ḥeqāṭ, I have not shut my ears to the words of truth.

27. Hail, Kenemti, who comest forth from Kenmet, I have not blasphemed.

28. Hail, Ȧn-ḥetep-f, who comest forth from Sau (Sais), I am not a man of violence.

29. Hail, Serȧ-kheru, who comest forth from Unȧset, I have not been a stirrer up of strife (or, a disturber of the peace).

30. Hail, Neb-ḥeru, who comest forth from Netchfet, I have not acted (or judged) with undue haste.

31. Hail, Sekhriu, who comest forth from Uten (?), I have not pried into matters.

32. Hail, Neb-ābui, who comest forth from Sauti, I have not multiplied my words in speaking.

33. Hail, Nefer-Tem, who comest forth from Ḥet-ka-Ptaḥ (Memphis), I have wronged none, I have done no evil.

34.

35.

36.

37.

38.

39.

34. Hail, Tem-Sepu, who comest forth from Ṭeṭu (Busiris), I have not worked witchcraft against the king (or blasphemed the king).

35. Hail, Ȧri-em-ȧb-f, who comest forth from Ṭebu, I have never stopped [the flow of] water.

36. Hail, Ȧḥi, who comest forth from Nu, I have never raised my voice (spoken arrogantly, or in anger?).

37. Hail, Uatch-rekhit, who comest forth from Sau, I have not cursed (or blasphemed) God.

38. Hail, Neḥeb-ka, who comest forth from thy cavern, I have not acted with arrogance (?)

39. Hail, Neḥeb-nefert, who comest forth from thy cavern, I have not stolen the bread of the gods.

40.

41.

42.

40. Hail, Tcheser-tep, who comest forth from the shrine, I have not carried away the *khenfu* cakes from the Spirits of the dead.

41. Hail, Ȧn-āf, who comest forth from Maāti, I have not snatched away the bread of the child, nor treated with contempt the god of my city.

42. Hail, Ḥetch-ȧbḥu, who comest forth from Ta-she (the Fayyûm), I have not slain the cattle belonging to the god.

The text of the Negative Confession in the Papyrus of Ani varies considerably from that of the older papyri, *e.g.*, the Papyrus of Nebseni and the Papyrus of Nu. The following rendering is from the Papyrus of Nebseni :—

1. Hail, Usekh-nemmt, who comest forth from Ȧnu, I have not committed sin.

2. Hail, Ḥept-Shet, who comest forth from Kher-āḥa, I have not robbed with violence.

3. Hail, Fenṭi, who comest forth from Khemenu, I have done no violence.

4. Hail, Ām-khaibitu, who comest forth from Qerrt, I have not stolen.

5. Hail, Neḥa-ḥāu, who comest forth from Rasta, I have not slain men.

6. Hail, Ruruti, who comest forth from heaven, I have not made light the bushel.

7. Hail, Ȧrti-f-em-ṭes, who comest forth from Sekhem (Letopolis), I have not acted deceitfully.

8. Hail, Nebȧ, who comest and goest, I have not stolen the property of the god.

9. Hail, Seṭ-qesu, who comest forth from Ḥensu, I have not told lies.

10. Hail, Uatch-nesert, who comest forth from Ḥet-ka-Ptaḥ, I have not carried away food.

11. Hail, Qerti, who comest forth from Ȧmenti, I have not uttered evil words.

12. Hail, Ḥetch-ȧbḥu, who comest forth from Ta-she, I have attacked no man.

13. Hail, Unem-snef, who comest forth from the execution chamber, I have not slain a bull which was the property of the god.

14. Hail, Unem-besku, who comest [forth from the Mābet chamber], I have not acted deceitfully.

15. Hail, Neb-maāt, who comest forth from Maāti, I have not pillaged (or laid waste) the lands which have been ploughed.

16. Hail, Thenemi, who comest forth from Bast (Bubastis), I have never pried into matters [to make mischief].

17. Hail, Āaṭi, who comest forth from Ȧnu (Heliopolis), I have not set my mouth in motion (*i.e.*, I have not slandered any man).

18. Hail, Ṭuṭuf, who comest forth from Ā (Āti ?), I have not been wroth except with reason.

19. Hail, Uamemti, who comest forth from the execution chamber, I have not debauched the wife of a man.

20. Hail, Maa-ȧnuf, who comest forth from Per-Menu, I have not polluted myself.

21. Hail, Ḥeri-uru, who comest forth from [Nehatu], I have terrorized no man.

22. Hail, Khemi, who comest forth from Aḥaui (?), I have not made attacks.

23. Hail, Sheṭ-kheru, who comest forth from Uri, I have not been a man of anger.

24. Hail, Nekhen, who comest forth from Ḥeq-āṭ,[1] I have not turned a deaf ear to the words of truth.

25. Hail, Ser-Kheru, who comest forth from Unes,[2] I have not stirred up strife.

[1] The Thirteenth Nome of Lower Egypt.
[2] The metropolis of the Nineteenth Nome of Upper Egypt.

26. Hail, Basti, who comest forth from Shetait, I have made none to weep.

27. Hail, Ḥer-f-ḥa-f, who comest forth from thy cavern, I have not committed acts of sexual impurity, or lain with men.

28. Hail, Ta-reṭ, who comest forth from Ākhkhu (Darkness?), I have not eaten my heart (*i.e.*, grieved or repented uselessly, or abandoned myself to remorse, or lost my temper and raged).

29. Hail, Kenemti, who comest forth from Kenmeṭ, I have cursed no man.

30. Hail, Ȧn-ḥetep-f, who comest forth from Sau, I have not acted in a violent or oppressive manner.

31. Hail, Neb-ḥeru, who comest forth from Tchefet, I have not acted [or judged] hastily.

32. Hail, Serekhi, who comest forth from Unth, I have not . . . . . . my hair [or skin?], I have not harmed (?) the god.

33. Hail, Neb-ābui, who comest forth from Sauti, I have not multiplied my speech overmuch.

34. Hail, Nefer-Tem, who comest forth from Ḥet-ka-Ptaḥ, I have not acted with deceit, I have not worked wickedness.

35. Hail, Tem-Sep, who comest forth from Ṭeṭu (Busiris), I have not done things to effect the cursing of [the king].

36. Hail, Ȧri-em-ȧb-f, who comest forth from Ṭebti, I have not stopped (or, fouled) the flow of water.

37. Hail, Ȧḥi-mu (?), who comest forth from Nu, I have not raised my voice (*i.e.*, spoken in a prideful or arrogant manner).

38. Hail, Utu-rekhit, who comest forth from thy house, I have not cursed (or, blasphemed) God.

39. Hail, Neḥeb-Nefert, who comest forth from the Lake of Nefer (?), I have not acted with insufferable insolence.

40. Hail, Neḥeb-kau, who comest forth from [thy] city, I have not sought to make myself unduly distinguished.

41. Hail, Tcheser-tep, who comest forth from thy cavern, I have not increased my wealth except through such things as are [justly] my own possessions.

42. Hail, Ȧn-ā-f, who comest forth from Ȧuḳer, I have not scorned [or treated with contempt] the god of my town.

APPENDIX

CHAPTER CXXV

ADDRESS TO THE GODS OF THE ṬUAT

[From the Papyrus of Nu (Brit. Mus. No. 10477, Sheet 24)]

[1 ...]

1. ... 2. ...

THE FOLLOWING ARE THE WORDS WHICH THE HEART OF TRUTH THAT IS SINLESS SHALL SAY WHEN HE COMETH WITH THE WORD OF TRUTH INTO THE HALL OF MAĀTI; THEY SHALL BE SAID WHEN HE COMETH TO THE GODS WHO DWELL IN THE ṬUAT; AND THEY ARE THE WORDS WHICH ARE [TO BE SAID] AFTER [HE COMETH FORTH FROM] THE HALL OF MAĀTI.

1. Nu, the steward of the keeper of the seal, whose word is truth, saith :—Homage to you, O ye gods who dwell in your Hall of Maāti! I know 2. you, I know your names. Let me not fall under your knives of slaughter, and bring ye not forward my wickedness to this

1 The passage within [ ] forms the title of the Chapter.

god in whose 3. following ye are. Let not evil hap (or, bad luck) come upon me through you. Speak ye the truth concerning me in the presence of Neb-er-tcher, for I have done what is right and just in Ta-Merȧ.[1] 4. I have not cursed the god (or, God), and my evil hap did not come upon him that was king in his day.

Homage to you, O ye who dwell in your Hall of Maāti, 5. who have nothing false in your bodies, who live upon Truth, who feed yourselves upon Truth in the presence of Horus 6. who dwelleth in his Disk; deliver ye me from Beba,[2] who feedeth upon the livers of the great ones (or, princes) on the day of the Great Judgment. 7. Grant ye that I may come before you, for I have not committed sin, I have done no act of deceit, I have done no evil thing, and

[1] An ancient name of Egypt.
[2] He was the first-born son of Osiris.

I have not borne [false] witness; **8.** therefore let nothing [evil] be done to me. I have lived upon truth, I have fed upon truth, I have performed the ordinances of men, and the things which gratify the gods. **9.** I have propitiated the god by doing his will, I have given bread to the hungry man, and water to him that was athirst, and apparel to the naked man, **10.** and a ferry-boat to him that had no boat. I have made propitiatory offerings and given cakes to the gods, and the "things which appear at the word" to the Spirits. Deliver then ye me, **11.** protect then ye me, and make ye no report against me in the presence [of the Great God]. I am pure in respect of my mouth, and I am clean in respect of my hands,[1] therefore let it be said unto me by those who shall behold me: "Come in peace, **12.** Come in peace."[2] For I have heard that great word which the

[1] *I.e.*, my speech is clean, *i.e.*, truth, and I have never soiled my hands by doing a false, or deceitful, or mean, or wicked act.

[2] *I.e.*, Welcome, welcome.

Sāḥu spake to the Cat,[2] 13. in the House of Ḥapṭ-ra. I have borne witness to Ḥer-f-ḥa-f,[3] and he hath given a decision (?) [concerning me]. I have seen the things over which the Persea tree 14. which is in Rasta, spreadeth its branches. I have made petitions to the gods, [and I] know the things [which appertain to] their bodies. I have come, travelling a long road, to bear righteous testimony, and to set the Balance 15. upon its supports within Åuḳert.

Hail, thou who art exalted high upon thy standard, thou Lord of the Atef Crown, who dost make thy name to be "Lord of the Winds," deliver thou me 16. from thy divine Envoys who punish and afflict according to [thy] decrees,

[1] Var. , etc.

[2] Var. "For I have heard the word which the Ass spake to the Cat."

[3] He was the ferryman who ferried righteous souls to the Island of Truth; his name means, "god with his face behind him."

and who make calamities to arise, **17.** and whose faces are without coverings, for I have done what is right and true for the Lord of Truth. I am pure. My breast is purified by **18.** libations, and my hinder parts are made clean with the things which make clean, and my inner parts have been dipped in the Lake of Truth. There is no single member of mine which lacketh truth. **19.** I have washed myself clean in the Lake of the South. I have rested myself in the City of the North, which is in Sekhet Sanḥemu (*i.e.*, the Field of the Grasshoppers), where the mariners of Rā wash themselves clean at the **20.** second hour of the night, and at the third hour of the day. The hearts of the gods are gratified (?) when they have passed over it, whether it be by night or whether it be by day, and they say unto me, "Let thyself advance." **21.** They say unto me, "Who art thou?" And they say unto me, "What is thy name"?

[And I reply], "Sepṭ-kheri-neḥait-ȧmmi-beq-f"[1] **22.** is my name. Then they say unto me, "Advance straightway on the city which is to the North of the Olive Tree. What dost thou see there?" The Leg and the Thigh. What **23.** dost thou say unto them? Let me see rejoicings in these lands of the Fenkhu.[2] What do they give unto thee? A flame of **24.** fire and a sceptre-amulet [made] of crystal. What dost thou do with them? I bury them on the furrow of M'nāat (*sic*), as things (*i.e.*, offerings) for the night. What dost **25.** thou find on the furrow of Māat? A sceptre of flint, the name of which is "Giver of winds." What now didst thou do with the flame of fire and the **26.** sceptre-

[1] *I.e.*, "He who is equipped with the *nehai* flowers, the dweller in his olive tree."

[2] A people who dwelt on the North-east frontier of Egypt, and who are by some identified with the Phoenicians.

amulet [made] of crystal, after thou didst bury them? I said a spell over them, and I dug them up. I quenched the flame of fire and I broke the sceptre-amulet, and I made 27. a lake of water. [Then shall the Two and forty gods say unto me]: "Come now, pass in over the threshold of "this door of the Hall of Maāti, for thou hast knowledge of "us." "We will not allow thee to enter in over us," say the bars of 28. this door "unless thou tellest us our names." [And I reply], "Tekh-bu-maā"[1] is your name. The right lintel of this door saith: 29. "I will not allow thee to pass over me unless thou tellest me my name." [And I reply], "Ḥenku-en-fat-maāt"[2] is thy name. The left lintel of this door saith: "I will not allow thee to pass over me 30. unless thou tellest me my name." [And I reply], "Ḥenku-en-ȧrp"[3] is thy name. The ground of this door

[1] *I.e.*, "Tongue [of the Balance] of the place of Truth."

[2] "Strengthener of the support of Maāt."

[3] "Strengthener of wine."

saith: "I will not allow thee to pass over me unless thou tellest me my name." [And I reply], "Àua-en-Ḳeb"[2] is thy name. And the bolt of this door saith: "I will not open the door to thee unless thou tellest me my name." [And I reply], "Sȧaḥ-en-mut-f"[3] is thy name. The socket of the fastening of this door saith: "I will not open unto thee unless thou tellest my name." [And I reply], "The Living Eye of Sebek, the Lord of Bakhau," is thy name. The Doorkeeper of this door saith: "I will not open to thee, and I will not let thee enter by me **31.** unless thou tellest my name." [And I reply], "Elbow of the god Shu who placeth himself to protect Osiris" is thy name. The posts of this door say: "We will not let thee pass in by us unless thou tellest our name." **32.** [And I reply], "Children

[1] The words within [ ] are from the Papyrus of Nebseni.
[2] *I.e.*, "Ox of Ḳeb."
[3] *I.e.*, "Flesh of his mother"?

of the uraei-goddesses" is your name. The Doorkeeper of this door saith: "I will not open to thee, and I will not let thee enter in by me 33. unless thou tellest my name. [And I reply], "Ox of Ḳeb" is thy name. [And they reply], "Thou knowest us, pass in therefore by us." The ground 34. of this Hall of Maāti saith: "I will not let thee tread "upon me [unless thou tellest me my name], for I am "silent. I am holy because I know the names of two feet "wherewith thou wouldst walk 35. upon me. Declare, then, "them to me." [And I reply], "Besu-Aḥu" is the name of my right foot, and "Unpet-ent-Ḥet-Ḥeru" is the name of my left foot. [The ground replieth]: 36. "Thou knowest us, enter in therefore over us." The Doorkeeper of this Hall of Maāti saith: "I will not announce thee unless thou tellest my name." [And I reply], "Discerner 37. of hearts, searcher of bellies" is thy name. [The Doorkeeper saith]

"Thou shalt now be announced." [He saith]: "Who is the god who dwelleth in his hour? Speak it (*i.e.*, his name)" [And I reply], "Āu-taui." [He saith]: "Explain who he is." 38. [And I reply], "Āu-taui" is Thoth. "Come now," saith Thoth, "for what purpose hast thou come?" [And I reply]. "I have come, and have journeyed hither that my name may be announced [to the god]." 39. [Thoth saith]: "In what condition art thou"? [And I reply], "I, even I, am purified from evil defects, and I am wholly "free from the curses (?) of those who live in their days, "40. and I am not one of their number." [Thoth saith]: "Therefore shall [thy name] be announced to the god." [Thoth saith]: "Tell me, who is he 44. whose heaven is of fire, whose walls are living serpents, and whose ground is a stream of water? Who is he?" [And I reply], "He is

[1] Here the scribe inadvertently repeats the passage beginning (l. 37).

Osiris." [Thoth saith]: "Advance now, [thy name] shall "be announced to him. Thy cakes shall come from the "Utchat (Eye of Horus or Rā), thy ale shall come from the "**46.** Utchat, and the offerings which shall appear to thee at "the word upon earth [shall proceed] from the Utchat." This is what Osiris hath decreed for the steward of the overseer of the seal, Nu, whose word is truth.

RUBRIC: **47.** THE MAKING OF THE REPRESENTATION OF WHAT SHALL HAPPEN IN THIS HALL OF MAĀTI. This Chapter shall be said by the deceased when he is cleansed and purified, and is arrayed in linen apparel, **48.** and is shod with sandals of white leather, and his eyes are painted with antimony, and his body is anointed with unguent made of myrrh. And he shall present as offerings oxen, and feathered fowl (*i.e.*, geese), and incense, and cakes and ale, and **49.** garden herbs. And behold, thou shalt draw a representation of this in colour upon a new tile moulded from **50.** earth upon which neither a pig nor any other animal hath trodden. And if this book be done [in writing, the deceased] shall flourish, and his children **51.** shall flourish, and [his name] shall never fall into oblivion, and he shall be as one who filleth (*i.e.*, satisfieth) the heart of the king and of his princes. And bread, and cakes, and sweetmeats, **52.** and wine, and pieces of flesh shall be given unto him [from among those which are] upon the altar of the Great God. And he shall not be driven back from any door in Åmentet, and he shall be **53.** led in along with the kings of the South and the kings of the North, and he shall be among the bodyguard of Osiris, continually and regularly for ever. [And he shall come forth in every form he pleaseth as a living soul for ever, and ever, and ever.]

[1] See Naville, *op. cit.*, Bd. II, Bl. 334.

CHAPTER XLII

[CHAPTER OF THE DEIFICATION OF THE MEMBERS]

PLATE XXXII

1. The hair of the Osiris Ani, whose word is truth, is the hair of Nu.

2. The face of the Osiris Ani, whose word is truth, is the face of Rā.

3. The eyes of the Osiris Ani, whose word is truth, are the eyes of Hathor.

4. The ears of the Osiris Ani, whose word is truth, are the ears of Up-uatu.

5. The lips of the Osiris Ani, whose word is truth, are the lips of Ȧnpu.

6. The teeth of the Osiris Ani, whose word is truth, are the teeth of Serqet.

7. The cheeks of the Osiris Ani, whose word is truth, are the cheeks of Isis.

8. The arms of the Osiris Ani, whose word is truth, are the arms of Ba-neb-Ṭeṭu.

9. The neck of the Osiris Ani, whose word is truth, is the neck of Uatchit.

10. The throat of the Osiris Ani, whose word is truth, is the throat of Mert.

11. The breast of the Osiris Ani, whose word is truth, is the breast of the Lady of Saïs.

12. The backbone of the Osiris Ani, whose word is truth, is the backbone of Set.

13. The trunk of the Osiris Ani, whose word is truth, is the trunk of the Lords of Kher-āḥa.

14. The flesh of the Osiris Ani, whose word is truth, is the flesh of Āa-shefit.

15. The belly of the Osiris Ani, whose word is truth, is the belly of Sekhmet.

16. The buttocks of the Osiris Ani, whose word is truth, are the buttocks of the Eye of Horus.

17. The phallus of the Osiris Ani, whose word is truth, is the phallus of Osiris.

18. The thighs of the Osiris Ani, whose word is truth, are the thighs of Nut.

19. The feet of the Osiris Ani, whose word is truth, are the feet of Ptaḥ.

20. The fingers of the Osiris Ani, whose word is truth, are the fingers of Sȧaḥ (Orion).

21. The toes of the Osiris Ani, whose word is truth, are the toes of the Living Uraei.

APPENDIX

THE CHAPTER OF THE DEIFICATION OF THE MEMBERS

[From the Pyramid of Pepi I, ll. 565 ff.[1]]

565. (sic)

566.

565. The head of this Meri-Rā is the head of Horus (?); he cometh forth therefore and ascendeth into heaven.

The skull of this Pepi is the Dekan star (?) of the god; he cometh forth therefore and ascendeth into heaven.

The brow of this Meri-Rā is the brow of . . . . . and Nu; he cometh forth therefore and ascendeth into heaven.

The face of this Pepi is the face of Up-uatu; he cometh forth therefore 566. and ascendeth into heaven.

The eyes of this Meri-Rā are the eyes of the Great Lady, the first of the Souls of Ȧnu; he cometh forth therefore and ascendeth into heaven.

The nose of this Pepi is the nose of Thoth; he cometh forth therefore and ascendeth into heaven.

The mouth of this Meri-Rā is the mouth of Khens-ur; he cometh forth therefore, and ascendeth therefore, and ascendeth therefore into heaven.

[1] See Maspero's edition, p. 221; Sethe's edition, Vol. II, p. 227.

The tongue of this Pepi is the tongue of Maāȧ (Truth)
567. in the Maāt Boat; he cometh forth therefore and ascendeth into heaven.

The teeth of this Pepi are the teeth of the Souls of [Ȧnu?]; he cometh forth therefore and ascendeth into heaven.

The lips of this Meri-Rā are the lips of . . . .; he cometh forth therefore and ascendeth into heaven.

The chin of this Pepi is the chin of Nest-khent-Sekhem (the throne of the First Lady of Sekhem); he cometh forth therefore and ascendeth into heaven.

568. The *thes* bone of this Pepi is the *thes* bone of the Bull Sma; he cometh forth therefore and ascendeth into heaven.

The shoulders of this Pepi are the shoulders of Set; he cometh forth therefore and ascendeth into heaven.

[The . . . . of this Pepi] . . . .; he cometh forth therefore and ascendeth into heaven.

[The . . . . . . of this Pepi] . . . . . . of Baābu; he cometh forth therefore and ascendeth into heaven.

569. The breast (or, heart) of this Meri-Rā is the breast of Bast; he cometh forth therefore and ascendeth into heaven.

The belly of this Meri-Rā is the belly of Nut; he cometh forth therefore and ascendeth into heaven.

[The . . . . of this Pepi] . . . . ; he cometh forth therefore and ascendeth into heaven.

[The . . . . . . of this Pepi] . . . . of the two Companies of the gods; he cometh forth therefore and ascendeth
570. into heaven.

The two thighs of this Pepi are the two thighs of Ḥeqet; he cometh forth therefore and ascendeth into heaven.

The buttocks of this Meri-Rā are like the Semktet Boat and the Māntchet Boat; **571.** he cometh forth therefore and ascendeth into heaven.

The phallus of this Pepi is the phallus of the Ḥep Bull; he cometh forth therefore and ascendeth into heaven.

The legs of this Meri-Rā **572.** are the legs of Net (Neith) and Serqet; he cometh forth therefore and ascendeth into heaven.

The knees of this Meri-Rā are the knees of the twin Souls who are at the head of Sekhet-Tcher; 573. he cometh forth therefore and ascendeth into heaven.

The soles of this Meri-Rā are like the Maāti Boat; he cometh forth therefore and ascendeth into heaven.

The toes of this Pepi 574. are the toes of the Souls of Anu; he cometh forth therefore and ascendeth into heaven.

Now this Pepi is a god, the son of a god; he cometh forth therefore and ascendeth into heaven.

This Pepi 575. is the son of Rā, who loveth him; he cometh forth therefore and ascendeth into heaven.

Rā hath sent forth Meri-Rā; he cometh forth therefore and ascendeth into heaven.

Rā hath begotten [this] Pepi; 576. he cometh forth therefore and ascendeth into heaven.

Rā hath given birth to Pepi; he cometh forth therefore and ascendeth into heaven.

This spell therefore is in the body of Meri-Rā; **577.** he cometh forth therefore and ascendeth into heaven.

This Meri-Rā is the Power, the Great Power, among the Great Council of Chiefs in Ånu; he cometh forth therefore and ascendeth **578.** into heaven.

He worketh the boat; Pepi cometh forth therefore and ascendeth into heaven.

[Pepi is] Horus, the nursling, the child; Meri-Rā cometh forth therefore and ascendeth into heaven.

579. Pepi hath not had union with Nut, she hath not given her hands to him; he cometh forth therefore and ascendeth into heaven.

Ḳeb hath not removed the obstacles (?) in his path; **580.** he cometh forth therefore and ascendeth into heaven.

No god hath smitten the steps of this Meri-Rā; he cometh forth therefore and ascendeth **581.** into heaven.

[Though] Pepi is not censed (?) is not mourned, hath not washed himself in the vessel, hath not smelt the haunch, hath not carried the meat-offering, hath not ploughed the earth, 582. hath not dedicated (?) an offering, he cometh forth therefore and ascendeth into heaven.

Behold, it is not this Pepi who hath said these things to you, O ye gods, 583. it is Ḥeka who hath said these things to you, O ye gods, and this Meri-Rā is the support which is under Ḥeka; he cometh forth therefore and ascendeth into heaven.

Every god 584. smiteth (*i.e.*, dedicateth) the feet of Pepi; he cometh forth therefore and ascendeth into heaven.

Every god giveth up to Pepi his throne in his boat; 585. he cometh forth therefore and ascendeth into heaven.

He plougheth the earth, he dedicateth an offering, he bringeth the vessel of [blood], he smelleth 586. the haunch, and he bringeth the meat offering; he cometh forth therefore and ascendeth into heaven.

Every god graspeth the hand of this Meri-Rā in heaven, 587.

He conducteth him to the House of Horus in the sky.
The word of his Double is truth before Ḳeb.

The above section from the text of Pepi I illustrates the poetical treatment which the Chapter of the Deification of Members received at the hands of the early scribes, and shows that each statement was followed by the refrain "he cometh forth therefore and ascendeth into heaven," which was probably sung in unison by a number of assistant priests. In the later treatment of the Chapter the refrain is suppressed, and in the Theban and Saïte Recensions the introductory matter, and the lines which follow the main section, prove that under the XVIIIth dynasty religious views of a totally different character were associated with it. This fact is well illustrated by the version of Chapter XLII written in the Papyrus of Nu, where we find that a title is given to the subject-matter of the main section which associates it with the great slaughter that took place in Ḥensu (Herakleopolis). The following is the text, with a translation :—

CHAPTER XLII

THE CHAPTER OF REPULSING SLAUGHTER IN HENSU

[From the Papyrus of Nu, Sheet 6]

CHAPTER XLII. 1. THE CHAPTER OF DRIVING BACK THE 2. SLAUGHTERS WHICH ARE PERFORMED IN ḤENSU (Herakleopolis). The Osiris Nu, whose word is truth, saith :—O thou land of the Sceptre! O thou White Crown of the divine form! O thou rest of the ferry-boat! I am the Child 3. (*Repeat four times*). Hail, Ȧbu-ur! Thou sayest daily: "The slaughter-block is made ready as thou knowest, and thou hast come to destruction." I am 4. Rā, who stablisheth those who praise him. I am the Knot of the god in the Ȧser tree, the twice beautiful one, who is more splendid to-day than yesterday (*Repeat four times*). I am Rā, who stablisheth those who praise him. 5. I am the Knot of the god within the Ȧser tree, and my appearance is the appearance [of Rā] on this day.

My hair is the hair of Nu. My face is the face of the Disk. My eyes are the eyes of 6. Hathor. My ears are the ears of Up-uat. My nose is the nose of Khenti-Khabas (?) My lips are the lips of Ȧnpu. My teeth are the teeth of 7. Serqet. My cheeks are the cheeks of the goddess Isis. My hands are the hands of Ba-neb-Ṭeṭ. My forearms are the forearms of Neith, the Lady of Saïs.

My backbone is the **8.** backbone of Suti. My phallus is the phallus of Beba. My reins are the reins of the Lords of Kher-āḥa. My chest is the chest of Āa-shefit. **9.** My belly and back are the belly and back of Sekhmet. My buttocks are the buttocks of the Eye of Horus. My hips and legs are the hips and legs of Nut. My feet are the feet of **10.** Ptaḥ. [My fingers] and my toes are the [fingers and] toes of the Living gods. There is no member of my body which is not the member of a god. Thoth protecteth my body **11.** altogether, and I am Rā day by day. I shall not be dragged back by my arms, and none shall lay violent hold upon my hands. And shall do me hurt neither men, nor gods, **12.** nor the Spirit-souls, nor the dead, nor any man, nor any *pāt*-spirit, nor any *rekhit*-spirit, nor any *ḥememet*-spirit. **13.**

I am he who cometh forth advancing, whose name is unknown. I am Yesterday. "Seer of Millions of Years" is my name. I pass along, I pass along the paths of the divine celestial judges. 14. I am the Lord of Eternity: I decree and I judge like Kheperà. I am the Lord of the Urrt Crown. I am he who dwelleth in the Utchat and in the Egg, and it is granted unto me to live therein. I am he who dwelleth in the Utchat when it closeth, and I exist by the strength thereof. I come forth and I shine; I enter in and I come to life. I am in the Utchat, my seat is 15. upon my throne, and I sit in the *ṭent* chamber before it. I am Horus. [I] traverse millions of years. I have decreed [the stablishing] of my throne, and I am the ruler thereof; and in very truth my mouth keepeth an even balance both in speech 16. and in silence. In very truth my forms are inverted. I am Un-Nefer, from one period

[1] From the Papyrus of Mes-em-neter.

even unto another, and what I have is within me. I am
17. the only One, who proceedeth from an only One, who
goeth round about in his course. I am he who dwelleth in
the Utchat. No evil thing of any shape or kind shall
spring up against me, and no baleful object, and no harmful
thing, and no disastrous thing shall happen unto me.
18. I open the door in heaven. I rule my throne. I open
the way for the births which take place on this day. I am
the child who traverseth the road of Yesterday. I am
To-day 19. for untold nations and peoples. I am he who
protecteth you for millions of years. Whether ye be
denizens of heaven, or of the earth, or of the South, or of
the 20. North, or of the East, or of the West, the fear of
me is in your bodies. I am he whose being hath been
wrought in his eye. I shall not die again. My moment is
in your bodies, 21. but my forms are in my place of

habitation. I am "He who cannot be known." The Red Fiends have their faces directed against me. I am the unveiled one. The period when the heavens were created for me **22.** and were enlarged the bounds of earth, and multiplied the progeny thereof, cannot be found out. They shall fail and not be united again. By reason of the speech which I address **23.** to you, my name setteth itself apart from all things evil which are in the mouths of men. I am he who riseth and shineth, a wall which cometh out of a wall, an only One who proceedeth from an only One. There is never a day that passeth without **24.** the things which appertain unto him being therein; passing, passing, passing, passing. Verily I say unto thee, I am the Plant which cometh forth from Nu, and my mother is Nut. Hail, O **25.** my Creator, I am he who hath no power to walk, the Great Knot who dwelleth in Yesterday. The might of my strength is within my hand, I am not known [by thee], but

I am he who knoweth thee. **26.** I cannot be held in the hand, but I am he who can hold thee in his hand. Hail, O Egg! Hail, O Egg! I am Horus who liveth for millions of years, whose flame shineth upon you, **27.** and bringeth your hearts unto me. I am master of my throne. I advance at this season. I have opened a path. I have delivered myself from all evil things. **28.** I am the golden dog-headed ape, three palms and two fingers [high], which hath neither arms nor legs, and which dwelleth in Ḥet-ka-Ptaḥ (Memphis). I go forth as goeth forth the dog-headed ape which dwelleth in Ḥet-ka-Ptaḥ.

RUBRIC TO CHAPTER CXXV

PLATE XXXIII

RUBRIC: **1.** Behold the Osiris Ani, whose word is truth, arrayed in fine linen, and shod with **2.** sandals of white [leather], and anointed with the very finest myrrh

unguent. There are offered unto him 3. a fine bull, and incense, and *ra* geese, and flowers, and ale, and cakes, and garden herbs. And behold, thou shalt draw a representation of a table of offerings 4. on a clean tile with pure colours, and thou shalt bury it in a field whereon no 5. swine hath trodden. And if a copy of this book be written upon it, he shall rise [again], and 6. his children's children shall flourish and prosper, like unto Rā, without cessation. He shall be in high favour 7. with the king, and with the *shenit* nobles of his court, and there shall be given unto him cakes and cups of drink, and portions of flesh, upon the altar-table 8. of the Great God. He shall not be thrust aside at any door in Åmentet; he shall travel in the train 9. of the Kings of the South and the Kings of the North, and he shall abide with the 10. followers of Osiris near Un-Nefer, for ever, and for ever, and for ever.

APPENDIX

The Vignette which follows the above RUBRIC apparently belongs to Chapter CXXVI, but the text of the Chapter is wanting; it is here supplied from the Papyrus of Nu, Sheet 24:—

1. The steward of the overseer of the seal, Nu, whose word is truth, begotten of the steward of the overseer of the seal, Åmen-ḥetep, whose word is truth, saith:—2. Hail, ye Four Apes who sit in the bows of the Boat of Rā, 3. who convey truth to Nebertcher, who sit in judgment 4. on the oppressed man and on [his] oppressor, who make the gods to be contented by means of the flame of your 5. mouths, who offer holy offerings to the gods, and sepulchral meals to the Spirit-souls, 6. who live upon truth, and who feed upon 7. truth of heart, who are without deceit and fraud, and to whom wickedness is an abomination, 8. do ye away with my evil deeds, and put ye away my sins [which deserved stripes upon earth, and destroy ye every evil thing which appertaineth to me], and let there be no

obstacle whatsoever on my part 9. towards you. O grant ye that I may make my way through the Åmeḥet,[2] let me enter into Rasta, let me pass through 10. the hidden pylons of Åment. O grant that there may be given unto me *shens* cakes, 11. and ale, and *persen* cakes, even as to the living Spirit-souls, and grant that I may enter into 12. and come forth from Rasta.

[The Four Apes make answer, saying:] Come thou, for we have done away with thy wickedness, and we have put away thy sin, along with thy sins upon earth which deserved stripes, and we have destroyed every evil thing

[1] Added from Brit. Mus. Papyrus No. 9913.

[2] Originally a chamber or place in the Kingdom of Seker, the god of Death, which was full of fire and boiling water; only the righteous could pass through this region unharmed. The gods held it in great awe, it was a place of mystery to the Spirit-souls, and it was a most fatal place for the dead. According to Chapter CXLIX the god of it was called SEKHER (?).

13. which appertained to thee upon earth. Enter, therefore, unto Rasta, and pass through the hidden pylons of Åmentet, and there shall be given unto thee *shens* cakes, 14. and ale, and *persen* cakes, and thou shalt come forth and shalt enter in at thy desire, even as do those who are favoured [of the God], and thou shalt be called [to partake of offerings] each day in the horizon.

CHAPTER CLV

THE CHAPTER OF THE ṬEṬ OF GOLD

PLATE XXXIII

CHAPTER CLV. 1. THE CHAPTER OF A ṬET OF GOLD. The Osiris Ani, whose word is truth, saith :—Thou risest up for thyself, O Still-heart! Thou 2. shinest for thyself, O Still-heart! Place thou thyself on thy base (?), I come, I bring unto thee a Ṭeṭ of gold, thou shalt rejoice therein.

APPENDIX

The version of this Chapter found in the Papyrus of Nebseni and in the Papyrus of Nu reads differently. Thus we have :—Rise up thou, O Osiris, thou hast thy backbone, O Still-heart, thou hast thy neck vertebrae and thy back, O Still-heart! Place thou thyself on thy base (?). I put water beneath thee, and I bring unto thee a Ṭeṭ of gold that thou mayest rejoice therein.[1]

[1]

RUBRIC: [1. From the Papyrus of Nu.]

[This Chapter] shall be recited over a Ṭeṭ of gold set in a stand made of sycamore wood which hath been steeped in a tincture of *ānkhamu* flowers, and it shall be placed on the neck of the deceased on the day of the funeral. If this amulet be placed on his neck he shall become a perfect Khu in Khert-Neter, and at the festivals of the New Year he shall be like unto the Followers of Osiris continually and for ever.

RUBRIC: [2. From the Turin Papyrus.]

[This Chapter] shall be said over a Ṭeṭ of gold fashioned out of the trunk of a sycamore tree, and it shall be placed on the neck of the deceased. Then shall he enter in through the doors of the Ṭuat. His words shall not be silenced. He shall place himself on his ground on New Year's Day among the Followers of Osiris.

If this Chapter be known by the deceased he shall live like a perfect Khu in Khert-Neter. He shall not be driven back from the doors of Åmentet. There shall be given to him the *shens* cake, and a cup of wine, and the *persen* cake, and slices of meat on the altars of Rā, or as some read, Osiris Un-Nefer. And his word shall be truth before his enemies in Khert-Neter continually, and for ever and for ever.[1]

CHAPTER CLVI

THE CHAPTER OF A TET OF RED STONE (CARNELIAN?)

PLATE XXXIII

1. 2. [2]

CHAPTER CLVI. 1. THE CHAPTER OF A TET OF CARNELIAN. The Osiris Ani, whose word is truth, saith:—The blood of Isis, the spells of Isis, 2. the magical powers of Isis, shall make this great one strong, and shall be an amulet of protection [against him] that would do to him the things which he abominateth.

[1] A fine collection of Ṭeṭs is exhibited in the Fourth Egyptian Room in the British Museum. Some are surmounted by crowns, , and . They are made of blue, or green, glazed faïence, lapis-lazuli, carnelian, agate, opaque blue glass, and one, a very interesting example (No. 20636), is made of stone and inlaid with lapis-lazuli, carnelian, plasma, and mother-of-emerald.

[2] The Papyrus of Nu has .

RUBRIC: [From the Papyrus of Nu.]

[This Chapter] shall be said over a Tet of carnelian, which hath been washed in a tincture of *ānkhamu* flowers, and is fashioned out of the trunk of a sycamore tree. It shall be placed on the neck of the deceased on the day of the funeral. If this be done for him the magical powers of Isis will protect his members. Horus, the son of Isis, shall rejoice when he seeth him. [No] road shall be blocked to him. His hand shall be to heaven, his hand shall be to earth, for ever. Do not let anyone see him. Verily . . . .

In the Saïte Recension the Rubric is a little fuller, thus:

[This Chapter] shall be said over a Tet of carnelian, anointed with tincture of *ānkhamu* flowers, made from the trunk of a sycamore tree. It shall be placed on the neck of the Khu. If this book be done (*i.e.*, written) for him, the magical spells of Isis shall protect him, and Horus the son of Isis shall rejoice [when] he seeth him. No road shall be blocked to him. His hand shall be to heaven, his hand shall be to earth . . . . If this book be known by him he shall be in the following of Osiris Un-Nefer, and his word shall be truth in Khert-Neter. The doors in Khert-Neter shall be opened to him. Wheat and barley shall be given to him in Sekhet-Åanru. His name shall be like [the names of] the gods who are there, the Followers of Horus who reap.

CHAPTER XXIXc

THE CHAPTER OF A HEART OF SEHERT STONE

PLATE XXXIII

1.

2.

CHAPTER XXIXc. 1. THE CHAPTER OF A HEART OF SEHERT STONE. The Osiris Ani, whose word is truth, saith:—I am the Benu bird, the Heart-soul of Rā, the guide of the gods 2. to the Ṭuat. Their Heart-souls come forth upon earth to do what their KAU (*i.e.*, Doubles) wish to do, and the Heart-soul of the Osiris Ani shall come forth to do what his KA wisheth to do.

The above Chapter is one of the many formulae which were composed with the view of protecting the heart, and it seems to have been drawn up for the purpose of inscribing upon hearts made of sehert, a stone which has not yet been satisfactorily identified. There is really no good reason for considering it as a variant of Chapter XXIXA or XXIXB, and it is only grouped with these because its subject matter is the heart. In the version of this Chapter published by Naville (*op. cit.*, I, Bl. 41), the text is somewhat fuller and reads :—

(*sic*)

For the texts and translations of Chapters XXIXA and XXIXB, see the description of the contents of Plate XV (*supra*, pp. 278 ff., Vol. I).

CHAPTER CLXVI

THE CHAPTER OF THE HEAD-REST, OR PILLOW

PLATE XXXIII

1\.

2\.

CHAPTER CLXVI. **1.** THE CHAPTER OF THE HEAD-REST [OR PILLOW], which is to be placed under the head of the Osiris Ani, whose word is truth. Awake out of thy sufferings, O thou who liest prostrate! **2.** Awake thou! Thy head is in the horizon. I lift thee up, O thou whose word is truth. Ptaḥ hath overthrown thine enemies for thee. Thine enemies have fallen, and they shall never more exist, O Osiris.

The above version of this Chapter is incomplete. The full text of it as found in the Papyrus of Nebseni (Sheet 21) is as follows:—

THE CHAPTER OF THE HEAD-REST [OR PILLOW]. Awake out of thy sufferings (or, pain), O thou who liest prostrate. They (*i.e.*, the gods) keep watch over thy head in the horizon. Thou art lifted up, thy word is truth in respect of the things which have been done by thee. Ptaḥ hath cast down headlong thine enemies. This work was ordered to be done for thee. Thou art Horus, the son of Hathor, Nesert, Nesertet, who giveth back the head after it hath been cut off. Thy head shall not be carried away from thee, after [it hath been cut off]; thy head shall not be carried away from thee, never, never!

With the head-rest, or pillow, the series of amulets which Ani regarded as all-important for his protection come to an end. In the Turin Papyrus several other amulets are figured, and the texts which were connected with them given. Thus the Vignette of Chapter CLVII is a vulture, with outstretched wings, holding in each claw the symbol of "life." This amulet was made of gold, and was laid upon the neck of the deceased; it symbolized the goddess Isis, and gave to the dead her protection. The deceased took the place of Horus, and, as Isis raised him from the dead in the papyrus swamps of the Delta, it was assumed that she would effect the resurrection of every one who worshipped her. The Vignette of Chapter CLVIII was a pectoral, with hawks' heads, which was made of gold and was placed on the neck of the deceased, to whom it assured the protection of Isis. The Vignette of Chapter CLIX is a sceptre 𓇅, which was made of mother-of-emerald. It was placed on the neck of the deceased, and secured for him the protection of the goddess Rennet. In the Vignette of Chapter CLX, we see Thoth giving the sceptre-amulet to the deceased, and it carried with it the protection and strength of the great god of words of power. The Vignette of Chapter CLXII is a cow. This amulet was made of fine gold and was placed on the neck of the deceased. The Chapter itself was written on a piece of new papyrus and laid under his head, and it was believed to keep in his body heat which resembled that which was in it when he was upon earth. In the Vignette to Chapter CLXIII we find a serpent with two human legs, and with a pair of horns and a disk upon his head. With it are two Utchats, each with a pair of wings and a pair of human legs. In the pupil of one Utchat is a hawk-headed figure of Menu, and in the pupil of the other is a figure of Menu with the head of Neith. These secured for the deceased absolute freedom and happiness in the Ṭuat, and abundance of food, and immunity from the calamities which Set could inflict. In the Vignette to Chapter CLXIV we have a figure of Mut, with three heads, viz., one of the goddess Pekhat, one of a man, and one of a vulture. Mut is provided with a phallus, a pair of wings, and the claws of a lion. With Mut are two fat dwarfs, each having a head with two faces, one of a man and the other of a hawk. The recital of the Chapter over these figures did away from the deceased the effects of death. In the Vignette of Chapter CLXV is a figure of Menu, with the body of a beetle and ithyphallic; he has a pair of plumes on his head, his right arm bears a flail, and is raised, and he wears a tail. With him is a human figure with a ram's head projecting from each shoulder. The figure of Menu is painted over the heart of the deceased and the other over his breasts. These caused the deceased to shine like the stars in heaven. In the Nebseni Papyrus (Sheet 22) the Vignette of Chapter CLXVII is an Utchat set upon the emblem of gold. The text of the Chapter refers to the bringing back to Rā his Eye, which had been carried off by Set. Thoth sought for the Eye, brought it back, and replaced it in the face of the Sun-god. As Thoth did this for Rā, so will he bring back the soul to the dead body of the man who is a loyal servant and worshipper of Osiris.

CHAPTER CLIa

THE TEXTS IN THE FUNERAL CHAMBER

PLATES XXXIII AND XXXIV

I. Speech of Isis. Isis saith:—I have come to be a protector unto thee. I waft unto thee air for thy nostrils, and the north wind which cometh forth from the god Tem unto thy nose. I have made whole for thee thy windpipe. I make thee to live like a god. Thine enemies have fallen under thy feet. I have made thy word to be true before Nut, and thou art mighty before the gods.

II. SPEECH OF NEPHTHYS. Nephthys saith unto the Osiris Ani, whose word is truth:—I go round about thee to protect thee, O brother Osiris. I have come to be a protector unto thee. [My strength shall be near thee, my strength shall be near thee, for ever. Rā hath heard thy cry, and the gods have made thy word to be truth. Thou art raised up. Thy word is truth in respect of what hath been done unto thee. Ptaḥ hath overthrown thy foes, and thou art Horus, the son of Hathor.][1]

III. SPEECH OF THE ṬEṬ. I have come quickly, and I have driven back the footsteps of the god whose face is hidden.[2] I have illumined his sanctuary. I stand near the god Ṭeṭ on the day of repelling disaster.[3] I watch to protect thee, O Osiris.

[1] The text of Ani is corrupt here, and the words within brackets are translated from the following text:

[2] Read:

[3] Var.

IV. Speech of Ḳestȧ (Mestȧ). I am Ḳestȧ, thy son, O Osiris Ani, whose word is truth. I come to protect thee. I will make thy house to flourish, permanently, even as Ptaḥ hath commanded me, and as Rā himself hath commanded.

V. Speech of Ḥāpi. I am Ḥāpi, thy son, O Osiris Ani, whose word is truth. I come to protect thee. I bind together thy head and the members of thy body. I smite down for thee thine enemies under thee. I give unto thee thy head for ever and for ever, O Osiris Ani, whose word is truth, whose word is truth in peace.

VI. Speech of Ṭuamutef. Ṭuamutef saith :—I am thy son Horus, who loveth thee. I come to avenge thee, O my father Osiris, upon him that did evil unto thee. I have set him under thy feet for ever and for ever, permanently, permanently, O Osiris Ani, whose word is truth, whose word is truth.

VII. 1. . . . 2. . . . 3. . . . 4. . . . 5. . . . (*sic*)

VIII. 1. . . . 2. . . . 3. . . .

VII. SPEECH OF QEBḤSENUF. Qebḥsenuf saith:—I am thy son, O Osiris Ani, whose word is truth. I come to protect thee. I have collected thy bones and I have gathered together thy members. [I have brought thy heart, and I have placed it upon its throne within thy body. I make thy house to flourish after thee, O thou who livest for ever.][1]

VIII. SPEECH OF THE FLAME. I protect thee with this flame. I drive him [the foe] away from the valley of the tomb. I cast (?) the sand about [thy feet]. I embrace the Osiris Ani, whose word is truth, in peace. [A better text gives: "I surround with sand the hidden coffer, and drive away therefrom those who would attack it. I shed light in the valley of the tomb, I illumine it. I traverse the roads to protect (Osiris)."][2]

[1] The text of Ani is corrupt. The passage in brackets is translated from another text which reads:

[2]

IX. Speech of the Flame. I come to hew in pieces. I have not been hewn in pieces, and I will not permit thee to be hewn in pieces. I come to do violence [to thy foe], but I will not permit violence to be done unto thee. I protect thee.

X. A soul saith :—The Osiris Ani, whose word is truth, praiseth Rā when he rolleth up into the sky in the eastern horizon of heaven.

XI. A soul saith :—The Osiris Ani, whose word is truth, in peace in Khert-Neter, praiseth Rā when he setteth in the western horizon of heaven, [and saith], "I am a perfect soul."

XII. Speech of Ani. The Osiris Ani, whose word is truth, saith :—I am a perfect soul dwelling in the divine egg of the Ȧbṭu Fish. I am the Great Cat which dwelleth in the Seat of Truth, wherein the god Shu riseth.

XIII. [Chapter vi.] The Chapter of not doing work in Khert-Neter.

1.

2. (*sic*)

3.

4.

XIII. Speech of the Ushabti Figure. [The Chapter of not doing work in Khert-Neter.] Illumine the Osiris Ani, whose word is truth. Hail, Shabti Figure! If the Osiris Ani be decreed to do any of the work which is to be done in Khert-Neter, let everything which standeth in the way be removed from him—whether it be to plough the fields, or to fill the channels with water, or to carry sand from [the East to the West]. The Shabti Figure replieth: I will do it, verily I am here [when] thou callest.

In the Papyrus of Nu and in the Papyrus of Nebseni, the speech of Ȧnpu, who is seen in the Vignette standing by the bier, forms a Chapter by itself, and is extant in two forms, which are as follows:—

Chapter CLIb. 1.

2.

1. Anubis the dweller in the mummy chamber, Governor of the Divine House, layeth his hands upon the lord of life (*i.e.*, the mummy), 2. the scribe, the draughtsman of Ptaḥ, Nebseni, the lord of fealty, begotten of the scribe and mason Thena, born of the lady of the house Mut-rest,

whose word is truth, and 3. devoting himself to him as his guardian, saith:—Homage to thee, thou happy one, lord! Thou seest the Utchat. 4. Ptaḥ-Seker hath bound thee up. Ȧnpu hath exalted thee. Shu hath raised thee up, O 5. Beautiful Face, thou governor of eternity. Thou hast thine eye, O scribe Nebseni, lord of fealty, and it is beautiful. Thy right eye is 6. like the Sektet Boat, thy left eye is like the Aṭet Boat. Thine eyebrows are fair to see in the presence of the 7. Company of the Gods. Thy brow is under the protection of Ȧnpu, and thy head and face, O beautiful one, 8. are before the holy Hawk. Thy fingers have been stablished by thy scribe's craft in the presence of the Lord of Khemenu, Thoth, 9. who hath bestowed upon thee the knowledge of the speech of the holy books. Thy beard is beautiful in the sight of Ptaḥ-Seker, and thou, O scribe Nebseni, thou lord of fealty, art beautiful before 10. the Great Company of the Gods. The Great

God looketh upon thee, and he leadeth thee along the path of happiness. Sepulchral meals are bestowed upon thee, and he overthroweth for thee thine enemies, **II.** setting them under thy feet in the presence of the Great Company of the Gods who dwell in the House of the Great Åged One which is in Ånu (Heliopolis).

CHAPTER CLIc. The following is a shortened form of Chapter CLIB :—

CHAPTER CX

THE CHAPTERS OF SEKHET-ḤETEPET (THE ELYSIAN FIELDS)

PLATE XXXIV

CHAPTER CX. 1. [HERE] BEGIN THE CHAPTERS OF SEKHET-ḤETEPET, AND THE CHAPTERS OF COMING FORTH BY DAY, OF ENTERING INTO AND COMING FORTH FROM KHERT-NETER, OF ARRIVING IN SEKHET-ÅANRU, 2. AND OF LIVING IN PEACE IN THE GREAT CITY, THE LADY OF WINDS. [The Osiris the scribe Ani, whose word is truth, saith :—] Let me be master there. Let me be a *khu* there. Let me plough there. Let 3. me reap there. Let me eat there. Let me drink there. [Let me beget there

] Let me do there all the things which one doeth upon earth. The Osiris Ani, whose **4.** word is truth saith :—Horus vanquished Set when [he] looked at the building (?) of Sekhet-Ḥetepet. [He] spread **5.** air over the Divine Soul in its Egg, in its day. He delivered the interior of the body of Horus [from the Åḳeru Gods]. I have crowned him in the House **6.** of Shu. His house is the stars. Behold, I take up my place in its nomes. He hath guided the hearts of the Company of the Firstborn Gods. **7.** He hath reconciled the Two Fighters (*i.e.*, Horus and Set), the guardians of life. He hath done what is fair, bringing an offering (?). He hath reconciled the Two Fighters with him that belongeth to them. **8.** He hath cut off the hairy scalp **9.** of the Two Fighters. He hath destroyed **10.** the revolts of [their] children. **11.** I have done away all the evil which attacked their souls. I am master in [Sekhet-Ḥetepet]. **12.** I know it. I have sailed over its lakes **13.** that I might arrive at the cities thereof. I have made strong **14.** my mouth. The Spirit-souls are ready [to fight], **15.** but they shall not gain the mastery over me. I am equipped in thy Fields, **16.** O god Ḥetep. What thou wishest thou shalt do, [saith this god].

The text of the above extracts from Chapter CX is full of mistakes, and the rendering here given is only a suggestion as to what Ani wished to say. The full text of the Chapter is given in the following Appendix, but it is very difficult to understand.

APPENDIX

CHAPTER CX

THE CHAPTERS OF SEKHET-ḤETEPET

[From the Papyrus of Nebseni, Sheet 17]

CHAPTER CX. **1.** HERE BEGIN THE CHAPTERS OF SEKHET-ḤETEPET, AND THE CHAPTERS OF COMING FORTH BY DAY; OF GOING INTO AND OF COMING FORTH FROM KHERT-NETER; OF ARRIVAL IN SEKHET-ÅARU; OF LIVING IN SEKHET- **2.** ḤETEPET, THE MIGHTY CITY, THE LADY OF

WINDS; OF HAVING POWER THEREIN; OF BECOMING A SPIRIT-SOUL THERE; OF PLOUGHING THERE; OF REAPING THERE; OF EATING THERE; OF DRINKING THERE; OF MAKING LOVE
3. THERE; AND OF DOING EVERYTHING THERE EVEN AS A MAN DOETH UPON EARTH. NEBSENI, THE SCRIBE AND DRAUGHTSMAN OF PTAḤ, SAITH:—

4. Set vanquished Horus, who was looking at the building in Sekhet-Ḥetepet. I set free Horus from Set. Set opened the paths of the Two Eyes (the Sun and Moon) in the sky. 5. Set ejected water with air upon the soul of his Eye (?), which dwelt in the town of Mert; he delivered the interior of the body of Horus from the hands of the Åḳeru Gods. Behold me! 6. I paddle this great boat over the Lake of the god Ḥetep; I seized upon it in the mansion of Shu. The mansion of his stars reneweth youth, reneweth youth. I paddle over 7. the Lakes thereof so that I may arrive at the towns thereof. I sail up to the town of the

god Ḥetep . . . . . Behold, I am at peace with his times, and with his guidance (?), and with his will (?), and with the Company of the Gods, **8.** who are his firstborn. He maketh the Two Fighters (Horus and Set) to be at peace [with each other], and to keep ward over the living whom he hath created in fair form, and hẹ bringeth peace; he maketh the Two Fighters to be at peace with those who watch **9.** over them. He cutteth off the hair from their divine fighters, he driveth away storm from the children (?). He guardeth from attack the Spirits. **10.** I have gained power therein. I know it. I have sailed over its Lakes so that I might arrive at its towns. My mouth is strong. I am equipped against the Spirits. They shall not gain the mastery over me. **11.** I am rewarded [with] these thy Fields, O god Ḥetep. What thou wishest that do thou, O lord of the winds. I shall be a spirit therein. I shall eat therein. I shall drink therein. **12.** I shall plough therein. I shall reap the grain therein. I shall be strong therein. I shall make love therein. My words shall be strong therein. I shall not be in subjection therein. **13.** I shall be a man of might therein. Thou hast made strong (?) the mouth and throat (?). Ḥetep Qettbu is its name. [It is] stablished upon the pillars of Shu, and is linked with the pleasant things of Rā. **14.** He is the divider of years, the hidden of mouth ; silent is his mouth, hidden is what he uttereth, he fulfilleth eternity, he taketh possession of everlastingness of existence as Ḥetep, Neb-Ḥetep. Horus **15.** maketh himself strong like unto a hawk which is one thousand cubits in length, and two thousand cubits in life (*sic*). He hath equipments with him, he journeyeth on, he cometh to the place where **16.** his heart would be, among the Lakes which are in its towns. He begetteth (?) in the birth-chamber of the god of the town (*i.e.*, the local god), he is satisfied with the food of the god of the town ; he doeth what ought to be done there, in the Field of Smas-er-Khet . . . . . everything of the birth-chamber **17.** of the god of the town. Now [when he] setteth in the [land of] life like crystal he performeth everything therein, [which things are] like unto the things done in the Lake Neserser, wherein there is none that rejoiceth, and wherein are evil things **18.** of all kinds. The god Ḥetep goeth in and cometh out, and marcheth hither and thither in the Field of Smas-er-Khet, the Lady of the birth-chamber of the god of the town.[1] [Let me] live with the god Ḥetep, **20.** clothed, and not despoiled by the Lords of the North (?), and may the Lord of things bring food (?) unto me. May he make me to go forward. May I come forth. May he bring to me my Power **21.** there, may I receive it, and may I be rewarded (or, equipped) by the god Ḥetep. May I be master of the great and mighty word in my body in (?) this my place. Make me to remember **22.** it. Let me [not] forget it. Let me go forward,

[1] The passage from "Now when he . . . . . the town," is repeated in the papyrus, as will be seen from the Egyptian text.

let me plough. I am at peace with the god of the town. I know the water, the towns, **23.** the nomes, and the lakes which are in Sekhet-Ḥetepet. I live therein. I am strong therein. I shine (?) therein. I eat therein. I . . . . . therein. **24.** I reap the harvest therein. I plough therein. I beget children therein. I am at peace therein with the god Ḥetep. Behold **25.** I sow seed therein. I sail about on the lakes thereof, and I arrive at its towns, O god Ḥetep. Behold my mouth is equipped, it possesseth horns (*i.e.*, teeth). Give unto me the abundance of the KAU (Doubles) and Spirit-souls. **26.** He who counteth me is Shu. I know him not (?) I come to its towns. I sail over its lakes. I walk about in Sekhet-Ḥetepet. Behold, it is Rā **27.** who is in heaven. Behold, it is Ḥetep [who is] its double offering of peace (?) I have advanced to its territory (or, land). I have put on my apparel. I have come forth.

I have given what **28.** it was upon me to give. I have made glad in [my] heart. I have conquered. I am strong. I have given directions to Ḥetep.

[Hail], Unen-em-ḥetep,[1] I have come to thee. My soul followeth **29.** me. The god Ḥu is on my hands. [Hail], Nebt-taui,[2] in whom I remember and forget, **30.** I have become alive. I have attacked none, let none attack me. I have given, give thou to me gladness. Make thou me to be at peace, bind thou up my veins (or, arteries? or sinews), let [me] receive air. **31.** [Hail], Unen-em-ḥetep, the Lord of Winds. I have come there. I have opened my head. Rā sleepeth. I watch not (?), [for] the goddess Ḥetemet is at the door of heaven **32.** by night. Obstacles have been put before me, but I have collected his emissions. I am in my city. O Nut-urt[3] (*i.e.*, Great City), I have

[1] The name of the first large section of the Elysian Fields.
[2] The name of a lake in the second section of the Elysian Fields.
[3] The name of a lake in the first section of the Elysian Fields.

come into thee. I have counted up my abundant stores. 33. I advance on my way to Uakh.[1] I am the Bull which is tied with a rope of lapis-lazuli, the lord of the Field of the Bull, the lord of the words of the god, the goddess Sepṭet (Sothis) 34. at her hours. O Uakh, I have come into thee. I have eaten my food. I am master of choice pieces of the flesh of oxen and of feathered fowl, and the birds of Shu 35. have been given unto me. I follow the gods, and I come [after the Doubles]. O Tcheft,[2] I have come into thee. I array myself in apparel, 36. and I gird about myself the *sat* garment of Rā. Behold the Court of the sky (or, heaven), [and] the followers of Rā who dwell in heaven. O Un-em-ḥetep, 37. the lord of the Two Lands, I have come into thee. I have plunged into the Lakes of Tchesert; behold, impurity of every kind hath removed

[1] The name of a lake in the second section of the Elysian Fields.
[2] The name of a district in the third section of the Elysian Fields.

from me. The divine 38. Great One flourisheth therein. Behold, I have found [him ?]. I have netted geese, and have fed full upon the finest of them. O Qenqentet,[1] 39. I have come into thee. I have seen the Osiris [my father]. I have saluted (?) my mother. I have begotten children. I have snared the serpents (or, worms), and I am delivered. 40. I know the name of the god who is with the goddess Tchesert, and who hath straight hair, and is equipped with horns [ready to gore]. He reapeth, and I both plough 41. and reap. O Ḥetemet, I have entered into thee. I have approached (?) the lapis-lazuli (sky ?). I have followed the winds of the Company of the Gods. The Great God hath given my head 42. unto me. He who hath bound my head on my body for me is the Mighty One, with eyes of lapis-lazuli (?), namely, Ȧri-en-ȧb-f ("He doeth as he pleaseth"). O Usert,[2] I have come into

[1] The name of a lake in the second section of the Elysian Fields.
[2] The name of a district in the third section of the Elysian Fields.

thee, to the house wherein food **43.** is brought unto me. O Smam,[1] I have come into thee. My heart watcheth, my head is equipped with the White Crown. I act as the guide of the celestial beings. I make to flourish **44.** terrestrial beings. There is joy of heart for the Bull, and for the celestial beings, and for the Company of the Gods. I am the god, the Bull, the Lord of the gods, who maketh his way over the turquoise (*i.e.*, the sky). O wheat and barley of the nome **45.** of the god, I have come into thee. I have come forward. I have lifted [you] up (*i.e.*, carried you), following the best offerings of the Company of the Gods. I have moored my boat to the tying-up post in the lakes of the celestial beings. **46.** I have pulled up the tying-up post. I have recited words, and I have ascribed praises unto the gods who dwell in Sekhet-Ḥetepet.

[1] The name of a district in the third section of the Elysian Fields.

CHAPTER CXLVIII

[THE CHAPTER OF PROVIDING THE DECEASED WITH MEAT, MILK, ETC.]

PLATE XXXV

1. The Osiris Aṅi, whose word is truth, saith :—Homage to thee, O Rā, 2. the Lord of Truth, the Only One, the Lord of Eternity and Maker of 3. Everlastingness. I have come before thee, O my Lord Rā. I would make to flourish 4. the Seven Cows and their Bull. O ye who give 5. cakes and ale to the Spirit-souls, grant ye that my soul may be with you. 6. Let him be born on your thighs. Let him be like unto one 7. of you for ever and for ever. Let the Osiris Ani, whose word is truth, have glorious power 8. in the Beautiful Åmentet.

[The Names of the Seven Cows and their Bull]

1. Ḥet-Kau Nebtertcher.
2. Åḳertkhentetåsts.
3. Khebitetsāḥneter.

4. Urmertusteshertshenti.

5. Khnemtemānkhānuit.

6. Sekhmetrensemābats.

7. Shenātpetuthestneter.

8. Kathaiḥemt.

ADDRESSES TO THE FOUR RUDDERS OF HEAVEN

PLATE XXXVI

Hail, thou Beautiful Power, thou Beautiful Rudder of the Northern Heaven.

Hail, thou who circlest, Guide of the Two Lands, Beautiful Rudder of the Western Heaven.

Hail, Splendour, Dweller in the temple of the Āshemu gods, Beautiful Rudder of the Eastern Heaven.

Hail, Dweller in the temple of the Red gods, Beautiful Rudder of the Southern Heaven.

Addresses to the Four Companies of the Gods

Hail, ye gods who are above the earth, ye Guides of the Ṭuat.

Hail, ye Mother-goddesses, who are above the earth in Khert-Neter, in the House of Osiris.

Hail, ye gods who guide Ta-tchesert, who are above the earth and are guides of the Ṭuat.

Hail, ye Followers of Rā, who follow in the train of Osiris.

APPENDIX

Rubric [from the Papyrus of Nu]:

Rubric: [These words] shall be said when Rā appeareth over [figures] of these gods written (or, painted) in colour upon a tablet, and thou shalt place offerings of *tchefau* food before them, cakes, ale, flesh, geese, and incense. They shall cause the deceased to enjoy the "offerings which come forth at the word [of command]" before Rā; and they shall give the deceased an abundance of food in Khert-Neter, and shall deliver him from every evil thing whatsoever. And thou shalt not recite this Book of Un-Nefer in the presence of anyone except thine own self. If this be done for the deceased Rā shall be a rudder for him, and shall be to him a strong protecting power, and he shall destroy all his enemies for him in Khert-Neter, and in heaven, and upon earth, and in every place whereinsoever he may enter, and he shall enjoy celestial food regularly and continually for ever.

In the Saïte Recension (ed. Lepsius, Bl. LXIX) this Chapter has a very long title which reads :—

1. The Book of making perfect the Khu in the heart of Rā, of making him to have the mastery before Tem, of magnifying him before Osiris, of making him mighty before Khent-Àmentet, and of setting awe of him before the Company of the Gods. It shall be recited on the day of the New Moon, on the sixth day festival, on the fifteenth day festival, **2.** on the festival of Uaḳ, on the festival of Thoth, on the Birthday of Osiris, on the festival

of Menu, on the night of Heker, [during] the Mysteries of the Ṭuat, during the celebration of the Mysteries in Àḳertet, at the smiting of the emissions, at the passage of the Funerary Valley, [and] the Mysteries . . . . . . [The recital thereof] will make the heart of the Khu to flourish (or grow) 3. and will make long his strides, and will make him to advance, and will make his face bright, and will make it to penetrate to the God. Let no man witness [the recital] except the king and the Kherḥeb priest, but the servant 4. who cometh to minister outside shall not see it. Of the Khu for whom this Book shall be recited, his soul shall come forth by day with the living, he shall have power among the gods, and it will make him irresistible 5. for ever and ever. These gods shall go round about him, and shall acknowledge him. He shall be one of them. [This Book] shall make him to know how he came into being in the beginning. This Book is indeed 6. a veritable mystery. Let no stranger anywhere have knowledge of it. Do not speak about it to any man. Do not repeat it. Let no [other] eye see it. Let no [other] ear hear it. Let no one see it except [thyself] and him who taught [it to thee]. Let not the multitude [know of it] **7.** except thyself and the beloved friend of thy heart. Thou shalt do (*i.e.*, write) this book in the *seḥ* chamber on a cloth painted with stars (?) in colour all over it. It is indeed a mystery. The dwellers in the swamps of the Delta and everywhere there shall not know it. It shall provide the Khu with celestial food in **8.** Khert-Neter. It shall supply his Heart-soul with food upon earth. It shall make him to live for ever. No [evil] thing shall have the mastery over him.

The addresses to the Four Rudders, etc., differ somewhat; they read :—

Hail, Power of heaven, Opener of the Disk, thou Beautiful Rudder of the Northern Heaven.

Hail, Rā, Guide of the Two Lands, thou Beautiful Rudder of the Western Heaven.

Hail, Khu, Dweller in the House of the Ākhemu gods, thou Beautiful Rudder of the Eastern Heaven.

Hail, Governor, Dweller in the House of the Ṭesheru Gods, thou Beautiful Rudder of the Southern Heaven.

Grant ye cakes, and ale, and *tchefau* food to the Osiris Ȧuf-ānkh, whose word is truth.

Hail, Father of the Gods! Hail, Mother of the Gods in Khert-Neter! Deliver ye the Osiris from every evil thing, from every evil obstruction, from every dire attack of an enemy, and from that deadly snarer with knife-like words, and from men, and gods, and Spirit-souls, and the damned, on this day, on this night, on this present festival of the fifteenth day, and in this year, and from the things of evil thereof.

CHAPTER CLXXXV

HYMN TO OSIRIS KHENTI-ÅMENTI UN-NEFER

PLATE XXXVI

1. The Osiris Ani, whose word is truth, praiseth Osiris Khenti-Åmenti Un-Nefer, and saith :—Hail, my Lord, who dost hasten through eternity, 2. whose existence is for ever, Lord of Lords, King of Kings, SOVEREIGN (Åti), God of the Gods, who live in their 3. shrines (?), ... gods . . . . men. Make thou for me a seat with those who are in Khert-Neter, who adore the forms of thy KA, and who 5. traverse (?) millions of millions of years. 6. . . . .

9. May no delay arise for thee in Ta-merȧ. 10. Let them come 11. to thee, all of them, great 12. as well as small. May this god give the power to enter in and to come forth from 13. Khert-Neter, without repulse, 14. at [any] door of the Ṭuat, to the Ka of the 15. Osiris Ani, [whose word is truth].[1]

The above Chapter is numbered here CLXXXV, because its contents somewhat resemble those of the Chapter in the Papyrus of Sutimes to which Naville has given this number, and its position at the end of the Papyrus of Ani suggests that it is a variant of it. The Papyrus of Sutimes reads:—

Sutimes, the libationer and president of the altar chamber of the Ȧpts, director of the scribes of Ȧmen, whose word is truth, praiseth Osiris, and doeth homage to the Lord of Eternity, and satisfieth the will of the God, and speaketh Truth, the Lord of which is unknown, and saith:—

Homage to thee, O thou Holy God, thou mighty and beneficent being, thou Prince of Eternity, who dwellest in thy abode in the Sektet Boat, whose risings are manifold in the Āṭet Boat, unto whom praises are rendered in heaven and upon earth. Peoples and nations exalt thee, and the awe of thy terror is in the hearts of men, and Spirit-souls, and the dead. Thy soul dwelleth in Ṭeṭu (Busiris), and the awe of thee is in Ḥensu (Herakleopolis). Thou settest the visible emblems of thyself in Ȧnu, and the majesty of thy transformations in the holy place. I have come unto thee. Truth is in my heart, and in my breast there is neither craft nor guile. Grant thou that I may have my being among the living, and that I may sail up and down the river among those who are in thy following.

1 The text of this Chapter is corrupt in many places.

CHAPTER CLXXXVI

[THE CHAPTER OF THE PRAISE OF HATHOR, LADY OF ÅMENTET]

PLATE XXXVII

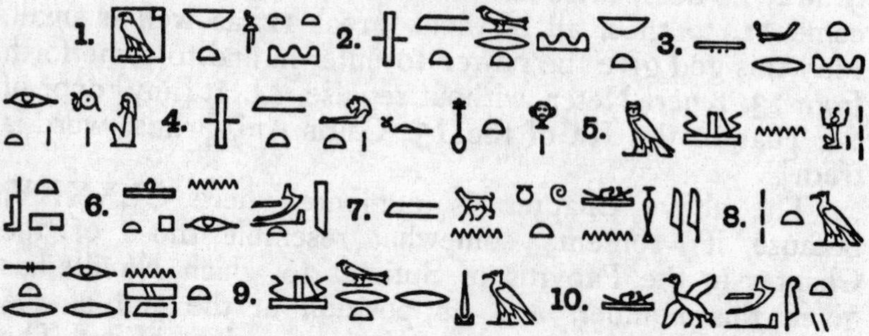

CHAPTER CLXXXVI. 1. Hathor, Lady of Åmentet, 2. the Dweller in the Great Land (*i.e.*, the Other World), the Lady 3. of Ta-Tchesert, the Eye of Rā, 4. the Dweller in his breast, the Beautiful Face 5. in the Boat of Millions of Years, the Seat 6. of Peace of the doer of truth, 7. [Dweller] in the Boat of the favoured ones . . . .

From the other papyri of the XVIIIth dynasty which contain the Vignette given on Plate XXXVII of the Papyrus of Ani, we learn that this last Chapter was devoted to praise of Hathor and another great Cow-goddess called Meḥurt. All the texts are more or less fragmentary, but it is clear that, after reciting the titles of the goddess Hathor and her praises, the deceased made a solemn declaration to her that he had not committed any offence in her country, that he had performed the commands of the king, whereby the gods were satisfied, and that finally he entreated her to let him live there in peace and happiness for ever.

APPENDIX

CHAPTER CXXXVII

THE CHAPTER OF THE FOUR TORCHES

[From the Papyrus of Nu, Sheets 26 and 27]

CHAPTER CXXXVIIA. 1. [1]

CHAPTER CXXXVIIA. 1. THE CHAPTER OF THE FOUR LIGHTED LAMPS WHICH ARE MADE FOR THE SPIRIT-SOUL. Behold, thou shalt make four rectangular troughs of clay 2. wherein thou shalt scatter incense, and thou shalt fill them with the milk of a white cow, and by means of these thou shalt extinguish the lamps. 3. The Osiris Nu, the steward of the overseer of the seal, whose word is truth, saith:— The fire cometh to thy KA, O Osiris Khenti-Àmenti! The fire 4. cometh to thy KA, O Osiris Nu, whose word is truth. The ordering of the night cometh after the day. 5. [The fire cometh to thy KA, O Osiris, Governor of those who are in Àmenti], and the two sisters (?) of Rā come

1 Added from the Papyrus of Nebseni.

likewise. Behold it (the fire) riseth in Åbṭu (Abydos), and it cometh; I cause it to come, 6. the Eye of Horus. It is set in order upon thy brow, O Osiris Khenti-Åmenti; it is set 7. in thy shrine and riseth on thy brow; it is set on thy brow, O Osiris Nu, 8. it is set on thy brow. The Eye of Horus protecteth thee, O Osiris Khenti-Åmenti, and it keepeth thee 9. in safety; it casteth down headlong all thine enemies for thee, and all thine enemies have fallen down headlong before thee. 10. O Osiris Nu, the Eye of Horus protecteth thee, it keepeth thee in safety, and it casteth down headlong 11. all thine enemies. Thine enemies have fallen down headlong before thy Ka, O Osiris Khenti-Åmenti. 12. The Eye of Rā protecteth thee, it keepeth thee in safety, and it hath cast down headlong all thine enemies.

13. Thine enemies have fallen down headlong before thy KA, O Osiris Nu, whose word is truth. 14. The Eye of Horus protecteth thee, it keepeth thee in safety, it hath cast down headlong for thee all thine enemies, and thine enemies have fallen down headlong before thee. The Eye of Horus 15. cometh. It is sound and well, it sendeth forth light even as doth Rā in the horizon. It covereth the powers of Suti with darkness, it mastereth him, and it bringeth its flame 16. against him by its own command. The Eye of Horus is sound and well, thou eatest the flesh thereof, thy body possesseth (?) it. Thou acclaimest it. The Four Fires enter into thy KA, O Osiris 17. Khenti-Ȧmenti, the Four Fires enter into thy KA, O Osiris Nu, the steward of the overseer of the seal, whose word is truth.

Hail, ye sons of Horus, Ḳestȧ, Ḥāpi, Ṭuamutef, 18. and Qebḥsenuf, ye have given your protection to your divine

Father (Grandfather?) Osiris Khenti-Åmenti, give ye your protection to the Osiris Nu, whose word is truth. **19.** Now therefore, inasmuch as ye have destroyed the Opponent of Osiris Khenti-Åmenti, who liveth with the gods, having smitten Suti with his right hand and arm when dawn came upon the earth, and Horus hath become master [of Suti], **20.** and hath avenged his divine Father himself; and inasmuch as your divine Father hath been made to flourish (or, germinate) through the union of the KA of Osiris Khenti-Åmenti, which ye effected, and the Eye of Horus **21.** hath avenged him, and hath protected him, and hath cast down headlong for him all his enemies, and all his enemies have fallen down before him, even so do ye destroy the **22.** Opponent of the Osiris Nu, the steward of the overseer of the seal, whose word is truth. Let him live with the gods, let him smite his enemy, let him destroy him, **23.** when light dawneth on the earth. Let Horus be master and avenge the Osiris Nu, and let the Osiris Nu flourish through his union with his KA which ye have effected. **24.** O Osiris Nu, the Eye of Horus hath avenged thee. It hath cast down headlong all thine enemies for thee, and all thine enemies have been cast down headlong before thee.

Hail, Osiris **25.** Khenti-Àmenti, grant thou light and fire to the perfect Heart-soul which is in Ḥensu (Herakleopolis). And [O ye Sons of Horus], grant ye power unto the living heart-soul of the Osiris **26.** Nu by means of his fire. Let him not be repulsed, and let him not be driven back at the doors of Àmentet! Let his offerings of bread and of linen garments be brought unto him **27.** among the lords of funeral oblations. O offer ye praises, as unto a god,

28.

RUBRIC:

29.

30.

31.

to the Osiris Nu, the destroyer of his Opponent in his form of Truth, and in his **28.** attributes of a god of truth.

RUBRIC: [This Chapter] shall be recited over four torches of *ȧtmȧ* cloth, which hath been anointed with the finest Theḥennu unguent, and the torches shall be placed in the hands of four men who shall have the names of the pillars of Horus written **29.** upon their shoulders, and they shall burn the torches in the beautiful light of Rā, and this shall confer power and might upon the Spirit-soul of the deceased among the stars which never set. If this Chapter be recited **30.** for him he shall never, never perish, and he shall become a living soul for ever. These torches shall make the Spirit-soul to flourish like Osiris **31.** Khenti-Ȧmenti, regularly and

[1] Var.

continually for ever. It is a struggle. Thou shalt not perform this ceremony before any human being except thine own self, or thy father, **32.** or thy son, because it is an exceedingly great mystery of Åmentet, and it is a type of the hidden things of the Ṭuat. When this ceremony hath been performed for the deceased, the gods, and the Spirit-souls, and the dead shall see him **33.** in the form of Khenti-Åmenti, and he shall have power and dominion like this god.

If thou shalt undertake to perform for the deceased that which is ordered in this "Chapter of the four blazing torches," each day, **34.** thou shalt cause the form of the deceased to come forth from every hall [in the Ṭuat], and from the Seven Halls of Osiris. And he shall live in the form of the God. He shall have power and dominion corresponding to those of the gods and the Spirit-souls **35.** for ever and ever. He shall enter in through the secret

pylons and shall not be turned back in the presence of Osiris. And it shall come to pass, provided that the following things be done for him, that he shall enter in and come forth. 36. He shall not be turned back. No boundary shall be set to his goings, and the sentence of doom (*i.e.*, guilty) shall not be passed upon him on the Day of the Weighing of Words (*i.e.*, the Great Judgment) before Osiris—never, never.

And thou shalt perform whatsoever [is written in] this book on behalf of 37. the deceased, who shall thereby become perfect and pure. And thou shalt "open his mouth" with the instrument of iron. And thou shalt write down these things in accordance with the instructions which are found in the books of Prince Ḥeruṭāṭāf, 38. who discovered them in a secret coffer (now they were in the handwriting of the god [Thoth] himself (*i.e.*, they were written in hieroglyphs) and had been deposited in the Temple of the goddess Unnut, the Lady of Unu)[1] during a journey which he was making in order to inspect 39. the temples, and the temple-estates, and the sanctuaries of the

[1] *I.e.*, Hermopolis, the city of Thoth.

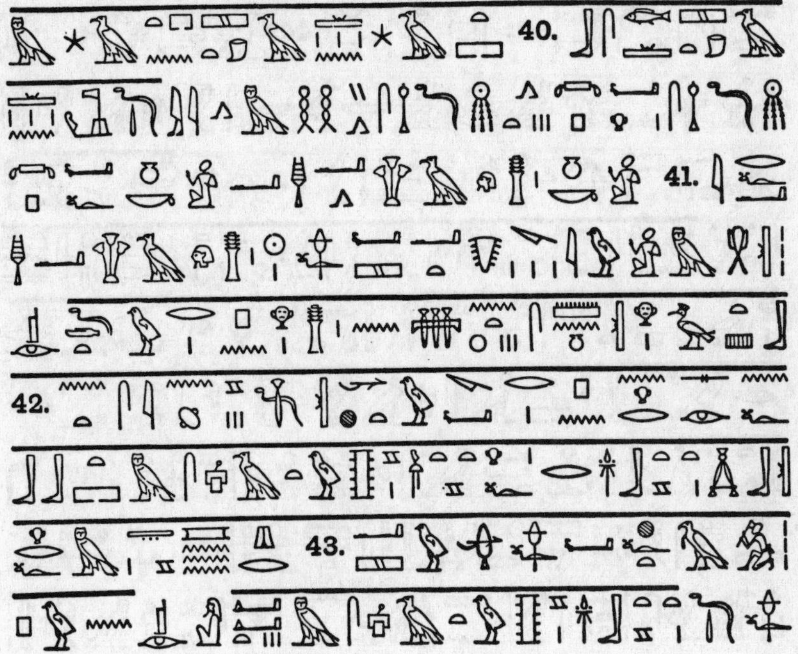

gods. And thou shalt perform these ceremonies secretly in the Ṭuat-chamber of the tomb, for they are mysteries of the Ṭuat, and they are **40.** symbolic of the things which are done in Khert-Neter.

And thou shalt say: I have come, I have advanced hastily. I cast light upon his (*i.e.*, the deceased's) footsteps. I am hidden, but I cast light upon his hidden place. I stand up close to the Ṭeṭ. I stand up **41.** close to the Ṭeṭ of Rā, I turn back the slaughter. I am protecting thee, O Osiris.

RUBRIC: This Chapter shall be recited over a Ṭeṭ of crystal, which shall be set upon a brick **42.** made of crude mud, whereupon this Chapter hath been inscribed. Thou shalt make a cavity in the west wall [of the tomb], and having turned the front of the Ṭeṭ towards the east, thou shalt wall up the cavity with mud which hath been mixed with **43.** the extract of cedar. This Ṭeṭ shall drive away the enemies of Osiris who would set themselves at the east wall [of the tomb].

44. 45. 46. 47.

And thou shalt say: I have driven back thy foes. I keep watch over thee. He that is upon his mountain (*i.e.*, Ánpu) keepeth watch 44. over thee ready for the moment when thy foes shall attack thee, and he shall repulse them for thee. I will drive back the Crocodile at the moment when it attacketh thee, and I will protect thee, O Osiris Nu. 45.

Rubric: This Chapter shall be recited over a figure of Ánpu made of crude mud mixed with incense. And the figure shall be set upon a brick made of crude mud, whereupon this Chapter hath been inscribed. 46. Thou shalt make a cavity in the east wall, and having turned the face of the figure of Ánpu towards the west wall [therein] thou shalt wall up the cavity. This figure shall repulse the enemies of Osiris, who would set themselves at the south (read, west) wall. 47.

And thou shalt say: I am the belt of sand round about the hidden coffer. I turn back the force of the blazing fire of the funerary mountain. I traverse the roads, and I

protect 48. the Osiris Nu, the steward of the overseer of the seal, whose word is truth.

RUBRIC: This Chapter shall be recited over a brick made of crude mud whereon a copy of this Chapter hath been inscribed. And thou shalt place a reed in the middle thereof, 49. and thou shalt smear it with pitch (or bitumen), and set light thereto. Then thou shalt make a cavity in the south wall, and, having turned the front of the brick towards the north, thou shalt wall the brick up inside it. [It shall repulse the enemies of the Osiris Nu] who would assemble at the 50. north wall.

And thou shalt say: O thou who comest to set fire [to the tomb or mummy], I will not let thee do it. O thou who comest to cast fire [herein], I will not let thee do it. I will burn thee, and I will cast fire 51. upon thee. I protect the Osiris Nu, the steward of the overseer of the seal, whose word is truth.

RUBRIC: This Chapter shall be recited over a brick of crude mud, whereon a copy of this Chapter hath been inscribed. [And thou shalt set upon it] a figure of the

deceased made of palm wood, 52. seven fingers in height. And thou shalt perform on it the ceremony of "Opening the Mouth." Then thou shalt make a cavity in the north wall, and having [placed the brick and the figure inside it], and turned the face of the figure towards the south, thou shalt wall up the cavity. [It shall repulse the enemies of thė Osiris Nu], who would assemble at the south wall.

And behold, these things shall be done by a man who is washed clean, and is 53. ceremonially pure, and who hath eaten neither meat nor fish, and who hath not [recently] had intercourse with women. And behold, thou shalt make offerings of cakes and ale to these gods, and shalt burn incense on their fires. 54. Every Spirit-soul for whom these things shall be done shall become like a holy god in Khert-Neter, and he shall not be turned back at any gate in Ȧmentet, and he shall be in the following of 55. Osiris, whithersoever he goeth, regularly and continually.

INDEX

A = Thoth, 134.
Āa, 270, 404.
Åāḥ, 479.
Åahet, 529, 530.
Åai, 158.
Åakebi, 147.
Āakheru, 137.
Āa-maakheru, 271, 407.
Åamḥet, of passing through, 483.
Āamu, 13.
Åāmu gods, 505.
Āapef, 198.
Āapep, the Great Devil, 49, 146, 147, 151, 152, 158, 159, 160, 166, 198, 233, 345, 392, 406, 495, 508; back of 30.
Åaqeṭqet, 262.
Åasen, 11.
Āa-sheft (shefit), 598, 608.
Åat of Spirit-souls, 139.
Åaṭes, 302.
Āaṭi, 583.
Åats, gods of the, 128.
Åats of the House of Osiris, 44, 45.
Åats, the Fifteen, 139, 354.
Åatqeṭqeṭ, 388.
Åatsetekau, 147.
Åat-shefshefit, 158.
Åb = heart, 176.
Ababi, 277.
Abd al-Laṭîf, 14.
Åbeth, 159.
Ablutions, 358.
Aborigines, Egyptian, 5.
Åbshe-åm-Ṭuat, 147.
Abstinence from eating meat and fish, and from women, 664.
Åbta, 158.
Åbṭu (Abydos), 25, 117, 166, 202, 230, 303, 350, 382, 422, 428, 520, 654.
Abṭu Fish, 298, 345, 502, 628.
Abu (Elephantine City), 569.
Åbu-ur, 607.
Abydos, 117, 143, 152, 166, 202, 224, 261, 281, 302, 313, 346, 353, 359, 364, 382, 402, 420, 421, 422, 429, 493, 519, 520, 522, 559, 604.
Abydos, Chapter of making to enter, 43.
Abydos, Lords of, 221, 361, 490.
Abydos, standard of, 43.
Abydos, Ṭuat of, 149.
Acacia tree, 264, 418, 492, 568, 569.
Adultery, 578.
Aelian, quoted, 108.
Åf, serpent, 152.
Åf-Rā (Åfu Rā, the body of Rā), 142, 143, 144, 145, 146, 147, 148, 149, 150, 151, 152, 153, 155, 156, 157, 158, 159, 160, 161.
Africa, 22, 114, 166, 205, 269.
Africans, 164.
Åfu, 146.
Åfu Åsår, 147.
Aged gods, 554.
Aged one, 112, 203, 250, 421, 444, 446, 560.
Aged one (Ptaḥ), 113.
Åḥ = Åaḥ, moon, 345.
Aḥ cake, 213.
Aḥani, 583.
Aḥet, 529.
Åḥi, 581.

Ahi mu, 584.
Āḥibit, 416.
Ahnas, 206, 360.
Āḥui, 519.
Air, 90, 143, 157, 166, 174, 284, 285.
Air, Chapter of giving, 35, 446.
Air, gift of Rā, 152.
Air, Chapter of breathing, 227, 456.
Air, Chapter of giving, 283, 447, 448.
Air, Chapter of snuffing, 448, 458.
Air in Other World, 34.
Aix in Provence, 11.
Aḳab, 282.
Aḳeb, 443.
Ākentaukhakheru, 137.
Akenti, 138.
Āḳert, Āḳerti, } 57, 204, 275, 327, 352, 423, 491.
Āḳert, Gate of, 160.
Āḳertkhentetȧsts, 644.
Ākeru gods, 93, 633, 635.
Ākhanȧrit, 156.
Akhekau serpents, 421.
Ākhemu gods, or statues, 649.
Ākhkha, 584.
Akhmîm, 203.
Akriu, 139.
Āksi, 140.
Alabaster, 441.
Al-Barshah, coffins of, 3.
Ale, 38, 518, 595, 613, 615, 616, 646, 649.
Ale, offering of, 12.
Alexander II, 117.
Alexander the Great, 117, 165.
Alexandria, 15, 23, 52, 267.
Al-Kâb, 493.
All Souls' Day, 292.
Altar, 11, 40.
Altars, gods of, 129.
Altars, Lords of, 419.
Ām-ā-f, 486.
Āmām, 236, 237, 418.
Āmamu, coffin of, 1.
Ām-ȧs, 251.
Āmeḥet, see Āmḥet, 37, 369, 615.
Amélineau, 24, 87, 103, 185, 200.
Āmen, god, 109, 110, 117, 167 194 ff.
Āmen of Ṣiwah Oasis, 165.
Āmen, seed of, 165.
Āmen-ḥetep, 614.
Āmen-ḥetep III, 26, 165.
Āmen-ḥetep, Papyrus of, 317.
Āmen-khat, 159.
Āmen-neb, 481.
Āmen-Rā, god, 111, 113, 165, 194, 198, 232, 233.
Āmen-Rā, his contract with Nesi-Khensu, 50, 111.
Āmen-Rā, Hymn to, 108, 195.
Āment, 129; river of, 366.
Āment, wife of Āmen, 194.
Āmenta, 199, 202.
Āmentet, 48, 139, 255, 364, 365, 372, 374, 376, 378, 379, 389, 439, 440, 455, 457, 473, 474, 480, 490, 494, 501, 542, 558, 578, 596, 613, 615, 616, 618, 652, 653, 657, 664; making a way in, 478.
Āmentet (Āmenti), the Beautiful, 223, 230, 327, 355, 452, 505, 644.
Āmentet, the Bend of, 395, 396.
Āmentet, Bull of, 445.
Āmentet, Souls of, 40.
Āmenti, 50, 52, 150, 292.
Amenti, festivals of, 44.
Āmenti, secret road of, 147.
Āmḥet, 139, 145, 224, 293.
Āmhetet-Rā, 234.
Ami Khent, priest, 250, 443, 479.
Āmi Ṭuat, 142.
Ām-Khaibit, 577, 582.
Ām-Khent-Ḥeru, 250.
Amkhiu gods, the Twelve, 149.
Ām-mit, 198, 236, 315, 373, 375.

Ȧmmi-unnut-f, 262.
Amnetuf, 160.
Ȧmset, 131, 191.
Ȧmset (south), 192.
Amsi, 188, 203.
Amta cake, 216.
Ȧm-Ṭuat, Book of, 359.
Amt-ur, 434.
Amulet, cow, 623.
Amulet, heart, 620.
Amulet, heart-soul, 290.
Amulet, pillow, 621.
Amulet, sceptre, 623.
Amulet, ṭeṭ, 616.
Amulet, tet, 618.
Amulets, 175, 323.
Ȧn, 353, 491.
Ȧnāf, 268, 391, 582, 584.
Ancestor, 368.
Ancestor-god, 118, 125, 243, 320.
Ancestors of Light, 519.
Ancestors of Rā, 304, 519.
Ancestors of the year, 304, 519.
Ancestress, goddess, 243.
Ȧneb-ḥetchet (White Wall, Memphis), 204.
Ȧn-em-hru, 263.
Ȧner, 509.
Ȧnerti, 509.
Angarêb, 244.
Angels, avenging, 200.
Angels, recording, 155.
Anger, 579, 581.
Ȧnhai, Papyrus of, 315, 373.
Ȧnḥer, 137, 271, 406.
Ȧn-ḥetep-f, 580, 584.
Ȧni, god, 110.
Ani, maxims, 103.
Ani, the scribe, his papyrus described, 217 ff.
Ȧniu, 491.
Ȧnkef, 11.
Ānkh, 233.
Ānkhamu flowers, 617, 619.
Ānkh-em-betu-mitu, 257.
Ānkhet Chamber, 174.
Ānkhfemfent, 270, 406.
Ānkhfemfentu, 137, 257.
Ānkhi, 159.
Ānkh-neteru, 149.
Ānkhti, 61.
Anku, 147.
Ȧnmutef, 225, 275.
Ȧnmutef, priest of, 422.
Ȧnp, 419.
Ȧnpu, 44, 45, 145, 182, 248, 262, 285, 386, 398, 407, 428, 429, 431, 438, 569, 571, 597, 607, 629, 630, 662.
Ȧnpu Khent Amenta, 12, 214.
Ȧnpu, Temple of, 457.
Ȧnqet, 173.
Ȧnruṭf, 203, 260, 492; gods of, 277.
Ȧnt, 166.
Ȧnṭ boat, 134.
Ȧnt fish, 292, 345, 502.
Ȧntch, 418.
Ȧntchet boat, 296.
Antechamber of Ṭuat, 149.
Ȧntef, coffin of, 1.
Antelope, 249.
Ȧn-ṭes, 203, 491.
Anthropomorphism, 120.
Antimony, 595.
Antioch, 201.
Ȧntiu gods, 159.
Ȧnu, chapter of going to, 37, 275.
Ȧnu, college of, 1.
Ȧnu, gods of, 88.
Ȧnu (Heliopolis), 24, 26, 57, 59, 69, 71, 111, 116, 117, 148, 156, 182, 203, 290, 302, 354, 357, 359, 366, 379, 390, 400, 406, 419, 424, 434, 445, 453, 482, 490, 491, 506, 520, 547, 548, 551, 553, 575, 604, 631.

Ȧnu, Souls of, 41, 78.
Ȧnu, Ṭuat of, 149.
Anubis, 85, 155, 182, 183, 235, 236, 238, 243, 245, 250, 253, 254, 275, 268, 313, 314, 315, 322, 373, 386, 393, 398, 407, 419, 420, 570, 629; son of Osiris, 54.
Anubis and the mummy, 34.
Anubis by bier, 29.
Ȧpa, coffin of, 2.
Ȧpȧ-ānkh, coffin of, 2.
Ape, 155; dog-headed, 235, 612.
Ape of Thoth, 236.
Āper, 63.
Āperḥernebtchet, 148.
Ape gods, 142, 158, 160.
Apes, 233.
Apes of the Lake of Fire, 42.
Apes, the three of the net, 45.
Apes, the two, 264, 398.
Apes, the four female, 120.
Apes, the four holy, 318, 614.
Apes, the four male, 120.
Aphrodisiac, 308.
Aphrodite, 186.
Apostates, 151.
Āpshai, 34, 199.
Ȧpt, 189.
Apts, 108, 110, 651.
Ȧpu, 188, 203, 204, 520.
Aqbi, 152.
Āqen, 156.
Aq-ḥer-ȧmi-unnut-f, 388.
Arabia, 95, 499.
Arabs, 121, 135, 203, 204, 206.
Archers, a group of stars, 93.
Architect of World, 170.
Ȧres, 153.
Ȧrfi-em-Khat, 577.
Ȧri-em-ȧb-f, 581, 584, 642.
Ȧri-su-tchesef, 274, 412.
Ārit I, 269, 402.
Ārit II, 269, 403.
Ārit III, 270, 404.
Ārit IV, 270, 405.
Ārit V, 270, 405.
Ārit VI, 271, 406.
Ārit VII, 271, 407.
Ārit, section of Ṭuat, 153.
Ārits, 354.
Ārits of Amenti, 44.
Ārits, the Seven, 137, 269, 402 ff.
Āriu gods, 526.
Armlets, 131, 232.
Arm rings, 94.
Arms, human, 234.
Arms of Ani, 598.
Aroeris, 179.
Arrogance, 581.
Artemis, 186.
Ȧrtifemṭes, 582.
Ȧsȧr (Osiris), see *passim*.
Asâsîf al-Baḥrîyah, 9.
Aser-tree, 607.
Ȧses, 139.
Ashebu, 137.
Āshemu, 645.
Asherah, 55.
Ȧshet, 325.
Āsh-ḥeru, 146.
Āshmiu fiends, 560.
Ȧsht fruit, 216.
Asia, 164.
Asiatics, 154.
Ȧsneteru, 147.
Aso, Queen, 54.
Asphaltites limen, 152.
Ass, 199.
Ass and Cat, 588.
Ass, Eater of the, 34.
Ass = Rā, 344.
Ass = Sun-god, 233.
Ȧssȧ, King, 22, 23.
Assembler of Souls, 457.
Assessors, the Forty-two, 576 ff.
Ȧst, 178, and see Isis.

Åsṭen, Åsṭenu, 188, 277, 429.
Åsṭes, 237, 386, 421.
Astronomy, 236, 343.
Aswân, 21.
Āṭ, 418.
Åṭebui, 494.
Atef Crown, 239, 241, 274, 276, 278, 365, 556, 588.
Åtek-tau-haq-kheru, 271.
Åtek-tau-kehaq-kheru, 406.
Atem, Atmu, } 110, 111, 112, 116.
Åter, 64.
Återt, South and North, 127.
Åṭesḥer, 271.
Åṭes-ḥer-åri-she, 406.
Āṭet Boat, 111, 128, 163, 342, 501, 502, 518, 524, 630, 651.
Atet cakes, 216.
Athribites, 307.
Åti, 59, 64, 342, 351, 579.
Åti (nome), 62.
Atlas, 175.
Åṭma cloth, 658.
Åtu, 140.
Åua-em-ḳeb, 592.
Åufānkh, 418, 419, 422, 495, 512, 520.
Åuheṭ, 529.
Åuḳert, 156, 348, 584, 588.
Åuḳert Khenti Åst, 126.
Åusårs (Osiris), 118.
Āu-taui, 594.
Aven, 203.

Ba, the, 76.
Ba of Kheperå, 118.
Ba of Temu, 114.
Ba-soul, 353, 472, 474.
Ba-soul in gold, 473.
Ba-soul in Ka, 345.
Baābu, 601.
Baba, 190
Båbå, 467.
Babat fruit, 216.
Babe, 446–448.
Babe = Ptah Tanen, 173.
Babu, 190.
Babylon of Egypt, 204.
Back of Nu, 608.
Backbone, 357, 406.
Backbone of Ani, 598.
Backbone of Nu, 608.
Backbone of Osiris, 319.
Baiti, 113.
Baiu shetaiu, 144.
Baiu Ṭuatiu, 143.
Bakau, 271.
Bakha, Mount, 130, 146, 340, 592.
Bakhet, 341.
Båkt, 63.
Balance, 42, 155, 182, 193, 234, 235, 238, 294, 315, 342, 362, 373, 391, 403, 439, 484, 588.
Bandlets, 94.
Ba-neb-Ṭeṭ, 207, 316, 598, 607.
Baqem, 277.
Barley, 109, 139, 172, 369, 370, 624, 643.
Barley, white, 518.
Bast, 187, 512, 578, 602.
Basti, 578, 584.
Bast in Ṭuat, 149.
Båta, serpent, 159.
Bati-erpit, 62.
Battle of the gods, 378.
Ba-ur-ṭeṭ, 22.
Beard, 630.
Beard, the African, 260, 276.
Bearer of the gods, 189.
Bears, 56, 201.
Beautiful Face = Rā, 108, 110, 630.
Beb, 190, 445.
Beba, 277, 303, 395, 586, 608.
Bebi, 431.

Bebti, 190.
Beer, 152, 212, 258.
Beer, imperishable, 88, 89.
Bees, 147.
Beetle, 33, 34, 141, 167, 339.
Beetle, god, 340.
Beetle in dusk, 150.
Beetle of Kheperå, 146, 148, 149, 160.
Beetle of the sky, 133.
Begetter of Millions of Years, 382.
Beginning, the, 112.
Beḥuṭet, 117, 180, 299.
Bekha, 203.
Bekhatet, 179.
Bekhkhi, 157.
Bel, 197.
Belly of Ani, 599.
Belly of Meri Rā, 602.
Belly of Nu, 608.
Benben stone, 156.
Bend of Åmentet, 395.
Bend of the Lake of Fire, 395.
Benu bird, 228, 258, 286, 287, 305, 309, 353, 379, 420, 569, 575, 620; of becoming, 38, 552.
Beq, 419.
Bergmann, 58, 73.
Besi, 159.
Bes-maa-em-ḳerḥ, 263.
Best-åru-ānkhetkheperu, 147.
Besu aḥu, 593.
Beṭ, incense, 216.
Bêth Shemesh, 24, 203.
Beṭshu, 64.
Birch, Dr., 9, 17, 18, 23, 57, 73, 78, 191, 255, 342, 355.
Birth chamber, 193, 637.
Birthday of Osiris, 647.
Birthplace of the gods, 354.
Bissing, F. W. von, 74.
Bitter Lakes, 142.
Bitumen, 214, 663.
Blacksmith, god, 171.
Blacksmiths, 346, 360.
Blasphemy, 151, 580, 584; of king, 581; of god, 581.
Blessed, Abode of the, 130.
Block, 140, 146, 287, 392, 395, 401, 453; the divine, 35; of avoiding, 466.
Blood, drinking of, 95.
Blood of Isis, 618.
Blood of Rā, 164, 383.
Blood of the dead, 146.
Blood watering, 263, 360.
Boat, Chapter of bringing, 39.
Boat, the divine, 356, 564.
Boat, magical, 325.
Boat of Åfu-Rā, 143, 144.
Boat of the Earth, 152.
Boat of Ḥai, 421.
Boat of Horus, 366.
Boat of Millions of Years, 124, 312, 472, 564, 652.
Boat of Nu, 506.
Boat of Osiris, 143.
Boat of Rā, 40, 90, 126, 166, 179, 183, 280, 296, 298, 300, 304, 305, 345, 346, 366, 475, 477, 507, 508, 614; of Rā Horus, 509.
Boat of Rā, Chapter of entering, 43; model of, 299.
Boat of Seker, 171.
Boat of the Sky, 133.
Boat with ape and pig, 155.
Body, Chapter for preventing decay of, 45.
Body of Ani, 598.
Body of the god, 565.
Body, reunion with soul, 228, 472.
Bodyguard of Osiris, 153.
Bodyguard of Rā, 147.
Boiling to avoid, 445.
Boiling water, Lake of, 152.
Book of Åmentet, 44.

Book of Breathings, 57.
Book of the Dead, 7; Recensions of, 1 ff.; title of, 3.
Book of Gates, 142, 150.
Book of him that is in the Ṭuat, 142 ff.
Book of knowing Rā, 117.
Book of opening the mouth, 3 ff.
Book of stablishing Ṭeṭ, 48.
Book of traversing eternity, 58.
Book of the Two Ways, 137.
Book of Un-Nefer, 328, 647.
Books, Hermetic, 267.
Boomerang, 149.
Bow, the double, 159.
Boxes, perfume, 246.
Boxes of purification, 252.
Bracelets, 131, 232.
Bread, 152, 258; offering, 12.
Bread cake, 215.
Bread, imperishable, 88.
Bread of eternity, 89.
Bread of Eye of Horus, 89.
Bread of Rā, 88.
Breast of Ani, 598.
Breast of Meri Rā, 602.
Breast-offering, 213.
Bride of the Nile, 142.
Broad Face, 453.
Brocklehurst Papyrus, 271, 294.
Brow of Meri Rā, 600.
Brugsch, Dr. H., 7, 18, 23, 28, 53, 57, 60, 71, 73, 99, 105, 174, 175, 185, 202, 205, 255, 340, 355.
Bryant, 116.
Bubastis, 187, 204, 578.
Bubastis, Ṭuat of, 149.
Bull, 195, 530, 613.
Bull, calf of red, 555.
Bull in Heliopolis, 108.
Bull, Lord of the gods, 643.
Bull of Åmentet, 356, 445, 534, 546.
Bull of Ånu, 24.
Bull of gods of Anu, 308.
Bull of the Seven Cows, 44, 127, 644
Bull of the Sky, 301.
Bull, pied, 240.
Bull, skin of, 370.
Bull, young, 112.
Bulls, bellowing of, 147.
Bulrushes, 55.
Bunsen, 7, 9, 23.
Buqem, 116.
Burial customs, 4.
Burial of the dead, 3, 4.
Burning, to avoid, 445.
Burning of the dead, 3, 4.
Burning of the wicked, 161.
Burton, Sir R., 14, 430.
Busca Papyrus, 275.
Bush, the African, 131.
Bushel, 574.
Busiris, 59, 142, 166, 205, 263, 276, 302, 303, 342, 351, 353, 357, 364, 366, 389, 390, 422, 425, 491, 517, 520, 525, 527, 531, 533, 547, 569, 570, 581, 651.
Buto, 55, 189, 205, 207, 214, 276, 302, 517.
Buttocks of Ani, 599.
Buttocks of Meri Rā, 602.
Buttocks of Nu, 608.
Byblos, 54, 55.

Cackler, the Great, 176, 446.
Caḥtân, 95.
Cairo, Old, 363.
Cakes, 38, 212, 596, 613, 646, 649.
Cakes of Osiris, 281, 437.
Cakes of Rā, the Four, 547.
Calendar, 54.
Calf = sun, 133.
Callisthenes, Pseudo, 165.
Canal in 14th Åat, 141.
Canal, underground, 140.

Cannibalism, 95, 295.
Canopic jars, 131, 243, 322.
Captives as sacrifices, 166.
Carthagena, 15.
Caster, 170.
Cat, 263, 264, 588.
Cat, the Great, 390, 628.
Cat of Bast, 187.
Cats, male, 147.
Cataract, 100, 137.
Cataract, the First, 163, 173, 174, 175, 293.
Cataracts, 542.
Cedar, 122, 448, 568.
Cedar, extract of, 661.
Cedar oil, 214.
Cemeteries, 129.
Censers, 228, 243.
Ceremonies, funeral, 5.
Chabas, 7, 8, 10, 54, 59, 101, 103, 178.
Chain, 159; of Ḳeb, 159.
Chair, 34, 155, 244.
Chamber, funeral, texts in, 47, 624.
Chamber of cows, 64.
Chamber of torture, 398.
Champollion-Figeac, 7, 105, 106.
Chaos, 144.
Chapel, divine, 433.
Chapel of Ka, 74.
Chapters of Book of the Dead, 1 ff.
Chapters of Coming Forth, 29.
Charms, 198.
Cheeks of Ani, 597.
Cheeks of Nu, 607.
Cheese, 211.
Cheops, 9, 14.
Chephren, 14.
Chequer board, 257.
Chest of Nu, 608.
Chiefs, 317, 364.
Chiefs, Council of, in Ånu, 604.
Chiefs of Osiris, 42, 224.
Child = Rā, 108, 607, 610.
Children, the divine, 569.
Children of Horus, 131.
Children of Revolt, 266.
Chimpanzee, 284.
Chin of Pepi, 601.
Choiak, 54, 56, 178.
Christianity, 52.
Chronologer, 183.
Cippi of Horus, 180.
Circles, 147; gods of, 42.
City of God, 268.
City of north, 589.
Civilization, Egyptian, 7.
Clay troughs, 653.
Clement of Alexandria, 23, 267.
Cleopatra, 238.
Coffer of Seker, 171.
Cold, 267.
Collar of Gold, 46.
College of Ånu, 1, 24.
"Coming forth by day," 47, 48, 255, 369.
Confession, 42, 576 ff.
Continence, 442.
Contract between Åmen-Rā and Nesi-Khensu, 111.
Copper, 418, 440.
Copper eye paint, 214.
Coprophagi, 167.
Coptos, 54, 200.
Copts, 200, 202, 203, 204, 206, 360.
Cord-master, 94.
Corn, treading out of, 324.
Corruption, to avoid, 227, 461.
Corruption, chapter of avoiding, 34.
Corvée, the celestial, 155.
Cosmogony, 163.
Cow, 178.
Cow of Hathor, 186.
Cow of Neith, 187.
Cow of Sky, 132.

Cow with plumes, 46.
Cows, the seven, 44, 327, 644.
Cows, the seven of Hathor, 126.
Cow goddess, 116, 172, 186, 330.
Cradle, or nest, 447.
Creation, 119.
Creation, an effort of will of Temu, 113.
Creation, book of, 107.
Creation of men, etc., 162.
Creation, riddle of, 117.
Crocodile, 55, 188, 198, 199, 209, 307, 662.
Crocodile, Chapter of becoming a, 39.
Crocodile, Chapter of repulsing, 33.
Crocodile god, 546.
Crocodile of Land of Truth, 370.
Crook, 239.
Crown, Double, 239.
Crown, red, 95, 148.
Crown, white, 95, 148, 153, 173, 177, 263, 299, 351, 510, 518, 606, 643.
Crown of North, 159.
Crown of South, 159, 296.
Crown of Victory, 31.
Crystal, 560, 591, 593, 638.
Curses, 577.
Cutting the dam, 142.

Dahomey, 360, 430.
Damned, the, 341; burning of, 267, 392.
Darkness, 144, 145, 163, 166, 181, 227, 311, 550.
Darkness, the outer, 136, 200, 520; solid, 149.
Dates, 284.
Daughters, the two, 543.
Dawn-goddess, 179.
Dawn, spirits of, 233.
Day, 211, 350; and night, 197.
Day, duration of, 159.
Day of destruction, 425.
Day of souls, 292, 475.
Day of weighing words, 357, 660.
Days, the 5 epagomenal, 53.
Day-sky, 131.
Day-sun, 159, 359.
Dead, abode of, 132.
Dead body sacred, 5.
Dead eaten by animals, 4.
Dead hacked to pieces, 146.
Dead, judgment of, 302.
Dead, kingdom of, 142.
Dead, land of, 222, 256, 268, 294, 341, 435.
Dead, revivified, 143.
Dead, spirits of, 130.
Death, 161, 292, 294, 313.
Death, of avoiding the second, 361, 454, 561; Chapter of, 34, 47.
Death, forms of, 200.
Death, kingdom of, 145.
Death, the second, 161, 226, 230, 288, 512.
Death-god, 145, 171, 358, 478, 483.
Decapitation, 226.
Decapitation, of avoiding, 289, 470; Chapter of, 34.
Decay in mummy, 286.
Deceit, 239, 578, 586.
Defilement, 579.
Deification of members, 318.
Dekan star, 600.
Dêkanos, 201.
Dekans, 491.
Delta, 157, 164, 166, 186, 187, 189, 205, 206, 223, 358, 538, 623, 649.
Delta, dwellers in, 328.
Delta, Eastern, 148.
Demon with knife, 32.
Demons, red, 415.

de Morgan, 7.
Dêr al-Baḥarî, 2, 9, 165.
Desert, Lord of, 395.
Devéria, 2, 57, 87, 220, 255, 341.
Devil, 343.
Devils, 199.
Devourer, the, 236, 237.
Dew, eldest born of, 108.
Dhura, 172, 369, 518.
Diocletian, 201.
Diodorus Siculus, 14, 23, 24, 54, 152.
Discerner of hearts, 593.
Disk, 31, 170, 172, 345, 607.
Disk, reconstruction of, 148.
Disk on tree, 36.
Disk winged, 132.
Dismemberment, 4.
Divine Face, 112.
Doctrines, solar, 1.
Dog, 182.
Dog star, 141.
Dogs track Osiris, 54.
Domain, Fiery, 395.
Doorkeepers of Pylons, 44.
Doors, the four of heaven, 46.
Doors, the hidden, 129.
Doors, keepers of, 129.
Doors of Ṭuat, 36.
Double, the, 341.
Dove, 216.
Dragon, 197.
Draught-board, 258.
Draughts, 31, 265; playing at, 376.
Drink offerings, 208.
Drowned, the, 148, 157.
Dual-soul, 291.
Duck, 249.
Dümichen, 22, 73, 208, 248.
Dwarf, 273.
Dwarf with two faces, 623.
Dweller in Busiris, 369.
Dweller in hearts, 450.
Ears of Ani, 597.
Ears of Nu, 607.
Earth, 174; digging of, 360.
Earth, gods of four quarters of, 150.
Earth, return to, 229.
Earth, reunion with, 29, 396.
Earth-god, 116, 118, 134, 309, 342, 390, 438; his tunnel, 152.
East, Chapter of avoiding, 39, 228, 288, 467.
East, Gods of roads of, 128.
East, Mountain of, 524.
East, rudders of, 645.
East, souls of, 40.
Eater of the Arm, 155, 486.
Eater of the Ass, 34, 344.
Eater of the Dead, 199, 236, 237, 238.
Eavesdroppers, 578.
Eclipse, 119, 133.
Edfû, 117, 299.
Egg, 176, 283, 367, 446, 447, 449, 551, 609, 612, 633.
Egg, the cosmic, 119, 173.
Egg, the life in, 109.
Egg of Åbṭu Fish, 628.
Egg of Neḳeḳ-ur, 458.
Egg of Rā, 120.
Egypt, Christians of, 52.
Egyptians, 154; origin of, 4; sacred books of, 23.
Eight Elements, the, 120.
Eileithyiaspolis, 189, 205, 493.
Êl, 115.
El-Assâsîf, 9.
Elements, the Eight, 120.
Elements, the Four, 174.
Elephantine, 22, 59, 173, 174, 569
Elephantine, Cavern of, 142.
Elsah, 115.
Elysian Fields, 183, 202, 206, 256, 323, 502.
Emanation of God, 307.

Embalmer (Anubis), 182.
Embalming, 70, 289.
Embryo, 283.
Enemies in the Other World, 30, 35; to attack, 485.
Ennur bird, 140.
Ephesus, Council of, 203.
Erman, Dr., 6, 10, 21, 22, 74, 116, 121, 194.
Erpā, 176; Erpāt, 350.
Erṭa Sebanga, 138.
Eshmûnên, 204.
Essence of primeval matter, 118.
Eternal life, 66 ff.
Eternity, 112, 177, 267, 378, 380, 490, 550.
Ethiopia, 23, 54.
Everlasting Devourer, 395.
Everlasting Gold, 62.
Everlasting One, 111.
Everlastingness, 267, 380, 490, 550, 551.
Evil Eye, 139.
Evil, Recollection of, 39.
Executioner, 268.
Executioner of Osiris, 287.
Eye brought by Thoth, 267.
Eye eaten by Pepi, 85.
Eye, eclipse of, 119.
Eye paint, 214.
Eye, white and black, 261.
Eye of Horus, 83, 89, 91, 125, 141, 198, 203, 207, 209 ff, 260, 293, 314, 384, 394, 399, 459, 471, 472, 474, 475, 476, 479, 480, 484, 531, 595, 599, 608, 654.
Eye of Khnemu, 192.
Eye of Lord One, 306, 528.
Eye of Rā, 109, 159, 261, 384, 385, 387, 394, 401, 480, 492, 560, 595, 652, 654.
Eyes of Ani, 597.
Eyes of Temu, 161; eye of, 468.
Eyes of Meri Rā, 600.
Eyes of Nu, 607.
Eyes of Rā, 109, 111, 124, 133, 272.
Eyes, the two, 635.

Fabre, J. H., 133.
Face, beautiful, 109.
Face, the divine, 111.
Face of Ani, 597.
Face of Nu, 607.
Face of Pepi, 600.
Faces, the hidden, 129.
Famine, 174.
Fan, 284.
Fate, 193, 235, 564.
Father of beginnings, 106, 169, 174.
Father of fathers, 169, 174.
Father gods, 328.
Father of the gods, 162, 169, 176, 650.
Father Tem, 382.
Fat-Ḥeru, 65.
Fayyûm, 582.
Feather, 238; *see* Ostrich feather.
Feathers, 178, 314.
Feet, lifting up of, 477.
Feet of Ani, 599.
Feet of Nu, 608.
Fecundity, 273.
Fenkhu, 593.
Fenkhu cakes, 574.
Fenṭi, 316, 582, 596.
Ferryboat, 280, 346, 607.
Ferryboat of Rā, 435.
Ferryman, celestial, 288.
Festivals, list of, 647.
Festival Songs of Isis, 57, 178.
Field labourers, 155.
Field labourers of Osiris, 148.
Field of Åaru, 22, 76.
Field of Offerings, 41, 88, 136, 142, 145, 154, 370, 374, 524.

Field of Peace, 76.
Field of Rā, 310.
Field of Reeds, 41, 44, 136, 142, 154, 157, 206, 354, 356, 365, 370, 502.
Field of the Bull, 641.
Field of the Grain-gods, 143.
Field of the Grasshoppers, 589.
Field of Smas-er-khat, 637, 638.
Fields, gods of, 128.
Fields of Osiris, 148.
Friends, 199.
Fiery-Eye, 155.
Fiery-Face, 154, 157.
Figs, 89, 176.
Fighters, the two, 184, 326, 633.
Fighting gods, 453.
Filth, of avoiding, 35.
Fingers of Ani, 599.
Fingers of Nu, 608.
Fingers, the two, 83, 301.
Fire, 139, 174, 445.
Fire, Chapter of kindling, 43.
Fire, Creation of, 120.
Fire, house of, 128.
Fire in Ṭuat, 144.
Fire, Island of, 280.
Fire, Lake of, 42, 93, 156, 157.
Fire of Åat No. 8, 140.
Fire, pits of, 149, 153, 161.
Fire, region of, 141.
Fire, river of, 145.
Fire-god, 470.
Fire-gods, 128, 159.
Fire-spitting serpent, 199.
Fire-water, 151.
Fish, 509; the Great, 307.
Fish of Horus, 546.
Fish-bait, 575.
Fishes, the two, 166.
Flail, 239, 624.
Flame, 521, 627, 628.
Flame, kindling of, 43.
Flame, Lady of, 265, 401.
Flame-gods, 358.
Flesh, 576, 646.
Flesh, offering of, 613.
Flesh of Ani, 598.
Flesh of Horus, 306.
Flood, legend of, 312.
Flour, 216.
Flowers, 613.
Followers of Horus, 159, 210, 242, 346, 374, 620.
Followers of Nu, 506.
Followers of Osiris, 617.
Followers of Rā, 159, 641, 646.
Followers of Thoth, 159.
Followers of Un-Nefer, 553.
Food, 166, 229; Chapter of, 36.
Food, celestial, 342.
Food of Rā, 304.
Forearms of Nu, 603.
Form of Kheperå, 147.
Form of Osiris, 147.
Form of Rā, 147.
Form of Tem, 147.
Formulae, 208.
Formulae, religious, 5.
Fornication, 574.
Forts, the seven, in Dead Land, 268.
Fortune, 193.
Forty-two judges, the, 572, 591.
Four apes, 614, 615.
Four bulls, 130.
Four cardinal points, 130.
Four forms of Neith, 148.
Four forms of Osiris, 146.
Four forms of Tathenen, 147.
Four geese, 130.
Four gods of cardinal points, 130.
Four Horus gods, 192.
Four Khus, 192.
Four lamps, 653.
Four pillars of sky, 130, 175, 192.

Four quarters of world, 130, 552.
Four rudders, 129.
Four sons of Horus, 127, 146, 159, 191, 262, 322, 346.
Frazer, Dr., 54, 55.
Frogs, 163.
Frog-headed gods, 120.
Funeral ceremonies, 207–216; chapter of, 355 ff.
Funeral procession described, 243 ff.
Furnaces, 153.
Fusṭât, 352, 363.

Gaga-Makheru, 9.
Gall bladder, 192, 281.
Gangers of Osiris, 155.
Gap at Abydos, 202.
Garment of purity, 47.
Gate of Ȧḳert, 160.
Gate of Tchesert, 383.
Gate of the Gods, 40.
Gate of north, 382, 383.
Gate of the Pillars of Shu, 383.
Gates, hidden, 129.
Gates of Sekhet-Ȧaru, 522.
Gates of Ṭuat, 128.
Gates, secret, of Osiris, 138.
Gates, the Ten, 138.
Gebel Ḳâf, 135.
Geese, 595, 642, 646.
Genitals, 384.
Genitals of Osiris, 240.
George, St., 197.
Girdle of Nu, 311, 559.
Giver of winds, 593.
Gîzah, 14, 341.
Gnostics, 173.
God, attributes of, 105, 106 ff.; chapter of becoming, 38; devotion to, 105; eating the, 156; greyhound-faced, 395; house of, 103; ideas about, 99; in his egg, 140; the invisible, 156, 391; the primeval, 111; of the hidden face, 625; of mysteries, 506; the self-created, 267; triune of resurrection, 241; visible emblem of, 164.
Gods, the age of, 445.
Gods, birthplace of the, 354.
Gods, descent from Rā, 150.
Gods, the Eight, 453.
Gods, the Fighting, 453.
Gods, the First-born, 633.
Gods, first companies of, 120.
Gods, the Forty-two, 314.
Gods, Great Company of, 136.
Gods, Heart-souls of, 93.
Gods, ibis-headed, 41.
Gods, jackal-headed 153.
Gods, killed and eaten, 94.
Gods, Little Company of, 126.
Gods, measuring, 154.
Gods, mountain, 150.
Gods, Spirit-souls of, 93.
Gods of Aats, 128.
Gods of altars, 129.
Gods of cardinal points, 342.
Gods of circles, 42.
Gods of fields, 128.
Gods of fire, 128.
Gods of grain, 128.
Gods of horizon, 128.
Gods of offerings, 128.
Gods of Thigh, 128.
Gods, origin of, 109, 114; rations of, 144; rowing, 147; the Seven, 418; of tomb of Osiris, 262; touring, 147; the Ḥeteptiu, 155; the Maātiu, 155; the twelve singing, 154; worship of instituted, 54.
Goddess, three-headed, 46.
Goddesses, the hour, 153.
Goddesses, the weaving, 148.
God-King, 346.

God-man, 121.
Gold, 110, 234; collar of, 46; ṭeṭ of, 45; vulture of, 45; used in decorating papyri, 51.
Golénischeff, Dr. W., 9, 178.
Goodwin, W., 8, 198.
Goose, 39, 168, 394.
Goose and Tetȧ, 10.
Goose-god, 134.
Goose-pens, 575.
Gorilla, 284.
Grain, 172.
Grain, the red, 518.
Grain-god, 305, 524; grain-gods, 128, 143.
Granaries, 221.
Grasshoppers, 195, 589.
Graves, varieties of, 4.
Great Balance, 484.
Great Bear, 292, 387; gods of, 128.
Great Cackler, 283, 285, 446, 447, 449.
Great Chiefs, 237.
Great Deep, 481.
Great God, 306.
Great Green, 172, 260, 381.
Great House (= tomb), 42, 128, 250, 416.
Great Knot, 611.
Great Lady, 600.
Great Light, 501.
Great Oasis, 183, 202, 349.
Great One, 470.
Great Peace, 344.
Great Power, 604.
Grébaut, 111, 194, 207.
Greeks, 207.
Greenfield Papyrus, 49, 240, 465.
Greyhound, 280, 394, 435, 436.
Griffith, F. Ll., 74, 101.
Guardian of Balance, 247.
Guardian of Earth, 466.
Guardians of Roads, 129.
Guide of Millions of Years, 382.
Guides of the Ṭuat, 558, 646.
Guieyesse, 8.
Guillotine, 287.

Ḥā joint, 216.
Haȧker, 415.
Hades, 52, 135, 202.
Haḥetep, 140.
Hahutiȧ msau, 257.
Hai, Boat of, 421.
Hair, 636; lock of, 172; of Isis, 54, 401.
Hair of Ani, 597; of Nu, 607; straight hair, 642.
Haker, 419, 428.
Hakheru, 269, 402.
Hall, the Great, in Heliopolis, 110, 301; of the god, 570; of Judgment, 340; of Maāti, 42, 186, 222, 229, 234, 313, 568 ff., 575, 585, 591, 595.
Halls of Ȧmenti, 44.
Halls, the Seven, 269, 659.
Ḥamemet spirits, 465.
Hammer, 360; great chief of, 171.
Hand, 160; colossal, 159.
Hand, the left = evil, 151.
Hand, the right = good, 151.
Hands of Nu, 607.
Ḥap, 131.
Ḥāpi, son of Horus, 41, 122, 190, 240, 386, 394, 414, 427, 443, 626.
Ḥāpi, or Ḥap, the Nile, 76, 144, 493, 518.
Ḥapsemus, 147.
Ḥapt-ra, 558.
Haram al-maṣṭabat, 20.
Hare, 267, 271.
Harmakhis, 179, 235, 341, 490.
Haroeris, 254.
Harpokrates, 172, 180, 295; and lotus, 310.

Harpoons, 158.
Harris Papyrus, No. 1, 49.
Harris Papyrus, No. 500, 10.
Hathor, 36, 37, 40, 43, 80, 116, 175, 189, 235, 321, 336, 347, 371, 377, 474, 548, 597, 622, 625, 652.
Hathor, the Seven Cows of, 126.
Hathor, House of, 547.
Hathor, Hymn to, 230.
Hathor, month of, 54.
Hathor, praises of, 652.
Hathors, the Seven, 185.
Ḥātshepset, 2, 165.
Ḥau, 143.
Haunch, 604, 605.
Hawk, 234, 394, 547; cry of, 147; divine, 37, 227, 525; golden, 227, 305, 306, 523; green, 90; human-headed, 76, 286; of Rā, 263; 1,000 cubits long, 637; of 7 cubits, 524.
He who cannot be known, 611.
Head (human), 45; chapter of not cutting off, 34.
Head of Meri Rā, 600.
Headdress, 90.
Head-rest, 46, 230, 621; chapter of, 321.
Heart (åb), 76; chapters of, 32, 36, 226, 281, 437, 439, 449, 450, 451, 453, 454.
Heart amulet, 451.
Heart and lungs, 192.
Heart of carnelian, 33, 321, 450.
Heart of Horus, 306.
Heart of Osiris, 396.
Heart of *sehert* stone, 620.
Heart, texts of weighing of, 371.
Heart, weighing of, 33, 42, 234.
Heart-case, 437, 449, 450, 451, 453.
Heart-soul, 35, 76, 90, 238, 439, 442; reunited to body, 290; visits body, 39.
Heart-soul of Rā, 620.
Heart-souls, 476, 502.
Heat, to keep in body, 46, 623.
Heath, Dunbar, 101.
Heaven, theories about, 130; four doors of, 46; four rudders of, 44; mansions of, 370; of stars, 298.
Ḥebent cakes, 216.
Ḥebnent, 216.
Hebrews, 203.
Ḥebt-bird (ibis), 551.
Ḥebt-re-f, 141.
Ḥeḥ, Ḥeḥet, 120.
Ḥeḥu, Ḥeḥut, 163.
Ḥeḥ-en-renput, 260.
Ḥeka, 134, 150, 355, 605.
Ḥeka, goddess, 309.
Ḥeken oil, 223, 511.
Heker, night of, 648.
Heliopolis, 1, 24, 108, 110, 111, 115, 141, 148, 156, 162, 167, 195, 203, 225, 264, 265, 301, 342, 344, 352, 357, 363, 379, 390, 400, 422, 424, 425, 434, 453, 482, 490, 491, 506, 520, 547, 548, 551, 553, 576, 579, 631.
Helios, 53.
Hell, 135; of fire, 200.
Ḥemat, 531, 533.
Ḥememet, 491, 508, 519, 520, 552, 560.
Ḥem-nu, 561.
Henå, 65.
Ḥenātiu gods, 159.
Ḥenbet Årqiu, 273.
Ḥenbiu gods, 154.
Ḥenket, 65.
Ḥenku-em-årp, 591.
Ḥenku-em-fat-maāt, 591.
Ḥenmemet, 287.
Ḥensu, 35, 59, 117, 206, 226, 256, 277, 317, 360, 377, 381, 396,

399, 492, 520, 565, 575, 577, 606, 651, 657.
Ḥenti, 526, 531; periods, 352.
Ḥenti requ, 138, 411.
Ḥenu Boat, 8, 37, 171, 360.
Ḥep bull, phallus of, 602.
Ḥep, Ḥepi, 127, 191, 192, 443.
Ḥepr, 190.
Ḥept-khat, 576.
Ḥept-shet, 582.
Ḥeqat, 580.
Ḥeqāt, 583.
Ḥeqet, 165, 193; thighs of, 602.
Herakleopolis, 34, 59, 117, 203, 206, 226, 256, 260, 277, 360, 381, 396, 431, 492, 520, 565, 570, 577, 606, 651, 657.
Heralds of Ārits and Pylons, 44, 137.
Herbs, 575, 613.
Ḥer-f-em-qeb-f, 257.
Ḥerfḥaf, 280, 288, 316, 435, 578, 584, 588.
Ḥeriqenbetef, 154.
Ḥerisepef, 395.
Ḥeriuru, 583.
Ḥerkhuf, 21.
Hermes, 23, 53.
Hermetic books, 9, 23.
Hermopolis, 8, 41, 59, 117, 204, 309, 373, 441, 448, 458, 554, 576, 660.
Hermopolis, 453; books found at, 23.
Hermopolis, souls of, 41.
Herodotus, 14, 24, 204.
Heron, 309; Chapter of, 38, 228, 554.
Herrt, serpent, 153.
Ḥerthesuf, 147.
Ḥeru-Beḥuṭet, 180.
Ḥeru-em-Khebit, 414 ff.
Ḥeru-ḥekenu, 123, 125, 180.
Ḥeru-ḥetep, 25; coffin of, 2.
Ḥeru-khent-ȧn-iriti (?), 179, 262, 358, 389, 426.
Ḥeru-khenti-khat, 179.
Ḥeru Khuti, 110, 179, 235, 341, 490, 491, 497.
Ḥeru-merti, 179.
Ḥeru-netch-ḥer-tef, 389.
Ḥeru-netch-tef-f, 188, 388.
Ḥeru-nub, 179.
Ḥeru-p-khart, 179, 180.
Ḥeru-shefit, 117.
Ḥeru Shemsu, 192.
Ḥeru-sma-taui, 180.
Ḥeruṭāṭāf, 10, 14, 89, 282, 441, 660.
Ḥeru-ur, 153, 166, 179, 188, 206, 254, 392, 579.
Ḥesat, 302.
Ḥesepti, 7, 8, 282.
Ḥet Benben, 156, 204.
Ḥetch, 254.
Ḥetch ȧbeḥu, 316, 582, 583.
Ḥetem wine, 216.
Ḥetemet, 147, 640.
Ḥetep, god, 154, 634, 635.
Ḥetep, 324, 530, 636, 638, 639, 640.
Ḥetepetnebs, 147.
Ḥetep-mes, 419.
Ḥetep-Qettbu, 637.
Ḥetepsekhus, 386, 387.
Ḥeteptiu, 151; the twelve, 155.
Ḥetepui, 146.
Ḥeth cake, 216.
Ḥet-Ḥeru, 185.
Ḥet-ka-Ptaḥ, 40, 204, 438, 439, 490, 577, 580, 612.
Ḥet-kau Nebertcher, 126, 644.
Ḥetu Āabi, 535.
Hide, 240.
Hidden doors, 129; Faces, 129; Gates, 129.
Hidden land, 367.
Hidden One, 173.

Hidden of forms, 431.
Hidden region, 146.
Hieratic character, 49.
Hieroglyphs, 660.
Hippopotamus, 141, 189, 199, 273, 329.
Hips of Nu, 608.
Holy Hill, 365.
Holy Land, 206, 364.
Horapollo, 168, 169.
Horizon, gods of, 128.
Horizons, the two, 341.
Horns, 293.
Horrack, de, 57, 68, 178.
Horse, black, 200.
Horus, 41, 43, 49, 55, 61, 76, 84, 85, 89, 91, 97, 100, 110, 117, 118, 125, 143, 145, 146, 148, 149, 159, 173, 178, 179, 180, 184, 185, 188, 192, 197, 209, 249, 250, 252, 292, 307, 326, 343, 358, 359, 364, 366, 371, 374, 385, 386, 393, 399, 404, 427, 450, 486, 503, 506, 509, 521, 528, 529, 531, 532, 534, 535, 552, 564, 565, 567, 568, 604, 609, 612, 619, 622, 625, 626, 633, 635, 637, 657.
Horus, his addresses, 47.
Horus and the ladder, 83.
Horus and Set, 197, 211.
Horus, the aged, 158; the elder, 374.
Horus, the steersman, 345.
Horus, avenger of his father, 426, 475, 477.
Horus, birthday of, 53.
Horus, the blind, 179.
Horus, the child, 179, 180.
Horus, dweller in the belly, 179.
Horus, the golden, 177.
Horus, cippi of, 180.
Horus, eye of, *see* Eye of Horus.
Horus, his fight with Set, 56, 384.
Horus, the four sons of, 32, 38, 42, 89, 655.
Horus gives his Ka, 86.
Horus, head of, 600.
Horus, Lake of, 489.
Horus of Beḥuṭet, 180.
Horus of Sekhem, 264.
Horus of the Urrt Crown, 126.
Horus, son of Isis, 176, 180, 239, 241.
Horus, the Sun-god, 180.
Horus-Seker, 241.
Horus-Sepṭ, 241.
Horus-Set, 159.
Hour gods and goddesses, 147, 153.
House, Chapters of building and seeing, 43, 45, 48, 294.
House of Aged One, 344, 357; of Anubis, 570; of Åsṭes, 421; of Darkness, 525; of Fire, 128, 437; of Ḥapt-ra, 588; of Hearts, 437; of Horus, 606; of Isis, 530; of Moon-god, 560; of Nemes, 528; of Osiris, 44, 256, 360, 532, 570, 646; of the Prince, 357; of Refreshing, 354; of Shu, 633; of Soul, 342; of the Ṭeṭ, 143.
Ḥu, 134, 183, 235, 267, 371, 383, 421, 527, 532, 549, 559.
Hukheru, 137.
Hunefer, 247, 248; his Papyrus, 57, 217, 220, 241, 258, 259, 261.
Hunger, Chapter of avoiding, 48, 88, 89, 161, 192.
Husbandry, 54.
Hyena, 435.
Hyksos, 194.
Hymn to Osiris, 31; to Rā, 31.
Hyvernat, 201.

Iamblichus, 23.
Ibis of Thoth, 305.
Idrîsî, 15.

I-em-ḥetep, 10, 187.
Image of gold, 505.
Immortality, 66, 121, 177.
Incantations, 136, 165, 167, 293, 305, 328.
Incense, 110, 209, 215, 243, 507, 569, 613, 646, 653, 662; of Nekheb, 209.
Inertia, 267.
Inert ones, 266.
Ink-jar, 562.
Inks, black and red, 236.
Insolence, 584.
Inundation, 124, 144, 174.
Iron, 250, 441.
Iron instrument, 253, 279, 434; vessel, 213.
Isis, 43, 54, 82, 85, 90, 116, 118, 121, 124, 125, 126, 131, 134, 140, 147, 165, 181, 192, 234, 235, 242, 250, 254, 259, 264, 302, 307, 322, 340, 349, 371, 374, 380, 400, 426, 427, 428, 456, 509, 510, 526, 530, 597, 607, 623.
Isis, as swallow, 55, 305; birthday of, 53; cuts off hair, 54; goes to Byblos, 55; sets Set free, 56; speech of, 624; her spells, 61; uterus and vagina of, 45; her words of power, 122.
Island of the Earth, 22.
Island of Fire, 280, 288, 435.
Island of Flame, 521.
Island of Maāti, 387.
Island of Nesersert, 367.
Island of Truth, 346, 435, 588.
Islands of the Blessed, 190, 346.
Iuâu, Papyrus of, 26, 29, 257, 295.

Jackal, 240, 271, 448; of jackals, 283.
Jackal-god, 316.
Jackal-headed gods, 153.
Jars, Canopic, 131.
Jawbone, 210, 240, 270, 271, 406.
Jehannum, 135.
Jéquier, 101.
Jerusalem, 25, 353.
Jews, 25, 196.
Judge of living and dead, 177.
Judge of Truth, 201.
Judges, the Forty-two, 316.
Judgment, Great, 586.
Judgment Hall, 121, 155, 234.
Judgment of Osiris, 144, 151.
Judgment Scene, 182, 185, 195, 221, 226.
Junker, Dr. H., 116, 175, 241.

Ka, 73 ff., 291, 341.
Ka, chapel of, 174, 251.
Ka, priests of, 174.
Kaenmutef, 124.
Kakaå, 165.
Kamui, 545.
Kam-ur, 204, 307, 313, 570.
Kamutef, 108.
Karbala, 353.
Karnak, 108.
Ḳasut, 301.
Kathaiḥemt, 645.
Kau, the Twelve, 153.
Kau, the washed, 155.
Kaui, 579.
Ḳeb, 16, 25, 43, 53, 57, 60, 61, 80, 85, 89, 94, 116, 118, 126, 134, 146, 159, 174, 175, 176, 180, 235, 283, 301, 340, 342, 350, 371, 390, 397, 420, 438, 439, 443, 446, 447, 450, 458, 465, 508, 510, 526, 548, 604, 606.
Keeper of the Balance, 439.
Keepers of Cemeteries, 129.
Keepers of Doors, 129.

Kefaiu, 420.
Kek, 120; Keket, 120.
Kekui, 163; Kekuit, 163.
Ḳem-ḥeru, 457.
Kemtet plant, 152.
Kenemti, 580, 584.
Ḳenḳenur, 447, 449.
Kenmet, 580.
Ḳerasher, 57.
Ḳerḥ, Ḳerḥet, 163.
Ḳestȧ, 41, 127, 386, 427, 626.
Kha, Lake of, 324.
Khā, Pyramid, 14.
Khāfrā, 14, 164.
Khaibit, 78.
Khalîg Canal, 142.
Khā-nefert, 204.
Khânês, 206, 360.
Khârgah Oasis, 152.
Khari, 290.
Khartûm, 308.
Khat, body, 69.
Khati, 158.
Khati gods, 421, 422.
Khebit-saht-neter, 126, 644.
Khebt chamber, 579.
Khem, 188, 203.
Khemenu, 8, 25, 41, 59, 117, 175, 204, 235, 265, 266, 267, 373, 377, 441, 453, 576, 630; the eight elements, 120.
Khemenu, Souls of, 41.
Khemi, 583.
Khemiu, 147, 579.
Khemmis, 188.
Khemta, 192.
Khenem beer, 216.
Khenfu cakes, 216.
Khensu, 94, 194, 302, 309, 553.
Khensu-ḥetep, 103.
Khensu-ur, 600.
Khent, King, 202.
Khenti (Osiris), 62.
Khenti Amenti, 91, 152, 153, 647.
Khenti Ȧmenti Un-nefer, 278, 650.
Khent-Ȧriti (?), 209.
Khenti-heh-f, 262.
Khenti-ḥerȧb-ḥet-ṭesheru, 127.
Khenti-Khabas, 607.
Khent-menut-f, 80.
Kheperȧ, 70, 109, 111, 113, 118, 119, 124, 145, 146, 149, 162, 167, 169, 172, 195, 232, 309, 339, 340, 394, 397, 398, 404, 461, 463, 497, 508, 549, 552, 609; alone, 118; in his boat, 264; standard of, 160.
Kheperkekiukhāmestu, 149.
Kheperta, 172.
Khepertchesef, 167.
Kheprer, 109.
Khepri, serpent, 158.
Khepriu gods, 525.
Kherāḥa, 141, 142, 204, 352, 363, 400, 491, 576, 598, 608.
Kherḥeb, 2, 208, 244, 249 ff., 255, 360, 363, 648.
Kheri-beq, 267.
Kheri-beq-f, 387.
Kherp sceptre, 241.
Khersek-Shu, 571.
Khert-khent-Sekhem, 84.
Khert-neter, 29, 50, 140, 223, 255, 256, 265, 275, 279, 281, 282. 286, 355, 376, 405, 422, 423, 424, 435, 436, 437, 439, 441, 442, 445, 446, 448, 449, 450, 451, 453, 454, 457, 458, 459, 460, 465, 470, 471, 473, 474, 478, 485, 495, 500, 501, 505, 507, 512, 520, 523, 551, 556, 558, 567, 617, 618, 620, 628, 629, 632, 634, 646, 647, 649, 650, 651, 661, 664.
Kheru-Ennutchi, the nine, 154.
Kheru-metauḥ, 156.

Khesef-aṭ, 270, 405.
Khesef-ḥer-āsht-Kheru, 137, 220, 405.
Khesef-ḥer-khemiu, 137.
Khesef-khemi, 271, 407.
Khnem-Nefert, 7, 8.
Khnemt-ānkh-Ȧniut, 127, 645.
Khnemu, 52, 165, 173, 174, 175, 184, 192, 193, 194, 273, 371, 440, 446; the seven forms of, 174.
Khu, 45, 79; chapter of perfecting, 49, 647; of raising, 47.
Khufu, 9, 10, 14, 164, 441.
Khu-ḥerȧb-ḥet-āshemu, 127.
Khu of Osiris, 550.
Khu of Temu, 114.
Khu-tchetf, 138, 274, 412.
Khuti, 151.
King, 342; of Truth, 348.
Kingdom of Osiris, 268.
Knees of Meri Rā, 603.
Knife of Horus, 141.
Knot, 607; the Great, 611; tying of knots, 158.
Knowledge, 109.
Ḳôm as-Sulṭân, 428.
Kronos, 53.

Labourers, 518.
Lacau, 3.
Ladder, 82, 141, 300; lord of, 83.
Lady of the Hour, 497, 503.
Lady of the House, 182.
Lady of Saïs, 598.
Lady of Winds, 632.
Lake, gods of, 91.
Lake Neserser, 563, 564, 638.
Lake of boiling water, 152.
Lake of Fire, 42, 93, 157, 237, 268, 312, 318, 395, 446.
Lake of Flowers, 437.
Lake of Ḥetep, 635.
Lake of Horus, 489.
Lake of Khemta, 192.
Lake of Life, 153.
Lake of Living Uraei, 153.
Lake of Natron, 260, 381.
Lake of Nefer, 584.
Lake of Salt, 260, 351.
Lake of Sekhet-ȧru, 444.
Lake of Serser, 563, 564, 638.
Lake of South, 589.
Lake of Tchesert, 641.
Lake of Testes, 349, 488.
Lake of the Thigh, 300.
Lake of Truth, 589.
Lake of Ṭuat, 148.
Lake of Unt, 395.
Lakes in Delta, 157.
Lamellicorns, 168.
Lameness of Horus, 180.
Lamentations of Isis and Nephthys, 57, 178.
Land, cultivated, 578.
Land of Eternity, 498.
Land of Everlastingness, 498.
Land of Holiness, 297.
Land of Life, 487, 500.
Land of the Dead, 243.
Lands of the gods, 499.
Language of gods and men, 304.
Lanzone, 131, 178, 179, 181, 182, 185, 186, 187, 188, 189, 190, 198, 340.
Lapis lazuli, 9, 110, 353, 447, 448, 560, 567, 641, 642.
Law (Maāt) 101, 108, 234, 343, 349, 498; of Osiris, 238.
Laws, Code of, 54.
Laws of heaven, 343.
Leather, white, 595, 612.
Ledrain, 2, 59, 180.
Leemans, 220.
Lefébure, 121, 200, 207, 232.

Leg, 590.
Leghorn, 15.
Legs, 474; of Meri Rā, 602; of Nu, 608.
Leopard, skin of, 243, 275, 278.
Lepsius, 2, 6, 8, 11, 19, 23, 69, 70, 72, 172, 198, 199, 328, 362, 647.
Letopolis, 59, 206, 276, 302, 358, 392, 426, 546, 552.
Letopolites, 206, 307.
Letters, 343.
Leyden, 230.
L'Hôte, 73, 342.
Libation vases, 246.
Libyan oil, 214.
Libyans, 154.
Lieblein, 7.
Lies, 577.
Life after death, 29, 481.
Life, eternal, 66 ff., 312, 563.
Life, fluid of, 209; germs of, 162; Lake of, 153; origin of, 119; out of death, 462; staff of, 108, 109, 172; symbol of, 162; tree of, 88.
Light, 143, 166, 181, 267, 280, 475.
Light and Darkness, 197.
Light, creation of, 120.
Light of Rā, 109.
Light-god, 203, 227, 292, 300, 304, 307, 310, 446, 448, 478, 481, 494, 527, 530; of turning into, 559.
Light-spirit, 162.
Lightning, 130, 384.
Lily, 228, 557; of becoming, 38.
Limbo of snakes, 198.
Linen, 595, 612; garments of, 148; offerings of, 12; white, 88.
Lion of To-day, 258.
Lion of Yesterday, 258.
Lions, 199, 201.
Lion-god, 112, 294, 484; double, 399.
Lion-gods, 370, 528, 529, 530.
Lips of Ani, 597; of Meri Rā, 601; of Nu, 607.
Litanies of Seker, 58.
Litany of Osiris, 31, 296.
Litany of Rā, 167.
Liturgy, 221.
Liturgy of Āapep, 198.
Liturgy of funeral offerings, 3, 207.
Liturgy of Soul-god, 359.
Liver, 192, 216; eaten, 95.
Livers, 586.
Living gods, 608.
Living uraei, 599.
Loin cloth, 275.
Loom, 186.
Lord of Eternity, 177.
Lord of Hearts, 450.
Lord of Life, 45, 62, 526.
Lord of Life (Ptaḥ), 169.
Lord of Light, 549.
Lord of Souls, 137.
Lord of Terror, 395, 396.
Lord of Things, 455, 541.
Lord of Truth, 177.
Lord of Two Arms, 551.
Lord of Winds, 588, 640.
Lord of Years, 550.
Lord One, 306, 518.
Lords of Eternity, 558.
Loret, 54, 56, 178.
Lotus, 36, 187, 190, 310, 557, 558; with four Sons of Horus, 241, 313; of changing into, 228.
Luck, 235; ill, 586.
Lungs, 281.
Luxor, 165.
Lying, 239.
Lynx, 240; goddess, 139, 147.

Maa-ȧntuf, 579.
Maa-ȧnuf, 583.
Maa-ȧtef, 262, 387.
Maa-em-ḳerḥ, 388.

Maā-kheru, 87, 341.
Maāt at Creation, 118; the Beautiful, 349.
Maāt-kheru, 59.
Maāt, Maāti, 65, 120, 126, 166, 170, 184, 185, 195, 199, 229, 236, 298, 308, 340, 343, 345, 403, 466, 488, 503, 568, 573, 578.
Maāt, Maāti, Maātet, a boat, 42, 601, 603.
Maāti goddesses, 236, 315, 340.
Maāti, Hall of, 42, 568; food, 151; furrow of, 594; gods, 403.
Maāti, nome of, 362; plant of, 354.
Maātiu, the Twelve, 151, 155.
Maāt-ka-Rā, 50.
Mābet chamber, 583.
Mābit, 578.
Macarius of Antioch, 201.
Macedon, 165.
Mafṭet, 139, 147.
Mâmûn, 14.
Man, ram-headed, 150.
Man-god, 166, 317; of Memphis, 360.
Manetho, 7.
Mankind, four divisions of, 154.
Mansions, the Seven, 269.
Mānthet Boat, 133, 160, 163, 342, 602.
Manu, Mountain, 130, 179, 205, 340, 341, 344, 488.
Marduk, 197.
Mariette, 1, 2, 7, 20, 103, 111.
Mariners of Rā, 112, 503.
Mark, St., 52.
Maspero, Prof. G., 2, 5, 13, 18, 50, 73, 87, 101, 111, 121, 183, 191, 199, 202, 342.
Maṣṭabah tombs, 3, 5, 11, 14, 18.
Maṣṭabat al-Far'ûn, 19.
Master of lords of furnaces, 153.
Masturbation, 574.
Mat, 241, 245, 261.
Mats, grass, used in burial, 4.
Maṭarîyah, 352.
Matchaiu, 108, 110.
Mātchet, 267, 393.
Māṭes, 395.
Māṭet, Māṭett, a Boat, 165, 345, 488, 496.
Mathematics, 236.
Matter, primeval, 118, 119.
Màu (Cat), 390.
Maxims of Ani or Khensu-ānkh, 103.
Measure, 154.
Meat offerings, 208.
Meçca, 25, 353.
Medicine man, 263.
Mediterranean Sea, 5, 157, 260.
Mêdûm, 14.
Meḥen, 148, 150, 159.
Meḥnet, 62.
Meḥtiemsaf, 6.
Meḥ-urt, Meḥt-urt, 37, 48, 124, 172, 186, 261, 385, 520, 652.
Mekes sceptre, 66.
Mekhir, 575.
Members, 84.
Memphis, 40, 59, 116, 145, 169, 170, 171, 172, 187, 204, 206, 219, 295, 348, 352, 360, 438, 478, 490, 570, 577, 580, 612.
Memphis, theology of, 117.
Men = Egyptians, 154; origin of, 109, 114, 119; the Two, 184.
Menȧ, 6, 7.
Menȧt, 170, 232, 261, 276, 308.
Mendes, 207, 342.
Menes, 6.
Menḥu, 401.
Menkaurā, 8, 14, 164, 238, 441 ff.
Men Nefer, 204.
Menthu-ḥetep, 7; coffin of, 2.

Menu, 172, 188, 203, 380, 518, 623; festival of, 648; with body of beetle, 46; with tail, 624; Prophet of, 76.
Menu-Åmen, 108.
Menu-Ḥeru, 419.
Menuqet, 139.
Mer-en-Rā, 20, 21.
Meri Rā, 600–606.
Meroë, 330.
Mert, 316, 598, 635.
Mert Seḥert, 189.
Merti goddesses, 34, 285, 456.
Mes-em-neter, 8, 609.
Mesentiu, 251.
Meskhen, 421.
Meskhenet, 165, 193, 236.
Meskhent, 240.
Meskhet tool, 246, 253.
Mesopotamia, 268.
Mes-peḥ, 135.
Mes Ptaḥ, 138, 272, 409.
Mesqen, 456.
Mesqet chamber, 267, 370, 398.
Mest, 216.
Mestå, 127, 240, 626.
Mestchem, 254.
Mesu Beṭesh, 267.
Metal worker, 170.
Metchet oil, 213.
Metchet-mu-nebt-Ṭuat, 146.
Metchet qa tutchebu, 148.
Meteriu, 155.
Meteshẹrari she, 137.
Metessen, 137.
Metiheh, 269.
Metternich stele, 178.
Mice, 109.
Midwife, 193, 238.
Mighty One of Souls, 473.
Milk, 211.
Milk of white cow, 653.
Millions of years, 381.
Miracle play, 202.
M'nāat, 590.
Monogenês, 169.
Monotheism, 106, 115, 196.
Monster, composite, 198.
Monsters, winged, 199.
Moon, 43, 85, 109, 111, 119, 131, 132, 184, 233, 385, 423; Chapter of the new, 504; hymn to, 508.
Moon, crescent, swallowed, 292, 343.
Moon, first day of, 229.
Moon, the new, 298.
Moon, spirit of, 293.
Moon, worship of, 164.
Moon-god, 112, 293, 309, 311, 479, 560.
Mother-goddess, 328, 350, 646.
Mother of emerald, 46, 623.
Mother of the gods, 178, 650.
Mother of mothers, 174.
Mother, veneration for, 104.
Mother-womb, 340.
Mount Manu, 340.
Mount of Sunrise, 146, 149.
Mourners, 387.
Mouth, Chapter of opening, 32; of giving, 32, 367, 368.
Mouth of Meri Rā, 600.
Mouth, opening the, 226, 433.
Mouths of Nile, 54.
Muḥammad, 95.
Muḥammad 'Alî, 308.
Muhammadans, 25, 196.
Mulberries, 216.
Müller, Max, 12.
Mummification, 5.
Mummy, 523; chamber, 45, 205, 229, 322.
Murder, 574, 577.
Muslims, 353.
Mut, 194, 348.
Mut-em-ua, 258.
Mut-ḥetep, Papyrus of, 2.

Mutilation, 158.
Mycerinus, 14, 16, 18, 20, 441.
Myrrh, 110, 140, 244, 442, 575, 612.
Myrrh of women, 570.
Mystery, 570; of God, 107; of Ṭuat and Åḳertet, 648; of Seker, 359.
Mut, three-headed, 623.
Mut-rest, 629.

Naaruṭf, 203.
Nȧk, 198, 349; conquered, 111; vomiting of, 109.
Name, 32; to remember, 436; the importance of, 81; of God, 103; of Kheperȧ, 118; secret, of Rā, 122.
Nāq, 156.
Nārt, 59.
Nārti-ānkh-em-sen-f, 257.
Natron, 210, 243, 299, 507.
Nature-god, 182.
Nāu, 140.
Navel-cords, 472.
Navel-string, 236, 238, 240, 381.
Naville, 2, 6, 8, 9, 23, 28, 29, 50, 70, 169, 198, 199, 217, 255, 271, 341, 355, 567, 577, 583.
Neb-ābui, 580, 584.
Nebeḥ bird, 448.
Nebertcher (Osiris), 62, 119, 188, 267, 351, 366, 378, 390, 392, 394, 396, 397, 425, 432, 522, 526, 527, 534, 535, 586, 614.
Neb-ḥeru, 580, 584.
Neb ḥetep, 637.
Neb-Maāt, 578, 583.
Neb-maāt-ḥeri, 314.
Neb-maāt-peḥti, 571.
Neb-nefu, 575.
Neb-peḥti-thes, 314.
Neb-qeṭ, 220.
Nebseni, 8, 26, 217, 219, 224, 225, 227, 265, 276, 281, 299, 314, 325, 326, 369, 372, 389, 391, 392, 394, 424, 439, 467, 476, 485, 517, 546, 576, 582, 616, 622, 624, 629, 630, 635, 653.
Nebt-āba, 155.
Nebt-ānkh, 111.
Nebtaui, 324.
Nebt-ḥet, 182, 234.
Nebtsemanifu, 147.
Nebts-tchefau, 153.
Nebt-taui, 640.
Nebu-khert, 152.
Necklace, 280, 281.
Neck of Ani, 598.
Needle, 251.
Nefer-Tem, 170, 187, 264, 310, 392, 558, 580, 584.
Neferu, 2, 228.
Nefer-uben-f, 2, 228, 282, 291, 317, 443, 444, 479.
Negative confession, 49, 229, 318.
Negroes, 154.
Neḥaḥāu, 316, 582.
Neḥa-ḥer, 143, 147, 577.
Nehai flowers, 590.
Nehatu, 579.
Neḥbet sceptre, 66.
Neḥebkau, 140.
Neḥeb-ka, 188, 394, 455, 581, 584.
Neḥeb-nefert, 581, 584.
Nehep serpent, 156, 157.
Neḥra cake, 216.
Neith, 186, 192, 205, 214, 316, 421, 602, 607; four forms of, 148; self-produced, 187; Ṭuat of, 149.
Neḳau, 138, 273, 410.
Neḳeḳ-ur, 458.
Nekheb, 189, 254; incense of, 209.
Nekhebet, Nekhebit, 189, 204, 259, 493

Nekhen, 205, 493, 580, 583.
Nekhen, souls of, 41.
Nekhen-sema-taui, 127.
Nekht, 441 ; the general, 347.
Nekht-neb-f, 165.
Nekhtu Amen, 365, 366.
Nemes bandlet, 246, 254, 528, 529, 530.
Nen, Nenet, 120.
Nent, 472.
Nenshem joint, 216.
Nepet, 216.
Nepert, 64.
Nephthys, 25, 82, 85, 90, 116, 118, 126, 132, 134, 140, 165, 180, 192, 234, 235, 240, 242, 254, 264, 302, 322, 340, 349, 371, 380, 400, 426, 456, 510; birthday of, 53 ; speech of, 625.
Neprȧ, 305, 524.
Neri, 138.
Nerṭā-nef-besef, 388.
Neruit, 272, 409.
Neruṭef, 303, 313, 382, 388, 395, 420, 421, 426, 431, 565, 570.
Neserser, 563, 638.
Nesersert Island, 367.
Nesert, 622 ; goddess, 321.
Neshem, 420.
Neshem Boat, 364.
Neshmen unguent, 214.
Neshmet, 570.
Nesi Khensu, 50, 111, 117.
Nesitanebtashru, 49.
Nest, the double, 381 ; the dwellers in, 283.
Nest-khent-Sekhem, 601.
Net, 159, 421.
Net, fishing, 45.
Nets, 158.
Net-Ȧsȧr, 144.
Neṭāt, 77, 90, 350.
Neṭbit, 64.
Netcheh-Netcheh, 262, 388.
Netchemȧb, 101.
Netchesti, 63.
Netchfet, 62, 580.
Neteqaḥer Khesefaṭu, 137.
Neter, 115 ; meaning of, 99.
Neterit, 151.
Neter Khert, 205.
Net-Neb-uā, 143.
Netru, 63.
New Moon festival, 647.
New Year, 617.
Nicholas, Emperor, 9.
Nifu-ur, 364.
Night, 119, 171, 212, 222, 380.
Night of battle, 391 ; offerings of, 358, 590 ; sky, 131, 132, 500 ; sun, 199, 359.
Nile, 54, 57, 109, 122, 124, 137, 141, 144, 157, 163, 172, 174, 195, 202, 204, 281, 284, 363, 424, 493 ; Blue, 308 ; celestial, 94, 190 ; flood, 173, 177.
Nile-god, 142, 174, 190, 324, 414, 518 ; the two, 190, 191, 274.
Nile, mouths of, 54 ; valley of, 164, 168.
Nine gods, 108 ; serpents, 146.
Nipple cakes, 211.
Nipple of Isis, 211
Nome of Maāti, 362.
North, city of, 589 ; Crown of, 189 ; gods of roads of, 128 ; Lords of, 638 ; rudder of, 645 ; wine of, 216.
Nose of Nu, 609 ; of Pepi, 600.
Nouti, 99.
Nu, god, 59, 112, 114, 118, 120, 125, 133, 144, 149, 157, 160, 161, 162, 163, 164, 265, 266, 267, 268, 271, 291, 308, 316, 340, 349, 377, 490, 499, 528, 549, 551, 564, 581, 597, 600, 607, 611.

Nu, the Aged, 172; girdle of, 311; sky, 435.
Nu and his papyrus, 125, 217, 238, 314, 328, 444, 448, 467, 481, 572, 575, 582, 606, 614, 616, 629.
Nubia, 23, 116.
Nubians, 110, 120.
Nursing goddesses, 364.
Nut, 16, 17, 22, 25, 36, 43, 53, 57, 60, 84, 85, 90, 116, 118, 120, 126, 134, 149, 163, 172, 175, 176, 180, 235, 285, 302, 317, 340, 348, 349, 356, 371, 377, 450, 458, 459, 466, 472, 488, 489, 491, 500, 504, 510, 522, 524, 531, 542, 544, 554, 599, 604, 608, 611, 624; belly of, 602; children of, 465.
Nut-urt, 640.

Oars, 242.
Oases, 183, 206.
Offering, Royal, 214.
Offerings, at the word, 595; to provide, 40; field of, 41; for the dead, 143; gods of, 128; the great value of, 151; how to make, 104; made to Ka, 76; scribe of, 220; spirits of, 151.
Oil, Libyan, 214; cedar, 214; oils, 214.
Ointment, 254.
Okapi, 181.
Olive tree, 590.
Olympias, 165.
Olympus, 342.
Ombos, 188.
Omens, 212.
On, 1, 203.
One, 109; One One, 111, 114, 196.
Oneness, 342.
Only One, 610, 611.
Opener-gods, 129.
Opener of roads, 254; of the ways, 182.
Opening the mouth, 170, 192, 245, 246, 278, 280, 359, 442; description of ceremonies of, 248.
Orion, 62, 86, 94, 317, 363, 599; the Giant, 279.
Osiris, 25, 43, 69, 101, 116, 117, 118, 145, 146, 153, 162, 174, 182, 187, 197, 206, 207, 425, 426, 510, 534.
Osiris and embalmment, 460; his court, 136; and Ladder, 301; and Satyrs, 231.
Osiris Ānkhti, 61.
Osiris the Avenger, 180.
Osiris the Begetter, 64.
Osiris, boats of, 143.
Osiris, body of, 53.
Osiris, bodyguard of, 152.
Osiris, chapter of being with, 48,
Osiris, chapter of knowing, 41.
Osiris, chapter of praising, 42.
Osiris, chiefs of, 42, 48.
Osiris, cult of, 125.
Osiris, death of, 178.
Osiris, the deceased, 339.
Osiris, drowned, 54.
Osiris eats the Eye of Horus, 141.
Osiris, enemies of, 155.
Osiris, festivals of, 359.
Osiris, fields of, 148.
Osiris, firstborn of, 190.
Osiris, forms of, 61, 177.
Osiris, Gates of House of, 138.
Osiris, Governor of eternity, 64.
Osiris, green-faced, 276.
Osiris, head of, 202.
Osiris, house of, 44.
Osiris, hymns to, 48, 59, 221, 229, 232, 295, 490.
Osiris, iconography of, 177.
Osiris, judged, 110.

Osiris Khenti Åmenti, 25, 125, 143, 248, 329, 420, 568, 653, 654, 656 ff.; with Un-Nefer, 230.
Osiris, Kingdom of, 121, 137, 171.
Osiris the Kinsman, 356.
Osiris, Legend of, 52.
Osiris meets Rā, 263.
Osiris = moon, 177.
Osiris = Nile-flood, 177.
Osiris, phallus of, 599.
Osiris, reincarnation of Temu, 118.
Osiris, relics of, 277.
Osiris, resurrection of, 178.
Osiris, rise of cult of, 5.
Osiris, Sacrum bone of, 45.
Osiris, Sāḥu of, 72.
Osiris Sekri, 63.
Osiris, supremacy of, 1.
Osiris Thoth, 343.
Osiris, throne of, 144.
Osiris, titles of, 57.
Osiris, tomb of, 147, 202, 350.
Osiris, trial of, 87.
Osiris = Ṭuat, 135, 149.
Osiris, union with Nephthys, 54.
Osiris Un-Nefer, 224.
Osiris, vassals of, 565.
Ostrich, 448.
Ostrich feather, 234, 235, 238, 246, 275, 340.
Other World, 135, 183, and see *passim*.
Outer darkness, 201.
Overlord, 306.
Ox of Ḳeb, 592, 593.
Oxen, 595; offering of, 12.

Pa Bast, 204.
Paddle of Rā, 445.
Paddles, 242, 298, 506.
Palette, 39, 183, 184, 236, 244, 259, 268, 323, 562.
Palm tree, 109, 518; wood, 664.
Pan, 188.
Pans, 54.
Panopolis, 154, 203, 520, 579.
Pantheism, 115.
Panther, 56.
Papyrus, 183, 190; boat, 55; swamps, 623.
Paqrer, 558, 559.
Parthey, 23.
Pāt beings, 109, 608.
Pat cake, 216.
Pautu the oldest god, 349.
Pe, 25, 62, 205, 370, 517; souls of, 41.
Pectoral, 623.
Peḥreri, 471.
Pekh grain, 216.
Pekhat, 623.
Pellegrini, 57.
Pelusium wine, 216.
Pen-seed, 236.
Penti, 466.
Pepi I, 6, 17, 19, 21, 22, 78, 81, 82, 85, 100, 191, 302, 600–606; pyramid of, 1.
Pepi II, 6, 20, 21, 22.
Per-åb-sen, 11.
Per Åsår, 205, 359.
Per Bast, 204.
Per Menu, 579.
Per Neser, 437.
Per Rā, 203.
Per Uatchet, 205, 207, 427.
Per-ur, 436.
Pericardium, 431.
Per Kheru, 87.
Peroffsky, Gen., 9.
Perring, 18.
Persea tree, 390, 588.
Persen cakes, 615, 616.
Persia, 268.
Pert, 44.
Pert-em-hru, 28, 355.
Peseshkef, 210.

Pesh-en-kef, 228, 246, 253.
Pesk-Rā, 63.
Pesṭit, 156.
Pesṭu, 148.
Peṭā-Ȧmen-apt, 2.
Petemenophis, 9.
Peten cakes, 266.
Pe-Ṭep, 302, 427; gods of, 276.
Pet-she, 63.
Phacusa, 558.
Phallus, 267, 288; of Ani, 599; of Mut, 623; of Nu, 608; of Osiris, 401; of Pepi, 602; of Rā, 379, 383, 401, 467, 468.
Pharaoh's Bench, 19.
Philae, 173, 175.
Philip, 165.
Phoenicians, 590.
Phoenix, 228, 259, 575.
Phusis, 99.
Pibeseth, 204.
Pierret, 105, 106, 355.
Pietschmann, 23.
Pig, 34, 155, 596.
Pigmy, 22, 23, 46, 172.
Pillar of Byblos, 55.
Pillar of Osiris, 55.
Pillars of Shu, 377, 391.
Pillars of sky, 130, 174, 175.
Pillow, 621; amulet of, 451; chapter of, 46, 221.
Pilot fishes, 166; gods, 142.
Pisentios, 200.
Pit of tomb, 245.
Pits of fire, 149.
Pitch, 663.
Placenta, 200.
Planets, boats of, 135.
Plant, 611; of truth, 155, 156.
Plaque, 46.
Pleyte, 121, 186.
Ploughing, 275, 325; in Other World, 277, 303.
Plumes, 131, 293; of Menu, 380; of Osiris, 64.
Plutarch, 53, 56, 61, 178, 182.
Polytheism, 115.
Porphyry, 168.
Poseidon, 200.
Potter, wheel of, 112, 173.
Power of Powers, 93, 94.
Powers, the Eight, 159.
Power, the vital, 80.
Prayer, 5, 103, 268; ascends on incense, 243; for the dead 143.
Priests, 14; of Ȧnu, 162; of Ka, 74; of Rā, 1, 115.
Prince, chapter of becoming, 38.
Prince, House of the, 357.
Prisse d'Avennes, 101; papyrus 185.
Procession, funeral, 29.
Protector, 111.
Proto-Semites, 5.
Proverbs, Book of, 118.
Ptaḥ, 52, 108, 116, 117, 120, 169, 184, 187, 206, 256, 279, 308, 310, 321, 342, 360, 433, 483, 487, 548, 558, 608, 625, 626, 629, 635, changing into, 38, 228, 546.
Ptaḥ-Ȧsȧr, 170.
Ptaḥ-Ḥāpi, 170.
Ptaḥ-ḥetep, 185.
Ptaḥ-neb-Ānkh, 62.
Ptaḥ-Nile, 170.
Ptaḥ-Nu, 170.
Ptaḥ-Seker, 170, 630.
Ptaḥ-Seker-Ȧsȧr, 170, 171, 241.
Ptaḥ-Seker-Tem, 170, 245, 490.
Ptaḥ-shepses, 12.
Ptaḥ-Tanen, 170, 172.
Ptolemaïs, 50.
Punishment, everlasting, 161.
Punt, 108, 195, 205, 499.
Purgatory, 161.

Purity, 442.
Pylons, 354; chiefs of, 229; hidden, 44; of Ṭuat, 129; the Seven, 44; the Ten, 409; their names, 272.
Pyramid Texts, 1, 3, 21, 23, 24, 27, 28, 52, 57, 67, 71, 76, 81, 85, 100, 162, 177, 183, 186, 191, 193, 194, 198, 199.
Pyramid tomb, 1, 14.
Python, 233; of darkness, 263.

Qa-ḥaḥetep, 140.
Qān, 156.
Qebḥ, 443.
Qebḥsenuf, 41, 127, 131, 191, 240, 386; speech of, 627; West, 192.
Qefṭenu, 63.
Qenna, 217, 220.
Qenqen, 325.
Qenqenet, 642.
Qerȧu, 401.
Qernet, 577.
Qerrt, 59.
Qerrti, 578.
Qerti, 174, 583.
Qetqet, 324.
Quadrupeds, 119.

Rā, 24, 41, 44, 48, 49, 80, 82, 86, 90, 101, 108, 111, 115, 116, 117, 119, 120, 124, 134, 139, 141, 144, 145, 149, 150, 151, 152, 160, 164, 167, 169, 172, 174, 177, 182, 187, 195, 197, 200, 266, 284, 340, 342, 357, 365, 377, 378, 379, 388, 391, 397, 398, 402, 404, 420, 431, 444, 451, 455, 459, 466, 467, 473, 474, 475, 476, 482, 486, 488, 498, 500, 503, 504, 506, 507, 511, 512, 521, 524, 547, 549, 553, 565, 567, 597, 603, 607, 608, 613, 626, 637, 640, 641, 644, 646, 647, 649, 658.
Rā and Isis, 121; Rā and the Ladder, 83; bitten by serpent, 122; boat of, 40; body of, 157; bodyguard of, 147; bread of, 88; of being near, 43; eye of, 154; father of gods, 479; Followers of, 156, 159; Hymn to, 221, 224, 295, 339, 347, 487, 496, 508; Litany of, 167; mariners of, 589; meets Osiris, 263; the mummy of, 150; name of, 122; of Heliopolis, 114; of Sakhabu, 165; priests of, 175; forms of, 167; smell of, 108; soul of, 157, 389; soul of Ȧnu, 41; two eyes of, 34; worship of, 164; worshippers, 154.
Rā goose, 613.
Rā-Harmakhis, 371.
Rā Ḥeru Khuti, 40, 125, 139, 341, 347.
Rā Horus, 509.
Rā Kheperȧ, 468.
Rā Tem, 66, 175, 177, 394.
Rā-user, 193.
Rain, 133.
Rain maker, 363.
Ram, 30; = Khnemu, 173.
Rameses II, 193.
Rameses IV, 167.
Ram-god, 38, 293, 359.
Ram, man-headed, 142.
Ram of Osiris, 359.
Rasta, 41, 62, 63, 64, 141, 145, 205, 260, 261, 270, 275, 278, 303, 358, 359, 364, 366, 382, 402, 403, 405, 406, 420, 421, 422, 423, 570, 577, 588, 615, 616; of emerging from, 41.

Rat, 196; Rats, 109.
Rations, 157; of the god, 144.
Raven, Mr., 15, 16.
Read, 116.
Reaping, 324.
Re-birth, 240.
Recensions of the Book of the Dead, 1, 3, 26.
Red fiends, 611; gods, 645.
Red goddess, 309; Pyramid, 15.
Red Sea, 260.
Reed, 663; mat, 264.
Reeds, Field of, 41, 44.
Reenqerr, 148.
Re goose, 216.
Reḥnent, 63.
Reḥti, 559.
Reḥti-merti, 573.
Reḥu, 264, 400.
Reḥui, 181, 404.
Re-incarnation, 118.
Reins of Nu, 608.
Rekhit, 608.
Religion, Egyptian, 115, 120.
Remorse, 578, 584.
Renenet, 193.
Rennet, 623.
Rennt, 236.
Repentance, 584.
Rera, 359.
Reri, 160.
Resȧb, 137.
Resḥer, 137.
Resnet, 62.
Resu, 62.
Resurrection, 121, 171, 222, 293; of Osiris, 53, 425; symbol of, 146; triune god of, 241.
Retḥu cake, 216.
Return to earth, 484.
Rhea, 53.
Right, God judges, 185.
Righteous, the, 151.
River of Åment, 366.
River of fire, 201.
River of Ṭuat, 136.
Roads, Guardians of, 129.
Roads, South, North, West, East, 128.
Robbery, 576.
Ropes, 158.
Rossi, 121.
Rotting, 460.
Rougé, de, 24, 28, 103, 145.
Rubrics, 49.
Rudder, 457, 647; the Four, 44, 127, 327, 645, 649.
Runner, 489.
Ruruti, 577, 582.
Ruṭ-ṭeṭt, 165.

Sa, 134, 150, 152, 235, 371, 383, 421; magical power of, 189.
Sa (Saïs), 205.
Sȧa, 183.
Saa, 62, 267.
Sȧaḥ, 363, 434, 599; en-mut-f, 592.
Sabes, 137.
Sacrifices, human, 165; propitiatory, 151.
Sacrum bone, 45, 243, 263, 357.
Sacy, de, 14.
Saf cake, 216.
Saffron cakes, 399.
Saḥ, 94; Orion, 62, 317.
Sāḥal, 174.
Sāḥit, 279.
Sāḥu, 29, 70 ff., 290, 306, 403, 408, 588; entering Ṭuat, 256, 365.
Saḥura, 165.
Sail, 34, 35, 40, 283.
Sailor gods, 148.
Saïs, 148, 186, 205, 214, 580, 607.
Saïs, Lower, 63; Upper, 64.
Saïs, Papyrus of, 2.

Saïs, Ṭuat of, 149.
Sait goddesses, 158.
Saïte Recension 50.
Sakhabu, 165.
Ṣaḳḳârah, 11, 12, 18, 19, 205, 359, 478.
Saḳtif, 273, 411.
Sallier Papyrus, No. 4, 54.
Sām-em-qesu, 257.
Sām-em-snef, 257.
Sameref, 225, 245, 251, 252 ff., 275, 423.
Sand, 154, 629; belt of, 662; Osiris on his, 64; wall of, 145.
Sandals, 88, 209, 612.
Saneha, 13.
Sar = Osiris, 155.
Saset serpent, 150.
Sashsa, 301.
Sat garment, 641.
Sata, 307, 544; chapter of, 38.
Satet, 569.
Sȧti, 64, 173.
Sati-ṭemui, 139.
Saturday, 201.
Satyrs, 23, 54.
Sau, 41, 264, 580, 581.
Sau, soul of Anu, 41.
Saut, 577.
Sauti, 580.
Scalding, 36.
Scales, 32.
Scarab, 442; green stone, 440.
Scarabaeus sacer, 133, 339.
Sceptre, 239; amulet, 591, 593; land of, 606; mystic, 148; of flint, 590; of mother-of-emerald, 46, 623; jackal-headed, 155.
Schack Schackenburg, 137.
Schiaparelli, 2, 21, 208, 249, 250.
Schweinfurth, 22.
Scorpion, 199, 200, 521; goddess, 305.
Scribe of gods, 183, 236.
Scribe, real, royal, 242.
Scribes, errors of, 27.
Sculptor, 170.
Seasons, 343.
Seat of truth, 573, 628.
Sebȧ, 144, 152, 156, 344.
Sebȧk, 188, 545.
Sebȧk-Rā, 188.
Sebaq, 273.
Sebȧu, 60, 343, 345, 356, 358, 370, 425, 467, 468, 488, 495.
Sebek, 40, 186, 387, 592.
Sebi, 160.
Sebqa, 410.
Seb-ur, 246, 247, 250, 253, 278.
Seed of Amen, 165.
Seer of millions of years, 609.
Seḥ chamber, 258, 376, 420.
Sehert stone, 451, 620.
Seḥertbaius, 147.
Seḥetep-taui, 518.
Seḥtet, 62.
Sekem, 158.
Seker, 37, 146, 170, 199, 205, 251, 260, 275, 292, 294, 313, 352, 358, 359, 360, 478, 483, 570, 615; boat of, 171, 397, 492; realm of, 145.
Seker Åsȧr, 205.
Seker-Khā-baiu, 12.
Seker Osiris, 326, 329.
Seker, Ṭuat of, 149.
Sekhem, 59, 60, 80, 206, 264, 302, 307, 358, 392, 426, 546, 552, 601; gods of, 276.
Sekhem-metenusen, 271.
Sekhem Nefer, 127.
Sekhem ur, 81.
Sekhenur, 138, 274, 412.
Sekher, 615.
Sekher-Åṭ, 139.
Sekhet-ȧanru, 206, 325.

Sekhet-åaru, 136, 137, 138, 139, 154, 181, 192, 229, 297, 354, 365, 369, 370, 383, 444, 502, 522, 624, 632, 634.
Sekheṭ-ḥer-āsht-åru, 137, 269, 402.
Sekhet-ḥetep (ḥetepet), 136, 154, 206, 238, 323, 370, 374, 424, 454, 524, 643; chapters of, 229, 632 ff.
Sekhet Nebt-Ḥetepet, 156.
Sekhet Saneḥemu, 589.
Sekhet Tcher, 603.
Sekhmet, 41, 170, 187, 229, 310, 317, 421, 422, 434, 438, 439, 599, 608.
Sekhmet-em-ṭesu-sen, 407.
Sekhmetren, 127, 645.
Sekhpetqraiu, 216.
Sekhriu, 580.
Sekri, 478.
Sektet Boat, 42, 111, 127, 163, 264, 296, 345, 349, 363, 408, 487, 489, 496, 498, 501, 503, 524, 630, 651.
Selene, 83.
Selk, 178, 189, 192.
Sem priest, 32, 208, 243, 245, 248, 249 ff., 255, 278, 359.
Sema, 84.
Semåti, 273, 411.
Semi, 159.
Semketi, 363.
Semktet boat, 133, 163, 602.
Semmån, 209, 210.
Semsu, 147.
Semti, 282.
Seneferu, 13, 14.
Senmut, Island, 175.
Senṭ, Senṭå, 11.
Senti of Horus, 427.
Senu, 304, 520.
Senu wine, 216.
Sep, 209.
Sepa, 386.
Sepṭ, 141, 302, 392, 558.
Sepṭet, 641.
Sepṭ-kheri-Nehait, 589.
Sepṭt Uauau, 152.
Sepu, 554.
Sepulchres of gods, 153.
Seqeṭḥer, 137, 269, 403.
Ser, 147, 176.
Serå-kheru, 580.
Serekh, 236, 273.
Serekhi, 584.
Seresher, 270, 404.
Serestepu, 270, 405.
Ser goose, 216.
Ser-kheru, 583.
Serpent, 197, 343; boat, 145, 146; of becoming, 38; five-headed, 146; gods, 120, 140; made by Isis, 122; with legs, 46, 623; the spitting, 158; to avoid bites of, 33; of repulsing, 33; fiery, 143; the Nine, 146; two-headed, 145.
Serq, 159, 179, 189, 192, 565.
Serqet, 147, 305, 597, 602, 607.
Sert, 457.
Serṭiu, 579.
Sesheta Circle, 147.
Seshetṭ chamber, 523.
Seshsesh, 158.
Sessi, 158.
Set, 25, 54, 84, 85, 87, 110, 116, 118, 144, 150, 160, 166, 179, 180, 184, 188, 189, 192, 209, 213, 214, 250, 261, 263, 271, 276, 277, 287, 292, 294, 301, 311, 316, 326, 343, 344, 350, 356, 357, 358, 374, 399, 404, 424, 425, 427, 430, 434, 443, 444, 446, 453, 466, 521, 532, 533, 552, 566, 568, 598, 601, 623, 624, 633, 635.
Set Åmentet, 150, 206, 378.
Set and Ladder, 83; birthday of, 53;

the eternal, 149; father of the gods, 480; fights Horus, 384; genital organs of, 267; greatest of gods, 564; heart of, 479; mutilation of, 141; skin of, 240.
Setemȧritf, 155.
Setem Priest, 208, 359.
Set goose, 216.
Set-Horus, 181.
Set (Isis), 134, 128.
Sêt, 180.
Set-ḥeḥ, 149.
Setesh (?), 180.
Setfiu gods, 159.
Seth ḥeb, 213.
Seth wine, 543.
Setḥer, 157.
Sethu, 159.
Seti I, 133, 162.
Seti II, 167.
Seṭ-qesu, 316, 577, 583.
Set (Semt), 62.
Set Tchesert, 365.
Seven ārits, 137; gods, 262; headed reptiles, 200; spirits, 262, 386, 387, 388; uraei, 552.
Seventy-two conspirators, 54.
Shabaka, 117.
Shabti, 322.
Shabu, 274, 406.
Shadow, the, 78, 144, 228, 292, 474; of the dead, 139, 140, 144; of Kheperȧ, 118; of a man, 39.
Shai, 193, 235, 238.
Shame, to drive away, 30.
Sharpe, S., 116.
Shas-ḥetep, 59.
Shȧt cake, 216.
Shau, 65.
Shebu cake, 216.
She-en-ḥesmen, 260.
She-en-maāt, 260.
Shêkh Abû Manṣûr, 20.
Shemsu Ḥeru, 374.
Shemti, 159.
Shen, 259.
Shenȧt-per-utheset-neter, 126, 645.
Shenit, 237, 440, 534.
Sheniu, 286, 372, 393, 395.
Shennu, 65.
Shens cake, 216, 615, 616.
Shenth, 25.
Shenti, 420.
Shenu powder, 570.
Shenuti, 200.
Sheol, 135.
Shept-temesu, 257.
Sheput, 189.
Sherȧ, Sheri, 11, 12.
Sheret Nenu, 520.
Shert-en-Menu, 422.
Shes cake, 266.
Shesmu, 94, 268, 287, 392.
Shesshes, 345.
Shetait shrine, 358, 584.
Shetatbesu, 159.
Shet-kheru, 579, 583.
Shet-pet, 210.
Sheṭu, star god, 149.
Shmin, 203.
Shmûn, 204.
Shoulder of Horus, 426.
Shoulder of Osiris, 358.
Shoulder of Pepi, 601.
Shrines, the, 12, 152.
Shu, 24, 25, 41, 43, 68, 85, 116, 126, 146, 149, 174, 175, 176, 184, 235, 275, 283, 300, 302, 340, 370, 371, 377, 390, 399, 425, 431, 434, 448, 462, 465, 481, 510, 530, 592, 628, 630, 635, 639, 641; with green face, 277; House of, 633; origin of, 168; pillars of, 637; Soul of Ȧnu, 41.
Shuttle, 186.

Silver, 110, 440; silver-gold, 353.
Sin, 576, 586; sins, 42.
Sinaitic Peninsula, 13.
Singer of Åmen, 221, 232.
Sistrum, 221, 233.
Sîwâh, 185.
Skertchley, 430.
Skia, 78.
Skin of animal in burial, 4; of bull, 240.
Skull of Pepi, 600.
Sky, 234; beetle of, 133.
Sky boats, 131, 132.
Sky cow, 132, 163.
Sky god, 160, 348, 435; goddess, 118, 134, 342.
Sky, pillars of, 130; theories about, 130; a woman, 131, 132.
Slander, 578.
Slaughter, of avoiding, 34, 606; in Ḥensu, 317; house of, 420.
Slaughterer, 463.
Sledge of Seker, 360.
Sleepers in Osiris, 156.
Sma, 444; Bull, 601.
Smaiu, Smait fiends, 425, 430, 510.
Smam, 643.
Smamti, 138.
Smamur, 397.
Smas-er-khet, 637, 638.
Smelter, 170.
Smen goose, 141, 249, 300, 547.
Smer, 249, 251, 252.
Smetti, 402.
Smeṭu, 137.
Snake, never sleeping, 201.
Snakes, the nine in Ṭuat, 257.
Sodom, 574.
Sodomy, 578, 584.
Soles, 603.
Somaliland, 205.
Son of Earth, 307; of fire, 289.
Sons of Horus, 191.
Sons of revolt, 344.
Sothis, 85, 86, 141, 178, 641.
Soul, to bewitch away, 282; to vivify, 47; in captivity, 228; Creator of Nu, 551; the Divine, 389, 473; Everlasting, 491; life of, in heaven, 82ff.; living, 31.
Soul, of Horus, 532; of Rā, 59, 113, 389; of Set, 564; of Shu and Tefnut, 390; of Souls, 494; of Temu, 228, 549; rest, 245; reunion with body, 228, 472; spirit, 162.
Souls, broken, 153; enter Sāḥu, 72; live in Gt. Oasis, 183; of Åmentet, 40, 159; of Ånu, 41, 78, 302, 434, 553, 600, 601, 603; of East, 40, 349; of God, 104; of Khemenu, 41; of Nekhen, 41; of Pe, 41; of Rā, 110; of Ṭuat, 143; of West, 40, 349; of Urnes, 143; the Twin, 603.
Soul-god, 293, 359; of becoming, 38; of Ṭeṭu, 308.
South, gods of, 128; roads of, 128; rudder of, 645.
Sovereignty, symbols of, 234.
Spear of Rā, 109.
Speech, excessive, 580.
Spell of Meri Rā, 604; of Tem, 152.
Spells, 136, 158, 166; of Isis, 618.
Sphinx, 180, 341.
Spirit, the primeval, 119; of the moon, 293.
Spirit-body, 53, 60, 67, 121, 483, 570.
Spirits, the Seven, 262, 386, 387; of dawn, 233.
Spirit-soul, 15, 35, 79, 90, 125, 472, 483; of perfecting, 40, 42; of God, 307; of Osiris, 295.

Spirit-souls, 140, 141, 146, 162, 476, 485, 502, 510, 519, 522, 527, 528, 547, 563, 567, 608, 614, 639, 644, 651, 659; 9 cubits high, 139; of Rā, 297.
Spitting serpent, 158.
Spittle, 122.
Staff, 32, 41.
Stanley, H., 22.
Star, boats of, 133.
Star-god, 149, 156, 159, 502, 509.
Stars, 131, 459; imperishable, 141; morning, 160; never resting, 496, 531.
Stau, 151.
Stealing, 576.
Steersman, 298.
Stele, funerary, 247.
Steps, amulet of, 175; at Abydos, 359; god of, 367.
Stibium, 214.
Still-heart, 410, 418, 616.
Stomach, 192.
Storm, 119, 133; cloud, 511.
Strabo, 24, 54, 202, 203, 204, 205, 206, 207.
Suan, 117.
Sûdân, 136, 152, 167, 204, 244, 268, 284, 305, 308, 323, 340, 499; Egyptian, 116; S.E., 108.
Sulphur springs, 152.
Sun, 109, 111, 114, 132, 233; boats of, 46; eclipse of, 119; fires of, 159; path of, 43; early views about, 131; temples of, 165; worship, 167.
Sunday, 201.
Sun-god, 1, 24, 148, 158, 163, 173, 255; the dead, 145; enemies of, 146; in Ṭuat, 142; of night, 150; spirit, 156, 165.
Sunnu, 62.
Sunrise, 222, 233, 234; described, 160; Mount of, 146, 149.
Sut, 181, 251, 560.
Sutekh, 180.
Suten-ḥenen (Ḥensu), 206.
Suten ṭā ḥetep, 247.
Suti, 294, 300, 397, 447, 454, 510, 566, 608, 655, 656; heart of, 483.
Sut-joint, 216.
Sutimes, 227, 228, 651.
Swallow, 216, 264, 304, 305, 521; of becoming, 38.
Swallow=Isis, 55.
Swathings, 214.
Sweetmeats, 596.
Swine, 613.
Sycamore tree, 285, 438, 619; wood of, 617.
Syene, 117, 216.
Syria, 164.

Table of food, 283; of offerings, 213, 215, 613.
Tablet of Destiny, 379.
Ta-ḥer-sta-nef, 352.
Tait, 547.
Taiti, 64.
Taiu-rekhti, 276, 302, 428.
Ṭaḳȧ, 25.
Tamarisk, 55.
Ta-merȧ, 569, 586, 651.
Tanent, 64, 206.
Tannt, 398, 399.
Tanut-Ȧmen, 558, 559.
Tape measure, 154.
Tareṭ, 584.
Tareṭiu, 578.
Ta-Sekri, 65.
Ta-she, 582.
Taskmasters, 148, 155, 157.
Ta-theser, 59, 186, 206, 353, 364, 421, 493, 502, 646, 652.

Ṭat (Ṭuat), 135.
Taten, 342.
Tatenu, 116.
Tathena, 146.
Tathenen, 342; four forms of, 147.
Tattoo, 239.
Ṭaṭtu, 59.
Tatun, 233, 309, 342, 584.
Taui-Rekhti, 357.
Ta-urt, 43, 189, 329.
Tchām, 251.
Tchatchau, 148, 152, 155, 157, 224, 225, 229, 237, 275, 286, 303, 364, 371, 393, 422, 423, 424, 425–432, 435, 439, 456, 507, 510, 517, 541.
Tchaṭiu, 159.
Tchefau, 342, 649.
Tchefet, 584, 641.
Tcheḥra, 51.
Tchen, 418.
Tcheràu-ur, 248.
Tcherti, 259.
Tchesef, 138.
Tcheser, 174.
Tcheser-tep, 94, 582, 584.
Tcheserit, 159.
Tchesert, 558; cake, 216; goddess, 642; Lake of, 641.
Tcheṭbi, 152.
Tears of Kheperà; 119.
Ṭebat-neterus, 147.
Ṭeb-ḥer-k, 406.
Ṭeb-ḥer-kehaat, 137, 270.
Ṭebti, 584.
Ṭebu, 581; Land of, 551.
Tebun, 468.
Teeth of Ani, 597; of Nu, 607; of Pepi, 601; white, 212.
Tefnut, 24, 25, 43, 85, 116, 126, 175, 176, 235, 276, 340, 370, 371, 425, 481, 510; origin of, 118.
Teḥuti, 183.
Teka-ḥer, 154.
Tekem, 370.
Tekh, 184.
Tekh-bu-uaā, 591.
Tell Basṭah, 187, 204.
Tem, Temu, 24, 25, 40, 41, 57, 59, 70, 85, 89, 93, 105, 113, 116, 124, 125, 126, 146, 152, 161, 162, 164, 169, 174, 183, 195, 235, 264, 265, 266, 275, 279, 284, 306, 308, 311, 328, 340, 370, 371, 376, 380, 381, 383, 399, 404, 419, 425, 434, 447, 448, 454, 461, 487, 488, 494, 499, 510, 527, 532, 534, 535, 541, 547, 548, 562, 563, 624, 647; Eye of, 468; Mystic form of, 149; soul of, 228, 549; standard of, 160: Ṭuat of, 149.
Tem Harmakhis, 347.
Tem Ḥeru Khuti, 341, 347, 489.
Tem Kheperà, 279, 435.
Tem Sepu, 581.
Tem-Sep, 584.
Tem, the young, 310.
Temān, 253.
Temānu, 246.
Temit, 162.
Temt, 162.
Temu-Rā, 58, 68, 85, 183.
Tenà basket, 359.
Tenait, 542; festival of, 359.
Tenbes cakes, 216.
Tenemiu, 578.
Tenen, 342.
Teni, 428.
Tenn-t, 366.
Ṭent chamber, 609.
Ṭep, 25, 207, 214; 370.
Ṭepi serpent, 159.
Ṭept cake, 213, 216.
Tepṭuf, 570.
Ṭepu, 64.
Terrible One, 366.

Ṭesamenmit, 147.
Ṭesertbaiu, 160.
Ṭesher-àriti, 262, 388.
Ṭeshert, 555.
Tesherṭ-t, 309.
Teshtesh, 358.
Ṭeskhaibitu, 147.
Ṭesṭes, 488.
Tesur, 63.
Tet, 243, 288.
Tet of amethyst, 145; of carnelian, 230, 618; chapter of, 320.
Ṭeṭ, 150, 209, 233, 234, 243, 255, 263, 276, 303; amulet, 451; chapter of, 319; house of, 143; in Ṭeṭu, 56; of crystal, 322, 661; of gold, 45, 230, 616; of Rā, 661; speech of, 625.
Tetà, 17, 19, 20, 21, 71, 72, 79, 82, 100, 191; pyramid of, 1.
Ṭeṭà the sage, 10.
Ṭeṭi, 357.
Ṭeṭ-seneferu, 10.
Ṭeṭu (Buṣiris), 28, 142, 263, 281, 293, 302, 351, 353, 357, 359, 364, 366, 389, 422, 426, 430, 491, 492, 517, 520, 525, 527, 531, 533, 546, 547, 569, 570, 581, 651; gods of, 276.
Ṭeṭun, 302.
Ṭeṭut, 207.
Thebes, 117, 167, 172, 195, 198, 217, 220, 221, 232, 244, 344, 346, 571; western, 189; Ṭuat of, 149.
Theḥenu, 658.
Thenà, 274, 629.
Thenemi, 583.
Theology, Heliopolitan, 1.
Thepḥet-shetat, 146.
Therp goose, 216.
Thes bone, 601.
Thigh, 444, 590; Great Bear, 292, 387; gods of, 128; of heaven, 478; of Osiris, 431; of Ani, 599; of Pepi, 602.
Things of the Night, 276, 426.
Thirst, 88, 89, 192.
This, 25, 428.
Thoth, 10, 41, 46, 47, 48, 56, 60, 84, 85, 86, 117, 120, 123, 128, 134, 145, 162, 183, 186, 188, 193, 208, 209 ff., 235, 236, 239, 255, 256, 261, 266, 267, 279, 282, 284, 293, 298, 301, 302, 305, 311, 315, 323, 340, 341, 343, 345, 356, 357, 358, 373, 374, 384, 385, 386, 392, 403, 404, 417, 424, 425, 426, 427, 428, 429, 431, 432, 434, 444, 453, 458, 479, 480, 487, 497, 499, 503, 509, 512, 551, 560, 561, 562, 594, 595, 608, 623, 624, 630, 647, 660; author of the Book of the Dead, 23; of being near, 39; followers of, 159; nose of, 600; a soul of Anu, 41; speech of, 372; Ten Addresses to, 278.
Thoth-Hāpi, 444.
Thothmes III, 70.
Thought, 114, 161; of Kheperà, 118.
Thoueris, 189.
Throat of Ani, 598.
Throne, 87; of Osiris, 157.
Thunder, 130; cloud, 133, 384.
Tiamat, 197.
Tiele, 115.
Tile, 613.
Time, 184.
Timekeepers, 155.
Tmu, see Temu.
To-day, 177, 258, 267, 378, 610.
Toes of Ani, 599; of Nu, 608; of Pepi, 602.
Tomb, 245, 291; chapter of opening, 39, 292, 474.
Tongue of Pepi, 601

Tool, 300.
Torches, the Four, 43.
Tortoise, 199, 309.
Tow rope, 148, 345.
Transformations, Chapters of, 37, 38, 39, 114, 304 ff., 521, 523, 525, 541, 544, 545, 546.
Tree of life, 88.
Tree worship, 285.
Triad, 118.
Tripping, 35.
Truth, 103, 108, 110, 111, 177, 234, 241, 310.
Truth = God, 107.
Truth, goddesses of, 222, 340.
Truth, plant of, 156.
Truth, speakers of, 151, 154, 156.
Truth, tongue of, 601.
Ṭuamutef, 41, 127, 131, 191, 240, 386; speech of, 626; east, 192.
Ṭuat, 29, 60, 111, 125, 135, 142, 143, 146, 170, 174, 199, 347, 354, 363, 465, 478, 483, 490, 495, 525, 526, 527, 528, 529, 532, 550, 617; chapter of, 31; Circle of, 147; gates of, 128; gods of, 531; Lake of, 148; Leaders of, 42; Pylons of, 129; river of, 136, 143; Valley of, 136; work in, 155.
Ṭuat Chamber, 244, 301, 661.
Ṭuat of Heliopolis, 156.
Ṭuati, 156.
Tuatu unguent, 214.
Ṭuiqauiāaui, 139.
Tum, 67.
Tun cake, 216.
Ṭunā, 278.
Ṭunḥāt, 137.
Tunnel, 152.
Ṭun-tet, 253.
Ṭura, 18, 228.
Turin Papyrus, 9, 18, 29, 285, 299, 362.
Turquoise, 353, 560, 643; light, 347.
Tut cake, 215.
Tuti, wife of Ani, 221, 231, 232, 234, 242, 245, 257, 274, 295, 313.
Ṭuṭu, 579.
Ṭuṭuf, 583.
Twin-gods, 389.
Two Fighters, 633, 636.
Two Lands, 108, 110, 111, 122, 123, 220, 347, 351, 352.
Tylor, E. B., 54, 55.
Typhon, 54, 189; dismembers Osiris, 55; made captive, 86.

Uāau, 137.
Uāb Priest, 359.
Uak festival, 60, 647.
Uakh, 641.
Uakha, 324.
Uamemti, 579, 583.
Uārt corridor, 350; Great, 522.
Uārt-ent-mu, 141.
Uast, 117.
Uatch-nesert, 583.
Uatch ointment, 254.
Uatch-rekhit, 581.
Uatchet, Uatchit, 189, 190, 259, 265, 316, 401, 598.
Uatchturȧ, 260.
Ubes-ḥer-per-em-khetkhet, 388.
Uganda, 270.
Umbra, 78.
Unȧs, 6, 18, 19, 20, 66, 67, 74, 77, 78, 83, 84, 89, 92, 100, 168, 181, 184, 189, 191, 193, 197, 301; eats his gods, 93 ff.; pyramid of, 1.
Unȧset, 580.
Unb, 453.
Underworld, 135; and see Ṭuat.
Unem-besek, 578, 583.
Unem-ḥauau, 137, 270, 404.

Un-em-ḥetep, 640, 641.
Unem-khaibitu, 316.
Unem-sāḥu, 257.
Unem-snef, 316, 578, 583.
Unes, 583.
Unguents, 12.
Unḥāt, 269, 403.
Un-Nefer, Unn-Nefer, 48, 54, 57, 61, 188, 325, 352, 364, 374, 419, 422, 431, 490, 553, 573, 609, 613, 620, 647; with Ḥeru-Khuti, 295.
Unnut goddess, 660.
Unpet, 593.
Unt, 141; Lake of, 395.
Unth, 584.
Unti, 159, 491.
Unu, 448, 458, 480, 554, 660; spirits of, 84.
Up-uatu, 84, 152, 183, 302, 419, 429, 597, 600, 607.
Up-reḥui, 184.
Urā, goddess, 214.
Uraei, 141; fiery, 148; Lake of the Living, 153; of Tem, 380; goddesses, 486, 518, 530.
Uraeus of Rā, 301.
Ur-ḥeka, 32, 245, 247, 278.
Uri, 583.
Urit, 579.
Ur-kherp-hem, 1, 360.
Urmertus, 127, 645.
Urnes, 143.
Urt-ȧb, 358.
Urrt Crown, 88, 90, 126, 351, 396, 404, 407, 475, 486, 492, 505, 510, 560, 609.
Urti, 324.
Usȧr, 352.
Usekh Hall, 214.
Usekh Ḥer, 453.
Usekh-nemmat, 315, 576, 582.
Userkaf, 164, 165.
Usert, 642.
Uset, 269.
Ushabti, 224; Chapter of, 30; speech of, 629.
Ust, 403.
Utchat, 595, 609, 610, 630; of bringing, 46; filling of, 44, 575, 576.
Utchats, 233; winged, 623.
Uten, 580.
Uṭen cake, 212.
Uterus of Isis, 45, 288.
Utes, 302.
Utcha-aābt, 282, 446, 447.
Utu-nesert, 577.
Utu-rekhit, 584.

Vagina of Isis, 45.
Valley, funerary, 648.
Valley, the Great, 403.
Valley of Ȧbṭu, 559.
Valley of the Nile, 136.
Valley of the Ṭuat, 136.
Vegetables, 152.
Vegetation ruled by moon, 119.
Vertebrae, 287.
Vestibule, the east, 160.
Vestibule, the west, 150.
Vestibules of Ṭuat, 142.
Vignettes of Book of the Dead, 29, 49.
Vipers, 199.
Virey, 87.
Viscera, human, 287; small, 192.
Vulture, gold, 45.
Vyse, Col. Howard, 15, 18, 19.

Washing of Kau, 155.
Watcher, 108.
Watchers, the, 392, 395, 397, 398, 472; of Ȧrits, 137.
Watchman, 157; of pylons, 44.

Water, 174; boiling, 141, 145, 151, 156, 318; celestial, 118; chapter of drinking and obtaining, 36, 227, 285, 443; of avoiding dirty, 35.
Water-god, 173, 266, 314, 348.
Water-goddess, 163.
Water jar, 244.
Water, primeval, 119, 162.
Watering with blood, 263.
Wax figures, 198.
Weeping in Ṭuat, 147, 152.
Weight, false, 574.
Well in Åat VIII, 140.
West, gods of, 128; roads of, 128; Rudder of, 645; souls of, 40.
Westcar Papyrus, 10, 165, 193.
Wet-nurse, 236.
Wheat, 108, 109, 139, 172, 221, 324, 326, 369, 370, 620, 643.
Wheat = Osiris, 156.
Whey, 211.
Whip, 299.
Whisk, 269, 270, 271.
White House, 417.
White Wall, 59, 204.
White Wine, 216.
Wicked, their fate, 151.
Wiedemann, Dr., 10, 11, 13, 82, 121, 156, 181.
Wife of Rā, 165.
Wig, 156, 241, 570.
Wind, 172; north, 283.
Wine, 89, 211, 596.
Wisdom, 109, 118.
Witchcraft, 581.
Witch doctor, 363.
Wolf-god, 316; wolves, 435.
Women, wailing, 357.
Word, the, 343; of Tem, 114; of Thoth, 120.
Words, magical, 83; of Isis, 123; of power, 10, 32, 178, 226, 245, 279, 435; weighing of, 74, 121, 150.
Work in Ṭuat, 155; to avoid, 30.
World governed by Spirits, 114, 115.
World Ocean, 163.
Worms, 464, 528; in Åmentet, 366; to avoid, 33; in Rastau, 365.
Wrist-rest, 244.
Writing, 4, 183, 236.
Writing reed, 184.

Year, symbol of, 260; 365 days of, 53.
Year-god, 260.
Yesterday, 47, 177, 258, 267, 309, 378, 552, 609, 610, 611.

Zakâzîḳ, 187.